COMMUNICATING AND ORGANIZING IN CONTEXT

Communicating and Organizing in Context integrates Giddens' structuration theory with Goffman's interaction order and develops a new theoretical base—the theory of structurational interaction—for the analysis of communicating and organizing. Both theorists emphasize tacit knowledge, social routines, context, social practices, materiality, frames, agency, and view communication as constitutive of social life and of organizing. Thus their integration in structurational interaction provides a coherent, communication-centric approach to analyzing communicating, organizing and their interrelationships.

This book will be a valuable resource for students and scholars as an orientation to the field of organizational communication and as an integration of organizing and communicating. It will also be useful for practitioners as a tool for understanding how social and organizational contexts influence both face-to-face and mediated communication.

Beth Bonniwell Haslett (Ph.D., University of Minnesota) is a professor in the Department of Communication at the University of Delaware. Her research and teaching interests span both organizational and interpersonal communication, and focus on issues of face, cross-cultural communication and the social impact of information and communication technologies.

Dr. Haslett has written three books (*Communication: Strategic Action in Context; The Organizational Woman*, with F. L. Geis and M. R. Carter, and *Children Communicating*, with W. Samter) and has published more than 30 articles and book chapters.

COMMUNICATION SERIES
Jennings Bryant/Dolf Zillmann, General Editors

Selected titles in Organizational Communication (Linda Putnam, advisory editor) include:

Canary/McPhee—*Communication and Organizational Knowledge*

Cooren/Taylor/Van Every—*Communication as Organization: Empirical and Theoretical Explorations in the Dynamic of Text and Conversations*

Cooren—*Interacting and Organizing: Analyses of a Management Meeting*

Kramer—*Managing Uncertainty in Organizational Communication*

Nicotera/Clinkscales with Walker—*Understanding Organizations Through Culture and Structure: Relational and Other Lessons From the African-American Organization*

Parker—*Race, Gender, and Leadership: Re-Envisioning Organizational Leadership from the Perspectives of African American Women Executives*

Putnam/Nicotera— *Building Theories of Organization: The Constitutive Role of Communication*

Taylor/Van Every—*The Emergent Organization: Communication as Its Site and Surface*

COMMUNICATING AND ORGANIZING IN CONTEXT

The Theory of Structurational Interaction

Beth Bonniwell Haslett

Routledge
Taylor & Francis Group

NEW YORK AND LONDON

First published 2012
by Routledge
711 Third Ave., New York, NY 10016

Simultaneously published in the UK
by Routledge
2 Park Square, Milton Park, Abingdon, Oxon OX14 4RN

Routledge is an imprint of the Taylor & Francis Group, an informa business

© 2012 Routledge, Taylor & Francis

Library of Congress Cataloging in Publication Data
Haslett, Beth.
Communicating and organizing in context: the theory of structurational interaction / Beth Bonniwell Haslett.
p. cm.
Includes bibliographical references.
1. Communication in organizations. 2. Communication. 3. Organizational sociology. I. Title.
HD30.3.H374 2011
302.3'5 – dc22
2011003870

ISBN13: 978-0-805-83895-4 (hbk)
ISBN13: 978-0-203-80937-2 (ebk)

Typeset in Bembo by Taylor & Francis books

Printed on acid-free paper in the USA

To my mother, Edna Stoeckmann Bonniwell, 1914–2010
A woman of unfailing generosity, amazing grace,
faith and courage.

To my children, Heidi Christine and Erik David
Sources of pride and delight.

And
To the "babies," my grandchildren
Hope for a bright future.

CONTENTS

List of Figures and Tables   ix
Acknowledgements   x
Preface   xi

SECTION I
A Framework for Organizing and Communicating   **1**

1. Framing Communicating and Organizing   3

2. A Frame System for Communicating   18

3. A Frame System for Organizing   57

4. Connecting Communicating and Organizing   74

SECTION II
Giddens' Structuration Theory   **99**

5. Giddens' Structuration Theory   101

6. Giddens: Context, Agency and Interaction   138

7. Applying Giddens in Communicating and
   Organizing   167

SECTION III
Goffman on Communicating and Organizing 207

8. Erving Goffman's Interaction Order 209

9. Goffman's Framing of Interaction 240

10. Goffman and Larger Social Institutions 267

SECTION IV
Toward a Theory of Structurational Interaction 311

11. Toward a Theory of Structurational Interaction 313

12. Applying Structurational Interaction 342

References 385
Index 422

FIGURES AND TABLES

Figures

2.1	Toward a Descriptively Adequate Model of Communication	53
2.2	A Process Model of Communication	54
3.1	Social Systems	71

Tables

1.1	A Model of Frame Analysis	14
3.1	Frame System of Organizing	60
5.1	Modalities of Structuration and Social Institutions	103
8.1	Goffman's Frame Analysis	215
9.1	Goffman's Interaction Process	243

ACKNOWLEDGEMENTS

Permission granted to cite material from Anthony Giddens' *The Constitution of Society,* 1984, copyright © by Polity Press. These rights are for the UK, Commonwealth, Europe and the rest of the world. Copyrights © for the North American distribution are granted by the University of California Press.

Permission granted to quote material from Erving Goffman's Felicity's Condition, *American Journal of Sociology,* 1983, *89,* 1, pp. 1–53, copyright © by the University of Chicago Press.

Permission granted to quote material from Erving Goffman's *Frame Analysis: An Essay on the Organization of Experience,* 1974, copyright © by HarperCollins Publishers.

PREFACE

This book represents somewhat of an odyssey, taking me beyond my earlier career interests, yet reflecting a continued focus on issues of discourse and context.

My communication career started in communicative development, with a strong interest in the "miracle" of communication—with no particular training, most two-year-olds acquire the rudiments of language and communication, enabling them to participate in social interaction. From the outset, my doctoral training and subsequent research has been interdisciplinary. At Wisconsin, I studied with Frederick Williams, who was very interested in social differences in language use and contributed to studies on Head Start and other language intervention programs. While completing my doctoral work at the University of Minnesota, I was fortunate to complete interdisciplinary work, studying with James J. Jenkins, a noted psycholinguist, Gene Piche, a sociolinguist and literary scholar, and William S. Howell, an early specialist in cross cultural communication. The collegial departmental atmosphere fostered by the "Old Buffaloes" was also an inspiring model of collegial respect. To these mentors, I owe an extraordinary debt for their support, their openness to alternative viewpoints and their eclecticism—it is a model I have tried to emulate! From them, my scholarly foundation was firmly grounded in discourse, context and social relationships.

Over time, I became very interested in the question of intentionality—unfortunately, not a topic that can be pursued with interactants as young as three- to five-year-olds! The old saying "what you see is what you get" can be reframed as "what you hear is what you get" for preschoolers. When asking them to think of how they might have said something differently, they would just repeat themselves. Asking them to think about alternatives simply had them treating me as if I were crazy, just what didn't I get the first time?

In order to pursue strategic communication, then, I pursued scholarship in organizational settings, in which I could also focus on my interests in discourse and context. Context, in particular, could be more precisely articulated in organizational settings. And there were also strong connections between developmental scholarship and organizational scholarship, particularly around issues of identity, socialization and negotiation.

Until recently, there has been a disconnect between communicating and organizing in organizational communication scholarship. Scholars would focus on organizational communication processes, treating the organization itself as a backdrop, or foreground the organization, paying scant attention to communication. Recently, under the rubric of communication-as-constitutive-of-organizing, integrating communicating and organizing has now become a focal point for research and theorizing, with multiple models being advocated (see Chapter 4 for an overview of such approaches).

As I became acquainted with Giddens' structuration theory and discovered his use of Goffman's interaction order as a basis for social integration in structuration theory, integrating their approaches appeared to provide a very insightful, valuable approach to organizing and communicating. Goffman's emphasis on the interaction order and his concepts of frames and framing provide a processual aspect to Giddens' structuration theory. Giddens' work, in turn, provides theoretical depth and breadth with his analyses of sociohistorical contexts, social institutions, and time-space distanciation that would extend Goffman's interaction order. Goffman's analyses provide a micro-level focus that will be useful in elaborating Giddens' perspective. Both theorists emphasize tacit knowledge, social routines, context, social practices, materiality, frames and agency in their views. Goffman's use of frames interconnects the different layers of context that Giddens provides; thus Goffman's lamination can link the most concrete specific actions to their larger social contexts. Both theorists use frames as ways of capturing agents' knowledgeability, understanding social contexts and enacting social practices.

Taken together, their synthesis provides a rich, multi-layered, integrated framework for analyzing the interrelationships between communicating and organizing. As such, based on their integration, this book moves toward a theory of structurational interaction. Both theorists view communication as constitutive of social life and of organizing, as an aspect of social life. Their joint focus on communication and its importance makes structurational interaction an ideal perspective from which to analyze the interrelationships between communicating and organizing. As such, this theory provides an integrated, coherent view of communicating and organizing and also enables more insightful analyses in terms of both breadth and depth. And finally, structurational interaction incorporates multiple levels of analysis and the use of multiple methods of analysis.

Through structurational interaction, I hope to theoretically integrate their work more fully, while accurately interpreting and extending the work of both. What is of particular value for communication scholars is the very central role interaction plays in both Goffman's and Giddens' theories. Communication is necessary for all shared social action, but our focus will be on exploring the interconnections between organizing and communicating and on understanding what types of organizing (and communicating) are necessary for organizations. That is, not all organizing leads to organizations. And I believe both Goffman and Giddens have valuable insights into these issues. As is well known, the scholarly contributions of both men go significantly beyond the synthesis proposed here, so major aspects of both men's work will not be examined in this book; only those aspects central to organizing and communicating will be discussed.

In pursuing the analysis of the interaction order and social organization, Smith observes that "other researchers and scholars ... may deploy methods and adapt his ideas in ways he could not have envisioned. In undertaking those enquiries, it may be necessary often to break with the letter of Goffman in order to keep faith with the spirit of Goffman" (1999, p. 16). And as Giddens comments, "If ideas are important and illuminating, what matters ... is to be able to sharpen them so as to demonstrate their usefulness, even if within a framework which might be quite different from that which helped engender them" (1984, p. xxii). It is my hope that the theory of structurational interaction will be compatible with their spirit of inquiry.

The book proceeds in four sections. In the first section, an introductory chapter establishes frame theory as an overarching metatheory for integrating Goffman and Giddens. Both use frames in a similar manner: as a way of discussing agents' knowledgeability; as interpretive schemas; and as varying layers of context. Chapter 2 develops a model of communication, focusing on intentionality, communicative contexts, actor's knowledgeability and agency. Chapter 3 focuses on traditional approaches to organizations, and discusses research on communicative processes in organizations. Chapter 4 discusses current research concerns in organizational communication, examines the communication-as-constitutive-of-organizations perspectives and foreshadows the application of structurational interaction to communicating and organizing.

Section II (Chapters 5–7) focuses on Giddens' structuration theory and its utility in studying organizing and communicating. Chapters 5 and 6 outline structuration theory (ST), and aspects of structuration theory such as distanciation of time and space, sociohistorical contexts (historicity), modalities of structuration and so forth. Chapter 7 reviews some of the organizational scholarship based on ST, including significant theoretical applications of his work, such as adaptive structuration theory, McPhee and Zaug's four flow model, and Orlikowski's work on social practices and genres of communication.

Section III (Chapters 8–10) focuses on Goffman's interaction order, and discusses Goffman's work on moves, frames, face, alignment, footing and so forth. I also review Goffman's work as it has been applied to larger institutional settings. (Goffman has been frequently criticized for focusing on micro-level interaction and ignoring institutional settings with unequal power distributions. Yet his work has been applied in institutional settings and some of his own work, most notably on total institutions, analyzed large institutions.)

Section IV (Chapters 11 and 12) deals with two significant issues, developing a theory of structurational interaction and applying it to existing organizational communication issues and research. Giddens relies on Goffman's interaction order as a foundation for his structuration theory. Because many scholars working with Giddens are not familiar with Goffman's work, the significance of this relationship has been overlooked. Through the theory of structurational interaction, their interconnections are highlighted and their valuable insights into organizing and communicating more clearly understood. As such, structurational interaction provides an integrated, in-depth, coherent approach to organizing, communicating and their fundamental interrelationships.

I hope those readers interested in either Goffman or Giddens, but not their integration, will find the sections on each scholar's work to be a comprehensive, communicatively oriented overview of their work. Although Goffman is primarily known for his interaction order, his work, such as *Asylums* and more generally *Frame Analysis*, provides substantive insight into communicative processes within organizational contexts. In similar fashion, although Giddens is known primarily as a social theorist and for his structuration theory, nevertheless his work has valuable insights into issues like identity, trust, risk and social relationships. As such, these chapters will be of interest to communication scholars generally. Structurational interaction itself has much to offer communication scholars generally, whether focusing on interpersonal or organizational communication. Scholars in mass communication will also be interested in the discussion of framing as well as the discussion of mediated communication.

It has been intellectually challenging, but also very rewarding, to investigate the corpus of work of both Goffman and Giddens. Both men were prolific writers, and their work can be re-read frequently, with new gems and insights being revealed in each new re-reading. Richter noted that "concepts of communication play an important role in Giddens's work. In structuration he conceptualizes communication as one of the three dimensions along which structure and agency are articulated. In his theories of modernity and late modernity, he assigns communication and information technologies special significance in the transformation of social relations across space and time. His recent work on politics repeatedly stresses the importance of dialogic democratic discourse" (2000, p. 367). Richter further argued that there is a "great deal of potential for continued structuration-influenced communication research ... Giddens's engagement with communication virtually spans our field. Surely we have something to say in reply?" (*ibid*). The proposed theory of structurational interaction takes a step in that direction by attempting to make Giddens' work more accessible, and its communicative implications more clear and relevant.

Goffman's importance seems equally clear and significant, and compatible with Giddens' work. As Colomy and Brown observe:

> The autonomy of the interaction order, however, should not be construed as a rampant situationalism. The sources for the orderliness observable in particular settings are not generated in them at the moment. These patterns partly reflect the prior experience of participants and the cultural assumptions actors

bring with them to the encounter. ... Because it is penetrated by macro environments that reach across time and space, the interaction order is not an entirely local production.

(1996, p. 371)

In many aspects their works are compatible, and their focus on communication provides rich areas for further investigation. I hope to develop some of these implications in this book.

My approach to analyzing discourse and to integrating communicating and organizing has benefited greatly from countless discussions and interactions with Chuck Berger, Patrice Buzzanell, Bob Craig, Don Ellis, Gail Fairhurst, Wendy Leeds-Hurwitz, Kathleen Krone, Bob McPhee, Scott Poole, Bob Sanders, Karen Tracy and JoAnn Yates, as well as Robert Hopper and James Bradac, both of whom are greatly missed. And I am especially grateful for the friendship of Linda Putnam, and for our many conversations over the years. I also wish to thank my students, whose questions, interest and enthusiasm for challenging ideas continue to stimulate my own work. Thanks especially to those graduate students, Steve, JP, Melissa and Kelly, who read and critiqued earlier portions of the book. I also greatly appreciate the support and encouragement of Linda Bathgate, senior communication editor at Taylor & Francis. A very sincere thank you to Bob Catalano, physical therapist extraordinaire, for helping me to remain healthy and able to complete this book. And I am grateful to the University of Delaware for awarding me a sabbatical during which I worked on this book.

Finally, I deeply appreciate the loving support and space given me by my husband, Dave, which enabled me to complete this project, and for the continued love and support of my family.

My mother's interest and support throughout this project helped sustain my efforts and always provided an important source of strength. The support and encouragement of my sister, Judy, is also greatly appreciated and is a continual reminder of the value of sisterhood.

Beth Bonniwell Haslett
October 2010

SECTION I

A Framework for Organizing and Communicating

1

FRAMING COMMUNICATING AND ORGANIZING

Modern organizations are complex, paradoxical and continuously evolving. For organizations to survive and flourish, effective communication is critical. Generally, organizational communication research has tended to focus on communication, without integrating those processes with organizational theory, or to focus on organizations, without integrating communication with organizational structures. Recently, research on communication-as-constitutive of organizations has begun to address these inter-relationships. However, this recent work is limited in its focus and scope of inquiry.

What is needed is a theoretical framework that integrates communicating and organizing, so that their complex interrelationships can be more fully understood. In this book, I will use frame theory to integrate the theoretical perspectives of two noted social theorists, Erving Goffman and Anthony Giddens. Their synthesis, developed in the theory of structurational interaction, will provide a coherent, integrated perspective for research on organizing and communicating. Because communication is essential for any shared social activity, it is important to under-stand the full range of interrelationships between communicating and organizing, and their mutual influence upon each other.

Frame Theory

Frame theory has a long history of use in both the humanities and social science. Generally, frames can be viewed as a perspective or frame of reference. Classic work by Taylor and Fiske (Fiske & Taylor, 1991) and Schank and Abelson (1977) have developed frames (scripts and/or schemata) as a way to conceptualize human knowledge and action. Among communication scholars, work by Bateson (1972, 1976) and Goffman (1974, 1981a) have used frames as a device for signaling how communication is situated and interpreted in context.

In her classic article on frames, Tannen (1979) outlined several ways in which frames had been used to understand discourse. After Bartlett (1932), she notes that memory is constructed. We use our general impressions to construct details, so that our memory is actively processing information from moment to moment, looking for developing patterns. Tannen suggests three major ways in which frames represent knowledge: frames as communicated content (Chafe, 1977); frames as structures for representing stereotyped situations (Minsky, 1977, 1979), and frames as contexts, which identify meaningful behavior (Bransford & McCarrell, 1977).

Frames are used in everyday interaction. On an interactional level, frames are dynamic and changing as the interaction proceeds. In order to understand ongoing discourse, participants rely on tacit knowledge gleaned from others and from their prior experiences. This interactive notion of frames, Tannen argued, enables us to know what activities we are engaged in and how speakers mean what they say. That is, as Perri 6 noted, frames organize experience—"they enable people to recognize what is going on ... crucially, frames define what counts as relevant for attention and assessment" (2005, p. 94). Frames also reflect a "bias for action; that is to say, they represent people's worlds in ways that already call for particular styles of decision or of behavioural response" (ibid.).

In Goffman's terms, interactants are seeking alignment based on the shared understanding of the context in which the communication is occurring. In discussing organizing and communicating, I will be using frames to represent tacit knowledge, to identify the context, and to signal intended meanings within interaction. (For an excellent discussion of different senses of frames and the varied ways in which frames have been used in interaction, see Tannen, 1981.)

Further support for utilizing frame theory to understand communicative processes is offered by Entman. Entman argued that "the concept of framing consistently offers a way to describe the power of a communicating text" and suggested that framing can be an integrating, overarching theory for communication (1993, p. 51). Most importantly for our purposes, Entman locates frames at four different positions in the communicative process: with communicators, receivers, texts and cultures. As he observed:

> ... ***Communicators*** make conscious or unconscious framing judgments in deciding what to say, guided by frames ... that organize their belief systems. The ***text*** contains frames, which are manifested by the presence or absence of certain key-words, stocks phrases, stereotyped images ... and sentences that provide thematically reinforcing clusters of facts or judgments. The frames that guide the ***receiver's*** thinking and conclusion may or may not reflect the frames in the text and the framing intention of the communicator. The ***culture*** is the stock of commonly invoked frames; in fact, culture might be defined as the empirically demonstrable set of common frames exhibited in the discourse and thinking of most people in a social grouping.
>
> *(Entman, 1993, pp. 52–53, bold italics in the original text)*

In this view, frames play a central role in communication, influencing the communicative process at multiple points in processing and interpreting information.

Within media studies, D'Angelo (2002) suggested that frames are used to signal how the news media intends stories to be interpreted. Media scholars have used frames in three distinct ways: (1) a cognitive use of frames, which captures the negotiation of meaning between a news text and an individual's tacit knowledge; (2) a critical use of frames, which analyzes the way in which stories are used to reflect dominant class interests; and (3) a constructionist use of frames, which views news as a way of constructing social reality. (See also D'Angelo & Kuypers, 2010, on news framing.) I will primarily use frames in the cognitive and constructionist use, reflecting the basic processes of how texts interact with an individual's tacit knowledge in making sense of ongoing events.

This brief overview of frames demonstrates the usefulness of frames as a conceptual tool for analyzing communication.[1] Throughout this book, I will be using frames to represent knowledge, to reflect contexts for communicating and organizing, and to signal intended meanings in texts. Thus frames have multiple functions and operate on varying cognitive levels. We also need to note that frames are not neutral in the sense that they always reflect a particular point of view, which may conflict with the frames of others. Next, we turn to a more specific discussion of frames as applied to understanding communicating and organizing.

Frames in Communicating and Organizing

Frames may be used to represent the conceptual, cognitive context in which organizing and communicating occurs. As such, frames incorporate pre-existing, shared knowledge about events, objects and activities that people use to make sense of their experience. Hodgson (2007) argued that individuals require a "cognitive frame to process and make sense of ... information. The acquisition of this cognitive apparatus involves processes of socialization and education, involving extensive interaction with others" (p. 98). Our sociocultural knowledge frames our experiences into distinctive contexts, which, in turn, help participants interpret what is going on. As Ross (1981) observed, frames are "structures of expectations" that organize our knowledge of the world, and form the basis for our predictions about future actions, events and relationships. Frames are dynamic, active and continuously being constructed and altered by our interactions with others.

Gumperz (1992a, 2001) suggested that frames—as implicit sociocultural knowledge—help participants draw appropriate inferences, and signal what is meant by what is said. Frames represent participants' shared presuppositions and tacit knowledge, which they

---

1 For a more complete overview of framing and its use in the humanities and social sciences, see Benford and Snow, 2000; Entman, 1993; Goffman, 1974; Koenig, 2006; Tannen, 1981; Tannen and Wallat, 1987; and Shank and Abelson, 1977. A more complete overview is beyond the scope of this book, but frames have been used in consistent ways to represent social knowledge, signal the intended meaning in a message, to establish the context for on-going activity, and to reflect overall themes in texts.

apply in any relevant situation: However, these presuppositions and tacit knowledge are activated as well as altered by interactions with others. Thus, both the social context and the interaction itself mutually establish the appropriate meanings for activities and events in a given instance. As Levinson (1983) observed, the text is integrated with the knowledge base (context) to produce meaning. Thus frames are always ambiguous and provisional, allowing flexibility in the flow of interaction to alter and/or reconfirm ongoing interpretations.

Such frames of interpretation rely heavily on shared, tacit knowledge of the participants. As Goffman (1964, quoted in Lemert & Branaman, 1997) pointed out:

> At the very center of interaction life is the cognitive relation we have with those present before us, without which relationship our activity, behavioral and verbal, could not be meaningfully organized. And although this cognitive relationship can be modified during a social contact, and typically is, the relationship itself is extrasituational, consisting of the information a pair of persons have about the information each other has of the world, and the information they have (or haven't) concerning the possession of this information.
> *(Lemert & Branaman, 1997, pp. 239–40)*

Thus, the interaction order is "predicated on a large base of shared cognitive presuppositions, if not normative ones, and self-sustained restraints" (Goffmann, 1964, as quoted in Lemert & Branaman, 1997, p. 240).

Gioia and Poole (1984) integrated frames with scripts in organizing. Both are cognitive structures, closely related to categorization (Rosch, 1978) and prototyping (Cantor, Mischel, & Schwartz, 1982), which enable individuals to process social information. Comparing frames and scripts "can be linked to a comparison of a 'snapshot' of a situation and a 'motion picture' depicting the dynamic events of the situation" (p. 457). Gioia (1986) further noted that frames are like a "built-up repertoire of tacit knowledge that is used to impose structure upon, and import meaning to, otherwise ambiguous social and situational information to facilitate understanding" (p. 56). Frames thus incorporate knowledge and behaviors associated with particular scripts.

Gail Fairhurst (Fairhurst & Grant, 2010a) utilizes the concept of framing as a way of understanding leadership and leadership behavior. She notes that there are a variety of ways in which frames have been used but they all share "the casting of framing as both a cognitive device and a communicative activity defined by selection, emphasis, interpretation, and exclusion" (Fairhurst, 2005, p. 167). Fairhurst encourages managers to reframe using the power of language, thought and forethought and contrasts how different styles of message design logics influence the use of framing strategies. Her two books, *The Art of Framing* (Fairhurst & Sarr, 1996) and *The Power of Framing* (Fairhurst, in press, b), apply framing specifically to leadership and management.

Frames also serve as implicit guidelines that organize and influence meanings for organizational activities (Fairhurst & Sarr, 1996; Giddens, 1984; Orlikowski & Gash, 1994; Weick, 1990, 2001). Frames include "assumptions, knowledge, and expectations, expressed symbolically through language, visual images, metaphors, and stories. Frames are flexible in structure and content, having variable dimensions that shift in salience and content by context and over time. They are structured more as webs of meanings than as linear, ordered graphs" (Orlikowski & Gash, 1994, p. 176). Frames not only enable interpretation (in ambiguous situations), but also constrain interpretation (as when a frame is unreflectively applied in a new context).

Groups have also been identified as having shared frames or scripts (i.e., the concept of collective mind; see, for example, Cooren, 2006a; Hutchins, 1995; McPhee, Myers, & Trethewey, 2006; Weick & Roberts, 1993). Research on social cognition supports the idea that "people tend to share assumptions, knowledge and expectations with others with whom they have close working relationships. Likewise, social interaction and negotiation over time create opportunities for the development and exchange of similar points of view" (Orlikowski & Gash, 1994, p. 177). Because different groups are also exposed to differing concepts, beliefs and meanings, differences in frames across different groups and within a given work group may also exist (Daft & Lengel, 1984; Hepburn & Wiggins, 2007; Schein, 2004). Although "frames are individually held, and hence inevitably reflect individual variation, it is nonetheless useful to distinguish those cognitive elements that—through socialization, interaction, or negotiation—individuals have in common. It is these collective cognitive elements that individuals draw on to construct and reconstruct their social reality" (Orlikowski & Gash, 1994, pp. 177–78).

Some empirical studies of frames. Tannen and Wallat (1987) argued that frames, schema, scripts and other similar concepts can be viewed as "structures of expectations" and reflect "interactive frames of interpretation." In their analysis of a pediatric interaction, they found mismatches in the frames for both health and cerebral palsy that contributed to interactional difficulties in talk between the mother and pediatrician. Their use of Goffman's concept of footing also illuminated the ways in which the pediatrician and mother aligned with one another.

In the context of emergency 911 calls, Tracy (1997b) found conflicting frames from the callers (who reflected a customer orientation) and emergency calltakers (who assumed a public service frame). Such differences created different expectations about the type and speed of service that could be provided.

Using situated cognition ("the interaction of cognitive schemas and organizational context"), Elsbach, Barr and Hargadon (2005) reviewed empirical case studies of organizations in order to examine situated cognition more closely. On the basis of their review of organizational case studies, they argue that existing schemas (rules, self and event schemas) interact with organizational contexts (institutional/cultural, artifacts, physical and socio-dynamic contexts) to create momentary situated cognitions. These situated cognitions may involve judgments about (1) option attractiveness—the desirability of a given choice; (2) distinctiveness of self-perceptions—perceptions of one's expertise and skills; (3) problem understanding—key variables, causal relationships; and (4) collectivist mindset—openness to collective vs. individual thinking (p. 425).

They found common patterns of interaction across cognition and context. For example, event schemas and institutional norms interacted to create situated cognitions about option attractiveness. And rule schemas interacted with the physical setting to influence how problems were solved (i.e., problems that arose, timing, evaluation criteria). They concluded that such situated cognitions are important in group practices and decision-making. More importantly, situated cognition suggests that "organizations learn by developing stable schemas or knowledge structures at the collective level by accumulating similar experiences in similar situations over time. It also centers attention on the content or outcomes of cognitive processes, not the cognitive processes themselves" (p. 431).

These processes may work across industries as well. Nadkarni and Narayanan (2007) applied collective mind (a frame concept) to an industry and found that the "cognitive construction of industry velocity" by firms helped shaped industry changes over a 20-year period. Social networks and collective assumptions helped shape collective strategy frames as well as aggregate actions (p. 690). Such a framework blends context and cognition, as I do in the present book, and also incorporates the physical and material context which has become increasingly recognized as an important component of both organizing and communicating (Goffman, 1974; Latour, 1996, 2005).

Frames have also been used to explain how organizational members respond to and use new technology (Orlikowski & Gash, 1994). They concur with Weick that "cognition and micro-level processes are keys to understanding the organizational impact of new technologies" (Orlikowski & Gash, 1994, p. 175) and go on to develop the concept of technological frames. Technological frames:

> are the understanding that members of a social group come to have of particular technological artifacts, and they include not only knowledge about the particular technology but also local understanding of specific uses in a given setting. This contextual dimension of frames is one we wish to preserve in our treatment of technological frames, as it is particularly significant.
>
> *(Orlikowski & Gash, 1994, p. 178)*

Their field study uncovered significant differences across two organizational groups, the technologists and users, in their technological frames. Three domains of technological frames were found—the nature of technology; technology strategy (the motivation or vision behind the adoption); and technology in use (the actual conditions of use). They found that technologists and users had differing expectations across these domains and this resulted in misaligned expectations, contradictory actions (i.e., technologists installing and operating a technology while users wait for training) and unanticipated consequences (i.e., spotty adoption).

As we have seen, frames have been used for analysis on multiple levels. In a study looking at cultural frames, Koenig (2006) argued that frames have been viewed as both intentional (Entman, 1993) as well as tacit (Goffman, 1974). He focused on uncovering tacit frames, and used a cross-national method of analysis to discover them. Koenig noted that frames are influenced by a *"discursive opportunity structure, which varies systematically by country"* (p. 62). Three master frames (content frames that incorporate high cultural resonances) were found: (1) the ethno-nationalist frame, based on ontological groups categorized by ascriptive criteria such as religion; (2) the liberal-individualist citizenship frame, based on the assumption of individual freedom and equality of all people with regard to the state; and (3) the harmony with nature frame, based on valuing nature intrinsically. A study by Gannon, Locke, Gupta, Audia and Kristof-Brown (2005) explored cultural metaphors or frames that served as a major point of reference for different cultures and their emotional and cognitive values. A key feature in identifying frames is that frames are represented in identifiable conceptual categories. (See also Sewell, 2010.)

In summary, frames have been widely used and applied at multiple levels of analysis. Generally, frames have been used to characterize tacit, background knowledge; to represent stereotypical situations; to identify contexts of varying scopes; to signal intended meaning; and to shape communicative content. Thus frames are essential in processing information and sensemaking, and thus impose structure and meaning in everyday interaction. Frames are both created by and altered by social interaction. Misunderstandings that arise through different frames may create conflict as well as new opportunities for growth. Scripts, as frames that incorporate action and behavior, also guide social practices and activities.

With this general overview in mind, we now turn to examine Goffman's use of frames and framing. Frames form a major part of Goffman's interaction order, and he utilizes frames on the individual, group and institutional level (although his work on institutions is less well known).

Frames and Framing: Goffman's Approach

Frames and framing, as developed by both Goffman (1974, 1981a) and Bateson (1972, 1976), reflect very important aspects of communication. As Goffman noted:

> My aim is to isolate some of the basic frameworks of understanding available in our society for making sense out of events and to analyze the special vulnerabilities to which these frames of reference are subject. ...
>
> And of course much use will be made of Bateson's use of the term "frame." I assume that definitions of a situation are built up in accordance with principles of organization which govern events—at least social ones— and our subjective involvement in them; frame is the word I use to refer to such of these basic elements. ...
>
> *(Goffman, 1974, pp. 10–11)*

Goffman's use of frame incorporates defining and altering contexts. As Goffman notes, a frame of interpretation is a routine, taken-for-granted projection.

> In sum, observers actively project their frames of reference into the world immediately around them, and one fails to see their so doing only because

events ordinarily confirm these projections, causing the assumptions to disappear into the smooth flow of activity.

(Goffman, 1974, p. 39)

These disappearing presuppositions capture the subtlety and power of frames as tacit knowledge.

In contrast, Bateson's use of frame refers to the way in which ongoing action in a situation was to be understood (i.e., signaled as playful or serious, or mock fighting as compared to an intentional attack) (Bateson, 1972). Bateson's signaling was taken up by Goffman in his discussions of what is "really" going on an encounter, and to illuminate issues such as fabrications and deceit (Goffman, 1974). As a way of gaining insight into our underlying presuppositions about routine interaction, Goffman also studied behavioral deviations in which frames were breached (see, for example, his work on mental illness in *Stigma* [Goffman, 1963b] and *Asylums* [Goffman, 1961a]).

Altering frames. Frames, of course, may be transformed, contested, not fully followed, and the like (Goffman, 1974). Keying refers to the "conventions by which a given activity is transformed into something patterned on this activity but seen as something quite different" (Goffman, 1974, p. 43). For example, the meaningful frame of a friendly kiss of greeting between two acquaintances is keyed into a sexual exchange by prolonging the kiss. It is important to note that the initial frame underlies the subsequent keying—the already meaningful frame is openly known, and cues had been given as to how to interpret ongoing action. From that meaningful base, keying and rekeying adds another layer of interpretation or lamination to the ongoing interaction.

Although the ways to key and rekey would appear to be unlimited, Goffman, in fact, suggests that there are five basic mechanisms for keying/rekeying: *make-believe*; *contests*; *ceremonials*; *technical redoings* (i.e., practicing an activity to improve one's performance); and *regroundings* (i.e., when work is performed, but with different motivations than usual, as in, for example, when a member of England's royal family sells nylons at a charity function) (Goffman, 1974, p. 74). Keying also varies in the extent to which the frame is transformed or recast.

Another way to recast frames is by fabrication. Fabrication is an intentional effort to induce a false belief about what is going on, such as in hoaxes or lying (Goffman, 1974). The intent is to have some participants accept the reality of a meaningful frame, while other participants know there is something else going on—as in, for example, when a practical joke is being played. Frames thus facilitate fluid, routine interaction as well as allow for fabrication and deception.

Goffman's aim, then, is to attempt to explain the underlying frames that enable fluid, routine encounters:

It has been argued that a strip of activity will be perceived by its participants in terms of the rules or premises of a primary framework, whether social or natural, and that activity so perceived provides the model for two basic kinds of transformation—keying and fabrication. It has also been argued that these frameworks are not merely a matter of mind but correspond in some sense to the way in which an aspect of the activity itself is organized—especially activity directly involving social agents. Organizational premises are involved, and these are something cognition somehow arrives at, not something cognition creates or generates. Given their understanding of what it is that is going on, individuals fit their actions to this understanding and ordinarily find that the ongoing world supports this fitting. These organizational premises—sustained in both the mind and in activity—I call the frame of activity.

(Goffman, 1974, p. 247)

As we have seen, a multiplicity of possible frames, and the use of multiple frames within and across encounters, are clearly incorporated into Goffman's work. In addition, frames are used to characterize activities as social practices as well as include material objects. For Goffman, frames are the "essential organizing devices for the performance of social action" (Brown, 2000, p. 40). Goffman also pointed out that these frames are merely in the mind, but also found in social activity.

Because Goffman's interaction order is the basis for interaction in Giddens' structuration theory, frames are implicated in Giddens' work. An actor's knowledge, discursive and practical consciousness, and the like, reflect frames as developed by Goffman. One could argue that the interactional dimensions of signification, domination and moral sanctions are frames for different aspects of interaction. They also frame different types of institutions. As such, frames provide a powerful analytic and applied tool for understanding social interaction and social life. In addition, these frames may reflect different contextual levels (Goffman's layering or lamination) that build upon one another. While Goffman acknowledges larger institutional forces, and closely analyzes them in some cases (i.e., total institutions), it is not a focal point in his theorizing.

My argument is that these overarching frames of organizing (like organizations and institutions as articulated in Giddens' structuration theory) influence the communicative processes within each organizing context. These interactions, in turn, may reproduce or recast the overarching organizing frame. In other words, I advocate a position very similar to Gidden's structuration. In my synthesis, the theory of structurational interaction, Goffman's interaction order is extended to institutional settings and, with respect to Giddens' work, I emphasize its reliance on the interaction order and more fully develop it as part of structuration. Through structurational interaction, the fundamental linkages between communicating and organizing can be more fully developed. This theoretical synthesis also provides an integrated, coherent perspective that permits a greater depth and breadth of analysis. In this manner, I extend both Goffman's and Giddens' work. I may utilize their work in ways that they would not, although I believe my integration of their work is consistent with their fundamental approaches.

Thus, frame theory provides a very rich, multi-level and multi-faceted approach to communicating and organizing. As such, frames are able to capture the complexity of organizing and communicating processes. Frames are conceptualized on an intermediate level of analysis, and can become more abstract and macro in orientation. Or, conversely, frames can move to a more micro-level of analysis, such as a question and answer sequence. In what follows, I will extend frame analysis to incorporate more macro- as well as micro-levels of analysis.

Lamination or Layering of Frames

Goffman's concept of lamination—that frames can be layered within or upon one another—reflects the fact that different contexts of understanding and interpretation can be present within a single encounter. As such, frames may vary in scope, abstractness and detail.

Metaframes. First, on a metatheoretical level, at the most abstract macro-level, *metaframes* reflect our human knowledge and thinking about the nature of life itself. For example, they reflect beliefs about animate versus inanimate objects, the nature of the physical world, and the relationship between mind and body. Some aspects of this knowledge reflect universal experiences, such as our experience in the physical world (i.e., humans die without food and water). Other aspects, such as beliefs about animacy, may vary across cultures (i.e., some cultures treat rocks and trees as animate objects).[2] In general, this level would be similar to Goffman's use of primary social or physical frameworks.

Frame systems. Immediately below metaframes, at a less abstract level, we use *frame systems* to represent a collection of related frames that have important shared thematic representations. For example, one's frame system of organizing could be viewed as a conceptual map that represents our general knowledge about organizing. Other examples of frame systems might be kinship frame systems (reflecting how cultures view familiar ties and relationships); religious frame systems (reflecting beliefs concerning deities, human existence and a potential afterlife); or legal frame systems (reflecting judicial practices and beliefs about human rights and obligations). Such frame systems represent a way in which a particular social group, like North Americans or the Chinese, might categorize their cultural beliefs and assumptions. Each frame system is comprised of major belief systems, which reflect concepts about how groups or societies organize themselves socially around important lifestyle issues.

As Goffman cogently noted:

> Say that there is in any given culture a limited conceptual resource for defining situations differently, a limited set of basic reinterpretation schema (each, of course, realized in an infinite number of ways), such that the whole set is potentially applicable to the "same" event. Assume, too, that these fundamental frameworks themselves form a framework—a framework of frameworks. Starting, then, from a single event in our own culture, in this case, an utterance,

---

2 For our purposes, the macro-level of analysis, metaframes, will not be of particular interest. This level was briefly outlined here to demonstrate the utility of frame theory on multiple levels of analysis.

we ought to be able to show that a multitude of meanings are possible, that these fall into distinct classes limited in number, and that the classes are different from each other in ways that might appear as fundamental, somehow providing not merely an endless catalogue but an entrée to the structure of experience.

(Goffman, 1976, p. 306)

This underscores the cognitive underpinnings of Goffman's work, and his use of frames to identify contexts that help people understand one another, and to achieve some degree of intersubjective understanding.

Although Goffman did discuss primary frameworks (similar to my use of frame systems), he did not develop them extensively. He refers to primary frameworks as an element of culture, and to a "framework of frameworks" as a culture's belief system (Goffman, 1974, p. 27). A framework of frameworks would incorporate metaframes (universal) as well as frame systems (culturally based, like kinship systems). These core beliefs may differ across individuals, and changing such core beliefs is very difficult, especially since many are tacit, taken-for-granted beliefs.

One specific frame system, an *organizing frame system*, I argue, represents how groups manage their institutional practices and customs. For example, every organization faces issues around survival, integration and adaptation (Schein, 2004). But groups may follow different social practices in confronting these issues. While an organizing frame system reflects these universal challenges (like survival), distinct organizing frames (such as Bolman and Deal's symbolic or political frame) may respond to these challenges in different ways. These frames reflect an intermediate (meso) level of analysis, and are a frequently used entry point for organizational analysis. (Because our focus here is on organizing and communicating, our illustrations will reflect those contexts. However, similar analyses on frame systems and frames could be undertaken within any frame system. For example, a religious frame system might incorporate distinct frames such as Judaism and Catholicism.)

Frames. Thus, multiple frames may be present within an overarching organizing frame system: each frame emphasizes particular aspects of organizing. Each distinctive frame, while sharing some features with an overarching organizing frame system—our sociocognitive knowledge of organizing—will emphasize some features of organizing, and de-emphasize other features. For example, a *political frame* for organizing focuses on competing interests and conflict in organizations while a *cultural frame* focuses on shared values and symbols that may unify organizational members (Bolman & Deal, 2008; also see Morgan, 2006, for different metaphors for organizing and organizations).

As we have seen, each frame emphasizes some communicative and organizing processes, while ignoring others. However, within each conceptual frame, communicating and organizing processes co-produce one another. As Putnam, Phillips and Chapman point out, "all organizational theories contain implicit notions about communication, and all communication theories, in turn, provide important insights about organizing" (1996, p. 396). For example, in the symbolic frame briefly

TABLE 1.1   A Model of Frame Analysis*

Most Abstract
MACRO

Metaframes—global organizing categories that reflect human knowledge and thinking about life (e.g., natural world, social world, etc.)

Frame Systems—a collection of related frames that have important shared thematic representations (e.g., kinship frame systems, legal frame systems, religious frame systems, organizing frame systems, etc.)

Frames—reflects knowledge and expectations about a given social situation; represents knowledge about contexts, and appropriate (expected) actions and meanings within that context

Framing—communicative practices applied by participants in an encounter within a given social context

MICRO
Most Specific

---

* I will be using these different levels of frame analysis to analyze organizing and communicating. Each level is embedded within the next, more abstract level; that is, framing occurs within a given frame; a given frame is embedded within a given frame system. For our purposes, the metaframe level will not be used.

---

introduced above, communicative processes would highlight values, symbols and rituals that create a strong organizational culture (Schein, 2004).

The interrelationships being developed can be diagrammed as shown in Table 1.1.

The overarching frame systems of organizing and of communicating reflect our general conceptual expectations about organizing and communicating. For example, our frame systems about organizing might include expectations about power, hierarchy, interdependence and people. Our frame systems about communicating might include expectations that communication is intentional, structured, occurs between at least two people, and conveys information as well as emotions.

Note that frame systems, as represented here, reflect some expectations that transcend cultures. For example, in any culture, organizing will be conceptualized as involving power and people, and communicating will be conceptualized as an intentional and structured activity. However, how power and communication are enacted in a given situation will be culturally specific. For example, power relations in the US might be informal, whereas in Japan power relations might be marked by formality. Much more comparative cultural analysis will be needed before making definitive statements about the universality of features of frame systems.

Within each particular organizing frame, such as a human resources frame or a political frame, some aspects of our frame systems of organizing and communicating will be emphasized, and others de-emphasized. What a frame may exclude is probably as important as what it may include. Each frame draws *relevant* sociocultural knowledge from the overarching frame systems of communicating and organizing. For example, a *political frame* would draw upon knowledge and expectations about conflict of interest and negotiation (as cognitive expectations contained within the frame system of organizing), whereas a *human relations frame* would activate knowledge about workers, their characteristics and relationships, as the most relevant and critical aspects of knowledge in that frame. Each frame thus highlights and makes salient certain features, and guides one's interpretation of ongoing events (Entman, 1993; Haslett, 1987).

Thus, in summary, frames can be conceptualized on multiple levels, representing knowledge at both the macro- and micro-levels. At the most abstract level, *metaframes* reflect our cultural knowledge and traditions as well as fundamental assumptions about the nature of life. At the next level, *frame systems*, knowledge coalesces around related themes, such as organizing, communicating, worshipping, and so forth. At the least abstract level, *frames* represent specific approaches to organizing and communicating; as such, these frames represent the contexts in which communicating and organizing mutually co-occur and shape one another.

At the most concrete, interactional level, participants rely on the specific context and their interactions to make sense of ongoing organizing and communicating. For example, given that participants are utilizing a political frame, an argument between two managers may be viewed as a power struggle for control over a particular activity. From a human relations frame, that same argument may be viewed as a personality conflict between managers. It is important to note that, within our framework of expectations and tacit knowledge at a given time, we seek to make sense of activities and events going on around us. Each frame offers alternative interpretations and thus different meanings for events; each frame provides a relevant, valid interpretation of ongoing events, but not necessarily the only valid interpretation. In fact, one could argue that multiple frames are needed to make sense of the complexity and evolution of organizing and communicating: That is the approach being developed here. However, in any specific instance of interaction, participants are seeking the most plausible interpretation of events, signaled by the specific frame activated in the immediate social context and confirmed or disconfirmed by the evolving text (what is being said).

Framing. It is at the most concrete level of analysis, when examining specific interactions, that *framing* reflects particular text features which signal the communicator's intended meaning (Goffman, 1974). Here Goffman's work makes important contributions to understanding communicative processes. He outlines specific devices, such as nonverbal cues or textual features (i.e., naming practices, formulaic expressions), that signal what is *meant* by what is *spoken* or *written*. It is at the level of framing that interactants align themselves with one another in order to accomplish goals within a given organizational frame. Frames reflect background knowledge, physical and semiotic resources of understanding, and the different social memberships being claimed by an actor. Finally, framing devices also bracket episodes within a performance, such as a teacher giving directions and answering questions within a lecture.

As we have seen, at the most abstract level, *metaframes* represent our basic world knowledge as well as our cultural values and experiences. Within a given, culturally shared metaframe, our *frame systems* of organizing and communicating are very general, taken-for-granted expectations, derived from our experiences and cultural knowledge. These frame systems reflect our cognitive representations of knowledge needed to conduct our lives, within our physical, mental and social worlds. It thus encompasses what has been called world knowledge, and our frame systems help categorize and integrate that knowledge in meaningful ways.

The next level of knowledge representation is more specific, in which *frames* represent particular expectations and assumptions about organizing and communicating in a specified manner, highlighting relevant features of that frame and ignoring other aspects. Within each frame, framing devices signal both the appropriate social context and how the text (interaction) is to be interpreted within that context. Only the most relevant, activated knowledge, signaled by various framing devices, is used to develop meaningful interpretations in our interactions. Note, however, that receivers may ignore or misunderstand intended meanings, and that communicators also may be ambiguous in their messages.

As noted previously, both Goffman's interaction order and Giddens' structuration theory use frames in their theories. Thus frame theory provides a basis for synthesizing their work, and also their interconnections, which goes beyond the use of Goffman's interaction order in structuration theory. Frames not only conceptualize their ideas, but also allow for multiple points of entry and multiple layers of context for analysis. Frames also move between contextual levels, from very abstract levels of analysis (such as metaframes) to very specific interactional moves in a given context (such as alignment or repair moves). In addition, frames provide a very useful way to represent communities of knowledge and social practices that develop and sustain organizations and societies. Thus, the synthesis of Goffman and Giddens, through frame theory, provides a very rich, powerful perspective from which to explore organizing, communicating and their interrelationships. And does so in a manner that reflects the dynamic, continuously changing interrelationships between communicating and organizing.

In subsequent chapters, I will use frame theory to conceptualize both communicating and organizing. Our frame systems for organizing and communicating represent generic expectations about both; as such, these frame systems are prototypical expectations. For example, our frame system of communicating might include ideas about communication occurring on the verbal and nonverbal dimensions, and that communication is intentional. Our frame system of organizing might incorporate the ideas of specialization and interdependence. In other words, frame systems incorporate our most tacit, fundamental expectations about communicating and organizing. When we discuss cross cultural communication or globalized organizing, we should keep in mind that some expectations about communicating and organizing are shared across cultures, while other expectations are not shared.

With this general overview in mind, I turn to a more detailed discussion of our frame systems of communicating and organizing in Chapters 2 and 3. These frame systems reflect our tacit, taken-for-granted ideas about communicating and organizing.

Put another way, these frame systems represent our generic, commonsense knowledge of organizing and communicating. If we are to integrate the processes of communicating and organizing, we need to have a clear conceptualization of what is meant by communicating and organizing, Finally, in Chapter 4, I will discuss some current alternative approaches to organizational communication, especially those views on communication-as-constitutive-of-organizations.

2

A FRAME SYSTEM FOR COMMUNICATING

Based upon the frame theory outlined in Chapter 1, we now turn to developing a frame system of communication, representing the underlying assumptions we bring to bear when interacting with others. But how these assumptions are enacted in any situation will reflect the cultural values of the participants, as well as the context(s) of interaction. As mentioned previously, it is important to fully articulate our models and assumptions about communicating and organizing in order to fully appreciate their synthesis in our integration of Goffman and Giddens.

Individuals bring prior knowledge and experience to every interaction. During interaction, individuals draw upon the knowledge and experience *relevant* to that given encounter. The conversations in a particular interaction signal participants' goals, and provide the basis for further interaction. In what follows, we will discuss these processes in more detail. But before we begin, a very brief historical overview of communication studies will be useful for clarifying the different strands of research surveyed in this book.

A Very Brief Historical Overview

Language, the symbolic code underlying human verbal communication, has been analyzed on syntactic, semantic and pragmatic dimensions (Gumperz, 2001; Van Dijk, 1997a, b, c). Traditional linguistic analysis has tended to assess the syntax (structural) and semantic (meaning) levels of language, while remaining largely uninterested in pragmatics (considered the "error" dimension, because it addresses how people *use language in context*). However, as Haslett (1987) noted, "the inability of transformational grammars models to deal adequately with the extra-linguistic context of utterances, anaphoric and definite reference, pronominalization, elliptical comments, and presuppositions became clear" (p. 5), and thus scholars moved beyond the grammatical level to focus on language use in interaction. In addition, scholars became interested in studying communicative processes, or connected utterances, as opposed to the traditional linguistic analyses of single sentences.

Over the past four decades, research on pragmatics, or communicative processes, has exploded and became a significant research trend in communication, sociology, psychology, and related disciplines such as business, education and management. I will use the term "discourse" as synonymous with interaction or communication, and the term "text" to refer primarily to symbolic, relatively permanent inscribed messages, such as memos, organizational constitutions, letters and minutes of meetings (see McPhee's 2004b discussion of texts). I do not, for example, regard memory of conversations as "text," as these memories are not permanently inscribed—however, stories about organizational life, routinely transmitted and shared over time, would constitute "texts" in the sense of expressing the culture of an organization and/or sets of beliefs about that organization.

Cicourel (1980) outlined three general models of language use that were emerging: the speech act model, the expansion model and the information processing model. Speech act models (such as Cooren, 2006b, c; Cooren & Fairhurst, 2004; and Searle, 1995) focus on an utterance's locutionary and illocutionary effect, but do not take account of the multiple meanings of utterances or indirect utterances. Expansionist models focus on the use of an utterance in context and its relationship to culture and nonverbal dimensions of meaning. Information processing models incorporate cognitive schemata in interpreting utterances; these models incorporate frames, scripts and other aspects of participants' commonsense knowledge.

Although Cicourel (1980) and Van Dijk (1981) argued that all these dimensions should be incorporated into an analysis of communication, most approaches focus upon a single dimension. Genres of communication or discourse include different types of texts, such as narratives (Czarniawska, 1997) or memos (Orlikowski & Yates, 1998) and have broadened speech act analysis to incorporate larger, more diverse units of discourse. Expansionist models include perspectives such as the ethnography of speaking (Hymes, 1972), Gumperz' contextualization cues (1992a; Gumperz & Hymes, 1972), sociolinguistic analyses (Bernstein, 1977; Scollon & Scollon, 2001), and other models that focus on contextual and cultural factors influencing discourse. Finally, information processing models have used frame analysis (Goffman, 1974), scripts and schemata to incorporate commonsense knowledge, and actors' knowledge of context in interpreting discourse (as discussed in Chapter 1). (See Alvesson & Karreman, 2000a, b; Fairhurst, 2004; Jian, Schmisseur & Fairhurst, 2008; and Tracy, 2001, for excellent discussions of different approaches to discourse analysis and how discourse analysis may focus on language itself, language use, or the production of text.)

More recently, differing levels of context have also been part of discourse or interactional analysis. Different approaches vary in scope when applied to organizing: (1) micro-discourse approaches focusing on a given context or encounter; (2) meso-level discourse assesses language in context but also goes beyond texts; (3) "grand discourse" focuses on ideologies and their influence on organizational frames (such as a set of related constructs in a given organizational culture); and (4) mega-discourses reflecting archetypes or cultural beliefs/values (Alvesson & Karreman, 2000b, p. 1133). Thus, communicative analyses have grown beyond single utterances to connected discourse, and to examine discourse in a variety of contexts and across varying knowledge domains (for example, incorporating "grand" discourse and mega-discourses).

Three fundamental principles underlie approaches to discourse (Potter & Edwards, 2001). First, discourse is the primary means through which actions are done, and interaction is coordinated—an "action" approach. But unlike speech act theory, which claims a one-to-one relationship between discrete acts and discrete verbs, these actions are embedded in broad social practices. Both Goffman and Giddens would agree with this focus on social practices and action. Second, discourse is grounded in three ways: sequentially, with uptake; institutionally, with situated identities and tasks that are relevant; and rhetorically, with descriptions that can be examined for how they counter "relevant alternative descriptions" (thus reflecting the monitoring of conversations). Again, both Giddens and Goffman incorporate uptake, situated identities and monitoring in their models of social interaction. Third, discourse is construction, both constructed and constructive. It is constructed from varied resources (words, categories, interpretive repertoires and so forth), and constructs different versions of the world, including different versions of actions, events, social structures, and organizations. Both Goffman and Giddens are congruent with these principles.

A somewhat different set of underlying assumptions, yet compatible with the principles outlined previously, has been developed by Alvesson and Karreman. As they note:

> the nature of language as context dependent, metaphorical, active, built upon repressed meanings, and capable of constituting "other" phenomena. They are all consistent with an understanding of language users as socially situated, discursively constituted, sensitive, and responsive to dominant cultural norms, social rules, and available scripts for talk, oriented toward the effects of language use.
> *(Alvesson and Karreman, 2000a, p. 154)*

These assumptions also underlie the synthesis of Giddens and Goffman being developed here.

Over the last four decades, research in these areas has expanded enormously, and enriched our understanding of communication and its complexity, yet failed to integrate these three aspects of discourse (as action, as situated and as contextual) in modeling human interaction. Most research is unidimensional, focusing on text, for example, or context, but not integrating them. In order to have a more adequate understanding of communicative processes, all three aspects need to be acknowledged. The communicative model developed in this book attempts to integrate these dimensions by recognizing the importance of context; acknowledging situated identity and its influence on communication; and articulating how communication accomplishes social action. As we shall see, the theory of structurational interaction incorporates all of these discourse dimensions and thus provides a powerful theoretical base for exploring communication.

Before proceeding to this synthesis, we need to articulate our model of communication and its underlying assumptions. It is to this task we now turn.

A Frame System of Communicating

A Working Definition of Communication

One of the best working definitions of communication was developed by noted nonverbal communication scholar, Albert Scheflen. Scheflen (1972) views communication as an organized, standardized, culturally patterned system of behavior that sustains, regulates and makes possible human relationships. Several important underlying assumptions are presupposed by this definition. First, communication is a shared activity that enables human relationships to be established and maintained. Second, communication occurs both verbally and nonverbally. Language is the symbolic code that underlies human verbal communication. Nonverbal communication, especially prosody, intonation and eye gaze, plays a central role in interpreting interaction (Duncan & Fiske, 1977; Gumperz, 1992a; Izard, 2009; Izard, Stark, Trentacosta & Schultz, 2008). Third, communication is structured and sequenced. For example, conversations are sequenced by initial greetings, an exchange of information and leave-taking. Finally, patterns of communication vary across cultures and within cultures (i.e., varying as a function of age, class, ethnicity). He concluded that we can "think of communication as the mechanism of social organization" (Scheflen, 1972, p. 26). Similarly, Birdwhistell (1970) viewed communication as the process or dynamic aspect of social structure and as the behavioral aspect which enables interaction on multiple sensory levels (i.e., eye gaze, gesture, kinesics). Such views are very compatible with the views of both Goffman and Giddens on the centrality of communication—in everyday life and for social order generally.

Communication, then, is a societal process, with interdependent members and patterns of meaningful behavior which transcend the individual (Sigman, 1987). Communication

> is the active or dynamic aspect of social reality, although this does not mean that all persons having membership in a group share identical vantage points on social reality … the suggestion that communication and social reality are related is not intended to mean that individuals, at particular moments of interaction, *construct* or *create* social reality. Instead, social communication proposes that interactants' behavior serves to *recreate* and *invoke* the historically prior and continuing social reality.
>
> *(Sigman, 1987, p. 6)*

While analysts may focus on single interactional events or texts within an interaction, it is also important to note that semiotic codes and social contexts maintain information flow and operate across multiple contexts, time and space (Giddens, 1984, 1990a; Sigman, 1987). These semiotic codes include language, artifacts, nonverbal dimensions of communication and so forth.

Communication thus occurs on multiple levels and serves multiple functions. These functions may vary from the development and continuity of social relations to monitoring of the environment to the transmission of one's social heritage (Birdwhistell, 1970; Haslett, 1987). But understanding social contexts allows us to interpret what is going on in an interaction. Goffman takes a similar view, arguing that different layers or laminations of frames provide context for interaction (Goffman, 1974, 1983a, b). And both Giddens and Goffman argue that interpreting ongoing interaction relies on participants' tacit knowledge and understanding of the communicative context.

We also need to distinguish communication from information. Communication refers to intentional and goal-directed language use, whereas information is language that is "informative and may be interpreted regardless of its intention" (Ellis, 1999, p. 85). Thus, we may glean information from others, but also from the environment (like the changing colors of leaves to signal the beginning of fall) or from events (smoke from a fire) that are not intentional, but informative. Some types of information, such as data sets or meters registering heat and pressure, may be primarily informative yet somewhat intentional as well (i.e., such systems usually have a designed function or purpose for human use). Like intentionality itself, distinctions between communication and information may shade off into one another.

Thus far, we have developed a working definition of communication and noted several important features, such as its processual and intentional nature. Communication also serves multiple functions across varying contexts. In order to more fully understand the complexity of communication, we next turn to an analysis of major underlying assumptions of our communicative model. These assumptions articulate a position on some of the most current controversial issues in communication, such as intentionality and agency. Throughout our discussion, when relevant, Goffman's and Giddens' positions on these issues will be identified.

Tacit Assumptions Underlying a Frame System for Communicating

Underlying this working definition of communication is a set of tacit, taken-for-granted assumptions about communication which form our frame system for communication. We expect, and act upon, the knowledge that communication is:

- inferential
- intentional
- strategic
- transformative

- conventional
- jointly negotiated between speakers and hearers
- variable according to context
- dependent upon commonsense knowledge
- sequential
- accomplished in real time and space, although communication may be mediated, and alter time-space relationships
- systematic
- interpretive
- variable according to the participants' social relationships
- concerns face
- presumed to be relevant

Many of these underlying assumptions are interrelated. For example, our taken-for-granted commonsense knowledge frequently provides a basis for interferences and for interpretive procedures used in evaluating interaction. Taken together, these assumptions present a coherent perspective on communication. While not exhaustive, these shared assumptions are significant conceptual foundations for a frame system of communication. In what follows, each assumption is developed more in detail.

Inferences. In general, inferences can be viewed as the implicit meanings humans assign to objects and events. We derive these meaning on the basis of what is said (i.e., through presuppositions, conversational implications), on the basis of the context and on the basis of commonsense knowledge. Cicourel defines inferences as the "tacit ways in which we link information from different sources to create coherency and relevance in our speech acts and nonverbal and paralinguistic actions" (Cicourel, 1980, p. 117). Schiffrin (1994) noted that implicatures are inferences based upon the literal meanings of words and communicative principles in particular situations—interactants used them to make sense of the ongoing interaction. Grice (1975, 1989) refers to the interpretive, inferential nature of communication when he suggests that interactants construct arguments that support one interpretation over another by using conventional meanings, the Cooperative Principle, conversational maxims and contextual knowledge. Within organizations, some of these inferences will be gleaned from past organization practices, relationships with colleagues and the nature of the task being undertaken. Inferences thus form an important part of background, contextual information which participants use to make sense of ongoing interaction.

Intentionality. Most communication scholars agree that communication, as a social act, is inherently intentional (Berger & Bradac, 1982; Grice, 1975; Van Dijk, 1981). Grice (1975) views talking as an instance of purposive, rational behavior. While communication is commonly viewed as intentional, there is little agreement on how to conceptualize or measure intentionality. Implicit in any discussion of intentionality are unresolved questions such as the degree to which individuals consciously plan their communication, the degree of cognitive monitoring humans are capable of, the degree to which humans can accurately report their intentions, and the like. (See Searle, 1995, for interesting discussions on these issues.)

Three classic approaches to communicative intentionality have developed. One approach, taken by Searle (1983) and others, views communicative behavior as motivated by the need for social communion and cooperation. Our intentions, from birth, are driven by these basic social needs. Another approach views communicative intentions from the standpoint of social control. Here our communicative purposes are tied to issues of social control and influence, whether over our own behavior (Langer, 1983) or a relationship (Rusbult & Van Lange, 2003).

A third approach, taken by researchers in artificial intelligence, views intentionality as goal-seeking; when we act, we act to accomplish some goal. Douglas (1970), following in the tradition of Schutz and Husserl, argues that "it is primarily intentions at any time—our purposes at hand—that order human thought, that determine the relevance of information and ideas about the world and ourselves" (ibid., p. 26).

Parisi and Castelfranchi (1981) define a goal as a state that regulates an individual's behavior. Kellerman (1992) notes that communication is goal-directed both intrinsically (the process of symbolic exchanges) as well as extrinsically (the reason for the communicative exchange). In conversation, speakers and hearers must adopt at least one goal in common. At a minimum, their mutual goal may be merely to engage in a conversation with one another. Within organizations, subunits may have goals that undermine overarching goals of the organization and individuals may experience goal conflict in terms of their own personal needs and organizational demands (Morgan, 2006).

Although these approaches represent major avenues of exploring intentionality, alternative views have been developed. Sigman (1987) uses the term "invocation" as a "neutral term with regard to an actor's consciousness of his/her behavioral performance(s)" (p. 70). He points out that moments of consciousness and intentionality are only moments "regulated by the larger, continuous communication stream" (ibid.). Acts, and their relationships to each other and/or the broader contexts, thus account for meaningfulness. Because of partial awareness of intentionality and the importance of acts to larger communicative streams, intentionality and motivation are not critical in Sigman's communicative model. Morris, Menon and Ames (2008) also suggest that agents' actions and intentions may be construed differently as a function of culture—some cultures, for example, viewing intentionality in terms of individuals' intentions, while other cultures focus more on collective intentionality and action.

Ellis (1999) broadens the scope of intentionality. He argued that:

> Intentionality is an inner state that represents the speaker at the moment of expression and includes his or her goals, strategies, purposes, and affective states. Intentions are substantive in that they are infused with the ideas, content, and empirical knowledge that the speaker uses to navigate the world ...

When a hearer encounters a message, he or she must reason from behavior to intention because this is the essential procedure involved in capturing the meaning of an action.

(Ellis, 1999, p. 78)

1. *Giddens on intentionality.* In yet another alternative view, Giddens (1984, 1998) views intentionality from the standpoint of human agency—the capacity to act otherwise. In sharp contrast to other views, however, Giddens views agency/intentionality as a process which unfolds in both time and space (i.e., actions unfold over time and we orient ourselves spatially to ongoing interaction) (1998, pp. 90–91). Also, Giddens noted that intentionality or agency often needs to be completed by the responses/actions of others; thus, agency is fundamentally a process involving others, not just one's own actions. Giddens' views, in my opinion, are significant from a communicative perspective because he builds upon and incorporates others' responses. For Giddens, then, intentionality characterizes "an act which its perpetrator knows, or believes, will have a particular quality or outcome and where such knowledge is utilized by the author of the act to achieve this quality or outcome … we have to separate out the question of what an agent 'does' from what is 'intended' or the intentional aspects of what is done" (1984, p.10). He goes on to note that agency is *doing* as well as *the capacity to do otherwise*, and that agency has both intended and unintended consequences.

Additionally, for Giddens, the reflexive monitoring of behavior and the rationalization of one's actions are important components of intentionality. As Giddens (1984) points out:

> 'Reflexivity' hence should be understood not merely as 'self-consciousness' but as the monitored character of the ongoing flow of social life. To be a human being is to be a purposive agent, who both has reasons for his or her activities and is able, if asked, to elaborate discursively upon those reasons (including lying about them). But terms such as 'purpose' or 'intention', 'reason', 'motive' and so on have to be treated with caution … because they extricate human action from the contextuality of time-space. Human action occurs as a *duree*, a continuous flow of conduct, as does cognition, purposive action is not composed of an aggregate or series of separate intentions, reasons and motives. Thus it is useful to speak of reflexivity as grounded in the continuous monitoring of action which human beings display and expect others to display.

(Giddens, 1984, p. 3)

For Giddens, this reflexive monitoring evaluates action in context, and to account for actions is "the principal basis upon which the generalized 'competence' of actors is evaluated by others" (1984, p. 4). The competency of actors, acknowledged by others, is also a significant aspect of Goffman's interaction order. Thus, for Giddens, intentionality becomes akin to monitoring and rationalizing action in context and serves as a frame of interpretation for ongoing interaction. *The rationalization of action is intentionality viewed as a process.*

For Giddens, agents act strategically.

> 'Action' is not a combination of 'acts': 'acts' are constituted only by a discursive moment of attention to the *duree* of lived-through experience. Nor can 'action' be discussed in separation from the body, its mediations with the surrounding world and the coherence of an acting self. What I call a *stratification model* of the acting self involves treating the reflexive monitoring, rationalization and motivation of action as embedded sets of processes.
>
> *(Giddens, 1984, p. 3)*

Thus, for Giddens, intentionality is reflexive agency and a process which involves others' responses to acts and/or events.

2. *Shotter on intentionality.* John Shotter has written extensively on intentionality and developed a view of intentionality within the perspective of ecological psychology. Shotter argues, like Giddens, that action is informed by the context into which it is directed:

> the duality of structure ... when linked to the concept of intentionality ... explains how human action can, *in the course of its own performance,* provide itself with the conditions for its own continuation ... Due to its ability to produce in its wake, so to speak, a structured context for its own continuation, an action can be informed, not so much by factors present in the source from which it issues, as by the context *into* which it is directed.
>
> *(Shotter, 1997, pp. 78–79)*

Shotter incorporates both memory and time into his conceptualization of intentionality. He suggests that it is "memory—not as the process of 'retrieving' something 'stored', but as the process by which past specification is linked to current specifiability—which makes for intentionality, and gives a 'directionality' to mental activities" (1997, p. 90). The duality of structure is such that "the continuously produced *product* of the process is the ever-present *means* (the formative cause) of its continuation *as the process it is*" (ibid., p. 91). Thus, action and intentionality are grounded in a continuous flow of human activity—as Shotter comments, "in genuinely temporal processes, their structure is always becoming another structure" (ibid.).

Agency relies upon the duality of structure as well as upon memory because this produces a "line of intentionality into the future determining the *style* of what is to come" (ibid.). What is meant here is the shaping of future possibilities and potentialities—constraints as well as enablements, as Giddens would argue—rather than a strong determinism. Or, in Shotter's terms, a "vision of reality is implicit in a practice ... all mediators work both as enablements and as constraints" (ibid.).

Shotter's view is consistent with both Goffman's and Giddens' views of actors and agents.

> To be creatures of intelligence rather than instinct, agents must be able to project themselves into the future, to act not as their circumstances require, but as they themselves require … The actions of intelligent agents must continually be mediated by mental activity, activity which must link their present action both to its possible future consequences and their own past experience.
>
> … For human beings as persons, as socially autonomous members of a society … they have got to act, not just intelligently but also intelligibly and responsibly. … In other words, they have a *duty* to direct their conduct in such a way that it both makes sense to others and relates in some way with what, overall, others are trying to do in their lives.
>
> *(Shotter, 1997, pp. 95–96)*

In order to accomplish this, people must be knowledgeable about themselves and others, and their respective positions.

Major debates within organizational communication have surfaced around intentionality and agency from the work of Latour (1993, 1996, 2005) on actor network theory and Czarniawska (2004) on action nets. Both emphasize how action is accomplished and suggest that actors/actants form connections or associations that enable them to act and thus have effects (i.e., fishing for scallops, herding sheep). What is important to note is that agency—or the capacity to act—is extended to non-human entities. As Czarniawska (2004) commented:

> I understand action as a movement or an event, to which an intention can be attributed by relating the event to the social order in which it takes place. … The intentions are not a priori states but a posteriori interpretative attributions; indeed, it is appropriate to talk about the grammar and the rhetoric of motives, i.e. the scripts underlying such attributions … Such attributions can be made about any type of actant: a human, a machine, a tree. Similarly, the intentions can be taken away—disattributed—even from human actants (who then no longer act but "behave," "react," "move instinctively").
>
> *(p. 782)*

Thus, material objects, like documents, memos and so forth, are also accorded agency because they influence how agents (people) act and how actions may be carried out (i.e., computers programmed to perform specific functions). (This will be discussed in detail in subsequent chapters, but it is important to note this departure from other models of agency and/or intentionality.)

As can readily be seen, considerable controversy surrounds intentionality, its definition and its importance. For our purposes, varying degrees of awareness of intentionality may be acknowledged in terms of choosing message strategies. However, the meaning of acts must also be considered in view of larger contexts, and the importance of discursive and tacit knowledge recognized. While material objects may be involved in action, I, as do Goffman and Giddens, reserve agency and intentionality to humans in their capacity to "choose to act/do *otherwise.*" Emerging themes seem to be that intentionality involves action, is situated, may have intended and unintended effects, and is part of a stream of behavior. Intentionality also involves reflexive monitoring of actions. We would also be well advised to heed Edwards' caution:

> the point is to loosen up the status of communicative goals-and-intentions as an obvious basis for analysts' explanations of discourse, and to encourage instead an analytical stance in which such matters are, in the first instance, participants' business ... to take seriously the nature of talk-in-interaction, which means examining how meanings are interactionally accomplished.
> *(Edwards, 1997, p. 107)*

Strategic. Because communication is intentional, it is also strategic. Interactants pursue different aims and purposes beyond that of just being accessible to one another. It may be strategic, in fact, to avoid communicating with another in order to avoid conflict, to delay some action and so forth. Participants may also be strategically ambiguous for a variety of reasons.

Strategic communication also reflects planned sets of messages and/or events such as in a public relations campaign or advertising. Fabrication and deception may also play a part in strategic communication. Goffman, for example, discusses impression management and how to strategically manipulate impressions (Goffman, 1969b). And Giddens' discussion of political dialogue, and issues of trust and risk would seem to implicate strategic use of communication.

Transformative. Communication itself is a powerful force for transformation. Through interaction, participants may gain new information, may engage in conflict or may debate with others whose views differ from their own. All of these encounters open up the possibility for transformation. Dialogue is fundamentally transformative because we engage others and thus our own world views may be altered. Self-awareness may also be enhanced by interacting with others.

Self-help programs, such as Alcoholics Anonymous or Gamblers Anonymous, may be strategically transformative in the sense that interaction plays a pivotal role in confronting problems and addressing them. Education and counseling might also be considered strategically transformative in that the knowledge acquired may act to change the individual or group.

Conventional. Most interaction is more routinized than commonly realized. Underlying these interactional routines are conventional rules and stereotyped patterns of behavior. Heritage (1984) notes that utterances are interpreted in light of the normal, conventional patterns of interaction that operate in a given setting.

Communication behavior, then, can be viewed as conventional; guided by shared lexical meanings, shared commonsense knowledge and shared social rules of behavior. Within organizations, as Argyris and Schon (1996) noted, public declarations of policies (espoused theories) may differ from practices actually followed (theories-in-use). The use of rituals and social practices, emphasized by both Goffman and Giddens, also highlights the conventional aspects of interaction. (See also Jian, 2008, and Orlikowski, 2007, on social practices.)

Tacit, commonsense knowledge. Commonsense knowledge is complex and multi-layered: it represents different levels of abstraction, specificity and breadth (Garfinkel, 1962, 1967b; Haslett, 1987; Heritage, 1984; Van Dijk, 1981, 1997a, b; Van Dijk & Kintsch, 1983). As Schutz (1962) cogently argues:

> For we will find that the world of everyday life, the common-sense world, has a paramount position among the various provinces of reality, since only within it does communication with our fellow-men become possible. But the common-sense world is from the outset a sociocultural world, and the many questions connected with the intersubjectivity of the symbolic relations originate within it, are determined by it, and find their solution within it.
>
> *('Symbol, Reality, and Society,' Schutz, 1962,* Collected Papers, 1, *p. 294)*

How is such knowledge shared? Schutz (1962) discusses the "natural attitude" which reflects the degree to which external reality is taken-for-granted by members of a society. According to Schutz, commonsense knowledge reflects a reciprocity of perspectives that is established in two ways. First, the interchangeability of perspectives allows us—if we were in the same position as another individual—to experience what another had experienced for all practical purposes. (This appears to be similar to the Reality Principle, postulated by Clark and Clark, 1977, through which we acknowledge the sameness of our experiences in the physical world.) For both Goffman and Giddens the physical world is a primary framework that grounds all of our actions. After Schutz, Heritage (1984) also suggests that individuals can "know" one another in four distinct ways: as human beings, as members of the same culture, as specific persons and as specific persons now-in-this-immediate-situation.

Given the reciprocity of perspectives, Schutz (1967) suggests that participants appear to share knowledge reflecting typical motives, identities, actions and evaluations of their social group. During their lifetime, individuals will belong to many different social groups, such as their families, religious organizations, varying friendship groups, professional groups, sports groups groups at work and so forth. Despite the vagueness and imprecision of this knowledge, participants rely on it in planning and interpreting interactions and behaviors.

Second, Schutz suggested that participants share congruent systems of relevances; that is, irrespective of our unique individual experiences, "for all practical purposes" we interpret objects and events in a similar manner. Generally, for members of the same cultures, one can argue this to be the case; for example, deep-seated cultural values would reflect congruency in systems of relevances. The operating procedures of organizations, for example, reflect their shared systems of relevances, although organizational members may not believe or adhere to them to the same degree. However, for many interactions, especially those in which participants are members of different cultures or in which different group identities are an issue (see, for example, Gudykunst & Kim, 2003), this second assumption becomes highly problematic. Yet one effect of globalization may have been to expand the range of individuals who may share congruent systems of relevance (see Giddens & Piersen, 1998, and Zhao, 2004).

Thus, as Sharrock (1999) observed, "The 'world in common' is irreducibly a social world because it is known by way of socially distributed knowledge ... [it] is encountered in the form of 'the world of daily life'" (p. 127). As such, situational definitions have the following qualities: it is presupposed; transcends the immediate situation to incorporate a broader sense of everyday affairs; is created by predecessors and prior social activity, and is not solipsistic (pp. 127–28). This routine, mundane, taken-for-granted background knowledge enables everyday social order and interaction. Such knowledge is also multi-faceted, complex and continually being revised. This knowledge, in Goffman's view, reflects the "bona fide socially sanctioned facts of life" (Sharrock, 1999, p. 128). And as both Goffman and Giddens note, such knowledge allows us to negotiate everyday life with relative ease.

Giddens identified mutual knowledge as both discursive knowledge as well as a matter of "practical consciousness"—our knowledge of how to get along in the everyday world. He suggested that most mutual knowledge is "practical in character: it is inherent in the capability to 'go on' within the routines of social life. The line between discursive and practical consciousness is fluctuating and permeable, both in the experience of the individual agent and as regards comparisons between actors in different contexts of social activity" (Giddens, 1984, p. 4).

Giddens also highlighted the importance of actors' knowledgeability in social interaction and in the monitoring of social interaction. As he noted, "It is the specifically reflexive form of the knowledgeability of human agents that is most deeply involved in the recursive ordering of social practices"—in our particular case, the social practices that constitute human communication (Giddens, 1984, p. 3). Some of this knowledgeability may be discursive (capable of being expressed), while other knowledgeability consists of practical consciousness (knowledge of how to "get along" which is largely out of our awareness). But both are fundamental stocks of knowledge used in daily interaction and play a critical role in the production as well as interpretation of human interaction. (See also Oswick & Richards, 2004.)

These stocks of knowledge are the frames which conceptualize commonsense knowledge and everyday experience. For Giddens, interpretive schemes represent the core of the mutual knowledge by which meaning is sustained through interaction. Giddens also makes an analytic distinction between mutual knowledge and common sense—he uses common sense to refer to "the propositional beliefs implicated in the conduct of day-to-day activities ... that is to say, common sense is mutual knowledge treated not as knowledge but as fallible belief" (ibid., p. 337). Thus, some aspects of mutual knowledge may not be expressed discursively or as propositional beliefs.

Many scholars investigating communication acknowledge the fundamental importance of some degree of shared, tacit knowledge (Cook & Gueraud, 2005). As Goffman pointed out, however, different frames may be used by different participants so full intersubjectivity is not being assumed, particularly since there may be differential access to information (Goffman, 1969b, pp. 72–73). Discourse episodes are also set into their sociohistorical context and situated as part of a larger, continuous flow of information (Giddens, 1984; Sigman, 1987).

Recent research has contrasted shared cognition versus a collective mindset: the former refers to overlapping knowledge structures among individuals whereas the latter reflects how individuals in groups come to think alike in a specific context (Elsbach, Barr & Hargadon, 2005; Thompson, 2005; Weick, 2001, 2004). Both facets of knowledge influence organizing and communicating, and are acknowledged in the views being developed here. A collective mindset is clearly implied in differing scopes of discourse (i.e., narratives, grand discourse and mega-discourse, see Alvesson and Karreman, 2000a, b). Van Dijk's view of knowledge management includes a K-device (knowledge device) that reflects the beliefs interactants have about each other's knowledge (Van Dijk, 2005).

While communication is not possible without such shared knowledge, communication itself also enables us to share knowledge. When interacting, participants assume that they share some common definitions of the situation, and they act upon the basis of these shared definitions. Van Dijk (1997a, b) observed that communicators shape messages based on their perceptions of recipients' knowledge and attitudes. These shared assumptions reflect taken-for-granted, commonsense knowledge about communication behavior and everyday life (von Raffler-Engel, 1977). Denzin noted that

> Everyday and problematic interaction exhibit a situated, constraining structuredness based on ritual, routine, and taken-for-granted meanings. These constraining features are woven through the structures of the social relationships and ensembles of action. ... As interactional structures, ensembles are reified, patterned regularities of thought, action and interpretation.
>
> *(Denzin, 1992, p. 27)*

Socialization practices in organizations, for example, would assist new members of the organization in understanding the tacit, commonsense social practices of the organization.

An aspect of world knowledge, often tacit, yet assumed to influence communication, is *habitus* (Bourdieu, 1977, 1994). Habitus refers to "embodied dispositions to act and to perceive the world that directly reflect the macrosocietal conditions, political and economic forces, and relationships of power in which they were acquired" (Gumperz, 2001, p. 218). Critical theorists argue that we are therefore limited in our perspectives and fail to acknowledge others' perspectives and points of view, and consequently hegemony may result. (See, for example, the work of Deetz, Mumby, feminist scholarship and other critical discourse analysts.) Increasingly, such scholarship helps identify sources of hegemony and repression, and this knowledge also filters into our world views.

Gumperz (2001) suggests that his model of interactional sociolinguistics (IS) bridges habitus and localized interactive processes. IS focuses

> on communicative practice as the everyday-world site where societal and interactive forces merge. ... To interact is to engage in an ongoing process of negotiation, both to infer what others intend to convey and to monitor how one's own contributions are received ... individuals participating in such exchanges use talk to achieve their communicative goals in real-life situations, by concentrating on the meaning-making processes and the taken-for-granted, background assumptions that underlie the negotiation of interpretation.
> *(Gumperz, 2001, p. 218)*

This view of communicative practices is very compatible with those of Goffman and Giddens.

Narrative psychology (Bruner, 1990) views narratives as related to cognitive plans and representations, and suggest that narratives help people "organize their experience in, knowledge of, and transactions with the social world" (p. 79). In Frye's (1957) analysis of four literary genres (comedy, tragedy, romance and satire), they are viewed as "deeply entrenched cultural models that people in Western cultures use and recognize, in anything from the writing and understanding of history, to everyday personal story-telling" (Edwards, 1997, p. 268). (See also the use of narrative in organizations by Czarnowski, 1997.) Many models of interaction acknowledge the importance of shared knowledge, whether that shared knowledge resides in frames, narratives or Grand Discourses.

Joint negotiation of interaction. Interaction requires coordinated communicative behavior between at least two participants. In conversations, taking turns, responding to the talk of other participants and the like, require joint management by participants. Interpreting utterances is also jointly managed, since hearers must ratify, disconfirm or otherwise respond to the speaker's utterance (Fitch & Sanders, 1994, 2005; Goffman, 1959, 1983a, b; Goodwin, 2003; Haslett, 1987; Hopper & Drummond, 1990; Levinson, 1983; Pomerantz, 1998; Schegloff, 1999). The jointly negotiated nature of interaction also allows for the indeterminacy of utterances; this indeterminacy is necessary for maintaining face and for allowing interaction to flow smoothly (Franck, 1981; Sigman, 1987; Van Dijk, 1997a, b).

Communicators are continuously adjusting their talk to one another during their interactions (Edwards, 1997; Goffman, 1983a, b; Haslett, 1987) and inappropriate behavior is usually marked and responded to (Buttny, 1993; Buttny & Morris, 2001; Garfinkel, 1967a, b; Pomerantz & Fehr, 1997; Van Dijk, 1997c). With the globalization of business, and increasing economic and political interconnectedness, cultural variability is an increasingly significant factor in both organizing and communicating (Carbaugh, 1996, 2005; Carbaugh & Berry, 2001; Giddens, 1990a, 1998; Ting-Toomey, 2005; Ting-Toomey & Kurogi, 1998).

In organizations, as Eisenberg (1984) points out, messages may be strategic as well as deliberately indeterminate. For organizing, the frame of the organizing activity (whether a political frame or a human resources frame, for example) provides the context in which this joint negotiation occurs. Most models of discourse and interaction assume that social interaction is fundamentally negotiated between participants and such issues as identity, conflict, access to resources, cooperation, face and the like are among key aspects being negotiated in interaction.

Variability as a function of context. One of the most widely shared assumptions about communicative behavior is that it varies across different contexts and different language users. Van Dijk suggested that communicative models need to incorporate multiple levels of context (the cultural level, the organizational level and the immediate social setting) as well as language-user characteristics such as age, sex, motivation, personal values and so on. As Van Dijk (1997b) suggested, context provided that which "we need to know about in order to properly understand the event, action or discourse" (p. 11). He also noted that "discourses and its users have a 'dialectic' relation with their context: besides being subject to the social constraints of the context, they also contribute to, construe or change that context" (ibid., p. 20).

Given the fundamental role context plays in language, communication and sensemaking, it is not surprising to find a rich diversity in approaches to context and to what context entails (Akman, 2000). Hymes' (1974, 1986) model of communicative competence (SPEAKING) sets out a sociocultural approach to context. Gumperz' interactional sociolinguistic model (1992a, b) uses the concept of contextualization cues to help participants focus on relevant aspects of the social context in their interpretations of what is going on. Weick (2001) attributes sensemaking to the resources of SIRCOPE (social setting, identity, retrospect, cues, ongoing development, plausibility and enactments; p. 461).

Gumperz (2001) aptly points out the importance of extracommunicative knowledge in human understanding (tacit knowledge and contextual knowledge):

> Garfinkel, by documenting the intrinsic incompleteness of everyday talk, and Grice, in claiming that listeners rely on assumptions about conversational cooperation to recast what is literally said, each in his own way argues for the importance of extracommunicative knowledge in human understanding … their perspective on interpretation is basically a dialogic one. The fundamental problem is not deciding on what an expression means but determining what a speaker intends to convey by means of a specific message. This view, that inferences are rooted in discourse as well as in the local circumstances in which they were produced, is by now widely accepted in discourse studies.
>
> *(pp. 216–17)*

In Van Dijk's analysis, context incorporated the sociocultural characteristics of participants, the setting, material objects, and participants' nonverbal actions, goals, plans, and frames. As Bavelas (1999) argued, communication scholars need to "identify and account for all relevant contextual features, wherever they appear" (p. 8). Within organizations, the interactional contexts reflect the organizational environment and the relational practices followed, such as the degree of formality or marking of status and power. For example, Alvesson and Karreman (2000a) note that

> terms such as *leader, decentralization, hierarchy, strategic, motives, participation, decision,* and so on do not have abstract, context-free meanings. ... Abstract definitions of leadership—in themselves seldom informative—say little about the specifics involved in these different situations. ... The accounts of informants in a case study may mean that leader and leadership may mean very different things every time the words are put into action. ... Through labeling somebody a leader, a particular version of the world is created, with political effects.
>
> *(p. 142)*

One's experience and sociocultural knowledge is also viewed as a central aspect of contexts. Two important dimensions of context are world knowledge and knowledge of language (Haslett, 1987). Buttny (1998) insightfully pointed out that context exists independently of any text, but is also created and recreated "in and through the text" (p. 46). This can be shown, for example, in how couples orient to therapy or to the use of reported speech. Goodwin (2003) makes a similar point about embedded contexts when speakers refer to events not part of the current interaction. Schegloff (1991a) distinguished between distal context (broader aspects of social life such as gender and ethnicity) and proximate context (the sequences of talk in a given situation, such as telling a story). Goffman's concept of frames and framing help identify the contexts in which encounters take place. Frames are both meta-communicative as well as representing distinct ways of looking at the world and thus framing different contexts of interpretation. Cicourel (1987, 1992) analyzed context in the sense of bureaucratic frames that shape institutional activities and set up interactions, as well as the more narrow sense of context in terms of the localized, specific, negotiated encounters with those broader institutional frames. Finally, Flowerdew and Leong (2010) discuss the importance of discursive knowledge in constructing identity.

Seeman (1997) discussed context as relevant to a given encounter in terms of five decisions that interactants face in defining their situation, and argued that these decisions are relevant to both individual as well as collective and/or institutional contexts. Defining context includes basic decisions about (1) the meaning and controllability of the interaction; (2) keying in a situation whereby ambiguity is resolved (similar to Gumperz' contextualization cues or Goffman's keying); (3) identifying norms that help constitute the situation; (4) deciding the boundaries of membership and one's degree of involvement; and finally, (5) deciding the goals and values attainable in the situation. Seeman's decisions reflect a broad view of context as well as its permeability and complexity.

A similar position is developed by Sillince (2007), who argues that when, where, as whom and why constitute the core dimensions of context. In examining talk at Enron, he found that organizational members, to achieve cross-contextual organizing in their work, used discursive means to place discourse from one context into another context. Discourse was located in terms of local vs. global dimensions, and the relationship of discourse to meaning. Through utilizing a structurational frame, Sillince suggests that people re-use old claims as premises for new arguments and thus mirrors the recursiveness in structuration theory. Intertextuality also occurs when texts are incorporated into subsequent texts and discussions. One discursive strategy used was that of reframing, or changing the point of a discourse. He argued that the dimensions of context he outlined can serve as a basis for operationalizing structuration theory.

In their study of Systech, Heracleous and Marshak (2004) found that to fully understand the actors' discourse, several frames of context were necessary, including the immediate interactional context, the organizational context and the broader industry context (p. 1301). Giddens' work on different types of social systems, such as legal or political institutions, will be particularly useful in exploring broader industry contexts.

Giddens observes that "Context includes the physical environment of interaction but is not something merely 'in which' interaction occurs. ... Aspects of the context, including the temporal order of gestures and talk, are routinely drawn upon by actors in constituting communication. ... the 'closure of meaning' of the polyvalent terminologies of everyday language ... can be grasped only by studying the contextual ordering of whole conversations" (1984, p. 71). Giddens also emphasizes that "'Context-dependence', in the various ways in which this term can be interpreted, is aptly regarded as integral to the production of meaning in interaction" (1976, p. 105).

Giddens' contextuality incorporates understanding of encounters as they occur as part of actors' daily time-space path, and the locales in which encounters take place. These locales, or settings, are also distributed throughout different regions and ultimately connect to broad interregional connections. Thus, context includes issues of body orientation, time-space considerations, and an appreciation of the regions in which encounters occur (i.e., kitchens are a location in which cooking occurs). Context, then, for Giddens, involves "(a) the time-space boundaries (usually having symbolic or physical markers) around interaction strips; (b) the co-presence of actors, making possible the visibility of a diversity of facial expressions, bodily gestures, linguistic and other media of communication; (c) awareness and use of these phenomena reflexively to influence or control the flow of interaction" (1984, p. 282). Thus, he concludes that the context of interaction is an integral part of that interaction. Context is also significant with respect to actors' monitoring of interaction: "Context, which includes the physical settings of action, has particular meaning in respect to the situated character of human activities, since it is deeply involved in their reflexive monitoring" (Giddens, 1990b, pp. 301–2).

Definitions of context also vary as a function of the analytic approach being taken and the inclusiveness of the definition (Dillard & Solomon, 2001; Tracy, 1998). Different disciplinary approaches may vary in terms of their focus on the text, on the situation, on the observable ways in which the context is revealed by the talk and so forth. While these approaches reveal the complexity of the concept of context, the approach taken here will emphasize a sociocognitive approach that recognizes participants' knowledgeability, the situatedness of the encounter and, most importantly, participants' views as to the relevancy of social and situational factors in the context. This approach is very similar to the approach of Van Dijk. Also critical in our working definition of context is the use of Goffman's frames and participants' knowledgeability, and discursive consciousness as developed by Giddens. (For an interesting discussion on context, see a series of journal articles discussing context in volume 31 of *Research on Language and Social Interaction*.)

Different conceptualizations of context all emphasize its fundamental importance in interpreting interaction. Most perspectives do not just focus on the immediate social setting (as does conversational analysis), but incorporate broader layers of context. The scope of these layers is a function of the analytic lens being used, with culture being the broadest conceptualization of context. Conceptions of context are also influenced by how frames define relevant aspects of a context, including the setting, situation, participants, their situated identities and so forth. Talk will also confirm or disconfirm understandings of the context and what we are doing.

The sequencing of communicative behavior. Schutz (1967), Cicourel (1980), Weick (2001) and others note that communication is both retrospective and prospective. Ongoing talk can retrospectively recast the interpretation of preceding turns as well as prospectively shape opportunities for future interactions (Boden, 1994; Giddens, 1984; Weick, 1995). The sequencing of utterances influences the interpretation of utterances as well as the general format of interaction (Duck, 2002; Heritage, 2005; Van Dijk, 1997c). For example, conversations are sequenced structurally; they begin with greetings, then the conversational topic is introduced, and finally, closings end the conversation.

In organizing contexts, messages may be direct and sequenced so that information required for the execution of tasks is readily available (Orlikowski & Yates, 2002; Weick, 1995). Management of information systems, and group decision-making support systems are frequently used to ensure timely message flow across organizations and organizational subunits (Poole & DeSanctis, 1992). In addition, information and objects connect in particular action sequences or activity systems across organizations in the production of good and services (Goffman, 1974, 1983a, b; Latour, 2005).

Communication across time and space. Adequate models of interaction must reflect real-world time limitations and spatial references, since interactions are limited by humans' ability to process language. Ellis (1999) argued that we process information and make decisions about the relevance, urgency, meaning and appropriateness of interaction under the restrictions of both time and human memory capacity. Psycholinguists have been particularly concerned with the analysis of language in terms of human perceptual and processing limitations. Van Dijk and Kintsch (1983), for example, in their model of discourse comprehension, emphasized the importance of time constraints on comprehension (see also Kintsch, 1988, 1998, for a reformulation of their comprehension model to incorporate more interpretive flexibility and a further elaboration by Sanjose, Vidal-Abarca & Padilla, 2006). March and Simon's (1958) classic work highlighted the difficulty people have in responding to information overload, and the subsequent errors or confusion that result.

The present time and place, of course, cannot be separated from past events and circumstances that have shaped the present context (Maines, Sugrue & Katovich, 1983). Building on Mead's notions of temporality, they noted that the past is represented in the present in several distinct ways—those aspects of the past that have been identified as relevant to the current situation; the actions and events in the past that shape possibilities for action in the present; the events that lead to existence of the present situation; and beliefs about useful actions to be pursued. Thus the notion of temporality, itself, evolves from distinct aspects of the past and projections about the future. (See also the work of Flaherty, 1991, 2003.)

Giddens' work (1984, 1990a, 1991a, b) incorporates the concept of distanciation, or communication and action over space and time when interactants are not physically co-present. Through the standardization of time, and modern systems of transportation and communication (including the storage of information), interaction can occur simultaneously across vast distances and different spaces. In addition, different interactions in different locations can be linked across time and space. These new conditions of communication, and their breadth of usage, constitute one of the major challenges facing communicating and organizing. (See Cooper, 2001. This issue will be developed and discussed in more detail throughout the book.)

To explore these time and space dimensions in interaction, Zhao (2004) developed a typology of differing conditions of communication in space and time. *Consociates* are those who interact with one another in real time and space—that is, they are physically co-present and thus share a "world within reach" and can influence one another in a physical "zone of operation" (pp. 91–94). These are the usual face-to-face (FtF) interactions we experience and through which we construct shared meanings through long-term, frequent interactions. *Contemporaries* are those that share world time (real time), but are spatially distant from one another—for example, with individuals from another country with whom we have no direct, co-present contact. Contemporaries have typified knowledge of one another and we establish trust across "objective meaning contexts"—so we trust that the postman will post our mail, and it will eventually reach its destination in the same way we trust the bank to accurately deposit and disperse our money (Giddens, 1990a, 1991a).

However, various telecommunication devices have created new spatial-temporal conditions of human contact (referred to as face-to-device communication, or FtD; Backhaus, 1997; Giddens, 1984; Goffman, 1963a; Meyerwitz, 1985; Suchman, 1987;

Tomlinson, 1997). Through inventions from the telegraph to instant messaging, mediated communication, especially electronic communication, has been "tearing space away from place" (Giddens, 1990a). Zhao pointed out that mediated communication extends human perception as well as the zone of operation (opening up a secondary zone of operation), although time will be somewhat "elastic" because of varying times taken to respond to messages.

When two or more "worlds within mediated reach" coincide, a new connection is forged, termed "telecopresence," during which interactants "stay within reach of each other's mediated senses" (Dertouzos, 1997). When people are in a situation of telecopresence, they are simultaneously in two meaning streams—one in real time and real space (geospace), and the other in real time, but distanciated space (cyberspace).

Individuals involved in telecopresence are, in Zhao's terms, *consociated contemporaries*. As Zhao (2004) notes

> The full conditions of telecopresence, therefore, consist in a situation in which individuals, though not mutually present in the same physical locale, are in each other's electronic proximity and capable of maintaining simultaneous contact with one another through the mediation of an electronic communications network. In the sense that they are positioned outside the range of one another's naked sense perceptions, the individuals are remote from one another (hence "tele"); but in the sense that they are able to reach one another in real or near-real time through electronic mediation, the individuals are together with one another (hence "copresence"). The term "telecopresence" thus captures the essence of the emergent condition of human interaction that brings distant people temporally together in cyberspace …
>
> In the sense that they share a community of time with one another, telecopresent individuals can be seen as consociates; but in the sense that they do not share a community of (physical) space with one another, these individuals should be regarded as contemporaries, telecopresent individuals are perhaps best described *consociated contemporaries*.
>
> *(pp. 98–99)*

Because organizing and communicating occur across multiple contexts, these differing contexts of communicating will need much more analysis and research. Giddens' work should be helpful with unpacking time-space distanciation while Goffman's work illuminates copresence.

In addition, time and spatial constraints have different effects in different mediums. The growing reliance on telecommunication systems in daily life significantly alter time and space constraints, such that thousands of individuals can simultaneously view an encounter thousands of miles away (i.e., a billion people watching the 2008 Olympics worldwide). We are just beginning to deal with the full range of implications of virtual communicating and organizing (DeSanctis & Fulk, 1999). However, modeling interaction should acknowledge the time and processing limitations under which it occurs, as well as the rapidly expanding knowledge base to deal with as a result of telecommunication and computer advances. (In subsequent chapters, we will discuss these issues in more depth.)

Systematicity. The systematicity of communication reflects both its sequential and structured nature. According to Kellerman (1992), systematicity is tied to communicators' choices, based on their desired goals in the interaction. Both normative and interpretive approaches to social behavior (including communicative behavior) assume that social behavior is systematic. Normative approaches stress the organized, socially sanctioned expectations individuals have about their social behavior. Within organizations, such sanctioned expectations would be reflected in corporate policies, handbooks and mission statements. Interpretive approaches emphasize the cultural patterning of social behavior and individuals' recognition of those patterns. Such patterning would reflect culturally based, commonsense knowledge about organizing as well as recognition of the corporate values highlighted in specific organizations (Schein, 2004). Goffman's work on rituals are examples of such systematicity.

Interpretiveness. The text, context, interactants and their mutual interrelationships determine how communicative behaviors are interpreted. The relative influence of each factor appears to be a function of the task and goals of the interaction. Within organizations, the product or service being provided, organizational size, organizational technology and task complexity would help shape the meaning of specific events and actions (Bolman & Deal, 2008; Donnellon, Gray & Bougon, 1986).

Additional complexity in interpretation is apparent when one considers that a text may have multiple meanings (Franck, 1981; Garfinkel, 1967a, b; Haslett, 1984, 1987; Sigman, 1987). In addition, texts build up over time, as interactants construct their own meanings based upon the unfolding interaction they are participating in (Ellis, 1999; Haslett, 1987; Schegloff, 2001). Sanders (1991) argued that participants use propositional content, the illocutionary force of utterances and conversational implicature to interpret utterances, but that only one aspect is usually emphasized.

Some argue that interpretive procedures must be analyzed independently of the decontextualized (literal) meanings of lexical items (Cicourel, 1980; Denzin, 1970; Douglas, 1970). These interpretive procedures are based upon taken-for-granted, commonsense knowledge about everyday life (Giddens, 1984; Goffman, 1974; Haslett, 1987). Communicator characteristics and the social relationships among participants appear to play a central role in the interpretation of ongoing interaction (Gudykunst & Kim, 2003; Haslett & Samter, 1997) and will vary across organizations and organizing frames (Boden, 1994; Bolman & Deal, 2008). Underlying these issues is the classical linguistic controversy over meaning and the degree to which meaning is shaped by syntax, semantics and/or language users (pragmatics).

There is also considerable debate around the closeness of the link between discourse and meaning. The multi-level, layered nature of communication within and across encounters may allow different frames of interpretation to be used or transformed: These transformations are systematically related to one another and enable multiple interpretations of a single event (Boden, 1994; Goffman, 1974). Alvesson and

Karreman (2000b) suggest that discourse and meaning vary along two intersecting dimensions: a very local, situational context versus a macro-system context, and discourse determination (discourse/meaning collapsed) versus discourse autonomy (where discourse/meaning are linked only in terms of the specific context, and thus not durable beyond the immediate context) (p. 1130). They also discuss different analytic perspectives one can take in analyzing discourse—an account, for example, can be viewed as a text (a story) separate from viewing an account as a "truthful testimony of a personal conviction" (p. 1143). Thus the relationships between discourse and meaning will be viewed differently depending upon the researcher's perspective and purpose. And so, too, will different interpretations be generated by participants, observers and scholars. (See also Giddens' comments on the double hermeneutic in science.)

Relational influences on communication. One of the most fundamental purposes of communication is to develop and maintain social relationships among individuals. Only through communication are individuals able to share information, create intersubjective worlds and coordinate their activities. As Shotter pointed out, "the primary human reality is conversational or responsively relational, that one's 'person-world' dimension of interaction or being exists within a whole melee of 'self-other' relationships or dimensions of interaction" (Shotter, 1993, p. 161). Scholars from a wide range of disciplines have acknowledged the fundamental role of communication in establishing social order, cooperation and social relations with one another (Cicourel, 1980; Douglas, 1970; Giddens, 1984; Goffman, 1974, 1976).

In organizing, control and coordination are made possible by communication. Within organizations, personal relationships may vary from friendship to superior/subordinate relationships which are marked by formal authority and designated job responsibilities. Communication plays an important role in the enactment of role-identities within organizations (Hepburn & Wiggins, 2007; Sanders, 1995). Recently, increasing attention is being directed at emotions in the workplace and how emotions influence both how work is done as well as how people are affected by the workplace (Fineman, 2000; Hochschild, 1979, 2000; Tracy & Tracy, 1998).

Over time, actors or agents may also assume different social identities and "the position-practice relations associated with them … they are associated with normative rights, obligations and sanctions which, within specific collectivities, form roles" (Giddens, 1984, p. 282). Some bodily attributes, like age and gender, are marked in all societies and also influence one's position-practices throughout the life-cycle. While there is a "unique" self—a continuity or biography of a particular individual—the most important consideration, for both Goffman and Giddens, is the set of social practices associated with that individual's position, not the person occupying it. Of course, both would acknowledge that others may or may not accept an individual's social competency in handling a particular position, so there will always be an evaluation of someone's ability to "carry off" a set of position practices.

Human relations and human interaction are both important features of Giddens' structuration model. As he notes:

A social relation is any tie that establishes some kind of bond between individuals or groups (such as a kinship relation), while social interaction refers to direct interchanges between them, whether face-to-face or mediated by other forms of communication.

Social systems are composed of social relations and social interaction, coordinated across time and space. Practices carried on in the contexts of co-presence (experienced by all actors as part of the *durée* of day-to-day life) are the 'stuff' of social interaction and the core elements of social reproduction generally. They constitute social systems, however, only insofar as they 1) regularly 'stretch' across time-space and 2) are mediated by communication other than of the face-to-face sort.

Social and system integration refer to the coordinating mechanisms that produce 'systemness' over different contexts of co-presence.

(Giddens, 1990b, p. 302)

Face. Face is also an integral aspect of any communication model. I shall be using Goffman's concept of face—"the positive social value a person effectively claims for himself by the line others assume he has taken during a particular contact" (Goffman, 1955, p. 213)—as a fundamental aspect of communication and, as Goffman states, it is a basic unit of social action. Face is emergent, interactional and jointly negotiated: a "person's face clearly is something that is not lodged in or on his body, but rather something that is diffusely located in the encounter and becomes manifest only when these events are read and interpreted for the appraisals expressed in them" (ibid., p. 214). "Face is ... a condition of interaction rather than an objective of interaction in most circumstances. When face claims are not supported, face becomes both a condition and the object of interaction until the face needs of the claimant are met" (Brown, 2000, p. 62).

During interaction, mutual understanding of the context is established and face claims are put forward by interactants. But this mutual understanding is fragile, momentary, and thus subject to continual negotiation and adjustment. At times, it will be routine and taken-for-granted, and, at other times, hotly contested. But the frames established will provide the interpretative basis for ongoing activity by participants.

With respect to the importance of face in communication, Tracy (1990) has proposed five tenets of face based on Goffman's work. These principles are that facework has identity implications; that face claims vary according to the situation, personality and culture; that encounters often involve tensions surrounding different aspects of face; that face threat is primarily a reflection of the actions people perform; and that any interaction potentially threatens face (pp. 215–22). As Goffman noted "there is no occasion of small talk so trivial as to not require each participant to show serious concern with the way in which he handles himself and others present" (1955, p. 226). That is, *face is always a relevant consideration in interaction*.

Relevance. If there is a fundamental premise of interaction, it is the expectation of relevance. When communicating with others, we expect their remarks to be relevant to the topic and goal at hand, and we work hard to "fit" their remarks within the scope of those goals. Three principles (relevance, cooperativeness and face-work) are, I believe, universal expectations of communication, with relevance being the most fundamental. Relevance is of central importance in communication because it connects actions to goals, and thus helps us interpret ongoing interaction.

Relevance is important because it explains two critical processes: (1) how we establish our specific interpretive frames from our more general frame systems and (2) how interactants in a given conversation develop a relevant knowledge base for interpreting messages (i.e., the framing of a specific encounter). Mason (2006) suggested that relevance is a function of inferencing and the "evolving, intra-interactional nature of context … a process of joint negotiation of contextual assumptions, even those of … divergent contexts may emerge among participants" (p. 359). A participant's choice of utterance will always be a strategic, contingent choice: Because participants must respond as the interaction proceeds; because their relevant knowledge bases are changing, fragmented and incomplete; and because their conversational goals are instrumentally tied to one another, such choices are always strategic.

Unger (2002, 2006) has also proposed a model of relevance-theoretic comprehension: Context is an important part of relevance, especially the culturally shared knowledge that influences people's expectations of what's relevant in a particular context, and thus highlights certain inferential processes, while ignoring others. Nuances in the discourse itself, like intonation or emphasis, will also hint at an utterance's relevance. Unger argued that relevance is critical for comprehension, and that coherence is a by-product of relevance. Conversational analysts also identify relevance as a key issue, but for them it is an issue framed by sequencing—"why that now?" (Maynard & Zimmerman, 1984; Schegloff & Sacks, 1973).

From a variety of perspectives, including the view of communicating developed here, relevance is a key principle. As Grice stated: "Under the category of Relation I place a single maxim, namely, 'Be relevant.' Though the maxim itself is terse, its formulation conceals a number of problematic issues—questions about what different kinds and foci of relevance there may be, how these shift in the course of a talk exchange, how to allow for the fact that conversational topics can be changed, and so forth" (Grice, 1989, p. 27). As Unger noted, some conversations have "drift," while others do not.

My use of relevance, as does that of Leech (1983), connects utterances with the conversational goals of participants. Given the importance of relevance (both in terms of the views set out here and in view of the degree to which the concept is relied upon in most analyses of verbal communication), it seems essential to clarify this concept. I propose, after Leech (1983), that "An utterance U is relevant to a speech situation if U can be interpreted as contributing to the conversational goal(s) of s or h" (p. 94). I am expanding this general definition of relevance to include knowledge and actions, as well as utterances. The formulation of this more inclusive concept of relevance is as follows: An utterance, action or unit of knowledge is relevant to a speech situation if it can be interpreted as contributing to the conversational goal(s) of the speaker or listener.

I use the term "unit of knowledge" to include any element of general knowledge, irrespective of how such units may be processed and represented in memory. Knowledge could be represented in the form of scripts, propositions, frames, communicative practices, practical reasoning or in some other format. As can readily be seen, this more inclusive formulation is needed because general knowledge and the relevant knowledge base derived in a particular social setting significantly influence our interactions. Utterances, as well as knowledge structures, objects and actions (i.e., nonverbal behaviors) are connected to conversational goals through relevance. Relevance connects text, context and participants, and thus enables us to interpret communicative behavior.

Another important aspect of relevance is that any communication is presumed to be relevant. For Sperber and Wilson, as well as the view taken here, "every act of ostensive communication communicates a presumption of its own optimal relevance" (Blackmore, 2001, p. 105). In other words, speakers try to be relevant and listeners try to connect utterances in some meaningful manner to the interaction at hand.

Speakers try to make their utterances relevant and then listeners work hard to make sense of them—this aspect of relevance is termed the cognitive principle of relevance; that is, humans tend to cognitively maximize relevance (Sperber & Wilson, 1995; Wilson, 1998). More generally, this might also be considered a fundamental aspect of sensemaking. As Blackmore (2001) notes, not all utterances succeed in being "optimally relevant" but listeners still try to connect utterances meaningfully to the interaction and context at hand.

A more limited view of relevance treats it as an aspect of coherence. That is, the issue of relevance is the "local" issue of how utterances contribute to the topic under discussion (Tracy & Moran, 1983). However, Blackmore (2001) advocated the view that coherence flows from relevance when she suggested that "hearers' intuitions about coherence can be explained as a consequence of the hearer's search for an interpretation that is consistent with the Principle of Relevance [Sperber & Wilson, 1986]" (p. 112).

While coherence is essential for interpreting utterances, such approaches fail to provide satisfactory accounts of how we construct meanings. The missing principle, once again, is that of relevance. Interactants try to be sensible (i.e., capable of being interpreted), not generally, but in a particular way (i.e., in a way contributing to their conversational goals). To be generally coherent (or sensible) provides a range of alternative meaningful interpretations; speakers go beyond (or try to go beyond) this potential range of meanings to signal to the intended or *relevant sense* of an utterance. Meaning-based approaches to relevance (such as those limiting relevance to this issue of topical relevance) can specify a range of plausible interpretations of what is said, but fall short of specifying what is meant by what is said.

While conversationalists try to make their utterances both relevant and coherent, relevance is the more fundamental in shaping interaction. This can be demonstrated in a number of ways. First, if an utterance is relevant, then it must also be coherent. This is, if the utterance is related to the general sense of the matters at hand in the conversation, then it also must be meaningful in some sense—namely, the sense in which it is relevant to the conversational matter at hand. However, an utterance may be coherent (i.e., meaningful), but not be relevant to the conversation. For example, one could retort (as many do) in an argument, "But that's not relevant to the issue." If we understand an utterance's relevance, we assume that, whatever people have said, it is somehow related to the matters at hand—otherwise, why say anything? In short, the issue is not meaning in general, but meaning for a specific purpose. And, as both speakers and listeners, we strive for relevance.

The issue of relevance, in my view, is the issue of pertinent information. How do we determine what is pertinent information? First, interactants' goals must be considered because those goals direct interactants' acquisition of knowledge. Second, in the context in which we are operating, our goals intersect with others to accomplish some purpose. When communicating within organizations, personal goals and organizational goals may be contested. In interaction, all participants' goals may be contested, and thus relevance is continuously in flux. Finally, it should be noted that what is relevant varies across time, circumstances and interactants—relevance is always contingent and evolving.

Thus far, we have developed frame theory as a basis for conceptualizing knowledge, representing context and signaling meaning—all essential components of communication. In addition, through the concept of frame systems, which represent core beliefs and assumptions coalescing around a single theme, like kinship systems or religion, we have developed the underlying beliefs and assumptions around communication in this chapter. While some may disagree with some of these assumptions, I think many would agree that these are important qualities of communication. I would argue that such general assumptions may be universal beliefs, but that *how they are enacted varies across cultures*. I am arguing that communication is inferential, intentional, strategic, transformative, conventional, and jointly negotiated by interactants. Communication varies across contexts, depends upon participants' commonsense knowledge, is sequential, and is extended and accomplished in real time and space. In addition, communication is systematic, interpretive and varies according to the social relationships among interactants. Two additional components—face and relevance—are of fundamental importance in communicating. And, it is important to lay out these fundamental assumptions for discussion and inquiry, in order to be clear about how communication is being developed in this book as well as to foster discussion about these assumptions among interested scholars and readers.

Throughout the development of this frame system of communication, I have indicated points of congruence between these assumptions and the work of both Goffman and Giddens. We can note important points of congruence, although these ideas will be developed more fully in subsequent chapters. Both Goffman and Giddens are interested in how social life is developed and sustained. Goffman argued for the foundational importance of the interaction order in creating and sustaining social life. Giddens uses Goffman's interaction order as the basis for social systems: as he notes, "Social systems are composed of social relations and social interaction, coordinated across time and space" (1990b, p. 302).

While Goffman focused primarily on communicative contexts where interactants were physically co-present, some of his work, most notably *Asylums*, provides illuminating insights into institutional settings. In contrast, Giddens focused on social systems, particularly those distanciated or stretched out over time and space, in which interactants are not physically co-present. Goffman's work develops and discusses the importance of accessibility, and people's ability to respond to one another, both verbally and nonverbally. Although it was not a focal point of his research, Goffman clearly envisioned communication expanding across time and space, and believed his model was compatible with such expansions (arguing that some communicative cues would be diminished or lost, such as facial cues being lost over telephones and the like). Finally, for both Goffman and Giddens, frames in actors' minds are believed to parallel the frames used in social activity and action.

Both Goffman and Giddens used frames to analyze actors' stocks of knowledge, to categorize social practices and contexts, and to signal meaning within interactions. While Goffman's frames capture communicative processes among co-present individuals and groups, Giddens' frames reflect both communicative as well as organizing frames, such as organizations of legitimation, domination or moral sanctions. As such, these contexts range greatly in scope, yet these contexts can be layered within one another (via lamination and rekeying).

Both recognize the importance of context in communication, with Giddens focusing on expanded, distanciated concepts of context whereas Goffman focused on the more immediate, physical setting. Both emphasized materiality in communicating, acknowledging the importance of physical props, regions and material resources in communicating. Both acknowledge the power of communication as a source of change, transformation and strategy.

Socially competent communicators are viewed as important. Goffman argued that communicative competence is a sign of a sane individual and both agree that honoring face is an important aspect of communication. Communication also varies and is interpreted by individual communicators, their social relationships with one another, and the context. Both men acknowledge the structured nature of communication via ritual and shared social practices.

Actors intentionally communicate to create certain impressions and to accomplish social action; as such, both Goffman and Giddens acknowledge the importance of social practices, agency and the community of knowledge built up around social practices. Both men recognize the importance of face and relevance, with face being a key concept in Goffman's work on communication. And, finally, time and space are important in both men's views of interaction, with Goffman being among the first to recognize the importance of the immediate material context for communication, and Giddens extending communication through time and space via distanciation and historicity.

Thus, as can readily be shown, the frame system of communication being developed here is compatible with the views of both Goffman and Giddens. In future chapters, we shall explore these linkages more fully in our synthesis of Goffman and Giddens and their approach to communicating and organizing.

We next turn a model of communication, specifically noting how many of the concepts we have developed can be incorporated into a model of communication.

A Communication Model

Interaction as a Process

Given these underlying assumptions in our frame system of communication, what occurs during an interaction? Important aspects of a communication model incorporate the shared, commonsense knowledge of interactants, the context, their social relationships with one another and their goals.

Among interactants, the basis of shared knowledge is richer and more complex for those who are friends, kin, or have an extended social or work relationship with one another. They are richer because we "know" one another as specific persons and as specific persons now-in-the-immediate-situation, rather than just as human beings and members of the same culture or the same organization. As interpersonal relationships develop, the information exchange among individuals becomes increasingly personal and idiosyncratic (Gudykunst & Kim, 2003). Cultural expectations for specific types of relationships may be activated as well, such as "what it means" to be a friend in the US, or to be a family member in China and so forth (Gudykunst & Kim, 2003; Kim, 1995; Oetzel, 2001). Within organizations, long-term members have more extensive relationships and knowledge than do newcomers. In addition, depending upon what particular organizational frame is operating, relationships may be a focal point (as in the human relationships frame) or simply background information (as in the structural or systems frames).

Participants' comments are assumed to be relevant to their goals. Using their relevant knowledge base and inferences about the probable goals of one another in the interaction, interactants coordinate their utterances and attempt to maximize the achievement of their own goals. Speakers try to be relevant as possible and hearers assume that the speakers' utterances are as relevant as possible (Haslett, 1987; Pomerantz & Mandelbaum, 2005; Sperber & Wilson, 1995).

Through communicative practices used by participants, inferences are made about what is going on in the interaction. Given the retrospective and prospective nature of interaction itself, these inferences are subject to continuous evaluation. But the crucial element is that of *relevance*—utterances are related to interactants' goals in that particular context, and are interpreted as being so related. In communication, signaling or accomplishing relevance is how one's actions are made sensible. No single communicative practice signals relevance, but rather the communicative practices taken as a whole, viewed against a general sense of what is being accomplished, renders a sensible account of what is meant. Taken together, communicative practices establish the interpretive, accountable nature of interaction. The relevant knowledge base of speakers and listeners is both the *interpretive frame* as well as the *jointly negotiated meaning* upon which *accountability* is established. This accountability in social action is inescapable (Buttny, 1993; Davidson & Friedman, 1998; Giddens, 1984; Goffman, 1974, 1981a; Haslett, 1987; Heritage, 2005; Massey, Freeman & Zelditch, 1997).

In what follows, I propose a model of the communicative process. For purposes of clarity, the process will be divided into pre-interactional variables, interactional variables and post-interactional variables. This process is continuous, and interaction itself may transform the frames that participants envoke in the immediate situation. Giddens' duality of structure is very applicable here, in that communication shapes interactional outcomes and those outcomes, in turn, shape future communication. That is, structure and agency recursively and mutually influence one another.

Pre-Interactional Variables

Pre-interactional variables represent the relevant knowledge base and goals that participants bring to bear on the ongoing interaction. Given our focus on organizing, we will apply this general process to organizational communication.

1. *Relevant Knowledge Base.* The relevant knowledge base of participants reflects their general knowledge of context, text and interaction processes, grounded in a particular culture and in a particular organization. As Gumperz noted, "participants' definition of what the relevant event is and what it means in an encounter emerges in and through the performance itself … we are dealing with schemata or frames, embodying presuppositions associated with ideologies and principles of communicative conduct that in a way bracket the talk, and that thereby affect the way in which we assess or interpret what transpires in the course of an encounter" (2001, p. 219). More specifically, this general knowledge includes:

A. *Commonsense knowledge.* Commonsense knowledge reflects ordinary social practices followed in a particular culture, as conceptualized by Schutz (1962), Garfinkel (1967a, b), Giddens (1984), Goffman (1959, 1974) and others. This commonsense knowledge is grounded in participants' real-world experiences, and shared in varying degrees by differing subcultural groups. Commonsense knowledge thus incorporates frame systems of organizing and communicating within a given culture. In cross-cultural encounters, these frame systems may differ significantly and thus message misinterpretation may be more likely. (This knowledge draws from our metaframes of organization and communicating, as well as the specific organizational frame being applied.)

B. *Interactional knowledge.* Interactional knowledge reflects cultural practices and norms for interaction in different organizations, institutions and social settings, as well as among different groups of participants. This knowledge may also be represented by scripts, routines and the like which reflect action and interaction sequences that accomplish a particular goal, such as conducting a business meeting (Giddens, 1984; Gioia, 1986; Goffman, 1974; Grant, Keenoy & Oswick, 1998). This knowledge draws on our experiences in framing—or actually carrying on—on interactions with others, and adjusting to different goals, individuals, moves and so forth.

C. *Linguistic knowledge.* Linguistic knowledge reflects knowledge of grammatical, semantic and pragmatic principles that govern use of a given language (Ellis, 1999; Haslett, 1987; Van Dijk, 1997a, b). From these three types of knowledge about how interactions are carried out within a given culture, and within a specific organization, participants derive a *relevant knowledge base.* In light of their goals, participants select, from their general knowledge of interaction, the knowledge most relevant to accomplishing their goals. Relevant knowledge thus includes (1) more detailed knowledge of the immediate social situation; (2) knowledge of the larger social context (the organization) within which the immediate social situation is embedded; (3) knowledge of standard interpretive practices in a given social setting, including material objects and both verbal and nonverbal practices; (4) knowledge of likely goals that can be accomplished in that particular social setting; and (5) knowledge of the specific participants involved.

This relevant knowledge base is a more detailed, specific subset of general knowledge: It is goal-directed, context-centered, and applies to specific social situations and participants. Specialized knowledge about participants incorporates the influence of the organization, social relationships among participants, and cultural differences. For example, if both participants have an enduring social relationship with one another—such as a long-term friendship or a long-term work relationship—the specialized knowledge provided by the relevant knowledge is particularized and adapted to that relationship. However, if the interactants are members of different cultures, then specialized knowledge of the other may consist only of stereotypes or typifications of the other's culture (Gudykunst & Kim, 2003) or each may simply react to the other as a human being (Schutz' most general level of knowledge of others).

From their relevant knowledge bases, participants develop a general set of hypotheses about how they expect the interaction to proceed; these hypotheses serve as framework of interpretation for the present encounter and guide for future actions. In Goffman's terms, these hypotheses enable participants to align themselves with others in the interaction. Framing, then, reflects the participants' strategies for achieving their own goals as well as aligning with the other participants.

Let me briefly demonstrate the difference between a general knowledge base and a relevant knowledge base. Suppose that you are a North American businesswoman who has been invited to a cocktail party by your superior. Your general knowledge base for cocktail parties reveals that polite behavior is expected (commonsense knowledge); that North American cocktail parties are used for social as well as business reasons (cultural knowledge); that a diverse range of topics can be discussed, from business to personal topics, but personal topics should not be overly serious or overly personal (interactional knowledge for the context of cocktail parties); and, finally, that formal language will be used (linguistic knowledge).

From this general knowledge base, a more specific relevant knowledge base can be drawn. You know that your superior gives very formal cocktail parties, with formal dress required (knowledge via past experience and information from other colleagues); that primarily business topics will be discussed, since your superior prefers to handle delicate negotiations in this manner (specific cultural practice in this organization, the Minedale Mining Company); that the specific topics likely to be discussed involve negotiations for raw materials (specific interactional knowledge regarding the topic); and that language is likely to be highly technical and legal (knowledge about the likely topic and areas of discussion). This more concrete, particularized, relevant knowledge base is the framework of interpretation that our North American businesswoman would enact at the cocktail party, and one that would enable her to formulate hypotheses about what has taken place, what is going on and what will be going on.

Some aspects of this relevant knowledge base will be similar for both speakers and hearers—but they need not be identical. The differing goals of speaker and hearer, for example, will produce different relevant knowledge bases. If the speaker and hearer share the same language and culture, the commonsense knowledge serving as a basis for social order in that culture will provide the necessary intersubjective basis for interaction. However, in culturally diverse encounters, such as transnational business encounters, the intersubjective bases for interaction may, in fact, have to be established before much interaction can take place. There may be significant differences in the frame systems for organizing and communicating held by members of different cultures (Ting-Toomey, 2005). For example, in diplomatic discussions, a significant amount of time may be spent on setting up protocols for subsequent talks.

In addition to this relevant knowledge base, participants have goals they wish to accomplish in any interaction. Multiple goals may be pursued by participants and may conflict with one another. As noted earlier, when we interact with others, we share a time and/or space for our mutual interaction, but no other common goal may be present.

2. *Goals.* For purposes of our discussion, I loosely define "goals" as what we hope to accomplish by our actions. As such, goals can be separated from intentions. Intentions are motives for actions; while I can never be certain of your motives, I can often infer your goals from your actions. (We do this by assuming that people are motivated to act, and that their actions are consistent with, or contribute to, the realization of their goals.) People's acts, of course, may be misdirected in the sense that they may not facilitate goal achievement; however, this does not

invalidate the general line of reasoning being pursued here. Action is a consequence of both knowledge and choice, and mistaken choices and mistaken knowledge frequently occur in an imperfect world.

Interactional goals may be quite difficult to analyze. First, individuals' awareness of their goals varies as a function of their monitoring skills (Berger & Bradac, 1982), their perceived control of events (Langer, 1983) and other factors. Second, goals themselves may be quite vague (i.e., I want to be sociable) or fairly precise (i.e., I want to write a grant proposal testing solid fuel injection systems). Third, multiple goals may be pursued simultaneously (i.e., I may want to be sociable as well as write the grant proposal). Fourth, some goals, like those concerning *impression-management* and *face*, may always be present in interaction (Goffman, 1955, 1974). Fifth, goals may also be closely tied to given contexts, and may not be attainable outside those contexts (Edwards, 1997; Tracy, 1990). Sixth, goals may also be weighted in importance relative to one another, of long- or short-term duration, and changeable over time. Finally, within organizational settings, goals may be constrained by the organizational context, and by competing goals and interests across organization subgroups. This last point is particularly crucial in organizations, and, in fact, forms a key component of the political organization frame. In short, goals appear to be as flexible and varied as the actions that support them.

Despite these complexities, however, people appear to act in ways that facilitate their goals. In interaction, participants make their utterances relevant to their conversational goals which, in turn, contribute to their personal goals (Tracy, 1991). Organizational members might be simultaneously pursuing their own goals, as well as their organization's goals. Speakers, then, try to be relevant, and hearers assume that speakers are trying to be relevant (see also Haslett, 1987, and Sperber & Wilson, 1995, 2002, who argue that speakers try to be as relevant as possible). It should be noted that speakers and listeners do not have to share goals: the only goal speakers and hearers must share is that of cooperating so that interaction between them may take place (Dascal, 1981; Tracy, 1991).

Two pre-interactional variables, the relevant knowledge base and participants' goals, mutually interact and influence one another. First, a participant's goals will control what aspects of general commonsense knowledge become activated and thus constitute part of that participant's relevant knowledge base. Second, as individuals acquire new information, their goals may change. And finally, as goals change, there will be corresponding changes in their relevant knowledge base.

Now that I have specified the nature of pre-interactional variables (the relevant knowledge base that participants use in an encounter, and their goals), I next discuss influential communicative variables that emerge during the interaction itself. During interaction, given the relevant knowledge base and participants' goals, participants talk and interpret others' remarks. Interpretations of another's comments are always tentative and projected; tentative because they are hypotheses about what is meant, and projected because speakers/listeners base their next remark on their interpretation of the preceding dialogue.

When applied to organizational settings at the micro-level of specific interaction, our frame systems for organizing and communicating, and our frames (i.e., structural, political), are incorporated into our commonsense background knowledge: On that basis, we are *framing* our interaction and aligning with others through goal-directed, communicative strategies, moment by moment, as the encounter proceeds. This framing, of course, is carried out with the expectation that knowledge may be incomplete and uncertain, due to unforeseen consequences of actions (Giddens, 1990a, 1991a).

Interactional Variables

The actual interaction involves the organizational frame, immediate physical setting, the participants, and the unfolding text or dialogue. The organizational frame is the background context in which the immediate social encounter takes place. The immediate physical setting includes the specific time, location, objects, and their arrangement (Gee, 1999; Goffman, 1967; Latour, 2005). Participants are influenced by four factors: their goals; their relevant knowledge base; their emotions (i.e., feelings and values about the interactional activity, other participants, and the like); and their interactional skill. Interactional skill refers to participants' ability to appropriately adapt their communication to different participants, and to satisfy different communicative demands across a diverse set of social situations.

The text or dialogue itself consists of the sequential order of utterances made by each participant, including their interruptions, overlaps, hesitations, and so forth. This text is both verbal and nonverbal. On the verbal dimension, the topics discussed, the conversational management practices used and the lexical items used (i.e., term of address, deictic elements such as "this") are of particular concern.

Textual variables act as relevance markers. Out of a set of potentially relevant contexts, the text marks the specific operative context for that interaction at that particular moment. As Goffmann (1974, 1981a, 1983a, b) notes, participants' framing of the interaction allows for continuous alignment as their goals shift. During the interaction, different contexts may become relevant. For example, as an amiable discussion turns into a heated argument, different goals may emerge, and different aspects of the topic may be emphasized. Such changes constitute a change in what the relevant context is for that interaction.

On the nonverbal level, interactional variables include paralinguistic features (like stress and intonation) that accompany utterances, as well as nonverbal behaviors (like eye gaze, touch, proximity and so forth). These nonverbal behaviors help convey, albeit indirectly, what is meant (most especially, the intensity of what is meant). (See, for example, Burgoon & Bacue, 2003; Burgoon, Buller & Woodall, 1989; Goodwin, 1981; Izard, 2009; Izard, Stark, Trentacosta & Schultz, 2008) for communication research combining both verbal and nonverbal features of interaction.)

Another important variable will be whether or not interactants are co-present with one another, or if some mediated communication channels will be used. As

Zhao (2004), Giddens (1984) and Goffman (1983a, b) have noted, face-to-face (FtF) interaction is different from face to device (FtD) interaction. Different sources of information will be accessible and thus influence the encounter.

Post-Interaction Variables

Interaction outcomes are very difficult to discuss since they are frequently unclear. If multiple goals are being pursued by participants, interactional outcomes may be further confounded. At a minimum, any response to a preceding remark could be considered an outcome. On the other hand, we could focus upon long-term outcomes, such as how a particular encounter shapes a relationship, influences decision-making, or alters goal attainment. Some interactional outcomes, for example, may be more critical for interpersonal relationships and organizational goals than others. However, little is known about these critical encounters. Frequently, they are not even readily apparent to the participants themselves, and become clear only in retrospect (Weick, 1995). Giddens (1984) suggests that interactional outcomes should be relatively confined to the immediate social context because, as one moves further from the encounter, the influence of unintended consequences and institutional forces come into play.

In view of the general lack of clarity in this area, and in view of some of the difficulties outlined above, let us simply consider any response to a preceding utterance as an outcome. As a pattern of responses or outcomes evolves throughout the interaction, participants develop a "global" sense about the encounter, and how it is proceeding (i.e., whether it is a hostile exchange; whether the project proposal seems complex and too expensive; whether she seems nice; whether we really have serious differences over our organizational goals). Over time, these global evaluations may influence how we approach subsequent encounters of a particular type (like interviews) or with particular individuals. For example, over time, we may build up an adverse attitude toward someone because past encounters have frequently been painful. Within organizations, negative patterns of interaction may be build up over time and influence current interactions (even though the circumstances and individuals who contributed to the negativity may no longer be with the organization). (Figures 2.1 and 2.2 are taken from Haslett, 1987.)

These three phases of interaction—pre-interaction influences, the interaction itself, and interactional outcomes—respectively parallel developing hypotheses, testing hypotheses, and confirming hypotheses. Prior to our interactions, we develop expectations (derived from our relevant knowledge base) about what might occur in a forthcoming interaction. During interaction, we test these expectations through our utterances and our interpretations of others' responses. As the interaction proceeds, our expectations are confirmed or disconfirmed; and we continually adapt or align our communicative behavior according to our conversational goals.

Although we have discussed communicative variables in terms of their influence as pre-interactional, interactional, or post-interactional influences, we must keep in

Pre-Interaction Variables	Interaction Variables	Post-Interaction Variables
Commonsense Knowledge/Tacit Knowledge		
Consists of:		*Consists of the responses*
Practical reasoning		interactants make to one another;
Cultural norms and values (regarding		goal achievement and short-term/
organizations, institutions and individuals)		long-term effects on their social
Interactional knowledge		relationship with one another
Linguistic knowledge		
$\rightarrow$		
Using the principle of relevance, determined partially by past experience and knowledge, goals in the interaction and knowledge of the other participants (if available) participants construct a *Relevant Knowledge Base*.		
$\rightarrow$		
Relevant Knowledge Base for Interaction (RKB)		
Consists of potential frames of interpretation to be activated by the text and immediate social context of interaction; context-centered, goal-driven relevant knowledge	IMMEDIATE SOCIAL/PHYSICAL SETTING	
	Interactant A $\nearrow$ TEXT* $\searrow$ *Interactant B*	
	RKB Verbal RKB	
	Goals Nonverbal Goals	
	Interaction Interaction	
	Skills** Skills	
	Affect*** Affect	

FIGURE 2.1 Toward a Descriptively Adequate Model of Communication

*Verbal text features would include topics, lexical items, deictic elements, presuppositions, entailment, implicature, accountability practices (like turn taking, presequences, etc.) and speech markers, like honorifics and so forth.

** Interaction skills would reflect features like communication apprehension, specially required skills such as those in interviewing, cross-examination and the like which are required in certain professions or settings, any communicative disfluencies such as stuttering, etc.

*** Affect reflects the attitude (positive, negative, etc.) of an interactant toward the context and participants—for example, a participant may like the other participant but feel very negative about the context of interaction and the topics discussed.

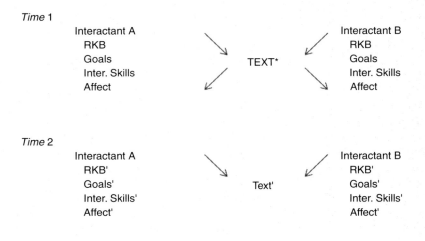

Time 1

Interactant A		Interactant B
RKB		RKB
Goals	TEXT*	Goals
Inter. Skills		Inter. Skills
Affect		Affect

Time 2

Interactant A		Interactant B
RKB'		RKB'
Goals'	Text'	Goals'
Inter. Skills'		Inter. Skills'
Affect'		Affect'

Time 3

(Cycle of interaction repeated, with new RKBs being produced, and potential changes occurring in interactants' goals, exercise of interactional skills and their affect)

FIGURE 2.2 A Process Model of Communication
*The initial text being considered here is a three-turn unit, rather than the more standard single utterance-response unit. Initially, the speaker makes an utterance s/he thinks is maximally relevant to his/her goal. The listener makes her/his response, on the basis of his/her projected interpretation of what the speaker meant by what was said. It is only upon the speaker's next utterance—the third turn—that some evaluation of the projected interpretations is rendered. That is, the speaker can confirm, reject or alter the listener's projected interpretation as displayed by his/her response.

mind that communication is a continuous, ongoing process. Participants' communicative practices signal an utterance's relevance; that is, they signal a speaker's intended meaning. The view of communicative processes developed here also emphasizes the role of commonsense knowledge and the relationship of such knowledge to participants' interactional goals. Finally, the view developed here focuses on the text, and the role of the text in signaling the relevant interpretive context.

In summary, participants try to accomplish their goals through interaction, and their comments are assumed to be relevant to their goals. Speakers try to maximize the relevance of their comments, and listeners, in turn, try to infer the relevant, goal-directed interpretation of the speaker's comments. Although speakers and listeners try to construct plausible interpretations of the ongoing interaction, what is critical is that the relevant operative interpretation intended by the speaker be taken up by the listener. In interaction, then, our conversational goal is to be understood (i.e., interpreted) in a particular way.

Although one's personal goals may never be completely known to others, or even well understood by oneself, conversational goals can be understood because the speaker publicly commits him/herself to being held accountable by virtue of his/her communicative practices (Garfinkel, 1962, 1967a, b; Schutz, 1962). What we say represents what we are willing to be "publicly accountable for" (Buttny, 1993). While we may not ever be certain of another's intent or motivation, the public record of interactions provides us with a basis of interpretation of ongoing interaction (Gee, 1999). Interactants signal how an utterance is to be understood through their use of socially shared, interpretive frameworks that govern everyday social interaction. As such, interactants display, through their utterances, their orientation to the ongoing talk (Gee, 1999; Goffman, 1974; Schegloff, 1991).

Relevant uptake is signaled, by both speakers and listeners, through their communicative practices, such as their conversational management practices (adjacency pairs, topic initiation, and so forth), contextual cues, speech markers, deictic elements, account-giving strategies, and paralinguistic/nonverbal behaviors relevant to text interpretation. All these communicative practices signal how the text is meant to be heard, and thus reflect ways of being held accountable for what has been said: This is the *framing level* of interaction. These communicative practices are part of our shared, culturally determined, commonsense knowledge. (For a comprehensive overview of such practices, in organizing contexts, see Boden, 1994; Gee, 1999; and Hutchby & Wooffitt, 1998.)

Everyday practical reasoning appears to operate on the principle of relevance. Actions are perceived and evaluated in terms of their relevance for accomplishing some desired outcome. These means-ends linkages are not unique, but represent relevant, shared social knowledge. Within organizations, the overarching organizational frame will provide some constraints on the legitimacy and appropriateness of various means-ends linkages.

Similar relevant linkages exist between goals and social situations; a situation may facilitate achieving some goals while prohibiting the attainment of others (Canary, Cody & Manusov, 2008; Tracy, 1990). Relevant knowledge can also point out "what not to do," and we can avoid mistakes through an analysis of past experience. And people's experiences are likely to be similar with respect to their trial-and-error efforts to accomplish their goals. Thus, the commonsense knowledge used by participants in their interaction is that knowledge which they find relevant to the matters at hand—not a vast array of knowledge, but knowledge relevant to accomplishing the participants' interactional goal.

The communicative processes being developed here are very similar to Maines' conceptualization of negotiated order (Maines, 1982). Maines suggests three levels of negotiation: (1) negotiations or types of interpersonal interactions; (2) the negotiation context, which involves aspects of the context that can be jointly negotiated; and (3) structural context, the overarching frames relevant to the encounter. In the model being developed here, framing would reflect negotiations and the negotiation context, while the structural context would reflect frames (i.e., in the case of organizations, the overarching frame systems of organizing, as well as the more specific organizing frames being invoked, such as the structural frame, human resources frame, and so forth).

It should be noted here that, while I am emphasizing verbal communication, this in no way denies the importance of nonverbal communication in determining a speaker's intended meaning. Nor does this model overlook the importance of material objects and settings as key components in interaction. Verbal and nonverbal communication systems, I believe, are redundant and complementary; an adequate account of what is meant cannot be established without reference to both systems, or to the material and mental contexts which surround the interaction. (See, for example, Cooren & Fairhurst, 2004; Goffman 1955, 1983a, b; Goodwin, 1981; Haslett, 1987; Izard, 2009; Izard, Stark, Trentacosta & Schultz, 2008; Manusov & Patterson, 2006; Pomerantz & Fehr, 1997.) Given the increasingly mediated global world, information gleaned from emails and the Internet are also incorporated in our commonsense knowledge, and thus into our communicative practices and products (Cooper, 2001; Giddens, 1990a, b).

Taken together, communicative practices establish the interpretive, accountable nature of interaction. *The relevant knowledge base of speakers and listeners is both the interpretive frame as well as the basis for public accountability.* This accountability in social action is inescapable; as Heritage (1984) noted, "normative accountability is the 'grid' by reference to which whatever is done will become visible and assessable" (p. 117). Heritage also noted that individuals do this routinely; only in breaches or violations of ordinary practices are things called into question (i.e., accounts must be given). For example, if the listener mishears a speaker's utterance, then the speaker may repair that mishearing by rephrasing her utterance.

Although communication generally becomes more unique and specialized as interpersonal relationships develop, nevertheless general patterns of communication can be observed as a function of the type of relationship (i.e., spouse, good friend, sibling, and so forth). Cultures and social groups have models for enduring social relationships, like marriage; such models may have their own conversational practices (such as, for example, the use of multiple naming among intimates). In a parallel fashion, organizations and professions also develop their own conversational practices for interaction (for instance, the use of professional titles such as doctor or professor).

Thus far, we have developed a general model of human communication, incorporating our frame system of communication and applying that to the everyday, specific interactions we experience daily (the framing level). Although we have referred to organizational contexts in communication, we have not explored them in depth. In the next chapter, I will develop a frame system of organizing itself, as well as discuss organizations and the communicative processes in organizations.

3

A FRAME SYSTEM FOR ORGANIZING

What is an organization? At the heart of this question lie issues of structure, agency, materiality, knowledgeability and the communicative constitution of organizations. On the one hand, everyone "knows" what an organization is and appreciates the fact that we are suspended in a web of organizations in our daily lives—a layperson's view of organizations, if you like. On the other hand, what are the boundaries of organizations? What are their interconnections? What are the relationships among various groups participating in the organization? These are questions less easily answered.

In what follows, I will develop a frame system of organizing, consistent with both Goffman's and Giddens' perspectives and examine a range of approaches investigating the question "what is an organization?" On a less abstract level, we can frame organizations in different ways, with each frame, or analytic lens, characterizing organizations along different dimensions. Each frame (such as a political or structural frame) assumes a particular perspective on organizing, and looks at a number of variables, including communicating, that influence that model. These frames incorporate substantive research on different ways of conceptualizing organizing, and the communicative processes involved in organizing.

Any organization, however, may be assessed by any of these frames—it depends upon the issues and questions being raised. For example, a structural frame may emphasize hierarchy and communicative flows along that hierarchy, while a cultural frame focuses on organizational values and communicating those values to organizational members and to the general public. The idea here is not to return to a "container" perspective of organizations, but to look at frames as the surrounding context in which organizing occurs. Effective leaders and managers, in fact, can shift among alternative frames in order to provide useful solutions to problems (Bolman & Deal, 2008). It should also be noted that any organization may have multiple frames present, and different frames may be envoked at different times within an organization (S. Kramarck, personal communication, April, 2010).

Recently, the role of communicating in organizing itself has become a focal emphasis for organizational communication research. Communication is being recognized as constitutive of organizing. That is, organizing is not possible without communicating. Not only is communication fundamental for organizing, but it is necessary for any socially shared activity. While communicating is essential organizing, however, not all organizing necessarily results in an organization. So the fundamental question, what *is* an organization, still remains.

In this chapter, I will propose a frame system for organizing and various definitions of an organization will be discussed. In subsequent sections, I will explore explore different frames for organizations and their concomitant communicative processes; and examine alternative definitions of organizations, especially that of Giddens. I will also briefly present some general findings in organizational communication research.

Generic Qualities of an Organizing Frame System

One basic assumption would be that organizing is a human activity (one that incorporates material objects) and that organizational members have specialized skills and talents used in their organizing activities. In order to provide a product or a service, organizational members may collaborate and work with one another, creating networks of interdependence among themselves. Some organizations may consist entirely of members whose training is very specialized, such as law or medicine, and thus organizational membership is limited only to those possessing those skills. Belonging to a particular organization is usually a matter of voluntary choice. Through membership in an organization, an individual contributes her time and talents to the organization for compensation, and tacitly agrees to follow the norms and practices of the organization (Schein, 2004). Organizational members identify with their organizations to varying degrees and negotiate their identities at work (Kuhn & Nelson, 2002; Lammers & Barbour, 2002; Zorn & Townsley, 2008).

Organizing also relies on control and coordination, established through communicative and social practices. Coordination is necessary because different processes and activities have to be appropriately sequenced, and control is necessary to execute this coordination. Control processes usually depend upon a hierarchy where different job functions and responsibilities are outlined, and different rewards are attached to each hierarchical level. Those individuals at the top of the organizational hierarchy typically exercise the most control within an organization. Such coordination and control is implicit in Weick's definition of organizing—"a consensually validated grammar for reducing equivocality by means of sensible interlocked behaviors" (1979, p. 3).

Organizations have sets of social practices—"the fine, delicate and largely hidden membrane that supports, connects, and binds social actors in a flexible web of patterned relations" (Boden, 1994, p. 2). While many organizational theorists have reified structure, we will emphasize the emergence of social practices in action and interaction by organizational members. Organizational members shape their activities, retrospectively with past actions in mind, so current activities appear appropriate. Simultaneously, they fit in their activities within the present context (looking "sideways" in Boden's terms), as well as prospectively (providing a foundation for future directions and actions). Such alignment is achieved collaboratively by multiple organizational actors, who have differing amounts of information, and who align themselves within the context of organizational social practices.

Organizations are also viewed as having boundaries—their powers and responsibilities are carried out within specified parameters and locales. Organizational membership may also be expanded to include stakeholders, who have a vested interest in the organization or can make demands upon the organization, although they may not play a direct role in its day-to-day operation. Stockholders in a company or university alumni would be good examples of stakeholders. Complex sets of legal and cultural practices may limit organizing activities. For example, surgeons are not allowed to practice law nor can lawyers operate on patients. Medical operations typically take place in hospitals and/or clinics. Generally, however, organizations also have permeable boundaries, as organizational membership changes and as information flows across organizational boundaries (Bolman & Deal, 2008; Mintzberg, 1979; Morgan, 2006; Schein, 2004).

Organizations typically have names and images which uniquely symbolize their identity. Significant attention is given to establishing and maintaining a unique identity which makes an organization widely recognized. Organizations also want to enhance their employees' identification with the organization so as to ensure loyalty and cooperate and facilitate higher levels of achievement. And, finally, organizational members struggle with competing identities—their identification with their work, their organization, their careers, their families and their leisure activities. These identity concerns also focus on the meaningfulness of work and the work/life balance for organizational members.

Organizations can also be viewed as having both internal and external aspects. As noted organizational theorist Edgar Schein (2004) observed, organizations must maintain internal cohesion and external adaptation in order to survive. Internal cohesion rests on a shared core mission, shared goals and means that support that core mission, a shared language and/or conceptual system, methods for measuring how well the organization is doing, and strategies for repairing mistakes or making needed changes.

Organizations must also adapt to their external environment, whether it be in the form of increased competition from other organizations, or increased levels of governmental control. Adaptation frequently involves research activities to develop and/or improve products and services, competition to hire the best organizational members, the development of a supportive organizational environment through compensation practices, and so forth. Adaptation itself is an increasingly important quality of organizing—the ability to innovate and change in order to respond effectively to new environmental demands.

We have briefly outlined some generic characteristics of organizing: qualities such as interdependent activities, forms of hierarchical control, group boundaries, group membership and identification, and a need for internal cohesion as well as external adaptation will not strike anyone as being terribly unusual. Such qualities reflect, as noted previously, many of our taken-for-granted expectations about organizational life. Such a generic list is not exhaustive because organizing is constantly changing and responding to new environmental demands. However, these generic characteristics are assumed to apply across cultures. For example, all cultures utilize hierarchical forms of control in organizing, although how those hierarchies operate varies from culture to culture. Listed below are the generic organizational qualities in the frame system of organizing developed here.

Cross-cultural dimensions of organizations. In addition to these generic assumptions that help constitute our frame system of organizations/organizing, we can also

---

TABLE 3.1   Frame System of Organizing*

Generic characteristics of organizing:
- Goals → the core mission(s) of the organization
- Membership (voluntary) → individuals who carry on the organizing activities
- Specialization of members → reflects the required skills and knowledge of organizational members
- Tasks and delegated responsibilities → reflects the division of labor within an organization
- Interdependence → individuals/units depend on one another to carry out the organizational goals
- Hierarchy → reflects the organizational structure, and may reflect the exigencies of the task as well as power relations
- Rewards/punishments → norms for rewarding/punishing organizational members
- Control → organizational activities usually require coordination and individuals who guide and command that coordination
- Power → organizational members may exercise both authority and influence
- Coordination → organizing activities usually require that tasks be sequenced and integrated with one another
- Communicative processes → communication is necessary for any shared, social activity
- Leaders → those exercising authority and/or influence
- Boundaries → organizational boundaries, although permeable, usually refer to those members who carry out the daily organizing activities that sustain the organization
- Stakeholders → anyone having a vested interest in an organization, such as investors or university alumni
- Relationships → organizational members develop relationships with one another at work, such as colleagues, supervisor/subordinate, etc.

---

* This list reflects consistent, general assumptions about organizations and organizing, culled from the research literature on organizations. It is not necessarily a complete or exhaustive list. It may be viewed as a set of necessary, but not necessarily sufficient, conditions for organizing. Organizing is assumed to be in flux and change, rather than static.

examine scholarship that assessed cross-cultural differences among organizations. As mentioned earlier, culture is the overarching context for both communicating and organizing. Substantive scholarship has documented cultural influences both on communicating (Gudykunst & Kim, 2003; Ting-Toomey et al., 2000; Ting-Toomey & Oetzel, 2001) and on organizing (Hofstede, 1980; Hofstede & Hofstede, 2005). Because nation-states are becoming increasingly culturally diverse, and immigration is changing cultural and personal identities, cultural influences are becoming increasingly blurred and integrated. Nevertheless, culture, as a source of both individual and group identity, remains an important influence on human behavior.

The interrelationship I want to suggest is that communication makes possible both culture and organizing, and as such, communication is foundational for both. People learn how to communicate within a given cultural milieu and those communicative patterns tend to reinforce that culture. Thus, cultural and communicative patterns recursively produce and reinforce each other. In a similar fashion, culture influences preferences for organizing and organizations. Thus, culture and organizing patterns recursively produce and reinforce one another. Both organizing and culture are thus instantiated in everyday interaction, and are both the medium and outcome of those interactive processes. (I am assuming, of course, that we are viewing communicating, organizing and culture from the perspective of modernity, but for an intriguing discussion of how societies [cultures] have altered over time, read Giddens' discussion of historicity and the shift from traditional to modern cultures.) In sum, cultural practices and beliefs create the overarching context in which communicating and organizing takes place.

Cultural differences influence the structure and functioning of organizations, and culturally diverse workforces provide complex motivational challenges for managers (Hofstede, 1980; Hofstede & Hofstede, 2005; House, Hanges, Javidan, Dorfman & Gupta, 2004; Ingelhardt, 1997; Ralston, Holt, Terpstra & Kai-Cheng, 1997; Schwartz, 1999). Briefly examining some of this research will shed more light on the issue of how organizations are viewed.

The work of Geert Hofstede and his colleagues is most widely known in this area. Hofstede (1980, 2001) conducted a multi-national investigation of work dimensions to explore how different cultures varied in their approach to organizing. Hofstede's work uncovered four universal dimensions on which cultures differed: uncertainty avoidance; power distance; collectivism/individualism; and masculinity/femininity. Of these, the dimension of collectivism/individualism has been the most widely researched and is generally regarded as a fundamental dimension for comparing cultures. However, because of individual variability within a particular culture, an individual's self-construal (how individuals view themselves) has been used to link cultural orientation with individual values and behaviors (Oetzel, 2001).

The first dimension, *uncertainty avoidance*, reflects a culture's tolerance for ambiguity— some cultures, like Japan, rely on relatively rigid rules and procedures at work, such that everyone knows their duties and what is necessary to do. In contrast, other cultures, such as the US, have more flexible, fluid social practices. *Power distance* measures the distance people desire between themselves and those in positions of power, such as supervisors. For example, North Americans tend to prefer a low power distance, while Latin Americans prefer more distance. *Femininity/masculinity* reflects a culture's flexibility and nurturing: Sweden is a feminine culture with significant role flexibility, whereas Saudi Arabia has a masculine culture with more definitive roles for men and women. *Collectivism/individualism* reflects the relationship between the individual and society: in collectivist cultures, individuals identify most strongly with the group's interests, whereas in individualist cultures, individuals identify most with their own self-interest. It is important to note that there is significant within-culture variation along any of these dimensions. For example, someone in Japan could be more of an individualist, while someone in the US could display collectivist values. More recent work by Hofstede and Hofstede (2005) incorporated a dimension measuring *time-orientation*, and the US culture reflects a short-term time-orientation. Such short-term time-orientations value freedom, thinking for yourself, and achievement.

Studies have also been conducted surveying more countries and grouping countries along these different dimensions. (See House, Hanges, Javidan, Dorfman & Gupta, 2004, for detailed discussions of the GLOBE findings and methodology.) Countries have been broadly grouped into seven regions, grouping similar cultures together: English-speaking countries; Protestant Europe; Catholic Europe; Africa; Latin America; Asia; and South Asia. The most basic contrasts are on traditional versus secular-rational values, and on survival versus self-expression values (Inglehart, 1997).

Another broad cultural distinction of interest is the contrast between high context and low context cultures. High context cultures rely heavily on nonverbal communication and the interpretation of the context. Low context cultures, like the US, rely on verbal expressiveness and explicitness to define the context and the individual's orientation to the context. High context cultures rely on communication that is indirect while low context cultures meanings are directly and explicitly stated (Hall, 1976).

Nation-states are a primary source for cultural identity, and thus for organizational identity as well. However, there are two other senses of culture which are relevant to organizing and communicating. First, organizations have a unique cultural identity as organizations—not only in terms of branding their identity, but also in terms of their organizational social practices. That is, organizational cultures refer to an organization's preferred set of social practices, values and beliefs. For example, Deal and Kennedy (1982) contrasted "work-hard/play-hard" organizational cultures with those having a family orientation.

Within an organization, different subunits may have distinctive cultures: for example, sales forces versus "techies" (those supporting the technology used in the organization). Some important trans-organizational cultures may also exist and provide important sources of identification with professional groups and standards rather than any particular organization. We also need to appreciate cultural diversity as it exists across generations, between urban versus rural areas, ethnicity, and so forth.

See the work of JoAnn Martin (2001) for excellent discussions of organizational cultures and their complexity.

In both communicating and organizing, it is vitally important to recognize cultural diversity, and to acknowledge voices that may be marginalized or largely ignored (Clair, 1993). Through globalization and telecommunications, all areas of the globe are intertwined, and our relationships with one another depend on recognizing our differences as well as our similarities. Cultural background is one of the most significant factors influencing human behavior, and one of the most complex because many cultural influences are part of our tacit knowledge and practical consciousness. Some cultural differences are very subtle and largely outside our conscious awareness. Because both communicating and organizing will be influenced by cultural patterns of knowledge and social practices, we need to incorporate cultural frames of reference, in multiple contexts, into our views of organizing and communicating. We need to incorporate them not only in research, but also in the "real world" of intersecting multinational organizations, and complex global economic and political contexts.

As you will recall, frame theory has been used on three levels: metaframes, which represent knowledge at the most abstract level, frame systems, which represent knowledge organized around interrelated themes such as organizing and communicating, and frames, which represent knowledge constituting the contexts in which organizing and communicating co-occur and mutually influence one another.

Thus far, we have developed a frame system for organizations based on the work of Schein, Hofstede and others. Frame systems incorporate our most tacit, fundamental expectations about communicating and organizing. And the coherence of organizing itself, or of a particular work project, relies heavily on tacit knowledge (Weick, 2004, pp. 188–90). While many assumptions about communicating and organizing in the frame systems developed here are shared across cultures, these expectations may be enacted differently across different cultures. For example, tacit knowledge is important for both communicating and organizing, but such knowledge varies across cultures, and is grounded in different cultural practices.

In this next section, frames will be used to conceptualize some distinct perspectives on organizations. Although frame systems capture tacit expectations about organizing and communicating, *frames reflect the surrounding contexts of organizing and communicating*. Frames thus reflect our interpretive schema and scripts for making sense of "what is happening" in a particular encounter. As Weick observed:

> Frames and cues can be thought of as vocabularies in which words that are more abstract (frames) include and point to other less abstract words (cues) that become sensible in the context created by the more inclusive words. Meaning within vocabularies is relational. A cue in a frame is what makes sense, not the cue alone or the frame alone. *Said differently, the substance* of sensemaking starts with three elements; a frame, *a cue, and a connection.*
>
> *(Weick, 1995, p. 110, italics mine)*

Framing devices (Weick's cues) are specific strategies that are used to signal a communicator's intended meaning in a specific context (thus establishing a connection among the frame, cue and context).

Weick's sensemaking also incorporates the concept of frames and cues as noted previously. As he argues, "the content of sensemaking is to be found in the frames and categories that summarize past experience, in the cues and labels that snare specifics of the present experience, and in the ways these two settings of experience are connected" (1995, p. 111). Weick's use of frames is consistent with both Goffman's use of frames and with Giddens' conceptualization of tacit knowledge (stocks of knowledge) and social practices (routines and schemata for action). Goffman's framing would reflect the cues and labels that are enacted in a specific context, and would parallel Giddens' processes of signification (meaning) in interaction.

Alternative Frames for Organizing

In this next section I want to focus our attention on different frames for organizing, and suggest how each frame highlights particular features of organizing along with their concomitant communicative features. For example, within a structural or classical organizational frame, communicative processes focusing upon hierarchy and authority are highlighted. What is distinctive about the perspective being developed here is the linking of organizing frames to communicative processes.

As Bolman and Deal (2008) point out, organizations are complex and ambiguous, and no single frame is able to capture all the richness and complexity of organizing. They suggest that effective leaders and managers must be able to reframe—that is, move from one frame of organizing to another—to enhance their effectiveness. Each major school of thought (a frame) contains important ideas about organizing, but may not be the most appropriate frame to apply when trying to solve a particular organizational problem. Like Bolman and Deal, I characterize different perspectives on organizing as frames. However, while Bolman and Deal use frames to enhance managerial effectiveness, I will be concerned with exploring the knowledge represented in frames, and linking those organizing frames with communicative processes.

Each frame, as Bolman and Deal observe, reflects a major school of thought about how organizations function. In addition to the four frames developed by Bolman and Deal, I would add several more frames. Two other frames, an ideological frame and a systems frame, also characterize a unique perspective on organizing. In what follows, I shall briefly outline each organizing frame.

Organic versus mechanistic frames. One of the earliest general distinctions between types of organizing contexts (or distinct organizing frames) was the distinction between organic and mechanistic organizations (Burns & Stalker, 1961). In their research, Burns and Stalker contrasted a rayon mill (reflecting a mechanistic frame) with an electronics firm (reflecting an organic frame). Organic organizations are more flexible, have less rigid hierarchical structures, have employees who are more fully committed to the organization, and who are able to respond more quickly to change and external challenges. In contrast, mechanistic organizations have very centralized coordination and control mechanisms, a tightly structured hierarchy, and are less responsive to change and external challenge.

Further work by Lawrence and Lorsch (1967) argued that different organizations require different types of organizing and that more turbulent environments require more open, flexible coordination and control. They applied this to variation across organizational subunits as well. Giddens (1984) also discussed differences in types of organizations (i.e., organizations of signification, legitimation, and domination). Over time, these broad contrasts shifted into more differentiated frames, such as those developed by Bolman and Deal (2008); different organizational configurations, such as those of Mintzberg (1979); or different organizational metaphors, such as those developed by Morgan (2006).

The structural frame. During industrialization, the structural or classical frame emerged as people developed ways to efficiently mass produce goods. The structural frame highlights the importance of organizational design, hierarchy, specialization, and power. According to Bolman and Deal (2008):

> the *structural frame* emphasizes goals, specialized roles, and formal relationships. Structures—commonly depicted by organizational charts—are designed to fit an organization's environment and technology. Organizations allocate responsibilities to participants ("division of labor") and create rules, policies, procedures, and hierarchies to coordinate diverse activities.
>
> *(pp. 13–14, italics in the original)*

This organizing frame seems quite familiar to us because it is the perspective that dominates Western implicit expectations and thinking about organizing. Communicative processes that are emphasized in this perspective would be formal channels of communication, top-down communication flow, an emphasis on task-oriented communication and centralization of power and information.

The human relations frame. An organizing frame focusing on human relationships places most emphasis on people, their needs and their relationships. People constitute organizations, and their motivations, their relationships with others, their values, and their systems of rewards and punishments are central themes in this conceptual frame. As Bolman and Deal point out, "the key challenge is to tailor organizations to people—to find a way for individuals to get the job done while feeling good about what they are doing" (2008, p. 14). In this frame, interpersonal relationships are key, and communication focuses upon relational issues, job satisfaction, identity and teamwork.

The political frame. In this frame, organizing and communicating are viewed as negotiations that take place across continuously changing coalitions, interests and tasks within an organization as well as between an organization and its external environment (Morgan, 2006). Issues around values, goals, power, and rewards and punishments are emphasized. The focal processes underlying the political frame are conflict, interdependence, and power. A political frame suggests that organizational members have pluralistic viewpoints that are often in conflict with one another. Furthermore, organizations may frequently conflict with environmental forces, such as governments, other organizations, and governmental regulations (Morgan, 2006). Bolman and Deal (2008) point out that conflict is an inescapable aspect of the political frame because people have different needs, perspectives, and resources. Negotiation and persuasion are important communicative processes because of the competition over resources, and the ability to persuade others to your point of view.

The symbolic frame. Focal expectations in the symbolic frame highlight the values, symbols, norms, and meanings embedded in organizing. On a macro-level, organizing is embedded in societal cultures; on a more micro-level, organizations as socially constructed entities transmit their preferred ways of organizing to new workers. Subunits in an organization may develop their own unique cultures as well. Meaning and interpretation are problematized in the symbolic frame. Symbols and values, both in organizing and communicating, may change, unify and/or fragment groups (Martin, 1992, 2001). Discourse surrounding meaning, values and identity are critical communicative processes.

The systems frame. A systems frame highlights the interdependence and inter-connectedness across various organizing activities and entities. Organizing is a delicate, continuously fluctuating balance between differentiation and integration. Organizations are continuously in flux, co-constructing their environments and responding to them. Key organizing issues are complexity, redundancy, equifinality (multiple pathways for action), dynamic homeostasis (stability during change), and summativity ("wholeness" of the organization). Key communicative processes are centered around maintaining strong networks across the organization as information needs to be channeled rapidly, clearly, accurately, and responsively.

Ideology as frame. An ideological frame explores the implict, fundamental assumptions and values that underlie dominant organizing themes, such as hierarchy, patriarchy, and capitalism, and the communicative processes that sustain such patterns. Critiques of various organizing frames have been developed, ranging from Marxist critiques to feminist and postmodern critiques. Ideology may be a force for reframing on a number of levels, as witnessed in new models of organizing, such as NGOs (non-governmental organizations), concepts about civil society, feminist organizations, and the role of discourses in organizations (Bourdieu, 1990). Issues of voice, discourse, identity, power and hierarchy are emphasized in this frame. Commitment, identity, voice and participation are key communicative processes, as well as critical commentary around organizing and organizations.

Weick also discussed several types of frames: ideology or societal beliefs; organizational frames (non-routine structures); paradigms (for accomplishing work); stories (frames of sequences and experiences); frames of tradition (past precedents); and frames of action (carrying out particular behaviors or actions). These frames can also incorporate different degrees of scope or breadth. For example, one can frame a particular activity (like prepping a car for painting), frame specific routines in constructing a product (like an assembly line in a car manufacturing plant) or frame an entire industry (like differentiating manufacturing cars from manufacturing paint).

These frames therefore represent distinctively different ways in which organizing can be conceptualized and operationalized. As Bolman and Deal (2008) noted, these frames represent fundamental coping mechanisms for organizing. Each frame highlights some communicative processes, while downplaying others. However, we should also keep in mind that frames are not static, but fluid and continuously evolving. Some of this evolution is a result of tensions within each frame that "stretch and flex" the frame to test its utility and boundaries. For example, the structural frame has tensions surrounding the tightness of the organizing form—how much control needs to be exerted by authority? Or, to "frame" the tension somewhat differently, how much flexibility needs to be "built in" for maximum efficiency?

Transforming Organizing Frames

Frames are continuously evolving and developing. As new people, new information and new experiences become part of individuals' lives, their frames and schema change and adapt. In a similar fashion, organizations also adapt and change. Some of this organizational change occurs as a result of inherent tensions and paradoxes within organizations.

Underlying tensions have always been part of organizing (Conrad, 2004; Deetz & Mumby, 1990; Morgan, 2006). These tensions, such as the tension between control versus participation, differentiation versus integration, constraint versus creativity, autonomy versus interdependence, flexibility versus rigidity, and the degree of participation in organizational decision-making also influence organizational frames (Bolman & Deal, 2008; Kanter, 1983; Morgan, 2006). A fundamental tension within organizations is the tension between the individual and the organization as individuals give up some independence for the interdependence in organizations (Bacharach & Lawler, 1980; Conrad & Poole, 1998).

Beyond the tensions inherent within each frame, there are powerful transformational forces altering the nature of work itself, and, more generally, organizing and communicating. Among the forces transforming organizing frames are new technologies, primarily information technology and telecommunication devices, which have altered the manner in which we connect and organize (Giddens, 1990a). Because our world is now more interconnected, we face issues around globalization and diversity that affect everyday life. We have yet to fully understand the way in which new technologies profoundly alter communication, organizations and organizing (DeSanctis & Poole, 1994, 1997; Orlikowski, 2002, 2007), As these transformational forces continue to alter organizing and communicating, the nature of leadership and change itself also pose significant challenges for organizing and communicating.

Paradoxes. Another concern in organizing and communicating are paradoxes. As individuals are expected to participate more in organizations, as well as in a greater number of organizations, pragmatic paradoxes arise. Stohl and Cheney (2001) noted that paradoxes are time- and context-dependent, and products of relationships. In paradox, "when the action implications are traced out ... the command nature undermines the message's substantive content" (p. 355). Stohl and Cheney discuss four different categories of participatory paradox: of structure, of identity, of agency, and of power. It is not surprising that these issues are major concerns in organizing and communicating. For example, in her discussion of the dilemmas of participation, Kanter (1983) noted that participation itself may be paradoxical when employees perceive the invitation to participate as an order that must be obeyed.

In summary, frames, as they have been conceptualized here, represent the overarching context in an organizing; such contexts provide for overall integration and coherence in an organization. Frames can be thought of as taken-for-granted knowledge, as well as an organization's preferred ways of doing things. It is important to note, however, that any organization may have several frames simultaneously present. Organizational tension and transformation may occur, in part, because of the tensions between competing frames within an organization (Bolman & Deal, 2008). Finally, organizational members may employ different frames in the same, or different, communicative situations. Bolman and Deal (2008) suggest that effective managers and leaders are skilled at moving across different frames, depending upon their relevance in a particular setting.

Frames are useful heuristic devices for analyzing organizational activities; they provide multiple perspectives on organizing, and each perspective reveals some of the complexity of organizing. Organizational members may also strategically utilize these frames when dealing with different organizational issues. What is particularly useful, for our purposes, is viewing frames as the overarching context in which organizing and communicating take place.

Even given these efforts, exactly what constitutes an organization remains problematic, especially its emergent, continually changing nature. Although we have outlined some generic qualities of organizing, problems still remain. For example, families as well as organizations share goals, some hierarchy, some boundaries, job responsibilities and reward systems. However, most organizations have voluntary membership, whereas family membership is not voluntary, but a matter of blood relationships, emotional bonds and legal responsibilities. Frames have further refined the context of organizing because the surrounding contextual frame influences the shape of organizing and communicating within that context.

As we have seen, organizing is a complex process. However, we can move to a more fine-grained analysis and explore how scholars have defined organizations themselves. We next turn our attention to closely examine the properties of organizations, moving from the abstract qualities of organizing to explore the qualities of organizations.

What is an Organization?

Defining an organization, or at least specifying some generic qualities of an organization, is critical because not all organizing results in an organization. Organizing usually implies some coordination and control over activities, but how do we distinguish between organizing a sandlot baseball game and organizing General Motors? Is it a matter of size? Complexity? Profit? Compensation for work? Or do we even need to concern ourselves with differentiating between the two?

As a discipline, we seem to have assumed this to be an unproblematic issue. In reality, however, it is a complex issue that needs to be addressed before we examine the relationship between organizing and communicating. We may not be able to answer it satisfactorily, or without considerable controversy, but it nevertheless must be addressed.

Alternative perspectives on organizations. Various scholars have proposed differing qualities of organizations. Hodgson (2007) defined organizations as subsets of institutions; institutions are "systems of established and embedded social rules that structure social interactions" (p. 96). Organizations thus have boundaries, a designated membership, principles indicating who is in charge, and command chains that outline responsibilities within the organization (ibid.). Language, for example, is an institution, but not an organization.

As he concluded:

> Organizations are bounded institutions with a relatively high degree of cohesion. Their characteristics of membership, sovereignty and responsibility enhance the possibilities for more intensive interactions between individuals and organizations. ... They carry a richer repertoire of mechanisms and opportunities for creating habits and thereby altering preferences and beliefs. The other side of the coin is that organizations themselves depend upon the existence of a complex of habits relating to rules concerning membership, sovereignty and responsibility.
>
> *(p. 110)*

As we shall see, Hodgson's emphasis on habits is very similar to Giddens' and Goffman's emphasis on routines and social practices.

Iedema and Wodak (1999) also discussed the most salient characteristics of organizations, particularly discursive and material dimensions of organizations. Organizational discursive practices are important, not only in terms of speech or writing, but also in terms of "the use of brick or electronics rather than (or as well as) voice and gesture to make meaning" (p. 11). They also paid particular attention to the process of recontextualization As they suggested:

> Recontextualization involves shifts in meaning and materiality away from their previous instantiations. ... Recontextualization is achieved by means of "technologies" such as ... writing, electronic, design and built construction. These technologies ensure that the recontextualization of meaning from one mode to another achieves both depersonalization and power.
>
> *(ibid.)*

They further suggest that "technologization alters (discursive) practices. ... Importantly, what previously relied on extensive specification now becomes a matter of (newly conceived) background assumption, redefining both the practice and the community constituted by that practice." Power (especially hierarchy and the ability to focus attention), the continuity of the organization, decision-making processes, and impersonalization are also considered salient qualities.

Both Latour (2005) and Czarniawska (2004, 2006a) focus on action in organizing and organizations. There is no discernible beginning to organizing because actants (both human and non-human entities) are in webs of action that involve translation (making associations or connections) among groups, individuals and entities that constitute a particular action or effect. For example, teaching at a university involves networks or associations among faculty, students, construction workers and the materials used to construct university buildings, traffic lights to control traffic flow around the university, and so forth. As such, given these networks or associations, a precise beginning to an organization is impossible to determine.

Czarniawska (2004) focuses on connected action over time. "What is being done, and how does this connect to other things that are being done in the same context? It is a way of questioning that aims at capturing the traces of the past but not per-mitting them to decide the future. ... " (p. 784). In particular, organizing involves narratives constructing identities and interrelationships, texts, and material objects such as computers and bricks, so that the organization has stability and durability over time. What is also critical is the identity of the organization—the collective sense of "we"—and those who speak on behalf of the organization (a macro actor or actant—logos, for example, may represent organizations in the same way a spokesperson does).

Ahrne and Brunsson (2008) suggest that organizations may differ in terms of their completeness. Key qualities of organizations are features such as membership, hierarchy, rules, monitoring, and sanctions. They suggest that, outside of formal organizations, only some of these critical elements are present, and thus those organizations are incomplete. Formal organizations, possessing these qualities, reflect the highest degrees of social order, and such organizations have contributed to a global order. Finally, Tsoukas (2008) suggests that organizations can be viewed as a representation (locating the logic or syntax of the system); as the nexus of practices; and as an emergent pattern of actions. Every organization has these three components, and tries to align them.

Among these alternative perspectives, several themes emerge. There is a focus on action (or activity), materiality, and embedded social rules/practices that char-acterize an organization. A sustained sense of cohesion, and stability and durability over time are also emphasized. Finally, organizations appear to have an identity or a sense of cohesiveness over time. Given the emphasis on structuration theory (ST) in this book, it is important to examine Giddens' view of organizations.

Giddens' view of organizations. Giddens (1989) views an organization as "a large association of people run on impersonal lines, set up to achieve specific goals" (p. 276). Organizations are social systems which have clear, yet permeable boundaries, and use "certain typical forms of resources (authoritative and allocative) within discursively mobilized forms of information flow" (Giddens, 1984, p. 203). Organizational members also identify with the organization, and there is an asymmetrical power distribution with the dominant party in control and coordinating organizational activities. Well-established organizations have a "high degree of reflexive coordination of the conditions of system reproduction" (Giddens, 1990b, p. 303).

Organizations may also be classified according to their dominant modality—signification, domination or legitimation—respectively identifying organizations as focused on meaning (like education or religious organizations); focused on power (like political and economic systems); or focused on sanctions (like legal institutions). All organizations utilize all three modalities, but one modality is clearly dominant in an organization.

Giddens also views discourse (interaction) as playing a key role in the social positioning of actors. Social positioning is "constituted within structures of signification, domination and legitimation, within which social interaction takes place" (Heracleous & Hendry, 2000, p. 1261). As such, discourse is framed by an agent's social position and may be used as well to change or alter social positions.

Giddens uses the term "social systems" to include a wide variety of groups. He distinguishes among various groups, as outlined in Figure 3.1 (adapted from Giddens, 1990b, Figure 22.3, p. 303).

Networks are system of varying sizes whose connections are predominantly those of social relations rather than regularized interaction (i.e., local kinship network, trading networks, military alliances). Networks "often form a basis for the consolidating of social interaction into collectivities or associations" (Giddens, 1990b, p. 303).

In contrast to networks, members of *collectivities* or *associations* have a "definite sense of identity—they recognize themselves to be part of a corporate entity" (ibid.). Collectivities are less fluid and more coordinated systems than are associations, which are more flexible. The most significant type of association is a *social movement*, like the environmental or peace movements. For Giddens, social movements are as important as organizations. *Organizations* typically operate in fixed locales,

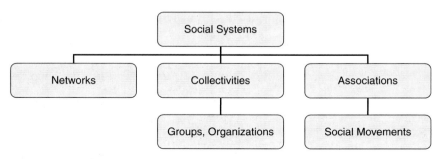

FIGURE 3.1 Social Systems

whereas social movements do not. Social movements also tend to be oppositional, and to confront organizations and associations (Giddens, 1984, p. 204).

Thus, for Giddens, an organization is also "a collectivity of some size, which has a high degree of reflexive coordination of the conditions of system reproduction. A distinctive feature of organizations is the regularized use of information, not just as a means of surveillance, but as a way of ordering social relations across time and space. Groups are smaller collectivities, quite often more ephemeral than organizations, and they ordinarily have a less developed reflexive component" (ibid.). In addition, when organizations are contrasted with other types of social systems, they are collectivities or institutions in that "the reflexive regulation of the conditions of system reproduction dominates other modes of system reproduction ... hierarchical relations of power are more prevalent mechanisms of coordination and control ... and ... roles are more clearly defined" (Sydow & Windeler, 1997, p. 472).

Giddens goes on to contrast the term "society" with the different social systems outlined previously. As he notes:

> A 'society' is a social system that includes all the other forms of social systems mentioned above. Yet 'include' is to a large degree a misnomer here, since many social systems cut across the boundaries of societies. Networks, as mentioned, may be global in character; organizations, like large business firms, may be located in many countries; social movements, like the contemporary peace movement, are frequently international in nature.
>
> *(Giddens, 1990b, p. 303)*

He further argues that the use of the term "society" must be carefully qualified because it may inhibit "the adequate interpretation of the distinctive properties of nation-states ... and [because] many forms of social interaction and social relation are not confined to any one society—this is particularly important in the current era, marked by a surge forward in the processes of globalization" (ibid.). Within the communication discipline, we are studying communicative processes in all types of social systems, and can usefully differentiate among them using structuration theory.

As Heracleous and Henry (2000) concluded, a structurational view of organizations entails (1) focusing on both action and the deeper structures guiding action; (2) recognizing the dynamic interplay of structure and action; (3) acknowledging social structures as the rules and resources agents use in daily interactions; (4) recognizing that social structures may be reproduced as well as changed in interactions and over time; and (5) treating agents as knowledgeable, active and reflexively monitoring their actions and the actions of others (p. 1260).

Organizations, as we have seen, are complex, multi-faceted social systems. Our review of alternative definitions have reflected that organizations are activity systems dedicated to a shared goal; that interaction is essential; that specialization, control and coordination are critical; and that individuals usually identify with the organization (to some degree).

In order to more fully understand organizing and organizations, the concept of frame systems has been used to discover our tacit assumptions about organizing and organizations. Some of these assumptions represent organizations as having regularized patterns of action and interaction (social practices) that control and coordinate activities directed at accomplishing a specific goal, such as producing cars or computers. Implied within these processes of control and coordination are issues such as hierarchy, power, boundaries, agency, and identity.

Frames have been used to explore organizing contexts, such as structural or political organizing contexts. Each frame highlights some aspects of organizing and communicating, while de-emphasizing others. Finally, we have looked at the defining qualities of organizations such as hierarchy, organizational members, goals, boundaries and communicative networks. In particular, we have examined Giddens' views of organizations, which emphasize structure, agency and interaction as properties of organizations.

While defining organizations is important, such definitions tend to treat organizations as outcomes—as a static product—rather than reflecting their emergent character and the underlying interaction processes that sustain both organizations and organizing activities. To complement this view of organizations as a socially structured product, we need to view organizations as emerging from organizing and communicative practices. Communicative processes are essential for organizing, and it is these communicative processes that provide organizations with their capacity to be created, sustained and altered. Communication, as action and agency, accomplishes organizational goals and provides the active component of organizing and organizations. In the next chapter, we shall investigate these processes more closely.

4

CONNECTING COMMUNICATING AND ORGANIZING

Broadly viewed, organizational communication may be viewed as the study of messages, information, meaning, and symbolic activity that constitute and make possible organizing (Putnam, Phillips & Chapman, 1996). Another very useful view of organizational communication is one emphasizing the trade-off between creativity and constraint; as Eisenberg and Goodall observe, organizational communication "is the moment-to-moment working out of the tension between individual creativity and organizational constraint" (1993, p. 30).

Conrad and Poole point out that organizational communication differs from interpersonal communication in the "complexity of the context and people dimension" (1998, p.9). Individuals communicating in organizations adapt their interpersonal relationships within the framework of organizational contexts. Within organizations, communication reveals the social hierarchy of organizational members, the amount and type of responsibility given to organizational members, and the creation and maintenance of the social division of labor. All of these perspectives place communication at the heart of organizing activities.

The paradigm shift from focusing on organizations (as containers of communicative processes) to focusing on organizing and communicating and their interrelationships has created a different set of research issues. The traditional view of organizational communication explores how communication functions within an organization and offers a static, or snapshot, view of communication. These classical approaches, utilizing a variety of research methods, treat communication as one of many variables influencing how organizations operate.

In contrast, recent scholarship emphasizes organizing and communicating as a process, and looks at how organizations emerge from communicating and organizing activities. Additionally, this view examines organizational social practices and activities, and focuses on action—perspectives also shared by Giddens and Goffman.

Such views are also exemplified in the communication-as-constitutive-of-organizations research.

In what follows, I shall first briefly overview research areas and findings in the traditional or classical approaches to studying organizational communication. This overview presents some of the communicative functions studied, but for a more thorough, comprehensive treatment of this scholarly tradition, readers are encouraged to read any one of a number of excellent organizational communication textbooks. Next, I will review the communication-as-constitutive-of-organizations scholarship and how Goffman and Giddens might address some of the concerns developed in this approach. Finally, I will discuss some major tensions and unresolved issues across these approaches.

Communicative Processes in Organizing

In classical or traditional approaches, the nature, or definition, of an organization is assumed to be non-problematic. Rather than viewing communication as constitutive of organizations, more traditional approaches emphasize communication as it occurs in specific tasks or functions. Communicating is examined as an internal as well as external process; as a function of task; and as a function of social relationships within an organization. We shall briefly review some of the communicative dimensions explored in the traditional approaches.

Level and scope of communication. In many organizations, communication occurs within dyads, groups, the organization as a whole, and between an organization and its surrounding environment. Dyadic communication may occur horizontally, such as interacting with colleagues or friends, or vertically across hierarchical lines, such as a supervisor reviewing the performance of a subordinate.

Group communication plays a key role in organizational communication (Frey, 1999). Increasingly, tasks are designed and executed by small groups making decisions and solving problems. Organizations are also frequently divided into larger groups, such as divisions and departments. Because significant work is accomplished by groups, it is especially important to understand group processes and group communication. Groups also vary in their autonomy, size, task complexity and its duration; such factors influence group communication.

Communication between an organization and its environment occurs in multiple ways, from communicating with other organizations to communicating with clients and the government. In many instances, communication with external publics is handled by spokespersons charged with that responsibility. Examples would include organizational lawyers responding to a governmental request, or public relations officers communicating with clients and advertising agencies.

Communication across an organization may occur in a number of different ways, ranging from company-wide memos to conferences involving the entire organization. Typically, such communication is handled by public relations and/or public information offices which handle both external communication and company-wide internal communication. Even this very brief overview illustrates the differing levels and contexts explored in organizational communication.

Organizational messages. Messages enable organizational members to coordinate, control and execute tasks. The complexity of an organization directly influences the type and complexity of message flow within that organization. For example, messages can range from exchanges between a doctor and a patient to exchanges in legal settings to a variety of other contexts assessing public dialogues (Hutchby, 2005; Tracy & Muller, 2001). McPhee and Zaug, as noted earlier, outlined four distinct message flows in organizations. Increasingly, research has also explored face-to-device (FtD) communication (Zhao & Elesh, 2008) in which various communicative mediums are analyzed, ranging from telephones, email, and Blackberries to other electronic forms of communication. Messages have also been contrasted between task-oriented messages and non-task-oriented messages which have no organizational purpose.

In sum, communication occurs across many different contexts, and may involve a wide range of organizational messages. Communication also occurs across multiple channels, including mediated and face-to-face (FtF) channels, formal or informal channels, and verbal or nonverbal channels.

Sensemaking in organizations. An article by Mengis and Eppler (2008) explores the role of face-to-face conversation for processing knowledge and sensemaking in organizations. They suggest that conversations—which provide flexible interaction and iterative forms of communication—build trust, strengthen relationships, and create and integrate knowledge that is essential for sharing tacit knowledge within communities (p. 1288). On the other hand, conversations may also negatively impact knowledge sharing through defensive arguing and/or unequal participation. They focus on conversational rules and review a wide range of studies talking about different communicative behaviors, such as skillful discussion and strategic communication, within different contexts, such as group meetings. They note that knowledge-intensive conversations have been studied with respect to knowledge management, organizational learning, decision-making and change management.

Their framework for conversation management in organizational knowledge incorporates many aspects of the communicative framework developed in Chapter 2 and the review of communicative functions in this chapter. Their framework reflects six different communicative dimensions: communicative messages, conversational intent, mental models of the participants, conversational processes, group dynamics and communicative background (i.e., the selection of people, time, space and organizational cultures). Like Goffman, their concept of messages incorporates verbal and nonverbal dimensions, as well as space. Like both Goffman and Giddens, their analyses incorporate the mental models (frames, resources and rules) and communicative background of participants. Finally, they make suggestions for specific conversational strategies based on a review of research strategies.

Formal and informal channels of communication. Organizational members may also communicate using both formal and informal channels of communication. Formal channels of communication handle an organization's public communication, both within the company as well as with its external publics. In addition, formal channels are used by organizational members to specify and carry out their particular job functions and responsibilities.

Messages sent across formal channels are usually initiated by those whose authority (job function and responsibility) legitimates their communication about particular issues. For example, a safety officer could send out notices concerning safety regulations in a manufacturing plant while a financial officer or custodian would not. Messages sent across formal organizational channels are usually public, focus on specific topics, and flow in a top-down fashion.

Finally, messages sent across formal channels are viewed as representing the public, legal stance of the organization on particular issues—in other words, what they are publicly (and perhaps legally) held accountable for. In many instances, therefore, formal messages might be reviewed by several different departments before being released. Examples of formal messages that routinely receive multiple reviews include advertisements for products, safety standards, and various company policies.

In contrast, informal messages flow in multiple directions across the organization. Informal conversations may cut across lines of authority, and their content is usually private (known only to those in that conversation). While formal channels may be used to cover topics of concern to the organization, informal channels may cover a wide variety of topics, including some that are personal and have no organizational purpose or goal.

Informal communication is a powerful tool for communicating because it may reveal the meaning contained in formal messages; that is, formal messages reflect "what is said" by legitimate authorities, while informal communication is often used to help organizational members "understand what is meant by what has been said" (Boden, 1994; Bolman & Deal, 2008). Thus, private, informal conversations often help organizational members interpret what is going on within the organization. However, it is often difficult to verify the accuracy of informal messages.

In summary, both formal and informal messages are important in organizing and communicating. These messages carry out and support the core functions within any organization, and help organizational members make sense of ongoing organizational activities. Effective organization members attend to both formal and informal communication, and use both to interpret what is going on. At various points, organizational members can act as gatekeepers and limit the flow of information to others.

Directionality of message flow. Organizational communication research has investigated the direction in which messages flow, whether upward, downward or horizontally. Downward communication flows from the top of the hierarchy to its lowest levels. Downward communication functions to send orders to subordinates, provide job-related information, evaluate organizational effectiveness, and inculcate organizational goals (Conrad & Poole, 1998). However, downward communication may also be overused, offer contradictory or unclear information, and reinforce power relationships in the organization (Kreps, 1990).

In contrast, upward communication, which flows from the bottom to the top of the organizational hierarchy, provides feedback about organization activities, and encourages participation by employees. Although upward communication can provide very useful information, frequently managers pay insufficient attention to it (Bolman & Deal, 2008), and employees may tend not to send bad news up the organizational hierarchy.

Horizontal communication enables organizational members to coordinate their activities, share relevant information, support one another's activities, resolve conflict, and solve problems (Kreps, 1990). Horizontal communication may be social as well as business-related. As Kreps noted, organizations may make it difficult for organizational members to use horizontal linkages (because these contacts may be regarded as primarily social, rather than business-related), and the boundaries between organizational units may limit such communication as well.

Face-to-face versus mediated communication channels. Early theorists and designers of organizations had little inkling as to the powerful new communication technologies that would transform organizations. Older organizational communication theories rested upon the premise of verbal, face-to-face communication (FtF), supplemented by written communication, and considerable time was needed to communicate across organizations (Yates, 1997). However, as new technologies and telecommunication systems developed, different channels of communication, such as email, voice mail and the intranet/Internet, transformed organizational communication. Fortune 100 companies, over a six-year period from 1991 to 1997, reported a decrease in print media, an increase in electronic mail and video, and about the same use of face-to-face interaction (USA Snapshots, USA Today, 1998). Of particular note was the approximately 700 percent increase in the use of email. Face-to-face communication remained steady at approximately 20 percent.

Burgeoning research demonstrates that electronic communication and the virtual connections between employees and organizations have transformed both personal and professional life. Research in adaptive structural theory (Poole & DeSanctis, 2004), genres of communication and sociotechnical frames (Orlikowski, 2000) and the linkages of human and non-human entities in work (Latour, 2005) are challenging the way we think about communicating and organizing. These issues will be discussed more thoroughly in subsequent chapters, especially Chapters 10 through 12.

Verbal and nonverbal communication. Both verbal and nonverbal channels of communication are important in understanding interaction. Most communicators respond to both channels of communication, and notice whether or not these channels are congruent or incongruent with each other (Burgoon, Guerrero & Floyd, 2010; Manusov & Patterson, 2006). Emotional expression in the workplace is now being researched (Fineman, 2000). Much emotional expression takes place nonverbally, and often will occur in "back regions" where there is some privacy. It is also necessary to note the importance of nonverbal communication represented in images, logos, icons and the like, as symbolizing both individuals and organizations.

Communicative tasks. What sets apart organizational communicative processes from more general patterns of interaction is its task-oriented focus, as well as its contextual constraints. Organizations produce goods and services, and expend considerable effort communicating about how best to provide them. Important communicative tasks include problem-solving, decision-making, conflict management, giving instructions, managing mergers, exploring and developing new markets, personnel evaluation, training and development, and so forth. Different organizing frames will emphasize some tasks much more than others, and accomplish them using different communicative strategies.

This brief overview has illustrated the range of communicative functions present in organizations. Depending upon the size and complexity of the organization, and its products, communication may also be more complex and multi-faceted. From this research base, as well as new theoretical developments in related areas, such as management and organizational behavior among others, increasing attention was directed toward communication as a critical component in organizing and organizations. This attention went beyond the functions of communication in organizing to a recognition of the foundational role communication plays in organizing. New research issues also emerged at this time, such as issues of identity (both personal and professional), the meaning and meaningfulness of work, work-life balance, participation and voice, materiality and others. Particularly challenging were the ways in which both organizing and communicating were altered through various mediated systems of communication, and their impact on globalization and our intertwined economies. Within organizational communication scholarship, the set of approaches collectively labeled as communication-as-constitutive-of-organizations focused on the foundational role of communication in organizing. Throughout our discussions, it would be helpful to keep in mind that approaches to organizational discourse may view organizations as a noun (an entity) and/or a verb (the processes of organizing). We now turn to a review of these approaches.

Communication-as-Constitutive-of-Organizations (CCO)

As mentioned previously, recent research in organizational communication has attempted to link interaction (discourse and texts) with organizing and organizations, and to generally articulate the role of communication in constituting organizations. A number of scholars have developed different approaches to this, and, in what follows, I will discuss some of these approaches.

Putnam, Nicotera and McPhee (2009) note that

> the typical definition of "constitute" and "constitution" highlights the forming, composing, or making of something in addition to describing the phenomenon that is constituted. ... Specifically, constitution connotes

one or all of the following notions of an organization, i.e., its historical emergence and contemporary reproduction, practices of organizing and participating, a body of knowledge about organizing, and the organization as a reified thing.

(p. 4)

Interestingly, structuration theory, as we shall see later, can incorporate all of those different approaches to organizations. The various CCO approaches outlined below focus on different aspects of constitution.

The Montreal School. The Montreal School, developed by James Taylor and his colleagues (Taylor, 2001a, b; Taylor, Cooren, Giroux & Robichaud, 1996; Taylor & Van Every, 2000), focuses on the interrelationships among texts, conversations and communication in constructing organizations. Although organizations contain multiple voices or points of view, the central process in constructing organizations is producing a "metanarrative that enfolds and transcends the narratives of the communities composing an organization" (Robichaud, Giroux & Taylor, 2004, p. 617). They outline several premises in their approach: that language supports collaborative activity; that sensemaking is retrospective and reflexive; that sensemaking has a narrative base; that organizational communication is rooted in communities of practice; that narrative closure grounds a community's identity; that language is recursive; and that conversations can exist with regard to other conversation only "if there is a voice to represent it" (ibid., pp. 617–23).

Discourse has two dimensions—"the *text* (what is said) and *conversation* (what is accomplished in the saying)" (ibid., p. 621). Through the sequential embedding of conversations within other conversations, a metaconversation is created that reflects an organization: "The metaconversation … is based on the existence of an implicit canonical script made of social and institutional rules and contracts" (ibid., p. 623). As new interactants are included, the metaconversation articulates new sets of rules and contracts.

The relationships formed are considered intercollective because they link different conversations. Individual actors are different from their roles, in which actions are scripted from the commonly agreed-upon organizational understandings. As such, "The constitution of an organization occurs in a metaconversation, where 'organization' refers to a language-based social entity composed of multiple communities of practice or cognitive domains" and the recursive conversational processes produce "higher-level discursive constructions providing continuity and stability (or discontinuity and change when megatexts are dropped and replaced" (ibid., p. 624). In this perspective, constituting organizations incorporates both a process and product view. When there are no contractual breaches, ordinary communication in organizations is routine (or imbricated; see Taylor, 2001b). Through the use of narrative-based interpretation, both individual and collective identities can be established. Of the four constitutive dimensions outlined by Putnam et al. (2009), their perspective appears to focus on the practices or organizing and participation and, to a more limited extent, on a body of knowledge about organizing (i.e., the emergent metaconversation).

Engestrom and activity systems. Engestrom suggests that discourse must be looked at in the context of the practical, productive, object-oriented activities of organizations. The production of objectives (goods, services or other outcomes) is the result of "an enduring, constantly-reproduced purpose of a collective activity system that motivates and defines the horizon of possible goals and actions" (1999, p.169, see also Engestrom, 1995, 1996). This also, in many respects, could serve as a useful definition of organizations. His scope of organizing includes the trajectory from raw materials, to product, to its eventual use by other activity systems; this view, like that of Latour (2005), Suchman (1987), and others, incorporates a network of connections (including non-human and human entities) across organizations in the production and use of objects.

Discourse needs to focus on "who is producing what in collection with whom by what kinds of machines" (Engestrom, 1999, p. 172). We need to integrate "talking out" with "acting out." Finally, Engestrom suggests that the basic unit of analysis should be the situated activity system (Goffman, 1961b). "Taking a situated activity system as the basic unit of analysis makes a whole range of phenomena available for integrated observation and analysis: physical inscriptions in public, material environment and artifacts, roles for different kinds of participants, rules differentiating successful from unsuccessful action, relevant tasks of seeing, moving and performing, and systematic language practices" (Goodwin, 1997, p. 172). Of particular note is the issue of relevance, as participants define their practical activities and outcomes in terms of accomplishing specific purposes. Engestrom's perspective would reflect a focus on practices of organizing and viewing organizations as reified things.

Four flow model. McPhee and Zaug (2000) view organizations as a "social interaction system, influenced by prevailing economic and legal institutional practices, and including coordinated action and interaction with and across a socially constructed boundary, manifestly directed toward a privileged set of outcomes" (p. 5).

According to McPhee and Zaug (2000), four types of message flow are communicatively constitutive of organizations. Complex organizations need to address four distinct audiences: *Membership negotiation* includes messages centering on relations among organizational members; *self-structuring* messages focus on control and coordination processes; *activity coordination* messages focus on various tasks and their connectivity; and *institutional positioning* reflects messages addressed to various external constituencies, such as governments and other institutions, and reflects processes of identity formation. After Giddens (1984), they suggest that "types of interaction constitute organizations ... insofar as basic features of the organization are implicated in the system of interaction" (p. 5).

Underlying the four message types is the legitimate authority of self-structuring, which incorporates reflexive design and control. Organizational self-structuring also involves the forming of boundaries and development of organizational identity.

Organizational knowledge, which outlines the relevance of messages to organizing activities, is also important. These message types also recognize that organizations are social forms that are culturally and temporally defined (Putnam, Nicotera & McPhee, 2009). Similar arguments are being made in this book, except frame systems, frames and framing are used as contexts which link organizing with particular types of interaction. And both models rely on relevance as a focal point of communication because it is the key to sensemaking and interpretation of messages, whether messages be primarily organizational or primarily interpersonal in nature.

Each flow or message type makes an important, yet distinct, contribution to organizing. And their complex interrelationships constitute particular organizational structures and communicative practices. While other theorists have focused on particular communicative tasks, such as decision-making or feedback (the activity-centered level in McPhee and Zaug), they provide an alternative, more inclusive way in which to look at organizational messages. McPhee and Zaug's four flow model appears to encompass all of the dimensions of being constitutive of organizations, and is the most inclusive perspective.

To closely examine the role of texts in organizing, McPhee also establishes some properties and features of organizations, which relate directly to the question posed at the beginning of this chapter. Organizations "are composed of people who impose and bring about relations and interaction among themselves as members" (2004a, p. 360). An organization is a "system of relations among its members" and these relations are usually stable, power-laden and artificially constructed (ibid.). Texts may reflect all these relations and enable the existence of multiple sites for organizations. Organizations are also considered multi-site, and each site—for example a shop floor versus managerial planning—has distinctive mindsets and practices (ibid., p. 362). Finally, organizations are reflexive social systems.

Kwon, Clarke and Wodak. Kwon, Clarke and Wodak (2009) developed a very comprehensive approach to organizational discourse by linking a discourse-historical approach to critical discourse analysis, within the framework of ethnography. They argue for "a critical and ecologically valid approach that articulates how discursive practices are influenced by, and in turn shape, the organizational settings in which they occur" (p. 273). Like the theory of structurational interaction, they seek to locate micro-level interactions within their broader organizational and socio-historical context. More specifically, Kwon et al. analyze power relationships as being partially determined by historical contexts, and suggest that executive teams be conceptualized as intersecting communities of practice as well as being a community themselves (p. 277).

Language/discourse gains power through three means: (1) power in discourse refers to the struggles of meaning, interpretation and access to meaning-making forums; (2) power over discourse refers to processes of inclusion and/or exclusion of organizational members, and (3) the power of discourses reflects the tacit, ideological aspects of discourse. These three discursive practices are located in four layers of context, from the immediate context, intertextual relationships, the extralinguistic social frames and the broader social, political and historical contexts. Like Giddens, they place discourse in a wide range of relevant contexts. Finally, they discuss different discursive strategies, such as mitigation, argumentation and so forth. As such, their model situates discourse in its varying layers of context, and with an analysis of the aspects of linguistic power and strategies being used in particular organizational practices. As such, this model looks at practices within an organization.

Cooren and Fairhurst. Cooren and Fairhurst (2004, 2009) argue that interactants, both human and non-human, contribute to organizing through enacting sequential templates of timing and spacing. This "*schema* or program [is] a generic form through which *any* coordination of activities potentially occurs" (Cooren & Fairhurst, 2004, p. 798). Greimas and others (Cooren, 2000; Greimas, 1987) have identified the following template: (1) a *manipulation* phase—having to do; (2) a *commitment* phase—wanting to do; (3) a *competence* phase—being able to do; (4) a *performance* phase—the doing; and (5) a *sanction* phase—assessing the performance (p. 798). As they note, "Based on co-orientation, there is a logical, problem-solving sequencing of events in a schema that provides actors with a basis for sensemaking. ... This generic form highlights the conditions of action (i.e., necessity, willingness, know-how, and means), the performance and its consequences" (ibid.). While this generic form can be applied to a variety of situations, it seems well suited to organizing because of its integration of knowing and doing.

In their analysis of police officers and dispatchers, Cooren and Fairhurst uncovered four defining features of an organizational schemata: various membership categorization devices were used; documents and vehicles were mobilized (an organization "can be *actualized* through the entities [humans and nonhumans] that officially act *in its name*") (p. 813); carrying out context-sensitive actions; and the implicit mobilization of procedures and protocols ("schemata are organizational to the extent that, in many respects, they are constrained in advance by these texts that also 're-present' [make present] the politic organization") (p. 814).

A related analysis by Cooren and Fairhurst (2009) raises the issue of how interaction contributes to the constitution of an organization. They criticize the McPhee and Zaug four flows because of its vacillation between two forms of agency (human vs. organizational) and its top-down analysis. However, I would argue that both are needed, and their analysis is not just top-down. They further note that studying organizing (a Weickian perspective) is not a complete answer to the question of what constitutes an organization. Here I would observe that, for the discipline, the issue of what is an organization still remains problematic. The lamination perspective (Boden, 1994) is also insufficient because it lacks features of organizational identity and agency (Taylor & Van Every, 2000).

To address these concerns, Cooren and Fairhurst developed the association thesis, based on the work of Latour. Essentially, they incorporate non-human entities in constructing an organization, and acknowledge their importance in hybrid agency (agency blended between humans and non-human entitites). They argue that interactions are never local, but rather dis-local—"That is, their local achievement is always mobilizing a variety of entities—documents, rules, protocols, architectural elements, machines, technological devices—that dislocate, i.e., 'put out of place' (Webster's Dictionary, p. 289) what initially appeared to be 'in place,' i.e., local" (p. 10). Such an analysis starts from the "bottom-up" and bridges the gap between macro- and micro-levels.

After Latour (1991, 1996, 1999), they argue that non-human entities (actants) provide the stable, enduring presence needed for organizations. Actor Network Theory (Latour, 2005) explicitly acknowledges the role of objects in constructing our social world, and extends agency to non-human entities. The stability and enduring presence of actants (non-human entities), in concert with human agency and action, enact organizations. In particular, non-human entities have the capacity to make a difference—to communicate something—that transcends time. While non-human entities are important in organizing (for reasons previously outlined), the view developed here, consistent with Goffman and Giddens, argues that non-human entities have affordances, but not agency.

As we have seen, communicating plays a key role in constituting organizations, being an essential element in creating and sustaining organizations. Common themes linking communicating and organizing reflect the importance of texts and message flows, and the central role of social practices in organizing. Texts also embody organizational knowledge and history and thus facilitate and shape organizational activities. The concept of association or connectedness also emphasizes the interconnections between the who, what, where and when in organizational activities.

Other consistent themes of the CCO perspectives, in discussing organizations and organizing, include an emphasis on action, or activity; a focus on interaction, ranging from narratives to texts to discourse; the importance of negotiating identity; competing views on agency; and an emphasis on materiality and the importance of non-human entities in organizations and organizing.

In evaluating some of these contrasting views on how communication constitutes organizations, I would argue that both forms of agency (human and organizational) are valuable. I would agree with the concept of hybrid agency—humans using material objects to act, although not with granting agency to non-human entities. Non-human entities have affordances, but not agency, because such entities cannot choose to do otherwise. (This argument will be developed more fully in subsequent chapters.) I would also agree that texts help provide a stable, enduring presence for organizations (and, in fact, are probably essential). Finally, I would not privilege a top-down or bottom-up analysis, but rather a meso-level entry point which incorporates both fine-grained analyses as well as more global, abstract analyses. Because I advocate the theory of structurational interaction, an integrated synthesis of Goffman and Giddens, like them, I support a duality of structure, with ever-widening layers of context, from the immediate concrete here-and-now situation to primary frameworks.

Regardless of the particular heuristic frame used, all organizing actions and activities are fundamentally grounded in talk. As Boden cogently remarked:

Talk ... is the lifeblood of all organizations ... it both shapes and is shaped by the structure of the organization itself. Through multiple layers of ordinary talk, people in organizations actually discover, as a deeply collaborative and contingent matter, their shared goals, many agendas, environmental uncertainties, potential coalitions, and areas of actual conflict. That mutual discovery, moreover, makes the durable features of the organization come alive—not just as fleeting details of the moment but as the elaboration of structure-in-action.

(Boden, 1994, p. 8)

While each of these frames, as Boden noted, is grounded in talk, the emphasis is on how a dominant frame, or perspective, influences communicative processes—and, reciprocally, how communicative processes shape actions and organizing.

The proposed synthesis of Goffman and Giddens, the theory of structurational interaction, is also grounded in talk. Social interaction (Goffman's interaction order) is a fundamental prerequisite for any social system, including institutions and organizations. The details of this synthesis will be fully developed in the remainder of this book. However, it should be noted that this synthesis will provide an integrated theoretical basis for exploring major themes—such as situated activity systems, materiality, social practices, various message types, agency and the like—which are highlighted in CCO research.

As noted previously, scholars have questioned the nature of organizing and the relationship between organizing and communicating. Scholars also have recognized the foundational role of communication in any shared social activity, most particularly in organizing. However, contrasting approaches to the nature of organizations, organizing, and communicating have raised many unresolved issues. These issues, tensions and paradoxes challenge scholars. In what follows, I will look at some of these contested issues.

Some Unresolved Issues in Organizing and Communicating

As Chia (2000) points out:

discourse is first and fundamentally the organizing of social reality. From this perspective, the idea of a discourse *about* organizations is an oxymoron. Discourse itself is a form of organization and, therefore, organizational analysis is intrinsically discourse analysis. Organization should not be thought of as something performed by pre-existing 'agents'. Instead the agents themselves, as legitimized objects of knowledge, must be understood as *effects* in themselves. The identity of the individual agent is constructed in the very act of organizing.

(p. 517)

Monge and Poole (2008) explore two additional perspectives to analyzing organizational communication: ecological/evolutionary theory and the organizational discourse perspective (in addition to the interpretive, critical and network approaches). After Grant et al. (2004), four domains of organizational discourse are conceptualized: (1) conversation and dialogue; (2) narratives and stories; (3) rhetoric or discourse for strategic purposes; and (4) tropes which capture the manner in which language creates meaning. These four domains cut across and relate to one another (for example, a narrative can be embedded within a conversation which, in turn, is part of a rhetorical, strategic plan of interaction). Two important dynamics operate across these dimensions: intertextuality which argues for the relationships across texts, and reflexivity on multiple levels. They argue for an integration of the ecological and discourse perspectives as a way of generating new insights into social construction and its relationship to evolutionary change.

And, Boden (1994) states, "It is through the telephone calls, meetings, planning sessions, sales talks, and corridor conversations that people inform, amuse, update, gossip, review, reassess, reason, instruct, revise, argue, debate, context, and actually *constitute* the moments, myths and, through time, the very *structuring* of the organization" (p. 8). All these scholars thus underscore the intricate connections between communicating and organizing, and the multiple ways in which these processes can be examined.

Emerging Issues

Although there is agreement about the fundamental linking of communicating and organizing, considerable controversy surrounds their interrelationships (as we have seen in discussing the communication-as-constitutive-of-organizations approaches). Some of the most contested issues in organizing and communicating concern the nature and role of text and agency. As I discuss these concerns, I will briefly fore-shadow the contributions that the theory of structurational interaction can contribute to these issues. These contributions will be more fully developed in Chapters 11 and 12. We begin this discussion with general concerns raised by Hardy, Fairhurst and Putnam, and Oswick et al.

Hardy. Hardy (2004) outlines three general issues in organizing and communicating: (1) "the constitution question of how local interactions develop organizing properties"; (2) "the scaling-up question concerning the identification of characteristics that imbue certain texts and their authors with agency"; and (3) "how grand discourses bear down on organizational life and how practices of consumption relate to acts of resistance" (p. 415). She argues that organizational discourse refers to "structured collections of texts that bring organizationally related objects into being as they are produced, disseminated and consumed" (p. 416).

She contrasts various approaches to organizational discourse analysis according to their focus on text or context, the degree to which context is proximal or distal, and whether or not the focus is critical or constructivist. She also notes that questions of agency are related to whether or not various texts have long-term durability, and thus help stabilize and reproduce organizational activities. The most influential texts are intertextual and interdiscursive in that they draw upon more broadly based meanings.

Finally, she focuses our attention on "The way in which texts become embedded—adopted and incorporated by other organizations—to become part of standardized, categorized, generalized meanings" (p. 416). This process provides a link between local conversations and the organizing properties of a larger organizational network. (See Cooren & Taylor, 1997; Phillips, Lawrence & Hardy, 2004.)

Fairhurst and Putnam. Fairhurst and Putnam (2004) suggest that organizational communication scholars strive for more clarity in their use of discourse approaches in analyzing organizations. They also argue for theories that simultaneously incorporate object, becoming and grounded-in-action orientations to organizations. An object orientation treats organizations as already constructed objects and explores communicative processes within that "container." (The general research overview outlined previously in this chapter reflects this object orientation.) In contrast, a becoming orientation explores how discourse and organizing mutually shape and influence one another. Finally, the grounded-in-action orientation explores how the organization is "anchored in the continuous flow of discursive conduct" (p. 18).

Fairhurst and Putnam also note two ways in which theorists have used discourse: discourse reflecting language-in-use, and discourses which reflect the logics, assumption, and patterns of thought characterizing cultures and intellectual eras (Foucault, 1972; Gee, 1999). The multitude of approaches to the nature of discourse (Alvesson & Karreman, 2000b) is matched by the differing views of the nature of text. In addition, there is the distinction between organizing and organization—when does the process become an entity? Fairhurst and Putnam conclude by encouraging discussions and integration across these alternatives to enrich our views of organizing and communicating. (For excellent coverage of the range of issues and approaches to organizing and organizations, also see Grant, Hardy, Oswick and Putnam, 2004.)

Oswick et al. Oswick, Grant, Marshak and Cox (2010) observed several waves of change in organizational discourse studies over the past decade. They note a move from "organizations and organizing" toward more specific discourse studies, focused on such issues as strategy, identity and change. Second, they see a shift toward a more pragmatic orientation, focused on issues such as actions, practices and materiality. These waves of change have led to discourses that focus on mythopoectic talk, frame talk and tool talk. Mythopoectic talk is "concerned with the big picture and setting broad, foundational parameters" (p. 9) and moving toward plurivocal constructivism. Frame talk provides the interpretive frameworks that guide meaning, and tool talk is the instrumental communication used in accomplishing tasks, which emphasizes practice. Finally, they argue for methodological pluralism, incorporating both qualitative and quantitative methods in pursuing these research areas.

In a forum critiquing the various CCO approaches, Bisel (2010) argues that such models included a range of views of what an organization entails (see also Sillince,

2010), which fails to adequately address materiality, and the role communication may play in disrupting and interrupting organizational action. In the same forum, Sillince (2010) argues that there is no consistency across views of organizations. He proposes that organizations emphasize context, switch among frames or perspectives, create consistency (repetition of practices and routines) and create purpose.

These brief overviews focus our attention on critical issues in organizational discourse, and the processes of organizing and communicating. Some of the CCO approaches address some of these contested issues, such as the nature of organizing. In what follows we shall explore more specifically some of the critical issues raised, such as organizations as entities, text, social practices, materiality and agency.

Organizations as Entities

This question returns us to the foundational questions about the nature of organizations, namely how do communicative actions become organizing activities leading to organizations and/or institutions. As we have seen, many focus on processes of organizing, rather than the organization itself.

Tsoukas (2000) looks at collective knowledge-in-action as a way of approaching the question of what is an organization. As he argues:

> An organized activity activity provides actors with a given set of cognitive catefories and a typology of action options. ... Since in a formal organization the behavior of its members is guided by a set of propositional statements, it follows that an organization may be seen as a theory—a particular set of concepts (or cognitive categories) and the propositions expressing the relationship between concepts.
>
> *(p. 108)*

This builds into a "community of practice, with specific contexts" (p. 109). As Tsoukas concludes, organizational knowledge is personal, propositional and collective (or cultural)—and this knowledge becomes the codified knowledge available in digital information systems (p. 110).

Tsoukas (2005) also observes such generalizing—"that types of behaviour in types of situations are connected to types of actors" (p. 124)—is a prototypical organizational practice. Such a view of organizations emphasizes its cognitive, collective basis, reflected in actors' knowledge as well as their practices.

King, Felin and Whetten (2010) focus on the "enduring, noun-like qualities of the organization" (p. 290). They argue that organizations are viewed as social actors, and that we attribute qualities and intentions to them as social actors. As they note, "Organizations are actors because society, not only legally but also practically and linguistically, grants them that status. Their status derives from the expectations of others, including the state, individual members of the organization itself, and other stakeholders and audiences who monitor and hold them accountable for their actions" (p. 292). Organizations also act intentionally and can choose to do otherwise; organizations have purposeful action and give rationales for their actions. As they point out, "The state, quite literally, treats the organization as a unitary actor and grants authority to the organization to erect membership barriers and to exert control over behavior within the organization" (p. 293). In some organizations, "personal preferences are set aside or ignored, and the collective considers what 'we' should do" (p. 293). Finally, organizations are also held accountable for their actions (hopefully so in the Gulf Oil spill, and other environmental disasters). If organizations are held accountable for their actions, this implies some agency for organizations: "organizations set strategy, pursue policies, and make other choices that play an important role in eventual outcomes" (p. 294).

Closely linked to organizational intentionality are claims about organizational identity. They argue that "identity claims become expressed as institutionalized mission statements, policies, and routines, they operate as the organization's social context, providing members and informed outsiders with a common set of phenomenological points of reference that guide consequential deliberation and organizational decision making" (p. 295). They conclude that understanding how organizations act will enable us to make valuable contributions to discussions about organizational agency and accountability, and that, once created, organizations act as social entities.

Developing a new paradigm of relationality and duality to analyze institutions, Mohr and White (2008) suggest that three types of social divides must be bridged—the issue of levels (micro, meso and macro), the divide between the symbolic and the material, and the agentic with the structural. Institutional resilience is related to the overall linkages across and within levels, while institutional change is related to the presence of multiple styles within an institution. Institutions are broadly defined and range across groups, organizations and broadly accepted cultural practices (like caste systems). As such, institutions represent "more enduring features of social life, that they tend to be reproduced and that they serve to structure and organize social action" (Mohr & Friedland, 2008, p. 421). Most importantly, social institutions are comprised of social networks across varying social relations and role systems. (This is very congruent with Giddens' view of institutions, as we shall see.) The concepts of relationality and duality are central to linking various social organizational levels as well as to linking various social orders with one another. Meaning and values are also enacted in daily social practices on both the individual and institutional levels. Individuals and institutions are coordinating their actions with others in order to exert control over their intermeshed activities. As Mohr and White (2008) argue, "agentic experience is characterized by a constant switching back and forth across a complex tapestry of institutional contexts" and contradictions and struggles are bound up in determining the appropriate relationships among actors and institutions (e.g., should the state, families or the church control education?) (p. 508).

Texts

Putnam and Cooren (2004) suggest that texts may refer to the "medium of communication, collection of interactions, and assemblages of oral and written forms" and that these varied forms of texts are constitutive of organizations and organizing. They argue that varied forms of language use, whether conversations or documents, reveal how organizations work, and, more importantly, form the foundation for organizing.

In interaction analysis (Fairhurst, 2004), texts emerge from predefined interaction codes that help interpret the patterns and sequences of talk-in-interaction, and their meanings. Cooren (2004), after Latour, suggests that texts can operate like machines and are thus decentered from, and external to, individuals' contributions to agency. As he argues, organizations are hybrids of both human and non-human contributions. In an analysis of problem-solving at a university undergoing financial crises, Castor and Cooren (2006) examine the hybrid nature of the problem-solving process by looking at the mutual transformations in various agents (non-human, textual, collective). Yet another view, by Taylor and Robichaud (2004), suggests that organizations are communicatively constructed by conversations and by texts (discursively generated interpretations of interaction, or sensemaking practices, of organizational participants).

Of particular interest is McPhee's analysis of texts (2004a) because of its application of structuration theory, and thus its direct connection to this book. I, like McPhee, argue that the term "text" has become so overused that we are ignoring important distinctions, and stretching "ordinary connotations beyond their actual range of validity" (p. 356). Thus, I will focus on the distinctions McPhee uses in his analysis of text. A "text" is "composed of signs or symbols, especially words and numbers" and, as such, excludes "most embodied performances and everyday social activities" (p. 357). In contrast, technologies are "studied, rule-governed courses of action that fashion material (speaking broadly) products with recurrent valued features," such as the minutes of a meeting. Some of these technologies are interpretive. But both technologies and texts have permanence in terms of "material inscription and the foundations for its interpretation, in knowledge and context, [which] endure far beyond the immediate setting of a communication episode" (p. 359). Finally, texts possess a certain level of coherence—necessarily incomplete, but still useful. Thus, texts are symbolic, have permanence, and some degree of coherence. McPhee notes that texts are important because of their accessibility to multiple parties, their preservation in legitimated forms, and their utility (ibid.).

Institutional reflexivity allows organizations to bracket space and time, and re-embed them in a redesigned manner (Giddens, 1984, 1991a, b). Three organizational features comprise institutional reflexivity—surveillance, knowledgeably designed locales, and time-space organizing features (such as schedules). Texts are essential for all these features. To these features, McPhee added another: that of organizational hierarchy. Formal relationships are outlined by the aforementioned features as well as by the discursive and textual expressions of formal structure and authority (i.e., legal statements around employment contracts, an organizational charter) (pp. 363–65).

As McPhee concluded, "a text is a relatively permanently inscribed symbolic formulation … it is a vital precondition for the development and continuing existence of organizations as we commonly conceive of them. An enduring inscribed record of organizational arrangements is a common if not necessary medium for stability of membership, relationships, and roles" (p. 365). Enduring texts are mediums for stipulating formal structures, and information storage and processing.

While there is strong agreement on the importance of texts, especially enduring, relatively permanent inscriptions, there are differences in terms of what scholars view as texts. Are conversations texts? Are material objects considered texts? As noted previously, my own preference is to retain the notion of text in its traditional linguistic sense—that of a written record, whether narrative, memo or email, which is a resource for organizational activities. And I agree with McPhee's views (2004a) on texts. To be so broadly inclusive of what counts as a text, as some scholars propose, will obscure important differences across various communicative mediums and conflate their effects with one another.

Materiality

The objects, resources, and the use of time and space are important emerging issues. Giddens suggests that "physical *milieux* of day-to-day life interlaces with routine and is deeply influenced in the contours of institutional reproduction" (1984, p. xxv). And Goffman's concepts of frontstage and backstage, and of co-presence intertwine materiality within their theories. Latour's work (2005) argues for hybrid agency, in which humans and actants exercise agency. Also, an emphasis on social practices combined social, cognitive and material aspects of organizing.

Pinch (2008) argues that both social skills (relational skills) and technical skills (i.e., scientific, instrumental and/or technical skills) are important in organizations. He and others have been important founders of the social construction of technology (SCOT); they build upon the work of Giddens and others and suggest that "it is important not to take either their constraining or enabling features for granted and study both how technologies could be different and how social interaction built around technologies could be different" (p. 469). Pinch uses the Moog synthesizer as an illustration of how design values and use shifted over time, and some of the factors behind its effectiveness. Finally, Pinch discusses the technological frames for both designers and users: "he [Moog] strived to understand what his users (his customers) wanted and he devised new ways to learn from them such that he could, in turn, discipline them more effectively" (p. 483). This, in turn, led to new uses and design features in the synthesizer, and such features, in turn, influenced social and cultural meanings and the economic development of electronic music. Pinch's work thus deals with many of the issues in organizational discourse, such as practices, materiality, agency and meanings.

Agency

Controversy surrounds agency in terms of its basic definition and its inclusiveness. Agency, for Giddens, lies in humans who have the capacity to choose to do otherwise. In particular, agents share mutual knowledge which allows them to meaningfully coordinate their activities. Agency reflects differing levels of consciousness and three processes—reflexive monitoring, rationalization, and motivation. (I shall explore these in more detail in upcoming chapters.) This is an internalist model of agency, but does not deny the impact or importance of material resources. As McPhee notes, a limitation in Giddens' model is that an agent may advocate a choice, but others may not listen, or be motivated to act (2004a, p. 366). This, however, is not unique to Giddens, but a potential weakness in any model of agency in which actions need to be collective and/or coordinated.

With regard to materiality, Giddens restricts agency to people—people use objects, both intentionally and unintentionally, in terms of the affordances of those objects. As Mingers (2004) noted, for Giddens,

> only people can actually undertake social activities. Systems, structures, practices or whatever do not, of themselves, act—only people can do that. ... This does not mean that such constraints do not *exist* independently of and prior to the activities of particular individuals. It simply means that the powers of the constraint are not actualized ... except through people. Nor does it mean that the actors involved have full transparency over the process ... it is quite possible for constraints to determine aspects of the contexts within which people find themselves and thereby shape the choices made without those involved being fully aware of it.
>
> *(p. 413)*

Mingers further notes that "Virtual rules and resources do exist; they are *real*; they are as Giddens says 'generative'—they do have causal effects; but they endure and underlie the events that they enable" (ibid.).

Conceptions of agency also have a cultural dimension, frequently ignored in our discussions of agency. A fascinating study by Morris, Menon and Ames (2001) explored cultural variations in conceptualizations of agency. While North American culture primarily regards agency as resting in individuals, other cultures conceptualize agency "primarily in terms of collectives such as groups or nonhuman actors such as deities or fate" (p. 169). These cultural perspectives on agency may exist in public forms, such as discourses and instititutions, as well as private forms (i.e., individual knowledge structures). For our purposes, they note that for organizational agency, "intentions, beliefs, and desires may correspond to internal states of the organization (i.e., policies, records, and strategic goals) rather than to mental states" (p. 170, fn 2). As such, they argue that social perception is influenced by implicit theories of agency (ITAs), which also acknowledge the influence of external factors on agency (i.e., autonomy). In their investigation of Chinese vs. North American perceptions of agency, they found North Americans had an individualistic view of agency as opposed to the Chinese view of collective agency (i.e., groups, families and organizations). Interestingly, they note that agency is different depending upon the domain of activity and that cultural institutions shape implicit theories of agency. For example, the North American legal system gives more freedom to individuals, and thus shapes expectations about individual actions, or, in the case of economies, "subsistence economies do not afford the expression of rampant individualism through material purchases" (p. 174). They also note that conceptualizations of agency may exist on different levels of abstraction: general conceptualizations would not be sufficiently detailed to guide specific actions and thus they "likely serve a belief-organizing function than a judgment-guiding function" (p. 171). Finally, they argue that ITAs are embedded within broader frameworks of institutions, practices, cultural representations and psychological tendencies (p. 180).

The broad-ranging discussion of different approaches to text, agency, organizing and organization has revealed some of the controversy over these issues. McPhee's conceptualization of text and agency is particularly important because of its application of Giddens' structuration. Heracleous and Hendry (2000) have extended structuration theory to an analysis of organizational discourse, which highlights other features of Giddens' approach and hints at some integration with Goffman's interactional order. In a broad-based discussion, Bisel (2009) points out that we need to employ multiple methodologies, and also look for negative cases, when communication has not worked well. I think these approaches are amenable to that, particularly in examining narratives, looking at strategic communication and negative cases. Jian, Schmisseur and Fairhurst (2008) also call for greater clarity and understanding of the diverse uses of "communication" and "discourse" across various disciplines investigating organizational communication. Cheney (2000) argues for growth in the field of organizational discourse by incorporating more different types of organizations, and expanding our views of sociohistoricity. Different external pressures need to be explored (such as varying forms of capitalism) and the ways in which globalizations may influence local practices.

Heracleous and Hendry. Heracleous and Hendry (2000) argue that, in an organizational context, agency is "ever present." Even texts are closely linked to their authorial context and rely on perceived instrumentality for their meaning. Language is viewed as a vehicle for conveying information as well as for constructing organizational and social reality.

In order to link structure and action on an organizational level, they turn to Giddens' work because the structurational perspective "provides a valuable meta-theoretical device … leading to a more sophisticated and productive view of organizational level discourse than can be obtained from any of the existing perspectives [interpretive, managerialist, or critical]" (p. 1253). They also view discourse as "any body of language-based actions, or language in use ... and 'text' in its linguistic sense to mean discourse fixed in writing" (p. 1258). While other metaphoric uses of text are valuable, "to include them in our definitions would only cause confusion and detract attention away from our central concern with structure and agency" (ibid.). My own usage and views, as well as those of Giddens (1984), are consistent with this position.

After Giddens, they argue that discourses exhibit "structural properties that are implicit, intertextual, trans-temporal and trans-situational ... the structural properties of discourse are instantiated in social interaction at the communicative level through the modality of agents' interpretive schemes. The two levels of discursive structure and communicative action are thus analytically distinct but practically interrelated" (p. 1263). Signification is the most important aspect to consider as it is most relevant to modes of discourse. Actors know, in order for their utterances to be viewed as legitimate and important, that specific modes of discourse must be used in particular contexts. Thus specific modes of discourse can be both enabling and constraining. For example, a lawyer or police officer not following appropriate forms of language might be viewed as incompetent, as well as failing to fulfill his or her legal obligations.

In the domain of discourse, Heracleous and Hendry suggest that structuration theory (ST) insightfully connects the surface structure of interaction, the communicative level, with the deep structure (signification or meaning). They argue that "deep structures are stable, largely implicit, and continually recurring processes and patterns that underlie and guide surface, observable events and actions" (p. 1266). Deep-seated meanings are "persistent features of discourse which transcend individual texts, speakers or authors, situational contexts and communicative actions, and pervade bodies of communicative action as a whole and in the long term" (ibid.). Some examples of structural features include central themes, root or generative metaphors, and rhetorical strategies in particular social settings. (These deep structures are represented in my communication model as tacit, commonsense knowledge.)

For a complete view of the relationship between communicative action and discursive structure, Heracleous and Hendry argue that a psychological perspective is needed to complement structuration theory. In particular, they look to apply "cognitive psychology so as to engage with the social and structural levels" (p. 1269). A key construct is that of schema. As they note,

> A schema can thus be seen as a psychological *frame* (Bateson, 1972, p. 186) providing the cognitive structuring necessary for actors to construct workable cognitive representations of the world and for consistency among cognitive elements and between these cognitive elements and actions. ... Schemata can operate at various levels of detail or abstraction, and can be both evaluative [and] descriptive. Schemata therefore have basic and vital functions in the interpretation of experience and indication of appropriate action.
>
> *(p. 1269, italics mine)*

Schemata are very similar to frames as developed in Chapter 1, and as used by Bateson, Goffman and others. As noted in Chapter 1, schemata and frames have been utilized in organizational research for quite some time.

For Giddens, interpretive schemes are "modes of typification incorporated within actors' stocks of knowledge, applied reflexively in the sustaining of communication" (1984, p. 29). As such, Heracleous and Hendry argue that "interpretive schemes are the modality through which discursive structures are instantiated at the level of communicative interaction, and though which communicative interaction can reproduce or challenge such structures" (2000, p. 1269). In essence, interpretive schemes operate as frames which link communicative action with discursive structures. They also note the importance of temporality and context in interpretive processes.

A similar point is made by Gioia (1986) when he argues that meaning is conveyed via symbols, and then "retained in a structured or schematic form via scripts. The scripts subsequently serve as a basis for action that further facilitates the meaning construction and sensemaking processes" (p. 50). As Heracleous and Hendry note, "interpretive schemes and agents' (communicative) actions are thus interrelated in a continual dialectic fashion: action arises out of interpretive schemes, and new experiences or reflections influence interpretive schemes and thus subsequent action" (2000, p. 1270).

Recall that Heracleous and Hendry (2000) call for a psychology to flesh out the details of structuration theory, and they suggest that schema theory or frames would be a way to do this. In synthesizing Goffman's work, with his emphasis on frames and framing, with that of Giddens, I believe that structuration theory can be usefully extended and lead to a theory of structurational interaction, which overcomes many of the limitations of various approaches outlined earlier. In fact, Giddens' work relies on Goffman's interactional order for his analysis of social integration, a fundamental requisite to system integration. With the core concepts of frames, communicating and organizing having been developed in the first four chapters of this book, I now turn to a detailed analysis of Giddens' structuration theory, then to Goffman's work, and, lastly, to an integration of their work and an extension of this synthesis. Of necessity, because of the sheer volume and diversity of both Goffman's and Giddens' work, only those concepts most relevant to organizing and communicating will be examined. However, readers will find that their ideas can be usefully applied in a wide array on contexts, as they already have been, and will continue to be.

Looking Forward

Although I have hinted at the potential benefits of a Giddens and Goffman synthesis, I would like to develop this in a bit more detail, so readers have an overall view of the remainder of the book. In this first section, I have established frame theory as a theoretical base for this synthesis.

Frame theory provides a robust, integrated approach for analyzing communicating and organizing. Frame systems enable us to explore the nature of communicating and organizing, and their interrelationships. Many of the underlying assumptions set forth might be widely acknowledged, such as assumptions that communication varies across different social relationships or that organizing requires control and coordination. Other assumptions, however, may be somewhat controversial, such as the nature of intentionality or the nature of agency. However, frame systems provide a way to clearly conceptualize organizing and communicating as they are being used in this book. Such conceptualizations must be clearly developed as the basis for our understanding of both communicating and organizing and as a basis for the theory of structurational interaction. Throughout these initial chapters, I have discussed points of congruence between my views on organizing and communicating, and Goffman's and Giddens' perspectives on communicating and organizing. These points of congruence will be further developed in my discussion of Giddens (Section II) and of Goffman (Section III).

Frames are used to define interactional contexts, to characterize the stocks of knowledge participants rely on to interpret ongoing interaction, and to signal participants' intended meanings. Both Giddens and Goffman use frames when discussing communicative contexts and interactants' knowledge about interacting. Framing devices, such as bracketing or alignment, help interactants to handle encounters in a routine, fluid manner and to make sense of what is going on.

Thus, frame theory provides an integrated, overarching theoretical perspective for analyzing communicating, organizing and their interrelationships. Frame theory also provides multiple levels of analysis and abstraction in analyzing these processes. In addition it provides a very rich examination of Goffman's and Giddens' work, and a coherent base for their synthesis.

Given this foundation, what lies ahead? A close analysis of Giddens' work demonstrates that he uses Goffman's interaction order as the basis for the integration of social systems. This fundamental connection between Giddens and Goffman has been largely overlooked. The purpose of this book is to explore this connection and to develop a theory of structurational interaction, and thus provide a rich, in-depth, communication-centered approach to organizing. Such a synthesis provides insight into the complexities of communicating, organizing and their interrelationships.

Both men's work will be discussed in-depth, focusing particularly on aspects of their work relevant to organizing and communicating. As such, those discussions can "stand alone" as succinct overviews of the communicative and organizational implications of each theorist. Because both Goffman and Giddens wrote extensively, and their insights on communication and organization were widely dispersed over a variety of publications, readers will find these sections a valuable overview of both men's work in these areas. These sections will be of interest to communication scholars exploring either Giddens or Goffman.

However, beyond each man's unique work, what benefits accrue from a theory of structurational interaction? Both men are social theorists focusing on how social life is established and maintained. For both, social interaction or communication is the foundation of social life. While Goffman focuses on communication as constitutive of social life, Giddens views communication as constitutive of organizing, as an aspect of social life. Goffman focuses on how the interaction order plays out in everyday interaction, while Giddens focuses on how the interaction order enacts social systems and their integration. Thus both theorists place social interaction or communication at the heart of their theories, and have valuable insights into communicating generally as well as in organizing.

Both theorists analyze a wide range of contexts. While Goffman focuses on the intricacies of communication in dyads, groups and institutions, Giddens talks about social systems, ranging from social movements to organizations to institutions to cultures. Taken together, the theory of structurational interaction allows us to analyze co-present interactants as well as interactions across time and space. In addition, Goffman's rekeying of frames allows us to assess frames within frames and thus move across differing layers of abstraction and complexity. (Perlow et al.'s analysis of nested structuration, discussed in Chapter 7, is an excellent example of this layering of organizing contexts.) Thus, structurational interaction enables us to analyze a wide range of contexts, of varying scope and complexity, with very fine analytic detail.

Flowing from these multiple levels of analysis, which, as Giddens remarks, "shade off" into one another, scholars are able to extend both the breadth and depth of their analyses. One may focus on a particular area in depth, but always be able to incorporate relevant aspects of broader contexts (or, conversely, hone in on more specific interactional details). (See also Nicholini, 2009.)

In sum, such a theory adds valuable insights into our understanding of communicating, organizing and their interrelationships. Each man's work is extraordinarily valuable on its own, but, taken together, each man adds rich insights into areas the other has not fully explored: Their synthesis enhances the impact of their work. In addition, this theory provides a communication-centered approach to organizing, and places communication at the heart of social life. Second, it provides a multi-level, integrated frame for exploring varying levels of complexity and context. Third, this theory promotes a wider range of research questions and the ability to pursue these issues in more depth, with awareness of the broader contextual influences that may impact a given organizing or communicative process. And finally, structurational interaction offers insights to major communicative and organizational issues, such as face, agency, identity, context, text and materiality.

SECTION II

Giddens' Structuration Theory

In his work, Giddens (1984) develops the theory of structuration, which addresses the relationship of the individual to society and, more specifically, examines the practices of social interaction which produce and reproduce social systems. Within the duality of structuration, social structure is instantiated by moment-to-moment interaction. In addition, structuration theory provides an understanding of the institutions that are needed in society, their changes over time, and their sociohistorical contexts of organizing. Finally, Giddens' differing levels and types of context and interaction may be viewed as frames, and thus consistent with frame theory.

For our purposes, because we are focusing on organizing and communicating, Giddens' work is significant. While Goffman focuses on face-to-face interaction, Giddens extends interaction to encompass social practices that are distanciated in time and space. As such, his work explores critical organizing and communicating issues such as agency, structure, power and change.

In Chapter 5, the basic constructs of structuration theory (ST) are discussed. The duality of structure, time-space distanciation, historicity, and the modalities of structuration are among the topics covered. In Chapter 6, Giddens' theory is further elaborated with consideration of the sociohistorical contexts of organizing, modernity, types of institutions, change, and globalization. And in Chapter 7, I discuss organizational research done using structuration theory as the theoretical framework for this research. Notable communication scholars applying structuration theory include McPhee, Poole, Seibold, and their colleagues, and Orlikowski and Yates with their work on new information technologies.

Through discussing structuration theory with a communicative focus, the close ties between Goffman and Giddens can readily be discerned. It is their synthesis, the theory of structurational interaction, that I believe will provide rich insights into organizing and communicating.

5

GIDDENS' STRUCTURATION THEORY

A Brief Overview

Giddens is arguably one of the foremost social theorists of our time. His work has influenced governmental policies as well as significantly influenced sociological theory and social science generally. His work responds to the intellectual divisions in the 1960s and 1970s surrounding social theory, critical social and historical analysis, and the move toward recognizing the active, reflexive character of human conduct. His focus on reflexivity acknowledged the fundamental role of language and cognitive faculties in human activity, and incorporated language and meaning into all spheres of activity. In terms of the continuing debate surrounding structure and agency, Giddens is considered by many to be the most important figure in this debate (Bryant & Jary, 2001a).

Giddens' structuration theory analyzed the larger political and economic environment in which organizing occurs, as well as the historical transition to modernity and postmodernity. Giddens also suggested the fundamental types of institutions which societies need in order to function, and incorporated material resources into his analyses of organizations. For our purposes, his focus on the duality of structure, which views interaction as the foundation for all organizing activities, is critical. In addition, he utilizes Goffman's interaction order as a foundation for his own work. Simply put, Giddens views structure as a characteristic of social systems which are produced and reproduced through social interaction; at the same time, interaction occurs within the structural properties of social systems. As such, both organizing and communicating recursively produce and reproduce one another.

I will focus on structuration theory and its implications for organizing and communicating. Structuration is an ontological theory, dealing with conceptions of human beings and human doings—"the situated activities of human agents, reproduced across time and space" (Giddens, 1984, p. 25). Action is always constituted through time and space, and "an ontology of time-space as constitutive of social practices is basic to the concept of structuration" (ibid., p. 3). And agents, through their actions, make a difference in the world (ibid., pp. 10–11).

The clash between objectivism and subjectivism is reframed by the duality of structure, which supports "an altered view of the intersection between saying (or signifying) and doing, offering a novel conception of *praxis*" (Giddens, 1984, p. xxii). For Giddens, the basic study of the social sciences is "neither the experience of the individual actor, nor the existence of any form of societal totality, but social practices ordered across time-space" (ibid., p. 2). Other aspects of his work will be addressed here only as they influence organizing and communicating, but it would be remiss not to recognize the wide-ranging contributions of his social theories.

One of Giddens' major contributions to the study of communication may be his emphasis on the sociohistorical context of interaction and the concept of time in communication. As Giddens noted,

> ... the relation between language and the 'context of use' are of essential importance to social theory. ... context cannot be treated as merely the 'environment' or 'background' of the use of language. *The context of interaction is in some degree shaped and organized as an integral part of that interaction as a communicative encounter.*
>
> *(Giddens, 1979, p. 83, italics in the original)*

Miller (1999) pointed out that through historical data we gain the ability to look at different social contexts, the ability to consider processes of organizational communication over long periods of time, and the retrospective distance to use these events in contemporary theory building. Not an easy task, but Miller argues that, by using frameworks such as structuration theory, social movement theory and symbolic convergence theory to enhance the interpretive interplay between history and theory, we gain a much richer perspective on organizing and organizations.

Social interaction, for Giddens, occurs in the intersection of individual time-space paths and their relations to other agents. Structure is reflected in the "binding" of time-space so that similar social practices can exist across varying time and space contexts, and can be viewed as systemic (Giddens, 1984, p. 17). For Giddens, "social practices, biting into space and time, are considered to be at the root of the constitution of both subject and social object" (Giddens, 1984, p. xxii). As such, Giddens' structuration theory deals with the "processual dynamic between structure and action" (Cohen, 1990a, p. 34) and larger patterns of information flow and interactional linkages are exposed through Giddens' analyses.

Structuration Theory

Gidden's theory of structuration developed a "hermeneutic interpretive sociology" which avoided both functionalism and structuralism:

> According to the theory of structuration, all social action consists of social practices, situated in time–space, and organised in a skilled and knowledgeable fashion by human agents. But such knowledgeability is always 'bounded' by unacknowledged conditions of action on the one side, and unintended consequences of action on the other. ... By the duality of structure I mean that the structured properties of social systems are simultaneously the *medium and outcome of social acts.*
>
> *(Giddens, 1981, p. 19)*

For Giddens, social life and social systems are recursive. As he noted, social practices are a mediating concept between agency and structure: we enact social practices and thus realize and act upon structures (Giddens, 1984, pp. 2–4). While social structures are reproduced through social interaction, there is always the possibility for change; change and continuity are always in tension with one another. In Giddens' view, then, social systems "comprise the situated activities of human agents, reproduced across time and space. Analysing the structuration of social systems means studying the modes in which such systems, grounded in the knowledgeable activities of situated actors who draw upon rules and resources in the diversity of action contexts, are produced and reproduced in interaction" (Giddens, 1984, p. 25).

The duality of structure is used to assess social practices on two levels—the interactional level and structural level (Sydow & Windeler, 1997). The interactional level consists of communication, power and sanction while the structural level consists of signification, domination and legitimation; elements within these levels interact with one another.

Various modalities connect these two levels of interaction and structure: the modality of interpretative schemes connects communication with *signification*; facilities connect power with *domination*; and norms connect sanctions with *legitimation*. All aspects of both levels are simultaneously present in every interaction. As such, competent agents apply interpretive schemes appropriate to the context in which they are operating, and mobilize facilities that they have access to in order to accomplish their purposes. Finally, agents apply sanctions to maintain actions they deem legitimate in a given context.

TABLE 5.1 Modalities of Structuration and Social Institutions

Social Institutions*	Symbolic	Political/economic	Legal
Structures	Signification	Domination	Legitimation
Modalities	Interpretive schemes	Facilities	Norms
Interaction	Communication	Power	Legitimation

*All social institutions use all modalities; however, they vary in what modalities are most important. From most important to least important, these modalities are ranked S-D-L in symbolic institutions; D-S-L in political and economic institutions, and L-D-S in legal institutions. (Adapted from Giddens, 1984, p. 31 and 1979, p. 82.)

Language provides an autonomous semiotic system that underlies verbal communication. Thus, in social interaction, "'messages' are always 'texts' in the sense in which they are generated from, and express a plurality of codes" (ibid., p. 99). For Giddens, structures of signification involve a system of semantic rules and codes (Giddens, 1976, pp. 123–24). When studying signification on the institutional level (the level of social systems), signification is reflected in modes of discourse and symbolic systems (i.e., world views, interpretative frameworks) (Craib, 1992, p. 53). Ideology, for Giddens, instantiates structures of signification that support the interests of powerful social groups (Giddens, 1979).

Modalities of structuration. Modalities are "the mediation of interaction and structure in the process of social reproduction" (Giddens, 1976, p. 122). These practices interact and intersect one another both as processes and as institutional forms (Giddens, 1984, p. 33). Every interaction contains aspects of meaning, power and moral sanctions. For Giddens, structure as signification reflects semantic rules; as domination it reflects unequal distribution of resources; and as legitimation it reflects evaluative rules. These three corresponding modalities of structuration—*interpretive schemes, facilities* (control over people and resources), and *norms*—link social action with social structure.

The distinctions among signification, domination and legitimation are primarily analytic. As Giddens pointed out, "If signification is fundamentally structure in and through language, *language at the same time expresses aspects of domination; and the codes that are involved in signification have normative force.* Authorization and allocation are only mobilized in conjunction with signifying and normative elements; and, finally, legitimation necessarily involves signification as well as playing a major part in co-ordinating forms of domination" (Giddens, 1979, pp. 106–7).

Interpretive schemes, stocks of meanings, and mutual knowledge not only enable mutual sensemaking among interactants, but also provide some structural constraints. Giddens distinguished between mutual knowledge, which refers to the "authenticity of belief" (Giddens, 1984, p. 336), and common sense, which refers to the "propositional beliefs implicated in the conduct of day-to-day activities" (ibid., p. 337). An agent's positioning, power, access to information and the unintended consequences of action are limits upon knowledgeability.

Norms link institutional structures of legitimation with moral sanctions and accountability in human actions. Such norms are the expected rights and obligations of participants interacting in a wide range of contexts (Giddens, 1979). But Giddens distinguished between the taken-for-granted (knowledgeability) and the accepted-as-legitimate. "Social life, in all societies, contains many types of practice or aspects of practices which are sustained in and through the knowledgeability of social actors but which they do not reproduce as a matter of normative commitment" (Giddens, 1981, p. 65).

There are also more calculated approaches in which agents weigh the costs versus the benefits of following certain social practices. For Giddens, such calculations may be limited by an agent's social positioning, how knowledge is developed and accessed, the validity of belief systems, and the dissemination of knowledge (Craib, 1992, p. 85). In modern societies, reflexivity is continuous because there are few traditions, and new information is always being produced.

Authorization and allocation are two resources that comprise the structures of domination. Authorization involves control over people (political institutions), while allocation involves control over material resources (economic institutions). Domination involves a system of resources, and legitimation involves a system of moral rules (Giddens, 1976, pp. 123–24). Finally, legitimation operates through sanctions which can be constraining or enabling, as well as coercive or inducing. As Storper noted, for Giddens the "web of different temporalities is woven together through the process of *legitimation*: it is a key to transformation and mediation relations among practices, on the one hand, and rules and resources, on the other ... legitimation is nothing more than the outcome of interaction" (Storper, 1997, p. 53).

Giddens (1979) suggests that four structures (that is, rules and resources in four areas) tie agents' actions to social systems:

1. *Signification*—structures of meaning and communication;
2. *Domination*—structures of control and power; there are *two* distinct aspects: authoritative control that commands others, and allocative command which refers to control over objects or material goods; and
3. *Legitimation*—structures conferring legal or normative sanctioning.

Every action reflects these four structures, and actors strategically select from these structures to conduct everyday life. As Kaspersen observed, an agent "uses communication, power, and legitimation in all ... actions" (Kaspersen, 2000, p. 61).

According to Giddens (1979), *signification institutions* (incorporating discourse, meaning and ideology) include churches, the media, and schools. *Authoritative institutions* include political institutions, while *allocative institutions* include economic institutions. *Legitimation institutions* include laws and jurisprudence. In order to have some degree of cohesiveness or social integration, societies must have all these types of institutions. And, in any analysis of social change, Giddens argues that one must look at all four institutions and their interrelationships in order to assess this change. These institutional distinctions provide a useful categorization for the institutions in a society (Giddens, 1979, p. 107). Thrift observed that different institutional orders—the political, symbolic, economic and legal—"will have different levels and distributions of contact in time-space" (Thrift, 1997a, p. 127).

All of these modalities operate simultaneously in interactions and social practices. According to Giddens, "structure cannot exist apart from the human actors who enact and interpret its dimensions" (Orlikowski & Robey, 1991, p. 149). In organizing and communicating, then, humans are knowledgeable actors (using interpretive schemes), exercising power (using resources), and are held accountable for their actions (using legitimation).

Orlikowski noted that structure is viewed as

> the set of enacted rules and resources that mediate social action through three dimensions or modalities: facilities, norms, and interpretive schemes. ... In their [agents'] recurrent social practices, they draw on their (tacit and explicit) knowledge of their prior action and the situation at hand, the facilities available to them (e.g., land, buildings, technology), and the norms that inform their ongoing practices, and in this way, apply such knowledge, facilities, and habits of the mind and body to "structure" their current action ... In doing so, they recursively instantiate and thus reconstitute the rules and resources that structure their social action.
>
> *(Orlikowski, 2000, p. 409)*

Thus "organizational reality can be analyzed in terms of the interlocking modalities comprising interpretive schemes, facilities, and norms" (Wilmott, 1981, p. 472).

These modalities can be bracketed for analysis, focusing on modalities as either features of social interaction (resources and rules) or as features of social systems. Modalities articulate the connection between the levels of action and system. As Giddens (1979, p. 81) puts it, the introduction of the level of modality provides "coupling elements" through which the bracketing of actors' strategic conduct or the properties of social systems are eliminated in recognition of their interrelation (Wilmott, 1981, pp. 472–73). As such, Giddens' structuration theory views structures as properties of social systems that are instantiated through social interaction and articulates "how interaction is accomplished by drawing upon the structural properties of social systems" (ibid., p. 473). Therefore, any and every interaction reflects an actor's strategic conduct as well as social structure—representing the duality of structure in which structure and agency co-occur.

> Every institutionalized practice or interactive relation is conceived in structuration theory to involve four structural properties: 1) rules pertaining to the constitution of meaning; 2) rules pertaining to normative rights, obligations and sanctions; 3) allocative (material) resources; 4) authoritative (non-material) resources. The analysis of properties in any given system (or multisystem collectivity) yields three analytic configurations: 1) structure of signification (semantic rules); 2) domination (authoritative and allocative resources); 3) legitimation (normative rules and sanctions). Alternatively these structural properties may be interrelated in differing orders of priority to yield four institutional orders: 1) symbolic orders; 2) political institutions; 3) economic institutions; 4) legal institutions.
>
> *(Cohen, 1990a, p. 43)*

As we have seen, interaction enacts both structure and action. In addition, every interaction incorporates signification, domination and sanctions. Through interaction, Giddens' structuration theory allows for both reproduction and change in social systems. We next turn to an analysis of the underlying assumptions of structuration theory.

Underlying Assumptions of Structuration Theory

Giddens (1983) outlined the major assumptions underlying his theory of structuration. Broadly, these assumptions can be grouped into two components, social integration and social systems. Social integration reflects a framework for interaction and builds upon Goffman's work. Social integration is required for system integration, in which different institutions and societies are intertwined. As Giddens noted:

> ... it is extremely important ... to emphasise that the systemness of social integration *is* fundamental to the systemness of society as *a whole*. System integration cannot be adequately conceptualised via the modalities of social integration; none the less the latter is always the chief prop of the former, *via the reproduction of institutions in* the duality of structure.
>
> *(Giddens, 1983, p. 77)*

I shall now examine social integration and system integration in more detail.

Social integration. The following assumptions are related to social integration or interaction.

1. Structures can be viewed as rules and resources, capable of transformation and mediation. Structural principles or basic "principles of organisation" across societies may be identified.
2. There is a *duality of structure* which reflects the recursive nature of social practices. "The concept of the duality of structure connects the *production* of social interaction, as always and everywhere, a contingent accomplishment of knowledgeable social actors, to the reproduction of social systems across time-space" (ibid., p. 77).
3. The knowledge that participants use in interaction is also the knowledge they draw on to give accounts of their purposes for interaction. Their practical consciousness of how to operate in interactions may only be partially discursively known to them, and must be distinct from unconscious motivation and cognition.
4. The duality of structure carries with it the properties for change, or dissolution— not just reproduction.
5. Social interaction involves components of power (domination), meaning (signification) and norms (legitimation).
6. Social systems are unified through social integration—a process represented in face-to-face interaction, and manifested as time-space presence in social organization. System integration (relationships among collectivities) presupposes social integration (ibid., p. 28). Social integration is presupposed for system

integration, but system integration also has some distinct mechanisms of integration.

Social Systems. For Giddens, the following assumptions apply to social systems.

1. A distinction is made between social systems and social structures. "Social systems are composed of patterns of relationships between actors of collectivities reproduced across time and space. ... Structures exist in time-space only as moments recursively involved in the production and reproduction of social systems" (Giddens, 1983, p. 26). Systems constitute situated practices, while structures have a "virtual" existence (ibid.).
2. Structuration is to be viewed within its contingent, historical place. That is, actors' knowledge is limited by unacknowledged conditions of action and unanticipated consequences of action within particular contexts. "The (bounded) knowledgeability of social actors is always and everywhere the medium of the continuity of institutions" (ibid.).
3. Three levels of time are implicated in structuration: (1) the immediate time of interaction, (2) the life-cycle of individuals on earth, and (3) "the long term reproduction of *institutions* across the generations, the contingency of the transformation/mediation relations implicated in structural principles of system organization. Institutions are practices which 'stretch' over long time-space distances in the reproduction of social systems" (ibid.). Contradiction (disjunction between structural principles of a social system) and conflict are features of social systems (Giddens, 1983, pp. 26–29).

The major underlying assumptions of structuration complement the underlying assumptions of the frame system of organizing and communicating being developed here. Both approaches emphasize social practices, practical consciousness and tacit knowledge and their collective importance for communicating and organizing. In addition, both acknowledge the importance of context for understanding both organizing and communicating, in terms of historicity as well as the immediate social situations in which interaction takes place. By the term "historicity," Giddens wishes to emphasize that we live in a world that is constantly exposed to change (Giddens, 1984, p. xxvii). Historicity represents "an active and conscious understanding of history as open to human self-transformation" (Giddens, 1981, p. 167). Both acknowledge the importance of time and space in communicating and organizing.

Most important, however, is that Giddens, Goffman and I acknowledge social interaction as a foundational core for organizing—without social interaction, no shared activity is possible. Organizing is not possible without communication, and organizing and communicating reciprocally shape one another. And, finally, we acknowledge the paradoxes, tensions and contradictions that influence organizing and communicating. In what follows, I will discuss social systems and institutions and their development in structuration theory.

Social Systems and Institutions

The theory of structuration examines the practices of social interaction which produce and reproduce social systems.

> Analysing the structuration of social systems means studying the modes in which such systems, grounded in the knowledgeable activities of situated actors who draw upon rules and resources in the diversity of action contexts, are produced and reproduced in interaction ... The constitution of agents and structures are not two independently given sets of phenomena, a dualism, but represent a duality. According to the notion of the duality of structure, the structural properties of social systems are both medium and outcome of the practices they recursively organize. ... Structure is not to be equated with constraints but is always both constraining and enabling.
>
> *(Giddens, 1984, p. 26)*

Furthermore, the reflexive monitoring of action both reliess upon and reenacts the institutional organization of a society (ibid.).

Agency and structure are thus interwoven in interaction. "Social structures are both constituted by human agency, and yet at the same time are the very medium of this constitution" and therefore, "structures are constituted through action, and reciprocally how action is constituted structurally" (Giddens, 1976, p. 121). As he emphasized, "it is not the case that actors create social systems; they reproduce them, remaking what is already made in the continuity of praxis" (Giddens, 1984, p. 171). Thus, studying "the structuration of a social system is to study the ways in which that system, via the application of generative rules and resources, and in the context of the unintended outcomes, is produced and reproduced in interaction" (Giddens, 1979, p. 66).

As Giddens concluded

> Structure, as recursively organized sets of rules and resources, is out of time and space save in its instantiations and co-ordination as memory traces, and is marked by an 'absence of the subject'. The social systems in which structure is recursively implicated, on the contrary, comprise the situated activities of human agents, reproduced across time and space.
>
> *(Giddens, 1984, p. 25)*

Social systems. Social systems are constituted by social practices, a reproduced *"interdependence of action,"* in which changes in one component may change other components. The smallest social system is that of the dyad. However, Giddens argued that we cannot assume that the workings of a dyadic system will reveal the workings of more inclusive social systems. His concepts of social integration and system integration contrast the various levels of interaction. According to Giddens,

'Face-to-face interaction' rather emphasises the significance of *space and presence* in social relations: in the immediacy of the life-world, social relations can be influenced by different factors from those involved with others who are spatially (and perhaps temporally) absent ...

(Giddens, 1983, p. 77)

Like Goffman, Giddens would argue that system integration cannot be collapsed into social integration, although the two are "loosely coupled," and social integration provides the foundation for system integration. However, as Giddens pointed out, unintended consequences of action extend beyond "the recursive effects of the duality of structure" (ibid., p. 78). Thus, system integration is influenced by a wider set of influential factors.

Social systems are patterns of action—relationships between actors and collectivities that are reproduced across time and space. Over time, as social practices are repeatedly reproduced, a pattern of social relationships emerges (in Giddens' terms, these repeated social practices are called "structural properties"). For example, such social practices were expressed in patterns of dominance between France and England and their respective colonies during the 1700s, and are continuously expressed in the use of money and capital to purchase goods and services. For Giddens, social relations can be studied on a syntagmatic dimension (the patterning of social relations involving the reproduction of situated social practices), and on a paradigmatic dimension ("involving a virtual order of 'modes of structuring' recursively implicated in such reproduction") (Giddens, 1984, p. 17).

Social systems, Kaspersen noted, can be said to have "reciprocal dependent action" (Kaspersen, 2000, p. 45). Intersocietal systems reflect a network of social systems that may cut across nation-state, societal, class, race and other boundaries. These intersocietal systems are the context in which social systems of many forms exist, and are extended across both time and space. Thus, social systems and societies are relatively permeable, and may be combined in multiple ways.

Societies. Social systems may be said to be *societies* if the following minimal conditions are met: (1) the system is associated with a locale; (2) the system has legitimate prerogatives over that locale, such as use of water, food, etc.; (3) the system has an "institutional clustering" of social practices among participants; and (4) participants have some awareness of identifying with an inclusive group (Giddens, 1983, pp. 45–46). As such, social systems may include societies that are nation-states, cultures and/or larger, geopolitical regions such as Latin America or Southeast Asia. Both time and space are relatively "elastic" concepts for Giddens because they may shift substantially as a result of whatever relevant context is being imposed by analysts.

Giddens also commented on the permeability of societal boundaries. As he noted, "'societies' rarely have easily specifiable boundaries. ... To help take account of that, I introduce the terms 'intersocietal systems' and 'time-space edges', referring to different aspects of regionalization which cut across social systems recognizably distinct as societies" (Giddens, 1984, p. xxvii). Time-space edges incorporate relations between different societies which bind time and space differently. Time-space concerns are critical for Giddens because the key to social order is "to explicate how the limitations of individual 'presence' are transcended by the 'stretching' of social relations across time and space" (ibid., p. 35).

Social systems can also be distinguished from one another by their fundamental structural principles; that is, by the most basic social practices which organize the system. Thus, Giddens distinguished tribal societies (village-centered) from class-divided societies and from modern nation-states associated with industrial capitalism (Giddens, 1981, pp. 158–68; Giddens, 1984, p. xxvii). A fundamental structural principle in class societies is "the disembedding, yet interconnecting, of state and economic institutions" (Giddens, 1984, p. 183). Disembedding separates social relations from specific contexts, especially through symbolic tokens (like money) and expert systems (e.g., the car mechanic, or the computer programmer, is an expert that an agent does not have to deal with directly). Thus modern institutions "disembed" social relations from local contexts of action. Disembedding means the "lifting out" of social relations from local involvements and their recombination across large spans of time-space.

The mechanisms of disembedding depend upon trust, where trust is defined as having faith in how system processes work, even though one has limited knowledge of such processes (Bryant & Jary, 1991, p. 209).

> Trust may be defined as confidence in the reliability of a person or system, regarding a given set of outcomes or events, where that confidence expresses a faith in the probity or love of another, or in the correctness of abstract principles (technical knowledge).
>
> *(Giddens, 1990a, p. 34)*

But trust is also very difficult because of the tensions and differences created by differing social systems as well as by differing stages of development across nation-states, cultures and regions.

As technology develops, expanded social control also creates more power within a society (Giddens, 1981). "Traditional practices are weakened (without disappearing altogether) through the penetration of day-to-day life by codified administrative procedures. The locales which formerly provided the settings for interaction in situations of copresence undergo a major set of transmutations ... replaced by a sprawling expansion of a manufactured or 'created environment'" (Giddens, 1984, p. 184). Surveillance—the coding of information relevant to the administration of subject populations, plus their direct supervision by officials and administrators of all sorts—becomes a key mechanism in facilitating a breakdown of social integration in a society. Dandeker (1990) noted that, when examining surveillance, we need to be aware of changes in supervisory power (moves to more strategies of personal affiliation as a way of extending authority), to be aware of information storage and retrieval, and to be aware of expertise as a form of surveillance (p. 217).

Institutions. Within the overarching context of social systems, Giddens also analyzed institutions. Institutions are standardized patterns of behavior which form a fundamental aspect of the time-space constitution of social systems; these patterns are continually constituted and reconstituted in daily social activity (Giddens, 1984, pp. 28–36). Organizations are actual operating institutions. For example, J. C. Penney's or Macy's are economic institutions, while the state of Minnesota is both a political and economic institution.

Giddens classified four types of institutions found in all societies, based on the universal structural characteristics of human interaction.

> All human interaction involves the communication of meaning, operation of power, and modes of normative sanctioning. These are constitutive of interaction. In the production of interaction actors draw upon and reproduce corresponding structural properties of social systems: *signification, domination* [authorization or allocation] and *legitimation.* ... These four structural features are implicated in the reproduction of all social systems ... providing a basic institutional categorization which at the same time recognizes the interrelation of structural components within concrete social systems or societies.
>
> *(Giddens, 1981, p. 46)*

Giddens argued that symbolic, political, economic, and legal/repressive institutions are found in all societies, although their forms and structural principles may vary widely across societies. In brief, Giddens' structuration theory viewed institutions as "basically practices through which the 'structural properties of society'—rules and resources—are instantiated and applied in the spatial-temporal setting of daily life" (Dallmayr, 1982, p. 21).

Levels of institutions. Within institutions, Giddens distinguishes three levels of analysis. At the most abstract level, *structural principles* are defined as the modes of differentiation and articulation of the institutions of a society (Giddens, 1981). These structural principles are "the most deeply embedded structural properties, implicated in the reproduction of societal totalities" (Giddens, 1984, p. 17). Such principles account for institutional alignments in a society. It is at this level that we can identify societal characteristics and differences (i.e., class-divided capitalism versus tribal societies).

Such structural principles organize society around consistent patterns of time-space distanciation; these different types of distanciation enable different types of societal integration. For example, Giddens suggests that tribal societies have low distanciation (interactions are face-to-face), whereas in capitalist societies, interaction occurs in "created environments" with a high level of distanciation (i.e., interaction can occur over different spaces at the same/different times) (Giddens, 1984, pp. 180–85).

At a mid-level of abstraction, *structural properties*, such as rules and resources, can be studied, along with transformation/mediation relations. Resources provide the material medium that may support an agent's actions, while rules are the taken-for-granted social practices which enable to us to go along in life and understand what is going on. Structural properties act to make possible, as well as to constrain, the potential for action. As such, structural properties reflect institutional features of social systems across time and space (Giddens, 1984, p. 185). As Giddens argued, rules and resources used in the production or reproduction of social action are simultaneously the means of system reproduction (Giddens, 1984, pp. 17–24).

For Giddens, rules of social life are "techniques or generalizable procedures applied in the enactment/reproduction of social practices. Formulated rules—those that are given verbal expression as canons of law, bureaucratic rules, rules of games and so on—are thus codified interpretations of rules rather than rules as such" (Giddens, 1984, p. 21). Social practices build upon overlapping and interconnected rules, and allow for flexible responses by agents (Giddens, 1979, p. 67). Thus, for Giddens, the basic unit of analysis for social systems is not the individual agent, nor society as a whole, but social practices as they occur across time-space.

As Giddens observed, "The structural properties of social systems exist only in so far as forms of social conduct are reproduced chronically across time and space" (Giddens, 1984, p. xxi). These structuring properties allow for "the 'binding' of time-space in social systems, properties which make it possible for discernibly similar social practices to exist across varying spans of time and space and which lend them 'systemic' form"—in other words, a virtual structure (ibid., p. 17). Thus, social systems, as recursively reproduced social practices, "do not have 'structures' but rather exhibit 'structural properties' and that structure exists, as time-space presence, only in its instantiations in such practices and as memory traces orienting the conduct of knowledgeable human agents" (ibid.). As Mingers noted, structural properties are the "most concrete, linking specific systemic occurrences with wider societal institutions. An example is the division of labor—a general structural property that is enacted within particular organizations. These are linked to dynamic processes of reproduction or change—what Giddens calls homeostasis and reflexive regulation or circuits of reproduction" (Giddens, 1984, p. 190, quoted in Mingers, 2004, p. 415). Finally, "those [social] practices which have the greatest time-space extension within such totalities can be referred to as *institutions*" (Giddens, 1984, p. 17). Such structures can be hierarchically ordered "in terms of the historical duration of the practices they recursively organize, and the spatial 'breadth' of those practices" (ibid.). Institutions can exist at varied levels, from schools to the Super Bowl to the U.S. government, and they are "built up and last over very long periods of time" and "provide stability to the systems and structures in society" (Poole & McPhee, 2005, p. 178).

In contrast, organizations and social movements are less deeply embedded social practices than institutions, and refer to existing social groups. Organizations and social movements are situated in a particular sociohistorical context and in time-space distanciation. Giddens (1984) further argues that organizations and collectivities try to alter the conditions of reproduction in social systems.

Structural sets are "the rule-resource sets, involved in the institutional articulation of social systems" (Giddens, 1984, p. 185). These modalities or structural sets reflect "clusterings" of transformation/mediation relations. As an example, in capitalistic societies, private property becomes transformed into money, money into capital, capital into labor contracts, and then into profit (Giddens, 1984, p. 186). Mediation and transformation together involve the mutual *convertibility* of rules and resources (Giddens, 1984, pp. 183–87). Money is a good example of this convertibility, both within and across societies. In education, the structural set would be as follows: private property; money; educational advantage; and occupational position (Giddens, 1984, pp. 185–86). That is, ownership of private property implicates money (wealth); wealth leads to educational advantage and thus implicates occupational position.

One can move from this structural set to more abstract structural principles (of capitalism) or to less abstract, specific rules and resources which outline particular institutions in a capitalistic society. Structural sets articulate structural principles (patterns of social relationships) and different structural sets reflecting different modalities of structuration. Three modalities of social systems are identified by Giddens—signification, domination, and legitimation (Kontopoulous, 1993, pp. 216–17). Rules and resources are properties of communities, while modalities are resources available to individuals in interaction (Bryant & Jary, 2000, p. 677).

The differentiations across these levels are primarily methodological, and "shade off" into one another depending upon the degree of abstraction involved in the analysis. As Turner (1986) observed,

> Through acts of human agency, structural principles produce "structural sets" that are, I sense, bundles or configurations of rules and resources that constrain the form of social relations across time and in space. As rules and resources are "transformed" by agents into general "structural principles" and "structural sets", such as "private property–money–capital–labor contract–profit", they become the "mediating vehicle" for producing and reproducing "structural properties" that are "institutional features of social systems, stretching across time and space."
>
> *(pp. 972–73)*

In summary, structural principles differentiate and articulate the institutions of a society as well as differentiate among different types of societies (tribes, class divisions and nation-states). These distinctions reflect different consistent patterns of time-space distanciation. Structural properties reflect the rules and resources drawn upon in social action and interaction. Forms of social conduct in social systems are reproduced across time and space, and also may be altered in social practices. Finally, structural sets reflect clusters of rule-resource sets, which act to mediate and transform social practices. An example would be how private property is converted into money, which reflects an educational advantage which leads to an occupation advantage. Analysts may move across these levels and begin their analysis at any level.

Interaction itself draws upon rules and resources via the modalities of communication (signification), sanctions (legitimation) and power (domination). Structure and agency mutually influence one another in every interaction as reflected in the duality of structuration. Individuals draw upon stocks of knowledge, discursive consciousness and practical consciousness in their interactions.

Praxis. Giddens has broadened the concept of *praxis* to encompass the production and reproduction of social life (Mendoza, 1997a, p. 253). For Giddens, praxis "refers to the constitution of social life as regularized practices, produced and reproduced by social actors in the contingent contexts of social life" (Giddens, 1982, p. 110). He argues that "Practices and institutions, which can be observed, must have rules underlying them for the activities to occur although these will not be observable save through the activities" (Mingers, 2004, p. 414). Thus, for him, social systems are patterns of relationships constantly produced and reproduced in social practices, and the scope of a social system is the span of time-space it incorporates or binds. It should be noted that "structural modes of conduct rather than historically specific acts [of individuals]" are critical for Giddens' theory (Cohen, 1990a, p. 36).

Giddens' position does not give primacy to either the individual or society; rather, he emphasizes the flow of social life and recurrent social practices. As he noted,

> 'Society' can be understood as a complex of recurrent practices which form institutions. Those practices depend upon the habits and forms of life which individuals adopt. Individuals don't just 'use' these in their activity but these life practices constitute what that activity is ... The structural properties of societies and social systems are real properties, but at the same time they have no physical existence ... *society only has form and that form only has effects on people in so far as structure is produced and reproduced in what people do.* This to me applies right through from the most trivial glance you might give someone to the most globalized of systems.
>
> *(Giddens & Pierson, 1998, p. 77, italics mine)*

Time and historicity. It is important to place the discussion of social systems and institutions in an appropriate sociohistorical context. Giddens (1983; Giddens & Pierson, 1998) pointed out that in pre-modern times, time-space was tightly connected to a given physical locale; both the "when" and the "where" were tightly bound to a physical location. With modernity, time and space were organized independently of each other, and removed from their traditional local contexts of action. As Giddens noted, "A feature of modernity is that distant events and actions have a constant effect on our lives, and a constantly increasing one too. That is what

I mean by disembedding, the 'lifting out' of forms of life, their recombination across time and space, but also the reconstitution of the contexts from which they came" (Giddens, 1998, p. 98). Giddens cited the example of an artisan whose work is no longer just "local," but globalized through the Internet and mass transportation. Today people live in a "post-traditional" world, with many competing traditions, and with the past providing a limited guide for the future.

Giddens conceptualized time in three distinct ways: First, there is time as experienced in the daily routines of life, reflecting the immediate temporal/spatial context of interaction. Second, time is a marker of human life and its passage (e.g., baby, teenager, middle age). Finally, time measures the long-term existence of institutions. Social changes occur in episodes (e.g., large-scale changes such as the formation of cities in agrarian states) and is reflected in "world time." World time reflects the varied social forms that cross various societies, geopolitical contexts, and sociohistorical *milieux* (Jary, 1997). World time thus captures the idea that sociohistorical context may affect the outcomes of similar episodes (e.g., industrialization in the US beginning in the 1800s in contrast to the industrialization of China beginning in the 1900s and continuing up to the present), and that what actors know about these developments may also influence outcomes (Bisel, 2009; Giddens, 1981). For example, developing countries may "know" about some of the consequences of urbanism as their countries experience these changes and that knowledge may influence the particular course of development those countries experience. Or developing countries may learn about the stages of HIV in humans from research in modern nation-states, and apply that medical knowledge for prevention and treatment of HIV in rural, tribal settings. These three aspects of time continuously interact with one another. (For a very rich discussion of time, see the special issue of *Time and Society*, volume 14, issues 2/3, 2005.)

Typically, time will also frame when activities may take place (e.g., parks and city offices may be open and accessible for certain periods of time, and closed for holidays). Social systems also allocate space (a resource) in which various social practices can be carried out (e.g., recreational parks, city municipal buildings, houses and grocery stores). In this way, time and space are inextricably bound to social practices that constitute and are constituted by social systems. Investigating the use of time in organizations, Perlow (1999) found that the sequence of organizational activities depended upon the social and temporal contexts in which they occurred; the organization's crisis mentality reflected both disruptive and heroic individual efforts in problem-solving. Software engineers experienced a consistent "time famine" (too much to do, too little time) as a part of their interdependent work practices.

Globalization. Although a thorough discussion of modernity and postmodernism is well beyond the scope of this book, Giddens' position is that of "radicalized modernity," in which a sense of dispersion and fragmentation contradicts global integration (Giddens, 1990a, p. 52). The four social systems most critical for modernity are the military, capitalism, nation-states, and information systems (Giddens, 1985a). Giddens utilizes the concept of re-embedding, in which disembedding mechanisms are linked to specific relations, in specific locales as a mechanism for globalization. For example, the disembedded monetary system is linked to specific institutions and organizations such as banks, loan offices, credit unions, and the like which may span the globe. And agents have access to disembedded mechanisms via specific locales (ibid., pp. 75–80). This modern time-span distanciation is a function of centralization, the ability to store information, the amount of surveillance, and the speed of communication within or across social systems. For Giddens, globalization transforms personal life and institutions, with many complex interconnections between them (Giddens, 1990a, 1991a, b). And global citizenship emerged in the 1960s and early 1970s because of the "intersections of satellite communication and computerization" (Rantanen, 2005, p. 66).

Globalization has enhanced disembedding, re-embedding and risk in created environments (and, for that matter, in physical environments as well). Generally, modernity is characterized by complexity, fragmentation, risk, and uncertainty (Bryant & Jary, 1997b, pp. 9–11). Uncertainty may pose a major challenge for making strategic choices and influencing institutionalized practices in organizations (Beckert, 1999). As Giddens concluded, "The reflexivity of modern social life consists in the fact that social practices are constantly examined and reformed in the light of incoming information about those very practices, thus constitutively altering their character" (Giddens, 1990a, p. 38).

Yet societies must have trust in distanciated institutions. As Rawls and David (2006) argued, given cultural diversity and multiple beliefs, trust is fostered by a shared commitment to social practices rather than by shared beliefs or lifestyles. Drawing on Giddens' views of trust, Kelly and Noonan (2008) found that work/practices established trust in an Ireland–India information offshoring relationship; a stable collaborative relationship was developed and helped contain a work crisis. In virtual teams, trust was found to influence perceptions of team cohesion and moderated the relationships between team communication and perceptual outcomes (Jarvenpaa, Shaw & Staples, 2004). An earlier study by Jarvenpaa and Leidner (1999) found that trust in virtual teams was fragile and temporal. In a set of interviews with university administrators, Goffman's and Giddens' work was used to conceptualize four trust development tactics: being visible, expressing sincerity, respecting face, and establishing routine activity (Gawley, 2007). (See also Gephart, Van Maanen & Oberlechner, 2009, Newell, David & Chand 2007, and a special issue on organizations and risk in late modernity in *Organization Studies,* 30, issues 2/3, 2009.)

As intersocietal connections become more extensive, institutions change, and their time-space edges are intertwined with other societies. Individuals become interconnected through the media of transportation and communication, as well as through the commodification of social life by means of money (Giddens, 1984). "As the world has globalized, so the technologies of self and cognition have also become more global: we can know others in ways that would not have been open to us before. Self and cognition have everywhere-mediated ... what we can regard as 'local' has changed, probably forever, and so have the conditions of theory and knowledge generation" (Thrift, 1997b, p. 58) The relationship of the individual to society becomes more complex as well, and questions concerning agency, continuity and change influence individual and institutional actions.

Within the context of modernization, Giddens suggested that capitalism and globalization depend upon regularized, routine market relationships that, in turn, depend upon a bureaucratic state and essential institutions, such as forms of monetary exchange and legal institutions. Both time and space are controlled in bureacracies, and written documents serve as resources for organizing and communicating. In the work environment, both managers and subordinates have an interest in working together to produce a good or service. The dialectic of control is present in their interactions, with managers having disciplinary power, yet also dependent on appropriate behavior by subordinates. Such mutual dependency, of course, varies across organizing settings and time-space, especially when the workers are distanciated in time and space (Giddens, 1984, p. 157).

Giddens' analyses of modernization suggested that time-space distanciation has created new types and forms of institutional orders. Such new forms "alter the conditions of social and system integration and thereby change the nature of the connections between the proximate and remote in time and space" (ibid., p. 144). Giddens argues that, with respect to globalization, "media and communications, and their role in promoting global interdependencies, is the most important dynamic force" because most global institutions would not be possible without them (Rantanen, 2005, p. 68). Some of these new institutional forms will be explored in Chapter 10. What is generally relevant for our purposes is awareness of those different connections, and their implications for organizing and communicating processes.

According to structuration theory, all social systems are instantiated through social practices and social interaction. Social practices and social interaction provide the context in which structure and agency mutually influence one another. It is to these fundamental processes we now turn, investigating the processes of social integration, which underlie social systems.

Social Integration: Rules, Resources, and Transformation

When assessing Giddens' structuration theory, Bertilsson pointed out that,

> Conceived within a time/space dimension, social institutions lay the foundation for orderly and reversible time: they exist independent of any particular action, but present individual action with its rules and resources necessary for its occurrence. Social institutions exist in their "absence", yet make the presence of action possible! On the system level, social institutions are the stations which bind time and space for generations of actors, thus enabling continuity. On the individual level, institutional frameworks define the openness and the closedness of action; the more diffused the institutional stations are, the

greater the degree of individual mobility, and thus time/space traveling. ...
The routinisation and habitualisation of action—our personal stations in life—bind
time and space, and help provide the "ontological security" without which
social life would be brutish and nasty.

(Bertilsson, 1997, p. 51)

As we have seen, Giddens' insights apply on different levels of analysis and reveal
the interconnections across levels. For Giddens, social reality reflects both subjective
human actors and institutional properties. People act in the context of past enacted
structures. These social structures shape interaction and action by providing contextual rules and resources that allow humans to make sense of their actions and
those of others (Orlikowski & Robey, 1991). In every interaction, modalities of
signification (interpretive schemes), domination (allocative or authoritative resources)
and legitimation (norms) operate. In this way, social structure and action constitute
each other recursively and continuously (Willmott, 1981).

These modalities are the processes of structuration and integrate the subjective
and objective aspects of human action (Giddens, 1979, 1984). According to
Giddens, "structure cannot exist apart from the human actors who enact and
interpret its dimensions" (Orlikowski & Robey, 1991, p. 149). In organizing and
communicating, then, humans are knowledgeable actors (interpretive schemes),
exercising power (using resources), and are held accountable for their actions
(legitimation).

In interaction, these three transformational modalities are enacted as facilities
(domination), interpretive schemes (signification), and norms (legitimation). As
Orlikowski noted, agents use

the set of enacted rules and resources that mediate social action through three
dimensions or modalities: facilities, norms, and interpretive schemes. ... In
their recurrent social practices, they draw on their (tacit and explicit) knowledge of their prior action and the situation at hand, the facilities available to
them (e.g., land, buildings, technology), and the norms that inform their
ongoing practices, and in this way, apply such knowledge, facilities, and
habits of the mind and body to "structure" their current action. ... In doing
so, they recursively instantiate and thus reconstitute the rules and resources
that structure their social action.

(Orlikowski, 2000, p. 409)

In applying structuration to organizing, "organizational reality can be analyzed in
terms of the interlocking modalities comprising interpretive schemes, facilities, and
norms" (Wilmott, 1981, p. 472).

Interpretive schemes are part of an actor's tacit knowledge, and are used in the
production as well as interpretation of utterances.

Communication, as a general element of interaction, is a more inclusive concept than communicative intent ... some philosophers ... have supposed that communicative intent is at best marginal to the constitution of the meaningful qualities of interaction, 'meaning' being governed by the structural ordering of sign systems. In the theory of structuration, however, these are regarded as of equivalent interest and importance, aspects of a duality rather than a mutually exclusive dualism.

(Giddens, 1984, pp. 29–30)

And signs "exist" only as the medium and outcome of communicative processes in interaction (Giddens, 1984, p. 31).

Domination involves a system of resources, and legitimation involves a system of moral rules (Giddens, 1976, pp. 123-24). Authorization is the resource that derives from control over people. Such control might be exemplified by person-to-person control, such as a parent disciplining his or her child, or a teacher teaching her students, or a police team maintaining crowd control. Authorization also flows from institutions, such as governments or the military exercising legal authority over its citizens. In contrast, allocation involves control over material resources, such as money, buildings, food or water. Legitimation, which involves a system of moral rules, applies sanctions which may be enabling, constraining, coercive or inducing. Some behaviors might be encouraged such as studying or working hard, while other behaviors, such as excessive drinking accompanied by disorderly conduct, might be punished by a stint in jail. All three modalities—authorization, allocation and legitimation—operate in every interaction.

These modalities can be bracketed for analysis, focusing on modalities as either features of social interaction (resources and rules) or on modalities as features of social systems (signification, domination and legitimation). "The significance of the level of modality is that it provides a means of articulating the connection between the levels of "action" and "system." Or, as Giddens (1979, p. 81) puts it, the concept of modality provides "the coupling elements" whereby the bracketing of actors' strategic conduct or the properties of social systems are "dissolved in favor of an acknowledgement of their interrelation" (Wilmott, 1981, pp. 472–73). As such, Giddens' structuration theory views "structure as a property of social systems that are reproduced through social interaction" and recognizes "how interaction is accomplished by drawing upon the structural properties of social systems" (ibid., p. 473). Thus, any and every interaction reflects both an actor's strategic conduct as well as social structure—representing the duality of structure in which structure and agency co-occur.

As Poole, Siebold and McPhee (1985) noted,

At the same time interaction draws on these institutions to constitute modalities, it is reconstituting the institutions. So, for instance, every social act draws on power, the capacity to alter a course of events by intervening, where "the course of events" may involve the activities of others. In this action, then, ... a peculiar institution—an order of domination—exists and is reproduced as it is drawn upon as a facility. Acts involving communication draw upon and reproduce an "order of signification," an institutionalized communication structure. And acts involving normative judgments draw upon and reproduce an order of legitimation, an institutional dimension which itself implies general, basic, and valid social value judgments.

(p. 79)

As an example, they point out that a group leader's calling a meeting to order involves group members' *interpretive schemes* (understanding and interpreting the leader's verbal behavior as leadership), *norms* (was the "call" carried out properly?), and *facilities* (does the leader have legitimate authority to conduct the meeting?) (ibid.).

An accurate description of social interaction, for Giddens, combines or interlaces meaning, normative elements and power, with contestation across each of these modalities. Accountability takes place at the intersection of interpretive schemes and norms, when we explain our actions in terms of rights and obligations owed to others as well as those owed to ourselves. The codes that produce meanings are found in language, in the ordering of social practices and in the understanding of how to "go on" in multiple contexts.

In sum, for both Goffman and Giddens, social interaction is a focal point and underlies social institutions (although this was never fully developed in Goffman's work). For both:

> All social interaction is *situated* interaction—situated in space and time. It can be understood as the fitful yet routinized occurrence of encounters fading away in time and space, yet constantly reconstituted within different areas of time-space. The regular or routine features of encounters, in time as well as in space, represent institutionalized features of social systems.
>
> *(Giddens, 1984, p. 86, italics in the original)*

As Kaspersen remarked, "the concept of duality of structure links the production of social interaction, conducted by knowledgeable agents, with the production of social systems across time and space" (2000, p. 43).

Rules play an important role in social interaction via rules of signification and legitimation. But rules also play a broader role in social systems. It is to an analysis of rules that we now turn.

Rules. The most important rules for social theory are those involved in the reproduction of institutionalized practices; they are deeply embedded in time-space and have the greatest time-space extension within societies. Two types of rules are *constitutive* rules (that govern or define basic activities) and *regulative* rules (that specify how something is to be done). Such rules may be contrasted as intensive/ shallow; tacit/discursive; informal/formalized; and weakly/strongly sanctioned (Craib, 1992, p. 46; Giddens, 1984, p. 22).

Intensive rules, like linguistic rules or rules for conversational turn-taking, are used daily. Both Goffman and Giddens would agree that "many seemingly trivial procedures followed in daily life have a … profound influence upon the generality of social conduct" (Giddens, 1984, p. 22). Mendoza observed that "Understood as intensive rules, structure reproduced via *duality of* structure is constitutive both of personality and routine" (Mendoza, 1997b, p. 300).

Within interaction, Turner (1986) noted that

> Rules operate in situations of interaction by specifying 'right and obligation' that are the bases for 'sanctions' and by providing 'interpretive schemes' and 'stocks of knowledge' that are necessary for effective 'communication'. Resources operate in interactional situations by providing 'allocative' (material) and 'authoritative' (organizational) 'facilities' for mobilizing 'power'. Thus, rules and resources are 'transformed' into power, sanctions, and communication among agents in interaction; in the process, they 'mediate' social relations.
>
> *(p. 972)*

Rules and resources are therefore used in every interaction. Rules are particularly important in forming, maintaining, ending and reframing encounters, and contribute to the sense of security we have in interacting with others.

According to Giddens, "awareness of rules, expressed first and foremost in practical consciousness, is the very core of that 'knowledgeability' which specifically characterizes human agents … such knowledge … provides for the generalized capacity to respond to and influence an indeterminate range of social circumstances" (Giddens, 1984, p. 22). For Giddens, practical consciousness can "enmesh rules and the 'methodological' interpretation of rules in the continuity of practices. … What Garfinkel calls 'ad hoc' considerations—the 'etcetera clause', 'let it pass', etc.—are chronically involved in the instantiation of rules, and are not separate from what those rules 'are'" (Giddens, 1993, p. 121).

Kaspersen (2000) used language to exemplify rules and resources. When we speak a language, we use certain rules of language to express ourselves, and also reproduce the rules of language. However, when we have motives or desires that cannot be expressed in a language, those rules become constraints. As agents act, they continually draw upon and reproduce these linguistic structures (structural properties) in their actions.

Giddens pointed out that knowing a language is also to understand and use "a range of methodological devices, involved both with the production of utterances themselves and with the constitution and reconstitution of social life in the daily contexts of social activity" (Giddens, 1987b, pp. 79–80). He suggests that structure is enacted through the things people do in regularized ways. This practical consciousness reflects our knowledge of how to go in life. And Giddens also noted that "what actors are 'able to say' about their activities is by no means all that they 'know' about them" (Giddens, 1982, p. 31). Like Goffman, Giddens would argue that "The knowledge of social conventions, of oneself and other human beings, presumed in being able to 'go on' in the diversity of contexts of social life is detailed and dazzling" (Giddens, 1984, p. 26).

Giddens suggests that "What agents know about what they do, and why they do it—their knowledgeability as agents—is largely carried in practical consciousness. Practical consciousness consists of all the things which actors know tacit about how to 'go on' in the contexts of social life without being able to give them direct discursive expression" (Giddens, 1984, p. xxiii). For Giddens, knowledgeability reflects what actors know about the context in which they and others act, and represents tacit as well as discursive knowledge.

Thus, for Giddens "agents draw on their awareness of the strategic context as they enact social practices. … Knowledgeability is always framed by a particular narrative inhabited by the agent involved, by a particular frame of meaning which includes wants and desires. … Skills are also involved in the enactment of practices or strategy … knowledgeability is, of course, implicated in both strategic conduct analysis and strategic context analysis" (Jary & Jary, 1997, pp. 189–90).

It is important to understand that structures, whether of social systems or of institutions, have only a "virtual" presence:

> … social systems, as reproduced social practices, do not have 'structures' but rather exhibit 'structural properties' and that structure exists, as time-space presence, only in its instantiations in such practices and as memory traces orienting the conduct of knowledgeable human agents.
>
> *(Giddens, 1984, p. 17)*

Thus, structural properties are internal, virtual, and part of the tacit knowledge of agents, which permits them to act as well as constrains their actions. "To regard structure as involving a 'virtual order' … implies recognizing the existence of (a) knowledge—as memory traces—'of how things are to be done' (said, written) on the part of social actors; (b) social practices organised through the recursive mobilisation of that knowledge; (c) capabilities that the production of these practices presuppose" (Giddens, 1979, p. 64).

Resources. All forms of interaction involve resources; *allocative resources* incorporate control over material resources or aspects of the material world, while *authorization* incorporates social resources, such as control over coordination in organizing. Allocative resources are of three types: material features of the environment (such as raw materials); means of material production (like technology); and produced goods (artifacts). Authoritative resources include organizing social use of time-space, organizing the relations among people in a society, and organizing life-chances (i.e., opportunities for self-development and self-expression) (Giddens, 1981, pp. 51–52).

Mediation and transformation. Mediation refers to the multiple ways in which interaction occurs across time and space in social systems. Giddens suggested that

"All interaction is 'carried' across time and space by media, organised structurally: ranging from the direct consciousness of others in face-to-face encounters to the modes in which institutions are sedimented in deep historical time, and in which social interaction is carried on across broad areas of global space" (Giddens, 1981, p. 53). A key characteristic of modernity is the disembedded, distanciated nature of interpersonal and institutional interactions.

For Giddens, sociohistorical conditions are the broad context in which social systems and institutions are enacted. The development of writing, according to Giddens, enabled social systems to move from traditional societies with high-presence availability and narrative histories to societies with time and space distanciation. Through writing, a society's storage capacity—of both material and authoritative resources—was expanded. When institutional forms persist across generations, they can extend their influence across time and space. Authorities can use this social storage capacity to retain control of knowledge and thus control social practices. If such knowledge is not questioned, it may become a significant source of power and domination (Giddens, 1981).

Reflexivity. In the late modern world, institutional reflexivity provides new means of monitoring and control, and is increasingly dependent upon knowledge systems (Giddens, 1990a, 1991a, 2003). Trust is not only essential in the interpersonal realm, but in institutions and knowledge systems as well. With both personal and institutional reflexivity, more changes in developing the self and self-identity are possible. As Giddens commented:

> The reflexive monitoring of activity is a chronic feature of everyday action and involves the conduct not just of the individual but also of others. That is to say, actors not only monitor continuously the flow of their activities and expect others to do the same for their own; they also routinely monitor aspects, social and physical, of the contexts in which they move ... actors— also routinely and for the most part without fuss—maintain a continuing 'theoretical understanding' of the grounds of their activity.
>
> *(Giddens, 1984, p. 5)*

Giddens argues that systems can be viewed as homeostatic causal loops, as self-regulating systems using feedback, and as involving reflexive self-regulation. Of these three levels of systemic processes, the feedback provided by information filtering and reflexive self-regulation is more complex than that provided by homeostatic systems. Feedback systems, for example, can be directive, not merely reactive (as in the case of homeostatic systems).

The reflexive monitoring of action by the self and institutional reflexivity are universal. However, with late modernity, the self becomes a reflexive project and institutional reflexivity is intensified because of expanded and conflicting knowledge bases (Bryant & Jary, 2001a, pp. 21–22). Giddens noted that modern reflexivity is intense because of its "presumption of wholesale reflexivity—which of course includes reflection upon the nature of reflection itself" (Giddens, 1990a, p. 39). Despite the plurality of divergent views, and in contrast to postmodern theories, Giddens suggested that new converging knowledge and views may develop (Giddens, 2003; Giddens & Pierson, 1998).

Knowledgeability and reflexivity. As we have seen, human agency and power are exercised by knowledgeable, reflexive agents. Giddens (1990a, 1992) developed two senses of reflexivity—one referring to the monitoring of action, and the other referring to knowledge and meaning. In these senses, reflexivity is used "to account both for the construction of autonomous personal styles and relationships at the level of everyday practical consciousness and for the appropriation of meanings and knowledge at the level of institutionalized discursive consciousness" (Hay, O'Brien & Penna, 1997, p. 94).

Reflexivity can also occur within practical and discursive consciousness: for example, everyday practical consciousness may be challenged by cross-cultural experiences and by knowledge of other lifestyles. This reflexivity and monitoring is also emphasized in Goffman's work.

Modes of regionalization. Regionalization referred not only to locales, but also to zones of time-space that are part of social practices. For example, a home contains different zones, such as bathrooms, closets, hallways, dens and bedrooms, and these are zoned temporally and spatially (e.g., some rooms are usually used at particular times, like bedrooms). Artificial lighting also permits activity "24/7" which is characteristic of modern societies. Thus work zones may have day or night shifts; "flex time" may allow for flexible scheduling but also may accommodate times when everyone's presence is required, weekdays may take on different characteristics than weekends, and so forth. Kidder (2009), examining the practices of bike messengers, argues that urban centers cannot be understood without an analysis of the relationship between space and social interaction.

Giddens suggested four parameters of regionalization: (1) *form*—the nature of the physical and/or symbolic markers that locate the region; (2) *duration*—length of encounters in a region (e.g., from 9 to 5); (3) *span*—the breadth of space and time incorporated into the region (e.g., the Northeastern US has distinctive geographical boundaries as well as characteristic social qualities), and (4) *character*—the time-space organization of locales which are located within more extensive social systems (e.g., the home in some societies is not only the locale for the family, but also for production, with closely connected gardens or shops). Giddens also noted that some locales are serial, in that activities and time in one area have implications for activities in other areas (e.g., preparation in the kitchen prior to serving a meal, getting required documents prior to leaving a country) (Giddens, 1984, pp. 120–22).

Within zones of activity in different settings, Giddens directed our attention to bodily positioning in different settings. The parameters of zoning include front and back regions, front regions referring to those in front of the body, and back regions referring to those areas behind the body. Generally, front regions represent visible zones that need bodily control, while back regions imply solitude or privacy (e.g., an entire group may claim a "relaxed aura" in a break room). Front regions are usually public, while back regions may be more private (e.g., front regions would be on the floor of a shop, while a back region would be a relatively private area for eating, storage of odd materials). Thus zoning seems to convey not only a sense of front and back, but also a sense of public and private spaces. This parallels spatial distinctions that Goffman has developed.

As can readily be seen, zoning provides a range of settings in which the tensions between public versus private, visibility versus invisibility, and autonomy versus surveillance can be accommodated. Giddens also observed that regionalization may be closely connected to sustaining basic ontological security. While Goffman's concepts of front and back stages have clearly influenced Giddens, Giddens has expanded these concepts into time-space distanciation and modes of regionalization.

Giddens noted that agents move in "physical contexts whose properties interact with their capabilities ... at the same time as those agents interact with one another" (Giddens, 1984, p. 112). Like Latour, Giddens acknowledged the importance of materiality. Movement in space has greatly accelerated over time; traveling from East Coast to West Coast took eight months on horseback; in 1910, this trip took four days by rail; and currently it takes about five hours by airplane. He also observed that the routine activities of agents, on a daily basis, follow a spatial path with varied locales or stations throughout (e.g., stopping at Starbucks on your way to work, dropping off your children at the daycare center, and arriving at your office). Thus locales have a serial character, bracketing time and space with different activities in different areas. (See also Low, 2008.)

While Goffman noted the importance of immediate, co-present, contextual features, Giddens suggested that even more attention needs to be directed to this aspect of social action. As Giddens noted, "Time-geography is concerned with the constraints that shape the routines of day-to-day life and shares with structuration theory an emphasis upon the significance of the practical character of daily activities, in circumstances of co-presence, for the constitution of social conduct" (ibid., p, 116). Locales provide interactional settings, and are usually internally regionalized (e.g., a coffee shop has a counter, an area for adding cream/sugar, and some seating areas; an office may have designated parking spaces, a reception area, and a conference room). As Giddens concluded, "Context thus connects the most intimate and detailed components of interaction to much broader properties of the institutionalization of social life" (ibid., p. 119).

Regionalization and time-space. According to Giddens, the concept of space has been less well developed and integrated into theories of social interaction and of social systems. All social interaction occurs in time and space, and intermingles the presence and absence of participants. As he notes

> All collectivities have defined *locales* of operation: physical settings associated with the "typical interactions" composing those collectivities as social systems ... common awareness of properties of the setting of interaction is a

vital element involved in the sustaining of meaningful communication between actors (as indexical features of communication). ... Locales are normally *regionalized* on a time-space basis. Regions are in some way 'set apart,' for certain individuals, or types of individuals, or for certain activities or types of activities.

(Giddens, 1981, pp. 39–40)

While human actors link activities via systemic locales, larger social systems (like societies or global organizations) need modes of system integration that use transportation and/or communication. Thus, for institutions and social systems there are spatial-temporal regionalizations of activities across extended locales and space which are connected by transportation and communication.

Regionalization is very similar to Goffman's concepts of front and back stage, and both theorists use the concept of presence-availability to discuss how participants have access to, and involvement in, interactions. Presence-availability ranges from co-presence (including gatherings, focused encounters and civil inattention) to mediated forms of co-presence (the use of telephones, computers, videos or a combination of media). As Turner noted, "as individuals interact, they use rules and resources to mark the geographical boundaries of their interaction, to connect their use of space to broader institutional patterns, to partition the space in which the interaction occurs, and to decide upon the time period during which space will be used" (Turner, 1988, p. 148).

Regionalization also applies to large spans of time-space, such as cities and industrial areas. And the designs of cities, buildings and other locales enables a lot of interaction or make interacting with others very difficult (i.e., the issue of both time and presence-availability). Giddens suggested that regionalization can be distinguished by dimensions of centered versus peripheral regions, and established individuals versus newcomers or outsiders. For example, cities are viewed as more central to a nation-state than villages, and those controlling resources are also more "central" than those holding few resources. Giddens pointed out that "the 'established' industrial nations of the Western 'core' maintain a central position in the world economy on the basis of their temporal precedence over the 'less developed' societies" (Giddens, 1984, p.131).

Regionalization, and time-space distanciation generally, play an important role in influencing social practices. Giddens summarized time-space and contextuality as follows:

All social life occurs in, and is constituted by, intersections of presence and absence in the 'fading away' of time and the 'shading off' of space. The physical properties of the body and the *milieux* in which it moves inevitably give social life a serial character, and limit modes of access to 'absent' others across space. ... In proposing the ideas of locale and of regionalization I want to formulate a scheme of concepts which help to categorize contextuality as inherently involved in the connection of social and system integration.

(Giddens, 1984, p. 132)

In Giddens' conceptualization of time-space, actors can move through daily time-space paths that reflect the distributions of encounters, the regionalization of locales, the contextuality of regions, and the intersections of locales. Social practices are closely tied to varying locales and time spans. During one day at work, I could drop off my children and get some coffee (daily time-space paths and distribution of encounters), then work at my office and meet with colleagues (regionalization of locales and contextuality of regions), and email our findings to the organization's worldwide headquarters (intersection of locales).

Time-space distanciation and contextuality are essential for understanding how encounters are carried out. Giddens argued that it is

> clear that no strip of interaction—even if it is plainly bracketed, temporally and spatially—can be understood on its own. Most aspects of interaction are sedimented in time, and sense can be made of them only by considering their routinized, repetitive character. … For the forming and reforming of encounters necessarily occurs across tracts of space broader than those involved in immediate contexts of face-to-face interaction. The paths traced by individuals in the course of the day break off some contacts by moving spatially to form others, which are then broken off and so on.
>
> *(ibid., p. 142)*

Thus, regionalization can link reflexive agents with distanciated social systems. Low (2008), using Giddens' structuration theory, suggests that "space can be seen as a *relational ordering of living entities and social goods*" (p. 35) and that space involves locating (situating people and materials) as well as synthesis (connecting people and materials across space).

Giddens suggested that the limitations of individual presence are transcended by the "stretching" of social relations across time and space (Giddens, 1984, p. 35). He points out that one's life-span is an irreversible flow, whereas daily life and institutional life is reversible. For Giddens, both the social practices of daily life and the institutional forms of societal organization influence the self. As he concluded, "All social systems, no matter how grand or far-flung, both express and are expressed in the routines of daily social life, mediating the physical and sensory properties of the human body" (ibid., p. 36).

More broadly, time and space also play a major role in societal evolution. For Giddens, different types of time-space distanciation—where interaction occurs at different locales and at different times, or where time and space are localized— influence the type of social practices and societal changes that are possible. For tribal societies, the village was the primary location for social practices. In modern times,

Western social practices may take place at different times and/or different spaces. That is, social systems are extended, or distanciated, over space and time. Social order, or societal integration in Giddens' terms, is a function of the type of time-space distanciation present in a society (Giddens, 1981, pp. 155–59). For example, Giddens argued that high time-space distanciation makes nation-states possible through written communication, rapid mass transportation and mediated communication.

Giddens drew our attention to the importance of time and space in organizing and communicating. This awareness enhances our understanding of organizing because the broader context of organizing—its historicity—is incorporated into our analytic frames. For example, we can assess the impact of modernization on traditional societies, or examine the impact of transitioning from modernity to high modernity on nation-states and their organizations. In addition, we can explore different types of organizing and communicating in different historical contexts. Distanciation allows us to explore the manipulation of time and space in our worldwide connections and interactions. Finally, the sense of time which individuals experience as they move through various career and family stages is also highlighted.

Power. For Giddens, interaction involves power as well as power being "instantiated in action, as a regular and routine phenomenon" (Giddens, 1979, p. 91). As he noted, the choice—the "could have done otherwise"—links action to power. For Giddens, power means "'transformative capacity', the capability to intervene in a given set of events so as in some way to change them" (Giddens, 1985a, p. 7). Power is also relational when the ability to secure outcomes "depends upon the agency of others" (Giddens, 1979, p. 93). In addition, "Unlike the communication of meaning, power does not come into being only when being 'exercised', ... because we can talk of power being 'stored up' for future occasions of use" (Giddens, 1976, pp. 111–12).

Power, according to Giddens, reflects relationships of autonomy as well as dependency in interaction. He views power as

> a sub-category of 'transformative capacity' [which refers] to interaction where transformative capacity is *harnessed to actors' attempts to get others to comply with their wants.* Power, in this relational sense, concerns the capability of actors to secure outcomes where the realization of these outcomes depends upon the agency of others. The use of power in interaction thus can be understood in terms of the facilities that participants bring to and mobilize as elements of the production of that interaction, thereby influencing its course. Social systems are constituted as regularized practices: power within social systems can thus be treated *as involving* reproduced relations of autonomy and dependence in social interaction. ... Power relations are relations of autonomy and dependence, but even the most autonomous agent is in some degree dependent, and the most dependent actor or party in a relationship retains some power.
>
> *(Giddens, 1979, p. 93)*

Giddens referred to this two-way nature of power as the "dialectic of control." For Giddens, even the most autonomous actor is somewhat dependent and the most dependent actor somewhat autonomous (ibid.). "Resources are the media whereby power is employed in the routine course of social action; but they are at the same time structural elements of social systems, reconstituted in social interaction" (Giddens, 1982, p. 39). He also views power as being situated both for individuals and for institutions; power is constituted and reconstituted in established conventions that individuals follow (Giddens & Pierson, 1998, p. 87). As such, an agent's strategies are contextually bound.

Power is both enabling and constraining. Power may also be hidden or unseen. For example, ideology may operate as power when a dominant group manipulates communication to advance their interests and/or when discursive forms of domination are part of agents' daily lives (Giddens, 1979, pp. 190–93).

Power is dependent upon allocative and/or authoritative resources. Such resources may range from raw materials to technology to the organization of life chances. Giddens argued that both material resources and allocative resources are critical for the expansion of power. For Giddens, structures of legitimation and signification are linked to power, and thus to structures of domination.

Agents are able to use a range of powers, including that of influencing the actions of others. The duality of structure captures this view of power as the capacity to achieve an intended end.

> Resources (focused via signification and legitimation) are structured properties of social systems, drawn upon and reproduced by knowledgeable agents in the course of interaction … the use of power characterizes not specific types of conduct but all action, and power itself is not a resource. Resources are media through which power is exercised, as a routine element of the instantiation of conduct in social reproduction. … Power within social systems which enjoy some continuity over time and space presumes regularized relations of autonomy and dependence between actors or collectivities in contexts of social interaction. But all forms of dependence offer some resources whereby those who are subordinate can influence the activities of their superiors. This is what I call the *dialectic of control* in social systems.
>
> *(Giddens, 1984, pp. 15–16)*

Power can be expressed, then, as the capability of the actor as well as the "mobilization of bias" built into institutions.

Subordinates may exercise power through manipulating resources in larger social systems and thus attain some autonomy from dominant agents. In larger social systems, however, actions are less controlled and intense. Tighter control is possible in face-to-face interaction than in larger social systems because the relations are more transparent.

Within encounters, differentials of power may also be influenced by turn-taking. Giddens observed that "All organizations involve the co-ordination of interaction in flows of time-space relations 'channeled' through regularized contexts and locales" (Giddens, 1984, p. 77). A courtroom is a good example of the interactional power of turn-taking as are doctor-patient interactions. As he observed:

> Notice also how intimately and fundamentally the 'facticity' of the institutional order is linked to power, which it both expresses and facilitates in the details of the interaction. For the 'acceptance-as-real' … is built into the mutually intelligible continuity of the interaction. … As a system of power relations, 'acceptance-as-real' has much more far-reaching implications than does the actual differential power that the participating agents are able to bring to the interaction to make their particular views count. … The fact that the conversation does not have a conventional turn-taking form is made intelligible by the mutual acknowledgement that the judge has a certain institutionalized social identity, allocating him definitive prerogatives and sanctions.
>
> *(Giddens, 1984, pp. 331–32)*

Thus power, for Giddens, is implied in action—it is an inherent, transformative capacity of action. And the "acceptance-as-real" is a critical component of interactional contexts and reflected in agents' commonsense tacit knowledge.

Governments and organizations may exercise a significant amount of power through their coordination of people's lives and through the sheer size of their organizing structure. Life-chances—for example, survival itself or the development of literacy—also influence power. And Giddens again underscored the importance of information and its storage:

> The storage of authoritative and allocative resources may be understood as involving the retention and control of information or knowledge whereby social relations are perpetuated across time-space. Storage presumes *media* of information representation, modes of information *retrieval* or recall and, as with all power resources, modes of its dissemination. Notches on wood, written lists, books, files, films, tapes—all these are media of information storage of widely varying capacity and detail. All depend for their retrieval upon the recall capacities of the human memory but also upon skills of interpretation that may be possessed by only a minority within any given population. … Moreover, the character of the information medium—as McLuhan, that now forgotten prophet, consistently stressed—directly influences the nature of the social relations which it helps to organize.
>
> *(Giddens, 1984, pp. 261–62)*

Thus, stored knowledge can shape future social practices, and with more sophisticated storage capacities (such as computerization), time-space distanciation and surveillance can be expanded (Giddens, 1981, pp. 93–96).

Surveillance is also an aspect of power via organizations and the modern state. First, states and organizations collect and collate information collected through a range of information technologies. Second, there may be also be direct surveillance of human activity in diverse bounded locales. Such surveillance can be in prison, at the workplace, while parking a car, or when purchasing a gift at a store.

Giddens also recognized that organizations themselves can be viewed as *"power containers"* (Poole & McPhee, 2005, p. 179). They bring together workers in areas where tasks can be controlled and coordinated. Specific schedules for work also enable surveillance of work. Finally, through distanciation, organizations can expand their power, especially through communication and transportation media, as well as through writing and information storage.

In contrasting Clegg and Giddens on their views of power, McPhee (2004a) suggested the following tenets in Giddens' approach to power: that power is important for, but not absolutely central to, structuration; that power is exercised in interaction and in the reproduced structures of institutional domination; that power is a prerequisite of agency; that power is the "essence of material practice in time and space"; that agents use authoritative and allocative resources in exercising power; that power is a dimension of interaction intertwined with meaning and norms; and, finally, that power always involves a dialectic of control (pp. 130–31). Rationalization of action and reflexive monitoring also play an important role in agency (and thus in the exercise of power). McPhee argued that the two views of power are complementary, with a major difference being their interpretation of modernity, with Giddens emphasizing high modernity (with its major institutions—capitalism, industrialism, surveillance and military power—and the processes of time-space distanciation, the disembedding and re-embedding of social systems, and the knowledgeable, reflexive monitoring of social relations). Leflaive (1996) also pointed out the fundamental role of power in agency and the ability to act.

Constraint and enablement. Giddens' critics have suggested that he gives insufficient attention to the idea of constraint, especially as a quality of social structure. This criticism derived from the "constraints" of social institutions which exist prior to an individual agent and often outlast the life of the individual agent. These reproduced practices, like language itself, are both *enabling and constraining at the same time*: some opportunities are opened up, while others are foreclosed. Giddens noted that

> Human societies, or social systems, would plainly not exist without human agency. But it is not the case that actors create social systems: they reproduce or transform them, remaking what is already made in the continuity of *praxis*. ... In general ... it is true that the greater the time-space distanciation of social systems—the more their institutions bite into time and space—the more resistant they are to manipulation or change by an individual agent. This meaning of constraint is also coupled to enablement. Time-space closes off some possibilities of human experience at the same time as it opens up others.
>
> *(Giddens, 1984, p. 171)*

In addition, constraint varies according to the "material and institutional circumstances of activity, but also in relation to the forms of knowledgeability that agents possess about those circumstances" (ibid., p. 179). These constraints in structure are also mediated by agents' motives and reasons (Giddens, 1990b). Thus, for Giddens, an actor's capabilities and the constraints within a given context, including the constraints of material objects, offer different opportunities for action: action always incorporates both constraint and enablement. For Giddens, then, "All constraints are also possibilities as it were so that all human life is involved in a mixture of possibility and constraints which is an inherent mixture" (Bleicher & Featherstone, 1997, pp. 19–22).

Some constraining/enabling qualities of action include the actor's physical body and the material aspects of the context: this refers to "the limits which the physical capacities of the human body, plus relevant features of the physical environment, place upon the feasible options open to agents" (Giddens, 1984, p. 174). Sanctions, such as coercion, threats, or disapproval, may constrain action as well. Sanctions derive from power relations and are often taken-for-granted aspects of social relations and the context. Sanctions themselves are represented as a contrast of tension between constraint/enablement and coercion/inducement (Giddens, 1981, p. 57).

An actor's access to resources will also influence constraint/enablement. For example, the societal position in which agents find themselves—a "facticity" which the agents did not bring about—will constrain action (Mendoza, 1997a, pp. 234–56). Thus, some structural constraints derive from the "the 'given' character of structural properties *vis-à-vis* situated actors" (Giddens, 1984, p. 176).

For Giddens, then, constraint/enablement may be material, a function of sanctions or structural. By structural enablement/constraint, Giddens means *"placing limits upon the range of options open to an actor, or plurality of actors, in a given circumstance or type of circumstance"* (Giddens, 1984, p. 177). As such, this includes differences in access to resources and the like, created by inequality of status, power and/or opportunity (Kilminster, 1997, pp. 95–98). The basic implications of these considerations, for Giddens, are profound: "all explanations [for social science] will involve at least implicit reference both to the purposive, reasoning behaviour of agents and to its intersection with constraining and enabling features of the social and material contexts of that behaviour" (Giddens, 1984, p. 179). To these constraints, Giddens added the constraint of the boundedness of knowledge, as well as the access to knowledge, which may be hindered by other agents (Giddens, 1987b, pp. 220–23). There is also the difficulty of agents being in different contexts: for some, certain actions may be controlled while, for others, those actions are something which just happens (ibid.).

Sources of both constraint and enablement also depend upon the basic modes of system regulation. Giddens (1979) discussed three modes of system regulation. First, homeostatic loops reflect the unintended consequences of daily activities (pp. 79–80). Second, self-regulation takes place through feedback, in which there is coordination but not necessarily complete control. Finally, reflexive self-regulation reflects intentional efforts by dominant political agents to use resources for control and coordination. As an example, Giddens pointed out that timetables reflect author-itative resources that control a large spatial-temporal sphere of activity. Office con-figurations may also be designed for survelliance and control (Giddens, 1985a). In sum, for Giddens, "All constraints on human action apart from those involved in the physical world derive from 'bounded rationality' and 'bounded power'" (Giddens, 1987b, p. 221).

Agency. Power is viewed as the capacity to do things, and if an agent is no longer able to do otherwise, she or he ceases to be an agent. "Power is instantiated in action, as a regular and routine phenomenon [and] resources are the media through which power is exercised" (Giddens, 1979, p. 91). While power enables action, it can also constrain action. And, as such, an agent's power will shift between autonomy or constraint (Giddens, 1984).

Reflexity is implied in agency, as actors evaluate their actions and its effects. Self-reflexivity is uniquely human because "human beings reflexively apply awareness of their historicity to modify the conditions of their existence" (Giddens, 1983, p. 80). Furthermore, "It is the specifically reflexive form of the knowledgeability of human agents that is most deeply involved in the recursive ordering of social practices" (Giddens, 1984, p. 3).

Giddens extended interaction to encompass institutions that are distanciated in time and space. He noted that

> The reflexive monitoring of action in situations of co-presence is the main anchoring feature of social integration, but both the conditions and the out-comes of situated interaction stretch far beyond those situations as such. The mechanisms of 'stretching' are variable but in modern societies tend to involve reflexive monitoring itself. That is to say, understanding the condi-tions of system reproduction becomes part of those conditions of system reproduction as such.
>
> *(Giddens, 1984, p. 191)*

Agents have power because they can implement flexible responses, as well as use rules and resources (Giddens, 1982, 1984). Creativity in practical knowledge—using rules in new ways—is possible because of different motivations and the agent's own reflexive monitoring of actions. As Llewellyn concluded:

> Giddens sees agents' capabilities residing in their knowledge and their power. In his schema there is a complex interplay between knowledge, rules, power and resources. Hence there is no absolute boundary between the knowl-edgeable, powerful agent and the organizational context for their action. Agential powers and agential knowledge encompass the rules and resources that agents (as organizational actors) are able to appropriate and make part of their constitution.
>
> *(Llewellyn, 2007, p. 151)*

Thus agency may reproduce structure or create new structures.

Structuration theory also allows for changing social practices, not just reproducing them. As Kaspersen noted:

> Ontological security, practical consciousness, reflexive monitoring of action, and rationalization of acting give the agency concept a recursive character, thereby providing both the concepts of agent and agency with a reproductive dimension. These elements help to explain why the same patterns of action are repeated and create the foundation for a social order. The concepts of transformative capacity, discursive consciousness, unintended consequences, and unacknowledged conditions of new actions are, however, aspects that may change existing routines.
>
> *(Kaspersen, 2000, p. 41)*

Social change may result from unintended consequences of actions, but actors may also intentionally change their actions. Through discursive consciousness, actors can reflect on their actions, incorporate new information and modify their actions.

Outhwaite (1990) outlined some major distinctions Giddens established concerning structure and agency. Giddens argued that structure is *both* enabling and constraining; that structural constraints are influenced by agents' motives; that structure influences both macro- and micro-levels of action; that agency refers not to intentions, but to the ability to carry out action; and that structures and systems are not identical (structures exist as rules and resources, and as properties of systems) (Giddens, 1990a, pp. 63–64). For Giddens, action and rules are inherently transformative, and social action draws upon and instantiates structure (Craib, 1992, pp. 35–42).

As we have seen, his work deals with critical organizing and communicating issues such as agency, structure, power and change.

Summary

For Giddens, structuration theory links social systems and individual agency through the recursive social practices of a society. As Giddens remarks, "Every competent member of every society knows (in the sense of both discursive and practical consciousness) a great deal about the institutions of that society: such knowledge is not *incidental* to the operation of society, but is necessarily involved in it" (Giddens, 1982, p. 37). Haugaard argued that, "Even though structures only exist at the moment of action, as rules and resources they can also order action by existing in potential form as knowledge of rules and resources ... social structures are 'carried'— exist in potential form—hence, structures are inherently both enabling (rules and resources) and, prior to action, exist as a form of constraint limiting the possibilities of future action" (Haugaard, 1992, p. 87).

Thus, for Giddens, social reality reflects both human actors and institutional properties. Social structure is enacted by humans; these structures shape interaction and action by providing contextual rules and resources that allow humans to make sense of their actions and those of others (Orlikowski & Robey, 1991). People act in the context of past enacted structures, and thus structure is objectified. In this way, social structure and social action constitute each other recursively and continuously.

To reiterate our earlier emphasis on social practices, structuration is not the "experience of the individual actor, nor the existence of any form of societal totality, but social practices considered across time and space" (Giddens, 1984, p. 2). As Thrift cogently remarked:

> each agent draws upon structure (that is, stocks of knowledge) to reproduce sets of spatially and temporally specific practices which in turn contribute to the total constitution of society at any one point in time in any one spatial location. Clearly, the spatio-temporal format of social systems intervenes quite strongly in the form that this recursive process takes, dictating a good part of the pattern of presence and absence to be found in the different contexts upon which particular agents can draw.
>
> *(Thrift, 1997a, p. 127)*

A major premise of structuration theory is that the "rules and resources drawn on in the production and reproduction of social systems are at the same time the means of system reproduction (the duality of structure)" (Giddens, 1984, p. 19). This parallels Goffman's argument that the social practices which create a particular interpretation of events (framing and keying) can also be used to reinterpret the events (or reframe and rekey them). For both Goffman and Giddens, social interaction is a focal point and underlies social institutions (although this was acknowledged, but never fully developed in Goffman's work). For Giddens, social integration is accomplished via face-to-face interaction, while system integration involves reciprocity across absent agents (collectivities or groups).

Structuration theory utilizes structural principles, structures and structural properties as explanatory concepts. Structural principles identify principles of organization of societies. Structures, viewed as rule-resource sets, reflect how social practices and institutions develop within social systems. The duality of structure requires the reflexive monitoring of action by agents and the structural properties of mediation and transformation. His work has also articulated the importance of historicity and time-space in social systems and social integration. His insights have also enhanced our understanding of power, reflexivity and knowledgeability in interaction.

As Turner noted:

> Giddens conceptualizes 'structure' as 'rules and resources' used by actors in interaction. Rules are 'generalizable procedures' and 'methodologies' that reflexive agents possess in their implicit 'stocks of knowledge' and that they employ as 'formulas' for action in 'social systems' (specific empirical

contexts of interaction). These rules of structure reveal a number of important properties: they are tacitly known; informal; widely sanctioned; and frequently invoked and used in conversations, interaction rituals, and daily routines. ... Structure also involves the use of resources that are the 'material equipment' and 'organizational capacities' of actors to get things done. ... Rules and resources are 'transformational' in that they can be created, changed, and recombined into different forms; they are 'mediating' in that they are what actors use to tie social relations together.

(Turner, 1986, p. 972)

With this overview of Giddens' structuration theory in mind, I will next take a close look at Giddens' concepts of the self, identity, and action/structure in interaction. These core concepts round out our organizing and communicating concerns.

6

GIDDENS: CONTEXT, AGENCY AND INTERACTION

With an overview of Giddens' structuration theory in mind, I now turn to a more thorough discussion of his views on agency, action and interaction and their implications for organizing and communicating. In particular, I will look at modernity as the context in which organizing and communicating take place. Through distanciation, disembedding, re-embedding, and communication and transportation advances, new forms of organizing and communicating are possible. In addition, I will discuss the challenges of interaction, agency, and the self in modern times, particularly in terms of identity, uncertainty and risk.

The Sociohistorical Context of Modernity

In discussing modernity, Giddens argued that the pace of change is so rapid and global that it is "discontinuous" with prior changes. Three sources for the dynamism of modernity can be traced. First, there is time-space distanciation: in traditional civilizations "systems of time and space are still closely connected with place. Time-reckoning never becomes completely separate from 'where' one is, while space remains infused with characteristics of localized milieux. In circumstances of modernity, time and space become 'emptied out' and distinguished from one another. The 'emptying' of time has priority in this process, because control of time, through abstract time-regulation, permits the coordination of activities across space" (Giddens, 1990b, p. 306).

The second source of dynamism is the disembedding of social systems, where social interaction and relations are "lifted out of" local contexts of interaction. The separation of time and space is essential for disembedding, and "disembedded activities promote a massive increase in time-space distanciation" (ibid.). For example, money—as a disembedding mechanism—allows economic relations across vast spans of time-space, and permits exchanges between people who will not ever meet.

Finally, there is the reflexivity of modernity, which Giddens argued goes beyond ordinary human reflexivity (i.e., keeping in touch with what is going on). For Giddens, the reflexivity of modernity "refers to the reflexive appropriation of the conditions of system reproduction—precisely one of the sources of social change. ... The reordering of time and space is again directly involved here. ... With the advent of modernity, reflexivity comes to permeate the very fundamentals of social reproduction, affecting the routines of everyday life as well as larger aspects of institutions. 'What was done before' has (in principle, and often in practice) no intrinsic connections with 'what is done now', save insofar as past practices can be defended in a rational way in the light of 'incoming knowledge'. ... In conditions of modernity, social practices are constantly examined and reformed in terms of novel information about their nature—in a process which has no intrinsic end-point" (ibid., pp. 306–7). Thus, reflexivity in modern life consists of continuously evaluating social practices in light of new information, and thus potentially altering these practices. These conditions, of course, heighten uncertainty and risk—and ontological security becomes more fragile, with knowledge being questioned and the self subject to increasing reflexivity (Hoogenboom & Ossewaarde, 2005). Reflexive organizations are thus needed for late modern society and are highly responsive to both institutional and technical environments.

The implications of time-space for modernity and for modern organizations are significant. As Giddens (1990a, 1991a, b) noted, the standardization of time and space supported the development of a rationalized organization. In turn, modern organizations connect the local and global in new, unprecedented ways and greatly extend their scope. With standardization, time and space constitute a world-wide frame of action and experience. Underpinning these changes, Giddens argues, is communication: "communications has become the driving force of successive waves of transformation of human society ... the simplest meaning of globalization is interdependence. We have started to be much more dependent on other people than ever before, and part of the reason is that we are constantly in communication with them all" (Rantanen, 2005, p. 73). Furthermore, with regard to globalization, Giddens sees "media and communications as having a fundamental role because most of the institutions we now associate with globalization would not be possible" without them (Rantanen, 2005, p. 68). As such, contexts are now global and distanciated in both time and space.

In addition, Giddens also specifically integrated talk into time-space contexts. As he noted,

> ... the contextuality of talk, like the contextuality of bodily posture, gesture and movement, is the basis upon which such phenomena are co-ordinated as encounters extending in time-space. ... Norms of talk pertain not only to

what is said, the syntactical and semantic form of utterances, but also to the routinized occasions of talk.

(Giddens, 1984, p. 83)

The frame theory of organizing and communicating being developed here, which emphasizes the importance of context and tacit knowledge, is again very similar to views of both Giddens and Goffman. Thus, for Giddens as well as Goffman, communication or interaction involves talk, context and bodily positioning. Interaction is situated in immediate contexts of action, but can also be extended in time and space, and placed within a world-history environment. Through time-space distanciation and the reflexivity of individuals and institutions, we have created the pace and magnitude of change that characterize modernity.

Globalization as change. As previously noted, one of the most important aspects of modernity, with its distanciation, standardization of time, and disembedding/re-embedding, is the sheer pace and scope of change—the way in which the "local" is also "global." As Giddens noted, "Globalisation concerns the intersection of presence and absence, the interlacing of social events and social relationships 'at distance' with local contextualities" Giddens, 1991a, p. 21). We all live locally because our bodies are situated in a given time and space, yet mediated experience alters our experience of the world.

He also observed that globalization is a dialectical process:

Globalization can thus be defined as the intensification of world-wide social relations which link distant localities in such a way that local happenings are shaped by events occurring many miles away and vice versa. This is a dialectical process because such local happenings may move in an obverse direction from the very distanciated relations that shape them. 'Local transformation' is as much a part of globalization as the lateral extension of social connections across time and space.

(Giddens, 1990a, p. 64).

In a subsequent interview (Bryant & Jary, 2001c), Giddens was asked to comment on the relation between the personal and the global: "We all experience the larger problems of the world in some part in personal terms, in the context of our own life situations; in turn, the changes we make in our own lives restructure larger issues ... every time you or I turn on our computers, we are contributing to globalization processes. That's structuration all over again" (p. 267). This dialectic involves everyone: "Transformations in self-identity and globalization, I want to propose, are the two poles of the dialectic of the local and the global in conditions of high modernity" (Giddens, 1991a, p. 32). Global awareness of certain issues, such as AIDS, global warming, poverty, and the like, may also shape lifestyle choices (Giddens, 1991a). However, as Tomlinson noted, these lifestyle choices also occur in a local context, which may complicate an actor's choices and motivation (Tomlinson, 1997, p. 125).

Giddens argued that societies have moved from simple modernity to reflexive modernity, in which we are confronting manufactured risks (i.e., those problems humans have created, such as pollution and global warming), as well as natural risks. A paradox confronts us because the means of sustaining life are simultaneously a major threat to planetary life, and this reverberates in every individual's connection to modern society (Giddens & Pierson, 1998, pp. 17–18). One's identity becomes a "moving projection through complex social, institutional contours of a globalized cultural system" (ibid., p. 19). He believes that dialogue is a key component in addressing the complexity of modern life (ibid., pp. 23–26). Modernity is more dynamic than other societal eras because of economic institutions, like capitalism; political institutions like democracy; the technological bases of modern societies, and the resultant openness of information exchange (Giddens & Pierson, 1998).

In their overview of Giddens' work on globalization and high modernity, Bryant and Jary (2001a) suggest four major themes surrounding globalization. First, there is an increasing spatial transformation of social relations, further stretching these relations across time-space. Second, communications have increased in intensity, reach, speed and influence. Third, new networks of knowledge, information and expert systems are available, and agents depend increasingly upon them. Finally, there is "a mediation of the global by the local" which eliminates any single dominant social system (pp. 24–25). And both individuals and institutions are influenced by these factors.

Giddens himself identified the complex pressures of globalization; the tension between the global and the local, the creation of new organizations, and the dissolution of nation-state boundaries. This is the context of organizing and communicating, and it alters the daily lives of all agents. For these interwoven social systems to be effective requires trust, despite high levels of uncertainty and risk (Giddens, 1991b, pp. 210–20).

Tomlinson (1997) suggested that modernity frees time and space from a particular place, thus allowing for distanciation and, most importantly, "the institutionalization of this distanciated interaction via the modern social *organization*. ... Organizations are, indeed, the prime instance of the potential for the *reintegration* of time and space which is characteristic of modernity" (p. 118). Through disembedding, the removal of social relationships from their local context and their restructuring across time and space, our interactions are increasingly influenced by "absent others." As Giddens commented, "locales are thoroughly penetrated by and shaped in terms of social influences quite distant from them ... the 'visible form' of the locale conceals the distanciated relations which determine its nature" (1990a, p. 19). For example, chain stores in malls, which are a feature in a local context, may exist, flourish or be removed by global market forces. Tomlinson argued that agents' awareness of complex socioeconomic and political systems is not central to agents' daily awareness. I would argue, in contrast, that agents might be quite aware of direct impacts of global forces—consider auto workers in Michigan and Ohio, farmers along the Rio Grande, or people ingesting tainted drugs or milk from China, to name just a few examples.

In summary, globalization in late modernity has changed both individual lives and institutional forms. For both individuals and institutions, distanciation, disembedding and re-embedding have altered relationships across time and space. One can be both here and there, and now and then. One's identities are also transformed as are institutions. One's local existence is inseparable from global activities and events. And both individual and institutional reflexivity enable evaluation of actions to an unprecedented degree. These challenges and changes, of course, bring increased risk with them and a great need for trust. Through modern communication networks and transportation, our worlds have become highly intertwined, and the pace and scope of change greatly extended and accelerated.

Globalization and mediated experiences. Globalization is also a phenomenon directly connected to mediated experience—and, as communication scholars, we are actively engaged in the study of communication systems and their impact. Giddens argued that print enabled the movement from traditional to modern societies, and various forms of mediated communication and transportation are characteristic of late modernity (Giddens, 1991a). For Giddens, language is the "prime and original means of time-space distanciation, elevating human activity beyond the immediacy of the experience of animals" (Giddens, 1991a, p. 23). He characterized the intrusion of the distant into everyday experience as the "openness of the world" in which "Distant events may become as familiar or more so, than proximate influences, and integrated into the frameworks of personal experience" (ibid., p.189). Because all experience is mediated, Tomlinson insightfully noted that we need to "appreciate the subtleties and complexities of different modes of experience available to human beings in conditions of modernity" and be aware of the qualitative differences across different types of mediation (Tomlinson, 1997, p. 123).

According to Giddens, globalization can be reflected in awareness of global influences in local markets, in awareness of world events via the mass media, and in awareness of the world as a single place, in which there are no "others" (Giddens, 1991a, p. 27). Problems, for example, in which there are high risks for all, are found in ecological problems such as global warming and water pollution. People recognized

> ... that reversing the degradation of the environment depends upon adopting new lifestyle patterns. Ecological problems highlight the new and accelerating interdependence of global systems and bring home to everyone the depth of the connections between personal activity and planetary problems.
>
> *(ibid., p. 221)*

While agents are aware of such issues, Tomlinson argued that the mass-mediated experiences of a global culture are more limited than those of a local culture. In local cultures, much more time and involvement has been invested in the development and maintenance of the culture, especially its symbolic and ideological underpinnings (Tomlinson, 1997, p. 130). For Tomlinson, dialogue is essential for the development of communal identity (ibid., p. 133).

A final important limitation of televised media experiences is that they are largely one-way and not dialogic: the Internet may be an exception to this in that it provides participation and the potential for dialogue. Giddens, like Tomlinson, suggested that "world building" is needed on the institutional level to build a communal identity. And Giddens has alerted us to the strength and pervasiveness of mediated experiences. For example, some global communities, such as Greenpeace, represent a community of common interests that transcend national boundaries. More scholarship will undoubtedly shed light on some of these issues, for they are clearly important issues in organizing and communicating in the modern era. And the role of dialogue is clearly central, whether face-to-face or mediated via the Internet, cell phones or other interactive media.

Change. While globalization is a continuous force for change, other factors have also fostered a continually evolving environment. Structuration theory identifies four types of change which may overlap with one another. They include:

1. system reproduction—changes due to the inherent indeterminacy of social systems;
2. system contradiction—changes resulting from clashes or struggles at the "fault lines" of social systems;
3. reflexive appropriation—changes driven by the reflexive examination of the conditions of social reproduction, and
4. resource access—changes produced by differential control of valued resources (Giddens, 1990b, p. 304).

At any given time in social reproduction, there may also be social change—such change is "usually *incremental* in character: a slow 'drift' away from a given practice or set of practices at any given location in time-space … by definition unintended and unplanned" (ibid.).

In addition, Giddens argued that social change is related to five concepts of structuration theory which help locate where change has occurred: structural principles; intersocietal systems; time-space edges; world time; and episodic characterizations. Episodes have specified beginnings and ends, and mark a sequence of changes to main institutions of society, like marking the emergence of agrarian states (ibid., p. 244). World time refers to historicity or the confluence of factors and social systems worldwide. Giddens also notes that social change may be altered by agents' reflexive monitoring of events, and knowledge of how similar changes have been carried out in previous times or societies. Change "depends upon conjunctions of circumstances and events that may differ in nature according to variations of context, where context (as always) involves the reflexive monitoring by the agents involved in the conditions in which they 'make history'" (Giddens, 1984, p. 245). For agents, reflecting on a distinction between the taken-for-granted and the accepted-as-legitimate may also create change through agents' reflexive monitoring of actions (Gregory, 1989, p. 200).

In discussing change, Giddens observed that agents alter something that precedes them. "Human societies, or social systems, would plainly not exist without human agency. But it is not the case that actors create social systems: they reproduce or transform them, remaking what is already made in the continuity of *praxis*" (Giddens, 1984, p. 171). Historicity also comes into play because "absent others include past generations whose time may be very different from that of those who are in some way influenced by residues of their activities" (Giddens, 1984, p. 37).

Giddens (1984) also argued that societal changes must be evaluated in the context of intersocietal systems. Some changes may be driven by external factors (e.g., a change in government in part facilitated by material support given by other countries to overturn that government). Examples on an institutional level would be changes in companies, or whole industries, as a result of outsourcing or pressure from foreign competitors. Change may also occur at time-space edges: these time-space edges are forms of contact that occur between structurally different societies. For example, an Indonesian tribal society may be changed by contact with Western countries. Globalization, generally, might be viewed from the perspective of time-space edges.

Change may also driven by managerial or organizational units. As Whittington pointed out, "Giddens does provide a theoretical scheme with considerable potential for understanding managerial agency. Although subject to routine and unintended consequences, organizations are capable of being governed purposively and reflexively through time. Their structural properties—the rules of conduct and allocation of resources—are drawn from the social systems in which their members participate. ... All actors—workers and managers—participate in a dialectic of control that allows them at least the power of defiance. They do moreover participate in other systems of activity from which they may carry into their firms quite different, often contradictory structural principles" (Whittington, 1997, p. 370). From such diverse forces of agency, change as well as contradiction may emerge within individuals as well as organizations, and, more broadly, institutions and social systems.

Giddens suggested a tension between unifying and fragmenting forces in modernity, but is optimistic that democratizing forces will prevail. As Spybey pointed out, "Giddens sees the empowered individual living in a society where there exists at least the capacity for 'people power'. ... As he puts it, the information environment embraces both rulers and ruled" (Spybey, 2001, p. 165). Some of Giddens' work in the area of democratic participation is outlined in his work on utopian realism and the third way. New life politics may create a "Utopian Realism" as a basis for a new social order. Much of Giddens' work in the late 1990s attempts to develop this perspective (Giddens, 1994, 1998). Communication scholars, like Deetz, Mumby, St. Clair and others, have articulated the need for participation in organizations.

In summary, change occurs from a variety of factors, ranging from globalization to change in resources to changes wrought by reflexivity. Change may occur at points of contact across different social practices, at time-space edges and in interactions across different societies and cultures. Changes may also be episodic and mark sociohistorical changes, such as the shift from agrarian to industrial societies. Different structural principles may also create opportunities for change. Finally, the speed at which change occurs, and its extensiveness, are also increased in modernity. Change itself is thus complex, and is also a result of contradiction within social systems.

1. *Contradiction.* Giddens incorporated contradiction as part of change in his structuration theory. He distinguishes two types of contradiction, an existential and a structural contradiction. The existential contradiction is that "life is predicated upon nature, yet is not of nature and is set off against [it]" (Giddens, 1984, p. 193). Structural contradictions refer to structural principles that "operate in terms of one another but yet also contravene each other" (ibid.). These structural contradictions may be primary (which enter into society's constitution) or they may be secondary, created by a primary contradiction. For example, the nation-state is a focal point of structural contradiction. Interestingly, the primary contradiction in capitalism is the tension between the private sphere (civil society) with the public sphere (the nation-state). A secondary contradiction in capitalism is the tension between the internationalizing of capital and the internal consolidation of nation-states. Two current examples would be the influx of foreign capital into the US as a result of other countries' economic turmoil (and thus creating additional concerns in the US over potential control over the U.S. economy by foreign investment), and immigration concerns which are inflaming debates about the economy and national security. Giddens suggests that existential contradiction is more prominent in tribal societies, whereas structural contradiction is more prevalent in class-divided societies. Structural contradictions have accelerated the processes of social change, and the establishment of varied forms of societies present today (Giddens, 1979, p. 199). Giddens also discusses the contradictions, in modernity, between "displacement and re-embedding, intimacy and impersonality, expertise and re-appropriation, and privatism and engagement" (Craib, 1992, p.105).

Contradiction mobilizes different interests within a social system, and different groups may actively conflict with one another, thus creating change. Reflexive appropriation may incorporate change that is "sequential and 'smoothly flowing,' but may also involve radical interventions, especially by social movements which may enter into a 'running dialogue' with organizations to which they are opposed, [and] as part of that very opposition, shaping and reshaping the respective outlooks of each" (ibid.). Finally, "differential access to resources generates differential power" and organized change may result from this (ibid.).

Contradictions do not necessarily lead to conflict. Agents are involved in conflict, and they may vary in their knowledge of their own interests, and also in their motivation and ability to act on them. Contradiction does not lead to conflict if agents fail to understand the contradiction; if there are multiple "fault lines" so that agents fail to act on some, or if there is direct suppression of a conflict (Giddens, 1979, pp. 140–46).

Because of the diversity across different organizations, modern organizations may contradict and challenge social systems. Multinational organizations create connections across a variety of nation-states, and may be influenced by the different social practices of other nation-states. The emergence of writing organizes, as well as reorganizes, time and space, and makes possible a "mobilizing reflexivity unavailable in oral cultures. As a result of this and other factors, change is no longer mainly of the incremental kind. Structural contradiction becomes a feature, with its associated tensions and struggles. ... Problems of resource access are magnified as the inequalities of various sorts become more marked" (Giddens, 1990a, p. 305).

As we have seen, the sociohistorical context of late modernity is a constantly changing, globalized environment. Distanciation and the disembedding of social practices, organizations and institutions have blurred the lines between local and global. Mediated communication has altered our awareness and opened up the world to us (Rantanen, 2005). This modern context has facilitated new social practices, new forms of reflexivity and new organizational forms as well as increased risk and uncertainty (Greener, 2008). We as individuals and organizational members face unprecedented challenges and Giddens' structuration theory has insightfully illuminated these issues (Wheeler-Brooks, 2009). With this broad context in mind, we now turn to examine interaction itself more closely, the source of both social order and social change.

Action and Interaction in Structuration Theory

Routine social practices and social interaction are emphasized by both Goffman and Giddens, with Goffman focusing on face-to-face encounters and Giddens focusing on how social practices constitute and reconstitute social institutions. In both theories, action and structure are intertwined in social interaction.

Jary and Jary (1997) underscored this link when they noted:

> If agents, and the hermeneutic and contingent nature of their everyday practices, are taken seriously, then what is "structural" about the structural context? Giddens's answer is, in effect, that the context is structural because it provides the foundations for an agent's next move. The context is "virtual" as it provides ideational knowledge of rules and resources, one's own and others, which inform and enable decisions to act. Elements taken from resources will, of course, be more imminently present within the action itself. This conception of structure means that it has to be mixed with agency at every turn in order to produce an action.
>
> *(p. 195)*

Social practices, for Giddens, incorporate the reflexive monitoring of action and the rationalization of action. As he pointed out, "These are crucial to practical consciousness; all (competent) actors in a society are expected to 'keep in touch' with why they act as they do, as a routine element of action, such that they can 'account' for what they do when asked to do so by others" (Giddens, 1981, p. 36).

As such, Giddens argued that the "duality of structure is always the main grounding of continuities in social reproduction across time-space. In turn, it presupposes the reflexive monitoring of agents in, and as constituting, the *durée* of daily social activity. But human knowledgeability is always bounded. The flow of action continually produces consequences which are uintended by actors, and these unintended consequences also may form unacknowledged conditions of action in a feedback fashion" (Giddens, 1984, pp. 26–27).

Individual agents (actors) are involved in interaction. Their actions (agency) constitute and reconstitute social practices and, when interwoven with others' actions, constitute and reconstitute organizations, institutions and societies. While social practices are key for Giddens, these social practices "build up" from the countless, daily routine encounters of individuals, whether others are co-present or absent, to create organizations and societies. When individuals reflexively monitor their actions and those of others, a social self emerges. The individual or social self is important because agency flows from an individual's actions. We now look more closely at the self, its emergence and agency in interaction, and, from Giddens' perspective, at the challenges humans face in the modern world.

The Self

Like Goffman, Giddens focused on the body and its location in time-space; both regard the body as the locus of the self, and gestures, facial expressions and bodily positioning as key in social interaction (or "social integration" in Giddens' terminology) (Giddens, 1984, pp. 41–43). Giddens also relied on the work of Erik Erikson on the development of the self.

The self has three dimensions: (1) a basic security system (ontological trust developed in infancy via care-giving relationships); (2) practical consciousness; and (3) discursive consciousness. For Giddens, interpretive schemes are embedded within each dimension of the self. As he noted, in relating agency to the self, that

> The constitution of the 'I' comes about only through the 'discourse of the Other'—that is, through the acquisition of language—but the 'I' has to be related to the body as the sphere of action. The term 'I' is in linguistic terms a 'shifter': the contextuality of social 'positioning' determines who is an I in any situation of talk. ... An agent who has mastered the use of 'I', as Mead says, has also mastered the use of 'me'—but only via concomitant mastery of syntactically differentiated language. ... The point is not just that these usages presume linguistic skills of a very complicated kind but also that they entail a ramified control of the body and a developed knowledge of how to 'go on' in the plurality of contexts of social life.
>
> *(Giddens, 1984, p. 43)*

Shotter also conceptualized selves as possessing a duality of structure—as having both a *me,* which looks at the self's current position/experience in society, and an *I,* which is able to act in an intended style or fashion (Shotter, 1997, p. 96).

Routine is critical for ontological security, and grounds us in the material world. Giddens argued that "Routinization is vital to the psychological mechanisms whereby a sense of trust or ontological security is sustained in the daily activities of social life … the apparently minor conventions of daily social life are of essential significance in curbing the sources of unconscious tension that would otherwise preoccupy most of our waking lives" (Giddens, 1984, p. xxiii). He concluded that "Routine is integral both to the constitution of the personality of the agent as he or she moves along the paths of daily activities and to the institutions of society, which are such only through their continued reproduction" (ibid., p. 60).

The self, then, is a narrative constructed throughout an individual's life-span. "Self-identity is continuously being developed or 'becoming,' and is strongly influenced by social integration with significant others, like parents, siblings and friends. Pure relationships—those entered into entirely for their own sake, and only as long as both parties are satisfied with the relationship—enter into self-identity so long as it is a positive contributor (Giddens, 2000, p. 151, cited in Kaspersen, 2000).

A self has multiple identities, reflecting social positions, exposure to mediated images of other lifestyles and choices, globalization, and a myriad of other influences (Giddens, 2004). For Giddens, "Self-identity is not a distinctive trait, or even a collection of traits, possessed by the individual. *It is the self as reflexively understood by the person in terms of her or his biography*" (Giddens, 1991a, p. 53) and in the ability to sustain a particular narrative. Substantial controversy exists over the influence of mediated communication in terms of how media images are received, interpreted, rejected, or incorporated into self-identity, as well as how different audiences respond to these images.

The self and consciousness. By agent, Giddens means "the overall subject located within the corporeal time-space of the living organism" (Giddens, 1984, p. 51). The self is viewed as the origin of action: the self "is the sum of those forms of recall whereby the agent reflexively characterizes 'what' is at the origin of his or her action" (ibid.). Like Goffman, Giddens emphasized the temporal and spatial aspects of early interaction as laying the foundation for ontological security as well as for further interactions. Stages of development in childhood move the child toward "autonomy, which should be understood as the foundation for the reflexive monitoring of conduct" (ibid., p. 57).

Based on the work of Laing and Erikson, Giddens focused on a child's coping with trust vs. distrust, engagement vs. disengagement, and initiative vs. guilt (Mendoza, 1997b). Basic ontological security is pre-linguistic and therefore remains at the unconscious level, but, as agents, young children negotiate their needs and desires with the external environment (ibid., p. 281). Ontological security is greatly facilitated by routinization, and helps curb unconscious tensions (Giddens, 1984, p. xxiv).

Through routine and interaction, children develop social practices which enable them to display their competence. Here Giddens relied upon Goffman's analyses of embarrassment, face and alignment (see Chapter 8). Facial expressions and body signals are viewed as particularly important signals of discomfort. As Mendoza pointed out:

> By citing the works of Goffman, Giddens wants to bring to the fore the important point that the sustenancy of trust, and hence ontological security, is not only based on the 'taken-for-granted' character of the duree of routine activities. ... Interaction therefore typically takes the form of a conscious undertaking actively built by actors by the use of skills and techniques of 'face work.' The 'power' of agents should not be purely seen as domination in the pejorative sense but as the capacity to 'save face.' Accordingly, the *competence* of the social actor is also judged by his ability to maintain self-esteem and ontological security by his actions.
>
> *(Mendoza, 1997b, p. 293)*

Social incompetence gives rise to feelings of shame, guilt, embarrassment or similar negative feelings that "flood through" from the unconscious (Giddens, 1984, pp. 50–60). (Much of this will be covered in our review of Goffman's work—suffice it to state that Giddens' emphasis on social integration rests directly upon Goffman's work. Some of the criticism of Giddens' work as being static, rather than processual, would be removed if scholars viewed Goffman's work as providing the processes of structuration through Goffman's model of social interaction—a point which we will cover in some detail later.) Mendoza raised an interesting point when he suggested that Freud, Bettelheim, Garfinkel, and Goffman all depict people as searching for meaning, where meaning stands not only for intelligibility, but also peace (ontological security) and worth (self-esteem) (Mendoza, 1997b, pp. 293–94). These are critical issues for Giddens as well.

For Giddens, not every act is motivated, nor does action necessarily involve a sequence of intentions. As he stated:

> ... rather than supposing that every 'act' has a corresponding 'motive', we have to understand the term 'motivation' to be a processual one. ... Ordinary day-to-day life—in greater or less degree according to context and the vagaries of individual personality—involve an *ontological security* expressing an *autonomy of bodily control* within *predictable routines*. ... Ontological security is ... maintained in a ... fundamental way by the very predictability of routine. ...
>
> *(Giddens, 1984, p. 50)*

Ontological security is the "Confidence or trust that the natural and social worlds are as they appear to be, including the basic existential parameters of self and social identity" (Giddens, 1984, p. 375). As an infant matures and becomes more autonomous, he or she learns how to "sustain the mutuality implied in trust via tact and other formulae that preserve the face of others" (ibid.). And trust, as we have seen, is a major aspect of interaction in our disembedded, distanciated social practices.

Over time, the infant/toddler increasingly recognizes the agency of others. Thus, for both Goffman and Giddens, humans are motivated to sustain mutual trust and a shared sense of "what is going on here." Without this mutuality and trust, social life is chaotic and unintelligible.

Through routinization, agents move through daily life and through societal institutions:

> Routine is integral both to the continuity of the personality of the agent, as he or she moves along the paths of daily activities, and to the institutions of society, which *are* such only through their continued reproduction. An examination of routinization, I shall claim, provides us with a master key to explicating the characteristic forms of relation between the basic security system on the one hand and the reflexively constituted processes inherent in the episodic character of encounters on the other.
>
> *(Giddens, 1984, p. 60)*

For Giddens, motivation is processual and "there is a generalized motivational commitment to the integration of habitual practices across time and space" (ibid., p. 64). Giddens also noted that actors have a significant affective involvement in routines because of the security provided by routinization. This is a viewpoint Goffman would also support, given his emphasis on face, its mutuality, and the sustaining of a working consensus of "what is going on here."

Personal relationships. For Giddens, in modernity, the self and society are intertwined in a global context. McPhee noted Giddens' reliance on Goffman's concepts of face and facework in reflexive monitoring and the rationalization of action, and in the mutual reflexive monitoring in conversation. Giddens also acknowledged Goffman's insights into "the spatiotemporal features of interaction processes" (McPhee, 1998, p. 93).

Although McPhee argued that social relations are viewed on the level of system integration, he failed to note that social relations fundamentally develop on the level of social integration, which Giddens argues always precedes and makes possible system integration. McPhee related structuration theory to personal relationships in four ways—the importance of trust; the viewing of identity as a reflexive, life-long project of searching for authenticity; the handling of fateful moments (like death) by experts; and selecting a lifestyle (referring to the vast choice of lifestyle options present in high modernity). Personal relationships have become "pure relationships" in which satisfaction is sought by both partners, and which continue as an intimate, enduring tie (Giddens, 1991a, 1992). In the context of the Internet as a new way of meeting others and forming relationships, Hardey (2004) examined how trust, authenticity and emotional communication are presented online.

As McPhee noted, Giddens recognized a number of tensions: between the conditional, temporary nature of relationships versus the trust and commitment for growth in relationships; between autonomy versus dependence; and between sexual exclusivity versus sexual openness and transience. McPhee concluded by pointing out the strengths of structuration theory in relationships, with its focus on self-consciousness, equality, trust and dialogue. In an empirical test of Giddens' pure love relationships, Gross and Simmons (2002) found that midlife North Americans experienced the rewards of freedom and happiness from such relationships, but did not experience many of the negative side effects (i.e., anxiety).

The self and self-identity is always in flux: Humans are always in the process of becoming throughout their life-cycle. Different stages of life bring forth different challenges and issues. Socialization also involves the reproduction of society, including the stages of infancy, adulthood, and death, and reflects the socialization of generations of agents over the course of time. As Giddens noted, a person's identity is "found in the capacity to keep *a particular narrative going*" (Giddens, 1991a, p. 54).

In recasting intimacy as a "'transactional negotiation of personal ties by equals," this may encourage the "*democratizing*" of both interpersonal and public domains (Giddens, 1992, p. 3). And intimate relationships are characterized as reflexive, open, contingent relationships in which there is self-actualization and trust (1990a, 1991a, 1992). However, given the disembedding of relationships and the reflexivity of modern life, ontological insecurity may occur, and the self balances trust against risk as part of modern life (Giddens, 1990a). For Giddens, with writing and thus information storage, dissemination and retrieval, tradition becomes just one possible way to deal with time and space (Giddens, 1987a, p. 277).

The increasing range of lifestyle choices, the more open and multiple contexts of action, and varied sources of authority provide agents with daily choices for constructing a narrative of identity (Giddens, 1991a, 1992). Through the increasing pace of globalization, especially new transportation and communication technologies, we have entered an era of radicalized modernity, with increasing connections to distant events (Giddens, 1991b, 1994, 2000). And with many distanciated relationships, trust becomes even more essential in interactions (Giddens, 1994).

Levels of consciousness. Consciousness is also viewed on several levels. There is the level of sensory awareness and functioning of the body that is presupposed by practical and discursive consciousness. Perception is viewed as monitoring a flow of activity integrated with the movement of the body in a particular time-space. Perceptual schemata continually process one's experience, and anticipate new incoming information. As Giddens suggested, "The main point of reference has to be neither the single sense nor the contemplative perceiver but the body in its active engagements with the material and social worlds" (Giddens, 1984, p. 47). Practical consciousness is the reflexive monitoring of action by human agents, while discursive consciousness is the ability to discuss and give an account of one's actions (ibid., pp. 44–45). Finally, Giddens noted that, when unconscious needs are under control, interaction and the reflexive monitoring of action proceeds relatively smoothly (Giddens, 1979, pp. 178–80).

Through discursive consciousness, individuals can reflect upon an activity and explain that activity. However, discursive consciousness only partially taps into practical consciousness (our tacit knowledge of routines and expectations). In contrasting discursive with practical consciousness, Giddens argued that "knowledgeability is founded less upon discursive than practical consciousness. ... All competent members of society are vastly skilled in the practical accomplishments of social activities. ... The knowledge they possess is not incidental to the persistent patterning of social life but is integral to it" (Giddens, 1984, p. 26). This emphasis is critical for Giddens to avoid the mistakes of structuralism and functionalism (i.e., ignoring actors' rationalization of action) and of phenomenology (i.e., regarding society as a "plastic creation of human subjects") (ibid.). For Giddens and Goffman, as well as in the theory of structurational interaction being developed here, tacit knowledge and context are important components of social interaction and social order.

As a competent agent, one draws upon mutual knowledge, conventions and resources when acting. This knowledge base consists of norms, facilities and interpretive schemes which are the means by which actions take place. And through their actions, agents produce and reproduce social systems. As Giddens argued:

> Reflexive monitoring of action both draws upon and reconstitutes the institutional organization of society. The recognition that to be a ('competent') member of society, every individual must know a great deal about the workings of that society, is precisely the main basis of the concept of the duality of structure.
>
> *(Giddens, 1979, p. 255)*

Thus action requires both knowledgeability and capability.

In summary, Giddens' model of social systems, including organizations, institutions and societies, presupposes social integration. This social integration takes place through social interaction in which the self develops. The self is a narrative of multiple identities, negotiated in a multitude of contexts over one's life-span. Individuals cope with the routinization of social practices, with issues of trust and risk, and with the demands of being a competent social actor, displaying practical and discursive consciousness and knowledgeability. Individuals also possess agency, or the capacity to do otherwise.

While these considerations might appear to be primarily interpersonal relationship issues, they are fundamental issues in organizing as well. As Giddens amply demonstrates, in modernity, the self and institutions are closely interwoven. Organizations present challenges with negotiating multiple identities and relationships, establishing trust, coping with risk and integrating one's actions with those of others. Giddens' profound insights enable us to see and understand the complexities in these issues as a result of modernity, time-space distanciation, disembedding and re-embedding.

With this understanding of the self, we next examine the individual-in-action. The issue of agency, or the capacity to act otherwise, and the relationship of agency and social structure, is a critical issue in social theory generally, but also in communicating and organizing.

Agency

Giddens recognized the interwoven strands of action and structure. As he stated:

> Understood as rules and resources implicated in the 'form' of collectives of social systems, reproduced across space and time, structure is the very medium of the 'human' element of human agency. At the same time, agency is the medium of structure, which individuals routinely reproduce in the course of their activities. All social life has a recursive quality to it, derived from the fact that actors reproduce the conditions of their social existence by means of the very activities that—in contexts of time-space—constitute that existence.
>
> *(Giddens, 1987b, pp. 220–21)*

Agency is conceptualized as a process, an ongoing series of practical, everyday social practices. Only when we reflect consciously and discursively are we noticing agency as a specific event or activity. Among other things, agents also have physical and contextual constraints limiting their actions. For Giddens, agency enables as well as constrains. As he noted:

> People ... do what they do in lots of different contexts, including physical contexts, which are strongly relevant to the possibilities and constraints facing any individual or group. ... The causal effects of structural properties of human institutions ... are there simply because they are produced and reproduced in everyday actions. Ultimately, they depend upon convention, which is both the means and outcome of such actions. Convention—what people do, what they do in their everyday lives—can have very severe constraining effects, of course, on what is possible for any individual ... technology is not different: it is constraining and enabling. It depends upon relationships between reasoning agents, who have various habits and conventions and do things. ... People can only act conventionally because of mutual understanding of convention. ... Use of convention, in language or more broadly, normally depends upon 'practical consciousness'—what Wittgenstein called our capacity to 'go on' in the diversity of contexts of social life.
>
> *(Giddens & Pierson, 1998, pp. 82–83)*

Individuals possess practical consciousness as well as agency and situated knowledge. According to Giddens, agency is the "capacity to have done otherwise" and is always involved in structure (as an expression of action).

> Structure only exists in so far as people do things knowledgeably and do them in certain contexts that have particular consequences. Those consequences are often ones that they don't themselves foresee or even know about—but it is their regular happening, their reproduction—which makes them structural and allows us to talk of structural effects. ... There isn't any other way in which population density, for example, has structural effects, except in so far as it *is organised through what people actually do.*
>
> *(ibid., p. 81, italics mine)*

Thus, only individuals have agency, and structures only have influence in terms of how they are enacted by human agency (i.e., the produced and reproduced effects of human action). When agents cease to have options, they cease to be agents but, as Giddens noted, in the majority of cases in social life, agents will have some control over their circumstances.

While agency is a central aspect of communicating and organizing, it is in organizations that *collective agency* is critical. As we have seen, social systems such as organizations and societies require coordination and control over a range of activities, usually carried out by a group of individuals. How does collective agency take place? It is to this critical issue we now turn.

Collective agency. As Giddens himself asked, " ... are collectivities actors? What does it mean to say, for example, 'The government decided to pursue policy X.' ... Action descriptions ... should not be confused with the designation of agency as such. Neither descriptions of action nor accounts of interaction can be given purely in terms of individual predicates. But only individuals, beings which have a corporeal existence, are agents. If collectivities or groups are not agents, why do we sometimes speak as though they were, as in the above examples? We tend to do so when there is a significant degree of reflexive monitoring of the conditions of social reproduction, of the sort associated especially with organizations, although not exclusive to them. ... It is important to understand that 'The government decided ... ' or 'The government acted ... ' are shorthand statements because in some situations it may matter a great deal which individuals were the main initiators or executors of whatever decisions were taken (or not taken) and whatever policies followed" (Giddens, 1984, pp. 220–21). Governments and businesses act as legal agents, and, as Giddens pointed out, "laws have to be interpreted, and applied; it takes human agents to do that, as well as to frame them in the first place" (Giddens, 1979, p. 272, fn. 3).

Giddens also observed that one can speak metaphorically of collective agency as, for example, in the case of firms that are oriented for profit (Giddens, 1984, p. 88). He also noted that the social constraints on actors apply to collectivities as well.

Usually business people accept the logic of the wider economy—which is a constitutive phenomenon. While Giddens allowed for collective agency, Goffman focused on individual agency. The theory of structurational interaction allows us to analyze both levels of agency, both of which are important in organizing.

Consistent with structuration theory, Mendoza pointed out that "Certain actions performed by certain individuals occupying certain 'position practices' assume significance for a collectivity as actions *of* such a collectivity or *for* such a collectivity, owing to certain conventions. These conventions form part of the *formulae* competent actors apply or follow in social activities" (Mendoza, 1997a, p. 228). Thus, for example, presidents and prime ministers sign agreements legally binding the activities of nation-states.

We also need to recognize collective agency as an effect of individual activities and actions. Through the binding of time-space, repeated social practices extend across varying temporal and spatial contexts, and become social systems. These social systems may be ongoing institutions, societies, social movements, nation-states and/ or part of civil society—collectivities of differing purpose and size. But repeated social practices, at multiple levels and instantiated in different contexts by human agents, enact these collectivities. Through their intermingled action and interaction, these collectivities produce effects and thus have agency. Such collectivities have boundaries, but mesh and interact with other collectivities at time-space edges. Such agency may also continue across the long duree of time. As Giddens notes, "Agency *is* history, where 'history' is the temporal continuity of human activities" (Giddens, 1987b, p. 220).

Intentionality. Actions create both intended (intentional) and unintended consequences. Intentionality is an inherent aspect of all human behavior and, according to Giddens, involves motivation, rationalization and reflexive monitoring of our actions. Motivation for action involves a potential for action and, in the case of routine activities, like brushing teeth, actions are not explicitly motivated, but more a matter of habit. Reflexive monitoring of action occurs continuously, as we evaluate what we are accomplishing, how others react to what we are doing, consider any adjustments to our behavior or the setting, and the like.

Rationalization of action reflects a process by which we tacitly understand the reasons for our actions. As Kaspersen noted, "Whereas reflexive monitoring of action concerns the intentional part of the action processes, rationalization of action primarily concerns the ability and the competence to evaluate the relationship between the action and its reason. In this way the agent also evaluates his own and others' competence" (Kaspersen, 2000, p. 38). While motivation may be unconscious as well as poorly understood, we need to acknowledge that "Partners in a collective structure share space, time, and energy, but they need not share visions, aspirations or intentions" (Weick, 1979, p. 91).

When individuals monitor and evaluate their activities, they are not completely aware of all the consequences of their actions—as Giddens suggested, unanticipated consequences provide the grounds for new actions. Giddens observed that the unintended consequences of action may produce unacknowledged conditions of action, and thereby influence future action (Giddens, 1984, p. 5). Reasons refer to the basis for acting, while wants refer to the motives for acting. For Giddens, a "major motivating force behind action [is] the necessity for 'ontological security' that arises from a need for a 'sense of trust.' Without a sense of trust and the resulting ontological security system, Giddens believes that actors suffer acute anxiety in their social relations" (Turner, 1986, p. 973). "However, motivation is not as directly bound up with the continuity of action as are its reflexive monitoring or rationalization" (Giddens, 1984, p. 6).

Intentionality thus operates within the context of reflexive monitoring of action, in conjunction with the unintentioned, unacknowledged conditions and outcomes of action (Giddens, 1979, pp. 41–42). However, while discursive and practical consciousness are permeable to each other, there are "barriers, centred principally upon repression, between discursive consciousness and the unconscious" (Giddens, 1984, p. 7).

Intentionality is viewed as a process: as such, agency "unfolds in time and therefore is a flow, not just an aggregate of individual actions ... temporality is bound up with human agency and so also is spatiality" (Giddens & Pierson, 1998, p. 90). For Giddens, routinization organizes interaction across time, while regionalization organizes interactional space. He suggested that routinization of encounters is of "major significance in bending the fleeting encounter to social reproduction and thus to the seeming 'fixity' of institutions" (Giddens, 1984, p. 72). Predictability in interaction is managed by practices such as the use of rituals like greetings; turn-taking; the use of tact (of special significance in Goffman's work); the use of status markers; and the use of frames for determining a range of appropriate behaviors (also central in Goffman's work).

Knowledgeability and accountability. There are many cases in which interactional routines or expectations are breached and, in those cases, actors are held accountable for their actions:

> The 'giving of accounts' — or 'supplying of reasons' — for action refers to this *discursive* capability and inclinations of actors, and by no means exhausts the connection between 'stocks of knowledge' and action. What actors are 'able to say' about their activities is by no means all that they 'know' about them. ... The knowledgeability involved in practical consciousness conforms generally to the Wittgensteinian notion of 'knowing a rule' or 'knowing how to go on.'
>
> *(Giddens, 1982, p. 31)*

By focusing on the human as "subject" and as "actor", Giddens argued that action (agency) required both capability and knowledgeability. Capability refers to the capacity to choose to do otherwise, as discussed earlier in Chapter 5. As Giddens argued, "Agency refers not to the intentions people have in doing things but to their capability of doing those things in the first place (which is why agency implies power)" (Giddens, 1984, p. 9). By knowledgeability, he included not only practical consciousness (noted above), but also discursive consciousness (that which we hold in our minds consciously), as well as the unconscious. He suggested that not all we "know" can be expressed discursively.

As Mendoza commented, "Structures figure in action only insofar as they are converted to *knowledgeability* or *formula* for doing social activities, i.e., only when they are filtered through the reflexive monitoring of conduct, applied to aspects of the knowledge used to secure desired outcomes in purposive conduct, either practically or discursively" (Mendoza, 1997a, p. 230). The validity of this knowledgeability is the degree to which actors can coordinate their actions with one another, and are able to go on (Giddens, 1984, p. 90). Such knowledgeability is relevant to a particular social context; what is known to one agent may be unknown to another.

Through practical consciousness, discursive consciousness, and agency, humans interact, establish, and maintain ways of getting on. Such interactional skills also rely on knowledgeable interactants, and much of this knowledge may not be discursively available to participants. As Giddens observed, the predictability of the social world and of interaction is

> 'made to happen' as a condition and result of the knowledgeable application of rules and resources by actors in the constitution of interaction. The 'accomplished' character of the social world always involves 'effort' on the part of social actors, but is at the same time for the most part done 'effortlessly', as part of the routine, taken-for-granted nature of everyday life. The relations between practical consciousness and the structural properties of social systems are founded above all in the *routinisation* of day-to-day life.
>
> *(Giddens, 1981, p. 64)*

Giddens cautioned us not to look at this routinization as either blind habit or as a normative commitment. It is, rather, " ... the everyday fact that social actors are knowledgeable about the conditions of social reproduction in which their day-to-day activities are enmeshed" (Giddens, 1982, p. 29). Furthermore, the connections between practical consciousness and the structural properties of social systems are found in the routinization of daily life. As he succinctly pointed out, "the prevalence of the routine or taken-for-granted rests precisely upon the casually employed but very complex skills whereby social actors draw upon and reconstitute the practices 'layered' into institutions in deep time-space" (Giddens, 1981, p. 65). Giddens (1984) observed that what people say about their actions is only one aspect of the substantial knowledgeability required in everyday living.

Knowledge is bounded because knowledge is usually differentially available (e.g., may be limited to those in power); because values may change and thus knowledge may be evaluated differently; because actions have unintended consequences; and because of modern reflexivity (e.g., experts, the influence of social science findings on social practices) (Giddens, 1990a, pp. 43–46). Giddens also articulated an important modern condition of system reproduction—namely, the attempt by actors to selectively filter information in regulating social systems.

Knowledgeability and accountability are part of discursive consciousness, but we know more (practical consciousness) than we can articulate. For agency, actors rely on both capability and knowledge. Structures influence action only to the extent they are reflected in knowledgeability and part of the reflexive monitoring of conduct. We coordinate with others in knowing how to go on, based on what is relevant to the context, even though participants may not share full knowledge with one another. We also rely on the importance of the routinization of social practices and taken for granted, tacit knowledge. These are "very complex skills whereby social actors draw upon and reconstitute the practices 'layered' into institutions in deep time-space" (Giddens, 1981, p. 65)

Here again, the importance of tacit knowledge, context and shared understanding are emphasized by Giddens. While Giddens argued that structuration theory was amenable to diverse methodologies, he also emphasized that any analysis must incorporate the full range of actors' knowledgeability, and recognize the significance of practical consciousness. Giddens also noted that unintended consequences flow from actions, and are dependent on many other contingent events and outcomes, and thus cannot be "something the original actor 'did'" (Giddens, 1984, p. 11).

Knowledgeable actors move through time-space, influenced by their stage in their life-span, relations with others and the organizations and institutions they encounter. Giddens refers to this trajectory through life as social positioning, a concept that locates the self in time-space as well as in terms of the self's multiple, overlapping and intersecting identities.

Social positioning. Social positioning has implications for institutional as well as social relationships, and must be placed within its sociohistorical context. Social systems are "organized as regularized social practices" and actors are "positioned" within these social practices (Giddens, 1984, p. 83). Social positions are constituted structurally as specific intersections of signification, domination, and legitimation. "A social position involves the specification of a definite 'identity' within a network of social relations, that identity, however, being a 'category' to which a particular range of normative sanctions is relevant" (ibid.). Thus, social systems are "structured 'fields' in which (as reproduced in the temporality of interaction) actors occupy define *positions vis-à-vis* one another" (Giddens, 1979, p. 117). I believe this is consistent with Goffman's view of roles, and the obligations and sanctions connected to roles in their appropriate social contexts.

Social relations concern the "positioning" of individuals within a "social space" of symbolic categories and ties. Rules involved in social positions normally have to do with "the specification of rights and obligations relevant to persons having a particular social identity, or belonging in a particular social category" (Giddens, 1984, p. 89).

Social relations are important in social interaction, "but are also the main 'building blocks' around which institutions are articulated in system integration" (ibid.).

Positioning, for Giddens, referred to being positioned with respect to the three types of temporality: the positioning of the body; the positioning of actors in their daily life; and their "simultaneous position within intersocietal systems whose broadcast span is convergent with the geopolitical distribution of social systems on a global scale" (Giddens, 1984, p. 84). Positioning refers also to movement through positions as individuals move through the life-cycle, and interact with different institutions, organizations, regions and intersocietal systems.

For societies in which social integration and system integration are relatively equivalent, positioning is "thinly layered." However, Giddens suggested that in contemporary societies, "system integration … increasingly relates the minor details of daily life to social phenomena of massive time-space extension" (ibid., p. 85). That is, the distanciation, re-embedding and disembedding in modern life has made social positioning vastly more complex. Most importantly, for our purposes, Giddens concluded that it is the "intersection between these forms of positioning and that within the *longue duree* of institutions which creates the overall framework of social positioning. Only in the context of such intersection within institutionalized practices can modes of time-space positioning, in relation to the duality of structure, be properly grasped" (ibid.).

Positioning goes well beyond individual actors because "institutionalized modes of conduct may be routinely reproduced for periods surpassing the participation of any given cohort of agents" (Cohen, 1990a, p. 41). Thus, "as agents reproduce systemic activities and articulations across time and space, they also regenerate the knowledge of practices (including the strategic use of resources) required to reproduce the system in the future. Structuration thus plays a crucial role in Giddens's conception of the constitution of order … [no] procedure of coordination and control would historically endure if all processes of structuration were to come to a halt: chaos and disorder would be rampant … continuities of structuration persist even in periods of radical change (i.e., restructuration)" (ibid., pp. 41–42).

In sum, social positioning incorporates a wide range of influences which extend beyond any individual's own life-span. Social positioning reflects one's own body-life activities as well as social relations with others. These activities and relationships are contextualized within time-space and within a specific sociohistorical moment and culture. One's identities are formed and re-formed within and across these social positions, reflecting both the local and global influences along the life-span trajectory.

Giddens' structuration theory offers profound insights into communicating, organizing and their interrelationships. Communication (social interaction) is the foundation for social practices which connect individuals together in a variety of social relationships, including those social practices which constitute collectivities. Structuration theory thus provides a basis for a communication-centric theory of organizing. In what follows, we explore these implications in greater detail.

Implications of Giddens' Structuration Theory

Giddens' structuration theory, in and of itself, offers significant insights into communicating and organizing. Communication in the form of multiple types of interaction, and in varied conditions of agents' presence and absence, plays a foundational role in Giddens' thinking. And organizing is central to his social theories; his concepts of social positioning, agency, the duality of structure, distanciation and historicity illuminate the processes of organizing. He argues that routinized social practices build into institutions, societies, and intersocietal systems, and bind time-space. His views expand our framework of understanding about communicating and organizing, and provide a multi-tiered level of analysis of social interaction.

The concept of agency, as a process in which a knowledgeable communicator strategically selects among various structures (rules and resources) to accomplish goals and to carry out social practices, expands our concept of social interaction. Giddens' concepts concerning tacit knowledge, discursive capacity, reflexive monitoring, and the importance of context are also major contributions to our insights into communicative processes. His expanded concept of context, extending beyond the immediate social context to sedimented institutional practices which encompass organizational settings, provides added depth to our understanding of organizations and organizing. These concepts address major issues in organizational communication such as the interrelationships between communicating and organizing, identity, globalization, agency, context and knowledgeability.

The distanciation of time and space, a core concept in structuration, is a significant feature of both organizing and communicating. For example, research on virtual teams used this concept to illuminate how dispersed work teams coordinate their tasks (see, for example, DeSanctis & Poole, 1994, 1997). Distanciation enables interaction across time and across space, and extends communication from face-to-face interaction to the "presencing" and "absences" of agents. The use of presences and absences will sharpen our analytic lens for understanding the processes of human interaction in multiple settings. The juxtaposition of Goffman's focus on co-presence and Giddens' distanciation might be especially insightful in exploring such issues. Issues of trust, for example, need further exploration as we increasingly rely on distant experts to carry on our daily life (e.g., bank tellers, medical researchers). Both "presences" and "absences" are becoming increasingly important in theories of communicating and organizing because many of our interactions, even intimate relationships, are occurring in conditions of "absences" (that is, people are temporally and spatially in different locales). Our interactions, of course, throughout our lives influence our social positioning and our complex, multiple identities.

Interaction may occur face-to-face, where participants are copresent at the same time and in the same space. Technology enables interaction when neither party is "present," but rather interactionally connected through mediation (e.g., through computers, telephones, blogs, video conferencing) where time and space has been coordinated to permit interaction. Because time and space has been standardized (i.e., latitude and longitude, and international time standards), it is possible to coordinate actions and interactions globally. This, of course, has permitted globalization as well as unprecedented economic and political coordination.

Giddens' focus on action is also shared by others who study discourse and organizing. Schegloff (2001) noted that "not only is action a relevant facet and upshot of the talk, but that *actions by other than the speaker are relevant to understanding a speaker's construction of discourse;* and, relatedly, that the absence of action by the recipient—*the absence of actions made relevant by the speaker's prior talk, the speaker's turn-so-far—may be crucial to understanding the speaker's further construction of the discourse"* (p. 241, italics in the original). Agency or action is coordinated through the process of interacting, and agents mutually influence each other during these interactions.

In both organizing and communicating, one of Giddens' core insights is the duality of structure: through interaction, participants produce and reproduce social practices. These repeated social practices enact institutions and societies: "the structured properties of social systems are simultaneously the *medium and outcome of social acts"* (Giddens, 1981, p. 19). As he further noted, "society only has form and that form only has effects on people in so far as structure is produced and reproduced in what people do" (Giddens & Pierson, 1998, p. 77). As Shotter noted, this duality of structure applies throughout daily life.

> ... the duality of structure relates the minor and seemingly trivial forms of daily social activity—the smiles, nods, and frowns, the utterances of individuals, their tones of voice and bodily posture—both to the structural properties of large scale social movements, to social history (moments) and social class (regions), as well as to the general evolutionary nature of the micro and macrophysical world.
>
> *(Shotter, 1997, p. 101)*

For analysts of institutional and organizational structures, the task, at the institutional level of analysis, is to examine the repeated social practices that characterize the particular institution (such as banking) or a particular organization (such as 3M). Analysts can further examine the impact of individual agents and their strategic conduct on particular tasks, organizations, groups or institutions. Structuration theory (ST) offers a "conceptual means of analyzing the often delicate and subtle interlacing of reflexively organized action and institutional constraint ... actors are at the same time the creators of social systems, yet created by them" (Giddens, 1991b, p. 204). Organizational actors, with their knowledgeability and transformative capacity, can act in innovative ways in conducting organizational work.

ST also helps us examine the relationship between institutional social practices and an actor's strategic conduct. As Livesay pointed out:

> Structures are the semantic and normative rules and power resources which, as abstract properties of communities, are used by social actors to produce the

skilled performances that constitute social life. They are the media of practical human activities, the tools of *praxis*. But through their very use in social practices, structures are *reproduced* as features of social communities, so that structures (as reproduced practices) are the outcome of practical activity. ... While the analysis of strategic conduct conceptualizes structures as generative rules and resources used in human *praxis*, institutional analysis understands them as reproduced practices ... any type of social production necessarily entails the (often unintentional) reproduction of the structures utilized in that action.

(Livesay, 1997, p. 351)

Giddens himself suggested the "following tenets as important in the analysis of strategic conduct: the need to avoid impoverished descriptions of agents' knowledgeability; a sophisticated account of motivation; and an interpretation of the dialectic of control" (Giddens, 1984, p. 289).

Another important insight from ST is that every act (interaction) incorporates the dimensions of power, meaning and norms, and their mutual influence. Frequently, our analyses focus on only one dimension, and overlook the enabling and/or constraining features of the other dimensions. Elaborating these interconnections will help illuminate the complexities of interaction, particularly the use of power and legitimation in social practices.

Mediation also draws our attention to the multiple formats and forms in which interaction takes place: we note not just presence or absence, but rules and resources and the role they play in interaction. Giddens' theory offers a way of unifying the various media and combinations of presence/absence that provides an integrative, holistic frame for human communication. In particular, his theory offers us useful insights into issues of trust, conflict, integration and change as these processes are influenced by different formats of communication.

Kilminster pointed out that Giddens' structuration theory shows how "the *actual process of interaction* by skilled, knowledgeable actors produces and reproduces the structure and widespread patterning ... of social relations ... the skilled interpretative exchanges of actors are not likely to be seen as taking place among peers (as Garfinkel implied) but are likely to be skewed or imbalanced by the distribution of power in society at large" (Kilminster, 1997, p. 115). Thus, ST offers a perspective for evaluating power differentials through differing rules, resources, and social positions available to agents. This is particularly important for research examining issues of voice, identity, participation and marginalization in organizing and communicating.

Finally, Giddens' work offers significant insights into change and contradiction. Change and contradiction are multi-faceted, often occurring at the time-space edges of contact between different societies and/or institutions. Change, particularly, must be understood in its temporal context and extant environmental conditions.

In brief, Giddens offers us a very rich, contextualized exploration of institutions and social life. Because his work regards human interaction as fundamental to social life and social systems, we can use his insights to assess human interaction in organizing. A similar focus on social interaction, in contexts of physical co-presence, is found in Goffman's work.

Some criticisms of Giddens' work. Although critics have suggested that Giddens has not provided any mechanisms for change (Stinchcombe, 1990), Cohen argued that Giddens' concepts of intended and unintended consequences, primary and secondary contradictions, and time-space edges allow for forces of change (Cohen, 1990b, p. 58). Our discussion earlier in this chapter outlined the many mechanisms of change that Giddens has developed.

Critics have also suggested (see Kaspersen, 2000) that Giddens does not have a concept of culture which would help explain differences among actors in terms of routines, social positions, access to information, and differences in meaning systems. However, I would argue that Giddens' concept of society is equivalent to culture; he uses the concept of a nation-state as an aspect of culture as well. These concepts, as well as his work on self-identity, suggest that our traditional notions of culture are no longer adequate. Increased reflexivity, both personally and institutionally, have complicated issues of identity, and because the self is a life-long, reflexive narrative, culture as a source of identity has become diluted. The concept of culture itself has also become more complex. However, as a response to globalization, we can also note the possibility of resurgent nationalism as a political (and cultural) force as well as increasing democratization (as Giddens outlined in the published Reith Lectures, *The Runaway World,* 2003).

Rather than ignoring culture, Giddens' work, taken as a whole, suggests how complex culture is. And his work highlights the changing shape of what the communication discipline recognizes as cultural differences (for example, Gudykunst and Kim's (2003) notion of cross-cultural communication as communication-between-strangers, and its contrast with relational/interpersonal communication). Also, research on self-construal suggests that a culture's influence on one is mediated by one's identification with that culture or subculture.

More recently, discussions of cultural differences have focused on identity issues. Differences within societies have been discussed in Giddens' publications in the 1990s, particularly *Modernity and Self-Identity* and *The Consequences of Modernity.* In Giddens' discussion of a possible new order beyond modernity, he highlighted the importance of life politics. He also highlighted emancipatory politics, and new forms of trust and organizations—in particular, social movements, like the peace, environmental, and human rights movements. Emancipatory politics concerns the alleviation of oppression, while life politics concerns a full, satisfying life for every-one (Giddens, 1991b, p. 213; see also *The Runaway World,* Giddens, 2003). Such issues are clearly central to any discussion of culture.

Another criticism, noted by a number of scholars, is that Giddens does not distinguish between levels of rules. Because Giddens' theory is an integrative synthesis, one should not necessarily expect precision in levels or layers of rules. Giddens did, for example, distinguish rules in contrasting structural principles with interactional rules, with the former defining societies and groups and the latter defining specific contexts and group practices. In addition, he observed that distinctions across social practices—rules and resources—often "shade" into one another and cannot be separated except for analytic purposes. The details of these levels of rules are to be worked out by scholars, working in different contexts and with different goals in mind.

Yet other critics have also argued that Giddens gives too much power to agency, and not enough to structural constraints. However, like Poole and McPhee (2005), I would argue that there is a balance between the two (enablement vs. constraint), with the balance being determined by the context and the social practices involved (p. 190). Conrad (1993) also pointed out that Giddens' analyses seemed to be one-sided in that it "focuses theoretical attention on processes through which state institutions exercise power over economic ones, and away from the processes through which organizations and organizational actors appropriate state power and shape political institutions for their own ends—what Deetz labeled 'corporate colonization'" (1992, p. 204). Conrad noted that Giddens responds to these concerns by arguing that the issue is "the relation between nation-states on the one hand and capitalistic control mechanisms on the other" (Giddens, 1989, p. 267). While not directly responding to Conrad's concerns, I would argue that more recent work by Giddens (1994, 2003), particularly on emancipatory politics and lifestyle choices, should begin to eradicate this one-sidedness.

Perhaps most significantly for our purposes in studying organizing and communicating, Giddens offers one of the most coherent theories for integrating micro- and macro-levels (terms, of course, which he eschews). Ritzer argued that what Giddens has done "is to redefine the linkage issue and focus on it relationally and dialectically rather than dichotomously. ... Giddens' inclusion of the time factor [is an] effort to make it dynamic rather than static; interested in social change rather than ahistorical structure ... it seems clear that the future development of micro-macro theory depends on its ability to work with both temporal and spatial variables" (Ritzer, 1990, p. 360).

Ritzer also noted that theories, such as Giddens', which incorporate aspects of existing theories and thus create new theories, are very useful. Particularly in the study of organizational communication, theories that span local, face-to-face interaction as well as interaction across social systems, such as multinational organizations within their institutional, sociohistorical contexts, are very important.

Applications to communication: some critical evaluations. In an interesting set of articles, Banks and Riley (1993) and Conrad (1993) discussed the usefulness of structuration theory for communication research and theory. They suggested three implications for communication research—that communication phenomena "must find their own form within the universe of structuration theory as it stands"; that multiple research methods can be applied to questions generated via structuration theory; and that contextual theories can be developed "without concern for the logical levels or generality of their ontological substrate, because the principal axis of structuration is human agency in real time-space/place" (p. 181). They went on to provide an excellent example of structuration research in organizing.

Banks and Riley offered exciting possibilities for applying structuration theory, and argued for a full appreciation of Giddens' work (rightly so, in my view). Conrad echoed that, but also argued that rhetorical/communication theorists should be applying communication research to fill the "gaps" and "inadequacies" in structuration theory. Conrad raised some issues that are of particular concern because they are driven by a focus on rhetorical/communication theory and issues. And I want to address them because the theory of structurational interaction addresses some of Conrad's concerns.

To begin, it is important to note two things. First, Giddens did not intend his structuration theory to be used directly as a research program, rather it can be used heuristically, and in parts, rather than as a whole; (although many scholars argue for its utility as a metatheory). Like Goffman's theory, Giddens' theory can be usefully applied and extended in a number of ways as has already been done (see Chapters 7 and 10). But careful attention must be paid, as Banks and Riley (1993) noted, to remain faithful to the tenets of structuration theory, and to explain its relevance and significance to the current work (thus avoiding the *en passant* problem) (p. 179). I echo their concern that, in much research, this has not been done—a "mention in passing" is insufficient grounding for applying/extending structuration theory or, for that matter, any of Goffman's work (research on face, for example, is rife with passing mention to Goffman, but with inaccurate or underdeveloped explanations of his views—see, for example, comments in Brown, 2000).

Second, some of the objections raised in both of these reviews, have, I think, been clarified by Giddens' subsequent work which, of course, does not reflect any weakness in the reviews—merely that, as many commentators have noted, by the time these criticisms get into print, Giddens has already answered the objections and moved on to other issues. For example, concerns that there was insufficient attention paid to motivation and personal relationships were addressed in subsequent publications (Giddens, 1990a, 1991a).

A third caveat needs to be mentioned. The purpose of this book is to demonstrate the utility of blending Goffman and Giddens, and, in part, Giddens already has done this through relying on Goffman's work. The theory of structurational interaction which I am developing answers many of the concerns raised by Banks, Riley and Conrad. Because Giddens himself acknowledged his reliance on Goffman, incorporating Goffman more fully into structuration theory is entirely consistent with the framework of Giddens' structuration theory. Thus, integrating these two scholars establishes a theory of structurational interaction, and in Chapter 11 and 12 I shall elaborate more on this.

In commenting on Giddens' career, Bryant and Jary concluded that

> Giddens' commentary on leading figures, schools and traditions is unsurpassed in volume, range and consistent quality. It would be a commendable

achievement even if he had done nothing else. But of course he has. ... It is arguable that of all the approaches to the agency-structure and macro-micro debates on offer. ... Giddens' is the most persuasive. ...

The principles of structuration have also proved useful to an impressive number of researchers in a dauntingly wide range of disciplines. In addition, Giddens has done as much as anyone to make concern for time-space an essential of social theory and empirical research design. ... Giddens has also played a leading role in establishing globalization and its concomitants as one of the biggest topics in contemporary social science.

(Bryant and Jary, 2001a, p. 33)

In order to fully appreciate Giddens' work, however, we need to examine how his structuration theory has been applied in a wide range of contexts. It has been applied in geology, business, sociology, communication, history, political science and architecture, using both qualitative and quantitative methods, but our concern here will be its application to communicating and organizing. I now turn to an examination of some of the applications of Giddens' structuration theory in communicating and organizing, in which a number of communication scholars have featured prominently.

7

APPLYING GIDDENS IN COMMUNICATING AND ORGANIZING

Clearly, the critics who suggested that structuration theory is too abstract to generate useful empirical studies were incorrect. (See Phipps, 2001, for an overview of empirical studies using structuration research.) Organizational scholars have applied Giddens' theory in a number of different areas (see Poole & McPhee, 2005, for a good overview of structuration applications in the communication discipline). Within the communication discipline, applications have focused on organizational culture, small group communication and argumentation, organizational processes, and adaptive structuration theory.

Poole and McPhee (2005) argued that structuration "encompassed both social structure and human action in a common framework that could explain individual behavior and the development and effects of social institutions ... [it] emphasized the role of processes in the constitution of society and, thus, fit well with conceptions of communication as a process ... encompassed stability and change ... [and] offered an understanding of how different levels of analysis—individual, group, organization, society—related to one another" (p. 173). They concluded that structuration "allowed powerful communication theorizing at a truly organizational level of analysis" (ibid.). And as Giddens (1987b) noted, organizations are particularly important in the modern age because of their power. In addition, Conrad noted that Giddens' structuration theory has value for communication scholars "because he views human beings as choice-making animals suspended in webs of their own making, views language and language use as central aspects of human experience, and strives to avoid the determinism and reification of traditional social and psychology theory" (Conrad, 1993, p. 205).

Sydow and Windeler pointed out that,

> By emphasizing structuration rather than structure, structuration theory neither takes rules and resources for granted nor simply seeks to measure

structural properties. Instead, it provides insights into the production and reproduction of structures in social interaction. *It also accounts for historically sedimented* habits, recurrently applied interpretative schemes, norms and facilities, thus bridging structure and process as well as structure and culture, all of which have generally been treated by orthodox organization theory as separate concepts. ... structuration views organizations as engaged in plural and overlapping social systems comprising other systems. ...

(Sydow and Windeler, 1997, p. 471, italics mine)

As such, ST presents an integrated view of organizing and communicating in social systems.

An added value of Giddens' work, as Bryant and Jary (1997b, 2001a, b, c) noted, may be to provide an intermediate theory that guides both new theory and empirical investigation. They argued that structuration provides concepts, frameworks and formulations of intermediate complexity. Cohen (1990a) suggested that a central advantage of Giddens' theory of structuration is its openness to praxis and historical change. It is also important to understand Giddens' work as a critical theory (Craib, 1992). In his analysis of modernity, Giddens explored the discontinuities in social change and commented on the "dark side" of such changes—like ecological destruction and possible nuclear annihilation.

Giddens regards his work as a sensitizing device that points toward research questions and issues. Structuration, for Giddens, is "an attempt to work out an overall ontology of social life, offering concepts that will grasp both the rich texture of human action and the diverse properties of social institutions. Some of these concepts should be useful as sensitizing devices for research purposes, while others help provide an explication of the logic of research into human social activities and cultural products" (1990b, pp. 310–11).

This chapter provides an overview of some of the research in which structuration theory (ST) has been applied to analyzing organizations. Readers may want to use some of these studies as a departure for their own scholarship, or to explore a topic in more depth. Coverage, of necessity, is limited to the research viewed as most relevant to our focus on organizing and communicating—thus, rich areas of application to political issues and to the study of modernity are not discussed. This is yet another reflection of the depth and breadth of structuration theory, and its utility as a social theory. While some studies have applied structuration theory broadly, others have selected aspects of Giddens' theory and applied it in their own area of research interest. Giddens himself has suggested that his theory may be used "piecemeal" with great utility.

Among communication scholars, Poole, McPhee, Seibold, and their associates, have been actively applying structuration theory to a range of communicative phenomena. They have applied structuration theory to small group research (Poole, Seibold & McPhee, 1985, 1986); Poole has examined decision-making in groups (Poole, 1999; Poole & DeSanctis, 1990, 1992); and Meyers and Seibold (1990a, b,

1991) have looked at persuasive arguments in small group research. Seibold and Meyers (2007) published an excellent overview of this work, and developed other facets of the structuration perspective for small group research. Mumby (1987, 1989) also used structuration theory to analyze power dynamics in organizations. In addition to the scholars previously noted, the work of Orlikowski, Yates, and institutional theorists on organizing and communicating will also be discussed.

Theoretical Extensions of Structuration Theory

A number of scholars have built upon or extended ST for use in analyzing organizing and communicating. Some have developed original extensions, while others linked ST with other theoretical approaches. I shall briefly overview these in the following section.

McPhee's Research

Using structuration theory, McPhee examined text, agency, organizations and structure. Texts are symbolic, inscribed as a relatively permanent medium, and have enough coherency in structure to be interpreted or processed (2004a, p. 355). Agency is viewed as an "internalistic" conceptualization, with agents having the power or capacity to do otherwise.

Of particular interest is McPhee's discussion of organizations. As you will recall, from Chapter 4, a major issue in organizing and communicating is how organizations are constituted. McPhee outlined several stable qualities of organizations. First, organizational members "impose and bring about relations and interaction among themselves as members" (p. 360). These relations are stable, artificially constructed, and reflect power alignments. Second, organizations are also multi-site, and different sites have different logics of action (e.g., shop floor operators have different activities and work flow than those in a planning office). Third, texts enable all of those previously mentioned organizing characteristics. As McPhee noted, "a text is a relatively permanently inscribed symbolic formulation ... it is a vital precondition for the development and continuing existence of organizations as we commonly conceive of them" (p. 365). Fourth, organizations are able to bracket time and space, and do so through the reflexive monitoring of system reproduction and articulating its discursive history. That is, through institutional reflexivity, organizational members develop, maintain and alter their organizing activities.

Giddens also placed organizations within their modern context, with time-space distanciation, the disembedding of institutions, and institutional reflexivity. Institutional reflexivity, as McPhee noted, "involves both the design of social settings to allow for knowledge and control, and the use of that knowledge to guide action within the settings" (ibid., p. 362). Institutional reflexivity also depends upon knowledgeably designed locales for administration and record-keeping: Such locations (for example, major cities in nation-states) are viewed as power containers

(Giddens, 1987a, b). Finally, organizations are time-space organizing devices, possessing such texts as schedules and plans, that organize both time and space. Hierarchy and power are reflected in these practices because "authorized members typically determine them, and authority is more or less clearly stipulated in formal documents that articulate organizational structure" (McPhee, 2004a, p. 365).

McPhee and Iverson argued that organizations are constituted in the same fashion as social systems—interactive episodes provide for coordinated action; such coordination can be stretched over time and space, and relations among contexts can be designed for purposeful control and monitoring (2009). Organizations, thus, are viewed as spatiotemporally distributed, material realities. Organizations are communicatively constituted by four flows of interaction—membership negotiation, reflexive self-structuring, activity coordination and institutional positioning.

Based on structuration theory, McPhee and Zaug (2000) analyzed communication-as-constitutive-of-organizations. Their "flow" model is multi-processual, incorporating different organizational sites, and including different people in different contexts. According to McPhee and Zaug, "Communication is a dimension of social interaction and practice, specifically the dimension in which meaning[s] are marshaled in the course of practice; communication draws on and reproduces the signification resources of a social system, but always in practical contexts" (2000, p. 6, cf. in Iverson & McPhee, 2008). McPhee and Zaug (2000) suggested that communication constituted organization in four distinct, yet interdependent "flows" (defined as circulating fields of evolving discourse). In a case study, McPhee and Iverson (2009) explored these four flows of organizing in the Communidad de Cucurpe, and its struggles to preserve the land rights of organizational members. These four flows illuminated different aspects of this legal and community struggle, with its shifting membership, changes in power and agency, and conflicts with ranchers.

Seibold and Associates

Like McPhee and Zaug, Seibold and Meyers (2005, 2007) view communication as a structurational process. Based on structuration theory (ST), they propose that communication is inherently a structuring activity and they explore how structures are appropriated, reproduced, and transformed through members' interactions. Recall that, in ST, structures are rules and resources used in interaction. Three mechanisms of structuring interactions are examined: (1) micro-level moves appropriating structures; (2) global patterns of members' use of structures; and (3) modalities of structuration.

Communication scholars have explored these structuring mechanisms. Seibold, Meyers and their colleagues, using a coding scheme developed by Canary et al. (2008), analyzed moves in group argumentation. Micro-level moves ranged from advancing "potential arguables" to "reason-giving arguables" to "disclaimers" and "counters." Each move relied on underlying rules and resources available to group members.

Such moves can be made individually or conjointly with others. Research exploring argument structures and patterning (Meyers & Seibold, 1990a, b), and investigating individual differences in message construction (Morris, Seibold & Meyers, 1991), have also been conducted. Another research context explored the minority/majority group contexts and argumentation structures (Lovaglia et al., 2005). (See Seibold and Meyers, 2007, for an overview of research findings.)

In analyzing more general patterns of structuring interaction, Browning and Beyer (1998) found that increased voluntary communication enhanced trust and cooperation among group members, and thus changed organizing processes for a SEMATECH consortium. Any interactional move simultaneously reflected the modalities of structuration (signification, domination and legitimation). Lewis and Seibold (1993) found that innovations (signification) in a food processing plant varied across work groups, and those innovations viewed as most effective (legitimation) enhanced the power of that work group (domination).

Seibold and Meyers (2005) concluded that viewing communicating as structuring interaction explained *"how* communication is central to the creation and transformation of social systems" (p. 148). It also permitted a more dynamic, fluid view of organizing and explored "how structuring interaction *occurs"* (ibid.). Finally, what appear to be exogenous factors (such as task type or technological support) can be directly incorporated into members' structuring practices (p. 150).

Integrating Structuration Theory with Institutional Theory

Whittington pointed out that structuration integrates well with an institutionalist perspective (generally, how social environments influence organizations). As he pointed out,

> It is my argument that the institutionalist perspective could be greatly enlarged if it were ready to make more than passing reference to Giddens. The structurationist conception of structural rules and resources offers a common framework for analyzing the disparate social influences—political, ethnic, domestic and professional—on managerial action. ... Structurationist acceptance of structural conflict and tension, rather than [the] institutionalist assumption of resolution and accommodation, gives leverage on the problems of uniqueness and change. Finally, the relationship of particular actors to society becomes less one of passive embeddedness, and more a matter of active engagement.
>
> *(Whittington, 1997, pp. 376–77)*

He concluded that

> Instead of treating the organization as a discrete entity within its environment, each firm and its activities should be examined as the expression of potentially

diverse social structural principles. It becomes necessary to identify the intersection within the firm of structural properties imported through multiple organizational memberships and superimposed by overlapping system boundaries.

(p. 381)

Some of those diverse social structural properties may be related to Giddens' discussion of different social institutions, such military, political, economic and legal institutions, and their importance in modernity.

In addition, Whittington (1992) suggested that managerial agency is influenced by the rules and resources contributed by agents through their multiple organizational ties, as well as by the ambiguity of rules influencing the production and reproduction of social practices (p. 704). He argued that managerial agency actively exploits "the tensions between divergent structural principles" created by the ambiguity of rules in complex systems, and by the contradictions between organizational principles and different organizational and personal values brought into the organization by other organizational members (ibid.). Such tensions are likely to increase because of globalization, and because of increasing interconnections across time-space edges.

Managers are "faced by a variety of conflicting rules of conduct, all legitimate and plausible, but, often, none with any obvious superiority. Choice is possible, even mandatory, because more than one course of action has systemic legitimacy" (ibid., p. 705). In addition, managerial agency must be able to access alternative structural principles; the legitimacy of these alternatives must be acknowledged, and some economic "slack" given for discretionary action. Whittington argued that ST allows institutional scholars to recognize and incorporate Giddens' "commitment to multidimensional social systems" (p. 707). Recognition of the multiple social identities of managers should also enhance our understanding of leadership and strategic choices. (See also Stevenson & Greenberg, 2000.)

Barley and Tolbert. In a classic article, Barley and Tolbert (1997) developed a model of institutionalization as a structuration process, and suggested methodological guidelines for testing these processes empirically. Institutional theory emphasizes cultural influences on decision-making, formal structures, norms, taken-for-granted knowledge, and the values of organizational members. As such, "institutions are socially constructed templates for action, generated and maintained through ongoing interactions. ... The patterned relations and actions that emerge from this process gradually acquire the moral and ontological status of taken-for-granted facts which, in turn, shape future interactions and negotiations" (p. 96). Although institutionalists acknowledged that institutions "arise from and constrain social action," they have focused mainly on institutional constraints on action (ibid.).

Institutions, as defined by Barley and Tolbert, represent "an existing framework of rules and typifications derived from a cumulative history of action and interaction ... To the degree that institutions are encoded in actors' stocks of practical knowledge (in the form of interpretive schemes, resources, and norms adapted to a particular setting which Giddens calls 'modalities'), they influence how people communicate, enact power, and determine what behaviors to sanction and reward" (p. 99). Daily interactions in institutions may be enacted through scripts (Barley, 1990), which also complements the communicating and organizing model being developed in this book as well as Goffman's frames. Scripts, from this perspective, refer to the "observable, recurrent activities and patterns of interaction characteristic of a particular setting. Scripts encode the social logic of what Goffman ... called an 'interaction order'" (1986, p. 108). Scripts also can be used at the interorganizational level of analysis, such as in the analysis of the dialogue between accrediting agencies and schools.

To study the process of change in an institution, Barley and Tolbert recommended selecting sites for change; charting flows of action at these sites and identifying scripts characteristic at different time periods; examining the scripts for evidence of change; and linking that observational data with other sources of change in the institution (p. 106). They also recommended the use of archival sources and other documentary data to identify institutional changes. Barley's 1986 study of changes in hospital radiology departments exemplified this type of study. They concluded that systematically exploring the relative impact of both behavioral and cognitive phenomena will enhance our understanding of both organizing and communicating. Lammers and Barbour (2006; Barbour & Lammers, 2007) have developed an institutional theory of organizational communication. While not based on structuration theory, all six aspects of their theory appear compatible with Giddens' theory.

While some critics (see Archer, 1990) suggested that Giddens conflates structure and action so they cannot be studied empirically, Barley and Tolbert disagreed. They suggested that defining scripts in behavioral terms and "treating them as pivots between an institution and action ... allows one to explicate the basis for one's inferences about systems of action, while simultaneously providing a point of reference for gauging the acceptability of deductions from transitional indicators of an institution and its implications for the logic of an interaction order" (p. 102). That is, scripts can simultaneously justify inferences for action; evaluate the acceptability of the action in an institutional context; and guide interaction in that given context. As such, ST enables the analysis of individual conduct within an institutional context which both constrains and enables action. (For an interesting contrast drawn between Archer and Giddens, see Llewellyn, 2007.)

Barley (1990, 1996) subsequently explored the concept of being a "technician" and how that shaped interaction and practices in organizing. Another study (Barley, 1990) outlined how new technology influenced agents' work roles and subsequently influenced interaction patterns and social networks at work. New distributions of status, new patterns of information giving, and new accessibility to information were noted. He suggested that researchers explore the interconnections across levels (from micro- to macro-levels) and map the flow of interactional influence across levels, noting both discourse and actions. Leonardi (2007) found changes in advice-seeking behavior after the introduction of new technologies, which, in turn, affected the social status of organizational members. Much of the work by Poole and his associates on Adaptive Structuration Theory sheds light on appropriation processes as well.

Structuration Theory and Self-Organizing Systems

Fuchs (2002, 2003) suggested that structuration theory is compatible with the concept of self-organizing social systems. Fuchs noted that Giddens explains structures and relates structures and actions dialectically, while Maturana relies upon consensual networks of interaction. As such, Fuchs concluded that ST has more explanatory power. Social systems can only be self-reproducing if human actors are viewed, as Giddens does, as both the "creator and created result of society" (Fuchs, 2003, p. 144).

Information is important in self-organizing systems as well as in structuration theory. "All self-organising systems are information-generating systems. Giddens' concept of storage mechanisms that allow time-space distanciation of social relationships helps to describe the relationship of information and self-organization in social systems" (p. 158). Fuchs (2002) suggests that the duality of structure allows for both individual and social information to emerge in an "interconnected interplay of structures and actors," thus giving rise to dynamic change and crisis (p. 30). Mechanistic causality is questioned by self-organization theories as well as by structuration theory (Fuchs, 2003, p. 157). Evolution is viewed as discontinuity and reflects the dialectics of chance, necessity and order. Given the parallels between ST and self-organizing systems, Fuchs concluded that Giddens' emphasis on the duality of structure and the centrality of interaction offered a strong perspective on the nature of self-organizing systems.

In addition, Mingers (1996b, 2004) noted the strong similarities between ST and autopoiesis. Both Maturana and Giddens emphasize the production and reproductions of systems and the view that systems can be recursively self-producing. He suggested that if a society or organization is viewed as autopoietic, then two issues must be addressed: first, the components of an autopoietic social system must be identified, and their processes of production described; and, second, the autopoietic social system must be constituted in time and space, and its boundaries demarcated (Mingers, 2004, p. 406). Mingers argued that the components of an autopoietic social system are the "elements of social structure— rules, positions, practices etc.—as potential components for social autopoiesis" (p. 417).

Giddens' concern with the continual, recursive production and reproduction of social systems clearly resonates with the concept of self-producing systems (autopoiesis). And both ST and autopoiesis argue that explanations "should be non-functionalist and non-teleological" (ibid.). Both differentiate between "that which is observable, having space-time existence, and that which is not but is still implicated in the constitution of a system (*structure/organization* for Maturana, *system/structure* for Giddens)" (p. 407). Finally, both identify similar relations: constitution/space, order/time and specification/paradigmatic (ibid.).

The second condition is more problematic in the sense of demarcating boundaries. Giddens used several circular feedback loops which, according to Mingers, can demarcate some boundaries—they are "homeostatic loops via unintended consequences of action, self-regulation through information filtering, and reflexive self-regulation involving conscious manipulation of social institutions" (p. 418). In the case of social systems, boundaries are complicated because two different strata—social structure and social action—are involved. Mingers suggested that we could examine society and uncover "an enormously complex inter-meshing of causal loops involving both observable activity and events stretching over time and space and the underlying structure of positions and rules. The difficult question, though, is to what extent such circuits can be said to form a boundary, or at least demarcate themselves from the background" (p. 418).

Giddens himself recognized the difficulty of boundaries: "It is important to re-emphasise that the term 'social system' should not be understood to designate only clusters of social relations whose boundaries are clearly set off from others. ... I take it to be one of the main features of structuration theory that the extension and 'closure' of societies across space and time is regarded as problematic" (1984, p. 165). Giddens' concept of historicity, time-space edges and time-space distanciation help illuminate some of these issues.

Mingers concluded that synthesizing Giddens' and Luhmann's theories might be very useful—distinguishing "between an observable system and underlying structure on the one-hand (Giddens), and, within the system, that between individual interaction and societal communication (Luhmann)—for analysis of the autopoietic properties of social systems" (p. 421). I would argue that ST, particularly integrating it with Goffman's work, which is already foundational to ST (and developed in the theory of structurational interaction), would provide an even more useful approach.

In brief, Giddens' structuration theory has been integrated and extended in a number of ways, demonstrating its richness and complexity. I have reviewed several scholarly contexts which have usefully explored structuration theory, ranging from communication flows in organizations to group argumentation to institutional theory. Other insightful extensions can undoubtedly be developed, as the breadth and depth of Giddens' work are more fully acknowledged.

ST developed the concepts of distanciation, the importance of time and space, knowledge, and the importance of information and information storage. All these focal points for ST are useful in analyzing mediated communication systems, particularly those extended over time and space. It is to this work I now turn, focusing on the work of Poole and his colleagues on adaptive structuration theory, and the work of Orlikowski and her colleagues on genres of communication.

Structuration Theory and Communication Technology

Two strands of research, by Poole, Orlikowski and their associates, have applied Giddens' structuration theory to new technology. These applications are particularly noteworthy because they take seriously the distanciation of time-space and its impact on new forms of organizations (virtual and dispersed), and the use of new technologies to support, alter and make possible new organizational arrangements. Orlikowski and her associates have developed the concept of duality in technology, and focused on social practices. Adaptative structuration theory, developed by Poole, DeSanctis, and others, has focused on how human agents adapt new technologies in their work, and on how these adaptations transform work. Some scholars are suggesting hybrid agency as a result of institutional and non-institutional discourses available through web-based communication. (For an interesting discussion of structuration theory in information technology, and a review of research methods, see Pozzebon and Pinsonneault, 2001, 2005. For an excellent review and evaluation of Giddens' structuration theory and its use by information systems scholars, see Jones and Karsten, 2008.)

Structuration Theory, Information Technology and Organizing

Orlikowski's work. A classic article by Orlikowski and Robey (1991) used ST to examine the relationship between information technology and organizations. Information technology is "both the product of human action as well as a medium for human action" and their research examined how information technology is "created, used, and becomes institutionalized within organizations" (p. 144). After Giddens, they argued that it is "more appropriate to speak of social systems *as exhibiting* structural properties that are produced and reproduced through the inter-action of human actors, rather than as *having* structures. But individuals ... call on the structural properties that were enacted in the past by prior human action (their own or that of others). In this way, the structural properties established by prior human action come to define and shape individuals' interaction, which in turn creates the structural properties anew" (ibid.). Giddens overcomes the problem of level of analysis, or point of entry, because through structuration "individual action and interaction constitute shared definitions of social structure" (p. 148).

They also suggested that "From an institutional point of view, interpretive schemes comprise structures of signification which represent the social rules that enable, inform, and inhibit the communication process. Thus in any interaction, shared knowledge is not merely background but an integral part of the communicative encounter, in part organizing it, and in part being shaped by the interaction itself" (p. 149). Information technology itself is a "medium for the construction of social reality" and formalizes and encodes standard ways of knowing and thinking (p. 155). Software technology, for example, can be viewed as an "interpretive scheme for translating human action into routines" (ibid.).

Resources constitute organizational structures of domination that are usually marked by asymmetry. As they noted, "the design and deployment of information technology, with its implications for information resources and enforcing rules, constitutes a system of domination" (ibid.). Because of information technologies (IT's) increasing importance as an institutional resource, conflict and challenge may arise around its use (Orlikowski, 1992a).

Finally, "Normative components of interaction always center upon relations between the rights and obligations expected of those participating in a range of interaction contexts. ... " (Giddens, 1984, p. 30). For institutions, "norms articulate and sustain established structures of legitimation" (Orlikowski & Robey, 1991, p. 149). Information technology can convey a set of valued norms and goals; monitor actors' compliance, and direct action and thinking in particular ways. Such technologies may also be used in ways not sanctioned by the organization (e.g., watching the Super Bowl at work). All these activities, of course, may be transformed and influenced by unintended consequences of action.

Orlikowski and Robey (1991) noted that there is an underlying duality in information technology. Information technology is a social product of human action in particular contexts while simultaneously providing "an objective set of rules and resources involved in mediating (facilitating and constraining) human action and hence contributing to the creation, recreation, and transformation of these contexts" (p. 151). Four key influences, operating continuously and simultaneously, influence technology and organizing: first, information technology implicates human action because "information technology is created and maintained by humans, and that information technology has to be used by humans to have any effect" (p. 153). (This is particularly important to remember in any discussions of materiality and its role in communicating and organizing.)

Second, information technologies *mediate* human action—information technology, from a structurational perspective, "does not *determine* social practices ... it has to be appropriated by human[s] ... and ... there is always the possibility that human[s] may choose not to use the technology or use it in ways that undermine its 'normal' operation. Thus technology can only condition, and never determine social practices ... technology both facilitates and constrains" (p. 153). Third, people's use of information technology is influenced by the institutional contexts in which they work; people are "constantly influenced by the values, interests, expertise, power, culture, and so on, that surround them. To act meaningfully in organizations, individuals draw on existing stocks of knowledge, resources, and norms to perform their work, often doing so only implicitly" (p. 154). Finally, information technology may reinforce, undermine or transform institutional structures.

It is essential to acknowledge the social context and social practices in which information technologies are used. Institutional resources, in terms of planning, scheduling and budgeting, are implicated in the use of IT. Developers and users of IT may depend upon shared signification, both personally and on an institutional level. And IT users may appropriate the technology in unanticipated ways. They concluded that "there is a tension between the knowledgeable action of human actors and the conservative, structural force of institutionalized practices. This dialectic is played out each day in every human interaction, and hence every context of interaction is punctuated by a certain indeterminacy" (p. 157). As such, ITs are not deterministic, but may have both intended and uintended outcomes.

They viewed structuration theory as a metatheoretic framework for "understanding the social factors pertaining to the development, use, and implications of information technology in organizations" (ibid.). They call for research in six areas—on systems' development processes; on the social consequences of information technology; on the relationship between systems development and social consequences; on the intended and unintended consequences of employing a particular technology; on how human action changes the technology; and on how given technologies may support or undermine institutional structures.

Jones and Karsten (2008) reviewed the use of structuration theory by information systems scholars. They note that a fuller, richer appreciation of Giddens' work would extend its usefulness to IS (information systems) scholarship. They suggest that some future directions for research would include the "interaction between technology and human action that may be significant for social practice" (p. 150), and the interpretive flexibility in the use of technology and its influence on social practices. The use of IS and its influence on social actors and social institutions also needs further exploration. As they note,

> The extent and variety of structurational processes in which IS may be significantly implicated, from individual identity maintenance through the temporal organization of work practices to the development of globalized high modernity, suggests a broader spectrum of potential topics and levels of analysis than IS researchers have traditionally studied. Tracing the dynamics of these interactions and their interconnectedness would seem to provide a significant challenge for IS research.
>
> *(p. 155)*

And, I might add, for organizing and communicating scholarship as well!

Structures and Genres of Communication

A significant body of work by Orlikowski, Yates, and their colleagues have used structuration theory to define genres of organizational communication as well as to explore communication patterns in distanciated time-space contexts (i.e., looking at new technology and virtual communication systems). Orlikowski (1992b) used a structuration model focusing on the duality of technology and its interpretive flexibility. As she noted,

Technology is the product of human action, while it also assumes structural properties ... technology is physically constructed by actors working in a given social context, and ... socially constructed by actors through the different meanings attached to it and the various features they emphasize and use.

(*Orlikowski, 1992b, p. 406*)

Genres, such as memos, proposals or meetings, are characterized by a similar form and substance, and respond to recurring situations (Yates, 1994, 1997; Orlikowski & Yates, 1998). Each genre possesses structural features, uses a particular medium, and relies on language as a symbolic system. Genres are rules, similar to Giddens' social rules, which connect form and substance with certain situations. For example, when agents write business letters, they draw upon genre rules for business letters and thus reinforce those rules through their actions. Genres thus shape and are shaped by communicative interaction, and interact systematically with various media.

They also discussed the historicity of shifts in genre practices over time, arguing that the need for internal communication reflected broad socioeconomic changes from 1870 to 1920, as well as changes in managerial philosophy. Earlier internal communicative genres, such as handwritten notes, telegrams and so forth, led to emails and other forms of electronic communication, such as JIT inventory management. Thus, genres are situated communicative action in a stream of social practices which shape and are shaped by them. As Orlikowski concluded, "the conditions influencing media use and the consequences of media use are tightly coupled in a process of structuration over time. ... Any time a new communication medium is introduced into an organization, we expect that existing genres of communication will influence the use of this medium, though the nature of this influence will reflect the interaction between existing genres and human action within specific contexts" (1992b, p. 406). In a study of genre repertoires in a group of distributed knowledge workers, Orlikowski and Yates (1994) found that group members developed an array of communicative practices (genres) as a response to media capabilities; time pressures from the task; project events and community norms; and that this array was a critical component of their organizing activities.

Genres look specifically at the communicative issues of why, what, who/m, when, where and how (Orlikowski & Yates, 1998). A genre system is established by participants and provides a schema for interaction among agents across media, time and space. They found that three teams in a high-technology company developed genres of mediated interaction and dissatisfaction arose when norms regarding the genres were violated (e.g., not responding to emails). Yoshioka and Herman (1999) explored the construction of a genre taxonomy that would identify recurrent communicative practices for organizations, such as memos and meetings.

Another study by Yates, Orlikowski and Woerner (2003) studied conversational threads in a year-long compilation of emails of a geographically dispersed software design organization. Conversational threads were defined as subsequent comments on an already introduced specific topic. *Simple threads* are tightly connected sequences that focus on a specific issue; *concurrent threads* reflect multiple simple threads interwoven over time and embedded within other ongoing interactions; and *compound threads* are simple threads linked together over time, focusing discussion on the same topic. These threads assisted organizational members in maintaining ongoing work and in focusing on the task, despite multi-party interactions, interruptions, and geographic separation. (See also McDaniel, Olson & Magee, 1996.)

Yates (1997) has also used Giddens' concepts of historicity and time as a way to understand the roles of both individuals and organizations in history. While one can assess an individual's single action in making a change, other actors and mechanisms might also be needed to bring about change. In her study, Yates analyzed changes in two organizations (Scovil and DuPont) as the result of technological change, such as written records, memos, and other forms of institutional communication that were developed (Yates, 1989). A new genre of web-based interaction, in which geographic location as well as specific features of a technology play a role in patterns of social interaction, may be observed in Internet sites such as Flickr and Jaiku (Erickson, 2010).

Structuration not only allows a useful analysis of technology, but also incorporates the historicity and social milieu surrounding these changes. While Orlikowski and Yates focused on organizational changes and IT, Poole and his associates explored how organizational groups have adapted ITs and how that adaptation has shaped group processes. Since a significant amount of organizational work is accomplished by groups, this is a major application of structuration theory and one that has great practical utility. (For an excellent review of applying Giddens' work to information technology, see Jones and Karsten, 2008.)

Adaptive Structuration Theory (AST)

Developed by Poole, DeSanctis, Fulk and their colleagues, AST applied structuration theory to the use of technology in organizing and communicating. AST focuses on the technical affordances provided by a technology, and the developing organizational structures flowing from human use of that technology (DeSanctis & Poole, 1994). Information technologies are of particular concern for us because of the premium modern organizations place on the rapid, efficient, and accurate exchange of information and its secure storage. Advanced information technologies range from electronic messaging to group decision support systems to other technologies for multi-party participation in information management (DeSanctis & Poole, 1994, p. 122). Considerable research supports the idea that "the effects of advanced technologies are less a function of the technologies themselves than of how they are *used* by people" (ibid.). AST thus assesses variations in how people adapt to and use information technology, and how technology influences organizational change. Structuration was examined on the micro-level (analyzing moves that appropriate, produce and reproduce structures) as well as on a global level (identifying patterns of structuration that depict an entire decision-making process) (Poole & McPhee, 2005, p. 183).

Two key aspects of AST include structuration and appropriation. The duality of structure (structuration) is "an interplay between the types of structures that are inherent to advanced technologies (and, hence, anticipated by designers and sponsors) and the structures that emerge in human action as people interact with these technologies" (DeSanctis & Poole, 1994, p. 122). In their study, DeSanctis and Poole examined small groups as they used a group decision support system (GDSS). Such systems provide computing, communication, and decision support capabilities to help groups generate ideas, plan actions, and solve problems. They concluded that AST considers the "mutual influence of technology and social processes" and thus corrects the imbalances of other approaches (p. 125). Appropriation is a key concept which refers to "the ways in which groups take structural features built into a technology, such as a voting feature in a GDSS, and use them in interaction" (Poole & McPhee, 2005, p. 183).

AST thus explores the interplay between advanced information technologies, social structures, and human interaction. Social structures refer to the rules and resources provided by institutions and by technologies for human activity (DeSanctis & Poole, 1994). Technology itself provides rules (like voting procedures and regulations about participation) as well as resources (such as public screens and data storage). They noted that "As these structures then are brought into interaction, they are instantiated in social life ... there are structures in technology, on the one hand, and structures in action, on the other. The two are continually intertwined; there is a recursive relationship between technology and action, each iteratively shaping the other" (p. 125). In order to understand how technologies are used in organizing, the social structures of technology must be analytically distinct from the social structures in interaction, and their mutual interrelationships assessed.

Structural features and the spirit of structural features are two different dimensions of a technology's social structure. Structural features reflect how information is gathered, stored and manipulated by users. Advanced information technologies (AITs) are noted for their multiple features; among the most important feature is that of restrictiveness. The more restrictive the technology, the fewer features that may be manipulated. Spirit is the "general intent with regard to values and goals underlying a given set of structural features" (ibid., p. 126). Spirit can be discerned by the design metaphor of the AIT: Its features; the nature of its interface with users; its training materials; and other help provided with an AIT system.

A technology also has the same modalities of structuration: (1) signification helps users understand the technology and its meaning; (2) legitimation provides users with a normative frame for appropriate behaviors with regard to the technology; and (3) domination is reflected in the influence moves provided to users by the information technology. Some technology may not provide a coherent spirit, and thus may provoke contradiction and conflict in its use. Some aspects of a technology's spirit might emphasize efficiency or leadership or tools for conflict management. Taken together, "the spirit and structural feature sets of an advanced information technology form its *structural potential*, which groups can draw on to generate particular social structures in interaction" (DeSanctis & Poole, 1994, p. 126). They suggested, for example, that in a formal group with a restrictive GDSS, group members might closely follow the agenda and procedures of the GDSS.

DeSanctis and Poole also suggested that other sources of structure for groups include the task, and the organizational environment. Given these factors, they set forth the following propositions for analysis:

1. To the extent that AITs vary in their structural features and spirit, different forms of interaction are encouraged by the technology;
2. AIT use may vary depending on the task, the environment and other sources of social structures;
3. As the technology, tasks and environmental structures are applied during social interaction, new sources of structure may emerge;
4. New social structures in group interaction will emerge as the rules and resources of an AIT are appropriated in a given context and reproduced over time; and
5. Group decision processes vary according to the nature of AIT appropriations.
(DeSanctis & Poole, 1994, pp. 128–30)

Factors influencing the appropriation of AITs could include members' interactional styles; their degree of knowledge and experience with the technology; and the degree to which members think other group members understand and accept the use of the technological structures. As DeSanctis and Poole noted, there is a "dialectic of control" between group members and the technology—this dialectic shapes the use of the technology and the new social structures that may emerge (ibid., p. 131).

Their proposals for studying the structuration of appropriation moves are of particular interest in terms of organizing and communicating: "Appropriation analysis tries to document exactly how technology structures are being invoked for use in a specific context, thus shedding light on the more long-term process of adaptive structuration" (ibid., p. 133). Appropriation assesses how technology and other social structures enter into human activity discursively, and can be assessed on the micro-, global, or institutional level. They observed that "written or spoken discussion about the technology is particularly important since this is evidence of people bringing the technology into the social context. From there, appropriation analysis can proceed to higher levels, global and institutional" (ibid.). Micro-level analysis can help explain why some groups use the technology successfully, and others do not. Further more, over time, micro-level appropriations influence institutional-level appropriations, and vice versa. Poole and DeSanctis (1992) developed a coding categorization of 37 appropriation moves, based on the number of structures involved and whether a move actively uses a structure, clarifies it, or is a response to another appropriation move.

Micro-level analysis can also examine speech acts, sequences of speech acts, and turns at talk, when organizational members use ASTs. They distinguished between faithful appropriations, those that are compatible with the technology and its spirit, while unfaithful appropriations create incompatible usages of the technology. Over time, micro-level appropriations build into global appropriation patterns. DeSanctis et al. (1992) found pure task and process groups, social and power-oriented groups, and mixed groups, in their analysis of groups' overall dominant patterns when using ASTs. While these analyses need to become more fine-grained, they nonetheless can be used as sensitizing devices to explore AST. (Goffman's frames and framing might also be usefully applied here.)

Poole and DeSanctis (1992) explored micro-level structuration in groups' usage of SAMM GDSSs in their work. As noted earlier, a GDSS facilitates group processes and decision-making. They found that GDSSs influence groups by structuring their activity, and thus mediating groups' decision-making. The restrictiveness of the GDSSs influenced structuration processes and thereby impacted the groups' consensus. They looked at individual structuring moves, extended sequences of moves (as sequences of bids and responses), and at junctural structuring events (episodes in which major directions for structuration are established) (p. 25).

Types of structuring (appropriation) moves included direct appropriation, substitution, combination, enlargement, contrast and constraint. A number of subtypes were measured as either faithful or unfaithful appropriations of the technology. Eighteen groups were studied, and their interaction was face-to-face. They found that technological restrictiveness (the lack of flexibility or choice in the GDSS) reduced the amount of structuring behavior focused on controlling the system and directed attention toward working with system outcomes. Eleven of the groups were faithful in their appropriations, while seven were not; faithful groups experienced high consensus change. Faithful appropriation groups tended to use the GDSS to monitor and to indicate where they were in their decision-making process. There were no significant differences in conflict between unfaithful and faithful groups.

Two interactional dynamics were found: (1) ongoing, continuous structuration (appropriation) processes, and (2) junctures at which major structural shifts occurred. They emphasize that their coding is only a sensitizing device and mainly valuable in spotting key events in the structuration process, like ironic appropriations, which could then be assessed qualitatively in more detail (p. 44). In such studies, using the theory of structurational interaction, especially frame analysis for unpacking meaning and the use of footing and alignment to track group members' changing views, would appear to be very useful analytic additions.

As they concluded:

> AST argues that advanced information technologies trigger adaptive structurational processes which, over time, can lead to changes in the rules and resources that organizations use in social interaction. ... Group members can

opt to directly use technological features, relate the structures to other structures, constrain or interpret the structure, or make judgments about the structure. The impacts of the technology on group outcomes depend upon: the structural potential of the technology (i.e., its spirit and structural features); how technology and other structures (such as work tasks, the group's internal system, and the larger organizational environment) are appropriated by group members; and what new social structures are formed over time.

(Poole and DeSanctis, 1992, p. 143)

The advantages of AST lie in its capacity to analyze between-group differences; to assess both the structural potential of technology and its use; and to enhance our understanding of groups generally.

A number of studies have explored the appropriation (use) of technology, with specific attention given to how agents have altered their practices and their routines in utilizing technology. Altering strategies frequently involved unintended consequences, such as altering the power hierarchy, access to information, and so on. Such studies flow from Giddens' structuration theory with its emphasis on resources, interaction, social practices, and knowledgeability of agents. As noted earlier, Orlikowski's research on technology-in-use exemplified these concerns. Barley (1986) studied the adaptation of CT scanners in two hospitals, and found that access to information, perceptions of expertise, and colleague relationships changed as a result of the new technology. The context of how work was accomplished in each hospital also shaped adaptive practices.

In a further extension of structuration theory in information technology, Chae and Poole (2005) explored the role of pre-existing information systems on the development and use of new emergent systems. They argued that pre-existing information systems influence emergent systems "through the material constraints and directions inherent in existing systems and through the experiences and learning from previous systems, which shape developers' approaches to building the new system" (p. 19). In Giddens' terms, developers have practical and discursive consciousness about pre-existing systems which influence their current design practices.

Critics have argued that the structuration of information systems (IS), in work such as Orlikowski's, are not sufficiently fine-grained to demonstrate adaptation to or design of ISs. Although Chae and Poole pointed out that this work has subsequently analyzed more generic processes of structuration, through use of metastructuring or a practice lens, they agree that more fine-grained analyses are needed. To address this need, Chae and Poole proposed an integration of structuration theory with actor-network theory. (I would argue that Goffman's interaction order would be an excellent tool for analyzing these interactions as well, and has the significant advantage in that Goffman's interaction order is central to Giddens' work.)

As they noted, "the actor-network is a socio-technical web that links together human and non-humans in a stable set of relations that align their interests" (p. 21). However, actor-network theory also has the shortcomings of (1) not differentiating the means through which actors and material objects structure action, and (2) viewing the interests inscribed to material objects as being fixed and static (ibid.). Pickering (1995) also criticized actor-network theory because both humans and material objects are treated in the same fashion. Pickering suggested that agency consists of three different types: *material agency* of the natural world, via natural laws; *human agency*, via individual intent, reflexive monitoring, and the meaning constitution of the social world; and *disciplinary agency*, via a discipline (such as systems design) which guides people through actions. These three senses of agency interact with one another in practice.

Chae and Poole argue that these three aspects of agency are necessary for the analysis and design of ISs. As they note, "The surface of emergence in IS development is a socio-technical construction constituted by human agents who draw on previously existing machines and disciplines" (2005, p. 23). They view an intranet as an example which draws upon these different agencies. Through using Pickering's concept of the mange of practice, they are proposing an integration of structuration theory with actor-network theory in a way that alleviated some of the problems associated with each theoretical perspective. In a detailed case study of the development of an IS in a major university, "it became evident that [the] pre-existing IS and institutions both within and outside ... played a critical role in its development" (p. 26). While a full discussion of this case study is beyond the scope of our concern, the reworking of AST enabled a fine-grained analysis of structuration during IS development.

Related studies. In an interesting study examining three global virtual teams from the same organization, Maznevski and Chudoba (2000) investigated their communication patterns using a qualitative, grounded theory approach with AST as a conceptual research template. Such teams are becoming increasingly important in multinational organizations, and little is known about how they effectively communicate with one another. Global virtual teams are geographically dispersed teams identified by their organization(s) as responsible for global business strategies, and rely more on technology-aided communication than face-to-face communication.

Data collection was conducted throughout a 21-month period. Interaction incidents occurred around information gathering, problem-solving, idea generating and comprehensive decision-making. These incidents varied in message complexity, in the communication medium selected, and in its duration. For effective teams, "function influenced form: The higher the level of decision process and/or the more complex the message, the more rich the communication medium used and the longer the incident's duration" (p. 16). In addition to interaction incidents, they found that effective teams were characterized by a strong repeating temporal pattern, established by intense coordination meetings which set the pace and tone of the global task. Pacing was more frequent when the task required more interdependence, and less frequent when the task was more autonomously configured. Finally, they found that organizational members' background and task context influenced media choice. They suggested that temporal patterning in groups is a significant issue to pursue in further research.

An exploration of AST by Contractor and Seibold (1993) added to that model through use of self-organizing systems theory (SOST). They utilized computer simulations to identify factors influencing the use of GDSSs, such as initial conditions for the appropriation of a GDSS and organizational members' awareness of norms around appropriation. Their model focused on "specifying boundary conditions under which a specific set of norms is more (or less) likely to be appropriated" (p. 558). Virtual decision-making groups which had training on group maintenance behavior experienced more social support, greater participation and greater satisfaction with the group than did groups without such training (Tullar & Kaiser, 2000). Attributions in virtual groups were influenced by perceived similarity/dissimilarity of situational constraints and perceived quality of others' performance (Bazarova & Walther, 2009).

The work of AST could be further extended by using the concept of frames. Orlikowski and Gash (1994) noted that "Technological frames have powerful effects in that people's assumptions, expectations, and knowledge about the purpose, context, importance, and role of technology will strongly influence the choices made regarding the design and use of those technologies. Because technologies are social artifacts, their material form and function will embody their sponsors' and developers' objective, values, interests, and knowledge of that technology" (p. 179). They noted that features, such as how work is divided, how much autonomy employees should have, and so forth, are built into the technology. They suggested that designers, managers and users will be among the critical social groups in using technology. Group context also influences the trust developed in computer mediated groups, with competitive groups experiencing more trust if there were introductory face-to-face meetings (Hill, Bartol, Tesluk & Langa, 2009).

Adaptation to new technologies can also be conceptualized as moving from individual sensemaking to group/social sensemaking and subsequently to actions, and then a new cycle of sensemaking begins (Griffith, 1999). She suggested that initial understandings of a technology—triggers for initial user understanding—can be placed in the context of later adaptation (AST). Her analysis rests upon a features-based theory of sensemaking (FBST) and she examined specific features of initial sensemaking from this perspective. These triggers include (1) the abstractness versus concreteness of the technology (e.g., the abstractness of genetically engineered food versus the concreteness of the tube of an MRI), and (2) the core versus tangential characteristics of the technology (e.g., connectivity of a telephone versus its external appearance). Griffith suggested that the FBST theory can help identify how users cognitively simplify a technology (via discrepancy, novelty and reflection), and how their responses may help organizations implement new technologies.

The Duality of Technology

Parallel to the duality of structure in structuration theory, Orlikowski argues that technology is shaped by human agents but also shapes human action in the duality of technology. As she noted, "Technology is created and changed by human action, yet it is also used by humans to accomplish some action" (Orlikowski, 1992b, p. 405). "This view starts with human action and examines how it enacts emergent structure through recurrent interaction with the technology at hand" (Orlikowski, 2000, p. 407). Another important assumption is that technology is "*interpretively flexible*, hence ... the interaction of technology and organizations is a function of the different actors and socio-historical contexts implicated in its development and use" (ibid.) Human agents are knowledgeable, reflexive actors and can create both direct, intended effects as well as unintended, unforeseen consequences. For example, while the use of email can speed and foster more organizational connectivity, it can simultaneously weaken status and social cues in the organization (Sproul & Kiesler, 1986).

The structurational model of technology also views technology as being potentially modified through its use and by surrounding institutional conditions. Orlikowski argued that human interaction with technology includes both a design mode and a use mode. That is, while the technology in question may be designed for specific uses, there is ample evidence that human agents modify, adapt, change, and use a given technology in many unintended ways. Technology may appear to be "stable-at-present" but it is continuously shaped by and shaping human use of that technology. Over time, social practices associated with a given technology may become routine, taken-for-granted aspects of organizational work.

Her structurational model of technology incorporated four interrelated aspects:

(1) Technology as a product of human action—elements of design, development, etc.;
(2) Technology as a medium of human action—technology facilitates/constrains human action through interpretive schemes, facilities, and norms;
(3) Institutional conditions of interaction with technology—factors such as professional norms, design standards, available resources, state of the art of materials, etc.; and
(4) Institutional consequences of interaction with technology—technology influences the institutional properties of an organization, through structures of signification, domination and legitimation.

Her field research study of Beta corporation found that technological tools included a set of rules and resources used by organizational members in their use of a technology, and that the knowledge embedded in the tools became part of the interpretive schemes constituting Beta's systems development knowledge. Technical consultants developed interpretive schemas of use which they legitimated and controlled. These practices supported Beta's institutional structure, and standardized language and norms of actions were developed so that consultants could easily switch from project to project. As she concluded, "there are strong tendencies within institutionalized practices that constrain and facilitate certain developments and deployments of technology ... understanding how different conditions influence the development, maintenance, and use of more or less interpretively flexible technologies would give insight into the limits and opportunities of human choice and organizational design" (Orlikowski, 1992b, p. 424).

Temporal patterning. Another study (Tyre & Orlikowski, 1994) explored the temporal patterning of technological adaptation in three organizations. They found a "window of opportunity" for change in adaptation for a brief time after implementation of a technology. Over time, practices surrounding the new technology became increasingly routinized, and the level of customization decreased. Approximately one year after implementation, they documented another period of adaptive activities. Other episodic adaptations occurred as a consequence of discrepant events or through new discoveries by users. They concluded that the process of technological adaptation is highly discontinuous.

Sociohistorical contexts of use. Like Giddens, Orlikowski believes it is important to contextualize human agency in its sociohistorical context. In a study investigating technological adaptation in the context of its use, Orlikowski et al. (1995) found that key organizational members shaped users' interaction with a conferencing technology; altered features of the technology; and controlled the context of use. Such activities, termed *technology-use-mediation*, direct attention and resources to adopting a technology to changing contexts. These direct, deliberate interventions acted to modify the context of use of the technology; facilitated the organization's effectiveness in utilizing the technology; and altered how users interacted with the technology. Such mediation strategies influenced the institutional practices, interpretive schemes, and rules and resources used in the technology. They concluded that this level of *meta-structuring* added another layer of structuration in which key mediators influenced other users, their attitudes and the institutional context. Another study by Orlikowski and Gash (1994) found that such mediators influenced the work habits and technological frames of meaning for agents. (I would also note that Goffman's lamination or layering of frames might be very useful in assessing this level of meta-structuring.)

Viewing technology as a social practice. Orlikowski (2000) extended the structurational perspective by linking it to social practice (a practice lens)—viewing technology use "as a process of enactment [which] enables a deeper understanding of the constitutive role of social practices in the ongoing use and change of technologies in the workplace" (p. 404). Dominant organizational interests are reflected in what technologies are used, how they are used, and in their legitimated organizational practices (for example, see DeSanctis & Poole, 1994; Latour, 1991, on inscription; and Poole and DeSanctis, 2004). As Giddens (1984) pointed out, "'materiality' does not affect the fact that such phenomena become resources ... only when incorporated within the process of structuration" (p. 33).

Orlikowski (2000) commented that "Technology structures ... are virtual, emerging from people's repeated and situated interaction with particular technologies. These enacted structures of technology use, which I term *technologies-in-practice*, are the sets of rules and resources that are (re)constituted in people's recurrent engagement with the technologies at hand" (p. 407). As an example, Orlikowski noted that when people use tax preparation software, not only does this reflect computer programming and the U.S. federal tax code, but they also draw upon their own expertise and experience with technology, as well as their rights and obligations as taxpayers.

From a practice lens, facilities, norms and interpretive schemes are rules and resources that support technologies-in-practice. Facilities refer to the hardware, software, buildings, etc. that agents utilize in a given technology. The norms refer to organizational practices such as training, protocol, etc., as well the agents' skills, experience and power. Interpretive schemes would incorporate "all the meanings and attachments—emotional and intellectual—that users associate with particular technologies, and their participation in a range of social and political communities" (ibid., p. 410). Ongoing enactment of a technology becomes routinized, and thus serves as a template for organizational use of that technology. Orlikowski also noted three different types of enactments—inertia, application and change—which examine the associated institutional conditions and consequences of technological practices. Over time, as an organizational community of users share technological practices, they may resist changing these practices.

Knowledgeability and knowing. Orlikowski (2002) further extended her social practice oriented perspective to focus on "knowing how to get things accomplished in an organization." In a study of a geographically dispersed high-tech organization, she found that competency in this organization required both collective and distributed knowing, grounded in the daily practices of organizational members. She developed a focus on knowing, rather than knowledge: "knowing is an ongoing social accomplishment, constituted and reconstituted in everyday practice" (p. 252). Agents' enactment of social practices and their reproduction of the "knowing" reflected in their practices is how "knowing" is reconstituted over time and in diverse contexts. Complex, geographically dispersed organizations rely on this knowing to function effectively.

Her study uncovered five types of knowing practices—two practices, shared identity and face-to-face interaction—"generate a knowing how to be coherent, committed, and cooperative across a variety of spatial, temporal, and political boundaries" (p. 256). Shared identity provided continuity in commitment and a common way of solving problems, while face-to-face interaction allowed organizational members "to constitute a sense of knowing their colleagues, of knowing their credibility in and commitment to specific issues, and of knowing how to collaborate with them" (p. 259). Accomplishing this required extensive travel at times, but rotating meetings helped alleviate this, and the end result—the building and sustaining of effective relationships across cultures and work groups—was considered well worth the effort. These practices, in particular, link face-to-face communication with mediated communication in the context of effective work practices.

Three other practices—aligning effort, learning by doing, and supporting participation—enabled organizational members to be "consistent, competent, and creative across a variety of technical, geographic, historical and cultural boundaries"

(p. 256). Giddens (1984), of course, considers knowledge a vital resource for understanding how to get along, and views writing and information retrieval to be a key way in which institutions expand their control.

Time-space distanciation. Orlikowski and Yates (2002) developed another theme in Giddens' work, that of time-space distanciation. In particular, they focus on how time is enacted in organizations. After Giddens, they argue that temporality is enacted in situational practices and reproduced through the influence of institutional norms, such as, for example, in "tenure clocks." Building from a practice model, they argue that "temporal structures [are] both the medium and outcome of people's recurrent practices" and thus time also exhibits a duality of structure. Both clock time (like hours or days, measured in linear, equivalent units) and event time (like rites of passage, graduations, careers) are linked to social practices.

Time reflects natural time as well as social time. Some social practices, like retirement, incorporate aspects of both—age as a natural time element, and age as a social time, such as when is an appropriate age for retirement, which shifts as a function of social and personal needs. They raised fascinating questions about temporal structuring in organizations and argued that a better understanding of how time is structured, by what criteria, and by what supportive mechanisms, will enhance our understanding of organizations. They concluded that an analysis of time will reveal that it is not a fixed entity, but a resource that can be shaped to enhance personal and organizational effectiveness. (Also see related work by Ballard and Seibold, 2003; Flaherty, 1991, 1993.)

Fusing Goffman with structuration theory. One article by Orlikowski (1996) is of particular interest because of her focus on micro-level changes that illuminate situated changes in organizations. Of particular interest is her fusion of Goffman (on the micro-level) with structuration—the focus of this book. Orlikowski argued that situated changes occur as agents improvise, adjust and innovate their work routines over time. She noted that this view is an alternative to the "strong assumptions of rationality, determinism or discontinuity characterizing existing change perspectives" (p. 63). Her study of the appropriation of new technology in a software organization over a two-year time span found that change was incremental and occurred "through the ongoing, gradual, and reciprocal adjustments, accommodations, and improvisations enacted by the CSD (customer support division)" (p. 69). New practices and new work routines developed and expertise in problem-solving was shared across managers and specialists.

Specialists were able to keep electronic records of service calls and their resolution; this data was shared and each specialist's work became "electronically visible and accountable" (p. 76). What was formerly private and back-region—their research in solving customers' problems—now became front-region (or front-stage) and specialists now were actively involved in impression management (Goffman, 1959). Specialists were aware of the accessibility and visibility of the database to their supervisors. As one participant noted, "I'm very guarded in what I put into the database. I am always concerned about being politically correct, professional, diplomatic" (p. 77).

Orlikowski related this self-regulation to Foucault's panoptic discipline: when agents are aware of visible surveillance, they assume "responsibility for the constraints of power" (Foucault, 1972, pp. 202–3, cited by Orlikowski, p. 77). Some specialists, as Orlikowski noted, used the system to embellish their work (Goffman, 1974).

> Specialists continually engaging with and contributing to such a transparent electronic text changed how they represented themselves to others, engaging in the construction of professional electronic personae. Such constitution of the self was facilitated by the cognitive and normative awareness of how different their work practices were when they were mediated by the technology.
>
> *(Orlikowski, 1996, p. 78)*

Process documentation and evaluation processes reflected this shift from private to public work space.

In developing a global support system, various local sites needed to develop common working assumptions and expectations. The collaborative work norms developed in the U.S. CSD area had not yet developed in the overseas CSD support areas, in part because they had used the system for less time. The CSD managers in each geographic region exchanged ideas and developed a set of guidelines for support and expectations globally. Overall, changes occurred in the nature and texture of work (becoming more public and structured); in patterns of interaction (from face-to-face to electronic); distribution of calls (based on expertise); in the mechanisms of coordination (becoming cross-functional, global and continuous), and in the nature of knowledge (from tacit to formal, procedural and distributed) (p. 89). This study is significant for its assessment of the micro, locally situated actions of agents that transformed work practices globally, and exemplies the power of both Goffman's and Giddens' work when integrated.

As we have seen, very rich applications of Giddens' work has developed in the area of information technology and organizations. Using ST, scholars have been able to integrate action and interaction in using technology; focus on social practices associated with IT and IS, and document changing social practices in use of technology in particular organizational settings. Of particular interest is the application of Goffman's work in such research and its utility in exploring communicative patterns. We now turn to a variety of other ways in which structuration theory has been used to analyze communicating and organizing.

Structuration, Organizing and Communicating

In all these studies, structuration has been used to illuminate a range of organizing and communicating activities. These studies range from overarching analyses of entire organizations, to analyses of specific features of organizing such as management or knowledge creation, to analyses of mediated forms of communicating and their organizational impact.

Andrew Pettigrew's *The Awakening Giant* (1985) analyzed an organization using structuration theory. Pettigrew's approach, after Giddens, emphasized the importance of contextual analysis. He examined how agents, particularly executives, managers, and groups, used both structure and context to achieve their goals. Pettigrew also separated context into inner contexts (organizational climate and politics) and external contexts (such as economic, political and market trends). While his analysis encompassed an overall view of that organization, most scholars have used aspects of structuration theory to examine specific organizational processes. In what follows, I shall review some studies which have applied ST in more specific organizational processes.

Nested structuration. A number of organizational theoretical perspectives (such as contingency theory, configuration theory and congruence theory) have focused on the "goodness of fit" among organizational structures, the task and the external environment. Perlow, Gittell and Katz (2004) developed a nested theory of structuration, in which "the process of structuration may occur on multiple levels simultaneously, with each level of the mutually reinforcing relationship between action and structure itself in a mutually reinforcing relationship with structures at the next level ... patterns of interaction and elements of the organizational context appeared to create a mutually reinforcing relationship, which itself, as an entity, appeared to be reinforced by elements of the larger institutional context" (p. 533). Individual action interacts with patterns of interaction, which in turn interact with the organizational context, which subsequently interacts with the institutional context. (This is similar to Goffman's lamination, and I suggest such integrated, nested relationships can also be assessed by a synthesis of Goffman and Giddens, with the use of frames to reflect differing layers of context.)

Their study explored patterns of helping in three different organizations, and they identified three distinct helping patterns—expertise centered, team centered, and managerial centered helping patterns. Cultural value orientations influenced institutional orientations, which subsequently influenced individual values—each level "nesting" the next level. They concluded that structuration theory provides a way of understanding the interconnections—at multiple levels—that shape patterns of interaction at work. Because many scholars dealing with structuration theory are not well grounded in communicative processes, many ignore the dynamic, fluid nature of structuration theory via its grounding in interaction. This study is a noteworthy exception.

Structuration and organizational identity. Organizational identity and commitment have been of significant interest to scholars, both in terms of its theoretical as well as practical implications. Scott and Myers (2010) use the duality of structure as a framework for exploring how communication is used in negotiating organizational membership over time. They balance structural features of negotiation with the active participation of organizational members, and develop testable propositions for further research. Scott, Corman and Cheney (1998) developed a structurational model of organizational identification. Their model argued (1) that structurational duality is a duality of identity and identification; (2) that regionalization is used as a metaphor for the size, compatibility, multiplicity and potential conflicts among identities; and (3) that identification is viewed as situated or contextualized.

Identity is conceptualized, after Giddens, as a set of rules and resources that function as an "anchor for who we are" (p. 303). Thus, identity reflects one's core values, beliefs and preferences—they are "stable characteristics that make up the self" (ibid.). Identity is shaped and revealed through discourse, and has to be recognized to be activated. "Identity represents a type of knowledge about a part of our self that helps to produce and reproduce behaviors in specific social situations. Thus, important parts of any identity are usefully thought of as "memory traces" (ibid.). Scott et al. also noted that many facets of identity may be institutionalized, and that one may "treat identity as a feature of organizations" (p. 304). Giddens (1991a) also suggests that the public realm is "expanding, giving more people opportunities to participate, to adapt available knowledge and skills to their own purposes, informed by their own experience, and to make informed choices about society. ... From this perspective, organizations offer one means of dealing with modern uncertainties and anxieties, and their costs have to be considered in relation to the expansion of autonomy, enabling people to participate in diverse social networks, and to acquire considerable social and technical skills and knowledge" (Webb, 2006, p. 188).

Identification, then, is "the process of emerging identity ... [it] represents the forging, maintenance, and alteration of linkages between persons and groups. ... Identifications are more readily subject to change than are more enduring identities (as structures) ... [and] signify some degree of attachment to various social collectives or other targets" (Scott et al., 1998, pp. 303–4). The duality of identity and identification "involves the appropriation of identities in the expression of identifications, which in turn serve to reproduce, regionalize, and unify identities" (p. 306). As such, identities available to organizational members are resources and rules (structure) that are used to produce identification (at the social system level) (p. 307). Christensen and Cheney (1994) noted that, while identities may be fixed in time and space, they may also be connected to internal drives to separate the self from the environment. Identities are also both constraining and enabling because they reflect certain choices, and eliminate other possibilities. Finally, attachment—or the modality of identification and identity—involves both individual action as well institutional structures (Scott et al., 1998, p. 310).

Giddens' concept of regionalization is used to explore multiple identities and their interplay. Agents have different identities that "correspond to different identification targets, or resources of identity" (Scott et al., 1998, p. 312). Agents may identify with the organization as an entity, with subgroups within the organization, with their professional or occupational group, with their task and so forth—thus ranging across multiple groups and layers within an organization. Scott et al. suggest that four especially relevant identities in organizations are individual, work group, organizational, and occupational/professional identities. These four aspects of regionalization include: (1) *form* represents the overlapping and unique regions of identity; (2) *character* represents the front and back regions which reflect the positive identifications (front) and the disidentifications (back); this is also connected to Goffman's concept of face; (3) *duration* represents the time over which facets of identity have been salient to the agent; and (4) *scope* of the identity is represented by its size and scale. An intriguing study by Kuhn (2006) looks at time involvement as a reflection of an individual's effort to display a positive, distinctive workplace identity.

Finally, identification is conceptualized as situated. In this way, changes in identification can be noted situationally and over time (see also Carbaugh, 1996). For Giddens, social interaction is located in time and space, or in particular contexts which he terms locales. Much of social interaction consists of routines in particular contexts. Scott et al. use Corman and Scott's (1994) reticulation theory, which links activity and identification via communication—"focused activities form the contexts that situate reproduction of network relationships in communicative interaction" (Scott et al., 1998, p. 323). As an example, they noted that an engineer might identify with his work group when a group goal has been met, but identify more broadly with the organization when the organization receives a large contract.

As Scott et al. concluded, "the activities that define our situations shape and are shaped by the social interaction that is so important in the identification process. The expression of identifications that shapes and is shaped by our identities varies situationally. ... Importantly, activity may serve to provide the situational context in which perceived memberships (identity) become instantiated in interaction with others (identification)" (p. 324). A study by Manning (2010) looked at the formation of project networks as an example of the mutual interplay of position and practice, or in Giddens' terms 'position-practice relations'. In the context of organizational reform, Llewellyn (2004) looked at how organizational members used their commonsense, social categorizations to judge the appropriateness of reform activities.

Alvesson (2010) identifies seven key images for organizational identity: self-doubters, strugglers, surfers, storytellers, strategists, stencils, and soldiers. Giddens' view of identity as a "reflexively organized narrative, derived from participation in competing discourses and various experiences" is captured in Alvesson's identity images of surfers, storytellers and strategists.

Kuhn and Nelson (2002), following the structurational approach to identity developed by Scott et al., view identity as "*structural* in the sense that it is medium and outcome of discursive acts; it is a source from which individuals construct expressions of self based on collectively generated identity types, such as 'social worker'" (p. 7). As such, identities are individual cognitions as well as properties of social structures. They note that "Identification ... is a *discursive process* implicating, shaping, expressing, and transforming identity structures that occurs during coparticipation in coordinated (i.e., organizational) activity. ... Identities, then, are both sources of, and targets for, identifications" (p. 7). Thus, both individual and organizational identity structures mutually shape one another.

In their longitudinal analysis of a planned organizational change, they found similar patterns of identification across members central to a communication network, and found that organizational members' explanations of a controversial event reflected structured interests and claims on collective identity. This approach assesses the multiplicity and duality of organizational identification by incorporating a relational and activity-based perspective as well as reflecting individual and collective identity structures. (See also Kraidy, 2002.)

Another important aspect of situated identity is the cultural context of identity. Das, Dharwadkar and Brandes (2008) examined the multiple social identities and multiple foci of workplace identities that face organizational members in emerging global workforces. After Giddens (1991a) they noted that "globalization is a form of an intrusion of distance into local, everyday lives" and that identity negotiations need to incorporate national and religious identities at work (p. 1500). Globalization effects also have to be explored in situations of non-traditional, non-face-to-face work arrangements (p. 1522). Their study of an international call center in India found that national identity centrality was negatively associated with workers' performance and positively related to their intention to leave. They concluded that organizational identity and occupational identity needed to be balanced with national identity centrality among employees.

Lammers and Barbour (2002) applied structuration theory to an analysis of physicians' identities in managed care arrangements in the US In their survey of physicians in three cities, they found that the region of the country influenced professional and managerial identities. Managed care varies throughout the US, and as physicians' status changed, their ontological security decreased. They found that professional commitment was strongest in areas where managed care penetration is lowest, although professional identity remained strong over all participants.

Identity and commitment also surfaced in considerations of work/life balance. In an analysis of work/family benefits, Kirby and Krone (2002) analyzed workers' discourse surrounding family leave and the contradictions between corporate policies and organizational members' behavior. Organizational members perceived negative responses from colleagues when taking family leave. Kirby, Wieland and McBride used structuration theory to conceptualize work/life conflict. Their overview of extant research linked individual interactions to societal concerns. As they noted, "microlevel interactions and macrolevel structures are mutually constitutive" (Kirby, Wieland & McBride, 2006, p. 328). They argued that work/life conflict occurred with respect to time, stress and behavior. Their findings reflect the interrelated influences of work and life on one another (i.e., looking at work-in-life [WIL] factors as well as life-in-work [LIW] factors). Stress in life has a negative correlation with job satisfaction and, similarly, low job satisfaction negatively influences life outside of work. In their suggestions for future research, Kirby et al. argued for the inclusion of more macro-level influences, such as economic, political, and cultural forces. A study by Tracy and Rivera (2010) also found male executives' treatment of women at work reflected their ambivalence toward and preference for gendered relationships in the private sphere. This ambivalence reflects a conflict over work-place identities for women. (See Butler & Modaff, 2008; Kirby et al., 2006; Knuth, 2000; Orlikowski, 2007; Pal & Buzzanell, 2008; and Nippert-Eng, 1996, for discussions about how new technologies have altered work.)

A structurational model of identification has many significant advantages. First, the process of structuration helps link identity and identification. It highlights the importance of communication in identification and the multiplicity of identities. Second, the contextualized nature of identification is also highlighted by structuration theory. Finally, a structuration model integrates many factors, such as culture, work/family balance, social positioning and so forth, and their influence on identity and identification.

Organizational culture. Organizational culture may be viewed as "contextually established modes of signification and legitimation" (Sydow & Windeler, 1997, p. 471). Using structuration theory, Riley's analysis of organizational culture (1983) looked at political images contrasting how two firms operated (both partnerships were owned by a parent corporation). Riley examined the material, action and verbal elements of the firms' discourse, and assessed them using Giddens' modalities of signification, domination and legitimation. At one firm, Riley found very high levels of politicking, with internal competition highly encouraged. She concluded that structuration theory was useful in identifying the differences in corporate culture across the two firms, and in locating contradictions within each firm.

A closely related aspect of organizations, organizational climate, was explored in a study by Bastien, McPhee and Bolton (1995), drawing upon earlier work by Poole and McPhee (1983; Poole, 1985) on climate. Climate was defined as shared activities and practices deemed important by organizational members and reflected in texts, discourse and action. In this case study, when examining changes after a newly elected CEO took over, Bastien et al. assessed kernel themes, surface themes, climate production processes, and processes of interpretation. Kernel themes (deeply held beliefs) emerged around issues of cost-cutting and secrecy. Cost-cutting decisions were made in secrecy, and thus the two kernel themes reproduced and institutionalized these practices. Surface climate themes of seduction and abandonment emerged in organizational members' stories about their organizational experiences. Finally, trust—an important issue in Giddens' analysis of modernity—emerged as a critical issue.

A study by Witmer (1997) explored deeply layered social interactions in a large chapter of Alcoholics Anonymous (AA), and the local chapter's relationship with the global organization. In particular, Witmer examined how the disembedded local chapter was transformed and recreated. Communicative actions were central to the transformational process, and included dyadic meetings, speaking at weekly chapter meetings, telephone conversations, and group discussions. The founder of the local chapter instantiated certain social practices (e.g., dress codes, shaking hands) which were not part of global organizational practices. The founder dominated the local chapter and instantiated a strong cultural identification with sobriety and service, but also acknowledged individual differences (i.e., individual members' narratives about their struggles).

Organizational knowledge. With the advent of the information age, rapid access to accurate, relevant knowledge has become increasingly important. Studies of new information technologies, reviewed previously, are part of that growing research area. Other scholars, however, are working on the acquisition of knowledge itself, and trying to understand how it is developed, shared and modified by organizational members. The model of communication developed in this book emphasizes, as does Giddens (and Goffman for that matter!), the importance of knowledgeable agents in organizing and communicating. (See also Nonaka & Krogh, 2009.)

A number of studies have pursued knowledge acquisition and management from a structurational perspective. Smoliar (2003) suggested that all three dimensions of Giddens' structuration theory (legitimation, signification and domination) can be usefully applied to managing knowledge rather than simply exchanging information. Using structuration theory, Berends, Boersma and Weggeman (2003) explored how organizational learning occurred in an industrial research laboratory. Social practices reflected organizational learning, and knowledge was distributed over a diverse range of practices, over time and space, and involved a number of organizational members. Members used rules and resources in changing their social practices. Studies by Parsons (2010) and Peters, Gassenheimer and Johnston (2009) explored organizational learning and knowledge in the context of marketing using a structurational approach.

Hargadon and Fanelli used structuration theory to develop an integrated perspective on organizational knowledge. Organizational knowledge is "the product of an ongoing and recursive interaction between empirical and latent knowledge, between knowledge as action and knowledge as possibility" (Hargadon and Fanelli, 2002, p. 290). Latent knowledge is reflected by schemata which identify representations of relevant situations, but also incorporate interdependent scripts, goals and the identities of others in these situations. Utilizing Goffman (1959) as well, they noted that individual identities relate to established roles, and that their identities shape the appropriate goals/scripts available to them. Such schemata are also "powerfully influenced by the surrounding social *milieu*, and as a result members of an organization often come to hold similar schemata" (p. 294). In an investigation of knowledge and innovation at two organizations, they found that while a variety of views may enhance novelty, at the same time it might weaken the "single-mindedness" needed for allocating resources. They concluded that firms may "need their clients for generating action as much as their clients need them for generating possibilities" (ibid., p. 299). Organizational knowledge, in their view, lies in the cyclical interaction between latent and empirical knowledge among organizational members. Accuracy in "knowing who knows what" was found to be more important to team effectiveness than accessing information from repositories (Child & Shumate, 2007).

Canary and McPhee (2009) combined structuration with cultural-historical activity theories in order to analyze how individuals develop policy knowledge. Their study explored how participants from various organizations and members of the general public interacted to construct their policy knowledge. Policy language, common metaphors, and various policy documents interpreted by professionals helped regularize practices and influenced parent-professional interactions on policy issues. Canary (2010) developed structurating activity theory (an integration of structuration theory and cultural-historical activity theory) to examine how policy knowledge is communicatively structured. Four theoretical aspects are developed: structuration through activity, mediation of social activity, intersections of activity systems, and contradictions. In particular, structurating activity theory "can potentially identify various knowledge constructing processes that depend upon and result in a variety of forms of knowledge" (p. 44).

In the context of public dialogue, Burkhalter, Gastil and Kelshaw (2006) propose that structuration theory provides a conceptualization of the self (reflexive, thoughtful and deliberative) that is a useful model for public, face-to-face deliberation. Utilizing Giddens' structuration theory, Kim and Kim (2008) suggest that "informal and nonpurposive everyday political talk, the practical form of dialogic deliberation, is the fundamental underpinning of deliberative democracy" (p. 51). Norton (2007) also argues that Giddens' structure-action model provides a useful platform for examining public participation in environmental issues.

Strategic communication. Giddens suggests that strategic conduct rests upon actors' knowledge. A number of studies have looked at structuration theory as a way of assessing strategic actions and agency. Strategic processes also involve administrative and other social practices (Jarzabkowski, 2005).

Framing strategic discourse as part of strategic decision-making, Hendry (2000) explored how alternative options were discussed, and strategic actions initiated and authorized. In particular, Hendry wanted to develop an integrated conceptualization that allows analysis of the choices, actions and interpretations in the strategy process. The interpretative perspective conceptualizes decision-making as a process of retrospective sensemaking (Weick, 1995). Through using Giddens' structuration theory, these processes of meaning creation may be viewed "as both creating and being constrained by the deeper social structures of language and signification, power and domination, legitimation and sanction. It is through the creation of decisions that strategic actions are defined and legitimated and the power structure of the organization maintained" (p. 962). Giddens' framework "incorporates elements of both social constructivism and individual intentional action" (p. 963) and can be used to explore emergent strategizing (p. 966). Hendry argues that strategy, when viewed as a social practice, relies on strategic discourse to mediate between cognition and action in the change process. Constant alignment of action and interpretation, through language, is necessary so that appropriate social structures and interactions for a new strategy can be created. Hendry argues that this structurational, discourse-oriented approach will offer a very rich conceptualization of strategy, in particular helping to develop a new way of talking about the changes being instituted.

A very intriguing study by Mantere and Vaara (2008) examined differences in discourse that encouraged or limited participation in strategy processes. In their study of strategy work in 12 organizations, Mantere and Vaara (2008) found three practices that encouraged participation (self-actualization, dialogization and concretization) and three discourse practices that limited participation (mystification, disciplining and technologization). They concluded that strategic processes in organizations may involve competing discourse practices.

Using an ethnographic analysis, Samra-Fredericks (2003) examined strategists' talk-based interactive routines and assessed their linguistic skills and forms of knowledge for strategizing. As Samra-Fredericks argued, a close analysis of language-in-use will reveal its connection to cultural resources, and the influence of particular strategists on the decision-making process. In particular, minor moves and lamination were examined to connect interaction with broader outcomes. Reframing the past in terms of potential future actions was found to be an important, influential strategic skill. (See also Samra-Fredericks, 2004a, b, for an analysis of managerial elites' discussion of shaping the strategic direction for an organization, and Samra-Fredericks, 2007, on social constructionism in organizations.)

A study focusing on the use of strategy teams found that "the acting and knowing of these teams is dynamic, collective and distributed within the multi-business firm" (Paroutis & Pettigrew, 2007, p. 99). In a longitudinal, three-year study of strategy teams, using both interview data and documentary evidence, they found that strategic practices across diverse areas of the organization were both recursive and adaptive. Within a single team, participants were executing, reflecting and initiating. Across teams, practices involved coordinating, supporting and collaborating. A final practice, shaping context, refers to activities that would eventually alter the structural and organizational context in which strategy was developed. They also found that strategy teams' activities evolved over time.

Inter-firm networks. Inter-firm networks span organizations and thus are characterized by dispersed, fractured social practices in which the dominant financial parties tend to exert most control (Sydow & Windeler, 1997). Firms try to calculate their potential advantages and, more than independent organizations, need to balance autonomy/dependence, trust/control, cooperation/competition, and stability/change. They also need to cope with contradictions among these dimensions and the economic context in which they operate. They concluded that structuration theory provided a knowledge base which enabled managers to more fully understand the structural features, rules of signifying and legitimation, and the resources of domination which characterize inter-firm relations.

Another study examined two structuration concepts—the duality of structure and the recursiveness of practice—and their influence on organizing networks. They concluded that inter-firm network processes can be viewed as "full of tensions and contradictions, governed by a dialectic of control. ... Thus tensions and contradictions, such as those between commitment and disagreement, ... efficiency and innovativeness, trust and control, cooperation and competition, stability and flexibility, autonomy and dependence, talk and action ... should be taken into account in interorganizational practices within interfirm networks" (Sydow & Windeler,

1998, p. 280). In addition, they emphasized, after Giddens, the importance of the sociocultural context surrounding the organization, especially economic practices in space and time.

Management studies. In a three-year case study of mill ownership, Spybey (1997) utilized Giddens' structuration theory to explore the distinct "frames of meaning" managers used to guide and to explain their actions. Through a series of open-ended interviews with 15 managers, a set of issues emerged which were common to all managers, such as relationships between manufacturing units and ownership/control of the firm. Two distinct managerial approaches were discovered, a traditional model advocating the values of the industrial wool-man, in contrast to younger managers who were professionally trained in other industries, and sought to apply more control over the manufacturing units.

Spybey contrasted the two groups of managers on their views of structural properties, modalities and structuration. The traditionalists were generally concerned with manufacturing standards and specialist skill while the professional group was focused more on investment return and managerial control. Disputes arose because of the differing perspectives and social practices sanctioned by each group. For example, the traditionalists did not see the value in the reporting documents established by the professionals. The case study tended to confirm the dominance and influence of financial capital, and the universalist values of professionals on profit return and control. Spybey concluded that structuration theory provides a very useful perspective on organizational culture, and on the systems of logic (frames of meaning or signification) that managers and subcultures utilize to account for their actions. (See also Spybey, 1984a, b for an analysis of frames of meaning used by managers.)

Whittington (1992, 1997) reviewed Giddens' contribution to analyzing managerial agency and leadership. While managerial control within organizations is likely to be incomplete because of the participation of diverse agents within the organization, purposive action is still possible (Giddens, 1985a, p. 186). Agents may also confront a variety of different structures that seem out of their control (Giddens, 1985b, p. 168). Yet organizations, which are purposive and reflexive, can collectively alter social systems. Whittington concluded that managerial agency included (1) the ambiguity and plurality of rules which can be followed at the manager's discretion, and (2) the contradictions which may arise from internal rules being challenged by cross-cutting systems of action and/or diverse perspectives being introduced as a result of managers' multiple organizational memberships (Whittington, 1997, p. 377).

After Giddens, Whittington outlined social systems (types of activity systems) and their structural bases for action. For example, given intellectual activity systems, the dominant structures are academic and professional; the basic resources are expertise and legitimacy; the basic rules are professional codes; and the major organizations consist of professional bodies and universities (ibid., p. 378). Furthermore, "Exploiting their own plural social identities, and those of others they need to influence, managers may exploit rules and resources from other systems in order to empower or legitimate their conduct at work" (ibid., p. 379). Thus managers draw on "resources and inspiration from all of their social identities" (p. 380).

Additionally, from a structurationist perspective, "leadership is not simply a matter of individual managers' personal psychological qualities ... but also dependent on the resources—capital, professional status, ethnic or gender privilege—made available by their specific social identities ... a manager's particular status within immediate social systems defines the symbolic resources at his or her disposal. Studies of organizational cultures should, therefore, not be made in isolation from the broader societies in which they are set, but rather explore the linkages between particular organizations and the social structural positions of their members. ... In this way, managerial agency can boil down to quite fundamental questions of social identity." (ibid., pp. 381–82).

Narratives. Narrative networks seek to highlight both the potential and realized interconnections between agents and actions. Building upon structuration, actor-network theory and organizational routines, Feldman & Pentland (2003; Pentland & Feldman, 2007) suggested that "Different interconnections make different stories, transforming the context. ... The networks we talk about, thus, are ... a means of making movement visible" (Pentland & Feldman, 2007, p. 781). After Simmel and Giddens, they view social forms in organizing as produced and reproduced in interaction. Their study of a narrative network sought to describe and compare patterns of interaction as they changed in the routine of purchasing airline tickets. Through purchasing an airline ticket, they created narratives from a number of different perspectives (e.g., the purchaser, technical support for computer systems, the airline representative) and thus linked actions across these narratives. They also noted alternative possible narratives and thus different routines. As they concluded, narratives "build in layers as are the processes in organizations ... the fragments are constructed through the actions of human and nonhuman actants. ... Increasingly, we find that organizational routines consist of modular, recombinable fragments that organizational designers, participants, and observers combine to create patterns that cohere through sequence, interdependence, and purpose" (Pentland & Feldman, 2007, p. 793).

Mumby (1987) used narratives to exemplify their role in legitimizing organizing practices. Narratives are a major symbolic form in which organizational ideology and power structures are constituted and expressed. His analysis of the IBM story pointed out that narratives do not "exist independently of the ideological meaning formations and power relations within which they are structured ... helping to position subjects within the historical and institutional context of the material conditions of existence" (pp. 125–26). Power is exercised through narratives because they "punctuate and sequence events in such a way as to privilege a certain reading of the world" (p. 126). Narratives have become increasingly recognized as important sources of information about organizing, as well as providing a lens through which to assess organizations. And, of course, stories are acknowledged as a major form of interaction, perhaps one of the most fundamental, in both oral and modern cultures.

Analysis of formal organizational channels of communication. McPhee (1988) explored vertical hierarchies or chains of command utilizing structuration theory. Such hierarchies were produced and reproduced on three different levels: (1) the executive level comprised a number of individual chain of commands and formal mechanisms were used to coordinate involvement at lower levels; (2) the next level—the managerial level—designed work for the group they supervised, and this provided them with a broader perspective on the organization than their subordinates; and (3) at the lowest level, workers assumed the formal structure, and often believed themselves misunderstood by upper layers of command. Miscommunication and misunderstanding occurred frequently across levels. As Poole and McPhee (2005) noted, "hierarchy is not the same system of rules and resources for people throughout the organization; it varies in a complex way and creates different milieus at different levels. Structuration theory thus leads us to think of formal structure in a new way, as the product of divergent perspectives relating differently to the abstract organizational schema" (p. 187).

Social practices and routines. As we have seen, Giddens emphasizes routines and action in structuration theory. Miettinen, Samra-Fredericks and Yanow (2009) argue that scholars need to understand practice "as taking place simultaneously both locally and globally, being both unique and culturally shared, 'here and now' as well as historically constituted and path-dependent" (p. 1310). Routines occur in interaction, and in social practices.

A number of studies have explored the importance of social practices in organizing— for example, in Orlikowski's practice lens, or in Feldman's study of incremental change (2000). Howard-Grenville (2005) investigated routines in a high-tech manufacturing firm. In assessing a routine termed roadmapping (a practice of generating detailed plans of action, including different alternatives, and incorporating criteria for making decisions), she found that the embeddedness of the routine and the power of agents influenced the routine's flexibility and potential for change.

Agency—through the different orientations and intentions of individuals—shape the performance of routines. In a field study of recruitment interviewers, Llewellyn and Spence (2009) analyzed job interviews as a distinctive activity, characterized by social practices and based on knowledge that organizational members utilize and orient to. Kuhn and Jackson (2008) developed a social practice framework to examine how organizational members frame and respond to problematic situations in a call center.

Organizational innovation. Using structuration theory, Lewis and Seibold (1993) explored the process of innovation. In particular, they argued that structuration theory can examine how user characteristics and their perceptions of an innovation may influence their use of rules and resources in adapting to the innovation. A case study of innovation illustrated the utility of the structurational approach.

An organization's adaptive capacity can also be better understood through linking structuration theory with the adaptive processes of multiplexity, redundancy, and loose coupling (Staber & Sydow, 2002). Structuration theory acknowledges that outcomes flow from interaction in which organizational members use structures of signification, domination, and legitimation. Managers can help provide an interactional context which facilitates the evolution of adaptive capacities.

The dialectic of control. The dialectic of control in structuration reflects a tension between autonomy and dependence, and a tension arising over access to resources. Sherblom, Keranen and Withers (2002) explored these tensions in a study of professional transition in a game warden service. Efforts to transform the service into a more culturally and ethnically diverse state agency created tensions in the role of the game warden (which was traditionally defined by independence and competence). The structural dualities of organizational practices that emphasized independence shifted to more dependence, with game wardens becoming more reliant on formal communication and monitoring established by the organization. Job priorities, role expectations, the need for coordination with other agencies, and the shifting expertise required, were all sources of tension among game wardens. Structuration theory assisted in the identification of surface changes as well as the deep-seated tensions of change and control.

Contradiction. Contradiction often occurs when companies are merging and rampant uncertainty exists. For example, primary contradictions may arise because of the political and economic contexts surrounding a merger. Using structuration theory, Howard and Geist (1995) explored the discursive responses of organizational members to a merger. Organizational members positioned themselves in a dialectic of control with management as the merger unfolded. Ideological positioning was influenced by agents' sense of empowerment or powerlessness. Contradictions developed as a result of tensions between change versus stability, empowerment versus powerlessness, and identification versus estrangement. As they concluded, "Invincibility, diplomacy, betrayal and defection, as discursive responses to the merger, represent different causal maps with varying interpretations of members' control in the face of the shifting ground of the proposed merger" (p. 129). They suggested that mergers reflect "a dialectic of the local and global where the transformations of tradition and place influence and interconnect with self-identity" (p. 127).

Agency. Another case study of a merger followed a team of core planners for the merger between a Swedish and a British firm, looking at agential positioning and agential powers. Llewellyn (2007) focused on agential powers on the individual level—taking a structurational perspective that looks at what agents do, how they accomplish it, and what the consequences of their actions are. The value of structurational theory in this case study was to reveal the differing rules the group members used to guide their actions. Managerial agency was also found to be related to the organizational structure but also to broader cultural practices (Sahay & Walsham, 2007).

In addition, a structurational approach revealed the "taken-for-granted knowledge" of executives by asking them to discursively lay out charters for their own positions, and to explain how their work fit into the overall merger. As such, organizational members were taking context into account in their actions.

Llewellyn concluded that understanding agential power/knowledge "must encompass organizational rules and resources" (p. 151). This appears to be particularly important when different cultures are being interwoven, and tacit social practices may be quite divergent.

Organizational change. Feldman (2004) viewed change processes which examined how resources may be used as changeable sources of energy. In her analysis of change within the governance of university residence halls, Feldman suggested that "Resources enable actors to enact schemas. Resourcing is the creation in practice of assets such as people, time, money, knowledge, or skill; and qualitites of relationships such as trust, authority, or complementarity such that they enable actors to enact schemas" (p. 296). Thus, resourcing cycles can be diagrammed as: resources > schema > actions > resources. And this cycle repeats itself.

In dealing with students' difficulties with bulimia, the residence staff members' actions "made resources available that constrained and enabled the building directors' abilities to deal with situations, like the bulimia incidents" (p. 303). Changes were made in centralization of information, hiring, in the feelings of acceptance, and in being perceived as team players. Resistance developed around these changes as well. She argued that structuration theory is useful in understanding resources as active and created by actions, and thus influencing change. Like the Barley study (1986), this study exemplified the importance of changes in social practices and organizational routines and their consequences, both intended and unintended.

Temporal issues in organizing. A substantive aspect of Giddens' structuration theory is his time-space distanciation. As noted earlier time and space, in Giddens' theory, are distanciated such that both time and space have been stretched and coordinated, and thus are simultanously local and global. Ballard and Siebold (2000) suggested that communication is the means by which time and work are coordinated. Work patterns are also influenced by timing and temporal constraints. For example, tight time schedules may create tense communication among group members. In further work, Ballard and Seibold (2003) have proposed a meso-level theory of organizational temporality which is compatible with, and partially based upon, structuration theory (Seibold, personal communication, April, 2008). Their model argues that ten dimensions of time (such as scheduling, flexibility, and scarcity) and three communication structures (coordination methods, workplace technologies, and feedback cycles) influence organizational members' perceptions of time. They generate a number of hypotheses for further research and testing.

In an excellent review of temporal perspectives on groups, Arrow, Poole, Henry, Wheelan and Moreland (2004) pointed out that structuration is notable for its emphasis on time, especially different views of time as well as time-space distanciation. A temporal perspective on groups reflects the following assumptions: that time is socially constructed; that time is a resource; that time is a fundamental issue for theory and research; that groups change systematically over time—they develop; that group processes have temporal patterning; and that groups are characterized by nonlinear dynamics (p. 75).

Complex theories, such as structuration, assume that groups are influenced by a multitude of factors; that groups are composed of multiple levels within the group and between the group and its environment, and that groups are often unpredictable (pp. 92–93). Researchers look for a "hidden order of structures and structuring processes underlying the observable group" (p. 94). They point out that two types of factors influence structuration: (1) the characteristics of the group and its situation (such as the task, members' understanding of structures, differential access, and distribution of resources), and (2) the dynamics through which different structural aspects interact with each other (p. 95). Exemplars of this approach include the analysis of arguments and social influence in groups (Poole, Seibold & McPhee, 1986); group use of information technology (AST and other studies discussed in this chapter); and jury decision-making (Keough & Lake, 1993).

We have seen that structuration theory has been very effectively applied in a wide range of organizational contexts. As this chapter, as well as the discussion of methodology in the Appendix shows, the criticism that ST is difficult to use in conducting research is clearly unfounded. In sum, research applying structuration in a wide variety of organizing contexts has been reviewed in this chapter. As we have seen, scholars have integrated Giddens with other theoretical perspectives, such as institutional theory, or have significantly extended Giddens' work, as have Orlikowski, Poole and their colleagues. As we have also seen, his work thus has great value for organizing and organizations.

While our concern is to review Giddens' applicability to the area of organizing and communicating, it is important to point out its application to other areas of communication. With regard to family communication, Krone, Braithwaite and others have applied structuration to family relationships and also connected familial social practices to larger global practices. (See, for example, Baxter, Braithwaite & Nicholson, 1999; Hochschild, 2000; Kirby & Krone, 2002; Krone, Schrodt & Kirby, 2006.) In addition, Giddens' work provides insight into the study of intimacy and pure relationships (1990a, 1991a, 1992).

Giddens also argued the structuration is linked to social critique. As such, researchers contribute new knowledge to members of a social group. To assess the duality of structure, research can be undertaken in two different ways, each focusing on a distinct area—these are viewed as different areas of emphasis which has no clear-cut line drawn between them. Research may be conducted on institutions and "structural properties are treated as chronically reproduced features of social systems" (Giddens, 1984, p. 288). Or, one may focus on strategic conduct and give "primacy to discursive and practical consciousness, and to strategies of control within defined contextual boundaries" (ibid.). The institutional context is taken as given, but acknowledged as being "produced and reproduced through human agency … the following tenets [are] important in the analysis of strategic conduct: the need to avoid impoverished descriptions of agent' knowledgeability; a sophisti-cated account of motivation; and an interpretation of the dialectic of control" (ibid., pp. 288–89). Giddens offers an analysis of two educational studies that demonstrate the methodological issues he discusses, and incorporate both qualitative and quantitative methods (see Giddens, 1984, Chapter 6).

I have argued that Giddens and Goffman have complementary theoretical perspectives. The value of each perspective is enhanced by integrating them into the theory of structurational interaction. Goffman adds a process dimension to Giddens' work through his focus on the interaction order, while Giddens adds breadth to Goffman's work through a rich analysis of agency and structure, institutional contexts, and time-space distanciation.

However, before exploring their integration and the theory of structurational interaction, we must turn to a detailed examination of Goffman's interaction order, how it complements structuration theory and provides a rich analysis of social interaction. Like Giddens, Goffman is a prolific scholar whose work is widely known in a number of disciplines. As we explore Goffman's work, we will see recurrent themes, such as interpretive schemes, frames, the importance of time and space, understanding the context in which organizing and communicating occurs, and other themes that also permeate Giddens' work.

SECTION III

Goffman on Communicating and Organizing

Thus far, frame theory has been used to analyze how humans process information, and thus make sense of the world. Frames not only reflect world knowledge or tacit, commonsense knowledge, but also categorize others' actions and identify social situations. We have also used frame theory to develop conceptualizations of both organizing and communicating. As mentioned previously, in order to provide an integrated framework for analyzing and understanding organizing and communicating, I will synthesize the work of Giddens and Goffman into a theory of structurational interaction. Giddens' structuration theory relies upon human interaction. As we have seen, Giddens argues that Goffman's interaction order is a necessary prerequisite for the integration of social systems, and thus his own structuration theory.

In this next section, I turn to the work of Goffman for a more precise analysis of communicative processes, for the framing of communicative contexts, and for understanding organizing contexts. I shall also review some of the research applying Goffman to analyzing organizations and organizational activities. We shall begin by looking more closely at Goffman's interaction order.

Goffman provides a detailed analysis of communicating. How do individuals interact daily with one another, and develop a mutual understanding of an encounter that allows them to live their lives? Goffman argues that actors (agents) align themselves with one another to accomplish their goals, and use face-work to present themselves to others. This micro-level of interaction Goffman terms framing, and at this level the concrete details of interaction are examined in specific social settings. Like Giddens, Goffman relies on commonsense knowledge or the knowledge of "how to go along" that underlies much of daily interaction.

In Chapter 8, key concepts in Goffman's frame theory will be discussed. Social integration (interaction) is essential for social systems, organizations and social institutions. Goffmanian constructs such as frames, alignment, footing, keying and rekeying, and so forth will be developed. In Chapter 9, concepts of the self, identity, face and face-work will be developed. Although Goffman has been criticized for ignoring social institutions in his theorizing, this is not the case. In Chapter 10, we will examine how Goffman's ideas have been applied in organizational settings, as well as taking a look at Goffman's own work on total institutions.

Communication is necessary for all shared social activity. It is Goffman's close scrutiny of daily interaction that illuminates the complex and continuous adjustments that such interaction requires.

8

ERVING GOFFMAN'S INTERACTION ORDER

An Introductory Overview

Erving Goffman is regarded as one of the leading sociologists of the twentieth century. His work continues to significantly influence ethnomethodology, symbolic interaction, discourse analysis and other areas within sociology, as well as being widely read and used in other disciplines such as political science, communication and history. It is to Goffman that we credit concepts such as the 'interaction order,' 'frames,' 'ritual,' 'the social self,' 'face,' 'the presentation of self' and 'performance' (See, for example, Goffman, 1956a, 1965, 1979 and 1983a). His writing was witty, brilliant and insightful.

What his contributions are, and will be, remain controversial, but his work continues to inspire significant scholarship on interaction. Branaman (2003) emphasized the importance of Goffman's work in providing "an integrative framework for considering the interrelationship of self, emotions, status structures, and resistance and agency … until another scholar emerges that equals Goffman's ability to provide the sustained and multifaceted analysis of interaction and inequality implicit in his work, I think much can be gained by returning to Goffman to 'compare notes' on theoretical conceptions and empirical research findings" (pp. 119–20).

Goffman himself characterized his overall purpose as analyzing

> the general cognitive issue that, moment to moment, individuals are (or can easily be made to be) concerned to identify what it is that is going on; that this involves a question as to what sort of activity is in progress, and whether deception is involved or open simulation; further, that activities of any kind, whether involving fabrication or keying or both or neither, are geared as such into the ongoing world, so that a characterization of how these activities are framed is not merely a participant's cognition. In developing this concern, I

focused on episodes of face-to-face activity, especially points where cognitive issues seemed most likely to occur: an episode's bracketing conventions, its laminative depth, its tolerance or intolerance for various types of out-of-frame activity, its potential for misframing, its vulnerability to disorganization. The warrant here is ... that our understandings of our own long-term relationships and commitments, and of our society's widely institutionalized enterprises, will be subject to confirmation and undermining during these occasions.

(Goffman, 1981b, p. 68)

(See also the work of Herrera Gomez & Soriano Miras, 2004a, b for discussions of Goffman and his views on daily life activities.)

Randall Collins, a leading scholar on Goffman's work, offered an excellent overview of Goffman's work, which incorporated his work on rituals, frames and the dramaturgical metaphor.

In Goffman's later work, especially *Frame Analysis* (1974) and *Forms of Talk* (1981), he describes quite complicated situational realities: frames around frames, rehearsals, recountings, debriefings, make-believes, lectures, broadcasting troubles, performer's self-revelations. These indicate the subtleties that make up the differences among formality and informality, relationships that take place on the frontstage and various kinds of backstages. Although the terminology is different, Goffman is in effect adding complexities to the basic model: situations are rituals calling for cooperation in keeping up the momentary focus of attention and thus giving respect both to the persons who properly take part and to the situational reality as something worth a moment of being treated seriously ... all these frames are ways in which attention is focused. This allows us to connect with the theatrical model. ... In effect the frontstage is the situation where attention is focused, incorporating some public who joins in the focusing; the backstage is where work is done to prepare so the focusing can be effectively carried out.

(Collins, 2004, p. 24)

Various kinds of relationships are analyzed with regard to the demeanor and deference shown across strangers, acquaintances, and the obligations of intimacy. In a four volume overview of Goffman's work, edited by Fine and Smith (2000), five core themes in his work are identified: the interaction order; the self; frames; stigma; and total institutions (see also Gronfein, 2000). All of these themes are relevant to our concerns about organizing and communicating, but let us focus primarily upon the interaction order, the self, and frames.

The Interaction Order

Erving Goffman was instrumental in establishing face-to-face interaction, the interaction order, as a specific area of study. He defined social interaction "as that which uniquely transpires in social situations, that is, environments in which two or more individuals are physically in one another's response presence" (Goffman, 1983a, p. 2). As Goffman noted, social life is a process of consciously and intentionally generating information to influence others (Goffman, 1959, pp. 3–4).

For our purposes, face-to-face interaction and social beliefs are critical features for organizing and communicating. When talk is viewed from an interactional perspective, Goffman stated that "it is an example of that arrangement by which individuals come together and sustain matters having a ratified, joint, current, and running claim upon attention, a claim which lodges them together in some sort of intersubjective, mental world" (Goffman, 1981a, p. 71). As Ellis pointed out, "Goffman's description of a frame is a social representation through which people structure experience, and these frames ... are the organizational principles and strategies by which situations are defined. What is important here is that social representations, situation prototypes in particular, move the self out of individual psychology and into the interactional world" (Ellis, 1999, p. 84).

Much of Goffman's work is concerned with the interactional order and the presentation of the social self in interaction. While his work has implications for social order, his primary interest focused on the interaction order, and how participants arrive at and maintain a "working consensus" that allows them to carry on their daily lives. As such, meaning "is an interactional achievement ... the product of a working consensus; a commitment to the interaction order" (Rawls, 2000, p. 261).

In social encounters, participants try to project "claims to an acceptable self" and to confirm "like claims on the part of others. The contributions of all are oriented to these and built up on the basis of them" (Goffman, 1967, pp. 105–6). Thus, Goffman notes that participants "are likely to find that they must accept the individual on faith, offering him a just return while he is present before them in exchange for something whose true value will not be established until after he has left their presence" (Goffman, 1959, pp. 2–3).

Goffman used frames to conceptualize the moment-to-moment "working consensus" participants develop as to "what is going on here." Frame analysis thus outlined the interactional devices people use in making sense of their lived experience.

> My perspective is situational, meaning here a concern for what individuals can be alive to in a particular moment, this often involving a few other particular individuals and not necessarily restricted to the mutually monitored arena of a face-to-face gathering. I assume that when individuals attend to any current situation, they face the question: "What is it that's going on here?" ... the question is put and the answer to it is presumed by the way the individuals then proceed to get on with the affairs at hand. ...
>
> My aim is to try to isolate some of the basic frameworks of understanding available in our society for making sense out of events and to analyze the special vulnerabilities to which these frames of reference are subject. ... I assume that definitions of a situation are built up in accordance with

> principles of organization which govern events—at least social ones—and our
> subjective involvement in them; frame is the word I use to refer to such of
> these basic elements as I am able to identify.
>
> *(Goffman, 1974, pp. 10–11)*

As Czarniawska (2006b) noted, for both Weick and Goffman, "no solid essence
in social life can actually exist. As long as there is life, it is moving and changing
shape" (p. 1662). Thus, social interaction requires continual alignment among participants. Instead of using breaches to uncover tacit understandings about rules of
conduct, Goffman focused on rules of irrelevance "which instruct participants about
what they should and should not make the focus of their attention during interaction" (ibid.). (See also Goffman, 1961b.)

The interactional order is usually circumscribed in space and time. It is clear that
individuals need to spend time in one another's presence, as in, for example, using
specialized equipment, sharing space in a public library or in a family setting, or
caring for a toddler. As Goffman observed

> When in each other's presence individuals are admirably placed to share a
> joint focus of attention, perceive that they do so, and perceive this perceiv-
> ing. … Speech immensely increases the efficiency of such coordination, being
> especially critical when something doesn't go as indicated and expected.
> (Speech, of course, has another special role, allowing matters sited outside the
> situation to be brought into the collaborative process.)
>
> *(Goffman, 1983a, p. 3)*

By being able to see and hear others, we are able to make two important
judgments: one is categoric (such as age or gender) and one is individual (for
example, are you John or Tom?). Thus, face-to-face interaction enables intimate
collaboration, correction of problematic understandings, and reference to other
distant contexts.

Gumperz (2001), like Goffman, viewed the interaction order or communicative
practices as a "distinct level of discursive organization bridging the linguistic and the
social" (p. 216). Gumperz noted that "Goffman has given us the outline of a communicative perspective on the social world. … Among the questions that concern
him are: how can we distinguish among various possible kinds of face-to-face
gathering? What are the observable interactive signs by which we can describe
the types of involvement that mark them? … he points out that 'framing' can be
viewed as something like a filtering process through which societal-level values and
principles of conduct are transformed and refocused so as to apply to the situation at
hand" (p. 217). Gumperz' concept of activity type, or activity, operates like
Goffman's frames in that they are both "abstract representations of the actions of
actors engaged in strategically planning and positioning their moves in order to
accomplish communicative ends in real-life encounters" (p. 222).

Talk is an important element of social interaction, but interaction analysis also needs to incorporate nonverbal actions as well as physical activity (Goffman, 1976, pp. 283–90). As Williams noted

> For Goffman then, the analysis of talk as a form of conduct is to be focused on moves and their organization within social encounters. We may legitimately go on to ask: what are the organising or structuring principles which lie behind patterns of moves such that they occur in the way that they do within such settings?
>
> An answer to this question requires us to take into account two direct principles of their structuring as well as a mediating condition. The two direct principles are those of communicative and ritual requirements, and the mediating condition is that of "context" or "frame."
>
> *(Williams, 1980, p. 219)*

Thus, for Goffman, moves reflect a "full stretch of talk or its substitutes which have a distinctive unitary bearing on some … circumstances in which participants find themselves" (1976, p. 272). It is important to note that moves can be nonverbal as well as linguistic.

The orderliness of the interaction order, as conceived by Goffman, is outlined by Colomy and Brown (1996):

> A diverse constellation of social and psychological conditions contribute to that orderliness—an ostensively pan-human need for face-to-face interaction rooted in universal preconditions of social life, the psychological untenability of participating in encounters that regularly break down and, more immediately, in what Goffman variously refers to as trans-situational regulations and expectations, information about situational proprieties as well as individual and categoric frameworks for classifying coparticipants, the cognitive relations between actors (what each can effectively assume the other knows), and a large storehouse of shared understandings and self-imposed restraints.
>
> *(1996, p. 308)*

In analyzing interaction, Goffman (1974) focused on frames and argued that "Frames are a central part of a culture and are institutionalized in various ways. They are subject to change historically. … Whatever the idiosyncrasies of their own motives and interpretations, they [individuals] must gear their participation into what is available by way of standard doings and standard reasons for doing these doings" (Goffman, 1981b, p. 63). Like language, frames are capable of generating a multiple set of responses across different contexts (Goffman, 1974, p. 236).

The interactional order highlighted the social practices and knowledge that allow people to develop a working consensus about what is going on here in this particular situation. Goffman's frame analysis is a rich analysis of context and the tacit knowledge we use when interacting. In *Frame Analysis* (Goffman, 1974), "core ideas struck a chord with social scientists and cognitive scientists" and they picked up on concepts of his prior work (Fine, Manning & Smith, 2000).

Frames are used to identify different types of activities in the Batesonian sense (Bateson, 1972) and are also used to establish genuine as well as fabricated activities, building from Goffman's use of dramaturgical, theatrical metaphors (ibid.). Frame analysis also incorporates elements of strategic interaction, and the use of moves to help define situations (ibid.). Finally, frames reflect occasions of interaction. These occasions have "a distinctive ethos, a spirit, and emotional structure, that must be properly created, sustained, and laid to rest" (Goffman, 1967, p. 19). In short, frames ask "about the central working principles that animate any particular mode of activity. 'Frame analysis' is the attempt to become cognizant of the rules of cognition and communication that are bound up with the production of any world" (Gonos, 1977, p. 858). Bloomaert et al. (2005) noted that "Frames are also the focus of interaction in the sense that Goffman invites analytic attention to the dynamics and flux of implicit and explicit spatial boundary marking as part of the monitoring and mounting of activities, often with short- or long-lived relationships of inclusion and exclusion as a result" (p. 207).

Social interaction occurs in social situations. And Goffman suggested that mediated situations, with the use of email and the telephone, provide a "reduced version" of the physical copresence, face-to-face interaction in social situations. It may be reasonable, then, to abstract principles from Goffman's analysis of the interactional dynamics of physical copresence, and to apply them to situations involving telecommunications and virtual presence. (As we shall see in Chapter 10, which focuses on applying Goffman's work in organizational settings, scholars have applied Goffman's ideas to mediated communication.) Goffman also cautions us to separate what is merely located in face-to-face encounters from that which cannot occur except in face-to-face encounters (Goffman, 1983a, p. 3).

Rawls (2000) suggested that Goffman has also addressed the agency–structure dichotomy which is a central concern in approaches to organizational communication and argues that elements of Goffman's interaction order deal with this dichotomy. These elements consist of the following. (1) Goffman argues that "a social self that is continually achieved in and through interaction … places constraints on the interaction order and supplies intrinsic motivation for compliance." (2) These constraints "define the interaction order, but also may resist and defy social structure." (3) "There is order and meaning to actions whenever there is an implicit commitment of concerted action." And (4) individuals "must commit themselves to the ground rules of interaction in order for selves to be maintained … [it] is a moral, not structural imperative" (Rawls, 2000, p. 253). Thus, Goffman argued that agency and structure are interwoven in interaction, and both constraint and enablement are possible.

Goffman also anticipated the post-modern subject with his emphasis on the social self, and the deconstruction of the individual self (Battershill, 1990). As Goffman noted, individuals or selves are a product of "joint ceremonial labor" (Goffman, 1967, pp. 84–85) and located in "manifold attachments and commitments to multi-situated social identities" (Goffman, 1961b, p. 142).

As can readily be seen with this brief overview, his work is very important in understanding communication and its complexities. His insights also apply to organizational settings, and he discussed, although not in great detail, how interactional practices vary in organized settings. In this latter respect, Goffman's work on total institutions and service encounters is very useful. As suggested previously, Giddens' work addressed questions surrounding organizing and organizations, and the socio-historical contexts of organizations, while Goffman provided us with a detailed analysis of ordinary interaction. In fact, Giddens (1988) himself suggested that the interaction order links macro-systems (like institutions and societies) with the individual. We now turn to a thorough analysis of Goffman's interactional order and frames as an approach to studying communicating. (See Table 8.1 for an outline of frames and framing covered in this chapter.)

TABLE 8.1 Goffman's Frame Analysis*

I. Underlying Assumption
  a. Felicity Condition
II. Interactional Principles
  a. Situational propriety
  b. Situational involvement
  c. Accessibility
  d. Civil inattention
  e. Keying, rekeying, and fabrication
  f. Anchoring
III. System and Ritual Requirements for Interactional Processes
  a. System requirements
  b. Ritual requirements
IV. Framing—interaction in social situations
  a. Interactional devices
    i. Anchoring devices
    ii. Moves
    iii. Embedding
    iv. Bracketing
    v. Participant status
      1. Speakers
      2. Listeners
    vi. Messages
  b. Interactional practices
    i. Projected lines
    ii. Ritual respect
    iii. Face and facework
    iv. Remedial practices
    v. Accounts
    vi. Territories of the self

* This attempts to include the most central aspects of Goffman's work with respect to interaction. Any errors in categorization are mine.

Elements of Goffman's Interaction Order

In his dissertation studying the community of Baltasound (Dixon), Goffman argued that interaction is one type of social order. Conversational interaction reflects a social order in that:

1. Different participants produce and exchange communicative acts.
2. Participants have expectations that limit the behaviors of the interactants.
3. Appropriate conversational contributions are motivated by immediate sanctions (i.e., approval or disapproval of behavior).
4. Conversational interactions occur within a wider social context.
5. When conversational rules are ambiguous or uncertain, embarrassment and social disorganization occurs.
6. Participants who break conversational rules create embarrassment; to avoid embarrassment, one uses the footing which gives him the least self-threatening position in the situation or the most defensible alignment possible.
7. People who offend, by not following appropriate conversational rules to establish the orderliness of the interaction, need correctives to restore the conversational order (i.e., apologies, accounts).
8. Participants use conversational rules to pursue private goals as well as the ends of the conversation itself. (These interactional elements are similar to those set out in our communication model, see Chapter 2.)

From the beginning of his career, Goffman set out his agenda for focusing on interaction in its own right, and laid the foundations for the centrality of communication in social life. As he noted

> Regardless of the specific roles and capacities which an individual employs when he engages in interaction, he must in addition take the role of communicator and participant; regardless of the particular content of the spoken communication, order must prevail in the flow of messages by which the content is conveyed.
>
> *(Goffman, 1953b, p. 345)*

Assumptions Underlying the Interaction Order

Based on a comprehensive review of Goffman's work, Manning (1992) suggested the following set of background assumptions or interactional principles in Goffman's work:

1. participants must display situational propriety;
2. participants must select an appropriate level of involvement;

3. participants must be accessible; and
4. participants must display civil inattention to strangers.

(pp. 78–79)

Underlying these background assumptions is the presupposition of felicity, which, for Goffman, states that interactants must demonstrate the meaningfulness and sanity of their actions (Goffman, 1983a, b). My use of relevance as a fundamental premise of communication is very similar to Goffman's use of felicity; when interactants try to be relevant (or search for an interpretation that *makes* an utterance relevant, they are, of course, assuming both meaningfulness and sanity).

Language was of particular concern for Goffman because it enables us to communicate across time and distance, to incorporate distant resources and to recreate past encounters. Our interactions require concentration, according to Goffman, because we need to competently control many aspects of communication such as tone, gesture, voice and message; because we are almost always monitoring others, and because our rewards come from others so we focus on our interaction with them (Erwin, 2000, p. 92). As noted by Mouzelis, "Passing from *langue* to *parole*, from the paradigmatic to the syntagmatic level, is like passing from normative expectations and dispositions conceived as 'memory traces' in the actors' minds to their 'instantiation' in specific interaction situations. This transition from the virtual to the actual, from rehearsal to performance, has been the primary focus of Goffman's work. It also is the most specific feature of what has been called the interaction order" (Mouzelis, 1992, pp. 127–28).

Felicity's Condition and presuppositions. For Goffman, presuppositions are an important aspect of felicity conditions. "A *presupposition* (or assumption, or implication, or background expectation) can be defined very broadly as a state of affairs we take for granted in pursuing a course of action. ... [social presuppositions incorporate] a double theme, namely our tacitly taking something for granted (whether aware of having done so or not), and also unabashedly, even unthinkingly, counting on others in the action doing likewise, at least enough, so they can easily interpret and understand our action accordingly" (Goffman, 1983b, pp. 1–2).

In interaction, Goffman focused on social presuppositions involved in verbal communication. We assume, almost always, that our messages will "get across" reasonably succinctly. With his usual wit, Goffman observed that " ... if we could not rely on our listeners grasping the point without extended elaboration, we could hardly afford the time to say anything; similarly, if they could not depend on one taking into consideration what they already know, they could hardly afford the time to listen" (Goffman, 1983b, p. 2). Those who disregard contextual factors because they are so complex need to keep Goffman's point very much in mind—humans quickly and accurately contextualize their interactions every day.

Such presuppositions are not infinite, but reflect a set of frames of interpretation utilized in interaction.

Say that there is in any given culture a limited set of basic reinterpretation schemes (each, of course, realized in an infinite number of ways), such that the whole set is potentially applicable to the 'same' event. Assume too that these fundamental frameworks themselves form a framework—a framework of frameworks.

Starting, then, from a single event in our culture … we ought to be able to show that a multitude of meanings are possible, that these fall into distinct classes limited in number, and that the classes are different from each other in ways that might appear as fundamental, somehow providing not merely an endless catalogue but an entrée to the structure of experience …

It is some such framework of frameworks that we must seek out; it is some such metaschema that will allow us to accumulate systematic understanding about contexts, not merely warnings that in another context, meaning could be different.

(Goffman, 1981a, pp. 68–70)

Goffman's "framework of frameworks" is conceptually similar to the concept of metaframes developed in our earlier discussion of frame theory (see Chapter 1). Substantial research has clearly demonstrated that individuals use frames (or schemas) to structure and interpret their experience (Bransford & McCarrell, 1977; Nisbett & Ross, 1980; Van Dijk, 1981; Van Dijk & Kintsch, 1983).

Goffman also noted that interactants identify when something is said or done that breaches or calls into question their interpretation of what is said (a quizzical look or a sarcastic tone of voice might key the realization that something else has been intended). When this breach occurs, conversational maxims, repairs and felicity conditions proposed by Searle, Garfinkel and others might help us address these problematic interpretations. However, Goffman's felicity condition refers to "what happens when these rereading rules, these presuppositions about presuppositions, are *themselves* breached. For when the … content of an utterance makes no sense in the context, *and* neither do conventional keyings, then a drastic interpretation must be made: namely, that the speaker is temporarily incompetent, or, if there is no corroborating evidence for that, that she or he is deranged" (Goffman, 1983b, p. 26).

The ritual obligation in interaction is to sustain a mutual focus on the interaction (if one is in a focused encounter or gathering, and one is also a participant rather than a bystander). This is such a fundamental expectation that "when these 'normal' ways of saying one thing and intending another, or acting as though the speaker has been misunderstood, do not plausibly account for what is in the mind of the individual in question, then a second interpretive step must be taken, and another order of explanation must be sought … Either their mind is fully and fixedly not where it should be or they presume the other's is where it is not reasonable to expect it to be, or both. Each utterance presupposes, and contributes to the presuppositions of a jointly inhabitable mental world, and even though such worlds last only as long as there is a warrant for a common focus of cognitive attention, one should not think one can go around failing to sustain them" (Goffman, 1983b, p. 26).

In short, the fundamental underlying presupposition in interaction is to display "our sense of what it is to be sane" (Goffman, 1983b, p. 27). My emphasis on relevance as a fundamental interactional premise rests on a similar logic—if a listener cannot make a relevant connection between the text and the context, even after repeated efforts, then the speaker's competence is called into question (see Haslett, 1987, and Chapter 2 for a more extensive discussion of this point).

These presuppositions—an understanding of what has been said previously, the joint situation interactants are in, and commonsense knowledge—are cognitive frames that help us uncover the relevant meaning of an utterance. But Goffman was also concerned about another interactional constraint, namely "the moral norms of considerateness which bind individuals qua interactants. Delicacy, courtesy, modesty, politeness—these are the sort of attributes that are involved" (Goffman, 1983b, p. 28). This latter constraint, the ritual or moral constraint, is one that governs who may ask what of whom, how they may ask and the like. Such considerations link the interactional order to social order, and are critical to understanding what is *meant* by what is said.

Ritual constraints. For Goffman, part of social propriety is whether or not the speakers are already acquainted because such relationships constrain what can and should be asked about. A good friend might ask about a family member's troubles while an unacquainted person would not (the unacquainted person might not know about the troubles or, if known, might not believe it appropriate to ask about them). "In brief, what we think of as a relationship is, in one sense, merely a provision for the use of cryptic expressions, a provision of what is required in order to allude to things economically. Certainly our obligation to keep the names of our friends in mind, along with other pertinent social facts concerning them, is more than a means of celebrating and renewing our social relationship to them; it also ensures a shared orientation for reference and hence talk whenever we come into contact with them. *What affirms relationships also organizes talk*" (Goffman, 1983b, p. 42, italics mine).

Goffman also pointed out that intimates can have taboo topics as well as a freedom to talk rather elliptically to one another. Indeed, to describe the reportability of event is to closely study the social relations of the people making the inquiry.

> In general terms, the communicative challenge interactants face is to utter something and to not disconfirm that we are sane requires that our saying be heard to draw appropriately on one array of presuppositions—that sustained by our hearers—and avoid being heard to make others—those which are not, although they may be persons not present. Responding to another's words, we must find a phrasing that answers not merely to the other's words but to the other's

mind—so the other can draw both from the local scene and from the distal, wider worlds of her or his experience. ... But there is not *analysis* of the taken-for-granted. No framework. Not even a simpleminded classifica- tion. ... The bearing of acquaintanceship and close ties, of the generation and intentional construction of joint biography, of being or not being in a state of talk, of the various locaters we employ to provide a framework for the statements we want to be in a position to utter succinctly—all these critical matters have been little studied. Behind all this, and linking these themes together, is the socially prescribed place of what is taken to be the operation of the mind. A question of who can say what to whom, in what circumstance, with what preamble, in what surface form, and, given available readings, will not be thought mindless in doing so. A question of what we can say and still satisfy Felicity's Condition.

(Goffman, 1983b, p. 48)

All these matters—being in a state of talk, locating and marking frameworks, and so forth—are core considerations in the communication discipline, and such issues have also been addressed as well by anthropologists, sociologists and psychologists. But no one has put these matters so insightfully, with their interconnections revealed, as Goffman. His insights challenge our research presuppositions and force us to look at what factors influence interactional processes.

Situational propriety. Situational propriety represents knowledge about how to carry out interaction in social settings. Such proprieties enable an aggregate of individuals to be in a defined social reality (Goffman, 1963a, p. 196). As Manning (2000a) notes, everyday life rules are contextual, so accounts of appropriate beha- viour must be grounded in context as well. This parallels our assumptions about the importance of commonsense knowledge and taken-for-granted, tacit knowledge in communicating and in everyday encounters. In order to proceed in an interaction, participants rely on a projected interpretation of the situation and the anticipated, appropriate behavior in those circumstances.

Goffman notes that:

Commonly, critiques of orthodox linguistic analysis argue that although meaning depends on context, context itself is left as a residual category, something undifferentiated and global that is to be called in whenever, and only whenever, an account is needed for any noticeable deviation between what is said and what is meant. This tack fails to allow that when no such discrepancy is found, the context is still crucial—but in this case the context is one that is usually found when the utterance occurs. (Indeed, to find an utterance with only one possible reading is to find an utterance that can occur in only one possible context.) More important, traditionally no analysis was provided of what it is in contexts that makes them determinative of the sig- nificance of utterances, or any statement concerning the classes of contexts that would thus emerge—all of which if explicated, would allow us to say something other than merely that the context matters.

(Goffman, 1981a, p. 67)

As such, Goffman reminded us that context is critical to interpretation and action, and needs to be accounted for.

Giddens also believes that context is vital for interpretation.

Many moves do seem to invoke rejoinders, but there are a variety of ways in which individuals can express intentions, provide approval or disapproval, or otherwise make their views known, without directly committing themselves to turn-taking within the conversation. A key aspect of all talk in situations of interaction is that both speakers and listeners depend upon a saturated physical and social context for making sense of what is said.

(Giddens, 2000, p. 165)

As Goffman concluded, in interpreting interaction, the whole situation must be taken into account.

Goffman's idea of context is embedded in his concept of frames. As such, frames "can be defined tentatively as the statement(s) required to place and to understand a strip of activity: 'on the beach,' 'play fighting' … and so on. Even if the actual frame is a nonverbal image, it can be represented in verbal form as a name, phrase, or proposition" (Scheff, 2005b, p. 381). Frames can be assembled and may require framing at different institutional levels. For Goffman, subjective context "usually involves more than a single frame. Rather, it is likely to be an assembly of frames, one fitting within, or merely added to the other" (ibid.). Thus Goffman regards the interaction order as a system of enabling conventions. As such, frames, for Goffman, represent the practices and conventions illuminating the immediate social setting of an interaction.

Whenever we interact in a social situation, our behaviors are bounded by that context (Goffman, 1983a). He pointed out that social situations "provide the natural theater in which all bodily displays are enacted and in which all bodily displays are read. Thus the warrant for employing the social situation as the basic working unit in the study of the interaction order. … the regulations and expectations that apply to a particular social situation are hardly likely to be generated at the moment there … quite similar understandings will apply to a whole class of widely dispersed settings, as well as to particular locations across inactive phases … public thoroughfares are behavioral settings that sustain an interaction order characteristically extending in space and time beyond any single social situation occurring in them" (Goffman, 1983a, p. 5). Goffman argued that quite general understandings apply across multiple social settings, and his development of frames elaborates this view of context.

Goffman suggested that rules govern appropriate conduct in social situations. These rules—"situational proprieties"—include common courtesies, appropriate spatial distancing, forms of address, and the like. As Goffman noted, the most fundamental rule is "the rule obliging participants to 'fit in' and 'not make a scene'" (Goffman, 1963a, p.11). Such rules can be adhered to, or disregarded, but they are "enabling conventions" that help interactants establish a set of expectations for that context. In addition, rules of relevance and irrelevance help participants sustain the social order by specifying what matters are to be attended to (Strong, 1988).

Goffman regarded social situations as small, local places which enable participants to mutually monitor one another and in which much of the world's work is accomplished. As Goffman noted

> ... it is mainly in such contexts that individuals can use their faces and bodies, as well as small materials at hand to engage in social portraiture ... It is here, in social situations, that the individual can signify what he takes to be his social identity and here indicate his feelings and intent—all of which information the others in the gathering will need in order to manage their own courses of action—which knowledgeability he in turn must count on in carrying out his own design.
>
> *(Goffman, 1979, sec. VI)*

Aspects of social structure, like class and gender, are considered but only in terms of the value they have in the situation at hand. For those in a gathering, "Cultural rules establish how individuals are to conduct themselves by virtue of being in a gathering, and these rules for commingling, when adhered to, socially organize the behaviour of those in the situation" (Goffman, 1964, p. 135). Rules may govern accessibility, focused encounters, initiation of talk, use of space, loudness of tone, and the like. As he concluded "Talk is socially organized, not merely in terms of who speaks to whom in what language, but as a little system of mutually ratified and ritually governed face-to-face interaction, a social encounter" (ibid., p. 136). For Goffman, talk cannot be separated from purposeful coordinated action (Fine, Manning & Smith, 2000).

In context, individuals can demonstrate deference (appreciation of and respect for others) by avoiding embarrassing topics and/or presenting positive appreciation such as compliments. Displaying appropriate demeanor means that one is comporting himself or herself as a reliable interactant in a particular setting. Both deference and demeanor are central to face-work. As Goffman observed, "individuals must rely on others to complete the picture of him of which he himself is allowed to paint only certain parts. Each individual is responsible for the demeanor image of himself and the deference images of others, so that for a complete man to be expressed, individuals must hold hands in a chain of ceremony. ... While it may be true that the individual has a unique self all his own, evidence of this possession is thoroughly a product of joint ceremonial labor" (Goffman, 1967, pp. 84–85). For Goffman, participants mutually accept each other's line as a basic assumption of interacting with one another (Goffman, 1967, p. 11). If face-work is aggressive and contentious, than interaction might reflect a "sustained disequilibrium" in which interactants "flounder in an interchange that cannot readily be completed" (ibid., p. 24).

Through examining improprieties and breaches that reveal the interwoven patterns of obligations and rights, Goffman's analyses highlight these underlying assumptions which make orderly interaction possible and, in fact, routine. However, we must also, as Goffman (1963a) pointed out, be careful to distinguish between "merely situated" as opposed to "situational" behavior: the latter applying to behavior which could only take place in face-to-face encounters while the former applies to behaviors which could easily be located elsewhere. In short, we must concern ourselves with what is intrinsic to interaction in a given context (pp. 21–23).

Situated co-presence. Goffman outlined four types of social settings or situated co-presence. A *social occasion* is a larger social context, such as a party, in which social gatherings and situations take place, typically marked by time, space and material props. *Social gatherings* are when two or more people are co-present, and are governed by prescriptive rules. *Social situations* refer to any interactions which have co-presence that allows for mutual monitoring of each other's behavior (Goffman, 1963a, pp. 18–19).

Gatherings may be unfocused mingling where two individuals are co-present but pursuing independent ends, like standing in line at the supermarket. In contrast, *focused gatherings*, or *encounters*, are when participants "openly cooperate to sustain a single focus of attention" like a chess game (Goffman, 1963a, p. 24). Encounters or focused gatherings thus offer participants a single focus of attention, a preferential openness to verbal communication, an ability to closely monitor the other's actions—all leading to a "we rationale" for what we are doing together (Goffman, 1963a, pp. 83–112). In larger gatherings, there may be multiple focused encounters as well as some individuals who are uninvolved or only peripherally involved.

Involvement. Involvement represents behavior that reflects an awareness of the needs of the occasion, but avoids self-consciousness, alienation, selfishness or calculation (Goffman, 1963a). "Involvement refers to the capacity of an individual to give, or withhold from giving, his concerted attention to some activity at hand … Involvement in an activity is taken to express the purpose or aim of the actor" (Goffman, 1963a, p. 43). Maintaining involvement is also a delicate balancing act: The individual's actions must satisfy his involvement obligations, but "in a certain sense he cannot act *in order* to satisfy these obligations, for such an effort would require him to shift his attention from the topic of conversation to the problem of being spontaneously involved in it" (Goffman, 1967, p. 115).

Goffman also discussed involvement contours—differing degrees of involvement—that individuals display throughout the day. *Main or dominant involvement* are aspects of the social setting that the interactant is obligated to recognize, such as observing appropriate military protocol when encountering a superior officer. *Side involvements* are activities that can be pursued while still addressing the main involvement, such as having a private conversation with a friend at a business meeting, but the obligations of the business meeting must be recognized as being dominant (i.e., the private conversation stops when the business meeting begins, or is conducted during a break in the meeting). People may also use "involvement shields," like newspapers or cell phones, to remain uninvolved or inaccessible (Goffman, 1963a, pp. 38–42).

It is also the case that "the individual must phrase his own concerns and feelings and interest in such a way as to make these maximally usable by others as a source of appropriate involvement; and this major obligation of the individual *qua* interactant is balanced by his right to expect that others present will make some effort to stir up their sympathies and place them at his command" (Goffman, 1967, p. 116). In sum, the individual "is expected to go to certain lengths to save the feelings and the face of others present" (ibid., p. 10).

According to Goffman, selecting an appropriate level of involvement, and engaging in side involvements, presents individuals with choices about their autonomy in the encounter (Goffman, 1961b). Involvement is signaled by outward expressions, and depends on the social occasion and situation (Goffman, 1963a, pp. 40–50). For Goffman, involvement is intertwined with euphoria, a sense of ease experienced within an encounter (Goffman, 1953b, p. 243). This euphoria translates into an ability to carry on in a situation and to display an appropriate involvement and commitment to the interaction. If an individual is too calculating or self-conscious it reveals an observing, rather than participating, alignment by an individual (Goffman, 1953b, pp. 250–60).

Interactants also need to avoid alienation and selflessness—either being distracted by external matters or appearing to lack character. As Goffman put it, "a delicate balance between involvement and self-control" must be maintained (Goffman, 1953b, p. 274). When composure is lost, one is said to be 'flooding out' and in some occupations, flooding out must be avoided at all costs (e.g., surgeons, police) (Goffman, 1961b, pp. 55–62). Goffman discussed the dialectic of involvement (too much or too little) when he noted that "Our sense of being a person can come from being drawn into a wider social unit; our sense of selfhood can arise through the little ways in which we resist the pull" (Goffman, 1953b, p. 320).

Goffman viewed involvement, and maintaining an appropriate level of involvement, as critical in interacting competently:

> When an incident occurs and spontaneous involvement is threatened, then reality is threatened. Unless the disturbance is checked, unless the interactants regain their proper involvement, the illusion of reality will be shattered, the minute social system that is brought into being with each encounter will be disorganized, and the participants will feel unruled, unreal, and anomic.
>
> *(Goffman, 1967, p. 135)*

But there is a paradoxical tension here, between what we are experiencing and what type of situational pressure might be being brought to bear (Ostrow, 2000,

p. 323). As Goffman expressed it, there is a "sensed discrepancy between the world that spontaneously becomes real to the individual, or the one he is able to accept as the current reality, and the one in which he is obliged to dwell" (Goffman, 1961b, p. 43).

Degrees of involvement are also a function of acquaintanceship. As Goffman pointedly noted, we need a reason to approach the unacquainted and an excuse as to why we may not approach, or interact with, an acquaintance. Acquaintances are recognized both cognitively and socially (Goffman, 1963a, pp.112–13). And some individuals, like the very old, very young or occupying service positions such as the police, are "open" to public interaction. Other service positions, like waiters, are frequently ignored during conversations with others.

While Goffman regards involvement as key to an encounter, he did not "privilege talk among the expressions given and given off in an encounter. Sometimes a nod or a wave can be interactionally equivalent to talk" (Smith, 2006, p. 40). And encounters can frequently be disrupted by external preoccupations, by self-consciousness or by focusing on outsiders.

Accessibility and civil inattention. Goffman's third principle of accessibility and civil inattention refers to the polite notice we give others in encounters, while not making them the focal point of our attention (Goffman, 1963a, pp. 82–85). This is very similar to notions of politeness (Brown & Levinson, 1987) and honoring face (Ting-Toomey, 1994; Tracy, 1990). Goffman suggested that civil inattention is necessary for social order and social solidarity, yet it also offered mechanisms for connecting with strangers (Goffman, 1981b). Lofland, in fact, argued that civil inattention makes possible "co-presence without commingling, awareness without engross-ment, courtesy without conversation" and smoothes interactions in public places like cities and parks (Lofland, 1998, p. 462). The significance of civil inattention is "that each individual implies to others that he or she has no reason to fear them, or *vice versa*" (Giddens, 2000, p. 162). Through civil inattention, others are recognized and given deference, yet everyone maintains privacy and safety.

Anonymous individuals are known only in categoric terms (i.e., older man, nurse), whereas personal knowledge of another reflects "anchored relations" which are reflected in tie-signs. "Tie-signs" such as handholding, walking in synchrony, and the like, signalled participants' togetherness or relationship in public places even though we may not know anything about them (Goffman, 1971, pp. 194–96). In public places and spaces, Goffman made us aware of "singles"—the unaccompanied person—as well as the "withs," those individuals accompanying one another (Fine, Stitt & Finch, 1984).

Social occasions must also be negotiated so that individuals may gain access to one another in an encounter. As Goffman noted, "'acquainted persons in a social situation require a reason not to enter' whereas 'unacquainted persons require a reason to do so'" (Goffman, 1963a, p. 124). Engaging another's attention is a deli-cate business because "the obligation to be properly accessible often covers a desire to be selectively quite unavailable" (Goffman, 1963a, p. 106). Interestingly, the constant management of attention may be one of the most important factors in interaction (Baptista, 2003).

While Goffman attempted to lay out a framework for analyzing frames, and the rules associated with them, it is important to remember that Goffman himself acknowledged that interaction is fluid, spontaneous and in continuous flux. For both Goffman and Giddens, rules act as resources for interaction, and can be used for a multitude of purposes. As Goffman noted, framing devices are "interactional devices people use in order to make sense of their lived experience" (Goffman, 1981b, p. 62).

Goffman (1983b) argued that social situations (frames) ought to be viewed as the basic unit of the interactional order because such situations require social management. There are *primary social frames* that constitute the central repertoire of a given culture (Goffman, 1974, pp. 21–27) and consist of rules that organize experience and everyday encounters. *Secondary frames* are keyings or rekeyings, independent of primary frames, which can reframe or alter the meaning of a strip of interaction. For example, participants rely on the immediate, specific context and their interactions to make sense of ongoing organizing and communicating activities. Yet every interaction offers alternative interpretations (rekeyings) and thus may provide different meanings for events. Thus, each alternative interpretation provides a valid interpretation of ongoing events, but not necessarily the *only* plausible interpretation.

In fact, one could argue that multiple frames or alternative interpretations are needed to make sense of the complexity and evolution of organizing and communicating, and that is the approach being developed here. Buzzanell (personal communication, 2006) suggested that alternative interpretations may be very valuable because they enable interactants to understand how others might react and thus predict their behaviors. (See also Bolman & Deal, 2008, who make a similar argument; see also the work of David Maines, 1993, 1996.) Tracy's discussion of the dilemmas of academic scholarly talk pointed out that "conversational moves that displayed a person to be taking an idea seriously were the same ones that might be used as evidence that a discussant was being self-aggrandizing or disrespectful" (Tracy, 2001, p. 733) and provides a nice example of alternative interpretations (reframing through rekeying). However, in any specific instance of interaction, participants are seeking the most plausible interpretation of events, signaled by the specific organizing frame being activated in the immediate social context and the text (what is being said).

Note that Goffman did not argue, as do social constructivists, that individuals create their situational definitions. Rather, individuals "assess correctly what the situation ought to be for them and then act accordingly" (Goffman, 1974, p. 2). Individuals adapt to situations; society creates definitions of situations, and these take precedence over individuals' constructions of meaning. Goffman further noted that social organization depends upon individuals' capacity to sustain one definition of a situation. Thus, for Goffman, social life reflects a process of producing information to influence others, and maintaining a common interpretive frame. We now turn to a more detailed analysis of frames and the framing process.

Frames and the Framing Process

Frames

In the preceding chapters, I have developed frame systems for organizing and communicating. These *frame systems* represent tacit, taken-for-granted knowledge and expectations about organizing and communicating. A more specific *frame* for communicating in organizations has also been developed, outlining some common interactional, organizational activities such as decision-making, and assessing different message types, distinct audience types and the like. A major theme running through these concepts has been that communicating and organizing co-produce one another; organizing frames provide the context for communicating, and subsequent interactions reproduce, alter and/or amend the organizing context. The new organizing frame produced, in turn, influences subsequent communication and the resulting outcomes again recast the organizing and communicating contexts. Thus, frames provide interpretative schemas for ongoing activity that reflect tacit knowledge of social contexts and social practices. As such, frames provide interpretive and contextual knowledge on multiple levels. (See also Vachstein, 2004.)

As noted in Chapter 1, these conceptualizations of frames are compatible with Goffman's use of frames. Primary frames are consistent with frame systems and frames are viewed as reflecting context, tacit knowledge and activity scripts. In what follows, I look more closely at Goffman's theoretical modeling of frames.

Primary and secondary frames. According to Goffman, primary frameworks are "the cognitive building-blocks of experienced social reality" (Crook & Taylor, 1980, p. 240). As Goffman suggests

> Taken all together, the primary frameworks of a particular social group constitute a central element of its culture, especially insofar as understandings emerge concerning principal classes of the schemata, the relations of these classes to one another, and the sum total of the forces and agents that these interpretive designs acknowledge to be loose in the world.
>
> *(Goffman, 1974, p. 27)*

Primary frameworks are either natural or social. Natural frameworks reflect direct, unguided physical experiences of humans. In contrast, social frameworks "provide background understanding for events that incorporate the will, aim, and controlling effort of an intelligence, a live agency, the chief one being the human being" (ibid., p. 22).

As such, social frameworks thus deal with guided doings. These guided doings by individuals reflect intelligence and purpose, and provide a context for understanding action and the relationship between mental states and behavior (Baptista, 2003). There are a substantial number of secondary frames, and they can be reframed and/or embedded in other, more complex frames (Goffman, 1974, pp. 248–50).

Frame status. One issue often raised is how Goffman views the status of frames: Namely, do individuals appear to utilize them in their lives? In response, Goffman made the following point:

> Here I want only to mention the belief that in many cases the individual in our society is effective in his use of particular frameworks. The elements and processes he assumes in his reading of activity often *are* ones that the activity itself manifests—and why not, since social life itself is often organized as something that individuals will be able to understand and deal with. A correspondence or isomorphism is thus claimed between perception and the organization of what is perceived, in spite of the fact that there are likely to be many valid principles of organization that could but don't inform perception.
>
> *(ibid., p. 26)*

Additionally, Goffman saw frames "as inhering in the organization of events and cognition ... I feel that play and a host of other keyings can be sustained with clear mutually-understood understandings as to what is going on, and no particular sense of instability" (Goffman, 1981b, p. 64). In many cases what the individual does in serious life, he does in relationship to cultural standards established for the doing and for the social role that is built up out of such doings. Some of these standards are addressed to the maximally approved, some to the maximally disapproved" (Goffman, 1974, p. 562).

Thus, "Goffman's favourite paradox—events on stage are 'not real', but their 'stagings' are—is caught and tamed through frame. Goffmanesque frames both classify activities, making them available to actors and interpret them, telling actors 'just what sort of status in the real world the activity has'" (Crook & Taylor, 1980, p. 244). Goffman suggested that people project their frames of reference to the surrounding world, but this was rarely noticed because events usually verified those projections (Goffman, 1974, p. 39). Both Goffman and Bateson would agree that "the frame is involved in the evaluation of the messages which it contains" (Bateson, 1972, p. 161). However, while Goffman used "frame" in the same sense that Bateson does, "it is clear that he differs from Bateson by virtue of his additional emphasis upon what we might call *frame-as-structure*, as distinct from the more interactionist *frame-in-use*. I frame my experiences, but the structure of frame is prior to my experiences" (Crook & Taylor, 1980, p. 245).

As Crook and Taylor (1980) concluded, there are three important features of Goffman's frame analysis: (1) different types of frames exist and some frames are more vulnerable than others; (2) individuals transform or rekey frames from the original frame identified; and (3) frames and rekeying are "systematically ambiguous between being passive and structure on the one hand and the active and structuring on the other" (p. 246). I would argue, however, that Goffman himself views frames primarily as active and structuring because frames direct our sensemaking activities.

They also noted that understanding what is going on is not "a metaphysical demand for an exhaustive account of every aspect of a situation described at every possible level of generality, it must be a demand for an account which is adequate to some practical matter at hand. Frame analysis cannot, and does not, aim to capture the activity-in-itself in all its infinite variety; *it seeks to account for the sense generated in activities which gives enough interpretation to enable actors to keep on acting*. In other words, frame analysis can only begin where accounts of activities begin ... to frame an activity is to offer an account of it which excludes other possible accounts" (Crook & Taylor, 1980, p. 248, italics mine).

Thus, Goffman's frame is not a model of rampant situationalism, and his concept of frames as both structured and structuring is consistent with our development of frame theory (see Baptista, 2003, and Chapter 1) as well as Giddens' concept of structuration (a key connection we will develop in subsequent chapters). This issue is especially important because many unjustly criticize Goffman's frames as "rampant situationalism"—however, what frames do is focus interactant's attention to the relevant aspects of any given encounter. As Goffman notes

> ... there is no occasion of talk so trivial as not to require each participant to show serious concern with the way in which he handles himself and the others present. ... An understanding will prevail as to when and where it will be permissible to initiate talk, among whom, and by means of what topics of conversation ... A single focus of thought and visual attention, and a single flow of talk, tends to be maintained and to be legitimated as officially representative of the encounter.
>
> *(Goffman, 1967, pp. 33–34)*

Interaction, then, is characterized by social rules; these social rules are tacit assumptions that constrain face-to-face encounters As he observed: "Face-engagements comprise all those instances of two or more participants in a situation joining each other openly in maintaining a single focus of cognitive and visual attention—what is sensed as a single mutual activity, entailing preferential communication rights" (Goffman, 1963a, p. 89).

It is critical to note that Goffman blends both cognitive processes (principles of organization of social events) as well as social practices in frames.

> ... these frameworks are not merely a matter of mind but correspond in some sense to the way in which an aspect of the activity is organized— especially activity directly involving social agents. Organizational premises are involved, and these are something cognition somehow arrives at, not

something cognition creates or generates. Given their understanding of what it is that is going on, individuals fit their actions to this understanding and ordinarily find that the ongoing world supports this fitting. *These organizational premises—sustained both in mind and in activity—I call the frame of the activity.*

(Goffman, 1974, p. 247, italics mine)

For Goffman, then, a frame is a "schemata of interpretation ... [which] allows its user to locate, perceive, identify, and label" their experiences (Goffman, 1974, p. 21).

Frames are thus anchored in the real world via individuals' activities. Activity that is "interpreted by the application of particular rules and inducing fitting actions from the interpreter ... itself is located in a physical, biological and social world" (Goffman, 1974, p. 247). Furthermore, "The very points at which the internal activity leaves off and the external activity takes over—the rim of the frame itself— become generalized by the individual and taken into his frame of interpretation, thus becoming, recursively, an additional part of the frame. In general, then, the assumptions that cut an activity off from the external surround also mark the ways in which this activity is inevitably bound to the surrounding world" (ibid., p. 249).

Both Goffman and Schutz utilized a "commonsense understanding mediated by the real world activities of persons as the proper focus of activity ... [however the] acculturated consciousness that is Schutz's starting point is very different from Goffman's social behaviorism that approaches questions about mind, self and consciousness from the objective world of human conduct" (Smith, 2006, pp. 58–59). In contrast to a semiotic approach, Goffman also "recommends treating apparent texts as part of the social world" (Crook & Taylor, 1980, p. 247).

In discussing *Frame Analysis*, MacCannell (2000) pointed out that

> Goffman undertakes, one 'world' at a time, a close analysis of the other ways in which meaning is molded to experience: benign deceptions, tests and trials ... and finally, *conversations*, the averred topic of phenomenological sociology. As always with Goffman, the description and analysis of these 'frames' (not 'world') is extraordinarily fine. ...
>
> Goffman presses his advantage by avoiding any tendency to interpret his material within a single frame where this would produce a distorted representation of experience, even, or especially, if the distortion is one that is prayerfully sustained by participants in the situation.
>
> Thus, for example, it may be necessary to apply several frames simultaneously to explicate the experience of being an experimental subject in psychological research. Here, in one sentence, Goffman (1974: 95) usefully employs five frames (hoax, non-hoax, experiment, test *and* intersubjective understanding): 'What has been pressed is that the hoax is not

quite a hoax, since the experimental frame does not so much create an environment in which subjects can be tested as it does create one in which they will actively attempt to discover what the experimenter wants of them, what it is that will make the undertaking successful for all concerned ... '

(p. 16)

Frames are nested within one another, and Goffman viewed conversations as occurring in a larger frame of interaction (contexts). A specific frame or situation can be understood by referring to adjacent, surrounding frames because when frames are keyed and rekeyed, they have a transformational relationship to one another. Goffman's transformations can move upward, to "conscious transformations into constructed realities," as well as downward to the physical primary framework in which actions take place (Collins, 1988, p. 62). Thus, frames may be layered or nested within other frames.

"Goffman is saying that talk needs to be analysed 'from the outside in', with the larger frame setting the conditions for what can emerge within it" (ibid., p. 51). Goffman's frame analysis also described them on three different levels or layers: The physical world, the social ecological level, and institutional settings (ibid., pp. 51–53). The physical world is primary, and communication, at this level, reflects how participants anchor themselves to their common physical world. The mental level is always based on the physical world, or primary frame. The social ecological level reflects Goffman's focus on physical copresence, and the awareness we have of one another's presence even though we may not be interacting with one another (e.g., standing in line waiting for a bus).

The institutional frames, which reflect the social contexts in which talk occurs, may range from lectures to church services to informal conversations. For Goffman, frames build upon or transform prior frames, and individuals themselves may frame an encounter in a variety of ways. Some contexts will enable a relatively fluid shift among frames, while other contexts (such as a radio talk show) will have less fluidity or "frame space" in which to change alignment. Collins suggested that these frame spaces act as norms as situations unfold, and participants feel compelled to act in a given way, or explain why they are not (e.g., apologizing, giving an account) (Collins, 1988, p. 57). Finally, the nesting of frames can represent the "multiple nature of reality," with "some frames being more fundamental than others" (Collins, 1988, p. 59).

Some of the institutional settings explored by Goffman range from mental hospitals (Goffman, 1961a) to various formats or forms of talk, such as radio shows, lectures and the theatre (Goffman, 1981a). Larger frames of organizing (such as the structural or human resources organizing frame) are also of particular interest to organizational communication scholars—as such, Goffman enables both the analysis, the tacit knowledge underlying such frames, and the analysis of their impact on communication.

Goffman also commented that frames tend to be reinforced and reproduced. As he noted:

> ... what people understand to be the organization of their experience, they buttress, and perforce, self-fulfillingly. They develop a corpus of cautionary tales, games, riddles, experiments, newsy stories, and other scenarios which elegantly confirm a frame-relevant view of the workings of the world ... And the human nature that fits with this view of viewing does so in part because its possessors have learned to comport themselves so as to render this analysis true of them. Indeed, in countless ways and ceaselessly, social life takes up and freezes into itself the understandings we have it.
>
> *(Goffman, 1974, p. 563)*

In brief, "'Frame analysis' is the attempt to become cognizant of the rules for cognition and communication that are bound up with the production of any world" (Gonos, 1977, p. 858). As previously noted, Goffman defined a frame as "principles of organization which govern events—at least social ones—and our subjective involvement in them" (Goffman, 1974, p. 10). Goffman also argued that frames reflect ways in which people organize and make sense of their experience and that frames reflect "the structure of experience individuals have at any moment of their social lives" (ibid., p. 11). As Baptista observed, "making sense is so fundamental a basis for maintaining the background assumptions of social reality that, even when a 'breakdown' does occur, individuals must rely on remedial interchanges ... which can be closely linked to a process of 'reframing'" (Baptista, 2003, p. 198). These views are consistent with the fundamental assumptions about communication and frames outlined in earlier chapters.

In addition, Gonos pointed out that there are a number of important characteristics of framed activity: (1) frames have a set number of key components with a specific arrangement and stable relations; (2) these components are complete and cohere; and (3) they suggest what "shall be taken by participants as real, and how it is that they should be involved in this reality" (Gonos, 1977, p. 860). In what follows, I will look at some component processes in framing—how frames are established, maintained or altered. Keep in mind that individuals may have more than one frame they apply to an encounter, and that frames may shift and/or break.

Framing

It is at the *framing* level—the everyday interactions within organizing—that these frames (for organizing and for communicating) mutually intertwine to enact organizational life. And Goffman's view of framing is among the most detailed and fully developed model of interaction, albeit developed in a number of works during his lifetime.

Framing refers to the use of particular text features to signal the communicator's intended meaning. Here Goffman's work, as does Bateson's, makes important contributions to understanding communicative processes. Their work refers to specific devices, such as nonverbal cues or textual features (e.g., naming practices, formulaic expressions), that signal what is *meant* by what is spoken or written. In particular, Goffman emphasized ritual, performances, frames and face-work (Denzin, 2002). His definitition of ritual referred to an activity, "however informal and secular, [which] represents a way in which the individual must guard and design the symbolic implications of his acts while in the immediate presence of an object that has a special value for him" (Goffman, 1967, p. 57). Rituals may include such things as salutations, compliments, and stereotyped, polite verbal interchanges. Although these appear meaningless, we can observe what happens when they are used and not used. This may be left out "When the situation is highly impersonal. ... But if they are omitted when there is a personal relationship of friendly acquaintanceship, the feeling is a social snub; failure to greet someone one knows, or not to ceremonially mark their departure, conveys the sense that the personal relationship is being ignored or downgraded" (Collins, 2004, pp. 17–18).

The framing process—the interactional process—reflects how everyday interactions are carried out. As Goffman put it, this is the "working consensus" interactants mutually sustain. Frames, for Goffman, are the principles of organization that structure an individual's perception of the social world and thus organize one's experiences. Goffman looked particularly at how actors sustained "any ritually organized systems of social activity" (Goffman, 1967, p. 45). In addition, Goffman focused on the social self enacted through interaction; this presentational self constrains the interaction order, and individuals commit to an interaction order for maintenance of the social self (Rawls, 1987, pp. 136–37). "We are *compelled* to have an individual self ... because social interaction requires us to act as if we do" (Collins, 1988, p. 50).

Framing is the enactment of the interactional order established by participants and is continuously changing as mutual working understandings are negotiated by participants. Goffman looked behind everyday activity to illuminate the frames that "invisibly govern it" (Gonos, 1977, p. 857). Frames must be negotiated because not everyone will apply a similar frame; some may contest a frame, misunderstand a frame, or misinterpret what is going on (for example, as in a fabrication). In what follows, I shall examine framing or the process of interaction in more detail.

Elements of Framing

Keying. Goffman viewed a strip of activity as a meaningful part of a frame, as defined by participants. A strip of activity can be framed in multiple ways, and transformed by keying and fabrication. Keying signals the way in which a frame might be alternatively interpreted (for example, by signaling humor during a critical comment given to another), while *fabrication* leads one to have a false impression about what is going on (Goffman, 1974, p. 83). Keyings and rekeyings may also be reversed (for example, a novel being transformed into a play, or a play being transformed into a novel) (ibid., p.79). As Goffman pointed out

> We face the moment-to-moment possibility (warranted in particular cases or not) that our settled sense of what is going on beyond the current social situation or within it may have to begin to be questioned or changed.
> *(Goffman, 1981b, p. 68)*

Although many scholars have discussed multiple realities and the complexities of the self, Goffman demonstrated how "different realities are *interrelated* ... by developing a systematic exploration of social laminations or keying" (Schmitt, 2000, p. 78). Mass media formats, such as soap operas, are "keyed" off of everyday life. Rekeyings are based "not simply on something defined in terms of a primary framework, but rather on a keying of these definitions" (Goffman, 1974, p. 81). (For an interesting discussion of studies based on keying as well as fabrication, see Schmitt, 2000.)

As Goffman noted, framing "does not so much introduce restrictions on what can be meaningful as it does open up variability. Differently put, persons seem to have a very fundamental capacity to accept changes in organizational premises which, once made, render a whole strip of activity different from what is modeled on and yet somehow meaningful" (Goffman, 1974, p. 238). Thus, variability, ambiguity, keying and fabrication are fundamental to Goffman's frame analysis. In fact, Goffman used the term "straight activity" to distinguish frames which are "real" and genuine, and perceived as such by participants (Goffman, 1974, p. 301).

In *Strategic Interaction* and in Goffman's subsequent books, his "earlier emphasis upon a functional coordination among social actors in upholding the fabric of social reality shifts over to a greater concern for the way in which this may be a conflictful situation among rival reality-constructors. At the end of this progression, we find the theme of multiple realities and the manoeuvring that is possible to contain one constructed reality within another" (Collins, 2000b, p. 316). Frames, and keying, become important ways in which multiple realities may be constructed or layered. Collins pointed out that Goffman's "frame model gives us a strong analytical grip on perhaps the key problem uncovered by Garfinkel and stressed by his most radical followers: The potentially infinite regress of levels of analysis and hence of levels of reality itself" (ibid., p. 313).

Goffman also argued that many felicitous conditions, such as those proposed by Austin, Grice, and Searle, are going to be continuously breached

> ... causing the hearer to reread the utterance as an expression of unserious-ness, sarcasm, under-statement, rhetorical question and the like. These "key-ings" provide something like a systematic convention-based means for shifting

from what is more or less literally said to what is meant, a presupposed interpretive repertoire that introduces reference and inference.

(Goffman, 1983b, p. 26)

A keyed frame is recognized by all participants as having been transformed: *keys* are "enabling conventions by which a given activity, one already meaningful in terms of some primary framework, is transformed into something patterned on this activity but seen by the participants to be something quite else" (Goffman, 1974, pp. 43–44). Keyings include *make believes* (rekeying a frame as play), *contests* (rekeying a conflictful aspect of everyday life), *ceremonials* (rekeying as a part of recognized ritual, such as a wedding), *regroundings* (rekeying by substituting one motive for another, such as a "shill" playing a role as a pseudo-gambler) and *technical redoings* (e.g., demonstrations, role-playing sessions). Finally, Goffman recognizes that keyed frames are reversible, and may themselves suggest further rekeying.

Schmitt (2000) extended Goffman's concept of keying through the concept of negative keying. Negative keying refers to situations in which the frames are ambiguous, blurred, or changing over time. Some examples include unequal group participation for minorities, the not-self (when an individual maximizes the self the individual accepts, and minimizes the self the individual does not accept) and ambiguous frames, as exemplified by parents of thalidomide babies who apply the normal child frame on some occasions, and the handicapped child frame in others. In negative keying the "transformations and the primary frame are perceived and overtly discussed by all the participants" (ibid., p. 86). He also suggests that "the most original and provocative instance of negative keying is when all persons are truly ambivalent about the problematic identity" such as "interactions surrounding a 'handicapped' child" (ibid., p. 88).

Smith (2003a) contrasted Goffman's frames along two dimensions: the presence or absence of keying, and the accuracy of participants' perceptions of the frames. Primary frameworks are not reworked, while both keyed and frabricated frames are. In primary and keyed frames, participants have accurate perceptions of what is going on, while in fabricated frames some participants are being deceived (for example, as in scams, hoaxes, cons and experimental tests). Benign fabrications, like practical jokes, do not harm the participants being deceived, but exploitative fabrications, like scams, harm the participants' self-interests (such as scams which defraud individuals).

Because social life is both fragile and changeable, Goffman assumed that different individuals may have different meanings for situations, and that these definitions are fluid, and continuously changing. Goffman also noted that ordinary troubles with frames occur because of ambiguity (such as vagueness or uncertainty), errors with framing, miskeying, misidentification of objects, misframing by different trackings, muffings and frame disputes (see Chapters 9 and 10 in *Frame Analysis* for extended discussions of how frames may be vulnerable and/or broken). With considerable wit and irony, Goffman suggested that

The box that conversation stuffs us into is Pandora's. But worse still, by selecting occasions when participants have tacitly agreed to orient themselves in stereotypes about conversation, we can, of course, find tight constraints obtain. ... But there are other arrangements to draw on ... In these circumstances the whole framework of conversational constraints—both system and ritual—can become something to honor, to invert, or to disregard, depending as the mood strikes. On these occasions it's not merely that the lid can't be closed; there is no box.

(Goffman, 1981a, p. 74)

While some actors may sustain situations, others may not, and thus frames may be altered.

Layering frames. Just as situations are dynamic and fluid, so too are frames. Although Goffman did not extensively treat the concept of embedded frames, he clearly viewed frames as being "laminated" (see Boden, 1994) or layered (Goffman, 1974, 1981a).

Goffman's vision is that conversation is always part of a larger frame of interaction. Only if the larger frame is properly handled can the conversation take place; and just how that larger frame is set will determine what kind of conversation proceeds within it. Most of the time we don't notice this larger frame, because it is routine and can be taken for granted ... Goffman is saying that talk needs to be analysed "from the outside in", with the larger frame setting the conditions for what can emerge within it.

(Collins, 1988, p. 51)

These larger frames provide the general social context, such as, for example, a business meeting. When integrated with Giddens' work, these general social contexts can become much more inclusive and broad in scope (e.g., sociohistoric contexts, different types of organizations, transnational organizations, and processes of globalization).

Larger frames include the physical setting and physical co-presence of participants in the encounter (see especially Kendon, 1988, for an excellent discussion of these issues), and the surrounding institutional frame (Collins, 1988). For Goffman, individuals do "not *create* 'definitions of situations' even though their society can be said to do so; ordinarily, all they do is to assess correctly what the situation ought to be for them and then act accordingly" (Goffman, 1974, pp. 1–2). While Goffman's work focused on how participants act "accordingly," he also noted that participants can deny or alter these frames through their actions. Like Giddens, Goffman would argue that people adapt to socially constructed situations and that social interactions may alter as well as reproduce social order.

Goffman's multi-layered concept of frame also applies frames to encounters, or situated activities (parallel to my use of frames to conceptualize immediate social settings). For Goffman, "Any situation, as it has become organized through social moves up to that point in time, constitutes a frame, a socially defined reality" (Collins, 1988, p. 54). As we have seen, Goffman also used the concept of "keying/rekeying" to elucidate the ways in which frames can be transformed and manipulated, such as with fabrications, or when frames are "broken" and repaired (e.g., radio talk-show hosts "breaking" frame when they make a gaffe and then apologize, and create circumstances even more humorous or embarrassing) (Goffman, 1981a). Goffman's "theoretical point is that frames build on previous frames, so that even errors do not so much destroy the social situation as give rise to a new situation, a transformation of the old. The complexity of reality (and of talk) comes from the 'emergent' quality" (Collins, 1988, p. 55).

Goffman's concept of frames and the rekeying of frames is very significant because it enables conversational participants (as well as analysts) to embrace moving from macro- to micro-levels and vice versa—a central issue for organizational scholars. For Goffman, frames, as they are keyed and rekeyed, may extend contexts to incorporate the entire organization (looking from the outside in) or focus on the immediate, physically copresent interaction between two organizational members. Through background tacit knowledge, framed at many distinct levels and boundaries, specific interactions take on meaning for both individuals and the organization. Thus, for Goffman, frames integrate interactions, at any level, into organizing and organizations.

I believe an appropriate interpretation of Goffman is found in his concept of keying and rekeying of frames, and the use of a hologram as a metaphor. Holograms represent all aspects of an entity in any single part, and thus any aspect captures the whole (Morgan, 2006). Like holograms, frames capture the meaning of organizing and of organizations, and may change, be broken, be rekeyed, and the like (and thus captures the contentiousness and power struggles of organizing in a way Boden's lamination metaphor does not). Scheff (2005b) makes a similar argument about the use of frames to unpack layers of context—namely, interactants' mutual awareness of the recursiveness of frames, and that this awareness "anchors" mutual understanding at a given point in time and enables consensus. Referencing Cicourel, Scheff notes that "the less we know about the larger context of discourse, the less able we are to understand it" (p. 378).

Frame space. Frame space—the flexibility of frames within which an encounter takes place—may be tightly structured, as in a radio talk show, or may be relatively flexible, as frames in ordinary conversation. As Goffman argued, the working consensus being developed may rely on complex layers of situational definitions at the same time. The importance of relevance to social intereaction is clearly established in Goffman's view: "we find ourselves with one central obligation: to render our behavior understandably relevant to what the other can come to perceive is going on. Whatever else, our activity must be addressed to the other's mind, that is, to the other's capacity to read our words and actions for evidence of our feelings, thought, and intent" (Goffman, 1983b, p. 51). A working consensus, in sum, is built upon notions of relevance and irrelevance (what is to be attended to or disattended to), mutual knowledge, an agreement as to claims that will be honored, and an agreement on the desirability of avoiding conflict (Goffman, 1959).

Frames are vulnerable and fluid because people frequently transcend them: humans may "pursue a line of activity—across a range of events that are treated as out of frame" (Goffman, 1974, p. 201). Perhaps this is the quality of multitasking— being able to simultaneously pursue a number of different activities. Even though one is involved in the main activity in an encounter, one is always able to circumvent deep involvement or give off a false sense of involvement (e.g., nodding of heads by students to indicate, at times falsely, their attention to a lecture). Yet an appropriate sense of involvement should normally be maintained because one's impropriety may be noticed and/or lead to similar improprieties by others (Goffman, 1974, p. 346). Levels of involvement should be appropriate in the context because inappropriate levels create frame tension, and may break frame.

Finally, Goffman suggested that frames can be broken, either in their application or internal structure. "Flooding in" occurs when a bystander becomes part of the frame, and "flooding out" occurs when one breaks frame by panic, uncontrollable laughter and the like. "Downkeying" takes place when mock acts become taken for real. "Upkeying" takes place when a participant loses a sense of reality about what is going on, and practices a type of "what-if" scenario (ibid., pp. 345–60).

In sum, frames organize our experiences and enable us to understand what is going on in particular encounters. Primary frameworks categorize our experiences into meaningful events: Natural primary frameworks represent the natural, physical world while social primary frameworks represent events socially constructed by humans. (Primary frameworks correspond to the level of metaframes, as developed in this book.) Primary frameworks can also be keyed, with this keying revealing how a particular interaction is to be interpreted (seriously or playfully, for example)—keying appears to operate as metacommunication (see, for example, Bateson, 1976).

Collins concluded that:

> Goffman wishes to show that everyday life is not at all simple, yet people are capable of dealing with complexities as a matter of ordinary commonsense.
>
> Goffman's *frames* are designed to support both these points: avoiding complete relativism, but showing multiple realities. This is done by a set of levels, each of which is built upon another. The multiple nature of realities comes from the way frames can be built upon frames, while the whole is anchored because some frames are more fundamental than others. These levels begin with 'primary frameworks': the natural world of physical objects in which people live, including their own bodies; and the social world of other people and their networks of relationships. At a higher level, a strip of activity in these primary frameworks can be transformed into make-believe, contests, ceremonials, or 'technical redoings'. ...Framing permeates the level

of ordinary social action. We live in a world of social relationships, in which roles are acted out, with various keyings and deceptions played upon them. This is the core of practical activities and occupations, of power and stratification.

(Collins, 1988, pp. 58–61)

Thus Goffman's use of frames allows for multiple layers of frames, moving across different levels of abstraction, and is consistent with the manner in which frame theory is being developed in this book.

Thus far, I have developed Goffman's concepts of frame, framing and the various layers of analysis they provide. This constitutes an overview of frame-as-structuring, a way of categorizing our social experiences, and how those frames are identified, maintained and/or altered. The value of Goffman's work in analyzing communicative processes and their role in constituting the social order is clear. We now turn to explore frame-as-use, and to investigate Goffman's interaction model.

9

GOFFMAN'S FRAMING OF INTERACTION

In Chapter 8, we examined the basic aspects of Goffman's frames as a knowledge system—what the various components of frames are, how they build upon and layer one another, and how they change. In this chapter, we shall explore how Goffman used frames to build a model of interaction. Here, we shall look at how frames are used to negotiate shared meanings in encounters. We shall explore interactional processes and devices, as well as Goffman's concepts of self and face, which are central to interaction. Thus, our emphasis here is upon frames-in-use.

While frames reflect the cognitive, contextual, tacit knowledge aspects of human experience, social practices, as frames, guide interaction. In what follows, we shall first look at the underlying principles sustaining Goffman's interaction order, and then explore the social practices participants use in their everyday encounters.

Interactional Processes

The interaction order, set forth by Goffman, is based on system and ritual requirements in interaction. These requirements are supported by interactional devices used in everyday encounters. These devices, such as anchoring and bracketing, help participants situate their interactional activities and responses (Davis, 1997). Let us begin by exploring the systematic and ritual requirements for interaction set out by Goffman, and then look more closely at interactional devices.

System and Ritual Requirements

System requirements. Goffman divided practices sustaining the interaction order into two general areas: system requirements and ritual requirements. Eight system requirements were developed by Goffman: (1) the capacity for speaker/hearers

(S/H) to both send and receive clear messages; (2) signals that acknowledge reception of messages; (3) signals that open up as well as close off talk; (4) signals for taking turns in order to respond to each other's remarks; (5) repair and interruption mechanisms; (6) metacommunicative signals to frame messages; (7) messages that are relevant to the ongoing talk; and (8) a distinction between those who are "in the encounter" as opposed to those who are not (e.g., eavesdroppers) (Kendon, 1988, pp. 32–33). Both Kendon and Goffman noted that messages can be both verbal and nonverbal. In addition, both argued that some "frame attunement" or orientation displaying a readiness for talk takes place prior to the interchange (ibid., p. 37). These eight system requirements are consistent with the underlying assumptions of the communicative frame system developed in Chapter 2.

In analyzing Goffman's work, Levinson suggested a somewhat similar set of system requirements which specified that participants need to be mutually oriented: to be monitoring and aware of the interactional environment; to be rational in the sense of means-ends reasoning; to be able to respond conditionally to preceding acts; to be aware of some relationship between the goals of the participants; and to be aware that each participant has the capacity for agency, and shares mutual commonsense knowledge about their situated activity (Levinson, 1983, pp. 44–45). System requirements thus outline the *minimal* conditions for interaction to take place.

Ritual requirements. In contrast to system requirements, ritual requirements refer to the social face and social order implied in face-to-face encounters. That is,

> ... social life is organized on the principle that an individual who possesses certain social characteristics has a moral right to expect that others will treat him/her in an appropriate way. In return, any individual who claims to have certain characteristics ought, in fact, to be what he/she claims. In consequence, then, when a person projects a definition of the situation and thereby makes a claim to be a person of a particular kind within it, a moral demand is made of others, obliging them to value and treat him/her in the manner persons of that kind have a right to expect.
>
> *(Williams, 1988, p. 67)*

In talking about such face-engagements, Goffman argued that they are viewed by participants as a "single mutual activity, entailing preferential communication rights" (Goffman, 1963a, p. 89). In organizing contexts, of course, an important component of the projected situation reflects the hierarchical positions participants have within the organization and their corresponding interactional rights and obligations.

In my view, the nature of Goffman's ritual expectations in interaction would appear to incorporate a number of formulations, such as Grice's Cooperative maxim, Goffman's felicity condition, and matters of face-engagement. In addition, ritual needs are sustained by a "set of rules—rules of relevance and irrelevance— which govern precisely which matters the participants may focus on and those which they must gloss over and ignore" (Strong, 1988, p. 234). Ritual expectations thus help participants maintain appropriate behavior within encounters.

Collins noted that ritual ties link a society. And Goffman added that

> Universal human nature is not a very human thing. By acquiring it, the person becomes a kind of construct, built up not from inner psychic propensities, [but] from moral rules that are impressed upon him without. These rules, when followed, determine the evaluation he will make of himself and of his fellow-participants in the encounter, the distribution of his feelings, and the kinds of practices he will employ to maintain a specified and obligatory kind of ritual equilibrium. The general capacity to be bound by moral rules may well belong to the individual, but the particular set of rules which transforms him into a human being derives from requirements established in the ritual organization of social encounters.
>
> *(Goffman, 1967, pp. 45)*

As we have seen, system requirements set out the necessary conditions for interaction to occur. In contrast, ritual requirements set out the social practices that will guide the interaction. It is important to note, however, that interactional frames may be reframed, altered or broken, while still preserving ritual requirements. We next turn to the interactional devices participants use to conduct their interactions.

Interactional Devices and Units

Interactional devices and units help us negotiate "what is going on here." They signal our understandings of events to others, and others, in turn, respond to those understandings by confirming or amending them. Some of these interactional devices have been closely investigated by ethnographers, sociolinguists, and discourse and conversational analysts. Goffman (1953b) argued that there are five elements to look at within an interaction. First, *messages* convey the information or content in utterances. With regard to messages, Goffman distinguishes between messages we "give off" (e.g., expressive communication such as grimaces, tension) and messages that are "given" (i.e., the linguistic message we utter). Speakers try to control both aspects of messages, but typically more control can be exerted over linguistic, rather than expressive, messages. Second, *ritual respect* reflects regard for others in the interaction; third, *face-work* reflects the self-respect taken up by the speaker. Fourth, *communicative constraints* are the conditions that must be met in order for moves to be understood (e.g., fulfilling felicity conditions in Searle's sense). And fifth, *framing instructions* indicate how moves are to be interpreted (i.e., metacommunication).

Goffman later developed the concept of interaction order and further refined his analysis of interaction. His last works analyzed frames as the foundation for the

TABLE 9.1 Goffman's Interaction Process

I. System and Ritual Requirements for Interactional Processes
   a. System requirements
   b. Ritual requirements
II. Interactional Devices
    a. Anchoring devices
    b. Moves
III. Interactional Practices
    a. Embedding
    b. Participant status
      1. Speakers
      2. Listeners
    c. Projected lines/footing
    d. Ritual respect
    e. Remedial practices
    f. Territories of the self
    g. Regions

interaction order, and emphasized talk as a key aspect of the interaction order. These units of interaction are similar to those outlined in Chapters 2 and 3. (See Table 9.1 for these interactional devices.)

Anchoring. Trust in a particular frame is maintained by anchoring. These anchors are interactional devices, like metacommunication, that underscore the intended way in which a frame is to be taken up. *Anchors* may frame a particular episode, or a socially organized activity, embedded in a stream of behavior. These episodes, according to Goffman, are viewed as part of how actual experiences are organized (Goffman, 1974, pp. 247–62).

These framing devices, such as anchors, clarify the intended meanings of participants and their interpretations of what is going on. *External brackets*, for example, tell us when episodes begin and end; interjections and jokes, for example, are often bracketed within longer discourse and set apart. In contrast, *internal brackets* are part of the structure of a specific social activity, such as taking a time out, and switching courts in a tennis match. Internal brackets may also characterize the structure of a conversation, such as conventionalized greetings, exchanges of information, and closings (Psathas & Waksler, 2000; Sacks, Schegloff & Jefferson, 1974). Goffman noted that there are temporal and spatial brackets around encounters as well as opening and closing brackets (Goffman, 1974, pp. 250–53). Courtrooms, homes, plays, offices and surgeries are different settings in which bracketing clearly delineates activities spatially and temporally. Differences in conventions for recognizing episodes will vary across cultures and over time.

Other anchoring devices include the *roles* that one assumes in the flow of ongoing activities, such as the role of a doctor in surgery. *Resource continuity*, the material traces left behind, such as rooms or written records, also help anchor the activity to the external world. As such, Goffman clearly recognized the importance of texts and material objects in interaction. We also use "unconnectedness" in anchoring frames—that is, we ignore aspects of the context that are not relevant to the ongoing activity, such as people in a meeting ignoring the caterers. And, finally, we assume that we are all alike in that we all have a physical, single self that spans many roles (Goffman, 1974).

In addition, anchoring devices help maintain involvement in a frame. Frames may be anchored by their connections to the broader social world, such as when one views an activity as "work" because one is compensated for it. Or, for example, when gamblers are able to concentrate on gambling because of the routine services supplied for them, such as food, drinks and bathrooms (Goffman, 1974, pp 80–90). Some resource continuity may enable individuals to view an activity as relatively enduring, and thus as "anchoring" one to a particular point of view (ibid., p. 290). However, many frames are anchored by layers of other frames. Branaman noted that the anchoring of frames "allows us to generate a *sense* of reality but does not render activity unframed and invulnerable to misconstruction" (Branaman, 1997, p. lxxv).

If errors in "framing" occur, a *frame trap* may ensue. That is, even though a corrective account may be given by the individual, "the world can be arranged (whether by intent or default) so that the incorrect views, however induced, are confirmed by each bit of new evidence or each effort to correct matters, so that, indeed, the individual finds that he is trapped and nothing can get through" (Goffman, 1974, p. 480).

While signaling of frames is done within and across encounters and episodes, framing also relies on meanings and tacit assumptions participants apply to the situation. This tacit knowledge may range from commonsense knowledge about gatherings and human agency to the knowledge we glean about close friends or our work environment. Anchors and tacit knowledge both clarify how the encounter is to be understood.

Moves. Within a particular interaction, Goffman viewed communicative or framing processes as a series of moves. According to Goffman, a move is a "structured course of action available to a player. ... [which] objectively alters the situation of the participants" (Goffman, 1969b, p. 145). Moves incorporate everything conveyed by an actor during a turn at taking action (Goffman, 1955, p. 20). Thus moves incorporate talk, actions, or a combination of them; some moves are visible, while others are concealed.

Goffman's use of moves also incorporates a wide range of responses in encounters. As he noted, a conversational move carves

> out a reference, such that the reference and the move may, but need not, be verbal. And what conversation becomes then is a sustained strip or tract of referencings, each referencing tending to bear, but often deviously, some retrospectively perceivable connection to the immediately prior one ...

sequences are thus involved, but these are not sequences of statement and reply but rather sequences at a higher level, ones regarding choice with respect to reach and to the construing of what is reached for. … In this way we could recognize that talk is full of twists and turns and yet go on to examine routinized sequences of these shiftings. Conversational moves could then be seen to induce or allow affirming moves or countermoves, but this gamelike back-and-forth process might be better called interplay than dialogue.

(Goffman, 1981a, pp. 72–73)

It is important to note here that Goffman is explicitly *not* concerned about a "sequence of statement and reply, but rather sequences at a higher level, ones regarding choice with respect to reach" (ibid.). Thus Goffman moves beyond the conversational analysts' focus on adjacency pairs and turn-taking to focus on broader aspects of meaning and context. In my view, this offers more analytic power and insight into communicative processes. Meaning becomes the issue, not a grammar of turn-taking. This is not to deny the valuable (but limited in my view) contributions of conversational analysis to understanding discourse.

Participant status. Within a specific encounter, Goffman (1981a) elaborated the broad distinction between speaker and listener. Speakers, for example, can be *animators* (expressing verbal and nonverbal actions); *authors* (in which they speak directly for themselves and not others); and *principals* (speaking for someone else or selecting a distinct identity and speaking from it—for example, that of a teacher speaking to a male student rather than a mother speaking to her son). Most analyses of communication assume that an individual speaks consistently with his/her role; but, as Goffman noted, that is not necessarily the case, as speakers appear to move seamlessly between different author and principal statuses. The principal perspective would appear to be particularly important in organizing, as frequently participants make reference to, or speak on behalf of, others, especially in organizational settings. These participant roles are not independent, but are dependent upon frames, and may be divided across different people (e.g., a spokesman and a stand-in represent a principal, but in very different ways) (McCawley, 1999). Leung and Gibbons (2008) found that interpreters' roles (i.e., different participant statuses) varied as a function of the task they were involved.

Listeners also have a variety of perspectives that can be assumed; they can be *ratified members* of the encounter, or they can be *"eavesdroppers"* or *"overhearers."* When they respond, listeners may also refer to private thoughts or reactions they had which they are now making public. Goffman incorporated these complexities in the concept of "participation framework," in which he indicated the multiple options both ratified and nonratified participants have in an encounter.

As different participation statuses are established, footing and alignment also change. Thus, like frames, participation status can be keyed and rekeyed. Goffman suggested that "The relation of any one such member to this utterance can be called the 'participation status' relative to it, and that of all the persons in the gathering the 'participation framework' for that moment of speech. The same two terms can be employed when the point of reference is shifted from a given particular speaker to something wider: all the activity in the situation itself ... an utterance does not carve up the world beyond the speaker into precisely two parts, recipients and non-recipients, but rather opens up an array of structurally differentiated possibilities, establishing the participation framework in which the speaker will be guiding his delivery" (Goffman, 1981a, p. 137). For example, different types of audiences—audiences at a political speech, or a lecture, or at a church service—have different expectations for participation and response (Goffman, 1981a, p. 138; Rae, 2001). Some audiences are imagined, while others are physically copresent. As such, participation status also provides a way of talking about how people may be marginalized or silenced in organizational and other communicative settings (Mumby, 1998; Mumby & St. Clair, 1997).

Not only do participation statuses vary, but Goffman also noted that participant arrangements can be embedded and re-embedded. "It turns out that, in something like the ethological sense, we quite routinely ritualize participation frameworks; that is, we self-consciously transplant the participation arrangement that is natural in one social situation into an interactional environment in which it isn't. In linguistic terms, we not only embed utterances, we embed interaction arrangements" (Goffman, 1981a, p. 153).

Levinson's modification. Goffman himself believed these categories had limited usefulness because they were too broad, based primarily on the assumption of dyadic interaction, and applied primarily to conversations (Goffman, 1981a, pp. 125–40). Briefly Levinson (1988) argues that there are participants and non-participants, and they can have production or reception roles. Levinson used four superordinate categories to explain a variety of production roles: (1) the speaker is Goffman's animator; (2) the composer is Goffman's author; (3) the motivator is Goffman's principal; and (4) the source is one who devises the form of the message. An ordinary speaker uses all four "production states." However, in contrast, a lawyer speaks for another in a prescribed format (using all the production states except number 2).

Superordinate categories for reception roles include recipient, addressee, participant and hearer (with varied channel-links enabling comprehension). An overhearer, for example, uses only the channel-link; in contrast, a "targeted overhearer" is both a recipient and uses the channel-link. As Levinson observed, "we are concerned with *what kinds* of categories we need to capture the assignment that we intuitively perform. There is little doubt that what is really interesting is precisely how such categories are invoked and manipulated, and what background expectations and linguistic and conversational devices play a role in these assignments" (Levinson, 1988, p. 192). (For an insightful discussion of these formulations, see Levinson, 1988, pp. 168–82.) It seems reasonable to assume that, for different organizing frames, different categories and conventions will be developed. Much of the work on membership categorization, developed in discourse and conversational analysis, would be of interest here.

Embedding. Goffman referred to communicative practices of *embedding*, in which participants change their relationships or alignment with one another, and their relationship to the ongoing talk (e.g., talking about the present moment, recounting a story from the past, presenting another person's point of view, or responding to another's remarks). Embedding is a form of speaking for another: "Indeed, it is as easy to cite what someone else said as to cite oneself" (Goffman, 1981a, p. 149). Much more empirical work needs to be done to note how these changes may be accomplished, with what effects and in what contexts.

Goffman referred to these changes in embedding as reframing the discourse; discourse can be reframed continuously and include different audiences and times (for example, interjecting discussion about a television program you saw a week ago in an ongoing encounter). At times, reframing may be done simultaneously, as when a pediatrican address her patient, the patient's mother, and an audience of pediatric residents who are observing the medical examination (Tannen & Wallat, 1987).

Footing. This is the general term Goffman used to refer to the projected line one takes up in an encounter, and his work explored how interactants alter their footings, and how others align to these footings. "A change in footing implies a change in the alignment we take up to ourselves and the others present as expressed in the way we manage the production or reception of an utterance" (Goffman, 1981a, p. 128). He developed differences among speakers (e.g., principal, animator) and different types of hearers (e.g., ratified and unratified) that provide insight into changes in footings.

Goffman referred to these activities as performances, in which participants establish a line (a projected self) which they try to maintain. In social encounters, a participant develops "what is sometimes called a line—that is, a pattern of verbal and nonverbal acts by which he expresses his view of the situation and through this his evaluation of the participants, especially himself" (Goffman, 1967, p. 5). All try to cooperate, as Goffman noted, working as a team to perform in ways that sustain the chosen impressions. "Performances consist of elements designed to enhance the audience's sense of 'realness.' These include a 'front:' the stage props, appropriate expressions, and attitudes that allow a performer to conjure up a desired self-image" (Fine & Manning, 2003, p. 34–35).

Ritual respect. Ritual respect is a matter of honoring face in the social circumstances at hand. Individuals who fulfill their interaction obligations simultaneously fulfill their moral (ritual) obligations. As Goffman noted, in interaction

A state where everyone temporarily accepts everyone else's lines is established. This kind of mutual acceptance seems to be a basic structural feature of interaction, especially the interaction of face-to-face talk.

(Goffman, 1967, p. 11)

These ritual requirements are maintained through the display of *deference* and *demeanor*. Deference is given when appreciation of, and respect for, the other participant is shown (Goffman, 1967, pp. 45–60). Deference can be shown, for example, by minor courtesies one extends (presentational rituals) or by avoiding face-threatening acts (avoidance rituals) (ibid., pp. 70–90). Deference can also be displayed by trust (accepting another into your home) as well as accepting expertise (accepting another's technical advice) (p. 59). For example, in a study of identity construction and trust building, Zhang and Huxham (2009) found the deference actions helped establish trust in Sino-Australian business collaboration.

Demeanor is displayed through dress, manner and attitude, which can convey desirable qualities about an individual. Appropriate demeanor is needed for interactants to be able to participate and to act in a manner that does not threaten others and facilitates their participation in an encounter (Goffman, 1967, p. 77). Deference and demeanor thus demonstrate basic interactional trust among participants. In Goffman's later work, he utilized an ethological approach to ritual that suggested "that displays are prospective in character, offering not so much communication as evidence of alignment" (Smith, 2006, p. 53).

Fundamentally, ritual respect is trust that interactants extend to one another in their encounters. For Goffman, the self and separation from a role are "the central analytical terms that support the spatially-defined scaffolding of the performance in a face-to-face interaction. *Both support ritual actions, social circles ritualized by people to confirm their own self where one['s] own expectation is balanced with the positive expectation of other people's behavior (the basis of the trust agreement that sustains and reproduces social interaction*" (Conte, 2008, pp. 378–79, italics mine).

Trust in others supports the routines of social life and social interaction (Goffman, 1983a). Giddens (1984) argues that this trust underlies Goffman's concept of civil inattention, in which people extend polite, non-threatening notice to one another in a variety of gatherings. (As we have seen, Giddens himself places significant emphasis on trust and risk in late modernity.) And, for Goffman, this trust extends to settings in which the "process dynamics of society devolve around trust as equivalent of the accepted social conventions and rules [that permit] … a great variety of projects and purposes to be realized by an automatic recourse to procedural forms" (Conte, 2008, p. 387). For both Goffman and Giddens, trust remains a critical issue in social interaction as well as system integration.

Remedial practices. "Remedial interchanges" are "both a category of interaction and an aspect of certain forms of interaction" (Giddens, 2000, p. 165). Goffman pointed out that a person

> … need not honour a rule of conduct that applies to him. He need not even provide virtual accounts, apologies, and excuses for his deviations. But at least he must be at pains to portray an advocable relationship to the negative judgment of him which results.
>
> *(Goffman, 1971, p. 186)*

When taking on a role, "the individual does not take on a personal, biographical identity—a part or a character—but merely a bit of social categorization, that is, social identity, and only through this a bit of his personal one" (Goffman, 1974, p. 286). What is important, in Goffman's view, is understanding what kind of person it is behind the role (ibid., p. 298).

In Goffman's work, accounts are viewed as a remedial activity (Buttny, 1993; Buttny & Morris, 2001). Accountability is directly linked to responsibility, for, as Goffman noted, "without knowing how those involved in an act attribute responsibility for it, we cannot in the last analysis know what it is that has occurred" (Goffman, 1971, p. 99). Accounts thus address the degree of offense, the agent's responsibility for it, and its impact on others. For minor offenses, most accounts are probably accepted (more a matter of ritual, such as when you excuse yourself for walking into someone inadvertently). However, more noteworthy breaches may call into question the speaker's account, and status and power may also come into play.

In sum, Goffman has proposed a communicative model in which participant status, alignment and remediation are central features. Such alignments take place within the working consensus that interactants have established. Participants project lines which are supported by others as a matter of ritualized trust. When those projected lines are not upheld, various forms of remediation may occur. Thus, for Goffman, the individual is a social self, developed through interaction, although possessing a biological history. Our model of interaction would not be complete without taking a detailed look at Goffman's concept of the self, and its emergence and maintenance in interaction. From an organizational perspective, the self assumes different roles, reflecting the different participation statuses which various organizational roles may require, and demonstrates the capacity to change footings in varied organizational contexts. It is to these processes that we now turn.

The Self

The Social Self

One of the major themes running throughout Goffman's work was a concern for the self. In looking at the trajectory of Goffman's work, Smith noted that

> His interest remained focused on the relation of the self to the interaction order ... the expressive capacities and ritual roles of the self set technical and moral constraints on the organization of the interaction order. ... Most fundamentally, the interactant's self is a "stance-taking entity," as is evident in the underlife and role distances essays, but reaches back to the early conception of the performer and is traceable right through to the dissection of agents (animator, author and principal) embedded in talk's production format.
>
> *(Smith, 2006, pp. 108–9)*

Clearly, in organizations, individuals take public stances and are held accountable for their actions and behaviors. One's interactions contribute to social practices of communicating and organizing as well as providing a vehicle for change.

Lest we think that interaction is only a matter of ritual obligation and thus limited choice, Goffman also reminds us that the self may resist the pull of society:

> Without something to belong to, we have no stable self, and yet total commitment and attachment to any social unity implies a kind of selflessness. Our sense of being a person can come from being drawn into a wider social unit; our sense of selfhood can arise through the little ways in which we resist the pull. Our status is backed by the solid buildings of the world, while our sense of personal identity often resides in the cracks.
>
> *(Goffman, 1961a, p. 280)*

For Goffman, the self is a presentational, social self. It is a product of joint ceremonial activities and reflects many conflicting roles. These roles are transitory, and intertwined in multiple commitments to multi-situated social identities (Goffman, 1961b, p. 142). The self enacts different roles, yet is also based on an individual's "continuing biography," which brings to bear past experiences on the present situation (Goffman, 1974, p. 287). There is a psychobiological dimension in developing the self because cognition, emotions and physical effort are involved in interaction. In interaction, we both express ourselves in a given way as well as try to impress others (Goffman, 1959, pp. 2–4). In our professional as well as personal life, we seek to manage the views others have of us.

Goffman's self is social in two senses: it is a performance that the individual puts on in social situations, as well as the capacity to sustain a dignified self-image with access to appropriate resources, displaying the appropriate traits and abilities associated with that image (Branaman, 1997, p. xlvi). The self, as a product of performance in social life, reflects crucial aspects of the self, such as gender, age and class; and we organize our activities in ways that express gender, age and class. Branaman, West and Zimmerman (1987), and others, credit Goffman's concepts of gender with influencing much of the work done on gender and its effects.

Throughout their lives, individuals are struggling with typifications, strategizing and maintaining definitions of situations. The self is a self intertwined and developed within a social matrix:

> ... each self occurs within the confines of an institutional system, whether a social establishment such as a mental hospital or a complex of personal and professional relationships. The self, then, can be seen as something that resides in the arrangements prevailing in a social system for its members. The self in this sense is not a property of the person to whom it is attributed, but dwells rather in the pattern of social control that is exerted in connection with the

person by himself and those around him. This special kind of institutional arrangement does not so much support the self as *constitute* it.

(Goffman, 1961a, p. 168, italics mine)

Social characteristics such age-grade, gender, class and race—these four statuses—"constitute a cross-cutting grid on which each individual can be relevantly located" and "our placement in respect to all four attributes is evident by virtue of the markers our bodies bring with them into all our social situations" (Goffman, 1983a, p. 14). (It is important to note that Goffman was aware that his analysis of these four statuses represented a middle-class, Western orientation—other cultures may recognize other statuses that may be used as "relevant locators".)

The self is also changeable, so social characteristics may also evolve, and therefore alter the self. As Goffman pointed out

> the self is not an entity half-concealed behind events, but a changeable *formula for managing oneself during them.* Just as the current situation prescribes the official guise behind which we will conceal ourselves, so it provides for where and how we will show through, the culture itself prescribing what sort of entity we must believe ourselves to be in order to have something to show through in this manner.
>
> *(Goffman, 1974, pp. 573–74)*

In this way, Goffman highlighted the negotiated, multiple identities that individuals display in interaction.

The social self, then, is intimately connected with organizing because the self is a product of systemic patterns of control and positioning. The social self is also intimately interwoven with communicating because the social self is an interactional, jointly created entity. Through interaction, the social self is continuously evolving.

The Communicative Self

Goffman's self is also a presentational self and thus simultaneously a complex, communicative self. As he noted

> Starting with the traditional notion of the individual as self-identified with the figure he cuts during ordinary interaction, I have argued some frame-relevant grounds for loosening the bond: That playfulness and other keyings may be involved which sharply reduce personal responsibility; that often what the individual presents is not himself but a story containing a protagonist who may also happen to be himself; that the individual's presumably inward state can be shared around selectively, much as a stage performer manages to externalize the inner feelings of the character he enacts.
>
> *(Goffman, 1974, p. 541)*

As Smith (2006) aptly commented, "Considerations of personal identity loom large in the interaction order, since it is here that social acceptance, character, reputation, composure and the like are enacted" (p. 99). And we continuously orchestrate these impressions.

> ... the individual does not go about merely going about his business. He goes about constrained to sustain a viable image of himself in the eyes of others. Since local circumstances always will reflect upon him, and since these circumstances will vary unexpectedly and constantly, footwork, or rather self work, will be continuously necessary.
>
> *(Goffman, 1971, p. 185)*

Smith also noted the dialectical tension in Goffman's work between information management and ritual, between the tactical and the tactful, and between the system and ritual requirements of the interactional order.

An authentic performance, as Goffman (1959) suggested, is a matter of whether or not the individual is authorized to perform in that manner: In other words, is the individual's projected line appropriate, or is the individual "out of face" and performing inappropriately? For example, does a car salesman have the authority to negotiate a car price, or a police officer the authority to give a sentence to a criminal? Any performance, of course, can be discredited if it is not supported or handled appropriately by others in the situation. "While it may be true that the individual has a unique self all his own, evidence of this possession is thoroughly a product of joint ceremonial labor" (Goffman, 1967, p. 85). However, whether individuals chose to present themselves with authenticity or with fabrication, "the presentational character of the social self is the primary constraint on the organization of social action" (Rawls, 2000, p. 256). It is through these interlocking presentational selves that social practices and social systems develop and evolve.

Thus, Goffman's self developed in the following ways: "(1) the self as socially determined and the dualistic socialized/unsocialized self; [and] (2) the individual as a strategic manipulator of impressions and the socially constrained, script-following social actor" (Branaman, 1997, p. xlviii). As Branaman noted:

> Goffman suggests that the self-as-performer is not merely a social product. The individual as performer is the thinking, fantasizing, dreaming, desiring human being whose capacity to experience pride and shame motivates him or her not only to perform for others but also to take precautions against embarrassment. ... Goffman emphasizes that the self-as-performer is not the same as the self as such, but rather is the basic motivational core which motivates us to engage in the performances with which we achieve selfhood. Thus, dualistic images of self do not contradict his idea that the self is socially constructed. As Goffman sees it, the socialized self, or the self-as-character,

represents a person's unique humanity. It is the socialized self, or the self-as-character, which is equated with the self in our society. ... Paradoxically, it is the self performed outwardly in social life and not the inner motivational core that we think of as the *inner* self.

(ibid., pp. xlviii–xlix)

Scholars assessing Goffman's work suggest that his view of the self may be interpreted both as trusting and compliant (the ritual self) as well as manipulative (the deceptive self). This raises the issue of how Goffman himself views the self, and whether or not the self is an authentic self (Chriss, 1995; Manning, 2000a). *The Presentation of Self in Everyday Life* (1959), *Encounters* (1961b) and *Strategic Interaction* (1969b) all contain analyses of deception, fabrication and counter-deception (see Manning, 2000a, for a fuller discussion of methods of deception and counter-measures). However, Goffman's fundamental point is that—whether being deceptive or authentic—people use the *same* mechanisms to present their line or footing. As Goffman aptly commented, "Whatever we use as a means of checking up on claims provides a detailed recipe for those inclined to cook up reality" (Goffman, 1974, p. 445).

Another issue Goffman focused upon was the issue of credibility; namely, the "ways in which people make their performances convincingly real" (ibid., p. 288). Both authentic presentations and fabricated presentations of the self need to be convincing to others in order to carry off the projected line. As such, Goffman's self is fundamentally a public self, whereby interactions, projected lines and the like present the self as social.

There is also continuity of the self across multiple contexts because Goffman refers to a biological self as well as to the history and continuity of a social self. In *Asylums* (1961a), Goffman explicitly outlined the ways in which inmates made secondary adjustments to protect and develop a self even under very harsh, negative circumstances. Goffman leaves the why of behavior essentially alone, except to argue that people appear to comply with ritual expectations because it is in their best interests to do so—social order is maintained and recognized, and thus embarrassment and shame are avoided. Perhaps an underlying issue of whether or not motives can ever be fully acknowledged—even by the actors themselves—is another reason why Goffman did not pursue this.

In view of the controversy around the authenticity of the self, I believe Goffman is clear on the following points. First, for a performance of the self to be authentic, it must be appropriate (i.e., legitimated by one's qualifications to act in that capacity—such as a priest or judge performing a wedding ceremony). Appropriate acknowledgment by others as to a credible performance makes authenticity a joint accomplishment. Second, the authentic performance of the self needs to be consistent over time and across roles—one's character should not be capricious. Third, the moves an actor makes to convey an impression are the same—whether one is being authentic or fabricating that impression. As Goffman noted, one uses the "same recipe" to cook up deceptions as well as authentic presentations. In addition, interactants may not ever really "know" whether a move is authentic or not, because agents may deceive themselves (i.e., be deluded). Fourth, one may move through different stages of belief, acceptance and/or denial regarding particular actions and the self is also in flux. In brief, judgments of authenticity appear to be a function of appropriateness (legitimacy plus credibility) and consistency. However, fundamentally, judgments of authenticity are limited because similar moves are used to both fabricate as well as convey authenticity.

The Expressive Self

Goffman also developed, in later publications, the concept of an individual as expressive and impulsive, not just as a socialized self. We are prone to act and speak impulsively, act in ways that breach the expectations of appropriate behavior in situations, and so forth. In *Asylums* (Goffman, 1961a) and *Stigma* (Goffman, 1963b), Goffman discussed the underlife of total institutions in which individuals develop resources to sustain a self, despite the mortification of individuals in such settings (e.g., treatment as a member of a batch, with no control over the time and resources by which we express our selves). Although these two books will not be discussed here, Goffman noted that it is frequntly in the contrasts—the normal self with the stigmatized self—that we understand what is hidden about the self and its emergence.

At issue, in every interaction, is the tension or balance between the informative and expressive aspect of communication. As Goffman observed, "as a source of information the individual exudes expression and transmits communication, but … in the latter case the party seeking information will still have to attend to expression lest he will not know how to take what he is told" (Goffman, 1969b, p. 9). When trying to conceal something, one may appear self-conscious and "it is this incapacity to inhibit warning signs of self consciousness that makes an individual relatively safe to be near" (Goffman, 1969b, p. 33). As communication research has shown, the "given off" behaviors are much more difficult to control than the given information. However, as Goffman noted, here everyone is "in the same boat" because deceptions often involve "a multiplicity of checks; everyone, in effect, is in a position to blackmail everyone else" (Goffman, 1969b, p. 77).

Rawls (2000) argued that people are motivated to comply with the interaction order. Goffman "argued carefully over the course of his career that there were interactional prerequisites and needs of self which places constraints on interaction. … Persons conformed with these [interactional ground rules] because if they did not their social selves would cease to exist. It was in their own self interest not to damage themselves and the interaction in which they were engaged" (Rawls, 2000, pp. 269–70, fn. 1).

Another important theme in Goffman's work is that individuals are constrained not to "overreach themselves" in claiming more worthiness than others are willing to accord them (Branaman, 2003, p. 109). This particularly applies in interactions involving stigmatized or marginalized individuals. Goffman also discussed the "good adjustment line" when stigmatized individuals interact with normals and are expected not to exaggerate their circumstances or disadvantage (Goffman, 1963b, pp. 114–17). In addition, Goffman cited examples where people's idealized selves are shifted downwards socially, such as poor families exaggerating their poverty for welfare authorities (Goffman, 1959, pp. 38–40). Interactional work to avoid such embarrassment renders the social structure invisible (Branaman, 1997).

The Psychological Self

For Goffman, the self is not entirely a social self. Goffman developed a dualistic sense of self in which individuals are driven sometimes to act in ways that do not support social norms (Branaman, 1997, p. xlviii). And there is also a biographical sense of self which carries over from situation to situation. In addition, individuals are able to strategically manage impressions in varying social settings. Thus, for Goffman, individuals are flexible in their choice of line, although not entirely free of social constraints; self-claims require "validation by social organizations and other participants" (ibid.). When projected lines cannot be supported, Goffman suggested that "cooling the mark out" addresses the need to help individuals accept a lesser or different status. For example, when one is not promoted at work, others bolster her spirits by lauding her great family and her mothering. This is done fairly frequently and easily because the self is constituted by many roles, and when one role (line) fails, another can readily be developed.

Individuals also distance themselves from some of the roles they play, and view some roles as unimportant to their personal identity. Goffman pointed out that the relationship between person and role "answers to the interactive system—to the frame—in which the role is performed and the self of the performer glimpsed" (Goffman, 1974, p. 573). When one claims a self, it must be consistent with the observable facts of one's social life. Embarrassment may result when interactants' claims about their various selves are not upheld. "Everyday conduct derives ... from ... being the kind of person who enacts and sustains the standards of conduct and appearance of their social group" (Smith, 2006, p. 43). And people can sustain embarrassment or loss in one role because they may be successful in others.

In addition, Goffman discussed a person's self-identity as his subjective sense of his own situation, his continuity and his character—separate from social identity. Our personal identities are defined by how others view us, and we try to maintain a "workable definition of self" that is linked to what others can accord to us (Goffman, 1971, p. 366). We do this through behaving consistently with the lines we have developed for ourselves. According to Goffman, mutual acceptance of each other's lines is a basic aspect of interaction (Goffman, 1967, p. 11). Giddens noted that, for Goffman, "The self consists in an awareness of identity which simultaneously transcends specific roles and provides an integrating means of relating them to personal biography; and a set of dispositions for managing the transactions between motives and the expectations 'scripted' by particular roles" (Giddens, 2000, p. 158).

"Agency", or the ability to act, is a key term for both organizing and communicating. According to Giddens, individuals as agents monitor and organize what they do, but they "must also be seen to 'demonstrate agency' to others" (Giddens, 2000, p. 161). He argued that Goffman approaches agency from three perspectives. First, agents understand what they are doing and they use that understanding "as part of the doing of it." These are "guided doings" in Goffman's terms. Second, individuals have to "chronically display agency to others. Routinely actors have to display competency in terms of control of bodily manoeuvring and positioning and the interpretation of communication from others" (ibid.). Finally, Goffman's "third sense of action" is "where the action is." For Goffman, "where the action is" is where an individual feels a sense of self-worth and involvement in the encounter.

Using Goffman's (1981a) concept of production format, Zidjaly (2009) explored how agency was constructed and jointly negotiated. In her ethnographic study, Zidjaly demonstrates that participants' shifted footing, and provided alternative options for action. This joint negotiation of agency, a collaborative effort to rewrite an official letter, revealed participants' use of past actions, counterarguments and expertise. She notes that "agency is best conceived as a collective process of negotiating roles, tasks, and alignments that takes place through linguistic ... or non-linguistic mediational means" (p. 178). Her ethnographic study demonstrated that exercising agency is a "mediated, collective process of negotiating alignments, tasks, and roles" and explored some of the linguistic strategies that participants use. Zidjaly's study is a necessary reminder that agency, even when exercised by individuals, is a joint achievement that depends on social rules and resources extending beyond that individual. This is especially so in organizational settings in which cooperative, collaborative and intermeshed action is necessary to exercise agency or, for that matter, in contentious disagreement as well.

Maintaining a line for one's self relies partially on impression management. In *Strategic Interaction* (Goffman, 1969b), Goffman discussed how we display approved attributes. Strategic interaction thus explores "the dynamics of interdependence involving mutual awareness ... basic moves [and] natural stopping points in the potentially infinite cycle of two players taking into consideration their consideration of each other's consideration, and so forth" (Goffman, 1969b, p. 137). As Goffman observed, "individuals will shape their expressive conduct to influence definitions of the situation and thus control how others present will respond to them" (Smith, 2006, p. 45). Misinformation or disinformation may arise as well, so there is always risk in interaction, and strong character indicates that one is able to maintain control in difficult situations (Goffman, 1967, pp. 218–20). It is also important to note that agents can act for themselves or others, and act as representatives of others (Goffman, 1969a). Agents' moves may vary from unwitting moves, to misrepresentation, to control moves (ibid., pp. 11–30).

Some critics have suggested that Goffman's self is a cynical, manipulative con man. In contrast, Giddens (2000) suggested that the balance of Goffman's writings portray a "highly moralized world of social relationships." As Giddens argued

> Trust and tact are manifestly more fundamental and binding features of social interaction than is the cynical manipulation of appearances. Thus people routinely shore up or 'repair' the moral fabric of interaction, by displaying tact in what they say and do, by engaging in 'remedial practices', and helping others to save face. If day-to-day social life is a game which may be on occasion turned to one's own advantage, it is a game into which we are all thrust and in which collaboration is essential.
>
> *(Giddens, 2000, p. 154)*

Giddens further argued that "Performances are however just as frequently used to reassure others of genuine motives and commitments as they are to disguise insincerities" (Giddens, 2000, p. 159). And Goffman pointedly reminded us that "When an individual speaks—formally or informally—sometimes what he seems to be doing is voicing an opinion, expressing a wish, desire, or inclination, conveying his attitude, and the like. These attestations of the existence of what are taken to be inner states have a relevant feature; they can be as little established as disconfirmed" (Goffman, 1974, pp. 502–3).

Individuals separate themselves from their roles to some extent. As Goffman argues, for individuals the "cycle of disbelief-to-belief can be followed ... starting with conviction or insecure aspiration and ending in cynicism ... because they can use this cynicism as a means of insulating their inner selves from contact with the audience. And we may even expect to find ... the individual starting out with one kind of involvement in the performance he is required to give, then moving back and forth several times between sincerity and cynicism before completing all the phases and turning-point of self-belief for a person of this station" (Goffman, 1959, p. 20). As these passages indicate, Goffman allows for both sincerity and cynicism, thus obviating the claims of many who study impression management that Goffman's self is primarily a cynical self.

As we have seen, Goffman has a very rich concept of self, incorporating the social self, communicative self, expressive self and psychological self. All these facets of the self are important for communicating and organizing. For Goffman, the self is a "joint ceremonial labor" that emerges through interaction, and these interactions are embedded within varying sets of social practices, reflecting both organizing and communicating processes. As such, the self is fundamentally interwoven with interaction. Goffman's discussion of alignment, footing, remedial repairs, projected lines and the like apply equally well to both interpersonal and organizational contexts. Issues, such as authenticity, identity and deception, also are valid concerns in both our personal and professional lives. As Goffman observed, there is continuity in the self across multiple contexts so we can anticipate that the richness and complexity of the self is relevant across multiple contexts. (See also Luhtakalio, 2005.)

Territories of the self. Included in Goffman's concept of self are territories of the self which involve physical objects, space, and privacy for the self (Goffman, 1971, pp. 30–40). The eight territories of the self include: (1) personal space; (2) the stall (a bounded space, like a library chair, which can be claimed completely for a short time); (3) use space (space immediately in front of you); (4) the turn (your place in a line, for example); (5) the sheath (your body and the clothing you are wearing); (6) possessional territory (like personal effects); (7) information preserve (the information you can control access to in the presence of others); and (8) conversational preserve (the ability to control who you converse with). These latter two would appear to be especially important in organizational communication.

Region. The region refers to the place in which the interaction occurs: The front region (frontstage) denotes the public arena for interaction where desirable impressions are being projected. In contrast, the back region (backstage) is private information that may be kept hidden because it may discredit or detract from the performance being given. For example, an employee projects support for a program (frontstage) but expresses serious reservations about it talking with a good friend (backstage). In some cases, a physical separation is needed between front and back regions, as in, for example, the kitchen (backstage) versus customer areas (frontstage) in restaurants, or the viewing versus preparation areas in funeral homes (Goffman, 1959, pp. 105–16). Everyone needs a backstage, however, for privacy for the self. According to Collins, Goffman conveyed "a sense of the potential fluidity and hence fragileness of social realities. Social life, under the functional constraints for people to uphold consistent definitions of reality both for oneself and for each other, is nevertheless forced into a two-sidedness: a frontstage and a backstage" (Collins, 2000b, p. 316).

In summary, the self is social, constituted by interaction with others, and by having one's lines supported by others. The self is also vulnerable and at risk in every interaction because one's projected lines may not be maintained by others. Multiple identities form the self, with some identities more central than others. There is a psychobiological aspect to the self as one carries with one's self the memories of past encounters and achievements, as well as one's corporeal body. In interaction, the self also confronts the tension between informative versus expressive needs. We also accept risk and rejection as a possible consequence of our actions and behaviors. And finally, the self claims territories, and utilizes both front and back regions.

As Goffman observed, as an aspect of ritual requirements, everyone is owed deference just by being human. Everyone should be accorded respect, as well as giving respect to others. This ritual respect is captured in Goffman's concept of face, which is a major facet of his concept of self, and central to his theory of the interaction order. We shall next explore Goffman's concept of face.

The Concept of Face

When interacting (the framing process), participants' social selves are open, accessible, and vulnerable to each other. In every encounter, Goffman argued that participants take a nonverbal and verbal line reflecting their view of the situation, and of others in the situation. Goffman regarded face as "diffusely located in the flow of events" and maintained by others in the encounter (Goffman, 1967, p. 7). It is in interaction that a "person protects and defends and invests his feelings in an idea about himself and ideas are vulnerable not to facts but to communications" and communications can be "by-passed, withdrawn from, disbelieved, conveniently misunderstood, and tactfully conveyed" (Goffman, 1967, p. 43). Face is the positive social value one assumes during a particular encounter—a self-image delineated in terms of approved social attributes—emerging through interaction and confirmed or disconfirmed by others.

For Goffman, face is supported by both ritual and strategic interaction. As Goffman argued, face maintenance is necessary for interaction—face-work refers to "actions taken by a person to make whatever he is doing consistent with face" (Goffman, 1967, p. 12). As Goffman notes, to understand face-work is to understand "the traffic rules of social interaction" (ibid.). Strategies can range from introducing positive information about the self, avoiding contact with those who might threaten the image one wants to project, or establishing a favorable balance in relationships with others (Goffman, 1967, pp. 10–20).

Face therefore is not a property of an individual, but is socially emergent—a combination of internally consistent acts that maintain a public projection of the self which is confirmed by others. Face is maintained when a projected self-image is accepted and supported by others. One's image is supported by one's own communicative efforts, but also needs to be supported by others in the situation. When an interactant establishes his own line, he must also honor the lines of others. Both interactants need to establish themselves as acceptable. "The contributions of all are oriented to these and built up on the basis of them" (Goffman, 1967, pp. 106).

Face-work. Face-work refers to actions necessary to establish a consistent face. As such, interactants contribute to an orderly flow of messages, and sustain the situational meanings of the encounter (the frames representing the immediate social settings). Mutual face, then, involves both the rule of self-respect and the rule of considerateness (Branaman, 2003, pp. 92–93). Goffman also emphasized the importance of social relationships with others in this process; as he notes, in a social relationship one is dependent upon trusting others to maintain one's self-image and to act in a tactful manner (Goffman, 1969a, p. 34). For Goffman, maintaining face is necessary for smooth interaction. Goffman observed that it seems to be characteristic in social relationships "that each of the members guarantees to support a given face for the other members in given situations" (Goffman, 1967, p. 42).

Face can be threatened either innocently (e.g., a gaffe), intentionally (e.g., an attack by another) or incidentally (e.g., an unintended consequence of an action or utterance). Individuals also act to avoid face-threatening situations, and may not choose to acknowledge face threats (e.g., ignoring put-downs, or acting as if an embarrassing action had not occurred).

Yet, at times, face-work becomes aggressive rather than being cooperative and interaction becomes contentious. In contentious encounters, sometimes discrediting information, snubs, insults, and the like occur (Goffman, 1967, p. 24). Face-work is needed to repair face, and to re-establish the line being taken. Corrective actions could include apologies, explaining that one's remarks were misunderstood, that one was just joking, and so on. Many times interactants may avoid face-threatening acts by avoiding sensitive topics or issues.

People interacting may act to preserve their own face, as well as the face of others in the encounter. Any group, Goffman argued, "must mobilize their members as self-regulating participants in social encounters. One way of mobilizing the individual for this purpose is through ritual: he is taught to be perceptive, to have feelings attached to self and a self expressed through face, to have pride, honour, and dignity, and to have considerateness, to have tact and a certain amount of poise" (Goffman, 1967, p. 44). This mutual regard for face provides the foundation for interaction; if face is threatened, there is social pressure to repair such threats, unless there is no desire to continue the interaction or preserve the social relationship. Cases of contentious face-work may not be resolved, as in the case of mutual exchanges of insults, with no repairs.

Face, then, enables interactants to smoothly and routinely interact in their social groups, including organizations and institution. Yet how face-work is carried out may vary culturally. Ting-Toomey (1988), Chen (1990), Economidou-Kogetsidis (2010) and Grainger, Mills and Sibanda (2010), among others, argue that face is a transcultural concept that varies in the nuances by which face-work management in carried out in different cultures. (See also Schimmelfrennig, 2002.)

Face, according to Goffman, is "on loan," and the commitment to preserve face makes "everyman his own jailer" (Goffman, 1967, p. 10). Ritual face-work makes participants "self-regulating participants in social encounters," and there are "feelings attached to self, and a self expressed through face" (Goffman, 1967, p. 44). Every interaction, no matter how trivial, contains the possibility for risk or gain. Goffman also noted that interaction in any culture has means for avoiding embarrassment and this may provide a basis for cross-cultural comparisons in interaction. In addition, face concerns are also emotional: "harm to another's face causes 'anguish,' and harm to one's own face is expressed in 'anger'" (Bargiela-Chiappini, 2003, p. 1458).

The maintenance of face also involves inhibition of responses, as well as participatory responses. Participatory responses are given spontaneously and candidly whereas inhibitory responses are more calculated. This early distinction, according to Chriss, later developed into his concepts of avoidance rituals and presentational rituals. In showing deference, avoidance rituals specify what not to do, while presentational rituals outline what is to be done (Chriss, 2003, pp. 188–90).

Face is maintained when the line one takes presents an image that is internally consistent and confirmed by others. Someone may be in *wrong face* when his or her line cannot be sustained by the information provided (Goffman, 1967, p. 8). *Being out of face* occurs when one does not have a readily available line of the kind participants in such situations are expected to have (ibid.). When face is threatened, a repair is needed to re-establish the interactional equilibrium. These interchanges consist of a challenge, an offering, acceptance, and gratitude although this sequence can be modified.

Goffman also acknowledged the delicate balance between maintaining one's own face, as well as that of others in an encounter, and he recognized that this must be accomplished "without any apparent effort, and without becoming material for the participants directly to consider" (Williams, 1988, p. 68). For Goffman, underlying face needs are the assumptions of Grice's Cooperative Maxim, and the assumption of rationality, or practical reasoning, "which guarantees inferences from ends or goals to means that will satisfy those ends" (ibid., p. 64).

According to Goffman, much of the support for mutual face is driven by the desire to avoid embarrassment. Goffman was concerned about the embarrassment that results when the self is discredited (Goffman, 1967, pp. 104–7). Moves in social status, even upwards, such as an employment promotion, may result in embarrassment if colleagues do not support the improved status. On the other hand, if one oversteps one's status, a resulting show of embarrassment will salvage the situation, and social order will be preserved. According to Branaman (2003), Goffman's work on the interrelationships among interaction norms, emotion, and social order has inspired subsequent work in the emerging subfield of the sociology of emotions (for example, in the work of Scheff, Collins, and Hochschild).

Brown and Levinson's extension of face. Based on Goffman's work, Brown and Levinson (1987) further developed the concept of face. Within the pragmatic tradition, they have developed a typology for the strategies interactants use in accommodating face needs. They suggested that face is an interactional universal, although expressed and manifested differently in different cultures. Like Goffman, Brown and Levinson suggested that interactants act in ways to preserve and honor face; it is in participants' best interests to do so in order that the fragile, working understanding that enables interaction is not disrupted.

Positive face strategies preserve the positive image claimed by interactants, while negative face strategies protect the freedom of action and freedom from imposition accorded to interactants. (In Goffman's terms, positive/negative face may be parallel, respectively, to Goffman's ideas of presentational moves or demeanor, and avoidance moves or deference.)

> In general, people cooperate (and assume each other's cooperation) in maintaining face in interaction, such cooperation being based on the mutual vulnerability of face. That is, normally everyone's face depends on everyone else's being maintained, and since people can be expected to defend their

faces if threatened, and in defending their own to threaten others' faces, it is in general in every participant's best interest to maintain each other's face.

(Brown & Levinson, 1987, p. 61)

However, Bargiela-Chiappini (2003) noted that Brown and Levinson's concept of negative face does not fit with Goffman's view of face, nor does their emphasis on the rational actor correspond to Goffman's view of face as an interactional state. (For excellent overviews of face and face-work, see Bargiela-Chiappini, 2003; Bargiela-Chiappini & Haugh, 2009; Brown, 2000; Chen, 1990; Holtgraves, 2001, 2009; Pfister, 2010; and Tracy, 1990).

Politeness. An overview of politeness by Holtgraves illustrated the variety of approaches taken to politeness, and focused on the dominant framework of a "face management view of politeness" (Holtgraves, 2001, p. 341). This approach argued that face concerns (Goffman, 1967) are the foundation for all politeness behavior, and that such concerns are present within encounters because one's face must be ratified or disconfirmed by others in the encounter. Research on politeness has been difficult because of the limitations of various classification systems for politeness strategies, and the multifunctionality of utterances (i.e., utterances may have multiple politeness strategies; see, for example, Tracy, 1990). Despite these difficulties, some findings appear consistent.

Brown and Levinson (1987) argued that politeness would vary as a function of the weightiness of a given act (determined by the intrinsic degree of imposition of the act, the power of the hearer relative to that of the requestor, and the social distance between them). Generally, there has been strong support for power as an influential factor, with higher speaker power being linked to less politeness in a wide variety of empirical and observational studies (Holtgraves, 2001, p. 347). Increasing imposition is also related to increases in politeness; positive face is associated with affiliation, while negative face is associated with autonomy (ibid.). Other factors influencing face and face-work include differences across individuals in terms of how concerned they are with face, an individual's self-esteem, and the use of indirect forms of communication. Other issues of concern include cultural influences on politeness, particularly in collectivist or individualistic cultures (see, for example, Spencer-Oatey, 2007), attention given to self-face versus other-face (Ting-Toomey, 2005; Ting-Toomey & Kurogi, 1998) and nonverbal expressions of politeness (emphasized by Goffman).

Mao (1994) argued that Brown and Levinson's concept of face, rather than applying universally, is biased with respect to a Western orientation to individualism. He linked Goffman's concept of face with the Chinese concept of face, and argued that both focus on the negotiated, emergent nature of face. Although Brown and Levinson acknowledged there are cultural variations in how face is accomplished, Mao suggested that their view still gives primacy to the self. Mao developed the Relational Face Orientation, which acknowledges the tensions between ideal social identity and ideal individual autonomy. However, these distinctions seem to mirror the distinction between collectivistic and individualistic cultures. Collectivist cultures value harmony and how individuals fit into the group, whereas individualistic cultures value the autonomy and independence of individuals.

In my view, Mao's comparisons highlight different ways in which public face may be developed and maintained. Mao observed that face in China includes both achievement and personal character. His findings suggested that we need to look for the manner in which face is conceptualized in different cultures, as well as look for distinctive cultural practices for honoring face. Finally, face may be a function of the roles people take, rather than reflect some essentialist notion of the self. I think Goffman's concept of face, as developed previously, is consistent with these concerns for cultural variability and for a socially emergent view of face. (See also Lerner, 1996, and Matsumoto, 1988.)

Yet another alternative model of face and face-work, Face Constituting Theory (Arundale, 2006, 2009, 2010), conceptualizes face as a dialectic of separateness and connectedness. As such, Arundale argues that face is relational, emerges through interaction, and applies cross-culturally—all consistent with Goffman's concept of face. Arundale goes on to argue that Goffman's concept of face is based on the individual and on rule-following actions. But face is both individual (the choice of a projected line) and interactional (that line must be supported or amended or challenged when interacting with others). As noted earlier, Goffman argues that face and face-work emerge in interaction and that face-work does not necessarily follow scripted rules; Goffman's own work provides for contentiousness in face and thus for contingencies that need to be negotiated in that situation. In part, Arundale's use of face may be viewed as an alternative framing of an interaction, one that may be keyed and rekeyed in a variety of ways. Another view on face, focusing on the tension between connectedness and separation, is O'Driscoll's Face Dualism Theory (O'Driscoll, 1996, 2007).

As we have seen, research on face and face-work has also widened beyond issues of politeness. Issues around face and identity, on self versus other versus mutual face (Ting-Toomey, 1988), and face concerns in various interpersonal and organizational contexts, are also receiving more scholarly attention (Haugh, 2009). Face can also be analyzed on multiple levels: on the individual level, through stocks of knowledge underlying interpretations of action, and attributions; on the interactive level, one can assess the implicit and explicit evaluations of participants that emerge; and at the sociocultural level, one can relate face to events over long time spans (Haugh, 2009, p. 17). Given the theoretical approach set out in this book, all these analytic levels could be accommodated. For a very rich, intriguing discussion of face-work cross-culturally, see Bargiela-Chiappini et al. (2007) on Eastern perspectives of face.

As Haugh cogently points out, face can "involve an awareness of one's position within a network ... can be associated with groups as well as individuals ... and be given or gained as well as sacrificed among other things" (Haugh, 2009, p. 2). A number of scholars have also called for returning to Goffman's original conceptualization of face (Bargiela-Chiappini, 2003)—a move I heartily endorse. Haugh (2009) argues that face is both constitutive of (i.e., necessary for) as well as co-constituted (i.e., jointly accomplished by participants) in interaction: this is a view that also reflects Goffman's conceptualization of face. Face-work reflects "the ritual attention that interactants must give to one another so that they can effectively participate in a social interaction. Face-work, then, is a requirement for social interaction, a mechanism that accounts for the emergence of orderly social interaction from the chaos of self-serving individuals" (Holtgraves, 2009, p. 193). In brief, face is required for and emerges within interaction. As such, face reflects the basic ritual respect and trust interactants extend to one another in their jointly achieved sense of "what is going on here." Haugh further notes that an analyst's approach needs to be "consonant with the understandings of participants" (Haugh, 2009, p. 9). Haugh concludes that "broadening the focus of analysis of face to include ways in which it is both co-constituted in as well as constitutive of interaction ... avoids divergence between the analyst's interpretation (second-order) and that of the participants (first-order)" (ibid., p. 15). (See also Tefkouraki, 2005.)

Increasingly, research is pointing out the complexity of identity and self-construal in social life (Gudykunst & Kim, 2003; Hacking, 2004). Tracy cogently summarized this complexity:

> Because people's self and other identity concerns are often complicated, many of the faces of facework may be visible in the same interaction. However, because language is multifunctional, serving other purposes besides face; because meaning is culturally situated and contextually cued; and because desired identities may be in competition, the job of claiming and inferring identities is a highly complex one.
>
> *(Tracy, 1990, p. 221)*

We might also view "claiming and inferring" face as equally complex.

In conclusion, framing, as we have seen, is an important aspect of guiding interactional behaviors in the moment-by-moment alignments among participants. Maintaining face is also an essential interactional component necessary for smooth, fluid interaction. Interaction also relies on mutual trust among participants because others confirm one's projected self-image. Finally, frames and framing moves rely on the taken-for-granted knowledge which sustains shared interaction and sensemaking. Goffman thus acknowledges the importance of the uses of frames being developed in this book: frames as representing the general social context ("basic frameworks of understanding"); frames as representing tacit knowledge ("standard doings and standard reasons for doing those doings"); and frames as representing immediate social settings ("definition of the situation").

Goffman's uses of frames and frame analysis have been developed as a way of analyzing the moment-by-moment alignment of participants in everyday encounters. Like Goffman, the theory of structurational interaction emphasizes the importance of context—the situated nature of talk—if we are to understand what is meant by what is said. In addition, we need to acknowledge the importance of shared commonsense knowledge, which undergirds every act of communication. To acknowledge these issues and their importance is not to descend into "rampant situationalism," but rather to understand, through frames, how people use everyday knowledge to interact with one another.

Goffman's unique, and frequently misunderstood, contribution is his argument for "the existence of social constraints and social facts which are not the effects of routinizations [expectations for future action created by the repetitition of action], not defined by social structure and not derived from individuals ... social facts [are] interactional, not social structural" (Rawls, 2000, p. 265). In this, Goffman and Giddens take similar positions—social facts and social practices are interactional.

Although some question the importance of frame analysis, Collins confronted these questions when he argued:

> A key characteristic of the realm of human culture, then, is precisely this feature of transforming ordinary actions into things seen in a different light. Even the nature of language itself might be interpreted in this way (although Goffman does not raise this point). ... Framing permeates the level of ordinary social action. We live in a world of social relationships, in which roles are acted out, with various keyings and deceptions played upon them. ... The nature of talk involves a complex shifting of frames, as people set up topics of conversation, manoeuvre over the implied relationships among the conversationalists, make jokes and insults, bargain, engage and distance themselves with their words and each other.
>
> (Collins, 1988, pp. 60–61, citing Goffman, 1974, pp. 496–559)

Turner (1988) constructed an implicit model of Goffman's work, linking macro-structural parameters with micro-level interactions. In any encounter, an agent brings shared cultural orientations on appropriate frames, rituals, and stagecraft (props and settings used in public performances)—all macrostructural parameters. Agents in encounters thus negotiate the meaning of what is going on three dimensions; incorporating the rituals, frames, and staging of both their own and others' performances. Goffman's substantial contribution was to acknowledge the impact of staging, ritual and framing in daily interchanges. As Turner concluded:

> I see Goffman as having made three important contributions to the study of interaction. First, his work was the first to recognize that everyday life is punctuated with rituals that mark group membership and that structure the sequencing of everyday interaction. Second, his earliest works were instrumental in conceptualizing the ecology and geography of interaction as crucial signaling processes. And third, his last major work transformed rather static

notions like 'definition of the situation' into a more active process of framing and reframing interaction settings.

(Turner, 1988, p. 95)

As such, Goffman's work is of significance in understanding communicating and organizing, and their interrelationships.

As we have seen, although Goffman's work was primarily focused on mundane daily encounters, his work has also discussed the impact of institutional orders on interaction. Because organizing and communicating are central foci of this book, it is to this aspect of his work that we now turn, looking at how Goffman's concepts have been applied in organizational settings.

10

GOFFMAN AND LARGER SOCIAL INSTITUTIONS

Although Goffman's work focused primarily on the interaction order and its properties, he did comment on the connections between the interaction order and other social orders, such as institutions. Beyond its foundational role in Giddens' structuration theory, we can directly connect Goffman's work to institutional contexts. There is much in his work to suggest that these linkages are possible, although Goffman himself did not develop these connections. McCannell suggested that Goffman tried to establish the interaction order as a social order in its own right, yet as he pointed out, "If there was ever a subject matter enmeshed in and determined by institutional arrangements … it is face-to-face interaction" (MacCannell, 2000, pp. 28–29). And Goffman himself noted that

> To confine ourselves to the large social formations resembles the older science of anatomy with its limitation to the major, definitely circumscribed organs such as heart, liver, lungs, and stomach, and with its neglect of the innumerable, popularly unnamed or unknown tissues. Yet without these, the more obvious organs could never constitute a living organism. On the basis of the major social formations—the traditional subject matter of social science—it would be similarly impossible to piece together the real life of society as we encounter it in our experience. Without the interspersed effects of countless minor syntheses, society would break up into a multitude of discontinuous systems. Sociation continuously emerges and ceases and emerges again.
>
> *(Simmel, as quoted in Goffman, 1953b, p. iv)*

While Goffman acknowledged the importance of societal institutions, he himself chose to work on the web of minor interactions which reflect and sustain those institutions.

Leeds-Hurwitz (2004) suggested that "an understanding of the relationship that holds between these levels [the interaction order and the social order] is necessary in order to fully understand and utilize Goffman's work" (p. 4). As she observed "Goffman assumes that social order is possible, and asks ... if we want to observe social order in action, at *what* do we look? ... *Order is seen as being a process through which behavior is systematized, a pattern which provides the structure for interaction, and which in turn is created through that interaction* ... Goffman assumes the questions of how and why coordination is achieved, asking rather what we should look at in order to observe that coordination in action. His answer, obviously, is everyday interactions" (ibid., p. 10, italics mine; see also Leeds-Hurwitz, 2008).

This perspective parallels the viewpoint of Giddens' structuration theory in which the duality of structure argues that interaction instantiates social structure, and that social structure reciprocally influences interactional patterns. As Giddens himself noted, in assessing Goffman's work, "The fixity of institutional forms does not exist in spite of, or outside, the encounters of day-to-day life but *is implicated in those very encounters*" (Giddens, 1998, p. 69, italics in the original).

For Goffman, social order is the "consequence of any act of moral norms that regulates the way in which persons pursue objectives" (Goffman, 1963a, p. 8). And he identified a variety of social orders, such as legal, economic, ritual, kinship and political orders, among others. Leeds-Hurwitz argued that these orders identify overlapping areas. As she concluded, "we study specific interactions in order to learn about the interaction order and, through it, eventually about the social order; we observe the micro level (the small and mundane) in order to comprehend the macro level (the large and meaningful). What intrigued Goffman were the implications of being able to observe social order only through individual examples of interaction" (Leeds-Hurwitz, 2004, p. 22). (I might add that even the mundane world of daily interaction is significant for negotiating face, identity, goals, and so forth.) In addition, interaction, for Goffman, serves as more than information transmission, but also serves a variety of communicative functions, such as fun, irony, sarcasm, and innuendo (Chriss, 1995, p. 556).

The Interaction Order and Social Order

Many scholars studying Goffman have noted the implications of his work for institutions and social structure, although he himself did not elaborate on this (Giddens, 1988; Manning, 1992; Scheff, 2005a, b). Goffman did, however, view social situations as the medium for the "loose coupling" of the interaction order to the social order:

> ... what one finds, in modern societies at least, is a nonexclusive linkage—a "loose coupling"—between interactional practices and social structures, a collapsing of strata and structures into broader categories, ... a gearing as it were of the various structures into interactional cogs. Or, if

you will, a set of transformation rules, or a membrane selecting how various externally relevant social distinctions will be managed within the interaction.

(Goffman, 1983a, p. 11)

This conceptualization parallels that of Giddens, with his use of modalities of structuration (signification, legitimation and domination).

Given Goffman's view of the self as managing shifting alignments within any interaction, he would obviously reject any simple type of determinism connecting the social order with the interaction order. He observed that "Social arrangements for the most part are inherently ambiguous, meaning here that the interactional facts are only loosely geared to structural ones" (Goffman, 1971, p. 224). Such a position is a natural consequence of the laminating or layered frames of interpretation in any encounter. Boden (1994), for example, utilizing Goffman's frame analysis, viewed organizations as a *"lamination"* of conversations, in which organizational layers are built up by decisions being *"talked* into being in fine yet layered strips of interaction" (p. 51). Societies may have either relatively tight or loose coupling between the interaction order and social order as in, for example, the distinctions between high-context and low-context cultures (see Hall, 1976), or restricted and elaborated codes (see Bernstein, 1977).

As noted earlier, although Goffman did not focus on macro-level social orders, he himself noted some fundamental linkages between interaction and institutions. One of the most fundamental of these is that any social organization (or social order) presupposes that individuals have the ability to maintain one definition of the situation—Goffman refers to this as "team playing," which involved rational actions (means-ends rationality) as well as control over information (Battershill, 1990, pp. 171–72). Thus Goffman, like Giddens, recognizes the centrality of communication in creating and maintaining social order.

Goffman also noted that, because complex organizations depend on people, and people can be harmed in situations, so too can their organizations. As Goffman observed, when organizational members can be intimated, persuaded or flattered, "here, too, the interaction order bluntly impinges on macroscopic entities" (Goffman, 1983a, p. 8). Through communication technology, these effects can be extended through time and space. Finally, Goffman noted that, for many organizations, situations center on people processing encounters:

Every culture ... seems to have a vast lore of fact and fantasy regarding embodied indicators of status and character, thus appearing to render persons readable. ... What is situational, then, about processing encounters is the evidence they so fully provide of a participant's real or apparent attributes while at the same time allowing life chances to be determined through an inaccessible weighting of this complex of evidence.

(Goffman, 1983a, p. 8)

Thus, the influence between interaction and social order appears to be both reciprocal and bi-directional. And in such situations, certainly power differentials are being explicitly outlined by Goffman. Thus Goffman, like Giddens, argued that social interaction can both reproduce the current social order as well as alter it.

In addition, as is generally agreed upon, social relationships influence participants' interaction and, within organizations, social relationships are likely to be influenced by one's categorical membership (e.g., institutional roles). It is especially significant to note participation frameworks in organizing contexts. When interacting, we identify people both categorically (age, gender, occupational role, institutional position, and so forth) as well as individually (as being friendly, self-confident, quiet, and so forth). Within organizations, categorical identification will often influence the manner in which interaction proceeds. For Goffman, both sources of identification are essential in all interaction (Goffman, 1983a, b).

Although Goffman suggested linkages between social organization and social interaction, he did not agree with those who find macrostructures embedded within the interactional order. As he noted, "they confuse the interactional format in which words and gestural indications occur with the import of these words and gestures ... How delicately or indelicately one is treated during the moment in which bad news is delivered does not speak to the structural significance of the news itself" (Goffman, 1983a, pp. 8–9). As Giddens observed, "Such a position, in Goffman's eyes, confuses the situation within which actions occur with the institutional consequences of those actions" (Giddens, 1988, p. 272). Macroscopic structures and processes can be subject to insightful microanalysis, but it is the type of microanalysis that explores critical differences between different industries, regions and so forth. Such differences would be, as I suggested elsewhere, of great interest to pursue (and a possibility offered by Giddens' institutions of signification, domination and legitimation).

Moreover, Goffman noted that one can specify the deference given to others in the broader social order. However, for the interactional order, Goffman suggested that, after this deference pattern has been noted, "one must search out who else does it to whom else, then categorize the doers with a term that covers them all, and similarly with the done to. And one must provide a technically detailed description of the forms involved" (1983a, p. 12). Thus for Goffman those intersections of the social order and the interaction order are useful and insightful, but one cannot expect that the "macrosociological features of society, along with society itself, are an intermittently existing composite of what can be traced back to the reality of encounters—a question of aggregating and extrapolating interactional effects" (1983a, p. 8).

Yet it is theoretically and analytically important to look at the interrelationships between the interaction order and social order because "neither the interaction nor the social order exists apart from observable behavior" (Sigman, 1987, p. 49). As Sigman pointed out, social structural considerations as well as momentary situational contingencies can influence the range of behavioral options appropriate at a particular time (ibid.).

Rawls notes that

> Interactions are not mini-institutions. The problem of achieving mutual understanding imposes its own constraints on interaction which are different from the constraints imposed by social institutions. ... a more satisfactory distinction between social forms draws a line between those aspects of encounters whose meaning is a constitutive achievement and therefore requires mutual commitment of a special sort, and those aspects whose meaning is defined with respect to pre-given framing considerations (e.g., institution, role).
>
> *(Rawls, 1989, p. 149)*

And Goffman argued that social structure helps select from the available repertoire of appropriate cultural displays (Goffman, 1983a, p. 11). For example, as Sigman noted, with respect to one's social status, in order to be relevant to some encounter, it must be "transformed into a *participation status*" (Sigman, 1987, p. 46).

More generally, Goffman emphasized that, although the social world contains complex levels, people nevertheless usually know, or could know, what level they are on. One is practicing for a game (a keying of a keying); or perhaps one is reminiscing conversationally about work experiences—both transformative keyings of the natural and social world. But "Goffman at least manages to capture both sides; not only the complexities and dynamics of the world, but also the ability of people (and of a sufficiently sophisticated sociologist) to settle on a clear reality much of the time" (Collins, 2000b, p. 334).

Thus, the social order and interaction order are intimately woven together in multiple ways. In addition, Goffman suggested that "society is organized on the principle that any individual who possesses certain social characteristics has a moral right to expect that others will value and treat him in a correspondingly appropriate way" (Goffman, 1959, p. 13). Furthermore, that same obligation exists for organizations: "Every organization ... involves a discipline of activity, but our interest here is that at some level every organization also involves a discipline of being—an obligation to be of a given character and dwell in a given world" (Goffman, 1961a, p. 188).

Ritual respect is a prime consideration in interaction, and organizational social practices may shape the manner in which ritual respect is displayed. Rawls also noted that

> ... every action and conversation takes place within an institutional context of some sort, and this context can always be brought to bear at the level of accounts. ... We construct sense in conversation through sequential implicativeness, but at any moment we may be moved to the level of accounts and forced back into our social positions.
>
> *(Rawls, 1989, p 169)*

While language has an order and referential meaning independent of social constraints, the *use of language—interaction—is always and everywhere subject to social constraints provided by institutional arrangements and one's positions in those arrangements.* Thus, Rawls is fundamentally incorrect in arguing that at any moment we may be moved into accountability, we are always and everywhere accountable socially. We use linguistic and other resources to present ourselves to others, gain desired ends, and the like, but linguistic resources are always socially contextualized.

Sigman (1987) suggested that a model integrating the contributions of both the interactional order and social order is required to adequately account for communication. I would argue that the communicative assumptions outlined previously and the theory of structurational interaction being developed here integrate knowledge of both the interaction order and social order, particularly in interactants' awareness of tacit knowledge, inferences and relevances that apply in particular social settings. Joint negotiation of encounters by participants allow social relationships to emerge, and new influences on both the interaction order and social order to emerge.

Goffman's concept of frames allows for multiple constraints and interpretations that acknowledge both social order and the interaction order (as you will recall, frames may represent structures of social organization). Goffman's work incorporates a much broader conceptualization of communicative processes, including frames and its rich layers of analysis; a concern for nonverbal aspects of communication, especially the use of space; an emphasis on routine and social practices; the importance of tacit knowledge, and, above all, a concern for the effects of communication on participants. In short, Goffman's work enables us to integrate meaning into the analysis of communicating which grammars of interaction, such as conversational analysis or speech act analysis, do not. The concept of grand Discourses, or meta-frames, can also be readily accommodated by frame analysis. While there is clearly value in studying grammars of interaction, they are limited in their ability to account for the richness and complexity of communicating and organizing. Goffman's broader perspective, incorporating both verbal and nonverbal dimensions of interaction, provides a stronger basis for assessing communicating and organizing. And my argument here is to suggest that Giddens' conceptualization of social order is compatible with Goffman's views, and that the theory of structurational interaction being developed here provides an insightful perspective on communicating and organizing.

Goffman's analysis of social systems (institutions). Although the social order was not a focal point of his scholarship, Goffman, as we have seen, clearly acknowledged the important interrelationships between the interaction order and the social order. And he clearly acknowledged that the social order was instantiated in interaction. While some critics have argued that he did not discuss the interaction order under conditions where power differences among participants was important, Goffman was aware of such differences and their impact on interaction. *Forms of Talk*, for example, analyzed institutional constraints on interaction.

Total institutions. One clear set of analyses relating the interactional order to larger institutional orders is Goffman's work on total institutions (see *Asylums,* Goffman, 1961a). Although a full review and appreciation of this work is well beyond the scope of this book, a brief overview will help flesh out some of the ways in which Goffman has pursued societal institutions such as mental hospitals and prisons in which inmates or patients are quite clearly separated from general society. As Goffman observed:

> Every institution captures something of the time and interest of its members and provides something of a world for them; in brief, every institution has encompassing tendencies ... some are encompassing to a degree discontinuously greater than the ones next in line. Their encompassing or total character is symbolized by the barrier to social intercourse with the outside and to departure that is often built into the physical plant, such as locked doors, high walls, barbed wire, cliffs, water, forests, or moors. These establishments I am calling *total institutions,* and it is their general characteristics I want to explore.
>
> *(Goffman, 1961a, p. 4)*

For Goffman, institutions were differentiated on the basis of how much time they take up from participants (Becker, 2003). Those institutions taking up almost all the time of participants were "total institutions." Total institutions (TIs) were further categorized on the basis of the participants' inclusion in TIs—they may not be able to take care of themselves, they may endanger others, or both, or they might be isolated for important work (such as military actions or a religious retreat) (p. 666). The language Goffman used was neutral and applied to institutions we may think about very negatively (such as prisons) or very positively (such as nunneries or monasteries) and thus illuminates the continuities and discontinuities across institutions, and in so doing solves the "problematic assumptions built into conventional thinking" (p. 668). Through Goffman's continuum, as Becker points out, "The total institution no longer stands out as aberrant—as though the social world was divided into institutions and practices that are 'ordinary' or 'normal' and do not ask for an abnormal commitment from a person, and then there is this strange one, completely different, which requires total control ... it is now just a different reading on a dial, another of the possible positions on this scale. This is not a trivial result" (p. 667).

Total institutions are designed to limit interaction among inmates (agents) as well as with the outside world. Other characteristics included: (1) locating all inmates in the same physical place and under the same authority; (2) all inmates are treated alike, and required to do things together; (3) activities are controlled by explicit formal rules under the direction of TI officials; (4) activities are tightly scheduled; and (5) organizational structure and activities operate under a single rational plan designed to fulfill the institutional goals. Some of these qualities,

Goffman noted, are shared by other institutions, such as educational institutions, but there are limits to the authority officials exercise (e.g., for controlling extra-curricular activities among college students). In TIs, ordinary boundaries around daily activities are removed so that sleeping, work and leisure activities occur in one setting and with the same group of inmates. There is very limited choice of activity or interpersonal contact for inmates.

Because TIs handle many human needs through a bureaucratic organizational structure which processes large groups of people, officials must develop tightly scheduled processing activities and routines. Staff supervise these routines but, as Goffman noted, this is really surveillance. Strict routines also enable infractions to be easily spotted and addressed. Such routines strip inmates of autonomy and choice. In addition, regimented activity, performed by many in a specified way, also strips away an individual's sense of self and identity. As Goffman noted, TIs are often "forcing houses for changing persons" (Goffman, 1961a, p. 12).

In prisons, for example, an individual becomes identified as an inmate, possessing a character and identity similar to others already incarcerated (e.g., people are categorized into groups such as dealer, drug addict, rapist). Personal identity, then, is lost in the membership categorization of "dealer," "drug addict," "alcoholic," and the like. This stereotyping fostered a distance between staff and inmates that preserved a barrier between them (Goffman, 1961a; Tracy, 2001). Staff, of course, have full access to one's records so one's past is visible and accessible to them. With respect to other inmates, Goffman noted that the footing or projected line the inmates developed—their explanation as to why they have been incarcerated—was generally taken at face value.

Further stripping away of the self ("mortification," as Goffman labeled this) occurred with the stripping of one's physical identity. Dress is prescribed as well as certain hair styles; one is subject to daily physical searches and there is no privacy. An institutionalized system of deference is to be observed at all times; as Goffman noted, this often required being attentive and continuously accessible to the ongoing activity (Goffman, 1961a, p. 21).

For inmates, then, the daily routines of a former existence are supplanted by a prison's privilege system of rules and routines. As one is admitted or processed, an individual is "shaped and coded" by administrative procedures. There is no voluntary departure from TIs; time must be served. Usually there is no "release" time—a time to be private, or to be inaccessible to the routine. And Goffman noted that reading materials, access to television and leisure time, may be severely constrained. These practices are in stark contrast to the "outside" world, where there is personal choice, privacy and less monitoring of behavior. (See also Malacride, 2005.)

In addition, Goffman wrote about asylums as total institutions, and his work helped lead to reforms in mental hospitals (Becker, 2003). Clearly, his work on total institutions revealed a deep insight into that type of social order. His work on gender advertisements and on radio talk shows also captured insightful aspects of their social orders. "It is no doubt significant that the only type of regularized organization which Goffman discusses in an extensive way is the total institution.

Other organizations seem to supply for him only the territories within which interaction is found and encounters occur. But the pressures of total institutions are such that proprieties observed elsewhere come under extraordinary strain" (Giddens, 2000, p. 166). Shenkar (1996) analyzed Chinese state enterprises in terms of Goffman's total institutions and found that such firms experienced "environmental penetration in a forceful, yet highly controlled and asymmetrical manner" which facilitated effective socialization and surveillance (p. 904).

While his illuminating analysis of total institutions reveals how those types of organizations/institutions operate, Goffman's ideas have general utility for organizing beyond that specific application. Goffman's work provides insight into organizations, and issues of order, trust and organizational underlife (Manning, 2008). First, Manning points out that Goffman's work focuses on doing—performances and social practices that help establish a working consensus for the encounter. Performances are always situated, and responses confirm or disconfirm the performance, in both its intended and unintended manifestations. Performances also have a public aspect (visible to others) and a private aspect (not open to others). Second, his work is centrally concerned with how "strangers treat each other with respect" (Manning, 2008, p. 680). Goffman views this trust and respect as a necessary "felicity condition" for interaction: "Social interaction is a communicative dance based on trust and reciprocity—the foundations of organizing" (ibid., p. 686). Clearly, a critical issue for social order, civility and relationships within organizations and groups is maintaining this fragile, emerging trust. Third, Goffman's theatrical metaphor is a "useful analogy ... the importance of this analysis is that organizations are not mini-theatres, but they supply the fronts, appearances, manner, routines and stimulate the necessary teamwork" (ibid., p. 680). And finally, Goffman's work is centered on social practices or the "doings" in organizational settings. All these facets of his work, then, may be usefully applied to organizational settings.

As does this book, Manning notes the fundamental significance of Goffman's interaction order for social order generally. For Goffman,

> ... society *is* interaction; without it, no business can be done; in fact there is no business that can be done. Interactions differ in purpose, and this purpose is in effect "laid on" by obligations and connections to larger social enterprises such as businesses. ... Interactional obligations are entangled with other stated aims and requirements. ... Goffman's aim is to show how situated constraints work on actions, whatever their setting.
>
> *(ibid., p. 681)*

There is, of course, resistance to these situational constraints. In *Asylums,* Goffman raises serious questions about the humaneness of treatment of patients which, Manning notes, may also apply to other marginalized groups.

Goffman defined a formal organization as a "system of purposively coordinated activities designed to produce some overall explicit ends. The intended product may be material artifacts, decisions, or information, and may be distributed among participants in a variety of ways" (Goffman, 1961a, pp. 175–76). As Manning notes, Goffman's "primary point is that organizations expect participants 'to be visibly engaged at appropriate times in the activity of the organization'" (Manning, 2008, p. 683). How this involvement is demonstrated and varies is an important aspect of organizational analysis.

Because action is always fluid and subject to change, Manning notes that organizational influences are often revealed by mistakes and judgments are made about what can and cannot be done "in the name of the organization" (Manning, 2008, p. 685). Organizational members may frame actions differently, and thus offer different explanations for actions, while still remaining consistent with the real events that took place. As Manning notes,

> Organizations are abstract entities, but organizing is a relational process of co-participants, and when these organizing processes come into contact with the hierarchical aspects of organizations, there may be conflict. Those in command segments can create limits by involving rules and procedures. These limits are marked, dramatized or expressed, in the options and nuances of what is said and done. The saying and doing in such marking is often shadowy because power blinds and binds relations and their scope. This power is rarely expressed (it is part of the "felicity condition") ... The rest comes as organizing ideas, designed to move and integrate people in groups, penetrate and shape what is done with the other.
>
> *(Manning, 2008, p. 688)*

Thus social relationships are key in organizing, and may be framed differently across organizational members.

In applying Goffman's concepts to his work on a theory of policing, Manning views organizations as actors or performers—as a "social object to which motives, purposes, aims and social features are attributed to and responded to by other actors. ... It could produce a line and create order in its audiences. ... Its existence as an actor is not constant but a product of the moves and definitions relevant to the situations in which action occurs" (ibid., p. 687). In his analysis of drug enforcement work, Manning found that trust was key (e.g., trusting your colleagues to back you up, in your sergeant to forgive/tolerate your mistakes).

Such work involves teamwork across many different situations, from raids to testifying in court. Drug units operated in a socially constructed environment, incorporating collective beliefs about the distribution and types of drugs, the problems associated with drug use, and so forth. Cases were viewed as open texts, which could be used by a variety of agents to pursue leads, and reduce uncertainty about the case. A "case" also referred to a variety of ideas, ranging from a future investigation to an informant's file to a written report of an arrest. What was recorded was "that which might be questioned in future about any decision ... [it is] a forward- and/or backward-looking formulation of decisions taken" (ibid., p. 691).

The drug enforcement units also took on a resemblance "by costume, manner, appearance and front" to the people they pursue and arrest (ibid., p. 692). As Manning concluded, his book, *Narcs' Game*, was an analysis of the "messy nature of formalized, purposive action. How is it that collective or joint actions are known and understood so that the organization can obtain an 'embracing concept of the members'?. ... As Goffman writes extensively, collective actions must include trust; without it, nothing goes forward" (Manning, 2008, p. 691).

In discussing organizations, Manning notes that various types of organizations exist, and they vary in their internal manner of encouraging compliance (such as money, loyalty or tradition), but all these "in Goffman's framework must be linked to the processes by which they are negotiated. ... *work is interactional work in whatever organizational context*" (ibid., p. 693, italics mine). Manning's work clearly demonstrates the validity and insight of Goffman's concepts when applied to organizational settings.

Talk at work. In discussing interaction in organizations, Goffman noted that much of organizational communication is task related and frequently interaction accompanies the performance of a task. In workplace settings, task priorities are often the dominant communicative focus, and other communication is expected to have minimal interference with task communication. Frequently, an "open state of talk" is created around tasks, in which long periods of silence might be broken by interjections, or is created in situations like brainstorming or group discussions, in which comments are freely given and the exchanges are relatively continuous.

When at work, an "open state of talk" is operating. When the task allows, individuals can talk, but there is no pressure to be involved in talk because the requirements of work might intrude at any moment. Thus patterns of talk and silence may take place that do not rely on ratified participation nor on bystanding (Goffman, 1981a, pp. 134–35). Keyton's concern with talk at work is clearly relevant here (Keyton, Messersmith & Bisel, 2008). As Goffman noted, "One clearly finds, then, that coordinated task activity—not conversation—is what lots of words are part of. A presumed common interest in effectively pursuing the activity at hand, in accordance with some sort of overall plan for doing so, is the contextual matrix which renders many utterances, especially brief ones, meaningful. And these are not unimportant words" (Goffman, 1981a, p. 143).

In institutions, the nature of footing and alignment may be distinct from that of conversation, and, like an open state of talk, may balance a variety of communicative considerations. Bonito and Sanders (2002), for example, found that participants in a collaborative writing task shifted footings both to avoid and to engage in conflict. Additional considerations were footings that moved from sub-task to sub-task (often implicitly understood), and participants who "shifted responsibility to manage disagreement while avoiding conflict" (p. 508).

In contrast, *fresh talk* is Goffman's term for referring to extemporaneous, ongoing forms of interaction in which participants' talk is not directly related to completing a task. In organizing contexts, then, a more detailed assessment of the participation framework(s) and their communicative flexibility is required. As Blommaert et al. (2005) suggested, "Goffman's set of distinctions between 'dominating/subordinate communication' and 'focal' and 'non-focal activity' not only emphasizes the complex multiplicity of simultaneous and sequentially-unfolding frame layers, it also encourages one to think in terms of hierarchical relationships subject to assessment, sanctioning and disciplining" (p. 207). In their study of multilingual classrooms, they found examples of teachers using different languages to invoke hierarchical relationships and to privilege one language over another. Hallett, Harger and Eder (2009) examined gossip as it operated in formal school meetings and explored its relationship to agency and interaction generally.

Marshak (1998) distinguished between *tool-talk* (the instrumental aspect of language), *frame-talk,* which creates the interpretive context for talk, and *mythopoetic talk*, which refers to meanings about the nature of reality captured within that talk. He argued that "tool-talk is contained or framed by frame-talk, and frame-talk is contained or informed by mythopoetic talk" (p. 22). Recent work in communication concerning participation, voice and the meaning of work are of interest here in examing mythopoetic talk.

Goffman also discussed *situated activity systems*; these encounters engage others in focused interaction. These activities are carried out out by groups in different areas. In Goffman's later work, he discussed the degree to which people who can respond to another may be considered copresent, even in encounters in which people are separated in space and/or time. Although bodily copresence may be eliminated, as in a transatlantic business call, nevertheless elements of focused involvement would remain. Given this work, and Goffman's moves toward a sociolinguistic perspective in his later work (Goffman, 1983a, b), his conceptualization of focused encounters and involvement appeared to be moving beyond the dimensions of physical copresence. A recent book by Jacobsen (2010), and work by Jenkins (2010) and Ling (2010), are examples of extending Goffman into mediated communicative encounters. In any case, such a move, in my opinion, would complement and extend his analyses, not contradict or undermine his arguments.

What is perhaps unique about embodied information is that "We are clearly seen as the agents of our acts, there being very little chance of disavowing having committed them; neither having given or received messages cannot be easily denied, at least among those immediately involved" (Goffman, 1963a, p. 16). Giddens noted that copresence, as defined by Goffman, does have certain qualities: "individuals become open to forms of psychic and physical molestation that cannot be operated at a distance. Given the inherent reciprocity of such interaction, others of course become equally vulnerable. Every case of interaction thus has an inherently confrontational character, but it is one typically balanced and managed by the resources individuals mutually apply to ensure respect and consideration for one another" (Giddens, 2000, p. 158).

Scheff, a noted Goffman scholar, argues that Goffman's idea of copresence "implies a model of solidarity as mutual awareness ... this concept of solidarity could be the main component of shared context, consensus, genuine love and social facts" (Scheff, 2007, p. 579). (See also Watson, 1999.)

As we have seen, Goffman himself articulated the connections between the interaction order and social order, arguing that both are reflected in daily interactions. He also analyzed organizations, most notably total institutions. In addition, Goffman analyzed the status of talk in organizations, through such concepts as participant status, fresh talk and so forth. Goffman's conceptualizations clearly provide insightful analyses of organizing and institutions. We next turn to other scholarship using Goffman's analytic framework in assessing organizing and communicating.

Goffman on Organizing and Communicating

Scholars have applied Goffman's concepts to organizational settings in many different ways. Some have analyzed different interactions within an institution, using frames, alignment strategies, differences in deference and demeanor, and so forth to illuminate organizational communication. Others have also utilized Goffman to explore general communicative qualities of institutions, such as strategic interactions, power, impression management and hierarchy. In what follows, I will present an overview of some of these applications.

Frames. Chreim used frames and frame appropriation to analyze control in organizations as well as to connect "micro-level discursive activities and wider discourses that enable and constrain such activities" (Chreim, 2006, p. 1261). After Heracleous and Barrett (2001), she viewed frames as "interpretive schemes that mediate between 'communicative action' arising 'out of the subjective meanings that individuals attach to situations and that orient their actions' and discursive structures that are 'persistent features of discourse that transcend individual texts'" (Heracleous and Barrett, 2001, p. 758, as cited in Chreim, 2006, p. 1263).

In her study, she connected individual frames to organizational (managerial) frames and institutional discourse. Change involved reframing, and as she noted, "frames elaborated in organizations, whether by managers or by employees, are seldom self-contained: they have a resonance with, or are derived, at least in part, from the wider institutional environment and occasionally shape the discourses in this environment. Thus, frames (individual and organizational) are intertwined with wider discourses that surpass the individual and the organizational meanings" (Chreim, 2006, p. 1265). Her case study analyzed organizational change and the tension between frame appropriation and alignment.

Chreim noted that her research tried to "integrate the notions of acceptance and resistance that are sensitive to the experiences of individuals with the notion of macro discourses that help shape individual and organizational frames" (ibid., p. 1266). Using interview data from 12 employees in two banks having undergone similar technological and sales changes over the last decade, Chreim explored their responses to these changes. Her findings indicate that institutional discourses provided a range of legitimating resources that employees used to account for their acceptance of, as well as resistance to, managerial frames.

Chreim concluded that wider discourses can impact micro instances of framing by constraining the meanings of employees as well as by providing them with resources that they can use to resist the frames proposed by managers. Her case study found that a "technological supremacy frame" was embedded in organizational discourse and was not openly contested. Thus, change processes appear to provide both opportunities for alignment and resistance.

Frames and social movements. Another set of studies utilized frames, on both the invidual and organizational level, to investigate social movements. As Collins noted, "social movement theory took a cultural turn toward examining movement frames, or group traditions and identities, and the flow of these cultural resources from one social movement to another. Mobilizing material and organizational resources, and using cultural resources are not incompatible in social movement" (Collins, 2004, p. 31).

In social movements, frames "assign meaning to and interpret relevant events and conditions in ways that are intended to mobilize potential adherents and constituents" (Snow & Benford, 1988, p. 198). As such, the goals and values of the social movement become congruent and aligned with individual values and beliefs. Communicative strategies included frame bridging, amplification, extension and transformation (this latter strategy involved reframing meanings and is compatible with Goffman's view of keying and rekeying and Gidden's concept of transformation). These processes of frame alignment are referred to *micromobilization* and incorporate the "various interactive and communicative processes that affect frame alignment" (Snow, Rochford, Worden & Benford, 1986, p. 464). Frame bridging enables connections between social movements themselves or with interested individuals; frame bridging is the primary frame alignment strategy (ibid., p. 468). Although each frame alignment strategy was used, they hypothesized there may be a relationship between various forms of alignment and particular goals for a social movement.

In analyzing social movements, Snow, Rochford, Worden and Benford (1986) argued that frame alignment processes (i.e., frame bridging, frame amplification, frame extension and/or frame transformation) were necessary for participation in movements. Frame alignment is a continuous, ongoing, interactional process necessary for participation. An analysis by Mathieu (2008) argued that the framing of social movements need to take into account the concrete, contentious settings in which such movements occur.

Studies of framing in social movements also found that the "mobilizing potency of a frame is affected by experiential commensurability and narrative fidelity" (Chreim, 2006, p. 1263). Experiential commensurability aligned a frame with an individual's personal experience while narrative fidelity addressed the alignment of a frame with wider cultural narratives. The culture and general environment provided resources, practices and values through which frames can be articulated and interpreted (Benford & Snow, 2000; Giddens, 1984; Goffman, 1974). While align-ment refers to an adjustment of frames, frame appropriation refers to an acceptance of the frame (it assumes something acquired as well as something invested in; see Cheney & Tompkins, 1987, p. 5). As we have seen, frame analysis has provided useful insights to communicating and organizing within social movements at multiple contextual levels (individual and group).

Encounters and organizing. Handelman (2005) utilized Goffman's concept of an encounter and Giddens' structuration in an extended case study. An encounter, according to Goffman, "provides a world for its participants but the character and stability of this world is intimately related to its selective relationship to the wider one" (Goffman, 1961b, p. 80). Handelman argued that "the idea of encounter ... opens space for the discussion of the emergence of structuration within the inter-action, relatively independent from macro domains. ... Giddens insists that Goffman's understanding of interaction has much more to do with the reproduction of macro institutions than he acknowledges" (2005, p. 70). Handelman further argued that, for Goffman,

> Rules of irrelevance focus participants on what should be paid attention to during focused interaction. Realized resources are concerned with the allo-cation and verification of locally understood identities and roles. Transformation rules suggest the modifications that will occur when elements previously defined as irrelevant are given recognition within the encounter. Together, these rules describe what happens to any element selected to become a con-stituent of the internal order of the encounter. Together, too, these rules bound and bind (indeed, frame, as Goffman [1974] later used the idea) the encounter through its own interactive dynamics—what is going on inside the encounter is somehow different from what is going on outside the encounter ...
> *(2005, p. 70)*

As Handelman argued, encounters are "emergent phenomena ... the very pro-cesses of interaction contain the potential to generate something other, something different, something unexpected, of small scale and consequence, of larger scale and consequence ... the encounter itself is *structuring*. ... Encounters are formed through the interaction of their creators, but they also shape this interaction as it is occurring. Therefore, encounters in general simply are not reducible to the contributions—the particular life conditions, decisions, strategies, moves, emotions—of the partici-pants"(ibid., p. 70). He also noted that encounters vary in their interior complexity and their ability to withstand rupture; and that their outcomes are "continuously reproducing and changing the shape of any given interaction order, even if in tiny ways" (ibid., p. 71).

Handelman applied these processes to assessing the emergence of social order through an extended case study, looking at encounters over time. The encounter, social situation and extended case are domains of social organization; such domains are those of "scale, ranges of power, and organizational capacity to structure other domains. ... " (ibid., p. 76). Added to these considerations is the issue of time and duration: Handelman argued for the "prospective perspective of encounters and of the extended case ... oriented toward the ongoing, continuous emergence of social life through its practices" (ibid.). As such, Handelman's perspective reflects a blending of both Goffman and Giddens.

Alignment. Maynard (2000) used frame analysis to assess plea bargaining discourse within the judicial system. He concluded that practitioners take up different alignments that connect with various organizational forms in which they are embedded, including relationships with others (such as witnesses), their own offices and colleagues, and other agencies (such as the police). People conduct themselves according to norms or ground rules which regulate their dealings with one another. He also noted, that "when one is engaged in researching talk within a singular setting, it may be desirable to involve the setting analytically" (p. 72). Giddens' analysis of the four types of organizations every society needs—including the legal institutions for a society—would be relevant here in providing that added contextual background.

Power and hierarchy. According to Goffman, power is an individual's capacity to influence others' action; "these powers may or may not be used and include the power to enforce, to cause something to occur, and the power to reveal and/or disrupt" (Goffman, 1963a, 1974, as cited in Rogers, 1980, p. 104, fn. 7). This conceptualization of power is quite similar to classic definitions of power as the capacity to have others act in ways they would not have otherwise acted (see, for example, Bacharach & Lawler, 1980).

Rogers (1980) argued that Goffman's work contains significant, implicit insights into power, hierarchy and social status. First, Goffman suggested that institutions set limits on face, status claims, autonomy and self-determination for organizational members. While not a focal emphasis in his work, Goffman was clearly aware of inequities and discussed the ways in which status degradation takes place (for example, see his work on total institutions as well as his remarks on encounters, such as performance appraisals, evaluating organizational members). For Goffman, "a social-structural matrix sets the limits to which 'face' and status claims can be ongoingly stabilized ... [it] variably extends or circumscribes opportunities for the autonomy and self-determination he deems necessary for the easeful, satisfactory maintenance of 'face' and self-respect" (Rogers, 1980, p. 101).

Goffman further argued that hierarchy limits autonomy for those on lower organizational levels, and that there is a tension between adjustment and conformity for both formal and informal social interactions (ibid.). Higher status individuals in an encounter will be more independent of the "good opinion of others," while a lower status individual will be more dependent on the support of others, especially superiors. The territories of the self that individuals claim and others respect are also influenced by deference and social status.

Finally, Goffman observed that organizations may prescribe displays of deference and demeanor, provide differential opportunities for risk and advancement, and control the social distribution of information (i.e., "false consciousness"). Goffman is concerned with the interaction order and, as Branaman pointed out, he thus did not emphasize questions of motivation and structural advantage/disadvantage.

> It is not that he denies their importance, but his concern is instead with the basic norms of everyday interaction and how these tend to stabilize established social orders ... the image that one is able to sustain in social interaction is a product of the place in a social hierarchy that persons with one's social characteristics tend to hold. Attached to social attributes such as class, race, and occupation are moral expectations concerning the appropriate treatment of the person to whom such attributes are ascribed as well as moral expectations about the appropriate lines that the person may legitimately take in social interaction ...
>
> *(Branaman, 2003, pp. 92–93, after Goffman, 1967)*

The degree to which one is accorded deference reflects the degree to which one possessed valued characteristics. As Goffman noted, "A status, a position, a social place is not a material thing, to be possessed and then displayed; it is a pattern of appropriate conduct, coherent, embellished, and well articulated" (Goffman, 1959, p. 75). Status claims, of course, will be relevant to face and to supporting face for the individual. Thus status, face and deference are a function of interaction, in which such projected lines are developed and either confirmed or disconfirmed.

Both situational and individual factors influence power. (Rogers referred to these as instrumental and infra-resources, 1980, p. 105.) For Goffman, individual resources included one's position, skills, character, composure, knowledge, information, and information states (Rogers, 1980, p. 105). Situational sources of power included perceptions of the situation, information and access. Perceptions of power are a function of the information (whether distorted or incomplete) and the experience one has with a given individual (such as character of the other and the degree of trust) (Goffman, 1974). Goffman also highlighted the importance of access to information as well as to territories (Rogers, 1980, p. 106).

According to Goffman, there is a distinction between interaction and strategic interaction (influencing others). Rogers argued that, for Goffman,

> interaction might be characterized as involving significant reciprocity, a relative absence of intentionality, and an ongoing modification of behavior which is distributed rather evenly among participants. Conceived as a type of interaction, influence involves relative one-sidedness, intentionality, and behavioural modification which is concentrated among the targets of influence.
>
> *(Rogers, 1980, p. 107)*

Notable influence tactics included fabrication, ambiguity, lies, innuendo, forms of concealment, omissions and denials (Goffman, 1974, pp. 80–110). Objects, space, and equipment can also be used to influence others as can the body itself (Goffman, 1959, 1974). Influence can also be exercised by the participation status of organizational members (which opens up an array of structurally differentiated possibilities, Goffman, 1981a, p. 137); those who have the highest participation status may also have more opportunities to influence and direct others (Gibson, 2003, 2005a, b; Rae, 2001). Using Goffman's analyses of regions, Hindmarsh and Pilnick (2002) explored the integrated spatial, embodied actions and coordinated social practices of anesthetic teams and found tightly organized, balanced, controlled movements among participants.

Goffman also acknowledged that different cultures and groups may use power in different manners. He concluded that

> ... forms of face-to-face life are worn smooth by constant repetition on the part of participants who are heterogeneous in many ways and yet must quickly reach a working understanding. ... All elements of social life have a history and are subject to critical change through time, and none can be fully understood apart from the particular culture in which it occurs.
>
> *(Goffman, 1983a, p. 9)*

Goffman also contrasted intentional with unintentional behaviors; intentionality involves conscious design by participants while unintentional behaviors are those participants are relatively unaware of, or uncalculated behaviors (Goffman, 1959, pp. 4–52). Rogers concluded that for Goffman intentional behaviors focus "on *interactional* goals, such as information control, impression management, and remedial results ... intentionality involves conscious goal-oriented activity which is rooted in the proclivities of actors to assess each other and their capacities to manipulate the objects of such assessments" (Rogers, 1980, p. 103). In strategic interaction, particularly in cases where special effort is needed to counter blocked or deflected actions, power, influence and control are called into play (Rogers, 1980, p. 104). Using Goffman's dramaturgical approach to interaction, the shifting of power and challenges to it were analyzed in British embassy meetings (Van Praet, 2009).

Goffman also discussed control, as both a process and effect (Rogers, 1980, pp. 107–10). The process of control is developed as the use of regulatory processes, such as sanctions enforcing institutional norms. Control is exercised by shaping and determining individuals' perceptions of a situation; examples of such control would include categorization, negative labels, labeling, ideology and stereotypes. Finally, an individual who cooperates with the definition of a situation is a "controlled member of a social system, whatever the motives for his conformity" (Rogers, 1980, p. 109).

Although Goffman's concept of control is difficult to distinguish from his concept of influence, nevertheless he drew attention to the ways in which "the day-to-day, routine conformity ... generally corresponds to the preferences of the most powerful, influential members of a social system. In his treatment of control Goffman provides not only conceptual grounds for attending to that phenomenon but also bases for identifying the relevance of labeling, belief systems, and the like to power ... his insights point to the ways in which those with power can exploit dominant belief and value systems to maximize their preferred outcomes without engaging in influence" (ibid., p. 110). Hegemony, for example, exemplifies these processes.

Individual choice and self-determination is a function of both external (social structural factors) and internal factors (one's biography). As Rogers (1980) pointed out

> the modes in which given *types* of people can effectively attempt to maintain face are considerably shaped by the social structures in which their dealings with one another routinely occur. ... self-image and social structure are complexly and dynamically intertwined as the notion of moral career so aptly suggests. ... Moreover, he [Goffman] is clearly sensitive to the unequal distribution of opportunities for face-maintenance as well as the ways in which social-structural factors render problematic the sense of self-determination.
>
> *(p. 115)*

Some occupations and organizations have more status and prestige than others (think of the popular television series *Dirty Jobs*, and pay disparities across occupations and individuals). Such disparities also influence one's opportunities for autonomy and self-determination.

> From Goffman's viewpoint, then, the hierarchical structure of formal organizations has profound implications. The strata comprising an organizational hierarchy are collectivities of people whose characters, officially available modes of self-presentation, and rights to deference are largely specified by their stratum membership. In fact, formal organizations *stage* differences among constructed categories of people, defining those categories in terms of purportedly actual differences in social worth and moral character. Over time membership in a given organizational stratum thus affects individuals' perceptions of their selves as well as of others in the organisation.
>
> *(Rogers, 1980, p. 116)*

Such staging differences might be reflected in more privacy for superiors (private offices, dining facilities), more space, more discretionary use of time and so forth to index social and organizational worth.

Using Goffman's concept of social grammars, Gordon, Stewart and Komberger (2009) found that "Ethics are enacted through these grammars which are used to decide whether behavior is acceptable or not ... [and] that historically shaped power relations frame ethics in practice. ... these power relations silenced critical voices and made ethics a matter of compliance" (pp. 84–85). The placement of social life in its sociohistorical context parallels Giddens' arguments on the importance of analyzing agency in its temporal, cultural and historical context (Giddens, 1984).

Carbaugh (1989, 2005) has developed the concept of cultural conversations, based partially on Goffman's interaction order and his use of ritual. As he noted, "Hearing conversation as ritualized draws to our attention several features: (a) the cultural sequencing of acts, (b) specific cultural terms being use, (c) the lexical structuring of the topic, (d) the tone of the discussion, and (e) folk genres of talk that these at once presume, create, and resist. Cultural variation in these shows deeper meanings about proper conversation itself and what it means to be a person" (Carbaugh, 2005, p. xxiv). As individuals try to restore or develop an expressive order in conversation, face threats may be created because of differing cultural patterns of interaction (ibid.).

Using Goffman's view on repairs of ritual disequilibrium, Carbaugh (2005) analyzed a strip of interaction in which Donahue interviewed Russian students on sexual practices. Almost immediately, corrective repairs were necessary because of differing cultural conversational norms for discussing such issues. What is at issue, as well, is the "creation, affirmation, and negotiation of shared identity" (Phillipsen, 1987, p. 279). Differences in cultural premises and conversational practices will make the process of social interaction even more fragile and fraught with opportunities for breaches and misunderstandings. Both institutions and interpersonal interactions are contextualized by the surrounding cultural milieux. A study by Allon-Souday and Kunda (2003) explored national, cultural identity as a resource in struggling with the job demands of globalization.

An insightful study by Hallet used Goffman's analysis of deference and demeanor to explore the power relationships in an educational institution, thus linking the interactional with the institutional. Hallet argued that deference is "symbolic power in potential form: once deference is acquired, it can be deployed as the symbolic power to frame actions, situations, and events in ways that induce compliance and constitute the social order" (Hallet, 2007, p. 149). Goffman clearly acknowledged power: "Regardless of the particular objective which the individual has in mind ... it will be in his interest to control the conduct of others. ... This control is achieved largely by influencing the definition of the situation" (Goffman, 1959, pp. 3–4, cited in Hallet, 2007, p. 151).

Hallet's ethnographic study of an urban public school explored a transition in administration and educational requirements, and its impacts on the staff. He found that the female principal's style precipitated a status dilemma, and that her aggressive, masculine style did not work effectively with the female staff. She lacked the necessary deference in order to make changes, and her demeanor was not viewed positively. Thus, she lacked the symbolic power to make changes "stick" although she clearly had the authority to do so.

Goffman's work on ritual is also implicated in analyses of organizational power. As Collins argued,

Why should rituals be important as a basis of power. ... Because the solid economic and political organizations of society must nevertheless be enacted. ... Empirical reality, in the most detailed sense, is made up by a succession of minute-by-minute encounters. 'Organisations' and 'positions' are thing-like in their solidity only because they are continuously and repeatedly enacted in a series of micro-situations. ... without the process of *continual* social definition, they cease to exist. ...

Organisations and stratified positions within them are prime instances of such things which take on a coercive reality because we collectively believe them to be so. Thus well-performed rituals create and re-create the stratified order, and hence underlie the distribution of material, power, and status privileges.

(Collins, 2004, p. 323)

In *Strategic Interaction*, Goffman appeared to support a model of limited human cognition, building upon Chester Barnard's classical work, in "which delegation of authority is inevitable, whether it is officially recognized or not. Hence real sources of power may be unofficial ones, and these exist wherever the outcomes of activities are most uncertain. ... It is impossible to attend to everything at once; so one suffices in most areas and optimizes only a few (Simon); one operates most basically upon expressions of real moves and judges the significance of explicit communications in this light (Goffman)" (Collins, 2004, p. 329).

Secondary adjustments. Despite pressures for conformity, people may "decline in some way to accept the official view of what they should be putting into and getting out of the organization and, behind this, of what sort of self and work they are to accept for themselves" (Goffman, 1961a, p. 304). While varied adjustments are possible, official norms may "expand a mere participation contract into a definition of the participant's nature or social being ... [thus] we begin to see the self-defining implications of even the minor give-and-take in organizations" (Goffman, 1961a, pp. 179, 186, as cited in Rogers, 1980, p. 119). Thus dialectical tensions exist between adjustment and conformity, and between the self and organizational roles.

Organizational members may use secondary adjustments to buffer themselves from organizational demands. Goffman defined secondary adjustments as "any habitual arrangement by which a member of an organization employs unauthorized means, or obtains unauthorized ends, or both, thus getting around the organisation's assumptions as to what he should do and get and hence what he should be" (Goffman, 1961à, p. 189). Secondary adjustments reflect ritual insubordination such as griping, making fun, being insolent and so forth. Disruptive adjustments are intended to abandon or radically change the organization, and contained adjustments seek to accommodate the organization (ibid.).

Rogers (1980) noted that people with substantive power make secondary adjustments (such as the use of expense accounts), as do individuals with little organizational power (as, for example, people employing a "work to rule" strategy and frequently disrupting the normal flow of work). Baptista (2003) suggested that the more formally organized an activity is, the more framing is vulnerable to disruptions. In *Stigma* and *Asylum*, Goffman discussed strategies by which deviant, lower status and stigmatized individuals maintain their self-worth and dignity.

In terms of adjustment or—perhaps more accurately—lack of adjustment, Goffman noted the false consciousness in social order. As he stated, "conventional persons often maintain the rules consistently enough to remain unaware of the situational obligations their conduct sustains" (Goffman, 1963a, p. 226). In other words, the expectations for social order might act against one's own interests or the group's interests. This also suggests hegemony in which the oppressed have no understanding of their oppression. Goffman's point, I think, is also that this frequently occurs in organizations where people do not have sufficient information to use in judging the potential risks and rewards of their actions, or non-actions.

But most scholars believe that such strategies do not officially challenge or disrupt the established social hierarchy (see Branaman, 2003, pp. 115–20 for a discussion of this issue). Goffman himself noted that, as long as public deference is maintained, subordinates are able to disregard their superiors. Nevertheless, "In rendering insight into the interactional 'tools' whereby hierarchies are built, maintained, and legitimated, Goffman provides a basis for the demystification of established social hierarchies. As a first step in challenging established social hierarchies, demystification, of course, is crucial" (Branaman, 2003, p.120).

Face and organizing. One of Goffman's major contributions has been the concept of face. Face has been further elaborated and applied in a variety of contexts (see, for example, Brown and Levinson, 1987; Ting-Toomey, 2005; Tracy, 1990). Face in organizations, of course, will be influenced by power, status, familiarity and task requirements (Holtgraves, 1992, 2009).

1. *Face threats.* Using Goffman's concept of face, Myers (2003) reviews how face threats may emerge during the discussion of risk issues, such as those between doctors and patients or clients and counselors. Such information might threaten face, both in terms of the risks themselves but also for recipients in placing trust in experts. Doctors and counselors, while presenting information concerning risks and decisions, must also be cognizant of how recipients are framing themselves. As Myers points out, "however the doctor and patient present themselves, whether the doctor is the authority figure or sympathetic advisor, whether the patient is hapless victim or active participant in the treatment, both participants have to work at maintaining the line, and repairing threats to face, if the encounter is to come off" (p. 216).

A study of face threat in negotiations found that individual differences in sensitivity to face threats (FTS) influenced negotiation outcomes in a variety of contexts (White, Tynan, Galinsky & Thompson, 2004). Job candidates with high FTS negotiated employment contracts with less joint gain, and the negotiating relationship was mediated by enhanced competitiveness of high FTS candidates. Generally the negotiator's FTS and his/her role in the negotiations influenced the negotiation process and outcome. Other studies have focused on the face tensions in 911 calls

(Tracy, 1997b; Tracy & Anderson, 1999; Tracy, K. & Tracy, 1998; Tracy, S. & Tracy, 1998) and the strategies by which callers and responders negotiate these tensions. In a face-threatening communicative task, bilingual speakers used footing and code-switching to negotiate interpersonal relationships (Su, 2009). In the workplace, Stewart (2008) found that ambivalent statements protected the speaker's face but allowed "highly face-threatening interpretations of what is said to circulate" (p. 50). In police interrogations, in which a coercive interaction is likely, suspects use strategic face-work to establish a socially acceptable face that deserves deference from the police (Sheffer, 2009).

2. *Face and politeness.* Some argue that face concerns (Goffman, 1967) are the foundation for all politeness behavior, and that such concerns are important in encounters because one's face must be ratified or disconfirmed by others in the encounter (Holtgraves, 2001). Research on politeness has been difficult because of the limitations of various classification systems for politeness strategies and the multifunctionality of utterances (i.e., an utterance may have multiple politeness strategies; see, for example, Holtgraves, 2009; Tracy, 1990).

Eelen (2001) argued that politeness theories are conceptually biased in that being polite is privileged over being impolite, speakers are privileged over listeners, and production of utterances is privileged over reception of utterances. Such concerns have led to the development of models of politeness based upon situated judgments of face and politeness (Watts, 2003) or upon face considerations in relationships (Spencer-Oatey, 2007). Yet others (Stewart, 2008) have argued for broadening the discussion of face and politeness to include wider participation frameworks (Goffman, 1981a) and to investigate the social embeddedness of politeness within varying cultural settings (Bargiela-Chiappini & Harris, 2006). In many analyses, Goffman's concept of footing (1981a) appears to be central to considerations of face and politeness: footing refers to the speaker's moves to establish the least personally threatening position possible. (See Hugles, 2009).

Despite these differing approaches, some findings appear consistent. Brown and Levinson (1987) argued that politeness would vary as a function of weightiness of a given act (determined by the intrinsic degree of imposition of the act; the power of the hearer relative to that of the requestor; and the social distance between them). Generally, there has been strong support for power, with higher speaker power being linked to less politeness, in a wide variety of empirical and observational studies (Holtgraves, 2001, p. 347). Increasing imposition is also related to increases in politeness. Although these variables are not additive in their effect on politeness, if one variable is quite large, the effects of other variables are reduced (ibid., p. 348). Other issues of concern include cultural influences on politeness, particularly in collectivist or individualistic cultures (see, for example, Spencer-Oatey & Jiang, 2003); attention given to self-face versus other-face, and nonverbal expressions of politeness (emphasized by Goffman).

3. *Face-attacks.* Goffman (1955, 1967) argues that communicators try to preserve one another's face during interaction through face-work. However, sometimes

comments may be viewed as intentionally rude or offensive. Face-attacks combine Goffman's concept of face threats with ritual affronts. Face-attacks are viewed as intentionally rude, as well as insulting (p. 173). Some face-attacks, like obscenities, name-calling and screaming, are "context-spanning face-attacks" and are viewed as rude and disrespectful across different situations (K. Tracy & S. Tracy, 1998).

In many contexts there is a need for conflict and expression of differing ideas, such as civic meetings on various topics (Tracy, 2008; Tracy & Durfy, 2007), situations around public services like 911 calls (Tracy & Tracy, 1998) and so forth. While in many circumstances, participants behave with politeness norms in mind, raising an objection to others' views may threaten their positive face (through challenging or questioning their views). Challenges nay also involve negative face (perhaps by denying others the right to speak or participate).

In order to have effective participation, interaction should allow for contentious exchanges: Tracy (2008) has developed the concept of "reasonable hostility"as a way of establishing situationally appropriate face-attacks. Using Goffman's concept of face, she distinguishes between reasonable and unreasonable forms of hositility (i.e., face-attacks). She develops a grounded practical theory which suggests that "attacking the face of others ... is appropriate in local governance sites when a set of people in the immediate public group or a larger public judge that critical, competence-challenging comments need to be uttered" (p. 188). What constitutes reasonable hostility is a function of who said what to whom, and grounded in the context, relationships among participants, and power, and "adorned with at least a piece or two of politeness jewelry" (p. 187).

An investigation of 911 calls by S. Tracy and K. Tracy (1998) uncovered a number of strategies used to protect the face of call-takers and to handle face-attacks by the callers. In addition, they connected context ("as concentric circles of influence") to strategy use, and reflected on alternative strategies in situations involving some type of negative emotion. Importantly, their analysis presents a framework for investigating 911 calls and a framework for analyzing responses, and thus providing practitioners with opportunities to reflect on their communicative behaviors.

Goffman and online communication. Although Goffman's work on face and presentation of self was based on co-present interaction, his work has usefully been applied to computer-mediated communication (Case & Pineiro, 2006; Rettie, 2009). Meyrowitz (1985), in applying Goffman to mediated communication settings, argued that Goffman's situation could be viewed as information systems or patterned access to information (p. 37). Boden and Molotech (1994) contrasted mediated and copresent interaction and suggest that most prefer the dense information, bodily cues and efficiency in face-to-face communication. Interestingly, Wilson, O'Leary, Metiu and Jett (2008) analyzed perceptions of closeness in co-present and virtual teams. Analyses and contrasts across various mediated communication systems also reflected the limits and advantages of the interactivity possible in each medium (Hutchby & Tanna, 2008). Although these comparisons and applications are yet in their infancy, I believe applying Goffman to mediated interactions will provide a very useful line of research. Some of the concepts explored are self-presentation, face, front and back regions, and framing.

For Goffman, mutual monitoring in face-to-face interaction allows for sustained, coordinated action (Goffman, 1983a, p. 3). As Rettie notes, in Goffman's interaction order "a shared definition of the situation creates the coherence of social reality: interactants share a physical location, a time-frame and a conceptual framework, coordinating their impression management through mutual monitoring and face-work" (2009, p. 424). If this shared sense of situation, or frame, is lost, then the situation may "collapse, disintegrate, go up in smoke" (Goffman, 1974, p. 302). (See also Gardner & Gronfein, 2005.)

Mediated forms of communication do not allow the same degree of mutual monitoring as do copresent, situated encounters. Rettie goes on to point out that

> Synchronous continuous media, such as phone calls and video links, enable a degree of ongoing mutual monitoring in real-time. Although the interactants are in different locations, they share a time-frame and a mediated copresence: as the interactants converse they collaborate on what we can call a *mediated encounter*. Using Giddens' (1984) concept of time-space distanciation, one can distinguish asynchronous mediated communication, which involves time-space distanciation, from synchronous mediated communication, which is spatially but not temporally remote.
>
> *(Rettie, 2009, p. 425)*

As Rettie argues, whether or not there is concurrent mutual monitoring influences the capacity of individuals to work together to support a "sustained, intimate, coordination of action." In asynchronous mediated communication there is no concurrent time-frame, and interactants cannot coordinate their actions as they could in an encounter. "Although asynchronous communication is organized, it is not situated in a common present and consequently does not afford continuous cooperative practice and the experience of a moment-by-moment intersubjectivity in a shared social reality" (Rettie, 2009, p. 426). She concludes that the asynchronous/synchronous distinction is not clear-cut because the use and perception of a medium "reflects socially shaped expectations" (ibid., p. 427). (We shall discuss these mediated encounters in more detail in Chapter 12, when we integrate Giddens and Goffman and their perspectives on mediated communication.)

In Rettie's analysis of mobile phone communication, she found that interactional norms shaped usage of mobile phones, rather than the features of the technology it afforded. She noted that "people on the phone are vulnerable [to be mediated and face-to-face contexts] because the 'person in the middle' can collude with the face-to-face interactant, who forms a 'concealed audience'" (Goffman, 1971, pp. 220–22, cited in Rettie, 2009, p. 427). Mobile phone usage involves two audio fronts, for example, one front being the person being addressed on the phone and the other front representing those who may hear the speaker's comments, and may be ratified or non-ratified participants. Rettie's example is that of a mother at work conversing with her daughter, using her daughter's name to inform her colleagues who she is talking with, or the mother might say how hard she is working to impress her employer (p. 428).

Rettie's qualitative interviews revealed that mobile phone calls and text message exchanges were perceived as different because of the lack of the presence of another person in text messaging. Some respondents believed the phone calls were like face-to-face interaction "with one's eyes shut" (p. 430). Respondents also associated more sociality and focused attention with phone calls. More cues as to the presentation of self were also available in phone calls rather than text messages (e.g., sighs, lengthy pauses). She concluded that interactional analysis needs to incorporate both mediated and unmediated interactions, as human communication increasingly includes both in a given situation: "Applying Goffman's concepts of the encounter, of the gathering and of front/back stages, both mediated and face-to-face interaction facilitates analysis of the complex interactional dynamics and participative frameworks created by the new media" (p. 436).

In an exploration of online social network sites (SNS), Tufekci (2008) used Goffman's presentation of the self to explore SNS usage. Tufekci distinguishes between the expressive Internet (i.e., technologically mediated sociality such as self-presentation, social monitoring and the maintaining of social ties) and the instrumental Internet (i.e., uses of the Internet for information seeking and non-social transactions such as banking). Use of SNS was influenced by two factors: attitudes toward social grooming (i.e., small-talk, general social information about others) and concerns about privacy. Non-users of SNSs were not interested in social grooming and indicated concerns about personal privacy. SNS users were heavier users of the expressive Internet, but there were no differences among students in terms of their usage of the instrumental Internet. Non-users of SNS were open to the possibility of genuine social interaction via online connections but were not interested in the social grooming aspects of the expressive Internet. Heath and Luff (1992) found interactants in computer/video media communication developed norms to organize their interaction and a sense of copresence in their shared, mediated environment. Jirotka, Luff and Gilbert (1991) used Goffman's participant roles to examine turn-taking behavior in computer mediated communication. (See also Nunes, 2007.)

An analysis of online exchanges among computer programmers demonstrated considerable face-work as they discussed their work and revealed differing technical, ethical and aesthetic concerns (Case & Pineiro, 2006). They discussed the relationship between coding aesthetics, identity and resistance revealed in programmers' exchanges. While management was most interested in functionality of the computer codes (its efficiency and accuracy), programmers were most concerned about the codes' intrinsic value. (See also Matsumoto, 1988, 2003.)

The use of mobile phones is an increasingly significant way in which to communicate with others in both personal and professional contexts, and which offer a wide range of video, texting and audio modes of interaction. Fortunati (2005) suggests that mobile phone use could influence social order by exposing backstage performances. The blurring of front and back regions in mobile phone calls may create overlapping performances, and lead to role conflict (Geser, 2004). Multiple front regions may emerge in combat information centers and thus create more difficulty in coordinating teamwork (Aoki, 2007). For young Japanese women, mobile phones establish some private space for interaction as well as opportunities for presentation of the self in terms of decoration for mobile phones and for phone carriers (D. Slater, personal communication, 2006).

Using Goffman's activity frames and participation frameworks, Aarsand (2008) explored classroom interaction among students in which students alternated between online and offline communication. Students switched frames (between online and offline) and used "tags" (nicknames) to maintain identity across frames. Hybrid interactions contain resources that may combine material, linguistic and/or visual resources, and interactants use frame management to utilize these resources. Aarsand conceptualizes the shifting between online and offline identities as borderwork. His analysis of how children use computers reveals that they considered both face-to-face interaction and computer interaction (using MSN Messenger) as social activities in which identity work occurs. Tags were used as identity markers which also signaled their competence in the use of the MSN systems.

A range of studies, exploring different contexts, examined mediated communication. Soukup (2006) used Goffman's dramaturgical perspective to analyze multimedia performance in a virtual community. Participants were able to creatively define and establish social settings, and collaboratively built an online community. Pearson (2009) found that participants on social networking sites (SNSs) created performances that play with identity, and alternate between the frontstage/backstage and public/private aspects of social connections. Ross (2007) found that an online community among London cabbies allowed peers a "back region" in which social comparisons were made, friendships formed and practice assessments were undertaken. Confidentiality on the online community allowed private disclosures which, if in a public front region, might have damaged one's reputation and judgments about competency. Perreta (2008) analyzed how people presented themselves in their MySpace profile pages. Most participants modified the template to add other textual information such as photos, video clips and music to create a virtual presentation. (See Ho & Okabe, 2005.)

These studies exemplify the ways in which Goffman's work has been usefully extended to computer mediated communication, including social networking sites as well as SMSs (short message systems). Their findings reveal the complexity of online communication and contrast it with face-to-face communication. Increasingly, as Rettie (2009) suggested and studies have documented, interactants will shift frames between mediated and non-mediated communication. Both personal and professional/workplace settings will reflect this blended communication. The synthesis of Goffman and Giddens (structurational interaction) will provide a very promising basis for exploring this blended communication and examining critical issues such as presentation of a/the self, the effects of specific mediums, social preferences in utilizing the media, and so forth. Although a more exhaustive review of this work is beyond the scope of this book, this work suggests the shape of very productive, future research in this area.

Impression management. Impression management (IM) research in organizations has explored Goffman's work in an attempt to understand whether or not a presented self is authentic, and what actions may stem from either an authentic or inauthentic self (Chriss, 1995, p. 561). As Goffman noted, "performers [are] making sure that as many as possible of the minor events in the performance, however instrumentally inconsequential these events may be, will occur in such a way as to convey either no impression or an impression that is compatible and constituent with the over-all definition of the situation that is being fostered" (Goffman, 1959, p. 51). Goodwin (2000, 2009) presents an excellent example of presentational research illuminating the different types of displays (social, cultural, material, sequential and embodiment) that underlie situated interaction. When one is able to control the definition of the situation, one can often control the behavior of participants in that situation. (See also Gardener & Matrnato, 1988.)

In his earliest work, as part of a grant to E. C. Hughes, Goffman explored the contradictions faced by people in particular roles. Goffman examined service station dealers in terms of how they viewed their work and status, their clients, and the company. The role difficulty experienced by dealers centered around their roles as businessmen, attendants and technicians. Goffman found that the dealers ranged from enthusiastic to apathetic, and they had developed views of good versus bad clients. Relationships with oil companies were problematic as the companies increasingly dominated dealers' activities. Even in the earliest part of his career, Goffman noted role contradictions and complexities, and how a larger organization impinged on the daily workings of service station dealers (Goffman, 1953a).

Goffman also noted that different organizational positions offer different interactional opportunities and responsibilities. Some are "exposed" or "open positions," like police, waitresses, and receptionists, which are open to approaches from others. Thus, different interactional opportunities are presented in different occupations.

The IM scholarship assumed that social actors have a hidden private agenda. IM research argues that people "present various images of themselves as a strategic move. Unlike Goffman's approach, this 'game' is not an end in itself but a *means to an end* of gaining benefits. It is a game of *misrepresentation*" (Tseelon, 1992, p. 116). Goffman also suggested "Communication techniques such as innuendo, strategic ambiguity, and crucial omissions allow the misinformer to profit from lies, without, technically, telling any" (Goffman, 1959, p. 62). Because Goffman's work discusses face and trust, as well as ambiguity and manipulation, clearly he believes both occur in the interaction order. Scholars suggesting that Goffman's work emphasized deception more than authenticity are, I believe, in error. For more discussion of Goffman and IM organizational research, see Welsh (1984), Willmott (1993) and Rosenfeld, Giacalone and Riordan (1995).

Others have used Goffman's work to discuss impression management (IM) in organizational settings. While many have criticized Goffman's approach as being inherently manipulative and cynical, others point out that the same tools that establish ritual (supportive) climates for interaction are also used for fabrication—thus, Goffman's model accounts for both uses of impression management (Cupach & Metts, 1994; Fairhurst & Sarr, 1996; Gardner, 1992). Manning (1991) argued that Goffman's dramaturgical metaphor changed over time, placing "less and less emphasis on the cynical aspects of impression management and focused more intensely on the importance of trust in everyday encounters" (p. 70).

Goffman's distinction between frontstage and backstage have been interpreted by IM researchers as contrasting a "false" or "inauthentic" public self with a "true" private self (Chriss, 2000). Yet Goffman discussed performance from the vantage point of teamwork, suggesting that participants play varied roles, from frontstage expressive performances to supporting backstage roles (Goffman, 1959, pp. 110–25). For front region or frontstage performance, Goffman argued that, "if an individual is to give expression to ideal standards during his performance, then he will have to forego or conceal action which is inconsistent with these standards" (ibid., p. 41). In other words, one will be judged on "the standards of conduct and appearance that one's social grouping attaches thereto" (ibid., p. 75). But we should recall that this consistency in impression management is essential in any public performance or given impression, whether insincere or authentic.

An interesting study by Greener (2008) explored gender differences in impression management among managers in the National Health Service (NHS) in England. Interviews were conducted with doctors and with high-level managers. Frontstage interactions tend to "be institutionalized and relatively fixed, leaning towards formal and highly ritualized behaviour" with little improvisation (p. 285). Backstage interactions reflected sites for hidden preparation. Outside-stage performances reflected interactions between some team performers and a selected audience.

Although senior management realized they had the coercive power to overrule the doctors, they believed it inappropriate to directly challenge the doctors, in part because managers also realized that doctors implemented the practices. Managers also realized that "it was easier to advance the agenda of the meeting if clinicians did not know the real situation and continued to believe that they were in charge. Face work was therefore about maintaining the long-term relationship between the two groups," and managers would acknowledge the real power "informally amongst themselves when backstage, but that deference had to be shown to the doctors in front-stage settings" (ibid., pp. 287–88). Both male and female mangers "engaged in face work necessary to preserve existing relationships to avoid a loss of face or prestige by the doctors" (ibid., p. 287).

In frontstage meetings, both female and male managers used persuasion and deference, and, when that failed, they used agenda-setting as a strategy. Men used that strategy to win the game, whereas women used to it "get the job done" (p. 289). Male managers used these strategies across all the stages, but women managers, when in outside-stage interactions (social gatherings, playing golf and the like), used mothering through language changes, acted with reduced deference, or played a "flirt role" (pp. 290–91). Such strategies were never used in frontstage interactions. Greener concluded that there was an "extraordinarily political environment" at the senior management level in NHS and that there were gendered differences in impression management strategies used by women and men managers, with women utilizing more varied strategies.

Impression management has also been used to examine a range of public interaction behaviors in a wide variety of contexts. Goffman's interaction ritual was used to analyze race, ethnicity and stylization in youngsters' use of "posh" and other linguistic styles in their impression management (Rampton, 2009). An interesting study of collaborative teaching (Preves & Stephenson, 2009) used Goffman's dramaturgical theory to analyze the ongoing negotiation of identity, roles and power among teachers during class. Veenstra (2008) developed the concept of "cultural talent," based on Goffman's impression management, and found that it was related to occupational skill and complexity.

In analyzing the cultural clash between young men and police officers, Peterson (2008) found that two distinct police groups followed different strategies in their negotiations with the young men, one police group seeking out confrontations or face contests (and thus dominating the streets), while the other group evaded such face contests (and thus projected a sharing of the street). An intriguing study by Nutch (2007) viewed a naturalist as the operator and tourists as the mark; the naturalist was "cooling the mark out" by foreshadowing the possibility of failing to sight whales during a commercial whale-watch. Interestingly, this "cooling out" was applied to a tourist group, rather than just an individual, and done in "anticipation of their likely experiencing a set of spoiled expectations" (p. 1783). (Having personally experienced such a spoiled expectation, I empathize with the tour group!)

1. *Emotion management.* Goffman's dramaturgical impression management has been used in Hochschild's emotional labor construct. When we manage impressions, according to Goffman (1955, 1956b, 1967), emotions arise in interaction—for example, we experience embarrassment when an interaction does not flow smoothly. In a study exploring emotions at work, Boyle (2005) examined emotionalized regions among emergency service workers. Emotions were expressed "offstage" primarily, with much of the emotional processing work done with spouses. Workers displayed softer emotions and affect with the public, often using humor or a caring attitude, while among the workers themselves such emotions were not displayed (most workers were male, and displayed a "stiff upper lip" demeanor). While clients were treated professionally, backstage workers frequently complained about patient and family attitudes. Thus, impression management lines were drawn between frontstage professional performances and backstage venting and complaints. Much of the emotional processing work, however, was done offstage and thus not considered part of the organization's responsibility. Boyle suggests that this might contribute to more on-the-job stress and turnover.

Hochschild (1979, 1983, 1991, 2000) extended Goffman's emphasis on interaction and impression management, through the concept of feeling rules. Feeling rules provide guidelines for how we should feel in given situations. Effective emotion management suggests that we manipulate our emotions to match feeling rules. In numerous service jobs, employees are expected to manage their feelings and affect in order to meet employers' demands for expressiveness and demeanor. Jobs in the hospitality industry or customer-oriented occupations, for example, require regulation of emotions (Hochschild, 1983). A study by Garot (2004) found that workers were sensitive to the emotional displays of applicants for housing places, despite "giving off" impressions of detachment and neutrality. In building a model of emotional labor, Kruml and Geddes (2000) identified dimensions of emotive effort and emotive dissonance (previously developed in the research literature of emotional labor). (See also Goss, 2005, on deference-emotion theory.)

Many jobs, of course, require emotional labor with differing levels of intensity and duration—consider jobs among medical personnel as opposed to receptionists as opposed to civil service positions (Zammuner & Galli, 2005). The work of Tracy on cruise ships (2000) and prison guards (Tracy & Scott, 2006) reveals a range of emotional labor management. Shuler and Sypher (2000) found that some workers thrive on doing emotional labor and found it fun, exciting and rewarding. Hochschild (1983) concluded that females do substantially more emotional work than do males. And, of course, Goffman's *Asylums* is rife with examples and illustrations of emotional labor, by both staff and inmates. (For a general review of emotions in organizations, see Fineman, 1993, 1996, 2000; Fineman & Sturdy, 1999; Hareli & Rafaeli, 2008; Meanwell, Wolfe & Hallett, 2008; and Rafaeli & Sutton, 1987; For a caution about the role of the researcher in being reflexive about their role in gender scholarship, see Lumsden, 2009.)

In analyzing the social influence of emotion in organizational settings, Hareli and Rafaeli (2008) suggest that emotion cycles occur in organizations, when organizational members respond to the emotions of others. Part of these emotional influences are captured by Goffman's concept of footing, where interactional elements may influence all participants in the setting, not just the intended recipients. They found that emotion cycles are influenced by both demographic variables and situational variables. Scheff's (2005b) deference-emotion theory argued that the emotions of pride and shame can motivate entrepreneurial conduct and may contribute to the volatility of such conduct. In an analysis of U.K. supermarkets, Fineman (1996) identified four emotional subtexts in encouraging "green supermarkets"—such emotional subtexts reflected enacting green commitment, defending *autonomy*, contesting green boundaries and avoiding embarrassment. External pressures from green activists were applied through techniques to create fear, shame and/or embarrassment.

2. *Impression management of embodied actions.* Goffman's work also concentrated on the nonverbal aspects of face-to-face interaction, noting the density of cues "given" and "given off" in encounters. Although substantive research has been conducted in this area, the scholarship reported here will focus primarily on workplace settings.

One aspect of bodily practices is gesture which, broadly defined, incorporates posture, dress, and choreographed activities—that is, it encompasses a "range of bodily practices that express social and cultural meanings" (Handler, 2009, p. 283). Goffman's analyses of the interaction order was among the first to focus on space and gesture, and their importance in the presentation of the self. Goffman's reflexivity of the self was reflected in "attention to the ways others are attending to self, and simultaneous strategic attention to the self one wishes to present to those others" (ibid., p. 286). As such, this is "the infinite regress of mutual consideration" (Goffman, 1963b, p. 18). Goffman also discusses people as vehicular units (to distinguish one's navigation through space) as well as participation units (people participating in interaction), and simultaneously attends to both (Goffman, 1971). Also, in *Stigma*, mixed contacts—those between stigmatized individuals and normal individuals—draw attention to the negotiation of personhood because a stigmatized person is not a complete interactional unit (Goffman, 1963b, pp. 5–12). These mixed contacts are scenes of "anxious unanchored interaction" (p. 13) because all participants are aware of the uncertainty about whether or not the "stigmatized" person's stigma should be ignored, recognized or made allowance for (Handler, 2009, p. 296). A normal human being is categorized, in part, by the tendency of large-scale bureaucratic organizations to treat all members as equal in some respects (1963b, p. 62). Goffman's attention to stigma thus furthers our understanding of our concepts of the self and bodily practices.

Napier (2007), in her analysis of interpreters, argued that successful interpretation rested on the ability of interactants to rely on their frames and to negotiate footing shifts through the use of cues like pausing, nods and eye contact. Patterson and Montepare (2007) examined the patterns of unfocused interactions (civil inattention) in Japan and the U.S. and found differences in smiles, nods, and greetings. Herzfeld (2009) analyzed his posture as he adapted to the Thai culture and progressed to a level of more approachable ease.

Roles and resources in organizing. Within organizations, there may be role sets; these sets incorporate all the various groups that one encounters in carrying out his/her typical role (i.e., a doctor's role set would include colleagues, patients, nurses, hospital administrators) (Goffman, 1969a, p. 45). In a similar fashion, individuals may participate in situated activity systems, such as doctors and scrub nurses participating in surgery, or students and teachers participating in a university lecture. Any individual has latitude in how they enact the role: that is, an individual organizes "his behavior *in relation* to situated activity roles, but ... in doing this he uses whatever means are at hand to introduce a margin of freedom and manoeuverability, of pointed dis-identification between himself and the self virtually available for him in the situation" (1969a, p.85). The social identity one takes on in organizing significantly influences the "weight" her/his utterances are given, what they may be able to discuss, and the like.

Roles in interaction, like professor and student, and resources, such as documents, also help us understand what is going on. Goffman noted that we should acknowledge the distance between the person performing a role and the role itself; people also may play multiple roles within an interaction. As he puts it, when taking on a role, the individual takes on "merely a bit of social categorization, that is, social identity, and only through this a bit of his personal one" (Goffman, 1974, p. 286). There also tends to be a loose fit between identity and role performance (Goffman, 1961a, b; Kossakowski, 2008; Spencer, 1987).

When speakers identify with particular institutional roles, they often select the relevant listening role for other participants. As Goffman observes

> ... the same individual can rapidly alter the social role in which he is active, even though his capacity as animator and author remain constant—what in committee meetings is called "changing hats." (This, indeed, is what occurs during a considerable amount of code switching, as Gumperz has amply illustrated.) In thus introducing the name or capacity in which he speaks, the speaker goes some distance in establishing a corresponding reciprocal basis of identification for those to whom this stand-taking is addressed. To a degree, then, to select the capacity in which we are to be active is to select (or to attempt to select) the capacity in which the recipients of our action are present. ...
>
> *(Goffman, 1981b, p. 145)*

Role distance enables one to perform a role as well as express one's own distance from, or disavowal of, a particular role (e.g., a subordinate who completes a task while complaining about it, or the organization). Kunda's ethnographic study of a high commitment culture (1992) used Goffman's frontstage/backstage concept to demonstrate the tension between role embracement (front stage behavior and identification) and role distancing (backstage feelings and disengagement). Other studies (Fleming, 2005; Tracy & Trethewey, 2005) have viewed "backstage" behavior as being authentic.

A note of caution, however, is in order: Goffman views the backstage as preparation for frontstage behavior and for concealment of props, behaviors and the like that might take away from the frontstage performance. Scholars need to assess, in every instance, whether or not such behaviors are indicative of preparation, of disidentification, of greater authenticity, of expressing a different range of behaviors, and so forth before making general claims about backstage behaviors being more authentic. For example, when emergency medical personnel "vent" their emotions away from patients, does this mean that such behavior is "more authentic" than the calm professionalism demonstrated before patients and their families—perhaps they are both "bits of social identity" that are equally authentic and sincere? And both sets of behavior may allow for distancing from the organizational tasks they are carrying out. For Goffman, "the performance of self continues backstage (albeit in a different role and to a different audience), and the same area may be simultaneously the front region of one performance and the back region of another" (Rettie, 2009, p. 427).

Resources may be material objects that can be drawn upon in interaction but also include items such as records and documents. As Goffman noted, "we all live in a world that we assume, by and large, has a permanent residual character … the assumption of resource continuity underlies our notion of faking and impersonation" (Goffman, 1974, p. 288). Elements in organizing such as establishing credentials, as well as assuring a steady stream of continuing material resources, are important. As we shall see, Giddens also views such resources as critical for interaction, organizing and social order.

With regard to resources, frames themselves are recursive and may become resources themselves. As Goffman notes, "The resources we use in a particular scene necessarily have some continuity, an existence before the scene occurs and an existence that continues after the scene is over. But just as this is part of reality, so conceptions that this is so become part of reality, too, and thus have an additional effect" (Goffman, 1974, p. 299). As such, organizational frames become part of the reality of ongoing organizational activities.

Identity. Substantial theoretical discussion centers around self-identity, identity work and the discursive resources that impact these processes (Giddens, 1991a; Sveningsson & Alvesson, 2003). Identity work involves "the mutually constitutive processes whereby people strive to shape a relatively coherent and distinctive notion of personal self-identity and struggle to come to terms with and, within limits, to influence the various social-identities which pertain to them in the various milieus in which they live their lives" (Watson, 2008, p. 129). As such, Sveningsson and Alvesson (2003) note that identity processes reflect the interaction of organizational discourses, role expectations, narrative self-identity and identity work. Such identity work involves fragmentation as well as integration between organizational discourses and identity (p. 1163). Another core issue has been "the extent to which human agency shapes self-identity in the context of wider discourses and other social structures—like race and class—that impinge on organizational members" (Down & Reveley, 2009).

For both Goffman and Giddens, individuals are reflexive, active agents in shaping interaction and action. Identities are "multiple, mutable, and socially constructed" (Ibarra & Barbulescu, 2010, p. 137; see also Goffman, 1959). For example, some view identity as changing as a function of multiple collaborations and cycles of interaction (Beech & Huxham, 2003). Finally, another critical issue is that of authenticity of identities—some scholars have used Goffman's backstage and frontstage behavior to help distinguish authentic from inauthentic identities. An intriguing article by Costas and Fleming (2009) overviews processes of disidentification, self-alienation and corporate colonization of authenticity. (For a very rich overview of identity negotiation at work, see Swann, Johnson & Bosson, 2009.)

A blend of Goffman's views on identity and narrative approaches to identity was developed by Down and Reveley (2009) in their analysis of a supervisor's construction of managerial identity. They argue that "self-narration on the one hand, dramaturgical performance and face-to-face interaction on the other hand—are processually co-dependent" (p. 380). Individuals use these processes simultaneously. They further argue that neither process alone is adequate to account for the construction of managerial identity because face-to-face interaction provides resources to confirm the narrative identities. Narratives and face-to-face interaction are mutually reinforcing: "interaction is fundamentally discursive in nature, and therefore has a narrational quality" (p. 383). However, "face-to-face interaction is a separable element of identity work that cannot be reduced to the self-narrational activities of individuals or the effects of external societal narratives or discourses upon them. Because of Goffman's insightful analysis of face-to-face interaction, his work should be brought to 'centre stage within management identity theory'" (ibid.).

They found that Wilson, a first-line supervisor, used "identity pegs" (Goffman, 1963b, p. 57), at the interpersonal level, on which to hang his self-narrative. "The main peg is successful self-presentation in front of peers and subordinates, by which he achieves self-verification. Episodes of successful self-presentation, in turn, become storyable items that Wilson then incorporates back into his identity narrative" (p. 381). They conclude that successful performances (presentations of the self) underlie identity work: "confirming one's identity by displaying oneself in front of others is central to identity formation" (Down and Reveley, 2009, p. 398).

Another study, by Ibarra and Barbulescu (2010), looked at narrative repertoires developed by individuals whose narratives developed within the frames of organizational norms. They suggest that identity studies need to specify "the interaction dynamics by which an individual's own narrative repertoire shifts in response to changes in the institutional environment so as to refinforce or transform work identities" (p. 149). Like Down and Reveley (2009), they link narrative to interaction which confirms, alters or disconfirms narratives. Also blending internal self-reflection with external discourses, Watson (2008) developed the concept of social-identities as a bridge between "socially available discourse and self identities" (p. 121).

Identity and social interaction in groups was analyzed by Patriotta and Spedale (2009). Sensemaking in groups develops in group interaction. Two processes are key: first, participants try to maintain a coherent self-image while also trying to influence group processes, and second, "face games" create an interactional order within the group that helps structure sensemaking within the group.

Relying on Goffman's concept of face and face-work, they focus on the process of interaction itself as sensemaking; as such, it reflects an "emergent and contingent process that results from the encounter of multiple actors, within a common space, at a specific time, and around a specific task" (Patriotta & Spedale, 2009, p. 1228). Group members are concerned "with making sense not only of their world but of themselves, the 'self' being a dynamic interpretative structure in response to self-derived needs for self-enhancement, self-efficacy and self-consistency. ... the establishment and maintenance of identity is a core preoccupation in sensemaking. ... Sensemaking is always influenced by the actual, implied or imagined presence of others and this characterizes it as an inherently social activity" (ibid., p. 1229).

Goffman's views on the presentation of the self, face and face-work illuminate the ways in which a group is able to form a "working consensus" that enables them to engage in sensemaking. As they note, "face is not the same as identity ... it is a basic construct that is entailed in the projection of impressions and line ... face expresses what the interacting 'others' take an individual to be in the context of their exchanges" (ibid., p. 1231). In their analysis of a consultancy task force, they found that the lines initially expressed by actors were resilient (adjustments to changing face were difficult) and shaped the subsequent social interaction—that is, "the initial framing of the sensemaking context affects the nature of sensemaking outcomes" (ibid., p. 1243).

Organizational discourses often create a dichotomy of fake vs. real identities for organizational members (Tracy & Trethewey, 2005). The self is a "practical everyday accomplishment" which implicates Goffman's view of an interactional, presentational self, but the self also negotiates among "discourses that construct employment and (subject) positions in institutional settings" (pp. 171–72). Organizational discourses and practices "produces four subject positions with both symbolic and material consequences: strategized self-subordination, perpetually deferred identities, 'auto-dressage,' and the production of 'good little copers'" (ibid., p. 168).

They present an intriguing discussion of the dichotomy of a real self/fake self in a number of different research traditions. They argue that identity is more appropriately understood as "constructed and constrained through various discourses of power" (ibid., p. 175). They conclude by arguing for "crystallized selves [which] have different shapes depending on the various discourses through which they are constructed and constrained" (p. 186). As noted earlier, Goffman himself suggests that one is continuously, reflexively assessing the self against a variety of roles and interactional opportunities, some of which reflect differing capacities for agency and action (i.e., the exercise of power). His position seems compatible with views of a crystallized self.

In her examination of tensions within occupational identity, Meisenbach (2008) found that organizational members framed their organizational activities in different ways to handle those tensions. Empowered occupational identity reflected an individual's ability to shift across six different power-laden and discourse influenced frames for fundraising activities. Their fundraising frames included financial, relational, educational, mission, coordination and magical frames; these frames "serve as correctives to each other and their associated discourses" (p. 280). Thus, identities appear to be fluid and shifting as organizational members pursue their tasks. Using Goffman's role-playing, Ligas and Coulter (2001) analyze the roles customers took in dissatisfactory, long-term service encounters. Roles that emerged included the helping, contented, discontented or disgusted customer. Interviews with three customers revealed both their backstage (behind-the-scenes contemplation) and frontstage behavior.

Frames and framing. Frames have been used to identify contexts, define actions and reflect tacit knowledge. Scholars have used frames in these senses to explore individuals' interpersonal and organizational behavior (Menand, 2009). A study by Markowitz (1998) explored the frames of meanings workers used to understand a union organizing campaign and the way workers related to the union. Two different campaign strategies were used, the blitz and the comprehensive campaign; both differed in the degree of worker participation advocated. Three stages of the campaigns (shared information, open communication, and common decision-making) were contrasted. Workers' frames of meaning influenced their actions across the organizations.

Framing was used to evaluate the "spirit of place" in identifying homey as opposed to institutional residential organizations for the elderly (Martin, 2002). Paradoxes associated with those frames, and the framing of staff and residents' views of bodily functions and death and dying were explored. Homey organizations used power to enhance residents' dignity and rights more so than did institutional organizations.

1. *Framing strategic planning.* A number of studies have used frames and framing to analyze the processes of strategic planning. A major article by Rasche and Chia (2009) integrates Goffman's work with an approach to strategy as a social practice. Rasche and Chia view strategy-as-practice, rather than viewing strategy as something organizations possess. As such, they incorporate the perspective of social theory and develop a view of strategy that places it in its historical-condition of creation (looking for the various tributaries that shape "practice theory"), assesses its different qualities, and uncovers its contextual aspects through ethnographic methods. Both Goffman and Giddens are utilized in their analysis, and their work centrally related to the practice turn in organizational research. As they note,

> Goffman understands mental schemes (i.e., "frames" that are necessary for the interpretation of a situation) as a *collective* phenomenon. These adopted frames allow actors to follow social practices to create social order and *at the same time* the identity of the individual. Social practices, thus, "frame" actors who, because of this framing, know who they are and how to act in an adequate and socially acceptable way … the trans-subjective frames reflect the background conditions necessary for this meaning production to take place. The frames, however, do not determine the performance of social practices. Rather … engaging in a social practice means to enact a situation through a frame to make use of the available stock of knowledge.
>
> *(Rasche & Chia, 2009, p. 719)*

Goffman also emphasizes the physical aspects of social practices, based on bodily movements, physical objects and props, and the use of space. As Rasche and Chia note, "Unlike Foucault and Bourdieu, Goffman starts from the subject-centred interpretative tradition and moves to 'de-centre' the subject and, consequently, shifts attention from purely mental activities to material social practices. The subject is not the ultimate locus of meaning production anymore, but understood as a participant of social practices who draws on certain shared cognitive presuppositions (i.e., 'frames') to understand the world" (ibid.). Thus, agents enact their shared understandings in their activities and actions.

Neo-interpretative social theorists assume that "collective knowledge schemes are a precondition to the constitution of the actor and his or her environment within social practices. Practices need to be based on knowledge schemes that transcend the individual because different actors perform social practices at different points in time-space" (ibid., p. 720). These assumptions complement the structurational theory developed by Giddens.

When investigating strategy practices, Rasche and Chia suggest studying bodily doings as well as bodily sayings. Routine practices are examined, and strategic activity is located in the "*patterns* of bodily doings and sayings that strategists perform" (p. 721). Studies might also investigate the use of PowerPoint, arrangement of physical spaces, the location of strategy sessions, use of materials like flip-charts and so forth. Strategists are also concerned with their credibility (Goffman's frontstage) and their positioning (footing and alignment) in discussions. They conclude with an interesting discussion of ethnographic methods, and second Goffman's emphasis on participant observation.

A study by Skaerbaek (2005) analyzed the framing of an annual report. The production and reading of an annual report reflects the relationship between the producers of the report (university officials) and those who read the report (parliament and government officials). Annual reports reflect the expectations of parliament and the government while avoiding the publication of any critical information that may create difficulty for the university. The annual report thus reflects different layers of meaning which are used for the management of impressions.

In a study of strategy, Sillince and Mueller (2007) found that management reframed accountability for planning and implementing a strategic initiative. When the initiative began to fail, changing goals reframed an initial focus on capability to a later focus on accountability. Framing and reframing demonstrated these shifts in strategizing. Tsoukas (2009) discusses background tacit frames and argues that conceptual reframing is a way to create new knowledge in organizations.

A fascinating study by Samra-Fredericks (2003) uses ethnographic analysis to look at strategizing as lived experience and as everyday interaction. One individual was particularly influential and his linguistic skills (i.e., questioning, displaying appropriate emotion, the use of metaphor and of history) and knowledge shaped strategic discussions. The framing process was intricate, dynamic, fragile and contentious (p. 168). Samra-Fredericks concluded by reflecting on the difficulty of ethnographic analysis and the need for interdisciplinary work on strategic practice—"embodied, emotional and moral *human beings* talking to each other" (p. 169). A study by Hample, Warner and Young (2009) tested the use of primary argument frames in evaluating arguments, although interconnections among frames, editing, and individual differences were more influential in editing arguments.

In an ethnographic study, Kaplan (2008) found that frames were "an integral part of how uncertainty was framed, and that contested frames were also part of the political process of strategizing. Managers used frames to conceptualize the market's movements, and when frames about a strategic choice were not congruent, actors engaged in highly political framing practices to make their frames resonate [with others] and to mobilize action in their favor" (p. 729). Frames are thus critical in viewing a situation as well as justifying actions, and allow for new power coalitions to form when frames are being contested. As she suggests, the framing contests represent "cognition as a dynamic, purposive, and politically charged process of meaning construction" (p. 730). She argues, like Goffman, that frames "are not simply tools to deploy, but rather 'schemata of interpretation,' which allow actors to make sense of ambiguous and varied signals ... frames shape how individual actors see the world and perceive their own interests. Actors make choices and act from within that understanding" (ibid.).

By corollary, framing also allows people to suggest what is going on to others. This process is "not necessarily seamless and inevitable" (ibid., p. 732). Actors have multiple frames to draw on at any point (Goffman, 1974), and through interaction, individual meaningfulness and collective meaning is negotiated. Kaplan argues that Goffman's ethnographic methods are a way to understand organizations through their daily practices, and also complements recent moves that take a practice-based view of organizations (Jarzabkowski, 2005; Orlikowski, 2000). As she concludes, actors have considerable agency that they exercise in their strategic choices and that "outcomes are mediated by the more or less skillful deployment of framing practices in organizational framing contests" (Kaplan, 2008, p. 747).

In an ethnographic analysis of a Japanese advertising agency, Moeran (2009) used frame analysis to capture the interactions among the differing professional groups hired to complete an ad campaign. Different teams, with differing frames, must work together to finalize the ad. Primary frameworks (Goffman, 1974) include competitive presentations, client workshops and studio shoots (Moeran, 2009, p. 969). The "guided doings" of the production shoot are determined by professional practices and norms. Tensions occur in the conceptualization and production of the advertising, which is contextualized by larger issues in the field of advertising as a whole, and the dual creative/administrative roles of participants. Creativity was thus enabled and constrained by various aesthetic, economic, material and social factors (p. 980).

2. *Framing leadership*. A number of scholars have examined leadership from the context of frames and framing. Most notably, Fairhurst has viewed framing from both a management and leadership perspective. *The Art of Framing* (Fairhurst & Saar, 1996) uses frames and reframing as techniques to help leaders problematize leadership issues. Subsequent work (Fairhurst, 2005; Fairhurst & Grant, 2010) applies both the cognitive and skill aspects of framing in leadership. Her forthcoming book, *The*

Power of Framing (in press, b) is designed to assist leaders and managers in applying framing with respect to their own communicative styles. This body of work contributes substantively to the use of frames and framing in leadership, and enriches our views of leadership.

Other scholars have used framing to assess particular leadership acts. Liu (2010) analyzed occasions of leadership failure and analyzed the framing strategies they used for apologizing. Leaders sought to manage impressions of them formed by multiple audiences and tried to project consistency across different frames. Sinha (2010) explored leadership from Goffman's presentation of the self. Impression management suggests that the leader enters into a pre-established social order and is held accountable to that order. Goffman's work encourages scholars of leadership to explore relationships among leader self-presentation, leader–follower trust and social tact (p. 199).

The Dramaturgical Perspective

Many organizational scholars have used Goffman's dramaturgical concepts and applied them in organizations in order to understand more about the dynamics of organizations. In the *Presentation of Self in Everyday Life*, Goffman (1959) outlined several of these concepts. First, performance refers to all activity by a given actor which influences other participants. Actors must sustain viable performances through props, actions, facial expressions and role attitudes. Second, performances involve teams and incorporate front regions (public spaces) as well as back regions (private spaces). Third, regionalization emphasizes the importance of spatial considerations in knowledge, power and space (Manning, 1991, p. 75). Fourth, "out of character communication" refers to the slippage in performance that reflects a discontinuity between the projected self and the presented self (Goffman, 1959, p. 206). For example, such slippage may involve contradictory information or reveal private backstage information. Finally, a performance concerns the impression management or line an individual wishes to develop. Impressions may be given (intentionally) or given off (revealing information inadvertently).

With the publication of *Frame Analysis* (Goffman, 1974), Goffman drew our attention to the differences between onstage interaction and interaction in real life (Manning, 1991, p. 82). Bodily alignment and tacit knowledge are two interactional aspects that are very distinct and highlighted onstage (respectively staged and articulated), while in real life, mutual body orientation and taken-for-granted knowledge are often assumed and not emphasized (ibid., p. 82). As Manning suggested,

> Understanding a performance, then, requires a practical or discursive knowledge of the frames that surround it. Frames are vulnerable. They can both … [be] *keyed*—that is, transformed from one schema of interpretation into another—and *fabricated*—that is, designed so as to mislead by others about

actual events … the implication of these different frame manipulations is that everyday life can tolerate extraordinarily complex frame structures with the same nonchalances concert pianists display in the midst of frighteningly difficult musical scores.

(p. 82)

Thus, the dramaturgical perspective evolved to incorporate frames and reframing. In addition, Goffman moved toward acknowledging that rules are resources and indeterminate guides to conduct (ibid., p. 85).

Performance as organizing. An aspect of Goffman's work that may apply particularly to organizational settings is his concept of performance. In looking at interactions through a dramaturgical or performance metaphor, Goffman stated that the "perspective employed in this report is that of the theatrical performance: the principles derived are dramaturgical ones. I shall consider the way in which the individual in ordinary work situations presents himself and his activity to others, ways in which he guides and controls the impression they form of him, and the kind of things he may or may not do while sustaining his performance before them" (Goffman, 1959, p. xi).

For Goffman, selves are embodied within performances, performances embodied in roles, and roles meaningfully embedded within frames; frames then become routine, and routines become strategic (Schoening, 1995, pp. 179–81; Schoening & Anderson, 1995). Actors simultaneously put forth a definition of the situation and their role within it. Goffman sensitized us to the performances in "front" regions where the audience cooperates with performers to bring off the performance (e.g., the collaboration and cooperation required to make a formal sales presentation to a board of directors, or a sales manager talking with his/her sales force). There are "back" regions where participants may prepare themselves or simply have privacy (e.g., offices, bathrooms). (See also Conte, 2008.)

Performances may be disrupted by challenges (e.g., a questioning of sales figures), revelation of private information (presumably protected by the performers) and "staging talk" (information given about the performance itself). The concept of cooperation by the team itself (the performers themselves), as well as the cooperation between audience and performer, is also highlighted.

Goffman also emphasized the importance of consistency among the setting, and the appearance and manner of the performer (Goffman, 1959, p. 25). As he cogently observed

A status, a position, a social place is not a material thing to be possessed and then displayed; it is a pattern of appropriate conduct, coherent, embellished, and well-articulated. Performed with ease or clumsiness, awareness or not, guile or good faith, it is none the less something that must be enacted and portrayed, something that must be realized.

(Goffman, 1959, p. 75)

Finally, throughout his work, Goffman argued that both authentic and fabricated performances utilize the same strategies of impression management. Because of this, his use of the dramaturgical metaphor is also useful in analyzing social interaction. As Goffman pointed out, "that deeply incorporated into the nature of talk are the fundamental requirements of theatricality" (Goffman, 1981a, p. 4). Some research has pursued the use of corporate theatre in which performances are staged to exemplify some of the difficulties an organization is experiencing; these staged performances allow the audience (organizational members) to view a controversy in a new way, and perhaps resolve some issues (Clark & Mangham, 2004; Clark & Salaman, 1996; Cornelissen, 2004; Mangham, 1990, 2005).

Using the theatre or dramaturgical metaphor of Goffman has also stimulated research on the "frontstage" and "backstage" of organizing. Using Goffman's metaphor, studies have explored operating "theatres," and examined the drama, scripting and learning lines, and changes between backstage and frontstage, in order to understand the role of operating room nurses and their tasks (Riley & Manias, 2005). An analysis of dying patients in a nursing home, developed from interviews with the staff, viewed dying as a three act play: *What If* (different treatments were used, new ones pursued); *Ready to Go* (completing unfinished business); and *The Look about Them* (well-known signs of imminent death) (Oliver, Porock & Oliver, 2006). (See also McLean, 2006.)

Dramaturgical metaphors. Goffman's work has also been used as a generative metaphor—by looking at social action as inherently dramaturgical (Oswick, Keenoy & Grant, 2001). They suggested that the dramaturgical metaphor can be used instrumentally (to study organizational processes) as well as used to establish a critical perspective on organizing. Several scholars, most notably Mangham and his colleagues (Mangham, 1998, 2005), have explored organizing, management and leadership using a dramaturgical metaphor. Gardner and Avolio (1998) have explored charismatic leadership utilizing a dramaturgical perspective: they found that framing, scripting, staging and performing are the basic phases in establishing charismatic leadership. They outlined testable research propositions, as well as discussed the practical implications of this approach.

Collins noted the value of the dramaturgical metaphor in cases of organizational conflict, emphasizing both the ritual and cognitive aspects of Goffman's work. He argued that "the publicly accepted definition of the situation is all-important, above all in cases of potential conflict; a clear definition of the situation creates an 'obvious' solution to the coordination frame, while the disturbance of this clarity can cause power to crumble. The stakes, then, in effective social dramaturgy are not only the general need for cognitive order of which Goffman speaks, they include the entire structure of domination" (Collins, 2000b, p. 330). The ritual model is especially useful because it can be presented in terms of variables, such as variations in "social density," which affect the strength and abstractness of shared symbols. Models of strategic interaction outlined the distribution of power and the potentials for its change (ibid.).

In an interesting extension of interaction rituals, extending both Goffman and Durkheim, Collins (2004) has developed an interaction ritual chain theory. This theory argues "that the social morphology that counts is the patterns of micro-sociological interaction in local situations" (p. 31). This theory adds value through its emphasis on situations themselves; situations are a process by which "shared emotions and intersubjective focus sweep individuals along by flooding their consciousness," and ritual is used to create cultural symbols. He also noted that situations that combine a strong mutual focus of attention with strong emotional entrainment, like 9/11, result in strong feelings of membership and also high emotional energy for participants (p. 42). Such moments are defining moments for both individuals and collectivities.

Summary

As we have seen, Goffman himself acknowledges the applicability of his concepts to institutional settings, and the loose coupling of the interactional order to the social order. His concepts of frames, framing, face, footing, alignment, deference and demeanor, front- and backstage, and territories of the self have provided insightful frameworks for analyzing communicating and organizing. Scholars have also utilized his dramaturgical perspective, presentation of self and impression management to develop major research streams investigating organizations.

In particular, his concepts of frames and framing have provided linkages between the interactional order and the social order. Although he did not explore such linkages in depth, as Gonos (1977) observed, "It remains for us to analyze the place of the frames of everyday life within political and economic systems, the frames at another level of organization. This is the possibility that Goffman's work affords" (p. 866). Although Goffman did not pursue links to more macro-structures (with some exceptions, such as his work on total institutions), his analyses of the interaction order are complementary to macro-level analyses, such as those of Foucault and Giddens.

Goffman would, in fact, argue that the interaction order is necessary for social order (a point that, I think, Giddens would agree with, given the centrality of interaction in his own work). Ytreberg (2002) noted that both *Asylums* and *Forms of Talk* "crucially focus on how discourses are conditioned specifically by their institutional context. In doing so, they indicate a link between the microsociological level and the macro level of society's institutions and their ideologies" (p. 495). As Hacking (2004) noted, our choices (agency) are possible by the blending of the immediate social situation (analyzed by Goffmans' work) and the sociohistorical context of that situation (analyzed by Giddens' work). Although Goffman did not pursue this link theoretically himself, nevertheless rich possibilities are suggested by his work.

According to Giddens, Goffman's preoccupation "with situations of co-presence leads him to underestimate the generalized importance of his theories for more 'standard'—that is, macro-structural—problems of sociology" (Giddens, 2000, p. 168). Yet, as Giddens pointed out,

> Who could dispute the fruitfulness of Goffman's decision to confine the realm of his investigations? In so doing he not only brought into view substantively new arenas of study, but he was able to explore questions invested with a new significance as a result of trends in social theory and philosophy over the past several decades. ... The routine and the mundane have a great deal to teach us about quite fundamental issues of human experience, action and consciousness.
>
> *(Giddens, 2000, p. 168)*

Although Goffman's use of frames is, as we have seen in this chapter, insightful, we can broaden the scope of frames which are of particular importance in analyzing organizing and communicating. As we have seen, Goffman's conception of frames can be embedded within other social systems, such as particular organizations, institutions, cultures, and technologies. As previously noted, Giddens' structuration theory incorporates interaction as the fundamental process in which structure, agency and action are intertwined. Through the theory of structurational interaction, we can begin to more fully explore the complexities of communicating and organizing. It is to these possibilities we now turn.

SECTION IV

Toward a Theory of Structurational Interaction

Given the overviews of both Goffman and Giddens, many points of similarity in their theories can be noted, well beyond Giddens' use of Goffman's interaction order as a basis for social integration. Shared emphases on social practices, agency, identity, the importance of context and actors' knowledgeability reflect some of the points of congruency between them. In addition, frames have been used by both theorists and can be used to interweave their theories even more tightly.

In Chapter 11, I will more fully integrate Goffman and Giddens, examining other ways in which their theoretical perspectives can be interwoven, while remaining consistent with both perspectives and moving toward establishing a theory of structurational interaction. In Chapter 12, I will apply structurational interaction to several existing research studies, and demonstrate how applying this theory could enrich those research findings. In addition, I will discuss ways in which we can extend this theory, and apply it to new areas of research.

11

TOWARD A THEORY OF STRUCTURATIONAL INTERACTION

There are four different ways in which their work can be integrated. First, I will use frame theory as a metatheory to link these two theorists, particularly since each theorist uses the concept of frames. Second, I will look at the foundational significance of Goffmans' interaction order for Giddens' structuration theory. Third, I will review Giddens' discussion of Goffman, and his incorporation of some of Goffman's constructs into his work. Fourth, I will develop some additional linkages between their work. And finally, I will outline some advantages of this blended theoretical perspective, which provides an integrated coherent perspective which integrates communicating and organizing.

Integration Through Frame Theory

In preceding chapters, I have discussed *frame systems* for organizing and communicating. These frame systems represent our tacit, taken-for-granted knowledge and expectations about organizing and communicating. *Frames*, more narrowly defined contexts for communicating and organizing, have also been discussed. Alternative organizing frames, like a structural or a political perspective, have also been discussed. Similarly, a frame for communicating in organizations has been developed, outlining some common interactional, organizational activities such as decision-making, the use of different message types and channels, and so forth. Finally, frames used to represent tacit, commonsense knowledge were also discussed.

Major assumptions underlying my discussion of frames and frame systems are (1) that communicating and organizing co-produce one another; (2) that organizing frames provide a context for communicating; (3) that organizing and communicating exist in the broader context of culture, and (4) that subsequent interactions may reproduce, or alter, both communicating and organizing. The new organizing contexts created, in turn, influence subsequent communicative practices, and the resulting outcomes again recast the organizing and communicating contexts. It is at the *framing* level—the everyday interactions within organizations—that these frames (for organizing and for communicating) mutually intertwine to enact organizational life. As such, frames and framing operate on multiple levels of analysis.

For our purposes, we must also ask how these frames become interconnected structures. As Czarniawska noted, "frames become enactments of situations that people will act upon, and they pick up their cues accordingly, describing them in words appropriate to a given frame or vocabulary. But how do they connect cued events into interlocking structures?" (2006b, p. 1670).

For answers, we turn to both Goffman and Giddens. On the level of social integration (or social interaction), Goffman's concepts of shared tacit knowledge, alignment and footing provide us with a moment-by-moment perspective on interlocked actions, while Giddens, through the duality of structure, binds structure and agency in interaction. Both scholars, via frames, establish differing layers of context, and thus provide the potential to connect actions with broader contexts of interaction (Goffman via frames, keying and rekeying, and Giddens via contextualization through the use of frames, rules, resources and distanciation). Taken together, the theory of structurational interaction provides a multi-level, multi-focal lens for assessing the richness and complexity of organizing and communicating. The fundamental unit of analysis is action (social practices), not the organization, the institution or the individual.

In what follows, I will integrate Goffman and Giddens through the use of frame theory, as developed in Chapter 1. The chart below outlines the levels of frame theory that were developed, and the primary ways in which their work is being utilized.

FRAME THEORY

Frame systems	Underlying related belief systems: Giddens & Goffman
Frames	
Institutional frames	Giddens' structuration
Contextual frames	Goffman & Giddens
Framing	Face-to-face encounters: Goffman & Giddens

Frame systems. Frame systems, reflecting underlying related belief systems, tap into human assumptions about the nature of human nature, the relationship of humans to the environment and so forth (Schein, 2004). How collectivities have answered such questions reflects their values and beliefs. While neither Goffman nor Giddens has discussed such belief systems in depth, both acknowledge the importance of cultural beliefs as a backdrop for organizing and communicating. Giddens' work focuses upon values and beliefs in his discussions of the transition from tribal to modern societies, in his discussions of issues like trust and risk in late modernity, and in his discussions of the contradictions and changes in social practices that accompany these transitions. Frequently, these beliefs are the tacit, taken-for-granted aspects of knowledge. While not a focal point for either theorist, it is important to recognize that frame systems are deeply embedded systems of beliefs and values that provide a contextual background for organizing and communicating.

In addition, the concept of a "frame system" has been used to explain the naïve, taken-for-granted assumptions humans have about communicating and organizing. Although this is in need of empirical verification, I would argue that the assumptions I have advocated are so generic and basic that they may apply across cultures. These assumptions, for example, reflect concerns about face and social relationships which appear relevant to all cultures. Although cultures vary in their social practices concerning face and social relationships, all cultures appear to have social practices dealing with these issues. And I would make a similar argument with regard to basic assumptions underlying communicating (see Chapter 2) and organizing (see Chapter 3).

Such frame systems capture our taken-for-granted knowledge that we rely on in our sensemaking activities. These basic assumptions are part of the "stocks of knowledge" and "interpretive schemes" that we utilize while interacting. Both Goffman and Giddens rely on knowledgeable agents in social interaction, and these basic assumptions form part of agents' knowledgeability. I believe these assumptions are consistent with both Goffman's and Giddens' theoretical positions. Examining these basic assumptions also expands our discussion about what is *meant* by organizing and communicating.

Frames. Giddens uses three modalities of structuration—signification, legitimation and domination—to frame the four types of institutions every society needs. Signification (meaning) frames social institutions, like educational systems and churches, that develop and foster core beliefs and values of a society. Domination frames two types of institutions, those governing economic and/or political systems. Legitimation frames institutions governing sanctions, such as the legal system of a country. Giddens' work allows us to frame various types of institutions and thus provides a more complete understanding of both their communicative and organizing processes.

Frames also reflect agents' knowledge of contexts and their interpretive schemas. Contextual frames enable participants to coordinate their talk and action, and to mutually sustain their interaction. Contextual frames also may cue or "key" what interpretive schemas might be relevant during a given encounter. Both men allow for varying scopes of context: Goffman via keying and rekeying and Giddens through distanciation and rules. Given these varying levels of context and interpretive frames, agents may acknowledge vary broad contexts (such as culture) or very focused, narrow contexts (what is going on right now in this particular encounter).

Frames, in both Goffman's and Giddens' work, enable us to utilize multiple levels of analysis, and to integrate analyses across levels. Thus we can study organizing, communicating, and their interrelationships and tensions at multiple levels. Giddens, in fact, builds upon Goffman's concepts of copresence, frames and routinization:

I have defined social integration as systemness in circumstances of co-presence. Several phenomena suggest themselves as being most immediately relevant to the constitution of social integration thus defined. First, in order to grasp the connection of social reproduction stretching away over time and space, we must emphasise how encounters are formed and reformed in the duree of daily existence.

Second, we should seek to identify the main mechanisms of the duality of structure whereby encounters are organised in and through the intersections of practical and discursive consciousness. This in turn has to be explicated in terms of both the control of the body and of the sustaining of rules and conventions. Third, encounters are sustained above all through *talk*, through everyday conversation. In analysing the communication of meaning in interaction via the use of interpretive schemes, the phenomenon of talk has to be taken very seriously, as constitutively involved in encounters. Finally, the contextual organisation in encounters must be examined, since the mobilisation of time-space is the 'grounding' of all the above elements. I shall undertake this latter task in terms of several basic notions, those of 'presence availability', 'locale', and the relation of 'enclosure/disclosure'.

(Giddens, 1984, pp. 72–73)

Thus, for Giddens, Goffman's interaction order is the foundation of social order. Both focus on everyday interaction or encounters; both emphasize frames as interpretive schemes and as interactional contexts. Such frames are used to "make sense of what is going on here." Finally, encounters are firmly grounded in time-space, bodily control and ritual (convention).

Goffman's use of frame is also integrated with Giddens' use of rules. In Giddens' view, "Framing may be regarded as providing the ordering of activities and meanings whereby ontological security is sustained in the enactment of daily routines" (Giddens, 1984, p. 87). As such,

Frames are clusters of rules which help to constitute and regulate activities, defining them as activities of a certain sort and as subject to a given range of sanctions. ... Framing as constitutive of, and constricted by, encounters "make sense" of the activities in which participants engage, both for themselves and for others. This includes the "literal" understanding of events but also the criteria by which it is made plain that what is going on is humour, play, theatre and so on.

(ibid.)

Thus both theorists recognize the routine, structured nature of encounters as frames. Craib also suggested that Giddens' concept of practical consciousness builds upon Goffman's notion of framing, which "in turn fits into an analysis of social reproduction of wider social systems through different types of encounter" (1992, p. 168).

Framing. Goffman's work is most central to framing—the specific moves and strategies used to negotiate encounters. Concepts such as face, alignment, footing, keying, rekeying, bracketing, secondary adjustments, front and back regions and so forth illuminate the complexity of everyday encounters. Yet, as both Goffman and Giddens suggest, humans appear to do this in an effortless fashion. And both regard the routinization of daily encounters to be essential for selfhood and ontological security.

As we have seen, both theorists have utilized frame theory in their work. Their mutual reliance on frames facilitates the integration of their work. But frame theory can also be used to more fully explain aspects of their work. For example, using frames to laminate or layer organizational contexts at different levels of hierarchy or inclusiveness. Or frames can be used to compare and contrast different types of institutions. Framing strategies can be used to explore conflict and strategy in different organizations. In many ways, then, frame theory can be used not only to integrate their work but also to further explore facets of their work. Using frame theory to integrate their work helps build the theory of structurational interaction which provides a rich, multi-level analysis of organizing and communicating.

Another useful way to explore the interrelationships of Goffman and Giddens is to assess their integration from the major approaches to organizational communication developed by Fairhurst and Putnam (2004).

Object, becoming and grounded-in-action approaches to organizational communication. Fairhurst and Putnam (2004) developed major contrasts across three different approaches to organizing and communicating—those with an *object* orientation, those with a *becoming* orientation, and those with a *grounded-in-action* orientation (previously outlined in Chapter 4). All these alternative orientations are reflected in different aspects within a theory of structurational interaction.

Object orientation. Within an *object* orientation, Giddens provides an excellent approach to looking at the way in which organizations are sedimented; institutions, he argues, are contextualized in a particular sociohistorical frame. Giddens, as a social theorist, discusses the nature of social systems, establishes four types of institutions that every society/culture uses, and explores broad historical forces, such as globalization and new technology, that continuously shape and develop institutions (Giddens, 1979, 1984). Such sociohistorical contextualization allows us more in-depth insights into how discourse occurs within particular organizations at a particular time as well as into organizational and institutional change over time. As a complement, Goffman's work is helpful in contextualizing interaction within particular organizational settings. His work on total institutions, asylums, radio talk shows, and the like, are insightful in probing these specific organizational arrangements.

Becoming orientation. Within the *becoming* orientation, scholars focus on language-in-use in the development and formation of organizations as well as on discourses centered around power and knowledge. Giddens and Goffman, like Haslett (1987), emphasize the importance of tacit knowledge and practical consciousness in sensemaking in interaction. As Boden (1994) argued, organizational members are simultaneously fitting in their comments retrospectively, prospectively, and at-the-current-moment. Both theorists provide insights on developing identity over an individual's life-span. In particular, Goffman's work enables us to examine the micro-actions and language-in-use that enable organizational actors to argue, persuade, negotiate, and the like in varied organizational settings. Both Giddens and Goffman provide an enriched perspective on how organizational members negotiate the details of everyday organizational activity.

Grounded-in-action orientation. Finally, within the *grounded-in-action* orientation, scholars examine how organizations/organizing "emerges and re-emerges in the ongoing stream of experience" (Fairhurst & Putnam, 2004, p. 19). Giddens' structuration theory and the duality of structure emphasizes the emergence of agency through the interaction of organizational members. As such, social interaction is both the medium and outcome of social structure. When exploring action within a particular social setting, Goffman's work, particularly frames and framing, allows us to analyze the moves, counter-moves, and negotiation of meaning among organizational participants. Differing degrees of participation, degrees of inclusion, and plurality of views are all developed within Goffman's approach.

Through structurational interaction, we can view organizing and organizations through all three orientations, simultaneously, and at multiple levels. Giddens explicitly deals with the issues of agency and structure, and, taken collectively, their work provides a layered contextualization of organizational activity. Frame theory provides the overarching architecture that strengthens this theoretical synthesis.

When both frame theory and the three orientations to organizational communication are integrated, we can explore the following interrelationships:

Frame Systems/Discourses/Object orientation/Giddens
Frames/Discourses and discourse/Becoming/Goffman & Giddens
Framing/Discourse/Grounded-in-action/Goffman & Giddens

On the macro-level of *frame systems*, both discourses and object orientations toward organizations are found in Giddens' work, particularly in his discussion of the sedimentation of organizations, their sociohistorical contexts, the types of organizations found in every society, and the characteristics of differing social systems. Social systems themselves, of course, as well as sociohistorical contexts, would reflect the discourses found in those societies.

Frame systems would also reflect discourses centered on communicating and organizing, as well as on other societal processes found in legal, political and economic systems and their organizations. Frame systems thus reflect the most tacit, underlying knowledge systems that maintain societal assumptions and beliefs. Goffman's work also focuses on tacit knowledge as a significant aspect of actors' knowledgeability. We may be, as Giddens noted, unaware, or only partially aware, of these knowledge systems. In the model of communication developed earlier in this book, I emphasized the role of tacit knowledge in communicative processes as does structurational interaction.

Frames draw upon the broad concepts within frame systems to create more narrow, well-defined and bounded social contexts for organizing and communicating. For organizing activities, three processes are especially significant: control, coordination, and culture. Control and coordination are necessary to achieve organizational goals and missions, and culture reflects the ways in which these control and coordination strategies work within a society or particular organization (thus we have two levels of culture, representing societal beliefs as well as specific beliefs and practices within an organization). Frames thus reflect various organizational cultures and their concomitant communicative practices (as suggested earlier).

In brief, both Goffman and Giddens utilize frames in ways consistent with frame theory as developed in Chapter 1. Both use frames as a way of capturing context and altering context; as interpretive schemes for understanding what is going on in the present situation; and as scripts for appropriate actions, both verbally and non-verbally. Frames, therefore, are key interpretive elements of interaction for both theorists. Frames also allow us to "scale up," "layer" or blend the macro-micro-levels through varying contextual brackets for interaction and action. Frames can be used to reflect aspects of tacit, taken-for-granted knowledge and practical consciousness, while framing reflects processes of interpretation that guide participants' behaviors.

Finally, on the *framing* level, structurational interaction provides an in-depth analysis of the moment-by-moment interactional processes in encounters. Giddens and Goffman both emphasize social practices as basic units of analysis. When interacting, actors enact structure and agency, and, through their actions, alter future encounters. Encounters may reflect misunderstandings, agreement, strategies, repairs, struggles over identity, and so forth. But it is in and through interaction that such issues are expressed and acted upon. It is at the framing level that we experience the impact of frame systems and frames.

Different interactional moves can be analyzed in different organizing and communicating contexts. In particular, structurational interaction can help illuminate the different types of "presence" across interactions and evaluate their impact. For example, how does teamwork develop in the contexts of copresence? In virtual contexts—with no face-to-face interaction? In hybrid contexts (a blend of FtF and FtD interactions)? Structurational interaction establishes an excellent base for exploring such issues, and given the impact of new technologies on communicating and organizing, this will be an increasingly significant area of research.

Thus far, we have illustrated the way in which frame theory can be used to integrate their work. However, Giddens explicitly uses Goffman's interaction order as a way of conceptualizing social integration. As you will recall, social integration is a prerequisite for social systems. As such, Goffman's interaction order provides a foundation for Giddens' views on social system integration. We next turn to an exploration of this critical interrelationship.

The Interactional Order as the Foundation of Social Order

Many scholars, in addition to Giddens himself, acknowledge the substantive role of Goffman's interaction order for social order. For example, Manning (1992) clearly pointed out the importance of social integration in unifying structure and agency in large social institutions. As he noted:

> For a sociological analysis to be satisfactory, Giddens argues that it must demonstrate a connection between face-to-face interaction and the organized pattern of role relationships that constitute a social system. In Giddens' vocabulary, sociologists must demonstrate a connection between "social integration" and "system integration". Social integration refers to the interactions between the different parts of a social system that produce a continual sense of social order over time. This distinction is not as abstract and forbidding as it appears at first. Consider a sociological analysis of a large corporation: system integration is maintained through the relationships between different roles in the corporation; social integration is maintained through face-to-face interaction.
>
> *(Manning, 1992, p. 180)*

In addition, Giddens' structuration theory also rests upon an implicit assumption of trust in social order of the sort outlined by Goffman (Manning, 2000a). According to Giddens, "Goffman's emphasis on trust and tact strikingly echoes themes found in ego psychology and generates an analytically powerful understanding of the reflexive monitoring of the flux of encounters involved in daily life" (Giddens, 1984, p. xxiv). Social integration is modeled in detail by Goffman, while Giddens looks comprehensively at system integration. As Giddens himself remarked,

> The study of interaction in circumstances of co-presence is one basic component of the 'bracketing' of time-space that is both condition and outcome of human social association. ... Relations in conditions of co-presence consist of what Goffman has aptly called *encounters*, fading away across time and space. No one has analysed encounters more perceptively than Goffman himself, and I shall draw heavily upon his work. ... He is one of the few sociological writers who treat time-space relations as fundamental to the production and reproduction of social life.
>
> *(Giddens, 1984, p. 36)*

Giddens also was influenced by the "profound difference ... between *face-to-face interaction and interaction with others who are physically absent*"—a concept thoroughly developed in Goffman's work, and pivotal to his thinking (Giddens, 1979,

p. 203). In structuration theory, social integration (developed via face-to-face interaction) is essential to the reproduction of institutionalized practices, and social integration is interwoven with system integration (Giddens, 1984). As Rawls (1988) concluded, "the interactional order is present as an organizational feature of all situations. It exerts some influence on all organizational features whether formal or not" (p. 127).

Hartland (2000) suggested that Goffman and Giddens are compatible in terms of their respective analytic endeavors:

> In Giddens' case, the systematic nature of Goffman's analyses of the interaction order flows from the way in which Goffman can be integrated into a larger theory of the constitution of social order. ... Goffman's work provides Giddens with an account of routine, which is a central piece in Giddens' sociological jigsaw by dint of the way it is used to relate psychological and structural phenomena.
>
> *(p. 292)*

Giddens himself puts this matter very strongly:

> Social institutions are formed and reformed via the recursiveness of social activity. The techniques, strategies, and modes of behavior followed by actors in circumstances of co-presence, even in the most seemingly trivial aspects of their day-to-day life, are fundamental to the continuity of institutions across time and space. In his studies of co-presence, Goffman demonstrates that the predictability of much of social life, even on a macro-structural plane, is organized via the practices involved in what he chooses to call the interaction order. But this order is never separate from either the ordering of behavior across contexts of co-presence, or the ordering of such contexts themselves in relation to one another.
>
> *(Giddens, 2000, p.172)*

Giddens also argued that mutual trust in interactional contexts extends to other contexts as well. "One might notice that analyzing the means of sustaining trust in settings of interaction in modern societies cannot be meaningfully kept separate from examining other modes of sustaining confidence across separated context. Money, for example, may be understood as a token of confidence, allowing transactions between individuals quite ignorant of one another, but who would otherwise be disinclined to have confidence in what the other or others might promise" (ibid., p. 172).

For Giddens, reflexive monitoring of an agent's own actions and others' actions is continuous, and the context of interaction is also monitored. In this respect, Goffman's work "on the ability of actors to maintain security and trust through the management of social action, assumes particular interest for Giddens" (Haugaard,

1992, p. 77). This knowledgeability and reflexivity of agents is fundamental in both Giddens' and Goffman's work. And both would agree that some of this knowledge is tacit or practical, and only partially discursive.

Giddens thus regards Goffman's analysis of social interaction as fundamental for structuration. For our purposes, the links between social integration and system integration are central to an analysis of organizing. As Giddens suggests,

> The connections between social and system integration can be traced by examining the modes or regionalization channel, and are channeled by the time-space paths that members of a community or society follow in their day-to-day activities. Such paths are strongly influenced by, and also repro- duce, basic institutional parameters of the social systems in which they are implicated … virtually all societies, no matter how small or seemingly isolated, exist in at least loose connection with wider 'intersocietal systems'.
>
> *(Giddens, 1984, pp. 142–43)*

As Giddens concludes, the "'systemness' of social integration is *fundamental to the systemness of society as a whole"* (Giddens, 1979, p. 77).

While Goffman's analysis is focused on face-to-face interaction, increasingly within complex (and even simple) organizations, communication is mediated, and links individuals who are distanciated in both space and time. In my view, it seems reasonable to assume that much of Goffman's work can be extrapolated and applied to mediated settings, primarily with respect to the rules, resources, and constraints within these settings, although some behavioral cues may be lost (e.g., eye gaze behavior is not available in telephone calls, unless such calls have video capability). For example, preliminary evidence already suggests that bracketing devices, footing and other features found in face-to-face interaction are already present in emails (Erickson, 2010). There is considerable disembedding and re-embedding among routine institutional relationships in modern life (e.g., we do not meet the payroll person for processing payments of a loan we may have). Some of these routines of insti- tutional interaction could be analyzed insightfully by Goffman's interactional order.

Although not explicitly developed in his work, Goffman certainly acknowledged, as noted earlier, the enabling/constraining influences of social structure (e.g., insti- tutions) on interaction. In fact, his studies of mental institutions can be viewed in that light. These studies explored the ways in which "normal" guiding interactional principles are violated in total institutions, and the ways in which mental patients, prisoners, and other participants modify the "rules" to allow for selfhood (Goffman, 1961b, 1963b).

An analytic example. Giddens' theory of structuration integrates both agency and structure in social systems. An example from Giddens of a small strip of courtroom interaction will clarify the compatibility and importance of social integration (Goffman's framework) for system integration (Giddens' framework). A judge, public defender, and district attorney are discussing what sentence should be given for a guilty plea in a second-degree burglary charge. Through a series of ten turns at talk, Giddens pointed out that participants' shared knowledge of the institutional features of the criminal justice system allowed them to have a meaningful exchange while reproducing this social system. As he noted,

> Each participant knows a vast amount about what a 'legal system' is, about normative procedures of law, about what prisoners, advocates, judges do, etc. In order to 'bring off' the interaction, the participants make use of their knowledge of the institutional order in which they are involved in such a way as to render their interchange 'meaningful'. However, by invoking the institutional order in this way—and *there is no other way* for participants in interaction to render what they do intelligible and coherent to one another— they thereby contribute to reproducing it. … They treat the system of justice as a 'real' order of relationships within which their own interaction is situated and which it expresses. And it is a 'real' (i.e., structurally stable) order of relationships precisely because they, and others like them in connected and similar contexts, accept it as such.
>
> *(Giddens, 1984, p. 331)*

Thus, from Goffman's work a close, detailed analysis of face-to-face interaction is provided, while Giddens' institutional analyses and the discussion of the intersections between social and system order provides an additional layer of interpretation. Thus structurational interaction can provide valuable insights into organizing and communicating on multiple levels.

I would argue that, in order to fully explore the complexity of organizing and communicating and their interrelationships, such integration is necessary—focusing on one dimension, and excluding the other, is insufficient. Giddens concluded that

> All social interaction is situated within time-space boundaries of co-presence (whether or not this be extended via media such as letters, telephone calls, etc.). Its situated character … is directly involved with the indexical nature of the "bringing off" of mutually intelligible communication. But the situated-ness of interaction is not a barrier to that institutional "fixity" demonstrated by institutional orders across time and space. It is its very condition, just as the existence of those institutional orders is the condition of the most transient forms of social encounter or conversation. The reflexive monitoring of social conduct is intrinsic to the "facticity" which the structural properties of social systems display, *not something either marginal or additional to it.*
>
> *(ibid., p.332, italics mine)*

Thus, the interaction order and social system order contextualize one another or, in Giddens' terms, reflect the duality of structuration. The theory of structurational interaction assumes this as a fundamental theoretical premise.

The interdependence of individuals and collectivities across time-space in social interaction and social relations is further acknowledged by Giddens when he pointed out that

> Social relations are certainly involved in the structuring of interaction but are also the main 'building blocks' around which institutions are articulated in system integration. Interaction depends upon the 'positioning' of individuals in the time-space contexts of activity. Social relations concern the 'positioning' of individuals within a 'social space' of symbolic categories and ties.
>
> *(Giddens, 1984, p. 89)*

Such symbolic ties and categories would reflect, of course, occupations, positions of legal authority, colleagues, family members, and the like. Individuals are thus aligning themselves in interaction as do groups and coalitions. Underlying this, of course, is their inescapable interconnection with one another. This interdependence may be only partially understood and is also a function of unanticipated consequences of action, whether of one's own actions or of others' actions.

Turner (1986) cogently summarized the relationship between Goffman and Giddens:

> For Giddens, "the routinization of encounters is of major significance in binding the fleeting encounter to social reproduction and thus to the seeming 'fixity' of institutions" (p. 72). Borrowing from Goffman but adding his own interesting phenomenological and ethnomethodological twist, Giddens proposes several basic procedures, or "mechanisms", that humans employ to sustain routines: Opening and closing rituals, turn taking in conversations, tact, spatial positioning, and framing. ... Interactions are also ordered in space as well as time. ... Agents use their stocks of knowledge to define "locales" that indicate the appropriate use of physical space as well as the relevant procedures to talk, tact, gesturing, and other interactive procedures. Giddens classifies locales in terms of their "modes" that order locales with respect to variations in their physical and symbolic boundaries, their duration across time, their span in space, and their ways of articulating an interaction context with larger institutional patterns. Locales also vary in terms of their requirements for high "public presence" (Goffman's frontstage vs. backstage regions) and their demands for "disclosure" or "enclosure" of self.
>
> *(p. 974)*

Giddens clearly did acknowledge the importance of the interaction order and relied heavily on Goffman's work. Most of the concepts mentioned above are common to both theorists. For our purposes in linking communicating and organizing processes, what is critical are "their ways of articulating an interaction context with larger institutional patterns." What is significant is that neither the interaction context nor larger institutional patters is privileged—both recursively shape one another. Thus, structurational interaction provides the basis for a coherent, integrated approach to organizing, communicating and their interrelationships in a way other theoretical approaches do not.

Both Goffman and Giddens (as well as other major social theorists such as Bourdieu and Foucault) were enmeshed in an intellectual milieu in which social theorists were reacting to tensions between structural determinism and individual voluntarism, and the underlying issue of social order. Both Goffman and Giddens focused on social order, and argued that social order is enacted in daily interactions across countless individuals and actions. For both, interaction instantiated social order, and, through interaction, social order is maintained or altered. Social order is both the *process* and *product* of interaction, and, reciprocally, interaction is both the *process* and *product* of social order. As such, interaction is the foundation of any social order. Both Goffman and Giddens acknowledged different types of institutions—for example, legal, meaning-centered, political, and economic institutions (and it is not surprising we acknowledge different frames or metaphors for organizing based on these different types of institutions). Both believed that the routinization of encounters was vitally important for ontological security, for the development of the self and social relationships, and for the establishment and continuity of social institutions and social systems.

Although these critical theoretical orientations were shared, Goffman and Giddens focused on different issues within the broad context of social order. Goffman was primarily concerned with establishing the interaction order as a distinct social order in itself, one that is foundational to all other social orders. Giddens, for example, argued that social integration (established by the interaction order) is necessary for any system integration (such as legal, political, economic systems or intersocietal systems). In contrast to Goffman, Giddens focused on the agency versus structure issue (voluntarism versus determinism) and argued that the duality of structure (instantiated in interaction) dissolves that distinction. A core process for both, however, is still interaction (communication). Both Goffman and Giddens present significant perspectives on the self and identity (Branaman, 2010). And both also acknowledge the possibility of change, transformation, and uncertainty in interaction.

Despite their shared critical emphasis on interaction, their interests in interaction were also divergent. Goffman's focus was on the fragile, momentary, shared inter-subjective social world established among co-present individuals, and the problematizing of how such fragile interactional worlds are sustained (e.g., face, face-work, trust and ritual). Giddens extended this interactional focus to distanciated contexts, which included contexts where people were not co-present, but separated by time and space, and explored how actions and activities could be "stretched" across time and space. Goffman, of course, speculated on such contexts (for example, there would be fewer cues "given off" for interpretation, and so forth) but did not develop this reasoning extensively. Thus both theorists acknowledged broader contexts of communication, with Giddens thoroughly developing such contexts through concepts such as distanciation, disembedding, re-embedding, and different types of institutions. The use of both theorists, in the theory of structurational interaction, provide a rich source of insight and analysis of mediated communication.

Both Giddens and Goffman would agree that the context of individual interactions are "loosely coupled" with broader social contexts. For Giddens, these links were developed through the duality of structure and structuration theory, while for Goffman these links are developed through layering or lamination of frames (both contextual as well as interpretive frames). Both would deny any reduction of social structure to any interaction, or interactional unit—the linkages, for them, are through transformational rules, acknowledging the different rules and resources available to interactants, and varying contextual categorizations (frames and rekeyed frames in interaction). Both would also deny the macro- versus micro- level distinction because social order is always present in any interaction (i.e., in the sense of tacit, commonsense knowledge, sociohistorical contextuality, material objects).

In brief, both Giddens and Goffman are compatible theoretically in a number of significant ways, particularly with respect to organizing and communicating, which is our focus here. Integrating their perspectives provides us with a much richer approach to organizing and communicating, capable of resolving issues of agency and structure, as well as extending our insights through a juxtaposition of their primary emphases. As we have seen, both Goffman and Giddens regard the inter- action order as foundational for both social order and system integration. Both theorists emphasize routines or social practices, social relations, and social interac- tion. Both view interaction as being carried out in contexts, although for Giddens such locales have been greatly extended. On the basic, foundational level of struc- turation theory, Giddens relies on Goffman's interaction order. For all of these reasons, I have integrated their perspectives and argued for a theory of structurational interaction.

Giddens on Goffman: Commentary and Reflection

Another way to assess the compatibility of Goffman and Giddens, is to examine what Giddens has said about Goffman's work. Because of Goffman's untimely death in 1982, the potential integration of their work through dialogue between them was not possible. Giddens regarded Goffman as a major social theorist: "there is a system of social theory to be derived from Goffman's writings, although some effort has to be made to unearth it and we cannot necessarily accept Goffman's own interpretations of his works in elucidating its nature" (Giddens, 1988, p. 250). Giddens provided a critical analysis of Goffman's work to "help us see how far they might be incorporated into a version of social theory that escapes the brackets he put around his own writings" (Giddens, 2000, p. 155). While Goffman investigated the tacit knowledge employed by actors and the practical consciousness that supported their actions, he has largely avoided any account of institutions. Giddens suggested that there is a need for an *institutional theory of everyday life* and Giddens himself integrated much of Goffman's analyses in his own work.

Points of Compatibility

In commenting on Goffman's work, Giddens noted Goffman's emphasis on focused interaction and his understanding that other activities, besides conversations (such as nonverbal gestures or props), may sustain the attention of the interactants. Giddens also commented on the distinctions between encounters and groups:

> All groups or collectivities, whether large scale or small, have some general traits of organization. These include a division between roles, provision for socialization, capability for collective action, and sustained modes of connection with the surrounding environment. Groups exist when their members are not together. Encounters, on the other hand, by definition only exist when the parties to them are physically in each other's presence. From such togetherness a range of characteristics flow.
>
> 'Examples of such properties include embarrassment, maintenance of poise, capacity for non-distractive verbal communication, adherence to a code regarding giving up and taking over the speaker role, and allocation of spatial position' (Goffman 1961a, p. 11). In focused interaction, the participants must maintain continuous involvement in the mutual focus of activity. This cannot be a property of social groups in general, precisely because of their persistence across different contexts of co-presence. Encounters may be a particular aspect or phase of the existence of collectivities, but to assimilate the two is to miss the very distinctive features of encounters upon which Goffman wishes to concentrate attention.
>
> *(Giddens, 2000, p. 156)*

While Giddens' points are well taken, I believe Goffman would not support the idea of continuous involvement, but would support instead the concept of continuous availability during which people may have side-involvements, and/or be otherwise distracted. In fact, Goffman himself discussed differing degrees of involvement in interaction. But, clearly, the different contexts of co-presence and distanciation are important aspects of organizations and groups, and Giddens' work addresses these issues, and thus complements Goffman's analyses. In my view, this contrast between co-presence and distanciation is a major research area in need of attention (and will be developed in more detail in Chapter 12).

The self. Concerning Goffman's view of the self and roles, Giddens pointed out that there is an enduring sense of self, as well as variety in how situated roles may be enacted. For Goffman,

The self consists in an awareness of identity which simultaneously transcends specific roles and provides an integrating means of relating them to personal biography; and a set of dispositions for managing the transactions between motives and the expectations 'scripted' by particular roles. All roles involve situated performances. But these are neither exhaustive of the role nor are they necessarily the same as the 'situated roles' that emerge in encounters. Situated roles may consolidate the expectations involved in a more encompassing role, or they may inhibit them.

(Giddens, 1988, p. 259)

Both would agree that selves have multiple identities and roles as well as an enduring corporeal body that occupies different time-space trajectories over an individual's life-span.

While critics have argued that Goffman's self is a cynical, manipulative actor, Giddens takes a quite different interpretation which, I believe, more accurately reflects the self in Goffman's work. Giddens argues that

What is striking about the interaction skills that actors display in the production and reproduction of encounters is their anchoring in practical consciousness. Tact rather than cynicism is inherent in the structuration of encounters. While the content of what counts as 'being tactful' may vary widely, the significance of tact in otherwise very different societies or cultures is impossible to dispute. Tact—a latent conceptual agreement among participants in interaction contexts—seems to be the main mechanism that sustains 'trust' or ontological security over long time-space spans.

(Giddens, 1984, p. 75)

Giddens (2009a) also comments that "knowing how to go on" is a collective enterprise—"very much also a matter of collective impression management" (p. 291). "'Society' is always and everywhere the creation of highly skilled and knowledgeable agents. Yet the continuous, minute, and amazingly complicated way in which we "bring off" social life with others at the same time depends fundamentally upon shared forms of tacit knowledge that can in no sense be reduced to the specific actions of individuals" (ibid., p. 292).

Monitoring interaction. Within interactional settings, Goffman pointed out that people routinely monitor the location as well as the people within it. Giddens also noted that the "time-space zoning of encounters is often fundamental to the performances that are carried on. The existence of back regions, for example, helps to explain a good deal of what goes on in 'public' settings of activity. ... The more formalized settings of interactions are those likely to be most closely linked with defined back regions, because in these regions control can to some degree be relaxed. ... All organizations in which formalized role relations are called for have areas, or sometimes only nooks and crannies, which allow such shelter" (Giddens, 1988, p. 261). Both theorists acknowledge the importance of front and back regions for public accessibility and privacy respectively.

Emotions are also a major facet of Goffman's work. Giddens points out that impression management is cognitive, but also involves emotions. As he notes, impression management, when "organized in the context of everyday rituals, and done in a collaborative way, it is the key to the continuity of the self and the containment of regulation of emotion" (Giddens, 2009a, p. 292). Tact and trust are also critical for managing anxiety (ibid.). (See also Gardener, 1992, 2000; Gardener & Gronfein, 2005; and Gardener & Martinko, 1988, on varied aspects of impression management.)

One of Goffman's major contributions, for Giddens, was to articulate the reflexive self-monitoring of the body in the coordination of interaction with others. As Giddens noted, such coordination involved an individual's reflexive self-monitoring of gesture, posture and bodily movement along with tact and respect for others. Such coordination is necessary to being seen as a capable agent, and thus intrinsic to agency itself. As Goffman remarked, "Bodily idiom, then, is conventionalized discourse ... there is typically an obligation to convey certain information when in the presence of others and an obligation not to convey other impressions. ... Although an individual can stop talking, he cannot stop communicating through body idiom" (Goffman, 1963a, pp. 34–35).

And for Giddens:

> Fundamental to social life is the positioning of the body in social encounters. 'Positioning' here is a rich term. The body is positioned in the immediate circumstances of co-presence in relation to others: Goffman provides an extraordinarily subtle but telling set of observations about face work, about gesture and reflexible control of bodily movement, as inherent in the continuity of social life. Positioning is, however, also to be understood in relation to the seriality of encounters across time-space. Every individual is at once positioned in the flow of day-to-day life; in the life-span which is the duration of his or her existence; and in the duration of 'institutional time', the 'supra-individual' structuration of social institutions. Finally, each person is positioned, in a 'multiple' way, within social relations conferred by specific social identities; this is the main sphere of application of the concept of social role. The modalities of co-presence, mediated directly by the sensory properties of the body, are clearly different from social ties and forms of social interaction established with others absent in time or in space.
>
> *(Giddens, 1984, pp. xxiv–xxv)*

It is this notion of positioning, Giddens wrote, that examines the "contextualities of interaction and allows us to spell out, in a direct way, the relevance of Goffman's work for structuration theory. All social interaction is *situated* interaction—situated in space and time. It can be understood as the fitful yet routinized occurrence of encounters, fading away in time and space, yet constantly reconstituted within different areas of time-space. The regular or routine features of encounters, in time as well as in space, represent institutionalized features of social systems" (Giddens, 1984, p. 87). Thus, Giddens extends Goffman's analysis of co-presence and routine encounters to the routinized encounters of institutions and social systems. And Giddens views these routinized encounters as the building blocks for institutions and social systems.

Giddens also points out the fundamental importance of Goffman's analysis of co-presence. As he notes, Goffman is "*the* theorist of copresence; much more than that, he explored the massively complex nature of what copresence actually is. *Copresence*—the behavior of subjects who are confined together for some while—has distinctive features that more impersonal connections necessarily lack. Yet it is Goffman's achievement to have shown that the grand institutions of society both operate through, presume, yet at the same time structure, the rituals that people follow when they are together in public places" (Giddens, 2009a, p. 291).

Furthermore, Giddens observes that copresence also reflects power—an idea not pursued by Goffman, but nevertheless implicit in Goffman's work. As Giddens argues, "The vast bulk of what frames situations of copresence is invisible—it consists of institutions, both taken for granted, but also drawn upon, by the parties to the interaction. This is most obvious in the case of language and communication, which presumes a vast apparatus of rules and signals displayed by a linguistic community. Yet it is also true of systems of power, which both structure, yet are reproduced by, everyday rituals of different sorts" (ibid., p. 293).

Agency. Giddens also discussed agency and action—"guided doings"—as implied in Goffman's perspective. A person must not only routinely monitor and organize their actions, but they must also "demonstrate agency" to others (Giddens, 1988, p. 262). According to Giddens, Goffman suggests that agency is demonstrated by three different types of action: (1) individuals need to understand what they are doing and convey that understanding to others; (2) individuals need to be aware, through the use of primary frameworks, that human action and action by other humans is different from natural action caused by nature; and (3) individuals need to discover the unique, distinctive qualities of "particular experiences and encounters" (Giddens, 1988, p. 262). The first is necessary to be viewed as a capable, competent actor; the second is necessary to be viewed as a knowledgeable actor; and the third, framing a particular context, is necessary for an actor to understand how to go on in that situation.

For both Giddens and Goffman, agency is the capability to act, and to act as a competent, knowledgeable agent in one's interaction with others. For both, actions include displaying a range of nonverbal behaviors and action, and the use of space and material objects. For both, agency involves actions, tasks or a combination of both.

The role of talk is also of special importance in Goffman's perspective. According to Giddens, the use of talk, rather than language, emphasizes its situated nature.

Furthermore, "The meanings which are deployed through talk are organized and specified by the whole range of subtleties of management of face, voice, or gesture and positions of body brought into play in circumstances of co-presence generally" (Giddens, 1988, p. 266). Moves are fundamental units of talk, and may cut across sentences, silences, interjections and a range of nonverbal behaviors. As Giddens concluded, interactants "depend upon a saturated physical and social context for making sense of what is said" (ibid., p. 267). As such, both Goffman and Giddens emphasize bodily positioning as well as talk in social interaction.

Some critical commentary. As Giddens noted, Goffman did not analyze many situations in which there are power disparities or in which decisions affecting hundreds are being made. While Goffman himself did not focus on such contexts, he was clearly aware of differences in power, access, and opportunity (see Chapters 5 and 6 in this book, and also Goffman's *Asylum* and *Stigma*). Other scholars have, in fact, used Goffman's work in looking at interactional differences across positions of varying power.

In brief, Giddens views Goffman's work as fundamental for structuration because of Goffman's analysis of social integration. For Giddens, Goffman's work is focused on "the intersections of presence and absence in social interaction. The mechanisms of social and system integration ... necessarily interlace with one another. ... The fixity of institutional forms does not exist in spite of, or outside, the encounters of day-to-day life but *is implicated in those very encounters*" (Giddens, 1984, pp. 68–69). Giddens also believes that the conditions of presence and absence outlined by Goffman apply across cultures or societies, although social practices will vary across cultures.

Giddens proposed a direct connection between "Goffman's analysis of co-presence with mechanisms of social reproduction across extended spans of time and space" (Giddens, 1988, p. 277). "This means relating the sorts of discussion Goffman provides with more extended analyses of the nature of the locales, and the modes of regionalization, whereby contexts of co-presence are conjoined" (ibid., p. 277). Through this book, I am attempting to point out ways in which these interconnections and extensions can be carried out through structurational interaction, and thus enrich our understanding of organizing and communicating.

As Giddens further noted:

> What is interesting and important here is not just the relation between co-presence and 'transcontextual' interaction, but the relation between presence and absence in the structuring of social life. 'Presence' by definition of course exhausts the limits of our direct experience. 'Co-presence' is not really some sort of subcategory of presence in general. It is rather a form of experience, which may be assumed to be characteristic of large parts of most people's day-to-day lives, in which others are directly 'available', and in which the individual *makes* him or herself 'available'—that is, demonstrates agency in Goffman's sense. ... But it is a mistake to see these as two opposed

forms of social connection. On the contrary, each interlaces with the other in a multiplicity of subtle ways.

(Giddens, 2000, pp. 172–73)

It is this interlacing of presence and absence that can be explored by integrating Goffman's and Giddens' perspectives, and is, I believe, one of the most significant advantages flowing from structurational interaction.

As we have seen, Giddens himself acknowledged his close theoretical ties to Goffman. While acknowledging these close ties, Giddens also made the case for extending their analyses, such as the one suggested above in terms of connecting differing contexts of presence and absence. As Giddens noted, "the fixity of institutional forms" is implicated in everyday encounters. Both theorists account for the self and varying roles; the importance of tact and trust; the significance of reflexive self-monitoring (which Giddens extends to institutional reflexivity); the impact of locales and modes of regionalization; and the importance of knowledgeable actors who are viewed as competent agents.

Toward a Theory of Structurational Interaction:

Integrating Goffman's Interaction Order and Giddens' Structuration Theory

A number of additional advantages to a theory of structurational interaction can be discovered by a closer analysis of their work and interrelationships. In what follows, I will more explicitly link these two theorists and thus provide a foundational link between communicating and organizing. In so doing, I will move beyond the integration provided by a frame metatheory, and by Giddens' comments on Goffman's work and its importance to structuration theory to argue for a theory of structurational interaction.

As Giddens observed, social integration, instantiated by Goffman's interaction order, is necessary for system integration. Communicating makes organizing possible, and organizing, in turn, influences the contexts for, and social practices of, communication. Giddens' distinctive contribution is to extend social order (enacted through the interaction order) through integrating social systems such as institutions, societies and collectivities, distributed throughout time-space. Both scholars offer perspectives that emphasize process or action, multiple modes of communication, multi-level analytic possibilities, and provide rich theoretical connections to other disciplines and areas of scholarship. Our models of organizational communication have not yet achieved a foundational integration of organizing and communicating. In what follows, I suggest that structurational interaction provides this foundation.

Perhaps the most critical point is that Giddens' structuration presupposes Goffman's interaction order. As Giddens commented, "The study of interaction in circumstances of co-presence is one basic component of the 'bracketing' of time-space that is both condition and outcome of human social association. 'Systemness' here is achieved largely through the routine reflexive monitoring of conduct anchored in practical consciousness. Relations in conditions of co-presence consist of what Goffman has aptly called *encounter*. ... No one has analysed encounters more perceptively than Goffman himself, and I shall draw heavily on his work" (Giddens, 1984, p. 36).

Social action is instantiated through social practices, and social practices are grounded in the co-presence of actors within an encounter, situating action in a particular locale (i.e., a particular time and space). Giddens also links co-presence with movement through time-space, a major premise of structuration. As actors go through their daily routines, they

> ... experience different contexts of co-presence as episodes within the time-space paths they trace out in the course of their day-to-day activities. Mediation between contexts in this sense—that is, the 'moving presence' of actors across time-space paths—strongly influences the nature of the encounters that are entered into.
>
> *(Giddens, 2000, p. 173)*

Thus both Giddens and Goffman rest their work on the foundation of an interaction order, and delineate its significance for social order, whether on a societal or institutional level.

Time and space are important for both Goffman and Giddens. Goffman acknowledges the importance of regionalization, frontstage, backstage and other zones of public/private encounters. Giddens extends space to distanciated locales, and time beyond the immediate present to distant locales. Goffman emphasizes the immediate present, although he would acknowledge the influence of distant people and events, if for no other reason than their being mentioned during interaction.

Together, their theoretical integration in the theory of structurational interaction offers a rich view of context. Frames, for Goffman, provide multiple layers of context in co-present encounters. For Giddens, contexts may be framed on a number of different levels, moving from a locale framed by a particular historicity in time-space (e.g., cultural tribes as opposed to modern nation-states) to frames provided by different types of institutions (e.g., legal, economic) to frames enacted by institutional leaders. Context, for both, is essential for interpretation of and participation in ongoing social life.

According to Giddens, there is blurring between co-presence, and what he calls "presence availability." As Giddens noted, in large gatherings people are

> 'available', in the sense that the individual might quite readily seek them out. But there may be more effort involved in so doing than in the case of individuals who are in adjoining rooms within a building, or in rooms on the

> same floor in the building. ... This means relating the sorts of discussion Goffman provides with more extended analyses of the nature of the locales, and the modes of regionalization, whereby contexts of co-presence are conjoined.
>
> *(Giddens, 2000, p. 173)*

This, again, provides an excellent example of the fusion of the two theorists, where time and space are integrated with co-presence and presence availability: presence availability is clearly a critical issue in globalization, and in transnational organizing and communicating. Goffman's own work commented on contexts in which others are not co-present, but nevertheless accessible or open to interaction. (See, for example, his discussion of how cues available in physical co-presence may be missing in mediated interaction, such as telephone conversations. Were his career not cut prematurely short, I am convinced he would have provided insightful comments on mediated communication as well.)

As such, together Goffman and Giddens provide us with analyses of a continuum of immediate co-presence to mediated relations and discourse that extends across time and space. We need to think more carefully about contexts of presence and absence, because even gatherings, for example, have blends of presence (e.g., the person in line with whom you are conversing and the other bystanders in line, a third person [absent] that the two of you are discussing, the presence or absence of material objects germane to the discussion, and the like). With structurational interaction, we can encapsulate a wide variety of contexts with varying presences and absences.

Social positioning within time-space also draws our attention to physical space, and the location of space. Goffman discusses regionalization of encounters, and Giddens regards this concept as highly important. As Giddens noted, "Locales are not just places but *settings* of interaction ... settings are used chronically—and largely in a tacit way—by social actors to sustain meaning in communicative acts. But settings are also regionalized in ways that heavily influence, and are influenced by, the serial character of encounters". Time-space also normally means social fixity; "the substantially 'given' character of the physical *milieu* of day-to-day life interlaces with routine and is deeply influential in the contours of institutional reproduction" (Giddens, 1984, p. xxv).

To recognize the power of positioning in time-space, we need only to think of the expectations with regard to varying time-space activities at home as well as at work. The rituals of institutions, such as the U.S. Presidential Inauguration; burials at Arlington National Cemetery; pleading a case before the U.S. Supreme Court; worshipping and facing Mecca daily; cleaning hospital surgical rooms; and using the "break" room at work, reflect powerful time-space rituals. In some instances, rituals are heavily protected against unwarranted intrusion, either spatially and/or temporally. An interesting contemporary time-space issue is the "working at home" phenomenon, and how that has redefined what work is, where it occurs, and the separation between one's work and private life.

Regionalization also has psychological implications with respect to disclosure and openness. Some information and some spaces are open and therefore disclosing, but others are enclosed and thus hidden. In Giddens' view, both Goffman and Foucault "accord great importance to the socially and historically fluctuating lines between enclosure and disclosure, confinement and display" (Giddens, 1984, p. xxvi).

Both theorists focus on processual or transformative models of interaction. Both emphasize the significance of social practices, and the importance of routinization which provides for interpersonal trust, ontological security, and intelligibility of action and discourse. The transformative processes for Goffman center around framing and keying, while rules and resources provide transformative opportunities within structuration. While Goffman reveals reframing in encounters, Giddens reveals transformation (reframing) in institutions and societies. For both, reframing or transformation is enacted through individual agency or institutional bias (Goffman clearly recognizes institutional agency, for example, in his discussion of total institutions, although it was not a focus of his theorizing).

Tacit knowledge, discursive consciousness, and practical consciousness are fundamental in their models. Actors rely on such knowledge to make sense out of what is going on, and to be able to participate competently in encounters. Actors will have different levels of knowledge at different times, and such knowledge may alter the effects of their actions. Routine social practices and social interaction are emphasized by both Goffman and Giddens, with Goffman focusing on face-to-face encounters and Giddens focusing on how social practices constitute and reconstitute social institutions.

Finally, both agree that the interaction order is loosely coupled with the social order. Both reject the distinction of micro versus macro as inappropriate and ill-advised. In addition, structuration theoretically dissolves any distinction between the agent and social structures. Both Giddens and Goffman acknowledge some of the mutual interplay and influence between individuals and larger institutions in a variety of contexts.

Research blending their perspectives. Several studies have blended elements of both Goffman and Giddens, although to a limited degree. Not surprisingly, most of this work has been done in the area of communicating and organizing with new technologies. Some scholars have contrasted various patterns of interaction, particularly face-to-face communication as opposed to distanciated communication, and in virtual organizations and multinational corporations. Again, both structuration and the interaction order were used in these studies.

Zack and McKenney (1995) studied the editorial groups of two newspapers and found that different groups were "using the same functional structure and performing the same task with identical communication technologies, but operating within different social contexts." As such, groups "appropriated the communication technology differently and in a way that was consistent with and reinforcing their existing social structure" (p. 394). They note that social context needs to be explicitly studied for its influence on the effects and outcomes of technologies.

Using Giddens' structuration theory and Goffman's interaction order as departure points, Leonardi (2007) explored the relationship between technology appropriation and informal advice networks. A large information technology organization implemented a new information technology (IT) service as a management tool. In this extensive ethnographic study, Leonardi documented changes in how technicians wrote up tickets (problem calls and their resolution); in how organizations developed a database of information about problems; in how technician expertise developed (for example, being known for their work on particular problems, or for their detailed tickets); and in how changes in the flow of information developed, especially informally. Front and back regions also played a role in that most work now became "frontstage" and consequently, agents became very aware of the widespread access to such information.

An intriguing study by Zhao and Elesh (2008) blended Goffman and Giddens in order to explore social contact in online public domains. Rather than arguing that online connectivity serves as open accessibility, they argue that regionalization of sociality occurs in the online world, with various blocks that restrict access and participation. For example, "email and IM are private domains for acquaintances, and chat rooms and MUDs are public social domains where many-to-most participants are strangers" (p. 575). Online users may put "involvement shields" (Goffman, 1967) in place to control engagement with others. They conclude that "online social connectivity is therefore an issue of normative regulations of the use of space, the regionality of social contact, the hierarchy of popularity and marginality, as well as affinity and animosity, privilege and intolerance. In the final analysis, it is linked to power relations" (ibid., p. 579).

Thus far, as I have demonstrated, a theoretical synthesis between Goffman and Giddens is clearly feasible and coherent. Indeed, specific linkages have been outlined by Giddens himself. Structurational interaction demonstrates the profound interrelationships between organizing and communicating as they contribute to social order. Although we can parse them analytically, in everyday life, these processes are intermingled. I now turn to a fuller discussion of the advantages of structurational interaction.

Advantages of Structurational Interaction

Giddens' work offers us a very rich, contextualized exploration of institutions and social life. Because his work regards human interaction as fundamental to social life and social systems, we can use his insights to assess human interaction in organizing. A similar focus on social interaction, in contexts of physical co-presence, is found in Goffman's work. When synthesized, their work provides a coherent perspective on organizing and communicating. Through this integrated framework, focusing on communication, we can study interaction within encounters, as Goffman did, but we can also extend our focus to social interaction and social practices in institutions and organizing, as Giddens did. As Giddens himself observed, Goffman's work contains much insight for analyzing interaction in organizations and in social systems, even though that was not Goffman's primary focus.

Structurational interaction offers significant advantages over current approaches to organizing and communicating. As we shall see, structurational interaction allows substantive depth and breadth in analyzing organizing and communicating. In addressing organizational communication, many perspectives focus on either communicating or on organizing, but rarely acknowledge their interrelationships. Structurational interaction enables us to focus on both aspects simultaneously, and to understand more completely how they mutually shape one another. Both Goffman and Giddens emphasize context; the mutual achievement of understanding in interaction; the taken-for-granted tacit knowledge that enables interaction; social roles; individual agency; and norms of interaction. While context, for Goffman, is primarily local and immediate, Giddens extends context to include locales and regions that are distanciated in time and space. Goffman's sense of time is bounded by the immediate encounter, while Giddens emphasizes the historicity of context, and the way in which situated action is embedded in the sedimented nature of social systems and institutions. As such, structurational interaction provides an extended analysis of time and of varied contexts, both immediate and distanciated.

Both rely on conventions in interpreting interaction; these conventions are matters of both practical consciousness and mutual knowledgeability. Both also separate the self and/or identity from the roles individuals play in various settings. Goffman, in particular, focuses on the line or alignment participants take with one another to preserve face. Finally, both allow for change and contradiction in interaction; Goffman looking more specifically at deliberate fabrication and keying, while Giddens looks at contradictions in terms of inconsistent structural principles.

Goffman focuses on the processes of co-present interaction, while Giddens focuses on interaction that is distanciated, disembedded and re-embedded. Goffman's work illuminates the complexity of face-to-face interaction, and both he and Giddens consider this to be the fundamental communicative context from which other forms of interaction build. Both also consider the total context in which human communication occurs, including nonverbal communication, space, time and physical/social setting.

Goffman and Giddens both regard encounters as routine, focused, co-present interactions. Giddens extends Goffman's encounters to "the fixity of social institutions." He argues that (1) encounters form and re-form over the course of daily existence; (2) the structuration of encounters is organized in and through the interface of practical and discursive consciousness; (3) talk is a significant component of encounters; and (4) encounters need to be contextualized by such factors as presence-availability, locale and enclosure/disclosure. *It is contextualization that grounds all of these elements in time-space.* Giddens concludes that, "In analyzing the communication of meaning in interaction via the use of interpretative schemes [frames], the phenomenon of talk has to be taken very seriously, as constitutively involved in encounters" (Giddens, 1984, pp. 71–73). Structurational interaction provides a rich analysis of encounters ranging across the routines and social practices found in organizing and institutional settings.

In addition, structurational interaction provides a number of distinct ways in which to evaluate encounters. Seriality, or the sequencing of encounters, is also emphasized by Giddens, consistent with his emphasis on the time-space dimension of interaction. Giddens views encounters as "the guiding thread of social interaction, the succession of engagements with others ordered within the daily cycle of activity" (ibid., p. 72). In addition to the openings and closings of talk as well as turn-taking, Giddens also incorporates Goffman's concept of bracketing for opening/closing temporal brackets and spatial brackets (Goffman, 1974, p. 252). Encounters may also be keyed, and thus transform encounters in a variety of ways for humor, deception, and so forth. Goffman's dramaturgical metaphor also highlights the serial nature of interaction as actions may be scripted and staged.

Giddens' structuration theory argues for the duality of structure and the recursiveness of interaction and social life. That is, as humans interact in their daily routines, we instantiate social structures and institutions. In particular, our interactions are situated in time and space, and influenced by the sedimented institutions that constitute our social life. Power, through authoritative and allocative resources, is available both to individuals and to institutions. Although Goffman's work, as Giddens noted, is primarily among participants of roughly equal footing, his work on total institutions—such as prisons and mental institutions—highlights the striking asymmetry of power in such organizations. Structurational interaction allows us to more fully understand the dynamics of rules and resources in our daily routines as well as to understand how institutions (collectivities) use rules and resources and how they shape our encounters.

Structurational interaction also challenges communication scholars to expand their own communicative frameworks. The concept of speaker and listener, as generally used in communication, is a primitive distinction between who has the floor and who does not. Goffman sensitizes us to the various roles speakers have as animators, authors, and principals. Listeners also have different statuses, depending upon whether or not they are ratified participants, overhearers, or eavesdroppers. As a consequence, the distinction between public and private—frontstage and backstage, and degrees of involvement—also provides a richer conceptual tool.

While communication scholars frequently refer to the importance of context, few have taken the difficult step of trying to "unpack" the concept and relate it meaningfully to communicative processes. Both Giddens and Goffman highlight the importance of contextual knowledge in interaction. Giddens expands our notion of context beyond the immediate setting to incorporate the historicity of the context, and the sedimented nature of institutions. For organizational communication scholars, this more extensive view of context is particularly important.

Like context, taken-for-granted tacit knowledge and practical consciousness has largely been ignored, yet the ability to achieve mutual understanding depends upon it. Both Goffman and Giddens emphasize the importance of knowledge about how to go along in encounters and, without apparent effort, to adjust to the normal flux and change in interaction. Mutual knowledge incorporates all the frames of knowledge thus far outlined, ranging from cultural knowledge to organizational knowledge to knowledge of specific others. Our models of communication must acknowledge this fundamental premise of shared tacit knowledge which underlies mutual understanding. As Giddens argues,

> ... most actors must be right most of the time; that is to say, they know what they are doing, and they successfully communicate their knowledge to others. The knowledgeability incorporated in the practical activities which make up the bulk of daily life is a constitutive feature (together with power) of the social world. ... Testing out just what it is that actors know, and how to apply that knowledge in their practical conduct (which actors engage in as well as social observers), depends upon using the same materials—an understanding of recursively organized practices—from which hypotheses about that knowledge are derived. The measure of their 'validity' is supplied by how far actors are able to co-ordinate their activities with others in such a way as to pursue the purposes engaged by their behaviour.
>
> (Giddens, 1984, p. 90)

What are some of the limits on actors' knowledgeability? Obviously, there are cultural limitations in knowledgeability, both in terms of discursive and practical consciousness. However, Giddens also notes other general limits. Access to knowledge is governed by an actor's social positioning, by the way in which knowledge is articulated, by the validity of knowledge claims, and by the means of disseminating the available knowledge. While all social actors have limits on knowledgeability because of their social positioning or milieu, through language we also know more than we can ever directly experience. Goffman, I believe, would support these views.

As Giddens points out, the way in which knowledge is articulated refers to how knowledge claims "are ordered in terms of overall 'discourse' and to the nature of different discourses" (ibid., p. 92). Here, although Goffman does not directly deal with different discourses, I believe his work would be compatible with different types of discourses, especially in light of how he transforms frames via rekeying. For example, one could reframe a discussion of power from a Marxist standpoint to a Foucaldian standpoint. Both would argue that modes of transmission may vary from oral to written cultures, and may vary in the use of mediated systems of communication. Thus, in many ways, structurational interaction reinforces the importance of knowledgeable agents, and illuminates the complexity of such knowledgeability.

Structurational interaction also permits a very comprehensive examination of face, and its crucial role in interaction. Both Goffman and Giddens argue that face is essential for agents to be acknowledged as competent, sane, social actors. We act to preserve trust and tact via face in our interactions with others. But face is also important from the perspective of bodily positioning. Many examples document this, such as facing people you are talking with, being disrespectful by turning your back on someone, and the primacy of a person's face in terms of expressiveness. As Giddens remarked, the "control of the body in fields of action in co-presence and the pervasive influence of face are essential to the whole of Goffman's writings ... co-presence is anchored in the perceptual and communicative modalities of the body" (ibid., p. 67). While Goffman mainly focuses on full co-presence, Giddens argues that "mediated contacts that permit some of the intimacies of co-presence are made possible in the modern era by electronic communications" (ibid., p. 68). Goffman himself observes that forms of mediated communication filter out some cues which are available in face-to-face interaction (FtF). Thus, I think it can be argued that Goffman's work can be usefully extended to incorporate mediated communication, and thus facilitate analysis of communicative processes in contexts of differing degrees of presence and absence. (In fact, scholarship has already extended Goffman's analyses to mediated contexts. See, for example, Dell & Marinova, 2002; Jenkins, 2010; Ling, 2010; and Ross, 2007 as well as work cited earlier.)

Structurational interaction offers a meaning-centered approach to interaction. Structurational interaction emphasizes the process of communication, with a dialogue among participants which reflects listeners' uptakes, accountability, the use of resources, and a reliance on mutual knowledge (or, in Giddens' terms, practical consciousness). Communication scholars often categorize types of messages, while ignoring how listeners respond to them (i.e., their "uptake"). In other cases, messages are evaluated without any reference to the social relationships among interactants or contexts. Or, given a certain type of social relationship, like a superior–subordinate relationship, scholars may generalize about their exchanges, while ignoring contextual influences.

All such analyses are limited in important ways and run the risk of serious errors of interpretation and evaluation. What is needed is a perspective that takes a holistic view of communication, emphasizing messages, social relationships, and context, both immediate and extended. Structurational interaction provides such a coherent, holistic view. Such holistic assessments also view intentionality and power as a situated, joint accomplishment of interactants, and thus offer a richer conceptualization of those issues as well.

In the theory of structurational interaction, interaction is conducted under conditions of felicity, where individuals are assumed to be sane and using shared conventions for communication. Communication is fundamentally supported by practical consciousness and the rationalization of actions; that is, interactants depend upon conventions and upon accountability as they communicate with one another. However, I would also add the concept of relevance—seeking connections between what is said and the ongoing flow of interaction, which is situated contextually, intentionally, and relationally. These assumptions allow interactants to achieve mutual understanding on a moment by moment basis.

The importance of communication as a process is also underscored in structurational interaction. Giddens, in particular, has a historical sense of time which incorporates the immediate context, the individual's life-cycle, and the sedimented time of institutional life (which may extend over generations and across space). Goffman looks at sequences or episodes of interaction as they unfold over time. While both use time and sequence to look at process, even more importantly, they use accounts, or rationalization of action, to unify dialogue and process. In other words, interaction is a process that unfolds as speakers/hearers negotiate their moment-by-moment mutual understanding. And both, of course, emphasize the substantial commonsense knowledge that underlies this process. In contrast, many communication scholars look at process primarily over a limited span of time (e.g., sampling group interaction over the course of a project), rather than as the unfolding of meaning as it is sequentially negotiated and confirmed (or disconfirmed).

Finally, structurational interaction allows a very detailed analysis of organizations, and places these institutions in a historical, cultural, and social context. In addition to framing institutions broadly, structurational interaction allows us to examine the communicative processes that produce and reproduce institutional and social structures. Power, through the mechanisms of resources, rules, and transformative capacity, can be examined closely for how it is instantiated in organizations. And through the distanciation of both time and space and consideration of presence and absence, we can examine the impact of new technologies and globalization processes on institutions.

The value of theory is often its ability to frame new issues to be addressed, and to illuminate tensions in current theories (Fairhurst & Putnam, 2004). One advantage of structurational interaction is the layering and integration of varying levels of contexts. New questions about the relationships across contexts and levels of analysis, a new way of framing complex issues such as agency, and the conceptual questions about organizing and communicating initiated by this theory will prove useful to theory development in organizational communication. And as Orlikowski and Robley (1991) note, structuration theory itself is "an emergent, process theory which accommodates multiple levels of analyses, is contextually and temporally situated, and avoids the blinders of ahistorical accounts of social phenomena" (p. 164).

As we have seen, when Giddens' structuration theory is blended with Goffman's insights into the interactional order, the theory of structurational interaction provides rich insights into organizing and communicating. In the next chapter, I shall provide some applications of structurational interaction that extend some research findings and point the way toward new areas of inquiry.

12

APPLYING STRUCTURATIONAL INTERACTION

In previous chapters we have explored both Goffman's and Giddens' work, and integrated their perspectives, relying on Giddens' own use of Goffman's work, discussing the compatibility of core concepts, and, for this integration, using frames and framing. One might ask: why bother? Although I have discussed its utility in prior chapters, I now want to turn to an in-depth discussion of the benefits of such a synthesis in thinking about organizing and communicating. First, I begin by discussing how this theoretical synthesis can address major issues raised in communication-as-constitutive-of-organizations (CCO) approaches and, more generally, in communication-centric approaches to organizing and organizations. Next, I evaluate four research articles and note how the proposed synthesis would enhance their scholarly findings. And, finally, I develop emergent issues for further exploration using structurational interaction.

Addressing Communication-as-Constitutive-of-Organizations (CCO) Issues

Initially, I want to recap the advantages of structurational interaction. First, and most importantly, structurational interaction offers an integrated, coherent approach to organizing and communication, and offers insightful perspectives on major issues in organizing and communicating, such as structure, agency, materiality, texts, context, and participants. This theory provides multiple points of entry for analysis, and supports multiple methods of research analysis. It suggests new approaches to dialectical tensions as well as suggesting additional sources of tension. In addition, structurational interaction enhances our understanding of identity and identity negotiation for both the individual as well as collectivities. In structurational inter-action, the theoretical weaknesses of both men are offset. For example, Goffman articulates the specific interactional devices Giddens is criticized for ignoring, while Giddens provides the range of contexts, such as institutional contexts, which Goffman is criticized for overlooking. Thus, their integrated perspective in the theory of structurational interaction offers a powerful theoretical base for exploring communicating, organizing and their interrelationships.

Second, the importance of context, in terms of both time and space, is carefully articulated. Their combined emphases on both time and space offer insightful conceptualizations for organizing and communicating, especially on the tensions between the local and the global, the relevance of sociohistorical contexts, and the different uses of time-space.

Finally, structurational interaction balances organizing processes with communicative processes, while not privileging one aspect over the other. This balance is a unique theoretical advantage in that their interrelationships can be more fully examined. This theory also provides insight into important developing issues such as communicating and organizing in different contexts of presence and absence, globalization processes and influences, and the influence of culture on organizing and communicating.

The use of frames as a vehicle for synthesizing their work also focuses our attention on critical communicating and organizing issues. Frame theory can be usefully employed to conceptualize both communicating (Chapter 2) and organizing (Chapters 3 and 4). Beyond this advantage, frames reflect tacit, commonsense knowledge and practical consciousness, and both Goffman and Giddens utilize frames in this sense. Frames also help define the contexts for organizing and communicating, and, through frames, contexts are layered or nested (Boden, 1994; Perlow, Gittel & Katz, 2004). Most importantly, frame theory links communicating and organizing processes so that their interrelationships can be more fully understood. Through interaction, structure and agency are intertwined, and organizing and communicating integrated.

With these advantages in mind, as a way of extending structurational interaction, I will discuss some of the ctitical issues emerging in the study of organizing and communicating, and their interrelationships. Structurational interaction will be used in developing responses to these critical issues; at times, I may rely more heavily on one theorist, but I will also demonstrate points of synthesis between the two men. I first begin by revisiting some of the issues in CCO as an approach to communicating and organizing. Next, I will briefly contrast structurational interaction with Latour's actor network theory, which incorporates the concept of hybrid agency. And finally, I will briefly explore four research exemplars and discuss the added benefits of structurational interaction in approaching this research.

Critical Issues in Communication-as-Constitutive-of-Organizations (CCO)

Putnam and McPhee (2009) argued that the varied approaches to CCO describe organizations and organizing along the following dimensions: (1) specific forms versus general forms; (2) necessary conditions versus characteristic processes; and (3) local communication versus contextually distant communication. Of the approaches they contrasted (McPhee and Zaug's flows, Browning et al's constitutive complexity, Cooren and Fairhurst's association and scaling up process, and Taylor and Van Every's theory of coorientation), all seem to support general forms over limited, specific forms and reflect a range of communication issues such as communication flow, nonhuman contributions, meanings aligned with rituals, tacit rules, and so forth.

Necessary conditions focus on the conditions required for communication to constitute organizing, while characteristic processes of organizations focus on how communication influences particular characteristic processes of organizations. The final contrast, that of local versus contextually distant communication, focuses on the role of context in the communicative composition of organizations. The five approaches examined vary across these two dimensions, and Putnam and McPhee's contrasts help clarify these varied positions.

From their comparisons, they argued that three important concerns emerged. The first is the importance of locating organizational communication in time and space. The second concern is the issue of representing and referencing organizations, and the third issue concerns materiality and embodied practices.

With regard to the first comparison, that of general versus specific forms, structurational interaction offers insight into both forms. Goffman's interaction order provides very specific, detailed analyses of focused interaction, yet also incorporates unfocused interactions and gatherings, which may include multiple sites of communication. With framing, interactions can be reframed, and contexts can be reconstituted and re-embedded in different locales and sites (i.e., distanciation). Thus frames and/or contexts can be nested within different social systems and constitute larger social systems.

Within larger social systems, different types of institutions exist (recall distinctions between institutions of signification, domination, and legitimation). Structurational interaction emphasizes routines and social practices and they can be conceptualized on multiple levels. For example, one might study organizational interviews and assess the routine of a job interview, but one might also study how that routine is incorporated, both materially and communicatively, into the larger routines of hiring, firing, socialization and so forth. Giddens' discussion of the Willis study (1984), on the education of English boys, is an excellent example of nested interactions and social practices that, when linked together, act to reinforce educational and job opportunities for young men.

With reference to focusing on necessary conditions versus characteristic processes, both can be analyzed using structurational interaction. As a general disclaimer, I would simply point out that organizational scholars have not yet determined what the necessary conditions for an organization are. That is, what makes organizing processes result in an organization? The most important point to make here is that structurational interaction argues for the fundamental importance of social interaction in social systems, and thus falls firmly into the CCO camp. Social interaction is necessary for any social order; among those types of social order are organizations and institutions. More specifically, Giddens' duality of structure is based on interaction, and he regards social integration (via social interaction) as a necessary condition for system integration (e.g., the constitution of larger social systems such as organizations, institutions, nation-states, and societies). Whatever the particular conceptualization of an organization—whether a flow model, institutional theory or some other conceptualization—social interaction will be a constitutive component of that conceptualization.

With regard to characteristic processes in organizing and their communicative constitution, structurational interaction offers various analytic strategies for conceptualization and research. For example, what are the "felicity conditions" underlying negotiation strategies? How do organizational members evaluate arguments? (See Seibold and his colleagues for structuration research relevant to this issue.) What constitutes the practical consciousness and discursive consciousness which contextualize a particular work practice? How are different genres of communication instantiated in differing organizational and institutional contexts? Characteristic communicative practices will always involve issues of framing, alignment, and contextualization, all of which are emphasized in structurational interaction. It is also important to note that these processes may play out differently in different types of institutions (i.e., institutions of signification, domination and legitimation) and in different cultures. (See also the work of Heracleous, 2001, 2004, 2006a, b for insightful discussions of discourse, frames and organizing.)

On the issue of local versus distanciated communication, structurational interaction would argue that social interaction is nested or framed within different contexts, such that the local and the global reflect one another. Giddens' discussion of shopping at a local mall and having the selection in available stores influenced by global processes (e.g., chains, foreign products, larger economic circumstances) is a good example of how the local and global enfold one another. Or Czarniawska's example (2006a) of an intimate conversation at a small table in a beer hall invoking film images of similar conversations for participants also illustrates how the local may merge with the global in material and performative ways.

Communicating across time and space. One area in need of further development is the conceptualization of time and space, which reflects Putnam's concern about locating organizational communication across time and space. Structuration theory's conceptualization of time-space and distanciation are important concepts which enhance our understanding of the capacity of telecommunication systems and mass transit to enable rapid, simultaneous, coordinated activities. While spatial concepts have not been as well developed, Goffman's use of front- and backstage and regions flesh out Giddens' emphasis on time-space distanciation. In addition, Giddens' concepts of social positioning, time-space trajectories and regionalization further integrate time-space and embodiment. Structuration theory also discusses the capacity—in modernity—to disembed and re-embed social episodes, encounters and organizations. In structurational interaction, both time and space are more developed than in any other approaches currently available. Structuration theory, in particular, has influenced work in archaeology and geography, while Goffman's work has influenced the analysis of arrangements of space in terms of private and public performances, and interactions. As such, structurational interaction provides a very rich approach to these concerns.

In addition, Giddens' concept of historicity—the different senses of time—are critical for studying the emergence of organizations and/or industries; the development of communicative genres; social positioning over one's lifetime in both personal and professional terms; and so forth. See the work of Ballard and Seibold (2000, 2003; Ballard, 2008) on time, which developed an approach, based on the work of Bourdieu (1977), on humans' experience of time. Although based on Bourdieu, their work is theoretically compatible with Giddens' discussion of time. While their meso-level model of organizational temporality is more explicit in identifying specific aspects of temporality than is Giddens' discussion, the breadth of factors taken into account (e.g., dominant cultural patterns, the organizational environment, work group norms) shares, with Giddens, a broad perspective on temporality. Hall (2003) suggested that time-space distanciation enables coordination of organizations, especially through the use of standardized, global time-space, although time-space orders are multiple and contradictory, and thus involve dialectical processes as well (Friedland & Boden, 1994).

As we have seen, structurational interaction offers a rich conceptualization of both time and space. An exciting application of this theory might be to explore differing sites of organizing across a multinational corporation in which the use of time and space is contrasted across cultures, work practices, and types of work. What types of conflict, tension, and paradox might develop at these time/space edges? Ancona, Goodman, Lawrence and Tushman (2001) suggested that using a temporal lens will help focus on social practices; their trajectories over time; the historical context of the organization; the timing of innovations; and both individual and organizational time orientation (past, present or future). Miller (1999) also noted the absence of sociohistorical contexts in organizational communication research, and argued that its addition will enhance our understanding of organizational processes. Structurational interaction, with its emphasis on time, especially in the sociohistoricity of social activity, will contribute substantively to such discussions.

Representing organizations. With regard to institutional identity, structurational interaction acknowledges actors speaking on behalf of an institution, organization, or an organizational entity (like a nation-state) representing a society. Structurational interaction would also acknowledge that there may be multiple voices, points of dissension, and controversy behind such spokespersons. The concepts of tacit knowledge, commonsense knowledge and shared social practices that underlie a collective mindset, represented by a spokesperson or a text (like the Global Warming Initiative or Geneva conventions for treatment of war criminals), are also elements of this theory. Structurational interaction thus offers excellent insight into the different "authors" a spokesperson might invoke (e.g., a principal, author). Institutional identity and its negotiation might be approached from the level of specific interactions between governments or organizations, or from the standpoint of negotiations across particular types of institutions (legal, educational and the like), or from relations between the general public and types of institutions (like the military)

Materiality. The final feature emphasized by Putnam and McPhee (2009) that of materiality and embodied practices—is also an aspect of structurational interaction. Structurational interaction acknowledges the material world and embodied practices as a significant aspect of social interaction. Goffman's dramaturgical perspective and Giddens' concept of resources invoke materials in interaction, and both focus on embodied practices and social routines. As such, structurational interaction acknowledges the multiple aspects of materiality and its importance as a source of stabilization, particularly in terms of written texts or other inscribed materials such as computer software or hardware. Gonos (1977) also noted that, for Goffman, various texts (spoken, written, painted, filmed and so forth) have distinct formal systems of social organization (p. 863). Giddens acknowledged that, in modernity, the storage of information and its inscription (especially in writing) made modern organizations possible, and led to the development of nation-states and the concentration of political and administrative power in cities. Goffman (1961b) incorporates materiality as well in his discussion of situated activity systems. With his concept of "fresh talk," Goffman acknowledged that, while much of the talk in organizations is centered around tasks and the material objects which may be involved in the task, some talk is not connected to the task, and thus relatively unconstrained (e.g., fresh).

At times, the discussion of materiality may incorporate a discussion of agency. For both Giddens and Goffman, agency—the choice to do otherwise—is a human capacity, exercised by other animals as well, but in more limited capacities. Humans create imaginary worlds and imagined ways in which to exercise agency, whereas other animals do not—or appear to have a very limited capacity to do so (play vs. non-play, as in Bateson's [1976] example). Many attribute humans' creative capacity to language.

Texts, such as documents, room arrangements and so forth, have "authority" accorded them by actors, but do not have agency. When actors recognize the authority of texts, such texts are given power—*but this is an affordance that must be legitimated by actors, and not assumed.* Thus, the U.S. tax code is accorded authority because society acknowledges its value and necessity, and sanctions are given for violating the code. But it does not have agency, because it (the tax code) has no power or choice to do otherwise: it is "what it is" until altered or re-interpreted (and/or arbitrated, probably in court).

In a similar fashion, material objects have "affordances," not agency. An affordance reflects the capacity in which an object can be used—how it is appropriated, of course, is partly a function of the material qualities of the object itself. While I can use a computer program in ways unintended by the designer of the system, the affordances to do so are limited by the capacity of that system—I cannot, for example, use a computer program to cut down a tree. While I agree whole-heartedly that material objects need to be included in our explanations of social practices, and agree with Latour that it is difficult (perhaps impossible) to identify the starting points of any action, I also agree with Goffman and Giddens that agency, in the sense of the capacity to choose to do otherwise, is a capacity of humans. Other sentient beings, while exercising agency, do so in a much more restricted fashion.

At this point, it might be useful to contrast structurational interaction with the work of Bruno Latour; his work has focused on hybrid agency and actants in organizing. Actants refer to both human and non-human entities, such as fences or ATMs, that can perform actions (limited, of course, by their affordances).

1. *Comparisons with actor network theory.* Latour rejected the idea of an everyday world: "We do not live at any scale and there is no everyday world! Focusing attention on one mundane local scale is exactly what we cannot ever witness or make intelligible. Action is always displaced, lopsided, shifted and scale never stable enough to offer a mundane grasp that would allow us to ignore the problems of social theory. What I call punctualizing and globalizing, sharing agencies with other actants who have different timings, tempos and properties, make it impossible to start and even more impossible to 'return' to one 'everyday world'" (Latour, 1996, p. 268). "What I am trying to focus on is a cross made by a double distinction: agency/structure, human/non-human" (ibid.).

Building on Latour, Cooren and Fairhurst (2009) suggest that organizations are "made of texts, but also of machines and architectural elements, its mode of existence, of course, also depends on the contributions of humans" (2009, p. 141). Each of the actors/actants can be seen as partly responsible for the product of the associations of texts and materials in organizing. Such action is a hybrid action (Latour, 1991, 1993, 1994, 2005) because it represents the association of many different actors who participate in what is going on. These actants are both human and non-human entities. As they note, "It is through this hybrid agency that organized forms and organizing take place" (p. 141).

Action is thus dislocal (in its capacity to produce an effect through space) and has mediacy (in its capacity to produce effects over time) (ibid.). As such, local actions can *scale up* and past actions can still have present-day effects. As Latour noted, "Everything in the definition of macro social order is due ... to technical mediation. Even the simple effect of duration, of long-lasting social force, cannot be obtained without the durability of nonhumans to which human local interactions have been shifted" (1994, p. 51). Generally, action nets and actor network theory have been part of a sustained interest in the impact of technology on organizing, and on discourse processes in organizational settings (see, for example, Button, 1987; Le Vine & Scollon, 2004). I will now respond to some points of complementarity and difference between structurational interaction and actor network theory, as developed by Cooren and Fairhurst with their specific focus on organizing.

2. *Points of convergence and divergence with structurational interaction.* Structurational interaction acknowledges the importance of material objects (non-human entities) in organizing and communicating, and in the constitution of organizations. Goffman was one of the first theorists to focus on the use of space in interaction (e.g., frontstage, backstage, regions) and to incorporate space as well as materiality as an element in interaction. For example, space can be used to signal physical co-presence, focused and unfocused encounters, gatherings and so forth. Material objects are frequently used in staging a performance of self. Giddens also acknowledges the importance of objects in terms of rules and resources used by interactants.

In addition, Giddens is clearly cognizant of the importance of texts. His distinctions between traditional and modern societies clarified the critical role of writing in this transformation. The storage of information itself, and the technology developed to store and process information, were also critical in developing modernity and concentrating administrative power. Thus, structurational interaction would also acknowledge effects through space and time (dislocality and mediacy in Latour), and, through time/space distanciation, structurational interaction would identify the processes by which this occurs. Giddens also very clearly acknowledged the technical mediation necessary for time/space distanciation. The very important contribution of actor network theory is to exemplify the varied ways in which humans and non-human entities interact in organizing and constituting organizations. As such, this is a very strong point of congruence between structurational interaction and Latour.

Another point of congruence is acknowledging what may pre-exist interaction or an organization. Both the model of communication developed in this book, as well as structurational interaction, acknowledge the influence of the past in terms of interactants' shared, commonsense knowledge and their understanding of the context in which they are interacting (this would include material objects as well, such as written documents and buildings). For Latour, this past is represented in a variety of texts, including documents, architecture, and the like. Both structurational interaction and Latour imply long stretches of time in capturing pre-existing social and material structures (for lack of a better word!). Giddens discusses historicity and the long duree of time as an influence, while Latour argues it is very difficult (or impossible) to identify the origin of an action.

This raises the question of boundaries—in Latour's view, boundaries cannot be determined because of the associated links of action across actants. However, in our ordinary, commonsense notions of an organization, some boundary is implied. Cooren and Fairhurst suggest that artifacts and space create some boundaries, and that is clearly the case. Goffman's concept of situated activity systems would also be useful in framing boundaries. I think an added value of structurational interaction in this regard is that access to *relevant* rules and resources might draw boundaries around an organization, thus implicating not only material structures, but also limiting the chain of associated actions. Knowing that bricks, made in Italy, were used to construct a particular building may make "no difference" to me as an actant in an organization located in that particular building, but if I were interested in the economic issues affecting that area, knowing that there was trade with Italy might be very relevant.

The issue of agency is a major contrast across the theorists. Both Goffman and Giddens reserve agency to humans, in contrast to Latour, who discusses hybrid agency as well as non-human agency. All would agree that objects and humans have effects—they can and do make a difference. And people use material objects to exercise power and create effects (hybrid agency). For Giddens, however, agency is more than making a difference—it is the ability to do otherwise, to have a choice. And I think Goffman would concur with this (consider, for example, his work on alignment, resistance in total institutions, and so forth). Here, then, is a critical difference. *Non-human actants cannot choose to "do otherwise"; they can break down and be repaired, but they cannot alter their physical capacities in terms of what they were designed to do* (e.g., the ATM cannot become a surveillance camera unless its original design incorporates this afforance). Non-human entities have "affordances" that can be used, adapted to, and modified in creative way by human users, as adaptive structuration scholarship has clearly demonstrated.

But the fundamental capacity in agency—the ability to choose to do otherwise—appears to be unique to humans. In addition, humans are creative; they can use objects to stand for any number of things, as anyone watching the average two- or three-year-old at play knows. This inventiveness or creativity is part of humans' initial engagement with objects as instruments of play as well as their subsequent understanding of object permanence—something we have perhaps overlooked in our theories. All entities have "affordances" (I cannot leap tall buildings in a single bound), but humans can exercise agency in creative, unique ways that non-human entities cannot. (I can imagine that those tall buildings are space aliens or a protective wall. Other animals do not seem to have this capacity.) Finally, for Giddens, Goffman, and myself, agency implies reflexivity—part of our capacity to choose to do otherwise rests on our monitoring of our own actions with an "eye" towards adjusting them if need be.

Another problematic area is in the definition of texts. The term, as frequently used, is so inclusive as to be vacuous. In particular, treating memory traces in the same way as one treats looking at architectural elements or barbed wire fences is problematic. These "texts" have very different affordances. There are issues not only of permanence and durability, but also of negotiated meanings. A written text, a memo, or minutes of a meeting, may be contested; but memory traces, I would argue, are much more "contestable" because they are not usually permanent or fully inscribed. Studies of rumor transmission are excellent examples of the permutations memory traces may go through as they are shared with others—in a way, and to a degree, that inscribed texts may not.

In addition, when discussing texts, Conrad (2004) noted that Cooren (2004) makes an "excellent case that members of organizations often respond to them [texts] as if they are [agents]. In this sense, when texts become de-authored, the original intent of their authors is both crucial, because at various points in the text's 'lifetime' that intent will become contested terrain, and irrelevant, because 'original intent' is necessarily constructed and reconstructed discursively" (Conrad, 2004, p. 438). As Conrad argued, organizational members use the "textual character of inanimate objects rhetorically and strategically," irrespective of the original intended usages (ibid.). Especially so, I might add, over time when a text becomes widely dispersed and invoked in multiple contexts.

Thus, a fuller explanation of texts and their different affordances would be useful. Because many scholars argue that organizations are built upon and rely upon texts—both individually and as representations of collective knowledge – in establishing social order and guiding social practices for organizations, a careful understanding of the different affordances of the different types of texts would seen necessary.

Finally, Cooren and Fairhurst argue that "if the idea of the communicative constitution of organization makes any sense, it is for us on the sole condition that the concept of 'communication' is extended to what nonhumans do. For instance, this means that we need to acknowledge that the sign indeed *tells* visitors what behaviors [have] to be adopted upon entering the building" (Cooren and Fairhurst, 2009, p. 142). This example reflects the transmission of information which can be conveyed verbally or nonverbally. However, this information may be acted upon in different ways depending on the purposes of human agent. A security system may or may not dissuade visitors from entering without checking in at the front desk. My decision (as an agent) about whether or not to check in depends upon my commonsense knowledge of how security systems work, and whether I am an employee whose purpose is to get to my office, or a thief whose purpose is to get in and out of the building undetected. These interpretive schemas and actions rest upon human agency, not upon the "agency" of the sign.

In brief, actor network theory clearly helps us understand the contribution of non-human entities to organizing, communicating, and organizations. Structurational interaction also help us understand the contributions of non-human entities. However, structurational interaction avoids the problematic issues raised by the concept of hybrid agency, boundaries, and the vagueness of texts. While clearly objects of varying ontologies should be folded into our theories of organizing, communicating, and organizations, a careful delineation of fundamental differences across non-human and human entities needs to be made.

Conrad's Critique of Discourse Centered Approaches to Organizing

Conrad's critique of organizational discourse also raised important concerns. After Alvesson and Karreman (2000a, b), Conrad (2004) suggested: (1) noting those aspects of discourse influenced by structural processes and those which are operating autonomously; (2) modelling levels of discourse, from specific contexts to patterns of discourse over time (from micro to meso to Grand to Mega-Grand Discourses); (3) incorporating social contexts and participants in analyses of discourse; and

(4) exploring the tensions among varying perspectives. Conrad goes on to discuss alternative perspectives, and evaluates them on these issues. What follows is a discussion of how structurational interaction addresses these issues.

Structural influences on discourse. All interaction is influenced by structure if context and relationships are considered structural mechanisms. Goffman would agree with this position, especially because all interaction is situated within cultural contexts and social relationships. (I will set aside the fact that language itself is structured.) Giddens, of course, argues that interaction is always structured via the duality of structure (e.g., structuration). The question then becomes an issue of relative tightness or looseness of the contextual/relational (structural) constraints. The relatively autonomous end of the continuum might be unfettered talk among intimates, with an unlimited range of topics, and with roughly equivalent stature among them (Giddens' concept of the "pure relationship" might be a good example). More tightly framed exchanges might range from casual exchanges between colleagues to the tightly controlled, prescribed investiture of a president of a country.

Once we move into organizational settings, however, context and relationships become defined institutionally, and the constraint/enablement aspects of interaction become less fluid and more fixed. Although one always has choice, in that one can choose to do otherwise, when we join organizations we have, as Bacharach and Lawlor (1980) observed, given over some of our decision-making to the organization, and given it some rights in ordering our actions in return for rewards of varying sorts (e.g., money, prestige, opportunity). Thus, institutional contexts reflect more tight interactional constraints and less enablement generally, although agency (the choice to do otherwise) always remains; some individuals, because of social positioning or "idiosyncratic credits," may have considerable discretion in their actions. We can, for example, explore interaction across a variety of settings, such as "fresh talk" as opposed to "task talk" in organized settings, in terms of their constraint/enablement, or examine forms of talk that vary in constraint/enablement across types of institutions (e.g., legal institutions as opposed to political institutions). Institutional contexts shape interaction, as well as being shaped by interaction.

Levels of discourse and context. This is an issue that has many guises. One way of framing this issue is as a "point of entry" decision for the analyst. The contextual scope of an analysis may vary from "micro-discourse" analyses, which focus on detailed analyses of a single encounter, to "mega-discourse" analyses, which examine patterns of discourse over space and time. The implication is that discourse processes are *altered* in some way by the point of entry selected (read *level* selected) and that these levels make a difference (e.g., the attempt to "scale up" to an institutional level). My question is a simple one. Do discourse or interactional *processes* vary across points of entry? And my answer is "no": interactants use the same fundamental processes—of interpretation, reflexive monitoring, and aligning with others—irrespective of the context and/or scope of context. Participants do not "invent" new interactional processes—align and reframe yes—but fundamentally create, no. However, the answer becomes "yes," if we consider the strategic interactional choices people make when interacting across different contexts. For example, I may readily interrupt a colleague, but not my superior.

Thus, the critical issue is not level of discourse, but the *framing of the context*. And both Goffman and Giddens offer insights on varying layers of context. Goffman's interaction order offers a range of concepts for analyzing encounters, such as alignment, footing, participant status, and frames. He also discusses a range of contexts, from focused encounters to gatherings, as well as different participant statuses for both speakers (e.g., author, animator) and listeners (e.g., overhearers, ratified participants). And Goffman's concepts are, I submit, valid and valuable at every contextual layer. In addition, through the concepts of framing, keying and rekeying, Goffman unpacks the manner in which contexts shift within episodes and across episodes, and how more expansive contexts can be incorporated via frames (e.g., framing and rekeying).

While his work did not focus on larger social institutions, Goffman was clearly aware of them—his work on total institutions, forms of talk, and so forth, reveal an appreciation of institutions as social systems and how discourse is patterned differently across different social systems. Goffman is also generally criticized for his lack of power analysis, although, in the aforementioned works, his detailed commentaries on the resistance of patients and prisoners to institutions reveal an insightful awareness and understanding of power dynamics. His book *Gender Advertisements*, is also noteworthy in these respects. (See especially Chapter 10, dealing with the application of his work in larger institutional settings.)

What structurational interaction incorporates is a wider range of contexts and contextual influences, including economic and political factors into discourse analysis. In addition, Giddens discusses the long *duree* of time as well as different types of institutions or social systems. The analysis of different types of institutions has been relatively neglected by organizational communication scholars, and I think it would be significant to study discourse differences across different types of institutions. (See, for example, the Courtright, Fairhurst Rogers [1989] study of organic versus mechanistic plant structures, and their respective communicative processes.)

Through structurational interaction, we can explore different types of institutions (of signification, domination, and legitimation), and conduct detailed contrastive analyses of how interactions are accomplished (e.g., what types of alignment, framing, and footing occur). Another area to explore would be McPhee and Zaug's four flows of discourse. For example, one could examine whether types of discourse and interaction vary across these flows, as well as investigate how these flows may vary within and across different institutions, such as legal, political or educational institutions. I suspect that substantial variation in interaction would be found. Giddens' discussion of time-space edges is clearly relevant to the study of institutional identification, and to discourse among "mega-actors."

While Goffman's analysis of context relies on frames, interpretive schemes, and framing in discourse, Giddens utilizes Goffman's interaction order as a basis for assessing context and adds rules and resources as major sources of structuration. While rules and resources would fit into Goffman's analysis as part of a frame or interpretive scheme, Giddens' use of resources emphasizes material resources (money, objects) more so than does Goffman's. But note the importance Goffman places on "props" and spatial arrangements that support co-present interactions. Thus, through structurational interaction, we have a broad range of contexts, multiple points of entry, and a use of historicity and resources neglected in many other approaches.

Mega-discourses (Potter & Wetherell, 1987), examining patterns of discourse over extended periods of time and space are similar to what many have labeled "world views" (Geertz, 1973, 1983; Haslett, 1987). The contextual scope for world views is cultural but some world views, like Jungian archetypes, may be pan-cultural or universal. Both Giddens and Goffman would acknowledge these world views as part of tacit knowledge or practical consciousness. (Some might argue that archetypes are part of the unconscious, but that debate is beyond the scope of our interests here.) Perlow et al.'s use of nested structuration is very relevant here because their model suggested that cultural world views provide an "envelope" which surrounds other levels of context (Perlow, Gittel & Katz, 2004). When institutions or individuals interact across differing cultural world views, difficulties arise because, in Giddens' terms, they reflect different time-space edges in the same way that globalization "confronts" traditional societies at time-space edges. Time-space edges thus provide a site for paradox and/or contradiction in organizing and communicating.

Finally, in looking at how discourse units or types of discourse may vary, some discourse types, like narratives, seem to operate in the same fashion across multiple contexts. In contrast, speech acts operate in very carefully prescribed contexts, and violating their felicity conditions invalidates their presumed effects. Both Giddens and Goffman would argue that such units would be "loosely coupled" to larger social systems, and that social systems, in turn, cannot be reduced to those elements. For Giddens, in part, this is so because of the unknown conditions and unforeseen consequences that surround every action. Both Goffman and Giddens would also argue that social practices are a basic unit of analysis, and we need to explore *how discourse operates in specific social practices—that is, in combination with time, space and objects utilized in that social practice.* It remains an empirical question to uncover which discourse types, or forms, operate in what fashion in what social context in a given sociohistoric context. And, in exploring these issues, we need to be aware of the double hermeneutic and our own research bias.

Context and participants. Numerous scholars (see Alvesson & Karreman, 2000a, b; Hardy, 2004; Haslett, 1987; Van Dijk, 1997a, b, c) have underscored the importance of not just focusing on talk, but also focusing on the context and participants. In the discussion above, I have already outlined the importance of context and its role in discourse and social interaction analysis. In discussing participants (in Goffman's terms, participant status), structurational interaction provides a rich perspective on participants. This theory discusses roles, and the capacity to separate oneself from various roles, assuming shifting identities and different social positions. In particular, Goffman's interaction order offers a rich discussion of different speaker-ship roles (e.g., animator, principal, authors). For those interested in institutional analyses of spokespersons, Goffman's principal concept investigates the distinctions between a spokesperson or speaking from a particular identity (e.g., that of a CEO, lawyer, social worker). Listeners' roles are also identified, including those who are ratified as participants and those who overhear.

Giddens' concept of social positioning discusses the movement of individuals throughout their lifetimes, and discusses the lifestyle choices individuals make in late modernity. In particular, conditions of late modernity involve trust and risk, both institutionally (in terms of trust/risk of institutions and the uncertainty of knowledge; Giddens, 2009b) and personally (in terms of lifestyle choices, choices about "pure relationships," and so forth). Again, the entry points for analysis and insight are varied. Social positioning, as developed by both Goffman (in terms of alignment and footing) and Giddens (in terms of time-space trajectories over one's lifespan), offers a rich perspective for analyzing identity and identification processes.

With regard to motivation, both Goffman and Giddens acknowledge it, but take the stance that intentions and motivations are largely unknowable. Although Goffman is criticized for portraying a cynical, manipulative agent (see, for example, research on impression management using Goffman's work on strategic action and pre-sentation of self), I think this criticism of Goffman is somewhat misguided. While he does talk about "cooling out the mark" and the work of spies, his larger point is that *the same strategies of impression management or presentation of self are used for authentic as well as inauthentic presentations of self.* Thus, he concluded that it is hard to discern the differences between authentic and inauthentic representations of the self. Only the individual actor may be aware of his or her "real" intentions, and intentionality may even be hidden from the self.

Goffman also alerts us to information that is "given off" which may be at odds with the impression being given. Here, Giddens' discussion of the role of the unconscious comes into play, and he would argue that some of our behavior is motivated by unconscious needs and goals. Both theorists emphasize the importance of controlling anxiety (and thereby avoiding embarrassment and shame), and maintaining a stable sense of self through interaction. (For a fuller discussion of these issues refer to Chapters 6, 9 and 10 and references to their work discussing these issues.)

Dialectical tensions. Finally, Conrad suggests the need for dealing with rhetorical tensions. Conrad (2004), citing Burke, defined "dialectical" as "meanings ... constructed through opposition and contrast. ... As social constructions of the meaning of one term develop and change, the meaning of the other changes as well—they are ever connected. The resulting tensions and contradictions can be managed in a number of ways ... but they never can be resolved" (p. 436). Some of the continuing ten-sions in contemporary organizational communication research are "action and structure; micro and macro; determinism and autonomy; modernism and postmodernism" (p. 436). Varied perspectives offer different responses to these dialectic tensions, some starting at the center looking toward both poles of the tension, while others "tack back and forth" in an iterative fashion between the dialectic poles (ibid.). The integrated theoretical perspective set out here addresses these issues.

In Giddens, the tensions between agency and structure become a duality in that structure is instantiated via interaction, and is both the medium and outcome of interaction. That tension dissolves in structuration as interaction is a form of agency. Both theorists would agree that agents' actions can provide constraint as well as opportunities for enablement, and thus balance the tension between determinism and voluntarism. Neither theorist would support the macro/micro distinctions, although both support varying layers of contextual frames surrounding interaction. In terms of the distinction between modernity and postmodernity, Giddens takes the position that we are in a period of late modernity.

One of Giddens' main dialectics, of course, is the dialectic of control, in which agency shifts back and forth between enablement and constraint. Goffman would be in agreement with this position. Giddens also discusses the tension between the local and the global, while generally observing that the local *is* global, especially with time-space distanciation, disembedding and re-embedding. There are also tensions at the edges of time/space, where different societies, institutions and social orders may conflict with one another. Finally, Giddens acknowledges that tensions occur because of inherent contradictions in system principles.

For Goffman, dialectical tensions are on the individual level with tensions between information management and the management of ritual; the tension between the tactful and the tactical; between involvement and non-involvement; and between the system requirements versus ritual requirements in the interaction order (Collins, 1988). As such, structurational interaction provides interesting insights into a range of dialectical tensions in social interaction.

As we have seen, structurational interaction responds to the critical issues that Conrad has raised. The macro/micro level is resolved in structurational interaction and multiple levels of analysis are available for research. A very rich, complex analysis of context and participants is also found in structurational interaction. Finally, the dialectical tensions developed by Conrad are addressed and added tensions exposed by structurational interaction.

Throughout our discussion of organizing and communicating, texts and their importance have been recurrent themes. However, there is substantive controversy in terms of defining texts, and some clarification might be useful.

Clarifying Texts

As mentioned previously, in the context of discussing organizing and discourse, there is a need for clarity in how people use and define concepts, such as discourse, texts, conversations, and narratives. Some very useful discussions are already available, and could serve as a basis for further discussion (see, for example, Corman & Poole, 2000; Fairhurst, 2004; Van Dijk, 1981, 1997a, b). Each scholar needs to articulate the intellectual context in which her or his views have been shaped. (See Tracy, 2001, for an interesting discussion of discourse in the communication discipline. More broadly, Grimshaw, 2001, discusses a plethora of approaches and different definitions of terms, and he strongly argues for clarity in terminology.) Some scholars have investigated differences between oral and written communication, and a brief consideration of these distinctions might further clarify what is meant by texts.

Written versus oral texts. One of the underappreciated distinctions among texts is that between oral and written communication. Written texts, such as documents, permit a larger system of coordination, more centralized control, and more "uniformity among different groups," because they provide a focus for interpretation (Johnson, 1999). As she noted, the more specifically a document describes who is to do what and when, the more uniformity there is. As she also observed, "there is less reciprocity in control by documentation than in control through speech and consequently the organizations they create are less adaptive; documents permit 'a kind of blind impartiality. ... Such design rules permit quick decisions as well as a kind of 'fairness'"(pp. 120–22). She concluded that "The process of formalizing involves creating constraints so that interpersonal structures are 'rationalized' in accordance with a paper design of human coordination ... because documentation is less personal, less adaptive, and less informative, its possibilities for creating coordination are limited" (pp. 122–23). Thus, organizing differences result from different formats used to carry out organizational taskss.

For Johnson, there are differences between oral and written communication, but almost no work has been done in how "they function differently in creating human relationships" (ibid., p. 120). Based on the work of Carroll Arnold, particularly his work on distinguishing oral from written rhetoric, Johnson suggested differences between organizing through speech and organizing through documentation. She suggested these differences lie across four dimensions—personality, adaptiveness, informativeness, and potential for editing. Speech carries a personal ethos, whereas documents are impersonal and carry the ethos of the organization. The greater adaptability of personal, verbal communication tends to give more information, while in documents, timing, form, and language are important. Documents can be edited, but our interpersonal "edits" may be awkward, and we may not be able to erase our mistakes from the minds of listeners. With documentation, it is easier to hold people accountable for their actions, while oral messages can be withdrawn, manipulated, or concealed (ibid., p. 121). As she noted, interaction is fluid, has a greater capacity to adapt, and is continuously negotiated, while documents remain the same, even though they may be edited at times.

To this, I would add that the enduring nature of texts—stability over time, interpretations over time—really comes down to how they are instantiated, and thus depends upon social practices and shared textual interpretations. (See also van

Gemert and Woudstra, 1999, for an interesting discussion of oral and written interaction in the document design process, and a useful literature review of a variety of research streams looking at these processes.)

Scholars need to refine and define their concepts concerning what constitutes a text and to fully explore the affordances of varying types of text (such as Johnson's discussion of oral versus written texts). Similar types of discussions, contrasting the use of different forms of mediated communication, are also needed to enhance our understanding of organizing and communicating. Such discussions are crucial because our world is saturated with hybrid forms of communication, interlacing offline with online interaction and virtual with face-to-face interaction. And, of course, structurational interaction is, as previously explained, well suited to this task in many ways.

Extending Some Research Studies

One of the major premises of this book is the value of applying an integrated Goffman/Giddens perspective to the study of organizing and communicating. Thus far, we have noted the compatibility of both theoretical perspectives, pointing out, in particular, Giddens' reliance on interactional processes and his emphasis on Goffman's work. We have also seen the value of Goffman's work when applied to organizational settings, as well as the value of Giddens' work for organizing and communicating. In this next section, I want to further develop the proposed synthesis, by exploring four studies, and applying structurational interaction to further enhance their results. Finally, I want to point out particular areas of emphasis within organizational communication which would benefit from applying structurational interaction. These suggestions will not be exhaustive—hopefully others will apply linkages in different areas of research—but rather suggest new approaches which will enhance our understanding of organizing and communicating, and their interrelationships.

Group Decision-Making

The first research example is an excellent programmatic essay by Poole, Seibold and McPhee (1985), which outlined a structuration approach to group decision-making, and demonstrates how structuration may be applied to organizing and communicating. They argued that structuration offers a metatheory which integrates both traditional and emergent analyses of small groups. Structuration focuses on social practices, and on how agents (actors) draw upon rules and resources in context, and over time. In addition, structuration views action as a "continuous flow of intentionality" which depends upon rationalization and reflexive monitoring (p. 77). Action is also temporal, situated in historical context, dependent on an agent's knowledgeability, and subject to unanticipated consequences. Structures also interpenetrate one another—for example, when managers give orders, positional power resources and language are drawn upon simultaneously, and thus both structures are altered and mediate one another (p. 80).

A second form of interpenetration occurs through contradiction. They noted that, for Giddens, contradiction may supply "fault lines" which create conflicts. Finally, they suggested a combination of quantitative and qualitative methods for structurational analysis. Dialectical explanations required an examination of the conditions surrounding action, and the nature of institutional orders and their interpenetrations—in other words, action is embedded in context, and that context must be understood (p. 81).

Stucturational conception of groups. First, Poole, Seibold and McPhee argued that groups, like people, "are real conceptual entities ... however ... both 'persons' and groups are real only due to production and reproduction processes in interaction" (p. 82). They suggested that a "structurational definition of a group will be cast in terms of action: a group is that which acts as a group. ... Only in the course of the group interaction process can one tell whether an act is leadership, individual deviance, or part of an ongoing pattern of differentiation" (p. 83). Because organizations can be viewed as a group of groups, these points are relevant to organizations as well.

Decision-making. Although their article focused on decision-making, Poole et al. pointed out that "Decision-making is but a single practice—more accurately, a single set of practices—suspended in a web of other practices, including the group's other ongoing work, its relations with other groups, and the emotional or social relationships among its members" (p. 84). In terms of decision-making, their structurational perspective conceptualized it as the "production and reproduction of *positions* regarding group action, directed toward the convergence of members on a final choice" (ibid.). This process involves three steps—the expression of preferences, argumentation, and strategic tactics. Every step reflect the three modalities of structuration—namely, meaning, norms and power. They noted that,

> As enacted through the three types of messages outlined above, group interaction invokes, constitutes, and reproduces *interpretive schemes* relevant to group decisions; decision rules serve as *normative structures* regulating the accumulation of preferences and reasons and "transforming" them into group decisions; and communication patterns and power structures are *facilities* that (among other things) shape input into and enable control over group decisions.
>
> *(p. 85)*

They argue that this formulation is a departure from (and I would add superior to) most group research because "these constructs are always mediated by interaction" (ibid.). This formulation is, I would argue, also advantageous for conceptualizing organizing and communicating.

Next, they set out a series of studies to explore group decision-making, including the temporal unfolding of preference distributions, frames for traditional structures for decisions and communication, and unintended consequences of actions in the group. They also wanted to extend their analyses to include contextual conditions for groups, such as the task, group size and group composition, which permit experimental manipulation of groups. Although clearly a more recent development, a structurational study of bona fide groups would greatly enrich our understanding of the context in which groups operate, such as their sociohistorical context, type of industry, the impact of time-space distanciation, and so forth.

Because structuration "is an *intersubjective* process—centered in interaction—and the subject is constituted as part of this process" (p. 90), Poole et al. focused on two aspects of a subject's positioning—negotiating a role and, more fundamentally, being constituted as an agent in interaction (as a coherent center of experience and action) (ibid.). They suggested that role development is thus a *"miscrostructuration"* process. Agents' comments have implications for the focus and flow of discussion, and, in turn, for the emerging group structure, and for group decisions. In terms of being viewed as a coherent agent, Poole et al. suggested that group members may affiliate themselves with certain beliefs, subgroups, etc., and thus indicate group membership in other groups. These referent groups may be invoked to exercise power and influence over other group members.

It is at this microstructuration level that structurational interaction could be usefully integrated within the structuration perspective. Clearly, concepts of face, alignment, footing, bracketing, front and back regions and framing would be useful with respect to both negotiating roles and establishing agential coherence. For example, how important is face in group discussion and decision-making? Are negative face strategies "frowned upon" or invoked regularly? How is the overall discussion being "framed"—as a contest between two powerful group members? As the expression of preferences develop, how do various group members align, re-align and position themselves? How does the social positioning of group members change over time and over the discussion, and how do such changes influence group interaction? Through a close analysis of ongoing interaction, one could observe the steps in decision-making unfold, as well as reveal critical "fault lines" of conflict. Structurational interaction can also shed light on the mediation of structures as well as on contradiction, and incorporate the analysis of bodily movements, gestures, and artifacts as part of group interaction.

A further article on the use of structuration to build group theory by Poole, Seibold and McPhee (1986) developed a broader application of structuration to group processes. Social practices are used as a basic unit of analysis for group processes and located both temporally and spatially (Giddens, 1984), In addition, social practices are located institutionally: "Clusters of practices constitute institutions, and in turn institutions provide the milieu for practices" (Poole, Seibold & McPhee, 1986, p. 244). As an example of the impact of institutional context, they cited differences in decision-making between juries as opposed to informal groups of teachers. Their discussion also highlighted the complexity of social practices:

As a central feature of culture, they are tied in a multiplicity of ways to members' experiences and traditions. ... There will always be unarticulated features behind any account of practice, either lay or scientific. Our capacity to describe and express practices is also limited because they are social phenomena, constituted in interaction and subject to a tradition. ... The life of a practice consists not in being carried out by a particular set of members but by existing through many repetitions by many different subjects. ... Practices are constituted by individual activities, but they also transcend any particular individual, just as group practices may be instantiated in collective activity and yet transcend any particular group.

(p. 246)

In structurational interaction, agents use rules and resources to constitute social practices. As they observed, it is not very useful merely to list rules and resources— but, because "they are meaningful only in relation to other rules and resources in an ongoing practice, it is not only necessary but more informative to study structuration than to attempt to isolate static structures" (p. 248).

Poole et al. (1986) developed a template for developing a structurational account of group decision-making. They established five core questions, developed from structuration theory.

1. Key aspects of group decision-making must be identified, and interrelated with the three modalities of structuration;
2. Key aspects must then be studied as both the medium and outcome of the structuration of a group's decision or non-decision;
3. The positioning of the agent in structuration must be assessed;
4. How structures (for example, of signification, domination or legitimation) mediate one another must be shown; and
5. How contradiction influences any of the aforementioned elements or structures must be indicated. (pp. 253–54)

Poole's work on decision sequences and Seibold's work on argumentation and decision-making exemplify research focusing on a particular social practice, and isolate key factors for future studies. Or researchers can look at well-established variables in the literature and look at that through a structurational perspective (ibid., p. 255). In each of these areas, Goffman's interaction order can provide insight into how these interactional processes are carried out, how participants establish and shift positions, and so forth. This will be of particular value in more fully understanding micro-structurational processes.

Taken as a whole, the structurational approach developed by Poole, Seibold and McPhee offers very useful insights into structuration theory, and its utility in research focusing on group processes. Collectively, their work stands as a very clear statement of Giddens' structuration theory and provides a guideline for analyzing communicative phenomena. They concluded that "the structurational perspective requires a commitment to the development of complex, multilevel theories ... [and] to the programmatic research effort necessary to explore the complex of influences on structuration" (ibid., p. 262). Because a substantive amount of organizational activity is conducted within groups, it is even more important to understand group processes from a very rich theoretical base. In keeping with this, through structurational interaction, we can also develop a more complete, complex view of interaction, as well as account for the role of institutions in interaction. For example, how are group processes framed and altered by institutional type (e.g., governments, economic institutions, legal and judicial systems)? Or, when assessing social practices during group conflict, how do various group members align themselves, enact power and so forth? Through structurational interaction a richer, more detailed perspective on social interaction processes in organizing is possible.

Our next illustrative research example is not a programmatic line of research, but rather a study dealing with an important contemporary workplace issue—namely, the social practice of working at home. Brocklehurst (2001) contrasted the positions of Foucault and Giddens in an effort to account for the efficacy of working at home.

Exploring Power, Identity, and Work

Brocklehurst (2001) explored the shift of several employees from an office site to working at home. As he pointed out, organizations become "stretched" when employees work at home, at a place and time of their own choosing. New forms of organizing, like home-working, have been primarily evaluated from the perspective of management and of quality of work life. Yet research has also documented shifts in power and identity as a consequence of working at home. Using Giddens' concept of the dialectic of control, Brocklehurst examined the power dynamics in working at home.

In terms of self-identity, Brocklehurst utilized Giddens' concept of reflexive self-identity in which identity is routinely created and sustained by the individual's reflexive activities (Giddens, 1991a, pp. 36–38). When new work practices need to be established, how does that affect self-identity and one's position at work? When working at home, time and space are distanciated and work time/space becomes disembedded, with consequences for social practices in the workplace as well as at home. Such changes have created more fragmentation and uncertainty. In contrasting Foucault and Giddens, Brocklehurst suggested that Giddens focused on agents as knowledgeable and reflexive, whereas Foucault viewed an agent as being in a historically located disciplinary process (and thus less reflexive) (Brocklehurst, 2001, p. 449).

With respect to the dialectic of control, research findings indicated that management appeared to be "pushing" a shift to home work, and workers were expected to accommodate this. A reluctance to enthusiastically embrace home work was noted, and, in one case, a unit manager was ultimately removed from his management position. Supervisory surveillance by management was also reduced by home work.

The interactional dynamics of the work group changed as well, with most feeling that "team spirit" had been lost. There were no opportunities to share social chatter, and group members believed meetings were a waste because there was little sense of identification with the group. A few respondents reported "stopping in at the office" even though this was not expected or required. Management rarely called people at their homes, respecting the home as a back region. In general, the team's social integration was disrupted and fragmented.

Interestingly, workers altered their home work spaces in a number of different ways. Some set off separate work spaces, with one participant demanding the same office materials that were available at the office site. At the office site, offices were appropriated by other units, so that, even when home-workers stopped in at the office, there was literally no space for the group to meet.

Home-workers devoted significant time and effort to "recreating a work identity that was convincing both to themselves and to others" (p. 456). These efforts included crafting both space and time for work while at home. Discipline was needed to accomplish work, as many respondents mentioned distractions at home. Part of their identity struggle concerned finding a name, "flexible working," that had none of the negatives implicitly attached to work at home. Interview comments clearly demonstrated that home-workers felt a decrease in status as a result of the move. The emphasis of Giddens on routine was underscored by the current study in that workers tried to "recreate the very same routines in the home" (p. 459).

Brocklehurst concluded that both Foucault and Giddens provide valuable insights into the process of adjusting to working at home. Giddens' structuration model focuses attention on space and time distanciation, and the need for adapting workplace social practices. This research study could have been more insightful had Giddens' concept of agency been utilized—agents have the capacity to make choices (i.e., exercise power), and this was unexplored in the study. Most importantly, however, Brocklehurst overlooked the interaction dynamics that had radically shifted as a result of the work changes—no small talk, no personal or group spaces, no common time for interaction, and the lack of interaction itself.

One could argue, from structurational interaction, that social system integration was destroyed, and that by utilizing Goffman's interactional strategies, one could examine how the disintegration of interaction led to system disintegration. For example, frame analysis could look at different interpretive schemes, and discover how different stakeholders approached these issues. A closer analysis of space would reveal the difficulties in establishing work space at home, and separating various home regions. And, if employees developed different relationships, one could explore how that occurred via interaction. Identity issues could have been more closely scrutinized, particularly in terms of social positioning and the resulting alignment of workers. What does work mean in the context of work/life balance issues? Is it easier—or more difficult—to achieve balance working at home or at an office? Thus, structurational interaction would have enriched this study and its findings.

Working at home or, in the case of academics, often working at the office as well as at home, is clearly a growing trend, and one that will need careful exploration, particularly for purposes of making public policy recommendations in this area. Clearly, the national context surrounding work at home is relevant here (see Kirby, Wieland & McBride, 2006, for an excellent discussion of structuration theory and work/life conflict).

Our third study features an analysis of new technology and some of its implications. Weick (1990) viewed new technologies to be "technology as equivoque," having multiple uses with plausible alternative interpretations for them. As he demonstrated, sensemaking in technology use is a highly complex process, and subject to influence by existing social practices. As we have already seen, significant research from a structurational perspective has been conducted on new technologies, particularly information and communication technologies. Weick's analysis extends to technology in general.

Technology as Equivoque

Weick argued that "New technologies mean many things because they are simultaneously the source of stochastic events, continuous events, and abstract events. ... They make limited sense because so little is visible and so much is transient, and they make many different kinds of sense because the dense interactions that occur within them can be modeled in so many different ways. Because new technologies are equivocal, they require ongoing structuring and sensemaking if they are to be managed" (Weick, 1990, p. 2). He argued that we can best understand these complexities if we use structuration, affect, and premise control to understand them.

Past studies have emphasized structural constraints while "Structuration pays equal attention to both sides of that structuring process (constraining and being constrained)" (p. 18). Weick cited Barley's 1986 study of two hospitals whose radiology departments adopted CAT scanners. Introducing a new technology "ratifies or alters scripts that have grown up as a result of previous structuring" (p. 19). Both hospital departments drew upon past social practices of institutionalized signification, domination, and legitimation. In one hospital, "the traditional pattern of technicians' deference to professional radiologists proved inadequate ... because radiologists had only modest understanding of the technology. The puzzling technology introduced slippage between the idealized patterns of dominance and legitimation built up from past practice and the immediate problem of trying to discover what the novel diagnostic signs meant. Given this slippage, new patterns of action emerged and were incorporated into scripts that made a lasting change in institutional structure" (pp. 19–20).

Weick pointed out that understanding how new scripts were created involved looking closely at the scripts that emerged "from actions involving the new technology" (ibid.). A detailed examination of these strategies, evaluating how these strategies were framed by the participants, how bodily actions and gestures and use of space were coordinated, and so forth, could be effectively done by utilizing structurational interaction. Patterns of deference could be illuminated by using the concept of face, while interactional changes could be assessed by shifting alignment and footing. As Weick noted, structuration treats technology use as an "ongoing redefinition among structure, action, and technology" (p. 21).

Premise controls are of particular importance because they reflect "managerial psychosocial assumptions" which are incorporated into technological and organizational designs (p. 35). Social practices, many of them tacit, influence how the technology is approached and used. One important practice concerns decision premises, because much of the work in operating technology is mental, and influenced by how operators are viewed (controlled by a technical system, or as "learning, self-organizing, and committed elements") (p. 36). Such issues could be addressed by exploring the frames of meaning managers and technicians use to guide their actions (i.e., incorporating a Goffmanian analysis into a structurational approach).

Weick himself encouraged such a focus when he concluded that "interactive complexity can be a social construction, as well as an indigenous feature of new technologies ... in their complex equivocality, they force us to grapple with a key issue in technology—namely, how to apply perceptual perspectives to a material world" (p. 39). This latter point, "how to apply perceptual perspectives to a material work," I believe, is a driving force behind Latour's work and clearly an issue organizational scholars need to address. Implications for affect also are discussed, and could be assessed using structurational interaction. Insights on the self, and issues surrounding identity, will surface in any discussions of affect. Notably, issues of face, deference, tact and trust play key roles in affect. Shifting alignment between management and technicians could also be investigated by structurational interaction. As technology itself is "stretched," as in telemedicine, various social systems may shift alignment as well. In presenting a coherent approach to these issues, structurational interaction can enrich research on the analytic dimensions outlined by Weick. (See also Drazin, Glynn & Kazanijian, 1999.)

A Sociolinguistic Approach to Globalization

Our final study focuses on globalization and its effects. In an intriguing sociolinguistic approach to globalization (as exemplified in an analysis of multilingual classrooms), Blommaert, Collins and Slembrouck (2005) argued that "situation-sensitive expectations and judgments about [communicative] competence can occur at a variety of scales and in light of diverse framings of communication" (p. 212). They further noted that "space is context and therefore a potential for semiotization ... it must be seen as something which generates indexical meanings. Such meanings ... are *scalar*, they involve important differences in order and scope, some being purely situational and others translocal. Furthermore, what happens in interaction is the deployment of spatially organized—scalar—indexicalities in ways that both reflect pre-inscribed conditions of use as well as opportunities for the interactional construction of meaning" (p. 213).

Their sociolinguistic approach assumed that people's "use of language is strongly influenced by the situation in which they find themselves ... and knowledge of language is rooted in situation and dynamically distributed across individuals as they engage in practices" (p. 205). "Focusing on space inserts language into semiotic complexes, including participation frames, topics, genres of discourse, material and symbolic resources, and so forth" (ibid.). Work emphasizing situated practice found that "the knowledge trajectory from novice to expert requires participation in groups, often beginning on the 'periphery' of spatial-action configurations, and that such groups often constitute communities of practice, i.e. communities that construct themselves around certain spaces in and for doing something: making cloth, making computer software, learning not to be a problem drinker, or learning the world of romance in college" (p. 206).

Goffman, of course, "insisted on the central importance of co-present others in spatial arrays for the practice and meaning of speech" (ibid.). Goffman's frame and footing concepts complement an analysis of space in which people traverse different spaces over the course of daily activity. This is also strikingly parallel to Giddens' concept of time-space paths or trajectories. Bloomaert et al. noted that "'frame' is a spatial metaphor" connecting space as *already there* (spaces already designed for certain activities), and space as '*inhabited, appropriated, shaped and (re) configured by occupants*' for varied social activities" (p. 206). Thus, frames encompass the pre-situational as well as the situationally produced.

When frame and footing are combined, analysis can move "from the observations of physical space and its constraints, over participant-configured (culturalized) activity contours and frames of reference, to the production and interpretation of sequentially-implicated moves in interaction ... [and] brings out the complex dynamics of interdependent participation frameworks, as organised by, around and within spatial delimitations" (p. 206). A structurational analysis of frames is also implicated when they noted that "Frame analysis draws attention both to how physical spaces are part of the conditions for establishing social activities ... but views the establishment of social activities equally as outcomes of interaction. In this sense, frame is at once locus, outcome and focus of situated interaction" (p. 207). A further structurational component may be added by exploring differences in interaction, framing, and "scales" in different institutions, such as economic, educational, political or military institutions. Also, if globalization is part of the research context, then structurational interaction can usefully be employed to assess cultural differences in social practices, conflicts at time-space edges in transnational work contexts, and so forth. This, again, underscores the substantive links between Giddens and Goffman, and their compatibility in my proposed synthesis.

Bloomaert et al. concluded that scales, in the sense of context and indexicality, implied "delicate but highly meaningful distinctions in 'rank' for particular spaces and the activities and repertoires valid there … These distinctions involve power differences: the higher-scale resources would typically be seen as more useful, more valuable than the lower-scale resources" (p. 208). In addition, while Goffman's analytical distinctions (centre/margin, permanent/transient, simultaneous/interdependent and focus/background) are applied in settings of co-presence, they argued that these distinctions can be applied to other scales, for example, in classroom seating arrangements. Finally, since spaces "come with preliminary restrictions on participation and repertertoires [this] raises the question of inclusion and exclusion" (p. 209). Clearly, this is an important component of power in need of further research. Who regularly inhabits a space, as opposed to "users" of the space, and who thus exhibits more control over the frames and framing activities? For example, doctors versus patients, or administrators versus clients, or workers versus customers? (See also Bloomaert, 2005, 2007.)

Thus, Bloomaert et al's sociolinguistic approach is very compatible with structurational interaction. Incorporating structurational interaction would provide additional insight into culture, social practices and interaction. Taken together, these four studies could be further developed through the use of the proposed synthesis in the ways that have been suggested. This last study has raised the issue of globalization and, clearly, structurational interaction would provide interesting insights into culture and its influences (Goffman through his emphasis on micro-level interactions and context and Giddens with his concepts of distanciation, disembedding and historicity). For example, an intriguing study by Fabros (2009) explores contested identities (personal, local and global) among workers in a global call center.

The issue of globalization also raises the fundamental issue: what is culture? This issue is important generally, but especially because communicating and organizing is now global in scope and influencing our everyday social practices. Scholarly views of culture have traditionally associated culture with nation-states, but with globalization and increasing immigration worldwide, that perspective may no longer be very satisfactory. Particularly because groups can maintain close connections via the Internet and other forms of communication technology, no matter where group members are physically located. And such concerns can be insightfully explored through structurational interaction.

Examining Culture and Globalization

Social integration occurs through co-present, face-to-face (FtF) interaction: we learn language and are socialized via such interaction. However, even in such FtF contexts, identities may be shifting and altered by many influences (see, for example, the research on first-, second- and third-generation immigrants, and their experiences in adapting to a host culture). And Giddens' ideas clearly highlight increasing uncertainty, fragmentation, and risk in modernity, and thus raises questions about basic values and identities. In addition, people in countries worldwide are experiencing more alienation, especially in the younger generations.

Giddens suggested that societies (cultures) need to share a way of communication (usually language(s)), share a way of life/values, possess control over a territory and its resources, and identify with the group. Through distanciation of time and space, the global has become local and the local global, and thus lines of cultural demarcation have become blurred. In addition, through distanciation we also may be very committed to a group or society, although we are not co-present in that group. Although I believe we must shift away from the "control over territory" as a definition of culture, clearly it is still a vital issue as we witness continual conflicts over territories. A sense of identification with and commitment to a group seems essential, and with this in mind, it seems reasonable to assume that shared beliefs and identification might be core concepts for culture (see, for example, studies on self-construal in cross-cultural communication). If that is the case, then modern telecommunication systems have been essential in forming and maintaining those commitments. Clearly Giddens' insights have forced us to address new issues in defining culture and identity, and together Goffman and Giddens suggest, as I explain later in this chapter, examining issues of identity as well as presence and absence in new ways.

What, then, is Goffman's view of the connection between social interaction and culture? According to Gonos (1977):

> The notion of frame allows Goffman a much different picture of culture and its consistency. Everyday activities are not simple reflections of the broader culture's organization and values. The boundary, or "membrane," between a focused activity system and the wider society is a screen which "not only selects but also transforms and modifies what is passed through it" (Goffman, 1961a, p. 33). ... Social action is contained, then, within micro-structures that have an integrity as systems in their own right. Society is a "framework of frames" (Goffman, 1974).
>
> *(Gonos, 1977, p. 861)*

This membrane, the "framework of frames," sifts through to every interaction, and influences that interaction; in turn, those interactions instantiate and recursively influence the broader framework of frames. For both Goffman and Giddens, and thus the theory of structurational interaction, social interaction enacts culture, and cultural practices, in turn, shape interaction.

Through globalization and modern communication technology, cultures can be distanciated in both time and space. Members of Greenpeace, for example, may be considered a culture because they share commitment to and identification with that group, even though they are not physically co-present in a particular location. However, culture usually is viewed as influencing our basic communicating and organizing styles, and Greenpeace may not have that type of tacit, wide-ranging influence. Greenpeace may alter our behaviors, but not fundamentally shape our self-identities or social practices. Or perhaps Greenpeace, like nation-state views of culture, are aspects of our self-identities that shift as we occupy different time-space, social positions. At the very least, structurational interaction raises some very profound questions about culture and globalization.

Revisiting and Reframing Contemporary Issues in Organizing and Communicating

Revisiting Contemporary Issues

In what follows, I will revisit some core emergent issues in organizing and communication, and suggest new research directions and conceptualizations for exploring these issues from the perspective of structurational interaction. In reframing core issues, I will suggest some new conceptualizations of important communicating and organizing issues.

Identity. One of the significant emergent themes in organizational communication is a concern for identity—the construction of identity in the workplace and its relationship to other aspects of identity. In modernity, agents are confronted with a variety of lifestyle choices, and participate actively in constructing their identity. In contrast, traditional communities have a more fixed range of experiences and materials to develop self-understanding and construct identities (Giddens, 1991a).

Given the modern media of communication, social relationships and symbolic resources are frequently disembedded from local contexts, and provide common modes of action, interaction and experience. With the expanded choices available, agents self-construct their lifestyle and identities, and balance trust versus risk. Trust/risk is an issue for social integration as well as for system integration. Increasingly, the overarching frame for these choices in late modernity are universal symbolic tokens (such as money), the emergence of expert systems, and exposure to mass culture through the communication media. As Hay, O'Brien and Penna (1997) point out, agents are internally referential, and individual and institutional relations can "undergo profound change in the face of new knowledge and information" (p. 87).

For Giddens, the self becomes a narrative of the choices an agent makes, and the corresponding risks that were assumed. And the context of high modernity—characterized by industrialism, capitalism, militarism and surveillance—provides the framework for the negotiation of self-identity (Giddens, 1985a). Using Goffman to closely analyze these processes of identity negotiation can reveal how issues of trust and risk are resolved (see, for example, Olufowote, 2008).

Social relationships are significant factors in developing and maintaining identities, both personally and professionally (Christensen & Cheney, 1994; Scott & Myers, 2010). Part of our identity is likely to reside in our cultural affiliations, and Giddens' and Goffman's emphasis on world knowledge incorporates cultural knowledge in their perspectives.

In structurational interaction, identities are multiple, shifting, contextual, salient (at a given moment) and of varying duration. Scollon and Scollon (2001) call for research on how identities and meanings are constituted through interaction and encourage scholars to ask how participants make culture a relevant category in their interactions (also see Wiley, 2004 and Womack, 2008).

Our identities are those aspects of the self that we choose to reveal to others and to be held accountable for. Slater (2008, personal communication) points to the concepts of "uchi" and "soto" among the Japanese—both are aspects of the individual, but uchi remains private and soto refers to those aspects of identity made public. Soto and uchi vary across different settings and relationships, but both are aspects of the self. Among intimates, for example, we open more facets of our identities, and we choose to remain more constrained and less open to strangers. Identity thus can be viewed as a mosaic—a coherent, consistent matrix which reveals different facets of identity across different relationships and contexts.

A National Communication Association preconference, titled "The Meaning(s) of Work Across Time, Culture and Systems: Exploring Work's Meaning(fullness) for Organizational Communication Research and Practice," November 2007, raised some important concerns about identity and meaning at work. These concerns ranged from the constructing of identity among professionals, the meaningfulness of work itself, analyzing work in appropriate sociohistorical contexts, and tracing the evolution of work practices. Especially in a climate of uncertainty and risk (Giddens, 1990a, 1991a), identity and identification processes are increasingly important. Through structurational interaction, we can enrich our understanding of the sociohistorical contexts of identity work and our understanding of the interaction processes used in forming identities, their maintenance, and their alteration and change. (For an excellent overview of identity processes, see Cheney, Zorn, Planalp & Lair, 2008.)

Agency. One of the key issues in social theory, and in organizational communication generally, is the concept of agency. What is agency? How can agency be a collective act? For example, we speak of the federal government as having passed taxation reform, and bailed out financial institutions. In an insightful review of agency over time, Emirbayer and Mische (1998) articulate the different components of agency, and the relationships of agency and structure. Their final conceptualization is remarkably similar to Giddens' view of agency:

> [We] reconceptualize human agency as a temporally embedded process of social engagement, informed by the past (in its habitual aspect), but also oriented toward the future (as a capacity to imagine alternative possibilities) and toward the present (as a capacity to contextualize past habits and future projects within the contingencies of the moment). The agentic dimension of social action can only be captured in its full complexity ... if it is analytically situated within the flow of time. More radically, we also argue that the structural contexts of action are themselves temporal as well as relational

fields—multiple, overlapping *ways of ordering time* toward which social actors can assume different simultaneous agentic orientations.

(pp. 963–64)

Because agents can be oriented to time differently within a given situation, or change their temporal orientations across contexts, "varying degrees of maneuverability, inventiveness, and reflective choice [can be] shown by social actors in relation to the constraining and enabling contexts of action" (p. 964).

According to Emirbayer and Mische, the past is reflected in the interational aspect; the present reflected in the practical-evaluative aspect; and the future reflected in the projective element. These distinctions are analytic, and aspects of these three elements are present within any concrete action. Of particular interest is the interational aspect, or the past, which reflects the significance of habit and routine in institutions. They note, as do institutionalist theorists, that "Institutional decisions do not develop through rational cost-benefits analysis, but rather are embedded in established routines and become 'rationalized' (and thereby legitimated) only through retrospective accounting processes" (p. 983).

Their view, like that of Bourdieu and Giddens, also recognized the creativity and improvisation of agents' actions. They suggest that, with projectivity, actors may orient "to the past through a retrospective-prospective process of *identification,* in which possible trajectories are located against a backdrop of prior typifications from experience, and relationships to the present through *experimentation,* in which alternative courses of action are tentatively enacted in response to currently emerging situations" (p. 988).

They also acknowledge that the concept of framing is similar to projectivity, in that framing is both "*diagnostic* and *prognostic*" (p. 993). "In proposing new social ends as well as different means for arriving at them, actors draw upon—and sometimes extend, rearrange, and transform—the master frames extant in the broader political culture" (ibid.) A key factor in the practical-evaluative dimension of agency—the present—is in the contexts of social experience, especially interaction with others (p. 994). Agents' self-reflexivity allows for critical judgment and imagining alternative actions that may free them from past interactive patterns, and may reframe their relationships to the current context (p. 1010). Their views support Giddens' views on agency, particularly in their emphasis on timing, self-reflexivity, and the potential for creative responses. Their views also connect directly with Goffman's concept of frames. Thus, their views as well as the theory of structurational interaction provide a richer, more complete analysis of agency than other perspectives offer, and one that can incorporate agents' differing analyses of the same situation.

Structure, action and agency. Giddens' structuration theory has focused on structure and agency as mutually constitutive, and separated only analytically. Some critics, most notably Archer (1990), have suggested this reflected a "fallacy of conflation"— that, for Giddens, structure and agency are so closely interwoven that one cannot examine their interaction (pp. 75–80). However, Emirbayer and Mische (1998) pointed out that central-conflationists assumed that this "constitutive relationship is held analytically constant" and thus these critics had overlooked that the "agentic orientations of actors (along with their capacity for inventive or deliberative response) may vary in dialogue with the different situational contexts to which (and by means of which) they respond" (p. 1004). Emirbayer and Mische go on to suggest a *"double constitution of agency and structure:* temporal-relational contexts support particular agentic orientations, which in turn constitute different structuring relationships of actors toward their environments. It is the constitution of such orientations within particular structural contexts that gives form to effort and allows actors to assume greater or lesser degrees of transformative leverage in relation to the structuring contexts of action" (p. 1004). They suggested that the empirical challenge is to locate and predict the relationships between different types of agentic processes and particular structuring contexts" (ibid.). *This is precisely what is possible through structurational interaction.*

In my view, this perspective is entirely compatible with Giddens' views and, in fact, different kinds of agentic processes and structuring contexts of interaction are already part of structuration theory. Consider, for example, Giddens' discussions of differences in power; the effect of different frames of meaning; the influence of position-place; the differences Giddens draws between traditional and modern societies; and, most importantly, his foundational reliance on Goffman's interactional order, and the differences among interactants and contexts developed within Goffman's theory. All these point to more creative agency than either Goffman or Giddens is generally credited with—social life is *not* just reproduced, but it is constituted in many distinct ways. Emirbayer and Mische suggested, for example, that it would be of interest to explore what types of contexts encourage actors to respond in routine ways, and what types of contexts facilitate more imaginative responses. For example, such inquiries may lead to insights into how and why social movements occur, and what maintains, sustains and/or alters them (ibid.).

In an explicit application utilizing both Goffman and Giddens, they suggested that actors have multiple agentic orientations. As Emirbayer and Mische noted, "we must recall that actors are always simultaneously located in a variety of temporal-relational contexts at once; this is reminiscent of Goffman's (1974) stress upon the multiple embeddings of situations in *different frames or vantage points on action.* We can extend Goffman's imagery by suggesting that it is possible to be (primarily) iterational in one frame, projective in another, and practical-evaluative in yet a third. Moreover, a switch in frames can reveal apparent contradictions in the reproductive or transformative consequences of action" (p. 1008). For example, they suggested that some professionals, who are experiencing a great deal of career success, might be able to creatively solve emerging difficulties in the workplace. However, in reframing their actions, they might also be privileged with respect to other career trajectories in the same social-cultural milieu. By their actions, they may be unintentionally reproducing larger schemas, and reinforcing social, political, and economic contexts, which, however unfair they may appear to be when viewed from an expanded perspective nevertheless favor the actors within their own personal and professional lives" (p. 1009; see also Blair-Loy, 1997).

I might also point out that both Goffman and Giddens would acknowledge that different agents—in the same contextual circumstances—may frame their interactions quite differently. In addition, different agents, acting in the same manner in the same circumstances, may account for their behavior in very different ways. And, I would argue, as do Emirbayer and Mische, that these issues apply equally well to collective entities, and that more research is needed to connect individual trajectories with sociocultural, political and economic trajectories. As they cogently concluded, this approach places agency within its own sociohistoric context.

The role of the unconscious. Marshak, Keenoy, Oswick and Grant (2000) suggested that scholarship ought to examine the "inner worlds from which discourse springs" (p. 245). They cited Alvesson and Karreman's conclusion that the linguistic turn in social science research is "consistent with an understanding of language users as socially situated, discursively constituted, sensitive, and responsive to dominant cultural norms, social rules, and available scripts for talk, oriented toward the effects of language" (2000, p. 154). They went on to note that "The possibility that motivation and meaning may also be influenced by subliminal cues or situated in the unconscious is not mentioned" (ibid.).

Marshak et al., in commenting on work by Lakoff and Johnson (1999) on the cognitive unconscious, noted that they argue that "Most of our thought is unconscious, not in the Freudian sense of being repressed, but in the sense that it operates beneath the level of cognitive awareness, inaccessible to consciousness and operating too quickly to be focused on" (1999, p.10). Their examples, such as monitoring participants' body movements and planning responses, appear to blend Giddens' practical and discursive consciousness. Marshak et al. also noted that is possible to study these unconscious processes through secondary means, such as metaphor and archetypes.

While Goffman clearly eschewed Freud and much of psychoanalysis, both he and Giddens would acknowledge the importance of tacit knowledge and commonsense knowledge, some of which may be influenced by the unconscious. More importantly, Giddens recognized the importance of the unconscious as a source of deep-seated anxiety, and argues that we manage that anxiety through social practices and routines. Goffman's work suggests that we rely on social practices and routines to avoid embarrassment and shame, and thus reduce anxiety. Giddens also incorporated Erikson's developmental stages in his later work, especially with regard to the development of the self and identity. Negotiation of identity is clearly important in organizations, and over the life-span of an individual. Views of organizations as psychic prisons (Morgan, 2006) may be relevant to some of these issues of anxiety and embarrassment.

Metaphors appear to capture subjective experience. As Lakoff and Johnson noted, "metaphors are based in sensorimotor experiences that through conflation come to be associated with other types of subjective experience. ... In short, we are literally 'wired' metaphorically. More complex metaphors result from conceptual blending and combinations of simpler or primary metaphors" (Lakoff & Johnson, 1999, p. 255). They cited a number of studies (Inns, 1996; Keenoy, 1991; Marshak, 1998) that have utilized metaphors, such as the journey metaphor, in analyzing organizational discourse and management. This seems a very fruitful line of analysis compatible with structurational interaction.

Reframing Some Critical Issues

Some consistent themes have emerged in the context of organizing and communicating, many incorporating some aspect of the nature of organizations, of materiality, and of time and space. From the perspective of structurational interaction, I would like to reframe those issues and expand our consideration of them.

Organizing and organizations. Communication is constitutive of all shared, social activity; it is a necessary condition for shared activity, and, in some cases, may be sufficient as well. Communication is thus fundamental for both organizing and organizations. Language is fundamental for verbal communication, and language is always organized and organizing. However, not all organizing (a process) results in an organization (a product). If I "organize" a picnic, my closet, a lunch with a friend, a baseball game with friends and neighbors, or a date with my spouse, this is clearly organizing, but such social activities do not constitute organizations. Leaving aside issues about materiality and actants (e.g., having a picnic means acquiring food, probably from a grocery store, and a grocer, in turn, may purchase it from wholesalers), I think most would agree these activities are not organizations.

While the discipline has begun to address communication-as-constitutive-of-organizations, in my view we need to try to first resolve the question "What is an Organization?"—the question posed at an ICA pre-conference in May 2008. This preconference was subtitled "Materiality, agency and discourse." While these issues were addressed in the context of organizing and organization, only a few papers directly addressed the issue of what we mean when we speak of an organization. In this respect, "organization" has much the same conceptual status as "communication"—since everyone has extensive experience with it, most assume that the concept is not problematic. However, the concept most assuredly is problematic.

If, as I am arguing, communication is required for organizing, and organizing does not necessarily result in (an) organization(s), then, in addressing the issue of how communication-is-constitutive-of-organizations, we need to stipulate what an organization is. In teaching, one way I try to encourage students to conceptualize what constitutes an organization is to initially ask them a series of questions trying to unpack their assumptions about organizations. For example, is a family an organization? A golf frisbee team? Why or why not? A chapter by Taylor et al. (2001) called for the study of how we conceptualize organizations and distinguish among different types of organizations.

In Chapter 3 on organizing, I presented a set of characteristics that seem to reflect our disciplinary view of organizations. Among these characteristics were control, coordination, purposeful activity, members, identity, materiality, and so forth: these generic characteristics, while articulated in many different ways, can serve as a departure point for further refinement. If we use a naïve perspective, and utilize commonsense views of organizations—how *ordinary people* view organizations— then comparative analyses might lead to more insights not only about the generic qualities of organizations, but also about their *distinct organizational forms*. From lists of organizations, such as those by Taylor et al. (2001), or by Stohl and Cheney (2001), let us contrast NGOs with governments; churches with international organizations such as the UN; or military organizations with social movements. This appears to be useful, both for refining the generic properties of organizations as well as for distinguishing differences across organizational forms (by this last point, I am referring to distinct organizational *forms* as opposed to differences in size, complexity, product, and so forth). For example, DeSanctis and Poole (1997) present an excellent overview on emerging organizations under new capitalism— featuring fluid, flexible, client-centered, connected networks of coordinated activities.

On the basis of our discussions about organizations and their distinct forms, we can address the issue of how communication-is-constitutive-of-distinct-organizational-forms, and we can view the intersection of communicating and organizing in constituting organizations. Let us address, for example, the issue of what communicative processes support and maintain particular organizational forms. To remain at the more abstract level of communicating and organizing, while valuable, leaves us at a level of vague generalities which have little, if any, explanatory utility (i.e., because all organizing involves communication, and all language is organized). Textbook definitions of organizations, or definitions advocated by particular theoretical perspectives, may be too general, or too specific (linked to the theoretical perspective being argued), to be of great value. (However, see overviews of alternative approaches to studying organizational communication, such as Corman & Poole, 2000; Mumby, 1997; and Putnam & Nicoltera, 2010.)

As previously mentioned, the concept of frames may be a very useful lens for examining organizations. If we "frame" or "contextualize" an organization as cultural, is the communication of values a core communicative process in that organization? If we "frame" or "contextualize" an organization as structural, is communication a predominantly vertical, hierarchical process? We can use framing to examine the interaction in different types of organizations, such as multinational corporations, NGOs, governments, and other standard forms of organizations ("standard" organizations in the sense that substantive literatures about differences across these organizational forms already exist). Through structurational interaction, we can explore social interaction in multiple settings and at multiple contextual levels; with structurational interaction, the contextual lens becomes much broader, spanning organizations across sociohistorical contexts (for example, incorporating traditional, transnational and modern organizations as well as changes across organizations over time; see, for example, Orlikowski, Yates, Okamura & Fujimoto, 1995; Yates, 1994). Different types of institutions can also be examined. For example, is organizing significantly different in an institution which is predominantly a legitimation organization (like a legal system) as compared to an institution which is predominantly one of signification (like an educational system)? Given the emphasis on social practices in structurational interaction, organizations can also be analyzed in terms of their activities (see Goffman's situated activity systems) or practices. The added value of structurational interaction is a comprehensive, coherent integration of communicating, organizing and organizations that is not found elsewhere—and this, in my view, is a profound advantage. We can then ask how communicating is constitutive of particular organizing forms, and how those organizational forms shape and transform communicative processes. We may, in fact, learn that there are genres of communication that are linked to genres of organizations. (See Mayes, 2005, for an interesting example and discussion of genres.)

While a definitive answer to "what an organization is" may be an unattainable goal at present, we can learn much about organizations by pursuing the aforementioned ideas. Others are already pursuing this question from different perspectives. McPhee and Zaug's (2000) four flow model may have identified some universal communicative processes inherent in any organization. (See Fairhurst and Cooren, 2004, for an interesting discussion on organizing and organizations from an interactional perspective.)

Another intriguing approach was presented by Ahrne and Brunsson (2008) in which they evaluate organizations on their orderliness and completeness. As such, they rank organizations on the basis of their inclusion of elements such as membership, hierarchy, monitoring and sanctioning. They also made the interesting point that the concept of "organization" has been replaced by constructs such as institution, network, regulation, and governance. Finally, I think there is value in asking ordinary people about how they would define organizations. And, in addition, to learn what they associate with organizations—like jobs, careers, work (Keyton, Messersmith & Bisel, 2008), compensation, identity, prestige, boredom, meaning (Zorn & Townsley, 2008), and the like. If our theories are to be practical (Craig, 1999, 2007; Craig & Tracy, 1995), to be applied (Cheney, 2000, 2007; Emirbayer & Sheller, 1998) and to identify practices, this would seem to be a useful approach as well (see also Jian, 2008.)

Materiality, organizing and communicating. The importance of materiality in organizing and communicating has been increasingly acknowledged (see, for example, Cooren, 2004; Knorr-Cetina, 1999; Pickering, 1995). For Latour (1991), "The main difficulty of integrating technology into social theory is the lack of a narrative resource. We know how to describe human relations, we know how to describe mechanisms, we often try to alternate between context and content to talk about the influence of technology on society or vice versa, but we are not yet expert at weaving the two resources together into an integrated whole" (p. 111). Giddens

(1989) also argued that social structure cannot be embedded in the technology of any material entity that is apart from society. As Giddens noted, "structure is what gives *form* and *shape* to social life, but is not *itself* that form and shape—nor should 'give' be understood in an active sense here, because structure only exists in and through the activities of human agents" (Pentland & Feldman, 2007, p. 795). In order to fully understand organizing and communicating, a number of scholars have been arguing for the integration of the social and the material.

Orlikowski (2007) noted that materiality has either been ignored or focused on as a specific technology. As she remarked, this creates conceptual difficulties because technology is treated as a separate, distinct phenomenon, and is viewed in terms of its leverage (historical and social effects) or in terms of humans interacting with the technology in different contexts (and the technology "vanishes"). In contrast, she argued that "the social and the material are *constitutively entangled* in everyday life" and that "*every* organizational practice is *always* bound with materiality. Materiality is not an incidental or intermittent aspect of organizational life; it is integral to it" (p. 1436).

Orlikowski argued that both materials and realities are relational. As she commented, "Humans are constituted through relations of materiality—bodies, clothes, food, devices, tools, which, in turn, are produced through human practices … these entities relationally entail or enact each other in practice" (p. 1438). As a consequence, she argued that organizational practices should be viewed as sociomaterial practices (Suchman, 1987). Two research examples included a detailed discussion of Google, and the page rank system for weighting web links which is "dynamic, relational and contingent" and which depends upon relations across designers, users, engineers and others to produce ever changing sources of information" (p. 1438). A second example looked at how the use of Blackberries has transformed the information flow and connections in a small private equity firm such that continuous availability has become a communicative norm (and problematic for the firm because of organizational members' fatigue and resistance to the demands of continuous accessibility).

While structurational interaction would complement these approaches, especially the constitutive entanglement of the social and the material, I believe they would both reserve "agency"—the capacity to do otherwise—to humans. Goffman reflects a human-centric view of materiality in his work (although we cannot speak to what his views may have been now; no doubt they would have contained some very useful and entertaining insights). Giddens actively incorporated material resources into his model, and clearly acknowledged technological mediation and transformation in a number of areas. Structurational interaction would acknowledge the interaction of humans and materiality, in terms of both the human body itself and other material aspects. So generally the move toward more consideration of materiality in both organizations and social life would be compatible with structurational interaction. And, from Giddens' work, the time/space distanciation, disembedding, and re-embedding are concepts that will help advance future work in this area.

Presence and absence, time and space. While new technologies have been altering communication and transportation for several hundred years, the scale and pace of change seems radically faster these days. The standardization of time, instantaneous and mobile communication, the disembedding and re-embedding of people and organizations, the interrelatedness of economic and political forces, and the capacity to be both here and there, and now and then, with our telecommunication systems, have transformed our lives. All of this has profoundly altered opportunities for communicating and organizing, as well as having altered our views of what communicating and organizing entails.

Zhao (2004) established a useful typology of differing contexts of communicating across co-present interactants, as well as across telecopresent interactants (see Chapter 2 for a full discussion of this typology). Briefly, co-present individuals (consociates) share real time and geospace, and thus establish shared, subjective meanings (for example, family members, or individuals in a small firm located in the same place/space). Contemporaries are those who share world time, but not geospace (for example, contemporaries from another country or city), and share "objective meaning fields," such as trust in external systems like banks. Telecopresent individuals share cyberspace, but not geospace and thus are temporally linked. Increasingly, organizations will be the sites of multiple communicative contexts, like those of co-presence, consociates and telecopresence. What is needed is an analytic framework to deal with these variations, and the broader issues of time and space.

I believe that structurational interaction provides a framework for analyzing a range of contexts in which co-presence, presence, and absence vary. Co-presence is fundamental—the social integration of co-presence is necessary for social order and system integration. Child development occurs within the context of co-present children and adults (not necessarily parents); that is how we develop ontological security, self/other distinctions, identities, and social relationships. In the context of co-presence, we learn to adapt, accommodate, use material objects (resources), and develop our sense of our material bodies. (See, for example, the developmental work of Erikson, 1950 and Haslett & Samter, 1997.)

As interaction unfolds over time-space, humans encounter a multitude of interactional contexts, involving co-present and mediated interactions. Social positioning over our lifetime exposes us to multiple social relationships, and to shifting identities and affiliations in the modern context of uncertainty, risk, trust, and power (Giddens, 1990a, 1991a). Although beyond the scope of this book, structurational interaction also has profound implications for social relations, families and intimate relationships. (See, for example, Callahan, 2004; Giddens, 1991a; Giddens & Pierson, 1998; Hartel, Zerbe & Ashkanasy, 2005; Planalp & Gavin-Doxas, 1994.) Increasingly, our lives will reflect hybrid relationships—offline interaction intermingled with online connectivity. Structurational interaction provides a very useful platform for these studies, and may be one of its most significant contributions to communicating and organizing.

Within organizations, we experience the same varied contexts of interacting, sometimes within a single organization, or sometimes across a series of organizations involving intertwined processes of activity (or, as Engestrom, 1999, expressed it, producing an object). Time and space may be stretched and extended in different ways. People around the globe literally work around the clock—stockbrokers in NYC coordinate their actions to coincide with other markets across the world. Neighborhoods experience globalization through foreign products purchased at a local mall as well as through unemployment, because jobs have been outsourced overseas. What is "absent" (i.e., the production of goods and services elsewhere) is now "present" in the products available at the local mall. We also have, thanks to electronic communication, the ability to be continuously accessible (and therefore, in some sense, to be continuously "present" through this accessibility) even though we are absent (see Orlikowski, 2002, for an interesting example of being continuously available at work).

Our modeling of presence and absence is built upon a corporeal body, materially anchored in a locale, and thus experiencing real time and real space, either alone or with others. It seems clear that our sense of presence and absence may be extended by the use of various electronic communication devices, such as the telephone, video-conferencing, and the Internet. As Zhao (2004) noted, we now can speak about extended human perceptual senses and extended zones of operation. And we need to think about the implications of this extension of time and space, and of presence and absence, for organizing, communicating, organizations, and for social order generally. For example, a study by Fiol and O'Connor (2005) explored these differing contexts when they analyzed teamwork in the contexts of FtF, hybrid and virtual groups.

Contextualizing presence and absence, time and space. In the broadest sense of presence, structurational interaction incorporates sociohistorical contexts, including social, economic, military and political forces, and different types of institutions, including those of domination, signification and legitimation. At this level, we are primarily focusing on interorganizational communicating and organizational/environmental interaction, across a range of organizations, such as multinationals, governments, NGOs, and social movements. One interesting question to pursue would be how different genres of organizations organize and communicate, both within the organization, and with its various constituencies.

Presence, at this level, can be both material and/or nonmaterial. For example, a U.S. presence in the Gulf might consist of a fleet of ships located in the Gulf, continuous diplomatic missions throughout the region, or both of these as well as other initiatives. Presence could also be reflected in a world view which recognizes colonization as an important sociohistoric force and legacy, whether for good or ill, which influences a particular region. In this case, although some material presence is not there, a social influence—a social presence—is clearly perceived and has consequences for actions in the region. Presence, in both the material and symbolic sense, enters into the discourse of a community and forms part of the context in which people act. Within an organization, for example, "presence" may be reflected by sets of professional standards or "best practices" which may establish mental models for actions and discourse by organizational members. Texts may also take on different degrees of "presence" as organizational members make judgments about their interpretation and relevance to ongoing organizational activities.

Within an organization, face-to-device communication (FtD) may vary across different contexts, but the emphasis here is on dialogue. One could also envision situations in which there is shared time but not shared space, as in a class taught simultaneously at the University of Delaware and in Turkey. Through video-conferencing, the class shared real time; although cyberspace is shared, real space is not. As such, the stream of meanings created might be said to be subjectively shared, and dialogue is possible. A second situation might be that of shared time and space, where two colleagues are co-present, yet communicate using cyberspace. If these colleagues are using an Internet chat room, then their dialogue may be available to anyone sharing cyberspace at that time (or perhaps later, if messages are retained). A third situation might be the same two colleagues, this time in their respective offices, instant messaging one another, so there is shared time and cyberspace, but not geospace (i.e., physical co-presence). Goffman's work is already being used to analyze mediated communication across a range of contexts (see, for example, Jenkins, 2010; Ling, 2010; and Ross, 2007).

Other scenarios could be invented, but this gives a thumbnail sketch of the different types of organizing and communicating contexts we currently experience. Knorr-Cetina and Bruegger (2002) distinguished between an embodied presence and response presence, where the latter might not be visible to an observer. Yet we know little about the impact of these differing contexts—how do organizational members collaborate, cooperate, connect, conflict, and compete with each other in these contexts? (For excellent discussions of these and other related issues, see Buttny, 1993, and LeVine and Scollon, 2004. See Flanagin, Stohl & Bimber, 2006, for a discussion of different collective action spaces.) We also need to explore the interrelationships between humans and communication/information devices (i.e., the affordances of varied devices) so that their mutual entanglement might be better understood.

A starting point might be to contrast various face-to-device (FtD) interactions with face-to-face (FtF) interactions, and here of Goffman's interaction order provides an excellent analysis FtF interaction. Short, Williams and Christie (1976) did an interesting analysis of FtF as opposed to telephone and telegraph messages, and similar analyses, contrasting FtF interaction with FtD interaction, might be conducted. Clearly, FtF is the foundational context in which humans learn to communicate, so other forms of communication can be usefully contrasted with that basic framework. (See Katriel, 1991, for some interesting examples and suggestions on how our views of communication may be altered by FtD interaction.) Co-presence, of course, occurs with rich nonverbal, verbal and contextual information accompanying messages. Decades of research have chronicled differences in nonverbal channels of communication (Ekman, 1993; Izard, 2009) and nonverbal behaviors in different situations, like deception (Burgoon, Buller & Goodall, 1989). The construct of media richness (Daft & Lengel, 1984) argues that communication media, including FtF, offer differing degrees of richness in terms of their ability to present complex information.

In situations involving conflict and/or trust, people may feel most comfortable in FtF interaction because of their access to nonverbal cues of deception (i.e., nonverbal leakage). Goffman's concept of face has been extensively studied as part of approaches to conflict (Ting-Toomey, 2005; Tracy, 1990), as well as to interaction generally. Given the range of studies already conducted on FtF communication, we can begin to contrast FtF with FtD and, most crucially, begin to understand how they complement or conflict with one another in interaction.

Here are some of the questions we might explore. In negotiating, the Chinese have a marked preference for long-term interactions and FtF discussions. Would FtD communication—for instance, using videoconferenceing prior to FtF meetings—"substitute" for some of the FtF meetings? Does FtF communication generate loyalty and identity more than FtD communication among organizational members? Is FtF required for organizational identification and interpersonal trust? Under what circumstances would FtD communication be preferred to FtF interaction? In some organizations, if you do not have sufficient "face time" with others in the organization, are you perceived as not doing your job, or as not being committed to the organization? What type of interaction opportunities are found in virtual as opposed to FtF encounters? (See, for example, Fayard, 2007, on environmental affordances for informal interaction.) What are common expectations regarding email, or flaming (a tendency to become more critical and harsh in email versus FtF interaction)? Are the expectations to honor face a part of electronic communication expectations? While individuals may fabricate information (Goffman, 1974), is this fabrication more difficult to maintain FtF? How might it be detected in FtD communication?

Another aspect of FtD communication is its influence on social relationships. As we interact with one another, we build up shared subjective meanings and a sense of one another. These issues are currently being explored across a variety of communicating and organizing contexts—from the development of interpersonal relationships in social network sites to the establishment of trust in virtual teams. How does communicating and organizing vary across different communication media? Would degrees of interpersonal trust, self-disclosure, and authenticity in FtF differ from that in FtD communication? Certainly, the identities one can assume in real life are distinct from those which can be assumed in cyberspace, as we have seen in blogging, chat rooms, and so forth: real life offers checks and consequentiality that cyberspace does not. To use one of Zhao's examples, it would be very difficult for an obese woman to portray herself as a slender boy in real life. Although we are not concerned here with virtual reality, but with virtual organizations, we must be aware of shifts in how people connect with one another in FtD organizational settings as opposed to FtF settings, and explore the relational consequentiality of alternative means of connecting with one another, and the identities we thereby develop.

Giddens (1987a) forecast these issues when he noted that

> Interaction in contexts of co-presence obviously has characteristics not found
> in "mediated" interaction ... But it is a mistake to see these as two opposed
> forms of social connection ... each interfaces with the other in many subtle
> ways ... individuals experience different contexts of co-presence as episodes
> within the time-space paths they trace out in the course of their day-to-day
> activities. Mediation between contexts in this sense—that of the "moving
> presence" of actors across time-space paths—strongly influences the nature of
> encounters that are entered into. ...
>
> The study of the mechanisms of ensuring presence availability has to be
> closely tied to analyzing what goes on in situations of immediate co-presence.
> This means relating [the] sorts of discussion Goffman provides with more
> extended analyses of the nature of the locales and modes of regionalization
> whereby contexts of co-presence are conjoined.
>
> *(p. 137)*

Structurational interaction appears uniquely suited for such investigations with its
blend of detailed analyses of social interaction in both FtF and FtD contexts and
with its sociohistorical and social positioning analyses further detailing those contexts. Indeed, we already are immersed in a mediated world and experiencing many
"hybrid" relationships (offline and online connectivity).

Research on such topics would enable us to more fully understand communicative complexity and its influences on organizing and organizations. And structurational interaction is uniquely positioned as a "common ground" platform for
research, providing us with multiple points of entry (Corman & Poole, 2000); a
diverse array of methodologies; and a coherent, overarching framework in which to
frame programmatic lines of research. Structurational interaction allows us to probe
the contours of presence and absence, time and space, with a breadth and depth
other frameworks do not allow.

Some emerging concerns. Recent emerging issues include face and identity. The
concept of face is receiving considerable attention and structurational interaction can
contribute to this scholarship. Many scholars are utilizing Goffman's concept of face
and developing research programs from that perspective. (See, for example, Haugh &
Bargiela-Chiappini, 2010; specific articles on face in the *Journal of Pragmatics,* 2010,
and its special 2007 issue on face.) Also, new conceptualizations of face, such as
Arundale's Face Constituting Theory (2006, 2009, 2010), which is partially based
on Goffman's work, are directing increasing attention to this area.

Face is also related to issues concerning politeness (Haugh, 2007), impoliteness,
politeness in computer-mediated communication (Locher, 2010) and in the workplace generally (Stewart, 2008). Some of this work on face and politeness has also
utilized a frame approach (Terkourafi, 2005).

Identity has also become a significant research issue as scholars deal with shifting,
multiple identities in conditions of uncertainty and risk. Structurational interaction

can contribute to these issues through the concepts of the self, ontological security, time-space positioning, face and historicity. Each of the major identity issues posed by Alvesson, Ashcraft and Thomas (2008)—those of why, who, what, when, where and how—can be addressed through structurational interaction and stimulate further research. Cross-cultural research in identity (Essers & Benschop, 2009) or examining identity in terms of personal predicaments (Watson, 2006, 2008) are research exemplars compatible with structurational interaction. Of special interest are approaches to identity which focus on self-other dialogue as an important source of identity development (Ybema et al., 2009). The importance of one's work identities, and the importance and meaningfulness of work itself, are important components of research on identity.

In conclusion, we might ask: What is the added value of structurational interaction in analyzing communicating and organizing? Extant research has generally focused on either communicating or organizing, and rarely incorporated each process in their research analyses. A major advantage of structurational interaction is that it integrates both aspects—organizing and communicating—into a coherent, comprehensive theoretical framework. This holistic, unified theory engenders a richer, fuller understanding of communicating, organizing and their interrelationships. Structurational interaction does not privilege either process, but focuses on how they mutually shape one another.

Scholars can utilize structurational interaction as a metatheory, or aspects of this theory can be used to generate new theoretical approaches. In addition, structurational interaction enables multiple points of entry and the use of multiple methodologies (i.e., qualitative, quantitative or critical) for scholarly analysis. Finally, structurational interaction is centered upon social practices and how those social practices are created, instantiated, reproduced and altered through discourse. In brief, structurational interaction provides a very powerful explanatory and analytic base from which to explore communicating and organizing. (For an example of a similar generative, metatheoretical orientation to the one proposed here, see Ridgeway, 1994, 2006, who conceptually links social structure and interpersonal behavior through ordering schemas, such as cultural schemas.)

Underlying assumptions for both communicating and organizing have been developed. The framing and reframing of context has been used to explain the levels or layering of organizations, and their interconnections. Frames may reflect actors' tacit knowledge and interpretive schemes, but these frames are discursively grounded: frames must be invoked (i.e., made relevant) through interaction and such frames may shift and be altered by interaction. Thus we have frames as knowledge structures but also frames in use which are fluid and changing in an interactional context. The centrality of social practices has been developed, and its role in constituting interactional routines and organizations clarified. Critical concepts such as agency, intentionality, context, tacit knowledge, the self, identity and relevance have also been developed.

Critical issues for organizational communication, among them issues of agency, materiality, time, space, power and texts, have been addressed and structurational interaction, as already demonstrated, can contribute substantively to the discussion of these issues. Time and space are fundamental concepts in structurational interaction and facilitate our understanding of time-space distanciation, the use of space as regions of activity, the use of space and material objects by interactants, social positioning across one's life-span and how interaction is sedimented in sociohistorical contexts. In the transition from tribal to traditional to modern societies, we also have a deeper understanding of the nature of social systems in those contexts as well as an understanding of the different types of institutions and organizations that emerge. In our modern era, structurational interaction provides insights into how globalization, new technologies and transportation have transformed both our personal and professional lives. The tensions and contradictions at time-space edges, where social systems, social relationships and social practices diverge, can be usefully investigated by structurational interaction.

In particular, emergent issues such as globalization, culture, multiple identities, trust, risk and emotion are also addressed by structurational interaction. Globalization has raised significant issues about the nature of culture, multiple and shifting identities, and the tensions of disembedded and re-embedded social relationships and social systems. Structurational interaction will also contribute significantly to discussions of FtF and FtD communication—which at present is transforming everyday life and will become an increasingly important area for future research.

The question of added value is clearly answered with a resounding yes. The theory of structurational interaction, as well as continued study of both Giddens' and Goffman's work, will advance our knowledge of organizing, communicating and their interrelationships. And it will continue to generate new theoretical approaches and insight into emerging issues.

As Clair (1999) noted,

> Communication—the narratives and the anecdotes, the traits and the styles, the monologues and the dialogues, the metaphors and the ceremonies, the colloquialisms and memorable messages, the strategically ambiguous and the outright deceptions, the decisions, the sarcasm, the irony, the promises, the voices, the images, the humor, the language and the silence of it all— exists simultaneously with organization. Organization—the production, the structure, the agency, the function, the connections, the relations, the economics, the needs, the corporations, the gangs, the rules, the resources, the consumption and commodification, the means and the methods—exist simultaneously with communication. They give life to each other. As the light gives substance to the shadows, the shadows define the light.
>
> *(p. 289)*

And, as I have attempted to demonstrate, structurational interaction illuminates both the light and the shadows.

REFERENCES

Aarsand, P. (2008). Frame switches and identity performances: Alternating between online and offline. *Text and Talk, 28*(2), 147–65.

Ahrne, G., & Brunsson, N. (2008). *Meta-organizations*. Cheltenham, UK: Edward Elgar.

Akman, V. (2000). Rethinking context as a social construct. *Journal of Pragmatics, 32*(6), 743–59.

Allon-Souday, G., & Kunda, G. (2003). The local selves of global workers: The social construction of national identity in the face of organizational communication. *Organization Studies, 24*(7), 1073–96.

Alvesson, M. (2010). Self-doubters, strugglers, storytellers, surfers and others. *Human Relations, 63*(2), 193–217.

Alvesson, M., Ashcraft, K., & Thomas, R. (2008). Identity matters: Reflections on the construction of identity scholarship in organization science. *Organization, 15*(1), 5–28.

Alvesson, M., & Karreman, D. (2000a). Taking the linguistic turn in organizational research. *Journal of Applied Behavioral Science, 36*(2), 136–58.

Alvesson, M., & Karreman, D. (2000b). Varieties of discourse: On the study of organizations through discourse analysis. *Human Relations, 53*(9), 1125–49.

Ancona, D., Goodman, P., Lawrence, B., & Tushman, M. (2001). Time: A new research lens. *Academy of Management Review, 26*(4), 645–63.

Anderson, R. J., Hughes, J. A., & Sharrock, W. W. (1987). Executive problem finding: Some material and initial observations. *Social Psychology Quarterly, 50*(2), 143–59.

Andersson, L. M., & Pearson, C. M. (1999). Tit for tat? The spiraling effect of incivility in the workplace. *Academy of Management Review, 24*(3), 452–71.

Aoki, P. M. (2007). Back stage on the front lines: Perspectives and performance in the combat information center. *CHI 2007*, San Jose, California. 717–26.

Archer, M. (1990). Human agency and social structure: A critique of Giddens. In J. Clark, C. Modgil, & S. Modgil (Eds.), *Consensus and controversy: Anthony Giddens*. London, UK: Falmer Press.

Argyris, C., & Schon, D. A. (1996). *Organizational learning, Vol. 2: Theory, method and practice*. Reading, MA: Addison-Wesley.

Arrow, H., Poole, M., Henry, K., Wheelan, S., & Moreland, R. (2004). Time, change, and development: The temporal perspective on groups. *Small Group Research, 35*(1), 73–105.

Arundale, R. (2006). Face as relational and interactional: A communication framework for research on face, facework, and politeness. *Journal of Politeness Research, 2*, 193–216.

Arundale, R. (2009). Face as emergent in interpersonal communication: An alternative to Goffman. In F. Barqiela-Chiappini, & M. Haugh (Eds.), *Face, communication, and social interaction* (pp. 37–53). London: Equinox.

Arundale, R. (2010). Constituting face in conversation: Face, facework, and interactional achievement. *Journal of Pragmatics, 42*(8), 2078–2105.

Ashforth, B. E., & Kreiner, G. E. (1999). "How can you do it?": Dirty work and the challenge of constructing a positive identity. *Academy of Management Review, 24*(3), 413–34.

Bacharach, S., & Lawler, E. (1980). *Power and politics in organizations.* San Francisco, CA: Jossey-Bass.

Backhaus, G. (1997). The phenomenology of telephone space. *Human Studies, 20,* 203–20.

Ballard, D. (2008). *Through time and space: Organizational communication message flows then and now.* Paper, Organizational Communication, Alta, UT.

Ballard, D., & Seibold, D. (2000). Time orientation and temporal variation across work groups: Implications for group and organizational communication. *Western Journal of Communication, 64,* 218–42.

Ballard, D., & Seibold, D. (2003). Communicating and organizing in time: A meso-level of organizational temporality. *Management Communication Quarterly, 16*(3), 380–415.

Banks, S., & Riley, P. (1993). Structuration theory as an ontology for communication research. In S. Deetz (Ed.), *Communication Yearbook, Vol. 16.* (pp. 167–96). Newbury Park, CA: Sage.

Baptista, L. (2003). Framing and cognition. In A. Trevino (Ed.), *Goffman's legacy* (pp. 197–215). New York, NY: Rowman & Littlefield.

Barbour, J., & Lammers, J. (2007). Health care institutions, communication, and physicians' experience of managed care: A multilevel analysis. *Management Communication Quarterly, 21*(2), 201–31.

Bargiela-Chiappini, F. (2003). Face and politeness: New (insights) for old (concepts). *Journal of Pragmatics, 35,* 1453–69.

Bargiela-Chiappini, F., Chakron, O., Lay, G., Jung, Y., Kong, K., Nair-Venugopal, S., et al. (2007). Eastern voices: Enriching research on communication in business: A forum. *Discourse and Communication, 1*(2), 131–52.

Bargiela-Chiappini, F., & Harris, S. (2006). Politeness at work: Issues and challenges. *Journal of Politeness Research, 2,* 7–33.

Bargiela-Chiappini, F., & Haugh, M. (Eds.) (2009). *Face, communication and social interaction.* London: Equinox.

Barley, S. (1986). Technology as an occasion for structuring: Evidence from observation of CT scanners and the social order of radiology departments. *Administrative Science Quarterly, 31,* 78–108.

Barley, S. (1990). The alignment of technology and structure through roles and networks. *Administrative Science Quarterly, 35*(1), 61–103.

Barley, S. (1996). Technicians in the workplace: Ethnographic evidence for bringing work into organizational studies. *Administrative Science Quarterly, 41,* 404–41.

Barley, S., & Tolbert, P. S. (1997). Institutionalization and structuration: Studying the links between action and institution. *Organization Science, 18*(1), 93–117.

Bartlett, F. (1932). *Remembering.* Cambridge, UK: Cambridge University Press.

Bastien, D., McPhee, R., & Bolton, K. (1995). A study and extended theory of the structuration of climate. *Communication Monographs, 62,* 87–109.

Bateson, G. (1972). *Steps to an ecology of mind.* New York, NY: Ballantine.

Bateson, G. (1976). A theory of play and fantasy. In J. Bruner, A. Jolly, & K. Sylva (Eds.), *Play: Its role in evolution and development.* London, UK: Penguin.

Battershill C. (1990). Goffman as a precursor to post-modern sociology. In S. Riggins (Ed.), *Beyond Goffman.* New York: deGruyter.

Bavelas, J. (1999). Come the millennium. *Research on Language and Social Interaction, 32*(1–2), 5–10.

Baxter, L., Braithwaite, D., & Nicholson, J. (1999). Turning points in the development of blended families. *Journal of Social and Personal Relationships, 16,* 291–313.

Bazarova, N., & Walther, J. (2009). Attributions in virtual groups. *Small Research Group, 40*(2), 138–62.

Becker, H. (2003). The politics of presentation: Goffman and total institutions. *Symbolic Interaction, 26*(4), 659–69.

Beckert, J. (1999). Agency, entrepreneurs, and institutional change: The role of strategic choice and institutionalized practices in organizations. *Organization Studies, 20*(5), 777–99.

Beech, N., & Huxham, C. (2003). Cycles of identity formation in interorganizational collaborations. *International Studies of Management and Organizations., 33*(3), 28–52.

Benford, R., & Snow, D. (2000). Framing processes and social movements: An overview and assessment. *Annual Review of Sociology, 26,* 611–39.

Berends, H., Boersma, K., & Weggman, M. (2003). The structuration of organizational learning. *Human Relations, 56*(9), 1035–56.

Berger, C. (1994). Power, dominance, and social interaction. In M. Knapp, & G. Miller (Eds.), *Handbook of interpersonal communication.* Beverly Hills, CA: Sage.

Berger, C., & Bradac, J. (1982). *Lanaguage and social knowledge: Uncertainty in interpersonal relationships.* London, UK: Edward Arnold.

Bernstein, B. (1977). *Class, control and codes: Vol. 3.* London: Routledge & Kegan Paul.

Bertilsson, M. (1997). The theory of structuration: Prospects and problems. In C. Bryant, & D. Jary (Eds.), *Anthony Giddens* (Vol. 1, pp. 44–60). New York: Routledge.

Bimber, B., Flanagin, A. J., & Stohl, C. (2005). Reconceptualizing collective action in the contemporary media environment. *Communication Theory, 15*(4), 365–88.

Birdwhistell, R. (1970). *Kinesics and context.* Philadelphia, PA: University of Pennslyvania Press.

Bisel, R. (2009). On a growing dualism in organizational discourse research. *Management Communication Quarterly, 22*(4), 614–38.

Bisel, R. (2010). A communicative ontology of organization? A description, history, and critique of CCO theories for organization science. *Management Communication Quarterly, 24*(1), 124–31.

Blackmore, D. (2001). Discourse and relevance theory. In D. Schiffrin, D. Tannen, & H. Hamilton (Eds.), *The handbook of discourse analysis* (pp. 100–118). Oxford: Blackwell.

Blair-Loy, M. (1997). *Career patterns of executive women in finance: An optimal matching analysis.* Unpublished manuscript.

Bleicher, J., & Featherstone, M. (1997). Historical materialism today: An interview with Anthony Giddens. In C. Bryant, & D. Jary (Eds.), *Anthony Giddens: Critical assessments, Vol. 1* (pp. 19–22). New York: Routledge.

Blommaert, J. (2005). *Discourse: A critical introduction.* Cambridge: Cambridge University Press.

Blommaert, J. (2007). Sociolinguistic scales. *Intercultural Pragmatics, 4,* 1–19.

Blommaert, J., Collins, J., & Slembrouck, S. (2005). Spaces of multilingualism. *Language and Communication, 25,* 197–216.

Boden, D. (1994). *The business of talk: Organizations in action.* Cambridge, MA: Harvard University Press.

Boden, D., & Molotch, H. (1994). The compulsion to proximity. In R. Friedland and D. Boden (Eds.), *Nowhere: Space, time and modernity.* Berkeley: University of California Press.

Bolman, L., & Deal, R. (2008). *Reframing organizations* (4th ed.). San Francisco: Jossey-Bass.

Bonito, J., & Sanders, R. (2002). Speakers' footing in a collaborative writing task: A resource for addressing disagreement while avoiding conflict. *Research on Language and Social Interaction, 35*(4), 481–514.

Bourdieu, P. (1977). *Outline of a theory of practice*. Cambridge, MA: Cambridge University Press.

Bourdieu, P. (1990). *The logic of practice*. Stanford, CA: Stanford University Press.

Bourdieu, P. (1994). Structure, habitus, power: Basis for a theory of symbolic power. In N. Dirks, & G. Eley (Eds.), *Culture, power/history: A reader in contemporary social theory* (pp. 155–99). Princeton, NJ: Princeton University Press.

Bourdieu, P. (2000). Erving Goffman: Discoverer of the infinitely small. In G. A. Fine, & G. Smith (Eds.), *Erving Goffman, Vol. 1* (pp. 3–4). Thousand Oaks, CA: Sage.

Boyle, M. (2005). "You wait until you get home:" Emotional regions, emotion process work, and the role of onstage and offstage support. In C. Hartal, W. Zerbe, & N. Ashkansay (Eds.), *Emotions in organizational behavior.* (pp. 45–66). Mahwah, NJ: Lawrence Erlbaum Associates.

Branaman, A. (1997). Goffman's social theory. In C. Lemert, & A. Branaman (Eds.), *The Goffman reader* (pp. xiv–lxxiii). Oxford, UK: Blackwell.

Branaman, A. (2003). Interaction and hierarchy in everyday life. In A. J. Trevino (Ed.), *Goffman's legacy* (pp. 86–126). New York, NY: Rowman & Littlefield.

Branaman, A. (2010). The protean Goffman: Erving Goffman and the new individualism. In M. Jacobsen (Ed.), *The contemporary Goffman* (pp. 232–56). New York, NY: Routledge.

Bransford, J., & McCarrell, N. (1977). A sketch of a cognitive approach to comprehension: Some thoughts about understanding what it means to comprehend. In P. Johnson, & P. Wason (Eds.), *Thinking: Readings in cognitive science*. Cambridge, UK: Cambridge University Press.

Brocklehurst, M. (2001). Power, identity and new technology homework: Implications for "new forms" of organizing. *Organization Science, 22*(3), 445–66.

Brown, K. J. (2000). *Communicating face: Exploring face performance in an organizational society*. Unpublished PhD dissertation, Salt Lake City, UT.

Brown, P., & Levinson, S. (1987). *Politeness: Some universals in language usage*. Cambridge, UK: Cambridge University Press.

Browning, L., & Beyer, J. (1998). The structuring of shared voluntary standards in the U.S. semiconductor industry: Communicating to reach agreement. *Communication Monographs, 64*, 1–25.

Bruner, J. (1990). *Acts of meaning*. Cambridge, MA: Harvard University Press.

Bryant, C. (1992). Sociology without philosophy? The case of Giddens' structuration theory. *Sociological Theory, 10*(2), 137–49.

Bryant, C., & Jary, D. (1991). Introduction. In C. Bryant, & D. Jary (Eds.), *Giddens' theory of structuration: A critical appreciation* (pp. 1–31). London, UK: Routledge.

Bryant, C., & Jary, D. (1997b). General introduction. In C. Bryant, & D. Jary (Eds.), *Anthony Giddens: Critical assessments, Vol. 1* (pp. 1–18). New York: Routledge.

Bryant, G., & Jary, D. (2000). Anthony Giddens. In G. Ritzer (Ed.), *The Blackwell companion to major social theorists*. Oxford: Blackwell.

Bryant, C., & Jary, D. (2001a). Anthony Giddens: A global social theorist. In C. Bryant, & D. Jary (Eds.), *The contemporary Giddens* (pp. 3–39). New York, NY: Palgrave.

Bryant, C., & Jary, D. (2001b). The body, self-identity and social transformation. In C. Bryant, & D. Jary (Eds.), *The contemporary Giddens.* (pp. 115–28). New York, NY: Palgrave.

Bryant, C., & Jary, D. (2001c). The reflexive Giddens: C. G. A. Bryant and David Jary in dialogue with Anthony Giddens. In C. Bryant, & D. Jary (Eds.), *The contemporary Giddens* (pp. 229–67). New York, NY: Palgrave.

Burgoon, J., & Bacue, A. (2003). Nonverbal communication skills. In J. Greene, & B. Burleson (Eds.), *Handbook of communication and social interaction skills.* (pp. 179–220). Mahwah, NJ: Lawrence Erlbaum Associates.

Burgoon, J., Guerrero, L., & Floyd, K. (2010). *Nonverbal communication*. Boston, MA: Pearson Education.

Burgoon, J., Buller, D., & Goodall, W. G. (1989). *Nonverbal communication: The unspoken dialogue.* New York: Harper & Row.

Burkhalter, S., Gastil, J., & Kelshaw, T. (2006). A conceptual defintion and theoretical model of public deliberation in small face-to-face groups. *Communication Theory, 12*(4), 398–422.

Burns, T., & Stalker, G. (1961). *The management of innovation.* London: Tavistock.

Butler, J., & Modaff, D. (2008). When work is home: Agency, structure, and contradictions. *Management Communication Quarterly, 22*(2), 232–57.

Buttny, R. (1993). *Social accountability in communication.* Newbury Park, CA: Sage.

Buttny, R. (1998). Putting prior talk into context: Reported speech and the reporting context. *Research on Language and Social Interaction, 31*(1), 45–58.

Buttny, R., & Morris, G. H. (2001). Accounting. In W. P. Robinson, & H. Giles (Eds.), *The new handbook of language and social psychology* (pp. 285–301). Chichester, UK: Wiley.

Button, G. (1987). Answers as interactional products: Two sequential practices used in interviews. *Social Psychology Quarterly, 50*(2), 160–71.

Callahan, J. (2004). Reversing a conspicuous absence: Mindful inclusion of emotion in structuration theory. *Human Relations, 57*(11), 1427–48.

Canary, D., Cody, M., & Manusov, V. (2008). *Interpersonal communication: A goals-based approach.* (4th ed.). New York, NY: St. Martin's Press.

Canary, H. (2010). Structurating activity theory: An integrative approach to policy knowledge. *Communication Theory, 20*(1), 21–49.

Canary, H., & McPhee, R. (2009). The mediation of policy knowledge: An interpretive analysis of intersecting activity systems. *Management Communication Quarterly, 23*(2), 147–87.

Cantor, N., Mischel, W., & Schwartz, J. C. (1982). A prototype analysis of psychological situations. *Cognitive Psychology, 14*, 45–77.

Carbaugh, D. (1989). *Talking American: Cultural discourses on Donahue.* Norwood, NJ: Ablex Publishing Corporation.

Carbaugh, D. (1996). *Situating selves: The communication of social identities in American scenes.* Albany, NY: State University of New York.

Carbaugh, D. (2005). *Cultures in conversation.* Mahwah, NJ: Lawrence Erlbaum Associates.

Carbaugh, D., & Berry, M. (2001). Communicating history, Finnish and American discourses: An ethnographic contribution to intercultural communication inquiry. *Communication Theory, 11*(3), 352–66.

Case, P., & Pineiro, E. (2006). Aesthetics, performaticity, and resistance in the narratives of a computer programming community. *Human Relations, 59*(6), 753–82.

Castor, T., & Cooren, F. (2006). Organizations as hybrid forms of life: The implications of the selection of agency in problem formulation. *Management Communication Quarterly, 19*(4), 570–600.

Chae, B., & Poole, M. (2005). The surface of emergence in systems development: Agency, institutions, and large-scale information systems. *European Journal of Information Systems, 14*, 19–36.

Chafe, W. (1977). Creativity in verbalization and its implications for the nature of stored knowledge. In R. Freedle (Ed.), *Discourse production and comprehension.* Norwood, NJ: Ablex.

Chen, V. (1990). Mien tze at the Chinese dinner table: A study of the interactional accomplishment of face. *Research on Language and Social Interaction, 24*, 109–40.

Cheney, G. (2000). Thinking differently about organizational communication: Why, how, and where? *Management Communication Quarterly, 14*(1), 132–41.

Cheney, G. (2007). Organizational communication comes out. *Management Communication Quarterly, 21*(1), 80–91.

Cheney, G., & Tompkins, P. (1987). Coming to terms with organizational identification and commitment. *Central States Speech Journal, 38*, 1–15.

Cheney, G., Zorn, T., Planalp, S., & Lair, D. (2008). Meaningful work and personal/social well-being: Organizational communication engages the meaning of work. In C. Beck (Ed.), *Communication Yearbook, 32* (pp. 137–85). Thousand Oaks, CA: Sage.

Chia, R. (2000). Discourse analysis as organizational analysis. *Organization, 7*(3), 513–18.

Child, J., & Shumate, M. (2007). The impact of communal knowledge repositories and people-based knowledge management on perceptions of team effectiveness. *Management Communication Quarterly, 21*(1), 29–54.

Chreim, S. (2006). Managerial frames and institutional discourses of change: Employee appropriation and resistance. *Organizational Studies, 27*(9), 1261–87.

Chriss, J. (1995). Habermas, Goffman and communicative action: Implications for professional practice. *American Sociological Review, 60*(4), 545–65.

Chriss, J. (1999). Role distance and the negational self. In G. Smith (Ed.), *Goffman and social organization.* (pp. 64–80). New York: Routledge.

Chriss, J. (2000). Habermas, Goffman, and communicative action: Implications for professional practice. In G. A. Fine, & G. Smith (Eds.), *Erving Goffman, Vol. 4* (pp. 262–90). London, Thousand Oaks, New Delhi: Sage.

Chriss, J. (2003). Goffman as microfunctionalist. In A. Trevino (Ed.), *Goffman's legacy.* (pp. 181–96). New York: Rowman & Littlefield Publishers.

Christensen, L., & Cheney, G. (1994). Articulating identity in an organizational age. In S. Deetz (Ed.), *Communication Yearbook 17* (pp. 222–35). Thousand Oaks, CA: Sage.

Cicourel, A. (1980). Three models of discourse analysis: The role of social structure. *Discourse Processes, 3,* 101–32.

Cicourel, A. (1987). The interpenetration of communicative contexts: Examples from medical encounters. *Social Psychology Quarterly, 50*(2), 217–26.

Cicourel, A. (1992). The interpretation of communicative contexts. In A. Duranti, & C. Goodwin (Eds.), *Rethinking context* (pp. 291–310). Cambridge: Cambridge University Press.

Clair, R. (1993). The use of framing devices to sequester organizational narratives: Hegemony and harassment. *Communication Monographs, 60,* 113–36.

Clair, R. (1999). Standing still in an ancient field: A contemporary look at the organizational communication discipline. *Management Communication Quarterly, 13*(2), 283–93.

Clark, H., & Clark, E. (1977). *Psychology and language.* New York, NY: Harcourt Brace Jovanovich.

Clark, T., & Mangham, I. (2004). From dramaturgy to theatre as technology: The case of corporate theatre. *Journal of Management Studies, 41*(1), 37–59.

Clark, T., & Salaman, G. (1996). Creating the "right" impression: Towards a dramaturgy of management consultancy. *Service Industries Journal, 18*(1), 18–38.

Cohen, I. (1990a). Structuration theory and social order: Five issues in brief. In J. Clark, C. Modgil, & S. Modgil (Eds.), *Anthony Giddens: Consensus and controversy* (pp. 33–45). London, UK: Falmer Press.

Cohen, I. (1990b). Interchange: Cohen replies to Stinchcombe. In J. Clark, C. Modgil, & S. Modgil (Eds.), *Anthony Giddens: Consensus and controversy* (pp. 57–59). London, UK: Falmer Press.

Collins, R. (1980). Erving Goffman and the development of modern social theory. In J. Ditton (Ed.), *The view from Goffman* (pp. 170–209). New York, NY: St. Martin's Press.

Collins, R. (1986). The passing of intellectual generations: Reflections on the death of Erving Goffman. *Sociological Theory, 4*(1), 106–13.

Collins, R. (1988). Theoretical continuities in Goffman's work. In P. Drew, & A. Wootton (Eds.), *Erving Goffman* (pp. 41–63). Cambridge, UK: Polity Press.

Collins, R. (2000a). The passing of intellectual generations: Reflections on the death of Erving Goffman. In G. A. Fine, & G. Smith (Eds.), *Erving Goffman, Vol. 1* (pp. 71–83). London, Thousand Oaks, New Delhi: Sage.

Collins, R. (2000b). Erving Goffman and the development of modern social theory. In G. Fine, & G. Smith (Eds.), *Erving Goffman, Vol. 3.* (pp. 307–37). Thousand Oaks, CA: Sage.

Collins, R. (2004). *Interaction ritual chains.* Princeton, NJ: Princeton University Press.

Colomy, P., & Brown, J. D. (1996). Goffman and interactional citizenship. *Sociological Perspectives, 39*(3), 371–81.

Conrad, C. (1993). Rhetorical/communication theory as an ontology for structuration research. *Communication Yearbook, 16*, 197–208.

Conrad, C. (2004). Organizational discourse analysis: Avoiding the determinism-voluntarism trap. *Organization, 11*(3), 427–39.

Conrad, C., & Poole, M. (1998). *Strategic organizational communication* (4th ed.). Orlando, FL: Holt, Rinehart and Winston.

Conte, M. (2008). Little naked pangs of the self: The real performance of the self and the function of trust in Goffman's action theory. *International Review of Sociology, 18*(3), 375–92.

Contractor, N., & Seibold, D. (1993). Theoretical frameworks for the study of structuring processes in group decision support systems: Adaptive structuration theory and self-organizing systems theory. *Human Communication Research, 19*(4), 528–63.

Cook, A., & Gueraud, S. (2005). What have we been missing? the role of general world knowledge in discourse processing. *Discourse Processes, 39*(2–3), 265–78.

Cooper, G. (2001). The mutable mobile: Social theory in the wireless world. In B. Brown, N. Green, & R. Harper (Eds.), *Wireless world: Social and interactional aspects of the mobile age* (pp. 19–32). London: Springer-Verlag.

Cooren, F. (2000). *The organizing properties of communication*. Philadelphia: John Benjamins B.V.

Cooren, F. (2004). Textual agency: How texts do things in organizational settings. *Organization, 11*(3), 373–93.

Cooren, F. (2006a). Arguments for the in-depth study of organizational interactions: A rejoinder to McPhee, Myers and Trethewey. *Management Communication Quarterly, 19*(3), 327–40.

Cooren, F. (2006b). The organizational communication-discourse tilt: A refugee's perspective. *Management Communication Quarterly, 19*(4), 653–60.

Cooren, F. (2006c). The organizational world as a plenum of agencies. In F. Cooren, J. R. Taylor, & E. Van Every (Eds.), *Communication as organizing: Empirical and theoretical explorations in the dynamic of text and conversation*. Mahwah, NJ: Lawrence Erlbaum.

Cooren, F., & Fairhurst, G. (2004). Speech timing and spacing: The phenomenon of organizational closure. *Organization, 11*(6), 793–824.

Cooren, F., & Fairhurst, G. (2009). Dislocation and stabilization: How to scale up from interactions to organization. In L. L. Putnam, & A. M. Nicotera (Eds.), *Building theories of organization: The constitutive role of communication* (pp. 117–52). New York: Routledge.

Cooren, F., & Taylor, J. R. (1997). Organization as an effect of mediation: Redefining the link between organization and communication. *Communication Theory, 7*(3), 219–59.

Corman, S., & Poole, M. (2000). *Perspectives on organizational communication: Finding common ground*. New York, NY: The Guilford Press.

Corman, S., & Scott, C. (1994). Perceived networks, activity foci, and observable communication in social collectives. *Communication Theory, 4*, 171–90.

Cornelissen, J. (2004). What are we playing at? Theatre, organization, and the use of metaphor. *Organization Studies, 25*(5), 705–26.

Costas, J., & Fleming, P. (2009). Beyond dis-identification: A discursive approach to self-alienation in contemporary organizations. *Human Relations, 62*(3), 353–78.

Courtright, J., Fairhurst, G., & Rogers, L. E. (1989). Interaction patterns in organic and mechanistic systems. *Academy of Management Journal, 324*, 773–802.

Craib, I. (1992). *Anthony Giddens*. London: Routledge.

Craig, R. (1999). Metadiscourse, theory and practice. *Research on Language and Social Interaction, 32*(1–2), 21–29.

Craig, R. (2007). Pragmatism in the field of communication theory. *Communication Theory, 17*, 125–45.

Craig, R., & Tracy, K. (1995). Grounded practical theory: The case of intellectual discussion. *Communication Theory, 5*(3), 248–72.

Crook, S., & Taylor, L. (1980). Goffman's version of reality. In J. Ditton (Ed.), *The view from Goffman.* (pp. 233–51). New York: St. Martin's Press.

Cupach, W., & Metts, S. (1994). *Facework.* Thousand Oaks, CA: Sage.

Czarniawska, B. (1997). *Narrating the organization: Dramas of institutional identity.* Chicago, IL: University of Chicago Press.

Czarniawska, B. (2004). On time, space, and action nets. *Organization, 11*(6), 773–91.

Czarniawska, B. (2006a). Bruno Latour: Reassembling the social: An introduction to actor-network theory. *Organization Studies, 27*(10), 1553–57.

Czarniawska, B. (2006b). A golden braid: Allport, Goffman, Weick. *Organization Studies, 27*(11), 1661–74.

Daft, R., & Lengel, R. (1984). Information richness. In L. Cummings, & B. Staw (Eds.), *Research in organizational behavior, Vol. 6.* Greenwich, CT: JAI Press.

Dallmayr, F. (1982). The theory of structuration: A critique. In A. Giddens (Ed.), *Profiles and critiques in social theory* (pp. 18–27). Berkeley, CA: University of California.

Dandeker, C. (1990). The nationstate and the modern world. In J. Clark, C. Modgil, & S. Modgil (Eds.), *Consensus and controversy: Anthony Giddens.* London: Falmer Press.

D'Angelo, P. (2002). News framing as multi-paradigmatic: A reply to Entman. *Journal of Communication, 52*(4), 870–88.

D'Angelo, P., & Kuypers, J. (Eds.). (2010). *Doing news framing analysis: Empirical and theoretical perspectives.* New York: Routledge.

Das, D., Dharwadkar, R., & Brandes, P. (2008). The importance of being "Indian": Identity centrality and work outcomes in an off-shored call center in India. *Human Relations, 61*(11), 1499–1530.

Dascal, M. (1981). Contextualization. In H. Parret, M. Sbisa, & J. Verschueren (Eds.), *Possibilities and limitations of pragmatics.* Amsterdam: John Benjamins B.V.

Davidson, M., & Friedman, R. A. (1998). When excuses don't work: The persistent injustice effect among black managers. *Administrative Science Quarterly, 43*(1), 154–83.

Davis, M. (1997). Georg Simmel and Erving Goffman: Legitimators of the sociological investigation of human experience. *Qualitative Sociology, 20*(3), 369–88.

Deal, T., & Kennedy, A. (1982). *Corporate cultures.* Reading, MA: Addison-Wesley.

Deetz, S. (1992). *Democracy in an age of corporate colonization.* Albany, NY: SUNY Press.

Deetz, S., & Mumby, D. (1990). Power, discourse and the workplace. In J. Anderson (Ed.), *Communication Yearbook, 13.* Beverly Hills, CA: Sage.

Dell, P., & Marinova, D. (2002). Erving Goffman and the internet. *Journal for Theory of Science, Technology and Communication,* 85–98.

Denzin, N. (1970). Symbolic interactionism and ethnomethodology. In J. Douglas (Ed.), *Understanding everyday life.* Chicago, IL: Aldine.

Denzin, N. (1992). The many faces of emotionality: Reading persona. In C. Ellis, & M. Flaherty (Eds.), *Investigating subjectivity: Research on lived experience.* (pp. 17–30). Newbury Park, CA: Sage.

Denzin, N. (2002). Much ado about Goffman. *American Sociologist, 33*(2), 105–17.

Dertouzos, M. (1997). *What will be: How the new world of information will change over time.* San Francisco, CA: Harper Edge.

DeSanctis G., & Fulk, J. (Eds.) (1999). *Shaping organization form: Communication, connection, and community*(1999). Thousand Oaks, CA: Sage.

DeSanctis, G., & Poole, M. (1994). Capturing the complexity in advanced technology use: Adaptive structuration theory. *Organization Science, 5*(2), 121–47.

DeSanctis, G., & Poole, M. (1997). Transitions in teamwork in new organizational forms. *Advances in Group Processes, 14*, 157–76.

DeSanctis, G., Poole, M., Lewis, H., & Desharnais, G. (1992). Using computing in quality team meetins: Some initial observations from the IRS-Minnesota project. *Journal of ·Management Information Systems, 8*(3), 7–26.

Dillard, J. P., & Soloman, D. H. (2000). Conceptualizing context in message-production research. *Communication Theory, 10*(2), 167–75.

Donnellon, A., Gray, B., & Bougon, M. G. (1986). Communication, meaning, and organized action. *Administrative Science Quarterly, 31*(1), 43–55.

Douglas, J. (1970). *Understanding everyday life.* Chicago, IL: Aldine.

Down, S., & Reveley, J. (2009). Between narration and interaction: Situating first-line supervisor identity work. *Human Relations, 62*(3), 379–401.

Drazin, R., Glynn, M. A., & Kazanjian, R. K. (1999). Multilevel theorizing about creativity in organizations: A sensemaking perspective. *Academy of Management Review, 24*(2), 286–307.

Duck, S. (2002). Hypertext in the key of G: Three types of "history" as influences on conversational structure and flow. *Communication Theory, 12*(1), 41–62.

Duncan, S., & Fiske, D. (1977). *Face-to-face interaction: Research, methods and theory.* Hillsdale, NJ: Lawrence Erlbaum Associates.

Economidou-Kogetsidis, M. (2010). Cross-cultural and situational variation in requesting behavior: Perceptions of social situations and strategic usage of request patterns. *Journal of Pragmatics, 42*(8), 2262–81.

Edwards, D. (1997). *Discourse and cognition.* Thousand Oaks, CA: Sage.

Eelen, G. (2001). *A critique of politeness theories.* Manchester, UK: St. Jerome.

Eisenberg, E. (1984). Ambiguity as strategy in organizational communication. *Communication Monographs, 51,* 227–42.

Eisenberg, E., & Goodall, H. (1993). *Organizational communication: Balancing creativity and constraint.* New York, NY: St. Martin's Press.

Ekman, P. (1993). Facial expression and emotion. *American Psychologist, 48*(4), 384–92.

Ellis, D. (1999). *Crafting society.* Mahwah, NJ: Lawrence Erlbaum Associates.

Elsbach, K. D., Barr, P., & Hargadon, A. (2005). Identifying situated cognition in organizations. *Organization Science, 16*(4), 422–33.

Emirbayer, M., & Mische, A. (1998). What is agency? *American Journal of Sociology, 103*(4), 962–1023.

Emirbayer, M., & Sheller, M. (1998). Publics in history. *Theory and Society, 27,* 727–79.

Engestrom, Y. (1995). Objects, contradictions and collaboration in medical cognition: An activity-theoretical perspective. *Artificial Intelligence in Medicine, 7,* 395–412.

Engestrom, Y. (1996). Interobjectivity, ideality, and dialectics. *Mind, Culture, and Activity, 3*(4), 259–65.

Engestrom, Y. (1999). Communication, discourse and activity. *Communication Review, 3*(1–2), 165–85.

Entman, J. (1993). Framing: Toward clarification of a fractured paradigm. *Journal of Communication, 43,* 51–58.

Erickson, I. (2010). Geography and community: New forms of interaction among people and places. *American Behavioral Scientist, 53*(8), 1194–1207.

Erikson, E. (1950). *Childhood and society.* New York: Norton.

Erwin, R. (2000). The nature of Goffman. In G. Fine, & G. Smith (Eds.), *Erving Goffman, Vol. 1* (pp. 84–98). Thousand Oaks, CA: Sage.

Essers, C., & Benschop, Y. (2009). Muslim businesswomen doing boundary work: The negotiation of Islam, gender and ethnicity within entrepreneurial contexts. *Human Relations, 62*(3), 403–23.

Fabros, A. S. L. (2009). Global economy of signs and selves: A view of work regimes in call centers in the Philippines. *Sociologie Du Travail, 51,* 343–60.

Fairhurst, G. (2004). Text, context and agency in interaction analysis. *Organization, 11*(3), 335–53.

Fairhurst, G. (2005). Reframing the art of framing: Problems and prospects for leadership. *Leadership, 1*(2), 165–85.

Fairhurst, G. (in press, a). Organizational discourse. In W. Donsbach (Ed.), *The international encyclopedia of communication.* Oxford: Blackwell.

Fairhurst, G. (in press, b). *The power of framing: Creating the language of leadership.*

Fairhurst, G., & Cooren, F. (2004). Organizational language-in-use: Interaction analysis, conversation analysis and speech act schematics. In D. Grant, C. Hardy, C. Oswick, N. Phillips, & L. Putnam (Eds.), *The Sage handbook of organizational discourse* (pp. 131–52). London: Sage.

Fairhurst, G., & Grant, D. (2010). The social construction of leadership: A sailing guide. *Management Communication Quarterly, 24*(2), 171–210.

Fairhurst, G., & Putnam, L. (1998). Reflections on the organization-communication equivalency question: The contributions of James Taylor and his colleagues. *Communication Review, 3*(1–2), 1–19.

Fairhurst, G., & Putnam, L. (2004). Organizations as discursive constructions. *Communication Theory, 14,* 5–26.

Fairhurst, G., & Sarr, R. (1996). *The art of framing: Managing the language of leadership.* San Francisco: Jossey-Bass.

Fayard, A. (2007). Photocopiers and water-coolers: The affordances of informal interaction. *Organization Studies, 28*(5), 605–34.

Feldman, M. (2000). Organizational routines as a source of continuous change. *Organization Science, 11*(6), 611–29.

Feldman, M. S. (2004). Resources in emerging structures and processes of change. *Organization Science, 15*(3), 295–309.

Feldman, M., & Pentland, B. (2003). Reconceptualizing organizational routines as a source of flexibility and change. *Administrative Science Quarterly, 48,* 94–118.

Fine, G., Manning, P., & Smith, G. (2000). Introduction. In G. Fine, & G. Smith (Eds.), *Erving Goffman, Vol 1.* (pp. ix–xlvi). Thousand Oaks, CA: Sage.

Fine, G., & Manning, P. (2003). Erving Goffman. In G. Ritzer (Ed.), *The Blackwell companion to major contemporary social theorists.* Oxford: Blackwell.

Fine, G., & Smith, G. (Eds.). (2000). *Erving Goffman,* Vols. 1–4. Thousand Oaks, CA: Sage.

Fine, G., Stitt, J., & Finch, M. (1984). Couple tie signs and interpersonal threat: A field experiment. *Social Psychology Quarterly, 47*(3), 282–86.

Fineman, S. (1993). Organizations as emotional arenas. In S. Fineman (Ed.), *Emotion and organization* (pp. 3–11). London: Sage.

Fineman, S. (1996). Emotional subtexts in corporate greening. *Organization Studies, 17*(3), 479–500.

Fineman, S. (2000). *Emotion in organizations* (2nd ed.). Thousand Oaks, CA: Sage.

Fineman, S., & Sturdy, A. (1999). The emotions of control: A qualitative exploration of environmental regulation. *Human Relations, 52*(5), 631–63.

Fiol, C., & O'Connor, E. (2005). Identification in face-to-face, hybrid, and pure virtual teams: Untangling the contradictions. *Organization Science, 16*(1), 19–32.

Fiske, S., & Taylor, S. (1991). *Social cognition* (2nd ed.). New York: McGraw-Hill.

Fitch, K., & Sanders, R. (1994). Culture, communication, and preferences for directness in expression of directives. *Communication Theory, 4*(3), 219–45.

Fitch, K., & Sanders, R. (Eds.). (2005). *Handbook of language and social interaction.* Mahwah, NJ: Lawrence Erlbaum Associates.

Flaherty, M. (1991). The perception of time and situated engrossment. *Social Psychology Quarterly, 54*(1), 76–85.

Flaherty, M. G. (2003). Time work: Customizing temporal experience. *Social Psychology Quarterly, 66*(1), 17–33.

Flanagin, A., Stohl, C., & Bimber, B. (2006). Modeling the structure of collective action. *Communication Monographs, 73*(1), 29–54.

Fleming, P. (2005). Metaphors of resistance. *Management Communication Quarterly, 19*(1), 45–66.

Flowerdew, J., & Leong, S. (2010). Presumed knowledge in the discursive construction of socio-political and cultural identity. *Journal of Pragmatics, 42*(8), 2240–52.

Fortunati, L. (2005). Mobile telephone and the presentation of self. In R. Ling, & P. E. Pedersen (Eds.), *Mobile communications: Re-negotiation of the social sphere* (pp. 203–18). London: Springer-Verlag.

Foucault, M. (1972). *The archaeology of knowledge.* (A.M. Sheridan Smith Trans.). New York: Pantheon.

Franck, D. (1981). Seven sins of pragmatics: Theses about speech act theory, conversational analysis, linguistics and rhetoric. In H. Parret, M. Sbisa, & J. Verschuren (Eds.), *Possibilities and limitations of pragmatics.* Amsterdam: John Benjamins.

Frey, L. (1999). *The handbook of group communication theory and research.* Thousand Oaks, CA: Sage.

Friedland, R., & Boden, D. (Eds.). (1994). *NowHere: Space, time, and modernity.* Berkeley, CA: University of California Press.

Frye, N. (1957). *Anatomy of criticism.* Princeton, NJ: Princeton University Press.

Fuchs, C. (2002). Some implications of Anthony Giddens' works for a theory of social self-organization. *Emergence, 4*(3), 7–35.

Fuchs, C. (2003). Structuration theory and self-organization. *Systemic Practice and Action Research, 16*(2), 133–67.

Gannon, M. J., Locke, E. A., Gupta, A., Audia, P., & Kristoff-Brown, A. (2005). Cultural metaphors as frames of reference for nations. *International Studies of Management and Organization, 35*(4), 37–47.

Gardner, C. B. (2000). Analyzing gender in public places: Rethinking Goffman's vision of everyday life. In G. Fine, & G. Smith (Eds.), *Erving Goffman, Vol. 2* (pp. 275–90). Thousand Oaks, CA: Sage.

Gardner, C. B., & Gronfein, W. P. (2005). Reflections on varieties of shame induction, shame management, and shame avoidance in some works of Erving Goffman. *Symbolic Interaction, 28*(2), 175–82.

Gardner, W. (1992). Lessons in organizational dramaturgy: The art of impression management. *Organizational Dynamics, 21*(1), 33–46.

Gardner, W., & Avolio, B. (1998). The charismatic relationship: A dramaturgical perspective. *Academy of Management Review, 23*(1), 32–58.

Gardner, W. L., & Martinko, M. J. (1988). Impression management: An observational study linking audience characteristics with verbal self-presentations. *Academy of Management Journal, 31*(1), 42–65.

Garfinkel, H. (1962). Commonsense knowledge of social structures: The documentary method of interpretation in lay and professional face finding. In J. Sher (Ed.), *Theories of mind.* New York, NY: Free Press.

Garfinkel, H. (1967a). *Studies in ethnomethodology.* Englewood Cliffs, NJ: Prentice-Hall.

Garfinkel, H. (1967b). Studies on the routine grounds of everyday activities. In H. Garfinkel (Ed.), *Studies in ethnomethodology.* Englewood Cliffs, NJ: Prentice-Hall.

Garot, R. (2004). "You're not a stone": Emotional sensitivity in a bureaucratic setting. *Journal of Contemporary Ethnography, 33*(6), 735–66.

Gawley, T. (2007). Revisiting trust in symbolic interaction: Presentations of trust development in university administration. *Qualitative Sociology Review, 3*(2), 46–63.

Gee, J. P. (1999). *An introduction to discourse analysis: Theory and method.* London: Routledge.

Geertz, C. (1973). *The interpretation of culture.* New York: Basic Books.

Geertz, C. (1983). *Local knowledge: Further essays in interpretive anthropology.* New York: Basic Books.

Gephart, R., Maanen, J., & Oberlechner, T. (2009). Organizations and risk in late modernity. *Organization Studies, 30*(2–3), 141–55.

Geser, H. (2004) *Towards a sociological theory of the mobile phone*. Retrieved April 2008, from http://socio.ch/Mobile/geser1.htm

Gibson, D. (2003). Participation shifts: Order and differentiation in group conversation. *Social Forces, 81*(4), 1335–80.

Gibson, D. R. (2005a). Opportunistic interruptions: Interactional vulnerabilities deriving from linearization. *Social Psychology Quarterly, 68*(4), 316–37.

Gibson, D. R. (2005b). Taking turns and talking ties: Networks and conversational interaction. *American Journal of Sociology, 110*(6), 1561–97.

Giddens, A. (1976). *New rules of sociological method*. London: Hutchinson.

Giddens, A. (1979). *Central problems in social theory*. Berkeley, CA: University of California Press.

Giddens, A. (1981). *A contemporary critique of historical materialism, Vol. 1: Power, property and the state*. Berkeley, CA: University of California Press.

Giddens, A. (1982). *Profiles and critiques in social theory*. Berkeley, CA: University of California Press.

Giddens, A. (1983). Comments on the theory of structuration. *Journal for the Theory of Social Behaviour, 13*(1), 75–80.

Giddens, A. (1984). *The constitution of society*. Berkeley, CA: University of California Press.

Giddens, A. (1985a). *The nation-state and violence*. Berkeley, CA: University of California Press.

Giddens, A. (1985b). Time, space and regionalization. In D. Gregory, & J. Urry (Eds.), *Social relations and spatial structures*. London, UK: Macmillan.

Giddens, A. (1987a). *The nation-state and violence*. Berkeley, CA: University of California Press.

Giddens, A. (1987b). *Social theory and modern sociology*. Cambridge, UK: Polity Press.

Giddens, A. (1988). Goffman as a systematic social theorist. In P. Drew, & A. Wootton (Eds.), *Erving Goffman: Exploring the interaction order* (pp. 260–288). Cambridge: Polity Press.

Giddens, A. (1989). Response to my critics. In D. Held, & T. Thompson (Eds.), *Social theory of modern societies: Anthony Giddens and his critics*. Cambridge, UK: Cambridge University Press.

Giddens, A. (1990a). *The consequences of modernity*. Cambridge, UK: Polity Press.

Giddens, A. (1990b). Structuration theory and sociological analysis. In J. Clark, C. Modgil, & S. Modgil (Eds.), *Consensus and controversy: Anthony Giddens*. London, UK: Falmer Press.

Giddens, A. (1991a). *Modernity and self-identity*. Cambridge, UK: Polity Press.

Giddens, A. (1991b). Structuration theory: Past, present and future. In C. Bryant, & D. Jary (Eds.), *Giddens' theory of structuration: A critical appreciation* (pp. 201–21). London, UK: Routledge.

Giddens, A. (1992). *The transformation of intimacy*. Cambridge, UK: Polity Press.

Giddens, A. (1993). *The Giddens reader* (Ed. P. Cassell.) Stanford, CA: Stanford University Press.

Giddens, A. (1994). *Beyond left and right—the future of radical politics*. Cambridge: Polity Press.

Giddens, A. (1998). *The third way—a renewal of social democracy*. Cambridge, UK: Polity Press.

Giddens, A. (2000). Goffman as a systematic social theorist. In G. A. Fine, & G. Smith (Eds.), *Erving Goffman, Vol. 4* (pp. 151–75). London, Thousand Oaks, New Delhi: Sage.

Giddens, A. (2003). *The runaway world*. New York: Routledge.

Giddens, A. (2004). Beneath the hijab: A woman. *New Perspectives Quarterly, 21*(1), 9–11.

Giddens, A. (2009a). On rereading the presentation of self: Some reflections. *Social Psychology Quarterly, 72*(4), 290–95.

Giddens, A. (2009b). Recession, climate change, and the return of planning. *New Perspectives Quarterly, 26*(2), 51–53.

Giddens, A., & Pierson, C. (1998). *Conversations with Anthony Giddens.* Cambridge, UK: Polity Press.

Gioia, D. (1986). Symbols, scripts and sensemaking. In H. P. Sims, & D. Gioia (Eds.), *The thinking organization* (pp. 49–74). San Francisco: Jossey-Bass.

Giola, D., & Poole, P. (1984). Scripts in organizational behavior. *Academy of Management Review, 9*(3), 449–59.

Glenn, H. (2008). The vernacular web of participatory media. *Critical Studies in Media Communication, 25*(5), 490–513.

Goffman, E. (1953a). *The service station dealer: The man and his work.* Social Research Inc., Chicago, IL.

Goffman, E. (1953b). *Communication conduct in an island community.* Unpublished Ph.D., University of Chicago,

Goffman, E. (1955). On face-work: An analysis of ritual elements in social interaction. *Psychiatry: Journal for the Study of Interpersonal Processes, 18*(3), 213–31.

Goffman, E. (1956a). *The presentation of self in everyday life.* Edinburgh, UK: Social Science Research Centre, University of Edinburgh.

Goffman, E. (1956b). The nature of deference and demeanor. *American Anthropologist, 58*(3), 473–502.

Goffman, E. (1959). *The presentation of self in everyday life.* Harmondsworth, UK: Penguin Press.

Goffman, E. (1961a). *Asylums.* Chicago: Aldine.

Goffman, E. (1961b). *Encounters: Two studies in the sociology of interaction.* Indianapolis, IN: Bobbs-Merrill.

Goffman, E. (1963a). *Behavior in public places.* New York: Free Press.

Goffman, E. (1963b). *Stigma: Notes on the management of spoiled identity.* Englewood Cliffs, NJ: Prentice-Hall.

Goffman, E. (1964). The negotiation situation. *American Anthropologist, 66,* 133–36.

Goffman, E. (1965). Embarrassment and social organization. *American Journal of Sociology, 62*(3), 264–71.

Goffman, E. (1967). *Interaction ritual: Essays on face-to-face behavior.* Chicago: Aldine.

Goffman, G. (1969a). *Where the action is.* London: The Penguin Press.

Goffman, E. (1969b). *Strategic interaction.* Philadelphia: University of Philadelphia Press.

Goffman, E. (1971). *Relations in public.* New York: Basic Books.

Goffman, E. (1974). *Frame analysis.* New York: Basic Books.

Goffman, E. (1976). Replies and responses. *Language in Society, 5*(3), 257–313.

Goffman, E. (1979). *Gender advertisements.* Cambridge, MA: Harvard University Press.

Goffman, E. (1981a). *Forms of talk.* Oxford: Blackwell.

Goffman, E. (1981b). A reply to Denzin and Keller. *Contemporary Sociology, 10*(1), 60–68.

Goffman, E. (1983a). The interaction order. *American Sociological Review, 48,* 1–17.

Goffman, E. (1983b). Felicity's condition. *American Journal of Sociology, 89*(1), 1–53.

Gomez, P., & Jones, B. C. (2000). Conventions: An interpretation of deep structure in organizations. *Organization Science, 11*(6), 696–708.

Gonos, G. (1977). "Situation" versus "frame": The "interactionist" and the "structuralist" analyses of everyday life. *American Sociological Review, 42,* 854–67.

Goodwin, C. (1981). *Conversational organization: Interaction between speakers and hearers.* New York: Academic Press.

Goodwin, C. (1997). The blackness of black: Color catgories as situated practice. In B. Resnick, R. Saljo, C. Pontecorvo, & B. Burge (Eds.), *Discourse, tools, and reasoning: Essays on situated cognition.* Heidelberg: Springer.

Goodwin, C. (2000). Action and embodiment within situated human interaction. *Journal of Pragmatics, 32*(10), 1489–1522.

Goodwin, C. (2003). Embedded context. *Research on Language and Social Interaction, 36*(4), 323–50.

Gordon, R., Stewart, C., & Kornberger, M. (2009). Embedded ethics: Discourse and power in the New South Wales police services. *Organization Studies, 30*(1), 73–99.

Goss, D. (2005). Entrepreneurship and "the social": Towards a deference-emotion theory. *Human Relations, 58*(5), 617–36.

Grainger, K., Mills, S., & Sibanda, M. (2010). "Just tell us what to do": Southern African face and its relevance to intercultural communication. *Journal of Pragmatics, 42*, 2158–71.

Grant, D., Hardy, C., Ostwick, C., & Putnam, L. (2004). *The Sage handbook of organizational discourse.* Thousand Oaks, CA: Sage.

Grant, D., Keenoy, T., & Oswick, C. (Eds.). (1998). *Discourse and organization.* London, Thousand Oaks, New Delhi: Sage.

Grant, D., Keenoy, T., & Oswick, C. (1998). Organizational discourse: Of diversity, dichotomy and multi-disciplinary. In D. Grant, T. Keenoy, & C. Oswick (Eds.), *Discourse and organization* (pp. 1–13). London: Sage.

Greener, I. (2008). Experts patients and human agency: Long-term conditions and Giddens' structuration theory. *Social Theory and Health, 6*(4), 273–90.

Gregory, D. (1989). Presences and absences: Time-space relations. In D. Held, & J. Thompson (Eds.), *Social theory of modern societies: Anthony Giddens and his critics* (pp. 185–214). Cambridge, UK: Cambridge University Press.

Greimas, A. (1987). *On meaning: Selected writings in semiotic theory* (Trans. P. Perron, & F. Collins). London: Frances Pinter.

Grice, H. P. (1975). Logic and conversation. In P. Cole, & J. Morgan (Eds.), *Syntax and semantics, Vol. 3, Speech acts* (pp. 41–58). New York, NY: Academic Press.

Grice, H. P. (1989). *Studies in the ways of words.* Cambridge, MA: Harvard University Press.

Griffith, T. (1999). Technology features as triggers for sensemaking. *Academy of Management Review, 24*(2), 472–88.

Grimshaw, A. (1987). Disambiguating discourse: Members' skill and analysts' problem. *Social Psychology Quarterly, 50*(2), 186–204.

Grimshaw, A. (2000). Erving Goffman: A personal appreciation. In G. A. Fine, & G. Smith (Eds.), *Erving Goffman, Vol. 1* (pp. 5–7). London, Thousand Oaks, New Delhi: Sage.

Grimshaw, A. (2001). Discourse and sociology: Sociology and discourse. In D. Schiffrin, D. Tannen, & H. Hamilton (Eds.), *The handbook of discourse analysis* (pp. 750–71). Oxford: Blackwell.

Gronfein, W. (2000). Erving Goffman. In G. Fine, & G. Smith (Eds.), *Erving Goffman, Vol. 3* (pp. 255–79). Thousand Oaks, CA: Sage.

Gross, N., & Simmons, S. (2002). Intimacy as a double-edged phenomenon? An empirical test of Giddens. *Social Forces, 81*(2), 531–55.

Gudykunst, W., & Kim, Y. (2003). *Communicating with strangers.* New York, NY: McGraw-Hill Higher Education.

Gumperz, J. (1992a). Contextualization and understanding. In A. Duranti, & C. Goodwin (Eds.), *Rethinking context: Language as an interactive phenomenon* (pp. 239–52). Cambridge: Cambridge University Press.

Gumperz, J. (1992b). Interviewing in intercultural situations. In P. Drew, & J. Heritage (Eds.), *Talk at work: Interaction in institutional settings* (pp. 302–27). Cambridge, UK: Cambridge University Press.

Gumperz, J. (2001). Interactional sociolinguistics: A personal perspective. In D. Schiffrin, D. Tannen, & H. Hamilton (Eds.), *The handbook of discourse analysis* (pp. 215–28). Oxford: Blackwell.

Gumperz, J., & Hymes, D. (1972). *Directions in sociolinguistics.* New York, NY: Holt, Rinehart & Winston.

Hacking, I. (2004). Between Michel Foucault and Erving Goffman: Between discourse in the abstract and face-to-face interaction. *Economy and Society, 33*(3), 277–302.

Hall, E. T. (1976). *Beyond culture.* New York: Doubleday.

Hall, P. (2003). Interactionism, social organization, and social processes: Looking back and moving ahead. *Symbolic Interaction, 26*(1), 33–55.

Hallet, T. (2007). Between deference and distinction: Interaction ritual through symbolic power in an educational institution. *Social Psychology Quarterly, 70*(2), 148–71.

Hallett, T., Harger, B., & Eder, D. (2009). Gossip at work: Unsanctioned evaluative talk in formal school meetings. *Journal of Contemporary Ethnography, 38*(5), 584–618.

Hample, D., Warner, B., & Young, D. (2009). Framing and editing interpersonal arguments. *Argumentation, 23*, 21–37.

Handelman, D. (2005). The extended case interactional foundations and prospective dimensions. *Social Analysis, 49*(3), 61–84.

Handler, R. (2009). Erving Goffman and the gestural dynamics of modern selfhood. *Past and Present Society, 4*, 280–300.

Hardey, M. (2004). Mediated relationships. *Information, Communication and Society, 7*(2), 207–22.

Hardy, C. (2004). Scaling up and bearing down in discourse analysis: Questions regarding textual agencies and their context. *Organization, 11*(3), 415–25.

Hareli, S., & Rafaeli, A. (2008). Emotion cycles: On the social influence of emotion in organizations. *Research in Organizational Behavior, 28*, 35–39.

Hargadon, A., & Fanelli, A. (2002). Action and possibility: Reconciling dual perspectives of knowledge in organizations. *Organization Science, 13*(3), 290–302.

Hartel, C., Zerbe, S., & Ashkanasy, N. (Eds.). (2005). *Emotions in organizational behavior.* Mahwah, NJ: Lawrence Erlbaum Associates.

Hartland, N. (2000). Goffman's attitude and social analysis. In G. Fine, & G. Smith (Eds.), *Erving Goffman, Vol. 2* (pp. 291–305). Thousand Oaks, CA: Sage.

Haslett, B. (1984). Communicative development: The state of the art. In R. Bostrom (Ed.), *Communication Yearbook, 8*, 198–267.

Haslett, B. (1987). *Communication: Strategic action in context.* Hillsdale, NJ: Lawrence Erlbaum Associates.

Haslett, B., & Samter, W. (1997). *Children communicating.* Mahwah, NJ: Lawrence Erlbaum Associates.

Haugaard, M. (1992). *Structures, restructuration and social power.* Aldershot, UK: Avebury.

Haugh, M. (2007). The discursive challenge to politeness research: An interactional alternative. *Journal of Politeness Research, 3*, 295–317.

Haugh, M., & Bargiela-Chiappini, F. (2010). Face in interaction. *Journal of Pragmatics, 42*(8), 2073–77.

Haugh, M. (2009). Face and interaction. In F. Bargiela-Chiappini, & M. Haugh (Eds.), *Face, communication and social interaction* (pp. 1–30). London: Equinox.

Hay, C., O'Brien, M., & Penna, S. (1997). Giddens, modernity and self-identity: The "hollowing out" of social theory. In C. Bryant, & D. Jary (Eds.), *Anthony Giddens: Critical ssessments, Vol. 4* (pp. 85–112). New York: Routledge.

Heath, C., & Luff, P. (1992). Media space and asymmetries: Communicative preliminary observations of video-mediated interaction human-computer interaction. *Sociological Theory, 7*(2), 315–46.

Hendry, J. (2000). Strategic decision making, discourse, and strategy as social practice. *Journal of Management Studies, 27*(7), 956–77.

Hepburn, A., & Wiggins, S. (2007). *Discursive research in practice.* Cambridge, UK: Cambridge University Press.

Heracleous, L. (2001). The contribution of a discursive view to understanding and managing organizational change. *Strategic Change, 11*(5), 253–61.

Heracleous, L. (2004). Boundaries in the study of organization. *Human Relations, 57*(1), 95–103.

Heracleous, L. (2006a). *Discourse, interpretation, organization.* Cambridge, UK: Cambridge University Press.

Heracleous, L. (2006b). A tale of three discourses: The dominant, the strategic and the marginalized. *Journal of Management Studies, 43*(5), 1059–85.

Heracleous, L., & Barrett, M. (2001). Organizational change as discourse: Communicative actions and deep structures in the context of information technology implementation. *Academy of Management Journal, 44*(4), 755–78.

Heracleous, L., & Hendry, J. (2000). Discourse, and the study of organization: Toward a structurational perspective. *Human Relations, 53*(10), 1251–86.

Heracleous, L., & Marshak, R. (2004). Conceptualizing organizational discourse as situated symbolic action. *Human Relations, 57*(10), 1285–1312.

Heritage, J. (1984). *Garfinkel and ethnomethodology*. Cambridge, UK: Polity Press.

Heritage, J. (2005). Conversational analysis and institutional talk. In K. Fitch, & R. Sanders (Eds.), *Handbook of language and social interaction*. (pp. 103–48). Mahwah, NJ: Lawrence Erlbaum Associates.

Herrera Gomez, M., & Soriano Miras, R. (2004a). Erving Goffman and the fragmentation of daily life. *Sistema 181*, 55–91.

Herrera Gomez, M., & Soriano Miras, R. (2004b). The theory of social action by Erving Goffman. *Revista De Sociologia, 73*, 59–79.

Herzfeld, M. (2009). The cultural politics of gesture. *Ethnography, 10*(2), 131–52.

Hill, S., Bartol, K., Tesluk, P., & Langa, G. (2009). Organizational contect and face-to-face interaction: Influences on the devleopment of trust and collaborative behaviors in computer-mediated groups. *Organizational Behavior and Human Decision Processes, 108*(1), 187–201.

Hindmarsh, J., & Pilnick, A. (2002). The tacit order of teamwork: Collaboration and embodied conduct in anesthesia. *Sociological Quarterly, 43*(2), 139–64.

Hochschild, A. (1979). Emotion work, feeling rules, ans social structure. *American Journal of Sociology, 85*, 554–75.

Hochschild, A. (1983). *The managed heart: Commercialization of human feeling*. Berkeley: University of California Press.

Hochschild, A. (1991). Ideology and emotion management: A perspective and path for future research. In T. Kemper (Ed.), *Research agendas in the sociology of emotion* (pp. 117–44). Albany, NY: University of New York Press.

Hochschild, A. (2000). Global care chains and emotional surplus value. In W. Hutton, & A. Giddens (Eds.), *Global capitalism* (pp. 130–46). New York, NY: The New Press.

Hodgson, G. (2007). Institutions and individuals: Interaction and evolution. *Organization Studies, 28*(1), 95–116.

Hofstede, G. (1980). *Culture's consequences: International differences in work related values*. Beverly Hills, CA: Sage.

Hofstede, G. (2001). *Culture's consequences*. (2nd ed.). Beverly Hills, CA: Sage.

Hofstede, G., & Hofstede, G. F. (2005). *Cultures and organizations: Software of the mind*. New York, NY: McGraw Hill.

Holmes, J., & Stubb, M. (2003). *Power and politeness in the workplace: A sociolinguistic analysis of talk at work*. London: Longman.

Holtgraves, T. (1992). The linguistic realization of face management: Implications for language production and comprehension, person perception, and cross-cultural communication. *Social Psychology Quarterly, 55*(2), 141–59.

Holtgraves, T. (2000). The linguistic realization of face management: Implications for language production and comprehension, person perception, and cross-cultural communication. In G. Fine, & G. Smith (Eds.), *Erving Goffman, Vol. 4* (pp. 342–69). Thousand Oaks, CA: Sage.

Holtgraves, T. (2001). Politeness. In W. Robinson, & H. Giles (Eds.), *The new handbook of language and social psychology* (pp. 341–55) Oxford: John Wiley & Sons Ltd.

Holtgraves, T. (2009). Face, politeness and interpersonal variables: Implications of language production and comprehension. In F. Bargiela-Chiappini, & M. Haugh (Eds.), *Face, communication and social interaction* (pp. 193–207). London: Equinox.

Hoogenboom, M., & Ossewaarde, R. (2005). From iron cage to pigeon house: The birth of reflexive authority. *Organization Studies, 26*(4), 601–19.

Hopper, R., & Drummond, K. (1990). Emergent goals at a relational turning point: The case of Gordon and Denise. *Journal of Language and Social Psychology, 9*, 39–65.

House, R. J., Hanges, P., Javidan, M., Dorfman, P., & Gupta, V. (2004). *Culture, leadership, and organizations: The GLOBE study of 62 societies.* Thousand Oaks, CA: Sage.

Howard, L., & Geist, P. (1995). Ideological positioning in organizational change: The dialectic of control in a merging organization. *Communication Monographs, 62*, 110–132.

Howard-Grenville, J. A. (2005). The persistence of organizational routines: The role of agency and organizational context. *Organization Science, 16*(6), 618–36.

Hughes, N. (2009). Changing faces: Adaptation of highly skilled Chinese workers to a high-tech multinational corporation. *Journal of Applied Behavioral Science, 45*(2), 212–38.

Hutchby, I. (1999). Frame attunement and footing in the organisation of talk radio openings. *Journal of Sociolinguistics, 3*, 41–64.

Hutchby, I. (2001). Technologies, texts and affordances. *Sociology, 35*(2), 441–56.

Hutchby, I. (2003). Affordances and the analysis of technologically mediated interaction: A response to Brian Rappert. *Sociology, 37*(3), 441–56.

Hutchby, I. (2005). Conversation analysis and the study of broadcast talk. In K. Fitch, & R. Sanders (Eds.), *Handbook of language and social interaction.* (pp. 437–60). Mahwah, NJ: Lawrence Erlbaum Associates.

Hutchby, I., & Tanna, V. (2008). Aspects of sequential organization in text message exchange. *Discourse and Communication, 2*(2), 143–64.

Hutchby, I., & Wooffitt. (1998). *Conversational analysis.* Cambridge, UK: Polity Press.

Hutchins, E. (1995). *Cognition in the wild.* Cambridge, MA: MIT Press.

Hymes, D. (1972). Model of interaction of language and social settings. In J. Gumperz, & D. Hymes (Eds.), *Directions in sociolinguistics: An ethnographic approach.* Philadelphia, PA: University of Pennslyvania Press.

Hymes, D. (1974). *Foundations of sociolinguistics: An ethnographic approach.* Philadelphia, PA: University of Pensylvania Press.

Hymes, D. (1984). On Erving Goffman. *Theory and Society, 13*(5), 621–31.

Hymes, D. (1986). Models of interaction of language and social life. In J. Gumperz, & D. Hymes (Eds.), *Directions in sociolinguistics: The ethnography of communication* (pp. 35–71). Oxford: Blackwell.

Hymes, D. (2000). On Erving Goffman. In G. Fine, & G. Smith (Eds.), *Erving Goffman, Vol. 1* (pp. 48–59). London, Thousand Oaks, New Delhi: Sage.

Ibarra, H. (1999). Provisional selves: Experimenting with image and identity in professional adaptation. *Administrative Science Quarterly, 44*(4), 764–91.

Ibarra, H., & Barbulescu, R. (2010). Identity as narrative: Prevalence, effectiveness, and consequences of narrative identity work in macro work role transitions. *Academy of Management Review, 35*(1), 135–54.

Iedema, R., & Wodak, R. (1999). Introduction: Organizational discourses and practices. *Discourse and Society, 10*(1), 5–19.

Inglehart, R. (1997). *Modernization and postmodernization: Cultural, economic, and political change in 43 societies.* Princeton, NJ: Princeton University Press.

Inns, D. (1996). Organization development as a journey. In C. Oswick, & D. Grant (Eds.), *Organization development: Metaphorical explorations* (pp. 110–26). London: Pitman.

Ito, M., & Okabe, D. (2005). Technosocial situations: Emergent structuring of mobile e-mail use. In M. Ito, M. Matsuba, & D. Okabe (Eds.), *Personal, protable, pedestrian: Mobile phones in Japanese life* (pp. 257–73). Cambridge, MA: MIT Press.

Iverson, J., & McPhee, R. (2008). Communicating knowing through communities of practice: Exploring internal communicative processes and differences among CoPs. *Journal of Applied Communication Research, 36*(2), 176–99.

Izard, C. (2009). Emotion theory and research: Highlights, unanswered questions, and emerging issues. *Annual Review of Psychology, 60,* 1–25.

Izard, C., Stark, K., Trentacosta, C., & Schultz, D. (2008). Beyond emotional regulation: Emotional utilization and adaptive functioning. *Child Development Perspectives, 2,* 156–63.

Jacobsen, M. (Ed.). (2010). *The contemporary Goffman.*.New York, NY: Routledge.

Jarvenpaa, S., & Leidner, D. (1999). Communication and trust in global virtual teams. *Organization Science, 10*(6), 791–815.

Jarvenpaa, S., Shaw, T., & Staples, D. (2004). Toward contextualized theories of trust: The role of trust in global virtual teams. *Information Systems Research, 15*(3), 250–67.

Jary, D. (1997). Society as time-traveller: Giddens on historical change, historical materialism and the nation-state in world society. In C. Bryant, & D. Jary (Eds.), *Anthony Giddens: Critical assessments, Vol. 3* (pp. 302–23). New York: Routledge.

Jary, D., & Jary, J. (1997). The transformation of Anthony Giddens. In C. Bryant, & D. Jary (Eds.), *Anthony Giddens: Critical assessments, Vol. 4* (pp. 137–54). New York: Routledge.

Jarzabkowski, P. (2005). *Strategy as practice: An activity-based approach.* London: Sage Publications.

Jenkins, R. (2010). The 21st-century interaction order. In M. H. Jacobsen (Ed.), *The contemporary Goffman* (pp. 257–74). New York, NY: Routledge.

Jian, G. (2008). *From the linguistic to the practice turn in organizational communication: Imagining the future of our field.* Paper, Organizational Communication Conference, Alta, UT.

Jian, G., Schmisseur, A., & Fairhurst, G. (2008). Organizational discourse and communication: The progeny of Proteus. Paper, Submitted to *Discourse and Communication.*

Jirokta, M., Liff, P., & Gilbert, N. (1991). Participation frameworks for computer mediated communication. *ECSCW 1991, 81–95.* Amsterdam.

Johnson, B. (1999). Communication for organizing: A typology of coordination formats. In P. Salem (Ed.), *Organizational communication and change* (pp. 99–124). Cresskill, NJ: Hampton Press.

Jones, M. R., & Karsten, H. (2003). Review: Structuration theory and information systems research. *Working Paper 2003/11,* Judge Institute of Management. Cambridge University.

Jones, M. R., & Karsten, H. (2008). Giddens' structuration theory and information systems research. *MIS Quarterly, 32*(1), 127–57.

Kanter, R. M. (1983). *The change masters: Innovations for productivity in the american corporation.* New York: Simon & Schuster.

Kaplan, S. (2008). Framing contests: Strategy making under uncertainty. *Organization Science, 19*(5), 729–52.

Kaspersen, L. B. (2000). *Anthony Giddens* (Trans. S. Sampson). Oxford, UK: Blackwell Publishers.

Katriel, T. (1991). Rethinking the terms of social interaction. *Research on Language and Social Interaction, 32*(1–2), 95–101.

Keenoy, T. (1991). The roots of metaphor in the old and the new industrial relations. *British Journal of Industrial Relations, 29*(2), 313–28.

Kellerman, K. (1992). Communication: Inherently strategic and primarily automatic. *Communication Monographs, 59,* 288–300.

Kelly, S., & Noonan, C. (2008). Anxiety and psychological security in offshoring relationships: The role and development of trust as emotional commitment. *Journal of Information Technology, 23*(1), 232–48.

Kendon, A. (1988). Goffman's approach to face-to-face interaction. In P. Drew, & A. Wootton (Eds.), *Erving Goffman: Exploring the interaction order.* Cambridge, UK: Polity Press.

Keyton, J., Messersmith, A., & Bisel, R. (2008). *Moving from talk about work to talk as work.* Position Paper, Organizational Communication Conference, Alta, UT.

Kidder, J. (2009). Appropriating the city: Space, theory, and bike messengers. *Theory and Society, 38*(3), 307–28.

Kilminster, R. (1997). Structuration theory as a world-view. In C. Bryant, & D. Jary (Eds.), *Anthony Giddens: Critical assessments, Vol. 1* (pp. 95–98). New York: Routledge.

Kim, J., & Kim, E. (2008). Theorizing dialogic deliberation: Everyday political talk as communicative action and dialogue. *Communication Theory, 18*(1), 51–70.

Kim, Y. Y. (1995). Cross-cultural adaptation. In R. Wiseman (Ed.), *Intercultural communication theory*. Thousand Oaks, CA: Sage.

King, B. G., Felin, T., & Whetten, D. A. (2010). Finding the organization in organization theory: A meta-theory of the organization as a social actor. *Organization Science, 21*(1), 290–305.

Kintsch, W. (1988). The use of knowledge in discourse processing: A construction-integration model. *Psychological Review, 95*, 163–82.

Kintsch, W. (1998). *Comprehension: A paradigm for cognition*. Cambridge, UK: Cambridge University Press.

Kirby, E., Wieland, S., & McBride, M. (2006). Work–life communication. In S. Ting-Toomey, & J. Oetzel (Eds.), *Handbook of conflict communication* (pp. 327–57). Thousand Oaks, CA: Sage.

Kirby, E., & Krone, K. (2002). "The policy exists but you can't really use it": Communication and the structuration of work-family policies. *Journal of Applied Communication Research, 30*(1), 50–77.

Knorr-Cetina, K. (1999). *Epistemic cultures: How the sciences make knowledge*. Cambridge, MA: Harvard University Press.

Knorr-Cetina, K., & Bruegger, U. (2002). Global microstructures: The virtual societies of financial markets. *American Journal of Sociology, 107*(4), 905–50.

Knuth, M. (2000). A dialogue on self and work. *Organization, 7*(3), 477–88.

Koenig, T. (2006). Compounding mixed-methods problems in frame analysis through comparative research. *Qualitative Research, 6*(1), 61–76.

Kossakowski, R. (2008). Between dramaturgy and totality: A call center in the perspective of Erving Goffman's sociology. *Studia Socjologiczne, 1*(188), 77–98.

Kraidy, M. M. (2002). Hybridity in cultural globalization. *Communication Theory, 12*(3), 316–39.

Kreps, B. (1990). *Organizational communication*. New York: Longman.

Krone, K. (2008). Forum introduction: Reflections on discursive and psychological approaches to leadership from around the globe. *Management Communication Quarterly, 21*(4), 508–9.

Krone, K., Strodt, P., & Kirby, E. (2006). Structuration theory: Promising directions for family communication research. In D. Braithwaite, & L. Baxter (Eds.), *Engaging theories in family communication* (pp. 293–308). Thousand Oaks, CA: Sage.

Kruml, S., & Geddes, D. (2000). Exploring the dimensions of emotional labor. *Management Communication Quarterly, 14*(1), 8–49.

Kuhn, T. (2006). A "demented work ethic" and a "lifestyle firm": Discourse, identity, and workplace time commitments. *Organization Studies, 27*(9), 1339–58.

Kuhn, T., Golden, A., Jorgenson, J., Buzzanell, P., Berkelaar, B., Kisselburgh, L., et al. (2008). Cultural discourses and discursive resources for Meaning/ful work: Constructing and disrupting identities in contemporary capitalism. *Management Communication Quarterly, 22*(1), 162–71.

Kuhn, T., & Jackson, M. (2008). Accomplishing knowledge: A framework for investigating knowing in organizations. *Management Communication Quarterly, 21*(4), 454–85.

Kuhn, T., & Nelson, N. (2002). Reengineering identity: A case study of multiplicity and duality in organizational identification. *Management Communication Quarterly, 16*(1), 5–38.

Kunda, G. (1992). *Engineering culture: Control and commitment in a high-tech corporation*. Philadelphia, PA: University of Pennslyvania Press.

Kwon, W., Clarke, I., & Wodak, R. (2009). Organizational decision-making, discourse, and power: Integrating across contexts and scales. *Discourse and Communication, 3*(3), 273–302.

Lakoff, G., & Johnson, M. (1999). *Philosophy in the flesh: The embodied mind and its challenge to Western thought.* New York: Basic Books.

Lammers, J., & Barbour, J. (2002). *Identity, institutions and structuration: The case of "managed care."* Paper, NCA Conference, New Orleans, LA.

Lammers, J. C., & Barbour, J. B. (2006). An institutional theory of organizational communication. *Communication Theory, 16*(3), 356–77.

Langer, E. (1983). *The psychology of control.* Beverly Hills, CA: Sage.

Latour, B. (1991). Technology is society made durable. In J. Law (Ed.), *A sociology of monsters: Essays on power, technology and domination.* (pp. 103–31). London, UK: Routledge.

Latour, B. (1993). *We have never been modern.* Cambridge, MA: Harvard University Press.

Latour, B. (1994). On technical mediation—philosophy, sociology, genealogy. *Common Knowledge, 3*(4), 29–64.

Latour, B. (1996). Pursuing the discussion of interobjectivity with a few friends. *Mind, Culture, and Activity, 3*(4), 266–69.

Latour, B. (1999). *Pandora's hope: Essays on the reality of scientific studies.* Cambridge, MA: Harvard University Press.

Latour, B. (2005). *Reassembling the social: An introduction to actor-network theory.* London: Oxford University Press.

Lawrence, P., & Lorsch, J. (1967). *Organization and environment.* Cambridge, MA: Harvard Graduate School of Business.

Leech, G. (1983). *Principles of pragmatics.* London: Longman.

Leeds-Hurwitz, W. (1989). *Communication in everyday life: A social interpretation.* Norwood, NJ: Ablex Publishing Corporation.

Leeds-Hurwitz, W. (2004). *Erving Goffman as a communication theorist.* Paper, ICA Convention, New Orleans.

Leeds-Hurwitz, W. (2008). Goffman, Erving. In W. Donsbach (Ed.), *The international encyclopedia of communication, Vol. 5* (pp. 2001–3). Oxfod: Wiley-Blackwell.

Leflaive, X. (1996). Organizations as structures of domination. *Organization Studies, 17*(1), 23–47.

Lemert, C. (1997). Goffman. In C. Lemert, & A. Branaman (Eds.), *The Goffman reader* (pp. ix–xiv). London: Blackwell.

Lemert, C. (2003). Foreword. In A. Trevino (Ed.), *Goffman's legacy* (pp. xi–xvii). New York: Rowman & Littlefield Publishers.

Lemert, C., & Branaman, A. (1997). *The Goffman reader.* London: Blackwell.

Leonardi, P. (2007). Activating the informational capabilities of information technology for organizational change. *Organization Science, 18*(5), 813–31.

Lerner, G. (1996). Finding "face" in the preference structures of talk-in-interaction. *Social Psychology Quarterly, 59*(4), 303–21.

Leung, E., & Gibbons, J. (2008). Who is responsible? Participant roles in legal interpreting cases. *Multilingua, 27*(3), 177–91.

LeVine, P., & Scollon, R. (Eds.). (2004). *Discourse and technology: Multimodal discourse analysis.* Washington DC.: Georgetown University Press.

Levinson, S. (1983). *Pragmatics.* Cambridge, UK: Cambridge University Press.

Levinson, S. (1988). Putting linguistics on a proper footing: Explorations in Goffman's participation frame works. In P. Drew and A. Wootton (Eds.) *Goffman: Exploring the interaction order.* Oxford: Polity Press.

Lewis, L., & Seibold, D. (1993). Innovation modification during intraorganizational adoption. *Academy of Management Review, 18*(2), 322–54.

Ligas, M., & Coulter, R. (2001). Changing faces in service relationships: Customers' roles during dissatisfactory encounters. *Advances in Consumer Research, 28,* 71–76.

Ling, R. (1997). One can talk about common manners. In L. Haddon (Ed.), *Themes in mobile telephony: Final report of the COST 248 home and work group.*

Ling, R. (2010). The "unboothed" phone: Goffman and the use of mobile communication. In M. H. Jacobsen (Ed.), *The contemporary Goffman* (pp. 275–92). New York, NY: Routledge.

Liu, H. (2010). When leaders fail: A typology of failures and framing strategies. *Management Communication Quarterly, 24,* 232–51.

Livesay, J. (1997). Normative grounding and praxis: Habermas, Giddens and a contradiction within critical theory. In C. Bryant, & D. Jary (Eds.), *Anthony Giddens critical assessments, Vol. 1* (pp. 344–63). New York, NY: Routledge.

Llewellyn, N. (2004). In search of modernization: The negotiation of social identiy in organizational reform. *Organization Studies, 25*(6), 947–68.

Llewellyn, N., & Spence, L. (2009). Practice as a members phenomenon. *Organization Studies, 30*(12), 1419–39.

Llewellyn, S. (2007). Introducing the agents. *Organization Science, 28*(2), 133–53.

Locher, M. (2010). Introduction: Politeness and impoliteness in computer-mediated communication. *Journal of Politeness Research, 6,* 1–5.

Lofland, J. (1980). Early Goffman: Style, structure, substance, soul. In J. Dutton (Ed.), *The view from Goffman* (pp. 24–51). New York, NY: St. Martin's Press.

Lofland, J. (1998). *The public realm: Exploring the city's quintessential public territory.* New York: Aldine.

Lofland, J. (2000). Erving Goffman's sociological legacies. In G. Fine, & G. Smith (Eds.), *Erving Goffman, Vol. 1* (pp. 156–78). Thousand Oaks, CA: Sage.

Lovaglia, M., Mannix, E., Sell, J., & Wilson, R. (2005). Conflict, power and status in groups. In M. Poole, & A. Hollingshead (Eds.), *Theories of small groups: Interdisciplinary perspectives* (pp. 139–84). Sage Thousand Oaks, CA.

Low, M. (2008). The constitution of space: The structuration of spaces through the simultaneity of effect and perception. *European Journal of Social Theory, 11*(1), 25–49.

Luhtakallio, E. (2005). Frame analysis in the study of gender representations in media images. [Kehysanalyysi mediakuvien sukupuolirepresentaatioiden tutkimuksessa] *Sosiologia, 42*(3), 189–206.

Lumsden, K. (2009). "Don't ask a woman to do another woman's job": Gendered interactions and the emotional ethnographer. *Sociology, 43*(3), 497–513.

MacCannell, D. (2000). Erving Goffman, 1922–82. In G. Fine, & G. Smith (Eds.), *Erving Goffman, Vol. 1* (pp. 8–37). Thousand Oaks, CA: Sage.

Maines, D. (1982). In search of mesostructure: Studies in the negotiated order. *Urban Life, 11,* 267–79.

Maines, D. (1993). Narrative's moment and sociology's phenomena: Toward a narrative sociology. *Sociological Quarterly, 34*(1), 17–38.

Maines, D. (1996). On choices and criticism: A reply to Denzin. *Symbolic Interaction, 19*(4), 357–62.

Maines, D., Sugrue, N., & Katovich, M. (1983). The sociological import of G. H. Mead's theory of the past. *American Sociological Review, 48,* 163–65.

Malacrida, C. (2005). Discipline and dehumanization in a total institution: Institutional survivors' descriptions of time-out rooms. *Disability and Society, 20*(5), 523–37.

Mangham, I. (1990). Managing as a performing art. *British Journal of Management, 1*(2), 105–15.

Mangham, I. (1998). Emotional discourse in organizations. In D. Grant, T. Keenoy, & C. Oswick (Eds.), *Discourse and organization* (pp. 51–64). London: Sage.

Mangham, I. (2005). Vita contemplativa: The drama of organizational life. *Organization Studies, 26*(6), 941–58.

Manning, P. (1991). Drama as life: The significance of Goffman's changing use of the theatrical metaphors. *Sociological Theory, 9*(1), 70–86.

Manning, P. (1992). *Erving Goffman and modern sociology*. Stanford, CA: Stanford University Press.

Manning, P. (2000a). Credibility, agency and the interaction order. *Symbolic Interaction, 23*(3), 283–97.

Manning, P. (2000b). Ritual talk. In G. Fine, & G. Smith (Eds.), *Erving Goffman, Vol. 4* (pp. 214–36). Thousand Oaks, CA: Sage.

Manning, P. (2000c). The decline of civility: A comment on Erving Goffman's sociology. In G. Fine, & G. Smith (Eds.), *Erving Goffman Vol. 1* (pp. 329–47). Thousand Oaks, CA: Sage.

Manning, P. (2008). Goffman on organizations. *Organization Studies, 29*(5), 677–99.

Manning, P. (2010). *Continuities in Goffman: The interaction order*. In M. Jacobsen (Ed.), *The contemporary Goffman* (pp. 98–118). New York, NY: Routledge.

Mantere, S., & Vaara, E. (2008). On the problem of participation in strategy: A critical discursive perspective. *Organization Science, 19*(2), 341–58.

Manusov, V., & Patterson, M. (Eds.). (2006). *The Sage handbook of nonverbal communication*. Thousand Oaks, CA: Sage.

Mao, L. (1994). Beyond politeness theory: "Face" revisited and renewed. *Journal of Pragmatics, 21*, 451–86.

March, J. (1976). *Ambiguity and choice in organizations*. Bergen, Norway: Universitetsforlaget.

March, J., & Simon, H. (1958). *Organizations*. New York: John Wiley.

Markowitz, L. (1998). After the organizing ends: Workers, self-efficacy, activism, and union frameworks. *Social Problems, 45*(3), 356–82.

Marshak, R. J. (1998). A discourse on discourse: Redeeming the meaning of talk. In D. Grant, R. Keenoy, & C. Oswick (Eds.), *Discourse and organizations* (pp. 15–30). Thousand Oaks, CA.: Sage.

Marshak, R.J, Keenoy, T., Oswick, C., & Grant, D. (2000). From outer words to inner worlds. Journal of Applied Behavioral Science, 36(2), 245–58.

Martin, J. (1992). *Cultures in organizations: Three perspectives*. New York: Oxford University Press.

Martin, J. (2001). *Organizational culture: Mapping the terrain*. Thousand Oaks, CA: Sage.

Martin, P. (2002). Sensations, bodies, and the "spirit of a place": Aesthetics in residential organizations of the elderly. *Human Relations, 55*(7), 861–85.

Mason, I. (2006). On mutual accessibility of contextual assumptions in dialogue interpreting. *Journal of Pragmatics, 38*, 359–73.

Massey, K., Freeman, S., & Zelditch, M. (1997). Status, power, and accounts. *Social Psychology Quarterly, 60*(3), 238–51.

Mathieu, L. (2008). Frames and cities: From the discourse order towards situated action. *Swiss Journal of Sociology, 34*(1), 55–70.

Matsumoto, Y. (1988). Reexamination of the universality of face: Politeness phenomena in Japanese. *Journal of Pragmatics, 12*, 403–26.

Matsumoto, Y. (2003). Reply to Pizziconi. *Journal of Pragmatics, 35*(10–11), 1515–21.

Mayes, P. (2005). Linking micro and macro social structure through genre analysis. *Research on Language and Social Interaction, 38*(3), 331–70.

Maynard, D. (2000). Frame analysis of plea bargaining. In G. Fine, & G. Smith (Eds.), *Erving Goffman, Vol. 3* (pp. 56–76). Thousand Oaks, CA: Sage.

Maynard, D., & Zimmerman, D. (1984). Topical talk, ritual and the social organization of relationships. *Social Psychology Quarterly, 47*(4), 301–16.

Maznevski, M., & Chudoba, K. (2000). Bridging space over time: Global virtual team dynamics and effectiveness. *Organization Science, 11*(5), 473–94.

McCawley, J. (1999). Participant roles, frames, and speech acts. *Linguistics and Philosophy, 22*, 595–619.

McDaniel, S., Olson, G., & Magee, J. (1996). Identifying and analyzing multiple threads in computer-mediated and face-to-face conversations. *Proceedings of the Conference on Computer Supported Cooperative Work* (pp. 39–47). Cambridge, MA.

McGinn, K. L., & Keros, A. T. (2002). Improvisation and the logic of exchange in socially embedded transactions. *Administrative Science Quarterly, 47*(3), 442–73.

McPhee, R. (1985). Formal structure and organizational communication. In R. McPhee, & P. Tompkins (Eds.), *Organizational communication: Traditional themes and new directions.* (pp. 149–78). Beverly Hills, CA: Sage.

McPhee, R. (1988). Vertical communication chains: Toward an integrated approach. *Applied Communication Quarterly, 1,* 455–93.

McPhee, R. (1998). Giddens' conception of personal relationships and its relevance to comunication theory. In R. Conville, & L. Rogers (Eds.), *Personal relationships and communication* (pp. 83–106). Thousand Oaks, CA: Sage.

McPhee, R. (2004a). Text, agency, and organization in the light of structuration theory. *Organization, 11*(3), 355–71.

McPhee, R. (2004b). Clegg and Giddens on power and (post) modernity. *Management Communication Quarterly, 18*(1), 129–45.

McPhee, R., & Iverson, J. (2009). Agents of constitution in communidad: Constitutive processes of communication in organizations. In L. Putnam, & A. Nicotera (Eds.), *Building theories of organization* (pp. 49–88). New York: Routledge.

McPhee, R., Myers, K., & Trethewey, A. (2006). On collective mind and conversational analysis response to Cooren. *Management Communication Quarterly, 19*(3), 311–26.

McPhee, R., & Zaug, P. (2000). The communicative constitution of organization: A framework of explanation. *Electronic Journal of Communication, 10.*

Meanwell, E., Wolfe, J., & Hallett, T. (2008). Old paths and new directions: Studying emotions in the workplace. *Sociology Compass, 2*(2), 537–59.

Meisenbach, R. (2008). Working with tensions. material, discourse, and (dis)empowerment in occupational identity negotiation among higher education fund-raisers. *Management Communication Quarterly, 22*(2), 258–87.

Menand, L. (2009). Some frames for Goffman. *Social Psychology Quarterly, 72*(4), 296–99.

Mendoza, J. D. (1997a). Structuralism and the concept of structure. In C. Bryant, & D. Jary (Eds.), *Anthony Giddens: Critical assessments, Vol. 1* (pp. 234–56). New York: Routledge.

Mendoza, J. D. (1997b). Ontological security, routine, and social reproduction. In C. Bryant & D. Jary (Eds.), *Anthony Giddens: Critical assessments, Vol. 2* (pp. 270–305). New York: Routledge.

Mengis, J., & Eppler, M. (2008). Understanding and managing conversations from a knowledge perspective: An analysis of the roles and rules of face-to-face conversations in organizations. *Organization Studies, 29*(10), 1287–1313.

Meyers, R., & Seibold, D. (1990a). Perspectives on group argument: A critical review of persuasive arguments theory and an alternative structurational view. In J. Anderson (Ed.), *Communication Yearbook 13* (pp. 268–302). Newbury Park, CA: Sage.

Meyers, R., & Seibold, D. (1990b). Persuasive arguments and group influence: Research evidence and strategic implications. In M. Cody, & M. McLaughlin (Eds.), *The psychology of tactical communication* (pp. 139–56). Clevedon, UK: Multilingual Matters.

Meyrowitz, J. (1985). *No sense of place: The impact of electronic media in social behavior.* New York, NY: Oxford University Press.

Miettinen, R., Fredericks, D., & Yanow, D. (2009). Re-turn to practice: An introductory essay. *Organization Studies, 30*(12), 1309–27.

Miller, K. (1999). The use of historical data in organizational communication theorizing. In P. Salem (Ed.), *Organizational communication and change* (pp. 175–88). Cresskill, NJ: Hampton Press.

Mingers, J. (1996). A comparison of Maturana's autopoectic social theory and Giddens' theory of structuration. *Systems Research, 16*(4), 469–82.

Mingers, J. (2004). Can social systems be autopoietic? Bhaskar's and Giddens' social theories. *Journal for the Theory of Social Behaviour, 34*(4), 403–27.

Minsky, M. (1977). Frame-system theory. In P. Johnson-Laird, & P. Wason (Eds.), *Thinking*. Cambridge, UK: Camridge University Press.

Minsky, M. (1979). A framework for representing knowledge. In D. Metzing (Ed.), *Frame conceptions and text understanding*. Berlin: de Gruyter.

Mintzberg, H. (1979). *The structuring of organizations*. Upper Saddle River, NJ: Prentice-Hall.

Moeran, B. (2009). The organization of creativity in Japanese advertising production. *Human Relations, 62*(7), 963–85.

Mohr, J., & Friedland, R. (2008). Theorizing the institution: Foundations, duality, and data. *Theory and Society, 37*(5), 421–26.

Mohr, J., & White, H. (2008). How to model an institution. *Theory and Society, 37*(5), 485–512.

Molotoch, H., & Boden, D. (1985). Talking social structure: Discourse, domination and the Watergate hearings. *American Sociological Review, 50*, 273–88.

Monge, P., & Poole, M. (2008). The evolutional of organizational communication. *Journal of Communication, 58*(4), 679–92.

Morand, D. A. (1995). The role of behavioral formality and informality in the enactment of bureaucratic versus organic organizations. *Academy of Management Review, 20*(4), 831–72.

Morgan, G. (2006). *Images of organization* (10th ed.). Thousand Oaks, CA: Sage.

Morris, A., Seibold, D., & Meyers, R. (1991). The influence of individual differences in message production on argumentation in group decision-making: Theory development and propositions. In D. van Eemeren, J. Grootendorst, & C. Willard (Eds.), *Proceedings of the second international conference on argumentation* (pp. 582–89). Amsterdam: International Society for the Study of Argumentation.

Morris, J. A., & Feldman, D. C. (1996). The dimensions, antecedents, and consequences of emotional labor. *Academy of Management Review, 21*(4), 986–1010.

Morris, M. W., Menon, T., & Ames, D. (2001). Culturally conferred conceptions of agency: A key to social perception of persons, groups, and other actors. *Personality and Social Psychology Review, 5*(2), 169–82.

Mouzelis, N. (1997). Restructuring structuration theory. In C. Bryant, & D. Jary (Eds.), *Anthony Giddens: Critical assessments, Vol. 2* (pp. 200–18). New York, NY: Routledge.

Mumby, D. (1987). The political function of narrative in organizations. *Communication Monographs, 54*, 113–27.

Mumby, D. (1989). Ideology and the social construction of meaning: A communication perspective. *Communication Quarterly, 37*, 291–304.

Mumby, D. K. (1997). Modernism, postmodernism, and communication studies: A rereading of an ongoing debate. *Communication Theory, 7*(1), 1–28.

Mumby, D. K. (1998). Organizing men: Power, discourse, and the social construction of masculinity(s) in the workplace. *Communication Theory, 8*(2), 164–83.

Mumby, D. (2000). Power, politics, and organizational communication. In F. Jablin, & L. Putnam (Eds.), *Handbook of organizational communication: Advances in theory, research and methods*. Thousand Oaks, CA: Sage.

Mumby, D., & St. Clair, R. (1997). Organizational discourse. In T. A. Van Dijk (Ed.), *Discourse as social interaction* (pp. 181–205). London: Sage.

Myerowitz, J. (1985). *No sense of place: The impact of electronic media on social behavior*. New York, NY: Oxford University Press.

Myerowitz, J. (1990). Redefining the situation: Extending dramaturgy into a theory of social change and media effects. In S. Riggins (Ed.), *Beyond Goffman*. New York: de Gruyter.

Myers, G. (2003). Risk and face: A review of the six studies. *Health, Risk and Society, 5*(2), 215–20.

Nadkarni, S., & Narayanan, V. (2007). The evolution of collective strategy frames in high-and low-velocity industries. *Organization Science, 18*(4), 688–710.

Napier, J. (2007). Cooperation in interpreter-mediated monologic talk. *Discourse and Communication, 1*(4), 407–31.

Newell, S., David, G., & Chand, D. (2007). An analysis of trust among globally distributed work teams in an organizational setting. *Knowledge and Process Management, 14*(3), 158–68.

Nicolini, D. (2009). Zooming in and out: Studying practices by switching theoretical lenses and trailing connections. *Organization Studies, 30*(12), 1391–1418.

Nippert-Eng, C. (1996). *Home and work: Negotiating the boundaries of everyday life.* Chicago: University of Chicago Press.

Nisbett, R., & Ross, L. (1980). *Human inference: Strategies and shortcomings of social judgment.* Englewood Cliffs, NJ: Prentice-Hall.

Nonaka, I., & Krogh, G. v. (2009). Tacit knowledge and knowledge conversion: Controversy and advancement in organizational knowledge creation theory. *Organization Science, 20*(3), 635–52.

Norton, T. (2007). The structuration of public participation: Organizing environmental control. *Environmental Communications, 1*(2), 146–70.

Nunes, J. (2007). Goffman's sociolinguistics and the mediated communication. *Tempo Social: Revista De Sociologia Da USP, 19*(2), 253–86.

Nutch, F. (2007). On cooling the tourist out: Notes on the management of spoiled expectations. *Qualitative Sociology Review, 3*(2), 64–81.

O'Driscoll, J. (1996). About face: A defense and elaboration of universal dualism. *Journal of Pragmatics, 25*, 1–32.

O'Driscoll, J. (2007). Brown and Levinson's face: How it can—and can't—help us to understand interaction across cultures. *Intercultural Pragmatics, 4*, 463–92.

Oetzel, J. (2001). *Managing intercultural conflict effectively.* Thousand Oaks, CA.: Sage.

Oliver, D. P., Porock, D., & Oliver, D. B. (2006). Managing the secrets of dying backstage: The voices of nursing home staff. *Omega, 53*(3), 193–207.

Olufowote, J. (2008). A structural analysis of informed consent to treatment: Societal evolution, contradiction, and reproductions in medical malpractice. *Health Communication, 23*(3), 292–303.

Orlikowski, W. (1992a). Knowing in practice: Enacting a collective capability in distributed organizing. *Organization Science, 13*(3), 249–73.

Orlikowski, W. (1992b). The duality of technology: Rethinking the concept of technology in organizations. *Organization Science, 3*(3), 398–472.

Orlikowski, W. (1996). Improvising organizational transformation over time: A situated change perspective. *Information Systems Research, 7*(1), 63–92.

Orlikowski, W. (2000). Using technology and constituting structures: A practice lens for studying technology in organizations. *Organization Science, 11*(4), 404–28.

Orlikowski, W. J. (2002). Knowing in practice: Enacting a collective capability in distributed organizing. *Organization Science, 13*(3), 249–73.

Orlikowski, W. (2007). Sociomaterial practices: Exploring technology at work. *Organization Studies, 28*(9), 1435–48.

Orlikowski, W. J., & Barley, S. (2001). Technology and institutions: What can research on information technology and research on organizations learn from each other. *MIS Quarterly, 25*(2), 145–65.

Orlikowski, W. J., & Gash, D. C. (1994). Technological frames: Making sense of information technology in organizations. *ACM Trans. Information Systems, 12*, 174–207.

Orlikowski, W. J., & Iacono, C. S. (2001). Research commentary: Desperately seeking the IT in IT research—A call to theorizing the IT artifact. *Information Systems Research, 12*(2), 121–34.

Orlikowski, W., & Robey, D. (1991). Information technology and the structuring of organizations. *Institute of Management Sciences, 2*(2), 143–69.

Orlikowski, W., & Yates, J. (1994). Genre repertoire: The structuring of communicative practices in organizations. *Administrative Science Quarterly, 39*, 541–74.

Orlikowski, W., & Yates, J. (July, 1998). Genre systems: Structuring interaction through communicative norms. *MIT Sloan School of Management WP #4030*, 1–15.

Orlikowski, W., & Yates, J. (2002). It's about time: Temporal structuring in organizations. *Organization Science, 13*(6), 684–700.

Orlikowski, W., Yates, J., Okamura, K., & Fujimoto, M. (1995). Shaping electronic communication: The metastructuring of technology in use. *Organization Science, 6*(4), 423–44.

Ostrow, J. (2000). Spontaneous involvement and social life. In G. Fine, & G. Smith (Eds.), *Erving Goffman, Vol. 2* (pp. 318–32). Thousand Oaks, CA: Sage.

Oswick, C., Grant, D., Marshak, R. J., & Cox, J. W. (2010). Organizational discourse and change: Positions, perspectives, progress, and prospects. *Journal of Applied Behavioral Science, 46*(1), 8–15.

Oswick, C., Keenoy, R., & Grant, D. (2000). Discourse, organizations and organizing: Concepts, objects and subjects. *Human Relations, 53*(9), 1115–23.

Oswick, C., Keenoy, R., & Grant, D. (2001). Editorial: Dramatizing and organizing: Acting and being. *Journal of Organizational Change Management, 14*(3), 218–24.

Oswick, C., & Richards, D. (2004). Talk in organizations: Local conversations, wider perspectives. *Culture and Organization, 10*(2), 107–23.

Outhwaite, W. (1990). Agency and structure. In J. Clark, D. Modgil, & S. Modgil (Eds.), *Anthony Giddens: Consensus and controversy* (pp. 63–72). London, UK: Falmer Press.

Pal, M., & Buzzanell, P. (2008). The Indian call center experience: A case study in changing discourses of identity, identification and career in a global context. *Journal of Business Communication, 45*, 31–60.

Paolucci, P., Holland, M., & Williams, S. (2005). The Mayberry Machiavellians in power: A critical analysis of the Bush administration through a synthesis of Machiavelli, Goffman, and Foucault. *Current Perspectives in Social Theory, 23*, 133–203.

Parisi, D., & Castelfranchi, P. (1981). A goal analysis of some pragmatic aspects of language. In H. Parret, M. Sbasi & J. Vershueren (Eds.), *Possibilities and limitations of pragmatics.* Amsterdam: John Benjamins, B.B.

Paroutis, S., & Pettigrew, A. (2007). Strategizing in the multi-business firm: Strategy teams at multiple levels and over time. *Human Relations, 60*(1), 99–135.

Parsons, E. (2010). Markets, identities and the discourses of antique dealing. *Marketing Theory, 10*(3), 283–98.

Patriotta, G., & Spedale, S. (2009). Making sense through face: Identity and social interaction in a consultancy task force. *Organization Studies, 30*(11), 1227–48.

Patterson, M., & Montepare, J. (2007). Nonverbal behavior in a global context dialogue questions and responses. *Journal of Nonverbal Behavior, 31*, 167–68.

Pearson, E. (2009). All the world wide web's a stage: The performance of identity in online social networks. *First Monday, 14*(3).

Pentland, B. T., & Feldman, M. S. (2007). Narrative networks: Patterns of technology and organization. *Organization Science, 18*(5), 781–95.

Perlow, L. (1999). The time famine: Toward a sociology of work time. *Administrative Science Quarterly, 44*, 57–81.

Perlow, L., Gittell, J., & Katz, R. (2004). Contextualizing patterns of work group interaction: Toward a nested theory of structuration. *Organization Science, 15*(5), 520–36.

Perretta, H. (2008). Presenting of self in MySpace.com, an online social networking site. *Masters of Abstracts International, 46*(1), 137.

Perri 6. (2005). What's in a frame? social organization, risk perception and the sociology of knowledge. *Journal of Risk Research, 8*(2), 91–118.

Peters, L., Gassenheimer, J., & Johnston, W. (2009). Marketing and the structuration of organizational learning. *Marketing Theory, 9*(3), 341–68.

Peterson, A. (2008). Who "owns" the streets? Ritual performances of respect and authority in interactions between young men and police officers. *Journal of Scandinavian Studies in Criminology and Crime Prevention, 9*(2), 97–118.

Pettigrew, A. (1985). *The awakening giant: Continuity and change in imperial chemical industries.* Oxford: Basil Blackwell.

Pfister, J. (2010). Is there a need for a maxim of politeness? *Journal of Pragmatics, 42*(5), 1266–82.

Philipsen, G. (1997). A theory of speech codes. In G. Philipsen, & T. Albrecht (Eds.), *Developing communication theories* (pp. 119–56). Albany, NY: State University of New York Press.

Phillips, N., Lawrence, T., & Hardy, C. (2004). Discourse and institutions. *Academy of Management Review,* 29(4), 635–652.

Phillips, T., & Smith, P. (2003). Everyday incivility: Towards a benchmark. *Sociological Review, 51*(1), 85–108.

Phillipsen, G. (1987). The prospect for cultural communication. In L. Kincaid (Ed.), *Communication theory: Eastern and Western perspectives* (pp. 245–54). New York, NY: Academic Press.

Phipps, A. (2001). Empirical applications of structuration theory. *Geografiska Annaler, 83*(4), 189–204.

Pickering, A. (1995). *The mangle of practice.* Chicago: University of Chicago Press.

Pinch, T. (2008). Technology and institutions: Living in a material world. *Theory and Society, 37*(5), 461–83.

Planalp, S., & Gavin-Doxas, K. (1994). Using mutual knowledge in conversations: Friends as experts on each other. In S. Duck (Ed.), *Dynamics of relationships* (pp. 1–26). Thousand Oaks, CA: Sage.

Pomerantz, A. (1998). Multiple interpretations of context: How are they useful? *Research on Language and Social Interaction, 31*(1), 123–32.

Pomerantz, A. & Fehr, B. J. (1997). *Conversational analysis: An approach to the study of social action as sense making practices.* In T. Van Dijk (Ed.), *Discourse as social interaction* (pp. 64–91). London: Sage.

Pomerantz, A., & Mandelbaum, J. (2005). Conversation analytic approaches to the relevance and uses of relationship categories in interaction. In K. Fitch, & R. Sanders (Eds.), *Handbook of language and social interaction* (pp. 149–74). Mahwah, NJ: Lawrence Erlbaum Associates.

Poole, M. (1985). Communication and organizational climates: Review, critique, and a new perspective. In R. McPhee, & P. Tompkins (Eds.), *Organizational communication: Traditional themes and new directions* (pp. 79–108). Beverly Hills, CA: Sage.

Poole, M. (1999). Group communication theory. In L. Frey, K. Gouran, & M. Poole (Eds.), *The handbook of group communication theory and research* (pp. 37–70). Thousand Oaks, CA: Sage.

Poole, M., & DeSanctis, G. (1990). Understanding the use of group decision support systems: The theory of adaptive structuration. In J. Fulk, & C. Steinfeld (Eds.), *Organizations and communication technology* (pp. 173–93). Newbury Park, CA: Sage.

Poole, M., & DeSanctis, G. (1992). Microlevel structuration in computer-supported group decision making. *Human Communication Research, 19*(1), 5–49.

Poole, M., & DeSanctis, G. (2004). Structuration theory in information systems research: Methods and controversies. In M. E. Whitman, & A. B. Woszezynski (Eds.), *The handbook of information systems research* (pp. 206–49). Hershey, PA: Idea Group Publishing.

Poole, M., & McPhee, R. (1983). A structurational theory of organizational climate. In L. Putnam, & M. Pacanowsky (Eds.), *Organizational communication: An interpretive approach* ed., pp. 195–219). Beverly Hills, CA: Sage.

Poole, M., & McPhee, R. (2005). Structuration theory. In S. May, & D. Mumby (Eds.), *Engaging organizational communication theory and research* (pp. 171–96). Thousand Oaks, CA: Sage.

Poole, M., Seibold, D., & McPhee, R. (1985). Group decision-making as a structurational process. *Quarterly Journal of Speech, 71,* 74–102.

Poole, M., Seibold, D., & McPhee, R. (1986). A structurational approach to theory-building in group decision-making research. In R. Hirokawa, & M. Poole (Eds.), *Communication and group decision-making* (pp. 237–64). Beverly Hills, CA: Sage.

Potter, J., & Edwards, D. (2001). Sociolinguistics, cognitivism and discursive psychology. In N. Coupland, S. Sarangi, & C. Candlin (Eds.), *Sociolinguistics and social theory* (pp. 88–103). London: Longman.

Potter, J., & Wetherell, M. (1987). *Discourse and social psychology*. London: Sage.

Pozzebon, M., & Pinsonneault, A. (2001). *Structuration theory in the field: An assessment of research strategies*. Paper, Global Co-operation in the New Milennium, 9th European Conference on Information Systems, Bled, Slovenia, June 27–29.

Pozzebon, M., & Pinsonneault, A. (2005). Challenges in conducting empirical work using structuration theory: Learning from IT research. *Organization Studies, 26*(9), 1353–76.

Praet, E. V. (2009). Staging a team performance. *Journal of Business Communications, 46*(1), 80–99.

Preves, S., & Stephenson, D. (2009). The classroom as stage: Impression management in collaborative teaching. *Teaching Sociology, 37*(3), 245–56.

Psathas, G., & Waksler, F. (2000). Essential features of face-to-face interaction. In G. A. Fine, & G. Smith (Eds.), *Erving Goffman, Vol. 4* (pp. 9–30). London, Thousand Oaks, New Delhi: Sage.

Putnam, L. (2000). *Shifting voices, oppositional discourse, and new visions for communication studies*. Paper, ICA Convention Presidential Address, Acapulco, Mexico.

Putnam, L., & Cooren, F. (2004). Alternative perspectives on the role of text and agency in constituting organizations. *Organization, 11*(3), 323–33.

Putnam, L., & Fairhurst, G. (2001). Discourse analysis in organizations: Issues and concerns. In F. Jablin, & L. Putnam (Eds.), *The new handbook of organizational communication.* (pp. 78–136). Thousand Oaks, CA: Sage.

Putnam, L., & McPhee, R. (2009). Theory building: Comparison of CCO orientations. In L. Putnam, A. Nicotera, & R. McPhee (Eds.), *Communication constitutes organization* (pp. 187–208). New York: Routledge.

Putnam, L., & Nicotera, A. (2009). *Building theories of organization: The constitutive role of communication*. New York: Routledge.

Putnam, L. L., Nicotera, A. M., & McPhee, R. (2009). Introduction: Communication constitutes organization. In L. L. Putnam, & A. M. Nicotera (Eds.), *Building theories of organization: The constitutive role of communication* (pp. 1–20). New York: Routledge.

Putnam, L., & Nicotera, A. (2010). Communicative constitution of organization is a question: Critical issues for addressing it. *Management Communication Quarterly, 24*, 158–73.

Putnam, L., Phillips, N., & Chapman, P. (1996). Metaphors of communication and organization. In S. Clegg, C. Hardy, & W. Nord (Eds.), *Handbook of organizational studies* (pp. 375–408). London: Sage.

Rae, J. (2001). Organizing participation in interaction: Doing participation frameworks. *Research on Language and Social Interaction, 34*(2), 253–78.

Rafaeli, A., Dutton, J., Harquail, C. V., & Mackie-Lewis, S. (1997). Navigating by attire: The use of dress by female administrative employees. *Academy of Management Journal, 40* (1), 9–45.

Rafaeli, A., & Pratt, M. G. (1993). Tailored meanings: On the meaning and impact of organizational dress. Academy of Management Review, 18(1), 32–55.

Rafaeli, A., & Sutton, R. I. (1987). Expression of emotion as part of the work role. Academy of Management Review, 12(1), 23–37.

Raffler-Engler, W. v. (1977). *The unconscious element in inter-cultural communication*. Unpublished manuscript.

Ralston, D. A., Holt, D., Terpstra, R., & Kai-Cheng, Y. (1997). The impact of national culture and economic ideology on managerial work values: A study of the United States, Russia, Japan, and China. *Journal of Applied Psychology, 28*, 177–207.

Rampton, B. (2009). Interaction ritual and not just artful performance in crossing and stylization. *Language in Society, 38*(2), 149–76.

Rantanen, T. (2005). Giddens and the "G"-word: An interview with Anthony Giddens. *Global Media and Communications, 1*(1), 63–77.

Rasche, A., & Chia, R. (2009). Researching strategy practices: A genealogical social theory perspective. *Organization Studies, 30*(7), 713–34.

Rattanen, T. (2005). Giddens and the "G"-word. *Global Media and Communications, 1*(1), 63–77.

Rawls, A. (1987). The interaction order sui generis: Goffman's contribution to social theory. *Sociological Theory, 5*(2), 136–49.

Rawls, A. (1988). Interaction vs. interaction order: A reply to Fuchs. *Sociological Theory, 6*, 124–129.

Rawls, A. (1989). Language, self, and social order: A reformulation of Goffman and Sacks. *Human Studies, 12*(1–2), 147–72.

Rawls, A. (2000). The interaction order sui generis: Goffman's contribution to social theory. In G. Fine, & G. Smith (Eds.), *Erving Goffman, Vol. 2* (pp. 252–74). Thousand Oaks, CA: Sage.

Rawls, A. W. (2002). Emergent sociality: A dialectic of commitment and order. *La Revue Du MAUSS,* (19), 130–49.

Rawls, A. W. (2003). Orders of interaction and intelligibility: Intersections between Goffman and Garfinkel by way of Durkheim. In A. Trevino (Ed.), *Goffman's legacy* (pp. 216–53). New York: Rowman & Littlefield.

Rawls, A., & David, G. (2006). Accountability other: Trust, reciprocity and exclusion in a context of situated practice. *Human Studies, 28*(4), 469–97.

Rettie, R. (2009). Mobile phone communication: Extending Goffman to mediated interaction. *Sociology, 43*(3), 421–38.

Richter, C. (2000). Anthony Giddens: A communication perspective. *Communication Theory, 10*(3), 359–69.

Ridgeway, C. L. (1994). Structure, action, and social psychology. *Social Psychology Quarterly, 57*(3), 161–62.

Ridgeway, C. L. (2006). Linking social structure and interpersonal behavior: A theoretical perspective on cultural schemas and social relations. *Social Psychology Quarterly, 69*(5), 5–16.

Riley, P. (1983). A structurationist account of political culture. *Administrative Science Quarterly, 28*(3), 414–37.

Riley, R., & Manias, E. (2005). Rethinking theatre in modern operating rooms. *Nursing Inquiry, 12*(1), 2–9.

Ritzer, G. (1990). Macro-micro linkage in sociological theory: Applying a metatheoretical tool. In G. Ritzer (Ed.), *Frontiers of social theory: The new syntheses* (Chapter 13). New York: Columbia University Press.

Robichaud, D., Giroux, H., & Taylor, J. R. (2004). The metaconversation: The recursive property of language as the key to organizing. *Academy of Management Review, 29*(4), 617–34.

Rogers, M. (1980). Goffman on power hierarchy, and status. In J. Ditton (Ed.), *The view from Goffman* (pp. 100–33). New York, NY: St. Martin's Press.

Rosenfeld, P., Giacalone, R., & Riordan, C. (1994). Impression management theory and diversity: Lessons for organizational behavior. *American Behavioral Scientist, 37*, 601–4.

Rosenfeld, P., Giacalone, R. A., & Riordan, C. A. (1995). *Impression management in organizations: Theory, measurement, practice.* London: Routledge.

Rosch, E. (1978). Principles of categorization. In E. Rosch, & B. Lloyd (Eds.), *Cognition and categorization* (pp. 27–48). Hillsdale, NJ: Erlbaum.

Ross, D. (2007). Backstage with the knowledge boys and girls: Goffman and distributed agency in an organic online community. *Organizational Studies, 28*(3), 307–25.

Ross, L. (1981). The "intuitive scientist" formulation and its developmental implications. In J. Flavell, & L. Ross (Eds.), *Social cognitive development.* Cambridge, UK: Cambridge University Press.

Rusbult, C., & Van Lange, P. (2003). Interdependence, interaction and relationships. *Annual Review of Psychology, 54*, 351–75.

Sacks, H., Schegloff, E., & Jefferson, G. (1974). A simplest systematics for the organization of turn-taking for conversation. *Language, 50*, 696–735.

Sahay, S., & Walsham, G. (2007). Social structure and managerial agency in India. *Organization Studies, 18*(3), 415–44.

Samra-Fredericks, D. (2003). Strategizing as lived experience and strategists' everyday efforts to shape strategic direction. *Journal of Management Studies, 40*(1), 141–76.

Samra-Fredericks, D. (2004a). Managerial elites making rhetorical and linguistic "moves" for a moving (emotional) display. *Human Relations, 57*(9), 1103–43.

Samra-Fredericks, D. (2004b). Understanding the production of "strategy" and "organization" through talk amongst managerial elites. *Culture and Organization, 10*(2), 125–41.

Samra-Fredericks, D. (2005). Strategic practice, "discourse" and the everyday practice of "power effects." *Organization, 12*, 803–41.

Samra-Fredericks, D. (2007). Social constructionism in management and organization studies. In J. Holstein, & J. Gubrium (Eds.), *Handbook of constructionist research*. New York, NY: Guilford Publications Inc.

Samra-Fredericks, D. (2010). Ethnomethodology and the moral accountability of interaction: Navigating the conceptual terrain of "face" and face-work. *Journal of Pragmatics, 42*, 2147–57.

Samra-Fredericks, D., & Bargiela-Chiappini, F. (2008). Introduction to the symposium on the foundations of organizing: The contribution from Garfinkel, Goffman and Sacks. *Organization Studies, 29*(5), 653–75.

Sanders, R. (1991). The two-way relationship between talk in social interaction and actors' goals and plans. In K. Tracy (Ed.), *Understanding face-to-face interaction: Issues linking goals and discourse* (pp. 167–88). Hillsdale, NJ: Lawrence Erlbaum Associates.

Sanders, R. (1995). The sequential inferential theories of Sanders and Gottman. In D. Cushman, & B. Kovacic (Eds.), (pp. 227–50). Albany, NY: State University of New York Press.

Sanjose, V., Vidal-Abarca, E., & Padilla, O. (2006). A connectionist extension to Kintsch's construction-integration model. *Discourse Processes, 42*(1), 1–35.

Schank, R., & Abelson, R. (1977). *Scripts, plans, goals and understanding*. Hillsdale, NJ: Lawrence Erlbaum Associates.

Scheff, T. (2000). Shame and the social bond. *Sociological Theory, 18*, 84–98.

Scheff, T. (2005a). Looking-glass self: Goffman as symbolic interactionist. *Symbolic Interaction, 28*(2), 147–66.

Scheff, T. (2005b). The structure of context: Deciphering frame analysis. *Sociological Theory, 23*(4), 368–85.

Scheff, T. (2007). A concept of social integration. *Philosophical Psychology, 20*(5), 579–93.

Schegloff, E. (1999). Discourse, pragmatics, conversation, analysis. *Discourse Processes, 1*, 405–35.

Schegloff, E. (2001). Discourse as an interactional achievement III: The omnirelevance of action. In D. Schiffrin, D. Tannen, & H. Hamilton (Eds.), *The handbook of discourse analysis* (pp. 229–49). Oxford: Blackwell.

Schegloff, E., & Sacks, H. (1973). Opening up closings. *Semiotica, 7*, 289–327.

Schein, E. (2004). *Organizational culture and leadership* (3rd ed.). San Francisco, CA: Jossey-Bass.

Schiffrin, D. (1994). *Approaches to discourse*. Oxford, UK: Blackwell.

Schimmelfennig, F. (2002). Goffman meets IR: Dramaturgical action in international community. *International Review of Sociology/Revue Internationale De Sociologie, 12*(3), 417–37.

Schmitt, R. (2000). Negative and positive keying in natural contexts: Preserving the transformation concept from death through conflation. In G. Fine, & G. Smith (Eds.), *Erving Goffman, Vol. 3* (pp. 77–93). Thousand Oaks, CA: Sage.

Schoening, G., & Anderson, J. (1995). Social action media studies: Foundational arguments and common premises. *Communication Theory, 5*(2), 93–116.

Schutz, A. (1962). *Collected papers, Vol. 1*. The Hague: Martinus Nijhoff.

Schutz, A. (1967). *The phenomenology of the social world*. The Hague: Martinus Niejhoff.

Schwartz, S. (1999). A theory of cultural values and some implications for work. *Applied Psychology: An International Review, 48*, 23–47.

Scollon, R., & Scollon, S. (2001). Discourse and intercultural communication. In D. Schiffrin, D. Tannen, & H. Hamilton (Eds.), *The handbook of discourse analysis* (pp. 538–47). Oxford: Blackwell.

Scott, C., Corman, S., & Cheney, G. (1998). Development of a structurational model of identification in the organization. *Communication Theory, 8*(3), 298–336.

Scott, C., & Myers, K. (2010). Toward an integrative theroretical perspective on organizational membership negotiations: Socialization, assimilation, and the duality of structure. *Communication Theory, 20*(1), 79–105.

Searle, J. (1983). *Intentionality.* Cambridge, UK: Cambridge University Press.

Searle, J. (1995). *The construction of social reality.* New York, NY: Academic Press.

Seeman, M. (1997). The elusive situation in social psychology. *Social Psychology Quarterly, 60*(1), 4–13.

Seibold, D., & Meyers, R. (2005). Communication as structuring. In G. Shepard, J. St. John & T. Striphas (Eds.), *Communication as … stances on theory* (pp. 143–52). Thousand Oaks, CA: Sage.

Seibold, D., & Meyers, R. (2007). Group argument: A structuration perspective and research program. *Small Group Research, 38*(3), 312–36.

Sewell, G. (2010). Metaphor, myth, and theory building: Communication studies meets the linguistic turn, in sociology, anthropology, and philosophy. *Management Communication Quarterly, 24*(1), 139–50.

Sharrock, W. (1999). The omnipotence of the actor. In G. Smith (Ed.), *Goffman and social organization* (pp. 119–37). London: Manchester University Press.

Sheffer, A. C. (2009). Facework in coercive interactions: Evidence from police field interrogations. *A Dissertation Abstracts International: The Humanities and Social Sciences, 70*(1), 166.

Shenkar, O. (1996). The firm as a total institution: Reflections on the Chinese state enterprise. *Organization Studies, 17*(6), 885–907.

Sherblom, J., Keranen, L., & Withers, L. (2002). Tradition, tensions, and transformation: A structuration analysis of a game warden service in transition. *Journal of Applied Communication Research, 30*(2), 143–62.

Short, J., Williams, B., & Christie, W. (1976). *The social psychology of telecommunications.* New York, NY: John Wiley.

Shotter, J. (1993). *Cultural politics of everyday life: Social constructionism, rhetoric, and knowing of the third kind.* Buckingham, UK: Open University Press.

Shotter, J. (1997). "Duality of structure" and "intentionality" in an ecological psychology. In C. Bryant, & D. Jary (Eds.), *Anthony Giddens: Ccritical assessments, Vol. 2* (pp. 78–103). New York, NY: Routledge.

Shotter, J., & Gergen, K. (Eds.). (1989). *Texts of identity.* London, Newbury Park, New Delhi: Sage.

Shuler, S., & Sypher, B. (2000). Seeking emotional labor. *Management Communication Quarterly, 14*(1), 50–89.

Shumate, M., & Fulk, J. (2004). Boundaries and role conflict when work and family are colocated: A communication network and symbolic interaction. *Human Relations, 57*(1), 55–74.

Sigman, S. (1987). *A perspective on social communication.* Lexington, MA: Lexington Books.

Sillince, J. A. (2007). Organizational context and the discursive construction of organizing. *Management Communication Quarterly, 20*(4), 363–94.

Sillince, J. A. (2010). Can CCO theory tell us how organizing is distinct from markets, networking, belonging to a community or supporting a social movement? *Management Communication Quarterly, 42*(1), 132–38.

Sillince, J., & Mueller, F. (2007). Switching strategic perspective: The reframing of accounts of responsibility. *Organization Studies, 28*(2), 155–76.

Sinha, P. (2010). The dramatistic genre in leadership studies: Implications for research and practice. *Leadership, 6*(2), 185–205.

Skaerbaek, P. (2005). Annual reports as interaction devices: The hidden constructions of mediated communications. *Financial Accountabillity and Management, 21*(4), 385–411.

Smith, G. (Ed.). (1999). *Goffman and social organization: Studies in a sociological legacy.* London: Routledge.

Smith, G. (2006). *Erving Goffman.* New York: Routledge.

Smoliar, S. (2003). Interaction management: The next (and necessary) step beyond knowledge management. *Business Process Management Journal, 9*(3), 337–53.

Snow, D., & Benford, R. (1988). Ideology, frame resonance and participant mobilization. *International Social Movement Research, 1*, 197–217.

Snow, D., Rochford Jr., E., Worden, S., & Benford, R. (1986). Frame alignment processes, micromobilization and movement participation. *American Sociological Review, 51*(4), 464–81.

Soukup, C. (2004). Multimedia performance in a computer-mediated community: Communications as a virtual drama. *Journal of Computer-Mediated Communications, 9*(4).

Spencer, J. W. (1987). Self-work in social interaction: Negotiating role-identities. *Social Psychology Quarterly, 50*(2), 131–42.

Spencer-Oatey, H. (2005). (Im)politeness, face and perceptions of rapport: Unpacking their bases and interrelationships. *Journal of Politeness Research, 1*, 639–56.

Spencer-Oatey, H. (2007). Theories of identity and the analysis of face. *Journal of Pragmatics, 39*, 639–56.

Spencer-Oatey, H., & Jiang, W. (2003). Explaining cross-cultural pragmatic findings: Moving from politeness maxims to sociopragmatic interactional principles. *Journal of Pragmatics, 35*(10–11), 1633–50.

Sperber, D., & Wilson, D. (1986). *Relevance: Communication and cognition.* Oxford: Blackwell.

Sperber, D., & Wilson, D. (1995). *Relevance: Communication and cognition* (2nd ed.). Oxford, UK: Blackwell.

Sperber, D., & Wilson, D. (2002). Pragmatics, modularity and mindreading. *Mind and Language, 17*, 3–23.

Spybey, T. (1984a). Frames of meaning: The rationality in organisational cultures. *Acta Sociologica, 27*(4), 311–22.

Spybey, T. (1984b). Traditional and professional frames of meaning in management. *Sociology, 18*(4), 550–62.

Spybey, T. (1997). Traditional and professional frames of meaning in management. In C. Bryant, & D. Jary (Eds.), *Anthony Giddens: Ccritical assessments, Vol. 4* (pp. 213–28). New York: Routledge.

Spybey, T. (2001). The constitution of global society. In C. Bryant, & D. Jary (Eds.), *The contemporary Giddens* (pp. 147–70). New York: Palgrave.

Staber, S., & Sydow, S. (2002). Organizational adaptive capacity: A structuration perspective. *Journal of Management Inquiry, 11*(4), 408–24.

Stevenson, W. B., & Greenberg, D. (2000). Agency and social networks: Strategies of action in a social structure of position, opposition, and opportunity. *Administrative Science Quarterly, 45*(4), 651–78.

Stewart, M. (2008). Protecting speaker's face in impolite exchanges: The negotiation of face-wants in workplace interaction. *Journal of Politeness Research, 4*, 31–54.

Stinchcombe, A. (1990). Milieu and structure updated: A critique of the theory of structuration. In J. Clark, C. Modgil & S. Modgil (Eds.), *Anthony Giddens: Consensus and controversy* (pp. 47–55). London, UK: Falmer Press.

Stohl, C., & Cheney, G. (2001). Participatory processes/paradoxical practices: Communication and the dilemmas of organizational democracy. *Management Communication Quarterly, 14*(3), 349–407.

Storper, M. (1997). The spatial and temporal constitution of social action. In C. Bryants, & D. Jary (Eds.), *Anthony Giddens: Critical assessments, Vol. 3* (pp. 36–59). New York: Routledge.

Strabheim, J. (2010). Relevance theories of communication: Alfred Schutz in dialogue with Sperber and Wilson. *Journal of Pragmatics, 42*(5), 1412–41.

Strong, P. M. (1988). Minor courtesies and macro structures. In P. Drew, & A. Wooten (Eds.), *Erving Goffman* (pp. 228–49). Cambridge, UK: Polity Press.

Su, H. (2009). Code-switching in manageing a face-threatening communicative task: Footing and ambiguity in conventional interaction in Taiwan. *Journal of Pragmatics, 41*(2), 372–92.

Suchman, L. (1987). *Plans and situated actions: The problems of human-machine communication.* Cambridge, UK: Cambridge University Press.

Sveningsson, S., & Alvesson, M. (2003). Managing managerial identities: Organization fragmentation, discourse and idenitity struggle. *Human Relations, 56*(10), 1163–93.

Swann, W., Johnson, R., & Bosson, J. (2009). Identity negotiation at work. *Research in Organizational Behavior, 29*(1), 81–109.

Sydow, J., & Windeler, A. (1997). Managing inter-firm networks: A structurationist perspective. In C. Bryant, & D. Jary (Eds.), *Anthony Giddens: Critical assessments, Vol. 4* (pp. 455–95). New York: Routledge.

Sydow, J., & Windeler, A. (1998). Organizing and evaluating interfirm networks: A structurationist perspective on network processes and effectiveness. *Organization Science, 9*(3, Special Issue: Managing Partnerships and Strategic Alliances), 265–84.

Tannen, D. (1979). What's in a frame? surface evidence for underlying expectations. In R. Freedle (Ed.), *New directions in discourse processing* (pp. 137–81). Norwood, NJ: Ablex.

Tannen, D. (1981). *Analyzing discourse: Text and talk.* Georgetown, VA: Georgetown Round Table.

Tannen, D. (1982). *Spoken and written language, Vol. 9.* Norwood, NJ: Ablex.

Tannen, D. (2009). Framing and face: The relevance of the presentation of self to linguistic discourse analysis. *Social Psychology Quaterly, 72*(4), 300–5.

Tannen, D., & Wallat, C. (1987). Interactive frames and knowledge schemas in interaction: Examples from a medical examination/interview. *Social Psychology Quarterly, 50*(2), 205–16.

Taylor, J. R. (1995). Shifting from a heteronomous to an autonomous worldview of organizational communication: Communication theory on the cusp. *Communication Theory, 5*(1), 1–35.

Taylor, J. R. (2001a). The "rational" organization reconsidered: An exploration of some of the organizational implications of self-organizing. *Communication Theory, 11*(2), 137–77.

Taylor, J. R. (2001b). Toward a theory of imbrication and organizational communication. *American Journal of Semiotics, 12*(2), 1–29.

Taylor, J. R. (2001c). What is "organizational communication"? communication as a dialogic of text and conversation. Communication Review, 3(1–2), 21–83.

Taylor, J. R., Cooren, F., Giroux, N., & Robichaud, D. (1996). The communicational basis of organization: Between the conversation and the text. *Communication Theory, 6*, 1–39.

Taylor, J. R., Flanagin, A., Cheney, G., & Seibold, D. (2001). Organizational communication research: Key moments, central concerns and future challenges. In W. B. Gudykunst (Ed.), *Communication Yearbook, 24* (pp. 99–137). Thousand Oaks, CA: Sage.

Taylor, J. R., & Robichaud, D. (2004). Finding the organization in the communication: Discourse as action and sensemaking. *Organization, 11*(3), 395–413.

Taylor, J. R., & Van Every, E. (2000). *The emergent organization: Communication as its site and surface.* Mahwah, NJ: Lawrence Erlbaum Associates.

Tefkourafi, M. (2005). Beyond the micro-level in politeness research. *Journal of Politeness Research, 1*, 237–62.

Thompson, M. (2005). Structural and epistemic parameters in communities of practice. *Organization Science, 16*(2), 151–64.

Thrift, N. (1997a). Bear and mouse or bear and tree? Anthony Giddens' reconstruction of social theory. In C. Bryant, & D. Jary (Eds.), *Anthony Giddens: Critical assessments, Vol. 2* (pp. 123–40). New York, NY: Routledge.

Thrift, N. (1997b). The arts of living, the beauty of the dead: Anxieties of being in the work of Anthony Giddens. In C. Bryant, & D. Jary (Eds.), *Anthony Giddens: Critical assessments, Vol. 4* (pp. 46–60). New York: Routledge.

Ting-Toomey, S. (1988). Intercultural conflict styles. A face-negotiation theory. In Y. Kim, & W. Gudykunst (Eds.), *Theories in intercultural communications* (pp. 213–38). Newbury Park, CA: Sage.

Ting-Toomey, S. (Ed.). (1994). *The challenge of facework*. Albany, NY: State University of New York Press.

Ting-Toomey, S. (2005). The matrix of face: An updated face-negotiation theory. In W. Gudykunst (Ed.), *Theorizing about intercultural communication* (pp. 71–92). Thousand Oaks, CA: Sage.

Ting-Toomey, S., & Kurogi, A. (1998). Face work competence in intercultural conflict: An updated face-negotiation theory. *International Journal of Intercultural Relations, 22*, 187–225.

Ting-Toomey, S., & Oetzel, J. (2001). *Managing intercultural conflict effectively*. Thousand Oaks, CA: Sage.

Ting-Toomey, S., Yee-Jung, K., Shapiro, R., Garcia, W., Wright, T., & Oetzel, J. (2000). Cultural/ethnic identity salience and conflict styles. *International Journal of Intercultural Relations, 23*, 47–81.

Tomlinson, J. (1994). A phenomenology of globalization? Giddens on global modernity. *European Journal of Communication, 9*, 149–72.

Tomlinson, J. (1996). Cultural globalisation: Placing and displacing the West. *The European Journal of Development Research, 8*(2), 22–35.

Tomlinson, J. (1997). A phenomenology of globalization? Giddens on global modernity. In C. Bryant, & D. Jary (Eds.), *Anthony Giddens: Critical assessments, Vol. 4* (pp. 116–36). New York: Routledge.

Tracy, K. (1990). The many faces of facework. In H. Giles, & P. Robinson (Eds.), *Handbook of language and social psychology* (pp. 209–26). London: Wiley.

Tracy, K. (Ed.). (1991). *Understanding face-to-face interaction*. Hillsdale, NJ: Lawrence Erlbaum Associates.

Tracy, K. (1997a). *Colloquinms: Dilemmas of academic discourse*. Norwood, NJ: Ablex.

Tracy, K. (1997b). Interactional trouble in emergency service requests: A problem of frames. *Research on Language and Social Interaction, 30*, 315–43.

Tracy, K. (1998). Analyzing context: Framing the discussion. *Research on Language and Social Interaction, 31*(1), 1–28.

Tracy, K. (2001). Discourse analysis in communication. In D. Schiffrin, D. Tannen, & H. Hamilton (Eds.), *The handbook of discourse analysis* (pp. 725–49). Oxford: Blackwell.

Tracy, K. (2008). "Reasonable hostility": Situation-appropriate face-attack. *Journal of Politeness Research, 4*(1), 169–91.

Tracy, K., & Anderson, D. (1999). Relational positioning strategies in calls to the police: A dilemma. *Discourse Studies, 1*, 201–26.

Tracy, K., & Durfy, M. (2007). Speaking out in public: Citizen participation in contentious school board meetings. *Discourse and Communication, 1*, 223–49.

Tracy, K., & Moran, J. (1983). Conversational relevance in multiple-goal settings. In K. Tracy, & R. Craig (Eds.), *Conversational coherence.* (pp. 116–135). Beverly Hills, CA: Sage.

Tracy, K., & Muller, H. (2001). Diagnosing a school board's interactional trouble: Theorizing problem formulating. *Communication Theory, 11*, 84–104.

Tracy, K., & Tracy, S. (1998). Rudeness at 911: Reconceptualizing face and face-attack. *Human Communication Research, 25*, 225–51.

Tracy, S. (2000). Becoming a character for commerce. *Management Communication Quarterly, 14*(1), 90–128.

Tracy, S., & Rivera, K. (2010). Endorsing equity and applauding stay-at-home moms: How male voices on work-life reveal aversive sexism and flickers of transformation. *Management Communication Quarterly, 24*(1), 3–43.

Tracy, S., & Scott, C. (2006). Sexuality, masculinity and raint management among firefighters and correctional officers: Getting down and dirty with "America's heroes" and the "sum of law enforcement." *Management Communication Quarterly, 20*, 6–38.

Tracy, S., & Tracy, K. (1998). Emotion labor at 911: A case study and theoretical critique. *Journal of Applied Communication, 26*, 390–411.

Tracy, S., & Trethewey, A. (2005). Fracturing the real-self-fake-self dichotomy: Moving toward "crystallized" organizational discourses and identities. *Communication Theory, 15*(2), 168–95.

Trevino, A. J. (Ed.). (2003). *Goffman's legacy*. New York, NY: Rowman & Littlefield.

Tseelon, E. (1992). Is the presented self sincere? Goffman, impression management and postmodern self. *Theory, Culture and Society, 9*(2), 115–28.

Tsoukas, H. (2000). Knowledge as action, organization as theory: Reflections on organizational knowledge. *Emergence, 2*(4), 104–12.

Tsoukas, H. (2005). *Complex knowledge: Studies in contemporary organizational epistemology*. New York, NY: Oxford University Press.

Tsoukas, H. (2008). What is an organization? *NCA Conference on what is an organization?* Montreal, Canada.

Tsoukas, H. (2009). A dialogical approach to the creation of new knowledge in organizations. *Organization Science, 20*(6), 941–57.

Tufekci, Z. (2008). Grooming, gossip, facebook, and myspace. What can we learn about these sites from those who won't assimilate? *Information, Communication and Society, 11*(4), 544–64.

Tullar, W., & Kaiser, P. (2000). The effect of process training on process and outcomes in virtual groups. *Journal of Business Communication, 37*(4), 408–26.

Turner, J. (1986). Review essay: The theory of structuration. *American Journal of Sociology, 91*(4), 969–77.

Turner, J. H. (1988). *A theory of social interaction*. Standford, CA: Stanford University Press.

Tyre, M., & Orlikowski, W. J. (1994). Windows of opportunity: Temporal patterns of technological adaptation in organizations. *Organization Science, 5*(1), 98–118.

Unger, C. (2002). *Cognitive-pragmatic explanations of socio-pragmatic phenomena: The case of genre*. Unpublished manuscript.

Unger, C. (2006). *Pragmatics*. New York: Palgrave Macmillan.

Urry, J. (1997). Time and space in Giddens' social theory. In C. Bryant, & D. Jary (Eds.), *Anthony Giddens: Critical assessments, Vol. 3* (pp. 128–46). New York: Routledge.

Vachstein, V. S. (2004). The book about the "reality" of social reality: I. Goffman. frame analysis: An essay on organization of experience. *Sotsiologicheskiy Zhurnal* (3–4), 178–87.

Van Dijk, T. (1981). *Studies in the pragmatics of discourse*. The Hague: Mouton.

Van Dijk, T. (Ed.). (1997a). *Discourse as social interaction*. London: Sage.

Van Dijk, T. (1997b). The study of discourse. In T. Van Dijk (Ed.), *Discourse as social interaction, Vol. 1* (pp. 1–34). Thousand Oaks, CA: Sage.

Van Dijk, T. (Ed.). (1997c). *Discourse as structure and process*. London: Sage.

Van Dijk, T. (2005). Contextual knowledge management in discourse production: A CDA perspective. In R. Wodak (Ed.), *A new agenda in discourse analysis: Theory, method and interdisciplinarity*. Amsterdam: John Benjamins.

Van Dijk, T., & Kintsch, W. (1983). *Strategies of discourse comprehension*. New York, NY: Academic Press.

Van Gemert, L., & Woudstra, E. (1999). Changes in writing in the workplace: Cycles of discussion and text. In *Organizational communication and change* (pp. 209–42). Creskill, NJ: Hampton Press.

Veenstra, G. (2008). Careers open to talent: Educational credentials, cultural talent, and skilled employment. *Sociological Forum, 23*(1), 144–64.

Watson, C. M. (2006). The presentation of self and the new institutional inmate: An analysis of prisoners' responses to assessment for release. *Life as theater* (pp. 183–85). New Brunswick, NJ: Transaction.

Watson, R. (1999). Reading Goffman on interaction. In G. Smith (Ed.), *Goffman and social organization*. London: Routledge.

Watson, T. (2008). Managing identity: Identiity work, personal predicaments and structural circumstances. *Organization, 15*(1), 121–43.

Watts, R. (2003). *Politeness*. Cambridge: Cambridge University Press.

Webb, J. (2006). Evaluating the concept of a productive subjectivity. *Organisations, identities and the self* (pp. 186–89). New York: Palgrave Macmillan.

Weick, K. (1979). *The social psychology of organizations*. (2nd ed.). Reading, MA: Addison-Wesley.

Weick, K. (1990). Technology as equivoque. In P. Goodman, L. Sproul, & Associates (Eds.), *Technology and organizations* (pp. 1–39). San Francisco, CA: Jossey-Bass Publishers.

Weick, K. (1995). *Sensemaking in organizations*. Thousand Oaks, CA: Sage.

Weick, K. (2001). *Making sense of the organization*. Oxford, UK: Blackwell.

Weick, K. (2004). How projects lose meaning. In R. Stablein, & P. Frost (Eds.), *Renewing research practice* (pp. 183–204). Stanford, CA: Stanford University Press.

Weick, K. (2006). Faith, evidence, and action: Better guesses in an unknowable world. *Organization Studies, 27*(11), 1723–36.

Weick, K., & Roberts, K. (1993). Collective mind in organizations: Heedful interrelating on flight decks. *Administrative Science Quarterly, 38*, 357–81.

Welsh, J. (1984). The presentation of self in capitalist society: Beuracratic visibility as a social source of impression management. *Humanity and Society, 8*, 253–71.

West, C. (2000). Goffman in feminist perspective. In G. Fine, & G. Smith (Eds.), *Erving Goffman, Vol. 4* (pp. 291–312). Thousand Oaks, CA: Sage.

West, C., & Zimmerman, D. (1987). Doing gender. *Gender and Society, 1*, 125–51.

Wheeler-Brooks, J. (2009). Structuration theory and critical consciousness: Potential applications for social work practice. *Journal of Sociology and Social Welfare, 36*(1), 123–40.

White, J. B., Tynan, R., Galinsky, A. D., & Thompson, L. (2004). Face threat sensitivity in negotiation: Roadblock to agreement and joint gain. *Organizational Behavior and Human Decision Processes, 94*(2), 102–24.

Whittington, R. (1992). Putting Giddens into action: Social systems and managerial agency. *Journal of Management Studies, 29*(6), 693–712.

Whittington, R. (1997). Putting Giddens into action: Social systems and managerial agency. In C. Bryant, & D. Jary (Eds.), *Anthony Giddens: Critical assessments. Vol. 4* (pp. 365–86). New York: Routledge.

Wiley, S. B. C. (2004). Rethinking nationality in the context of globalization. *Communication Theory, 14*(1), 78–96.

Williams, R. (1980). Goffman's sociology of talk. In J. Ditton (Ed.), *The view from Goffman* (pp. 210–32). New York, NY: St. Martin's Press.

Williams, R. (1988). Understanding Goffman's methods. In P. Drew, & A. Wootton (Eds.), *Erving Goffman* (pp. 64–88). Oxford: Polity Press.

Willmott, H. (1981). The structuring of organizational structure: A note. *Administrative Science Quarterly, 26*, 470–74.

Willmott, H. (1993). Strength is ignorance, slavery is freedom: Managing culture in modern organizations. *Journal of Management Studies, 30*(4), 515–52.

Wilson, D. (1998). Discourse, coherence and relevance: A reply to Rache and Giora. *Journal of Pragmatics, 29*, 57–74.

Wilson, J., O'Leary, M., Metiu, A., & Jett, Q. (2008). Perceived proximity in virtual work: Explaining the paradox of far-but-close. *Organization Studies, 29*(7), 979–1002.

Witmer, D. (1997). Communication and recovery: Structuration as an ontological approach to organizational culture. *Communication Monographs, 64*, 324–49.

Womack, D. (2008). *Global theorizing for global communicating: Managing multiple identities in the twenty-first century*. Paper, Organizational Communication at Alta, Revised: Reflection, Synthesis and Engagement.

Yates, J. (1993). *Control through communication: The rise of system in American management*. Baltimore, MD: John Hopkins University.

Yates, J. (1994). Evolving information use in firms, 1850–1920: Ideology and information techniques and technologies. In L. Bud-Frierman (Ed.), *Information acumen: The understanding and use of knowledge in modern business* (pp. 26–50). London, UK: Routledge.

Yates, J. (1997). Using Giddens' structuration theory to inform business history. *Business and Economic History, 26*(1), 159–82.

Yates, J., & Orlikowski, W. (1992). Genres of organizational communication: A structurational approach to studying communication and media. *Academy of Management Review, 17*(2), 299–326.

Yates, J., Orlikowski, W., & Woerner, S. (2003). Virtual organizing: Using threads to coordinate distributed work. *Proceedings of the 36th Hawaii International Conference of System Sciences,* Big Island, Hawaii*, 36,* 1–8.

Ybema, S., Keenoy, T., Oswick, C., Beverungen, A., Ellis, N., & Sabelis, I. (2009). Articulating identities. *Human Relations, 62*(3), 299–322.

Yoshioka, T., & Herman, G. (October, 1999). Genre taxonomy: A knowledge repository of communicative action. Unpublished paper, 1–25.

Ytreberg, E. (2002). Erving Goffman as a theorist of the mass media. *Critical Studies in Media Communication, 19*(4), 481–97.

Zack, M. H., & McKenney, J. L. (1995). Social context and interaction in ongoing computer-supported management groups. *Organization Science, 6*(4), 394–422.

Zammuner, V., & Galli, C. (2005). The relationship with patients: "emotional labor" and its correlates in hospital employees. In C. Hartal, W. Zerbe, & N. Ashkansay (Eds.), *Emotions in organizational behavior* (pp. 251–86). Mahwah, NJ: Lawrence Erlbaum Associates.

Zhang, Y., & Huxham, C. (2009). Identity construction and trust building in developing international collaborations. *Journal of Applied Behavioral Science, 45*(2), 186–211.

Zhao, S. (2004). Consociated contemporaries as an emergent realm of the lifeworld: Extending Schutz's phenomenological analysis to cyberspace. *Human Studies, 27*(1), 91–105.

Zhao, S., & Elesh, D. (2008). Co-presence as "being with": Social contact in online public domains. *Information, Communication and Society, 11*(4), 565–83.

Zidjaly, N. (2009). Agency as an interactive achievement. *Language in Society, 38*(2), 177–200.

Zorn, T., & Townsley, N. (2008). Introduction to the forum on Meaning/ful work studies in organizational communication: Setting an agenda. *Management Communication Quarterly 7, 22*(1), 14–151.

INDEX

Aarsand, P. 293
Abelson, R. 3
action and interaction in structuration theory 146–48
adaptive structuration theory (AST) 180–6
advantages of Goffman/Giddens synthesis 332–41
agency 150–5, 330–32
Ahrne, G. 70, 376
Akman, V. 33
Allon-Souday, G. 286
Alvesson, M. 20, 31, 34, 39, 87, 194, 300, 354, 373, 383
Ancona, D. 346
Aoki, P. 293
Archer, M. 173, 178, 205, 295, 297, 361, 371
Argyris, C. 29
Arrow, H. 204
Arundale, R. 263, 382
Ashcraft, K. 383
Ashkanasy, N. 378
Audia, P. 9
Avolio, B. 308

Bacharach, S. 67, 282, 352
Bacue, A. 51
Ballard, D. 190, 204, 346
Banks, S. 164–65, 279, 378
Baptista, L. 226, 228–29, 232, 288
Barbour, J. 58, 173, 195

Barbulescu, R. 300–01
Bargiela-Chiappini, F. 260, 262–64, 289, 382
Barley, S. 188–89, 172–73, 184, 204, 364, 386
Barr, P. 7, 31
Barrett, M. 279
Bartlett, F. 4
Bastien, D. 196
Bateson, G. 3, 9–10, 94–5, 214, 228, 233, 238, 347
Battershill, C. 214, 269
Bavelas, J. 34
Baxter, L. 205
Bazarova, N. 186
Becker, H. 117, 273–4
Beckert, J. 117
Beech, N. 300
Benford, R. 280–81
Benshop, Y. 383
Berends, H. 197
Berger, C. 23, 50, 285
Bernstein, B. 19, 269
Berry, M. 33
Bertilsson, M. 118–19
Beyer, J. 171
Bimber, B. 380
Birdwhistell, R. 21–2
Bisel, R. 87, 93, 116, 277, 376
Blackmore, D. 43
Blair-Joy, M. 373

Bleicher, J. 133
Blommaert, J. 214, 278, 365–7
Boden, D. 36, 39, 55, 59, 77, 83–6,
  236–37, 269, 290, 318, 343, 346
Boersma, K. 197
Bolton, K. 196
Bonito, J. 277
Bosson, J. 300
Bourdieu, P. 31, 303, 325, 346, 371
Boyle, M. 296
Bradac, J. 23, 50
Braithwaite, D. 205
Branaman, A. 6, 209, 244, 250, 252, 259,
  261, 283, 288, 325
Brandes, P. 196
Bransford, J. 4, 218
Brown, P. 261–2, 288–9
Browning, L. 171, 344
Bruegger, U. 380
Bruner, J. 32
Bryant, C. 101, 111, 114, 117, 124, 144,
  165–6, 168
Buller, D. 51, 381
Burgoon, J. 51, 78, 381
Burke, P. 355
Burkhalter, S. 198
Burns, T. 64
Butler, J. 196
Buttny, R. 32, 34, 47, 55, 249, 380
Button, G. 348
Buzzanell, P. 226

Callahan, J. 378
Canary, D. 55, 170, 197–98
Canary, H. 197–8
Cantor, N. 6
Carbaugh, D. 33, 194, 286
Carroll, G. 357
Case, P. 290, 292
Castelfranchi, P. 24
Castor, T. 90
Chae, B. 184–85
Chafe, W. 4
Chand, D. 117
Chapman, P. 13, 74
Chen, V. 260–62
Cheney, G. 67–8, 93, 192–93, 281,
  369–70, 376–76
Chia, R. 85, 303–04
Child, J. 197
Chreim, S. 279–80
Chriss, J. 253, 260, c268, 294–95
Christensen, L. 193, 369

Christie, W. 380
Chudoba, K. 185
Cicourel, A. 19, 23, 34, 36, 39–40, 237
Clair, R. 63, 144, 246, 384
Clark, E. 29
Clark, H. 29
Clark, T. 308
Clarke, I. 82
Clegg, S. 132
Cody, M. 55
Cohen, I. 102, 106, 115, 159, 163, 168
Collins, R. 210, 231, 233–4, 236–7, 239,
  241, 258, 261, 265, 271, 280, 286–7,
  308–9
Colomy, P. xv, 13
communication 18–56; model of 46–56;
  underlying assumptions of 23–45
communication as constitutive of
  organizations 75–88, 169–170, 342–8
communicative processes in organizing
  47–56, 75–97
Conrad, C. 67, 74, 77, 164–5, 167,
  350–52, 355–6
Conte, M. 307
Contractor, N. 186
Cook, A. 31
Cooper, C. 56
Cooper, G. 37
Cooren, F. 7, 19, 56, 80, 83, 87, 90, 344,
  348–51, 376
Corman, S. 192, 194, 357, 375, 382
Cornelissen, J. 308
Costas, J. 300
Coulter, R. 302
Courtright, J. 353
Cox, J. 87
Craib, I. 104–05, 121, 135, 145,
  168, 316
Craig, R. 376
Crook, S. 227–30
Cupach, W. 295
Czarniawska, B. 19, 27, 70, 212, 314, 345

Daft, R. 7, 381
Dallmayr, F. 112
Dandeker, C. 111
D'Angelo, P. 5
Das, D. 195
Dascal, M. 50
David, G. 117
Davidson, M. 47
Davis, M. 240
Deetz, S. 32, 67, 144, 164

Dell, P. 340
Denzin, N. 31, 39, 233
Dertouzos, M. 38
DeSanctis, G. 36, 38, 67, 78, 160, 168, 176, 180–84, 188, 375
Dharwadkar, R. 195
Dillard, J. P. 36
Donnellon, A. 39
Dorfman, P. 61–2
Douglas, J. 24, 39–40
Down, S. 301
Drazin, R. 365
Drummond, K. 32
duality of technology 178–80, 186–191
Duck, S. 36
Durfy, M. 290

Economidou-Kogetsidis, M. 260
Eder, D. 278
Edwards, D. 20, 28, 32, 50
Eelen, G. 289
Eisenberg, E. 33, 74
Ekman, P. 380
Elesh, D. 76, 336
Ellis, D. 22, 24–5, 36, 39, 40, 211
Elsbach, K. 7, 30
Emirbayer, M. 370, 372–3
Engestrom, Y. 81, 378
Entman, J. 4, 8, 18
Erikson, E. 147–8, 373, 378
Erickson, I. 180, 322
Erwin, R. 217
Essers, C. 383

Fabros, A. 367
face 259–64; 303–6
Fairhurst, G. 6, 19, 56, 83, 86–7, 90, 93, 295, 305, 317–18, 341, 344, 348–53
Fanelli, A. 197
Fayard, A. 381
Featherstone, M. 133
Feldman, M. 201–02, 204,
Felin, T. 88
Finch, M. 225
Fine, G. 225, 247
Fineman, S. 40, 78
Fiol, C. 379
Fiske, S. 3
Fitch, K. 32
Flaherty, M. 190
Flanagin, A. 380
Fleming, P. 299

Flowerdew, J. 34
Fortunati, L. 292
Foucault, M. 87, 191, 303, 309, 325, 335, 362–63
frames 1–22
framing 242–50
Freeman, S. 47
Friedland, R. 89, 346
Frye, N. 32
Fuchs, C. 174
Fulk, J. 38, 180

Galinsky, A. 288
Galli, C. 297
Gannon, M. 9
Gardner, C. 294
Gardner, W. 295, 308
Garfinkel, H . 29, 32–3, 39, 47, 55, 122, 149, 162, 218, 235
Garot, R. 297
Gash, D. 6–8, 186, 188
Gastil, J. 198
Gavin-Doxas, K. 378
Gawley, T. 117
Geddes, D. 297
Gee, J. 51, 55
Geertz, C. 354
Geist, P. 203
Gephart, R. 117
Gergen, K. 416
Geser, H. 293
Giacalone, R. 294
Gibbons, J. 245
Gibson, D. 284
Giddens, A. 99–207; the self 147–53
Gilbert, N. 292
Gioia, D. 6, 48, 95
Giroux, H. 80
Gittell, J. 192
Goffman 207–311; accessibility 225–7; civil inattention 225–7; communicative self 251–4; dramaturgical perspective 306–9; embedding 247; expressive self 254–55; face 259–64, 288–291; framing 232–39; Gidden's comments on 326–332; identity 300–02; impression management 294–6; interaction at work 279; interaction order 210–215; interaction order and social order 268–79; interactional units 242–49; online communication 292–4; presence and absence 378–82; psychological self 255–8; ritual requirements 219–241;

social self 249–51; system requirements of the interaction order 240–49; total institutions 273–75
Gomez, P. 210
Gonos, G. 214, 232–33, 309, 347, 368
Goodall, W. 381
Goodman, P. 346
Goodwin, C. 32, 34, 51, 56, 81, 294
Gordon, R. 285
Goss, D. 297
Grainger, K. 260
Grant, D. 6, 48, 86, 305, 308, 373
Greener, I. 146, 295
Gregory, D. 143
Greimas, A. 83
Grice, H. 23, 33, 42, 234, 241, 261
Griffith, T. 186
Grimshaw, A. 357
Gronfein, W. 211, 329
Gross, N. 151
Gudykunst, W. 30, 39, 46, 48, 61, 163, 264
Gueraud, S. 31
Gumperz, J. 5, 18–21, 31–5, 47, 212, 299
Gupta, A. 9
Gupta, V. 61–2

Hacking, I. 264, 309
Hall, E.T. 62, 269
Hall, P. 346
Hallett, T. 278, 286, 297
Hample, D. 304
Handelman, D. 281–82
Handler, R. 298
Hanges, P. 61–62
Hardey, M. 151
Hardy, C. 86–7, 354
Hareli, S. 297
Hargadon, A. 7, 31, 197
Harger, B. 278
Harris, S. 289
Hartel, C. 378
Hartland, N. 321
Haslett, B. 15, 18, 22, 29, 32–4, 39, 46–56, 219, 317, 354, 378
Haugaard, M. 135, 321
Haugh, M. 262–65, 382
Hay, C. 125, 369
Heath, C. 292
Hendry, J. 71, 93–5, 198
Henry, K. 72, 204
Hepburn, A. 7, 40
Heracleous, L. 35, 71–2, 93–5, 279, 345

Heritage, J. 28–9, 36, 47, 56
Herman, G. 179
Herrera Gomez, M. 210
Herzfeld, M. 298
Hil, S. 186
Hindmarsh, J. 284
Hochschild, A. 40, 205, 261, 296–97
Hodgson, G. 5, 69
Hofstede, G. 61–3
Holt, D. 61
Holtgraves, T. 262, 264, 288–89
Hoogenboom, M. 139
Hopper, R. 32
House, R. 61–2, 116, 213, 274
Howard, J. 202–03
Howard, L. 95, 203
Howard-Grenville, J. 202
Hughes, N. 289
Hutchby, I. 55, 76, 290
Hutchins, E. 7
Huxham, C. 248, 300
Hymes, D. 19, 33

Ibarra, H. 300–01
Identity 192–6; 300–02
Iedema, R. 69
Inglehart, R. 62
Inns, D. 374
institutional theory 171–3
Intentionality 155–6
interaction order; and social order 268–79
Ito, M. 293
Iverson, J. 170
Izard, C. 21, 51, 56

Jackson, M. 202
Jacobs, A. 278
Jacobsen, M. 278
Jarvenpaa, S. 117
Jary, D. 5, 111, 114,. 116–17, 123–24, 140–41, 146, 165–66, 168
Jarzabkowski, P. 198, 305
Javidan, M. 61–2
Jefferson, G. 243
Jenkins, R. 278, 340, 380
Jett, Q. 290
Jian, G. 19, 29, 93, 376
Jiang, W. 289
Jirokta, M. 292
Johnson, B. 300, 357–58, 373–74
Johnston, W. 197
Jones, B. 176, 178, 180

Kai-Cheng, Y. 61
Kaiser, P. 186
Kanter, R. M. 67–8
Kaplan, S. 305
Karreman, D. 19–20, 31, 34, 40, 87, 354, 372
Karsten, H. 176, 178, 180
Kaspersen, L. 105, 110, 121–22, 135, 148, 155, 163
Katriel, T. 380
Katz, J. 192, 343, 354
Keenoy, T. 48, 305, 373–74
Kellerman, K. 24, 39
Kelly, S. 117
Kelshaw, T. 198
Kendon, A. 236, 241
Keranen, L. 203
Keyton, J. 277, 376
Kidder, J. 127
Kiesler, S. 187
Kilminster, R. 133, 162
Kim, E. 198
Kim, J. 198
Kim, Y. 30, 46
King, B. 88
Kintsch, W. 29, 37, 218
Kirby, E. 195, 364
Knorr-Cetina, K. 376, 380
Knuth, M. 196
Koenig, T. 8
Kossakowski, R. 299
Kraidy, M. 195
Krone, K. 195, 205
Kruml, S. 297
Kuhn, T. 58, 194, 202
Kunda, G. 286
Kurogi, A. 33, 262
Kuypers, J. 5
Kwon, W. 82

Lair, D. 370
Lake, R. 205
Lakoff, G. 373–74
Lammers, J. 58, 173, 195
Langa, G. 186
Langer, A. 24, 50
Langer, E. 24, 50
Latour, B. 8, 27, 36, 51, 70, 78, 81, 83–4, 90, 126, 188, 348–50, 376
Lawler, E. 67, 282
Lawrence, B. 65, 87, 346
Lawrence, P. 65
Leech, G. 42

Leeds-Hurwitz, W. 268
Leflaive, X. 132
Leidner, D. 117
Lengel, R. 7, 381
Leonardi, P. 174, 336
Leong, S. 34
Lerner, G. 263
Leung, E. 245
Leung, T. 240
LeVine, P. 380
Levinson, S. 5, 32, 225, 241, 246, 261–62, 288–89
Lewis, L. 171, 202
Ligas, M. 302
Ling, R. 278, 340, 380
Liu, H. 306
Liu, M. 306
Livesay, J. 161–62
Llewellyn, N. 134, 173, 194, 202–04
Llewellyn, S. 134, 203–04
Locher, M. 382
Locke, E. 9
Lofland, J. 225
Lorsch, J. 65
Lovaglia, M. 171
Low, M. 126
Luff, P. 292
Luhtakallio, E. 258
Lumsden, K. 297

Maanen, J. 117
MacCannell, D. 230, 267
Maines, D. 37, 55, 226
Malacrida, C. 275
Mandelbaum, J. 46
Mangham, I. 308, 390
Manias, E. 308
Manning, P. 194, 214, 216, 220, 222, 247, 253, 268, 275–77, 295, 306, 320
Mantere, S. 198–99
Manusov, V. 55–6, 78
Mao, L. 262–63
March, J. 37
Marinova, D. 340, 380
Markowitz, L. 303
Marshak, R. 35, 87, 278, 373–74
Martin, J. 63
Martin, P. 66, 303
Mason, I. 42
Massey, K. 47
materiality 83–5
Mathieu, L. 280

Matsumoto, Y. 263
Mayes, P. 376
Maynard, D. 42, 282
Maznevski, M. 185
McBride, M. 195, 364
McCarrell, N. 4, 218
McCawley, J. 245
McDaniel, S. 180
McKenney, J. 335
Mclean, A. 308
McPhee, R. 7, 76, 79, 81–3, 90–2, 99,
   113, 120, 132, 150–51, 164, 167–70,
   181, 196–97, 202, 205, 344, 353,
   358–61, 376
Meanwell, E. 297
Meisenbach, R. 302
Menand, L. 303
Mendoza, J. 115, 122, 133, 148–49,
   155, 157
Mengis, J. 76
Menon, T. 24, 92
Messersmith, A. 277, 376
Metiu, A. 290
Metts, S. 295
Meyers, R. 168–71
Meyrowitz, J. 290
Miettinen, R. 202
Miller, K. 102, 346
Mills, S. 260
Mingers, J. 92, 113, 115, 174–75
Minsky, M. 4
Mintzberg, H. 59, 65
Mische, A. 370–73
Mischel, W. 6
Modaff, D. 196
Moeran, B. 305
Mohr, J. 89
Molotoch, H. 290
Monge, P. 85
Montepare, J. 298
Moran, J. 43
Moreland, R. 204
Morgan, G. 13, 24, 59, 65–7, 237,
   373
Morris, G. H. 24, 32, 92, 171, 249
Morris, J. 117
Mouzelis, N. 217
Mueller, F. 304
Muller, H. 76
Mumby, D. 32, 67, 144, 169, 201, 246,
   375
Myerowitz, J. 37
Myers, G. 7, 192, 288, 369

Nadkarni, S. 8
Napier, J. 298
Narayanan, V. 8
Nelsen, N. 58, 194
Newell, S. 117
Nicholson, H. 205
Nicolini, D. 97
Nicotera, A. 79, 82
Nisbett, R. 218
Nonaka, I. 197
Noonan, C. 117
Norton, T. 198
Nunes, J. 292
Nutch, F. 296

Oberlechner, T. 117
O'Connor, E . 379
O'Driscoll, J. 263
Oetzel, J. 46, 61
Okabe, D. 293
Okamura, K. 376
Oleary, M. 291
Oliver, D. 308
Olson, G. 180
Olufowote, J. 369
Organizations; alternative frames 64–7;
   communicative functions in 75–9;
   cultural differences in 61–3; generic
   qualities of 58–60; Gidden's view of
   70–1; transformation and paradoxes in
   67–8
Orlikowski, W. 6–8, 19, 29, 36, 67, 78,
   100, 105–6, 119, 136, 169, 175–80,
   186–191, 205, 305, 377, 379
Ossewaarde, R. 139
Ostrow, J. 224
Oswick, C. 48, 86–7, 308, 372
Outhwaite, W. 35

Padilla, O. 37
Pal, M. 196
Parisi, D. 24
Paroutis, S. 199
Parsons, E. 197
Patriotta, G. 301
Patterson, M. 56, 78, 298
Pearson, E. 293
Penna, S. 125, 369
Pentland, B. 201, 377
Perlow, L. 97, 116, 192, 343, 354
Perretta, H. 293
Perri 4
Peters, L. 197

Peterson, A. 296
Pettigrew, A. 192, 199
Pfister, J. 262
Philipsen, G. 286
Phillips, N. 13, 74, 87
Phipps, A. 167
Pickering, A. 185, 376
Pierson, C. 115, 123, 130, 141, 153, 156, 161, 378
Pilnick, A. 84
Pinch, T. 91
Pineiro, E. 290, 292
Pinsonneault, A. 176
Planalp, S. 370, 378
politeness 262–65
Pomerantz, A. 32, 46, 56
Poole, M. S. 6, 36, 67, 74, 77–8, 85, 99, 113, 120, 132, 160, 164, 167–8, 174–6,180–85, 188, 196, 202, 204–5, 357–61, 375, 382
Porock, D. 308
Potter, J. 20, 354
Pozzebon, M. 176
Praet, E. 284
Preves, S. 296
Psathas, G. 243
Putnam, L. 13, 74, 79–82, 86–7, 90, 317–18. 341–44, 347, 375

Rae, J. 246, 284
Rafaeli, A. 297
Raffler-Engler, W. 31
Ralston, D. 61
Rampton, B. 296
Rattanen, T. 17–18, 139, 146
Rawls, A. 117, 211, 214, 233, 252, 254, 265, 271–2, 321
reflexivity 124–5
Rettie, R. 290–1, 293, 299
Reveley, J. 300–01
Richards, D. 70
Richter, C. xiv
Ridgeway, C. 383
Riley, P. 164–5, 196, 308
Riordan, C. 294
Ritual constraints 219, 241
Rivera, K. 195
Roberts, K. 7
Robey, D. 105, 119, 136, 176–7
Robichaud, D. 80, 90
Rochford, Jr, E. 280
Rogers, E. M. 282–285, 287, 353
Rogers, L. 353

Rogers, M. 280, 282–5, 288
Rosenfeld, P. 294
Rosch, E. 6
Ross, D. 218, 293, 340, 380
Ross, L. 5
Rusbult, C. 24

Sabelis, I. 383
Sacks, H. 42, 243
Saffold, G. III
Sahay, S. 203
Salaman, G. 308
Samra-Fredericks, D. 199, 202, 304
Samter, W. 39, 378
Sanders, R. 32, 39–40, 277
Sanjose, V. 37
Sarr, R. 6, 295
Schank, R. 3
Scheff, T. 221, 237, 261, 268, 278–9
Scheflen, A. 21
Schegloff, E. 32, 34, 39, 42, 55, 161, 243
Schein, E. 7, 13–14, 39, 58–9. 63, 314
Schiffrin, D. 23
Schimmelfennig, F. 260
Schmisseur, A. 19, 93
Schmitt, R. 234–5
Schoening, G. 307
Schon, D. 29
Schrodt, P. 205
Schultz, A. 21, 51, 56
Schwartz, J. 6
Schwartz, S. 61
Scollon, R. 19, 348, 370, 380
Scollon, S. 370
Scott, C. 192–4, 297, 369
Searle, J. 19, 24, 218, 234
Seeman, M. 34
Seibold, D. 99, 168–72, 186, 190, 202, 204–5, 345–6, 358–61
self organizing system 174–5
Self; the communicative self 251–4; the expressive self 254–5; the social self 249–51
Sewell, G. 9
Shapiro, R. 61
Sharrock, W. 30
Shaw, T. 117
Sheffer, A. 289
Sheller, M. 376
Shenkar, O. 275
Sherblom, J. 203
Short, J. 380
Shotter, J. 26–7, 40, 148, 161

Shuler, S. 297
Shumate, M. 197
Sigman, S. 21–2, 24, 31–2, 39, 270–72
Sillince, J. 35, 87–8, 304
Simmons, S. 151
Simon, H. 287
Sinha, P. 306
Slembrouck, S. 365
Smith, G. 210, 214, 222, 225, 230, 235, 248–9, 252, 255–6
Smoliar, S. 197
Snow, D. 280–1
social integration 268–79
social positioning 158–9
Soriano-Miras, R. 210
Soukup, C. 293
Spedale, S. 301
Spence, L. 202
Spencer, J. 299
Spencer-Oatey, H. 262, 289
Sperber, D. 43, 46, 50
Sproul, L. 187
Spybey, T. 144, 200
Staber, S. 202
Stalker, G. 64
Staples, D. 117
Stephenson, D. 296
Stevenson, W. 172
Stewart, C. 285, 289, 382
Stewart, J. 285
Stewart, M. 282, 289
Stinchcombe, A. 163
Stohl, C. 67–8, 375, 380
Storper, M. 105, 120
Strong, P.M. 222, 242
structuration theory; agency 134–7; change in 143–6; communication technology 176–80; globalization 140–3; identity 192–6; implications of 160–4; intentionality 155–6; knowledgeability in 156–8; modalities 104–7; personal relationships 150–2; power 129–34; reflexivity 124–5; self-organizing systems 174–5; social integration 118–21; social positioning 158–9; social systems and institutions 109–10; structural properties 112–13; structural sets 114; time and historicity 115–16; time-space 126–9; structurational interaction; addressing communication as constitutive of organizations 342–51; advantages of 336–41; agency in 370–73; application

to group decision-making 358–62; application to technology 364–5; clarifying texts 356–8; culture and globalization 367–69; identity 369–70; integrating the interaction order and social order 332–336; integration via frame theory 313–20; interaction order and social order 320–26; power, identity and work 362–4; reframing critical issues 374–76
Sturdy, A. 297
Su, H. 289
Suchman, L. 37, 81, 377
Sutton, R. 297
Sveningsson, S. 300
Swann, W. 300
Sydow, J. 72, 103, 167, 196, 199
Sydow, S. 202
Sypher, B. 297

Tanna, V. 290
Tannen, D. 4, 7, 247
Taylor, J.R. 80, 83, 87, 90, 344, 374–5
Taylor, L. 227–30
Taylor, S. 3
Tefkourafi, M. 264
Terpstra, R. 61
Tesluk, P. 186
Thomas, R. 383
Thompson, L. 288
Thompson, M. 288
Thrift, N. 105, 118, 136
time and historicity 143–4, 160, 175–80, 354
time-space edges 110–111, 118, 334, 353–4, 366, 384
Ting-Toomey, S. 33, 49, 61, 225, 260, 262–3, 288, 381
Tolbert, P. 172–3
Tomlinson, J. 38, 140–5
Tompkins, P. 281
total institutions 273–5
Townsley, N. 58, 376
Tracy, K. 7, 19, 41, 43, 50, 55, 78, 225–6, 262, 264, 274, 288–9, 290, 297, 302, 357, 376, 381
Tracy, S. 36, 40, 195, 289
Trethewey, A. 7, 299, 302
Tseelon, E. 294
Tsoukas, H. 70, 88, 304
Tufekci, Z. 292
Turner, J. 114, 122, 127, 136, 156, 265–6, 324

Tushman, M. 346
Tynan, R. 288
Tyre, M. 188

Unger, C. 42
Urry, J. 128

Vaara, E. 198–9
Vachstein, V. 229
Van Dijk, T. 19, 23, 29, 31–3, 36–7, 48, 218, 304, 357
Van Every, E. 80, 83
van Gemert, L. 358
Van Lange, P. 24
Veenstra, G. 296
Vidal-Abarca, E. 37

Waksler, F. 243
Wallat, C. 7, 247
Walsham, G. 203
Walthers, J. 186
Warner, B. 304
Watson, C. 383
Watson, R. 279
Watson, T. 300, 383
Watts, R. 289
Webb, J. 193
Weggman, M. 197
Weick, K. 6–8, 31, 33, 36, 52, 63, 66, 155, 198, 212, 364–5
Welsh, J. 294
West, C. 250
Wetherell, M. 354
Wheelan, S. 204
Wheeler-Brooks, J. 146
Whetten, D. 88
White, H. 89
White, J. 288
Whittington, R. 144, 171–2, 200

Wieland, S. 195, 364
Wiggins, S. 7, 40
Wiley, S. 370
Williams, B. 380
Williams, R. 213, 241, 261
Willmott, H. 119, 294
Wilson, D. 43, 46, 50
Wilson, J. 290
Windeler, A. 72, 103, 167–8, 196, 199
Withers, L. 203
Witmer, D. 196
Wodak, R. 69, 82
Woerner, S. 179
Wolfe, J. 297
Womack, D. 370
Wooffitt, I. 55
Worden, S. 280
Woudstra, E. 358
Wright, T. 61

Yanow, D. 202
Yates, J. 19, 36, 78, 99, 169, 178–80, 190, 376
Ybema, S. 383
Yee-Jung, K. 61
Yoshioka, T. 179
Young, D. 304
Ytreberg, E. 309

Zack, M. 335
Zammuner, V. 297
Zaug, P. 76, 81–3, 170
Zelditch, M. 47
Zerbe, S. 378
Zhang, Y. 248
Zhao, S. 30, 37–8, 52, 76, 336, 378–9
Zidjaly, N. 256
Zimmerman, D. 42, 250
Zorn, T. 58, 370, 376